ABOUT THE AUTHORS

Thirty-year veteran journalist **George Cantor** was a baseball writer and assistant city editor for the *Detroit Free Press* before becoming their travel editor in 1973. A sports columnist at the *Detroit News* from 1991–1993, Cantor is currently a senior reporter. An award-winning newspaper columnist and sports-writer, he has contributed to Visible Ink's acclaimed *The Olympic Factbook.*

Mickey Lolich, author of the foreword, pitched in the major leagues with the Detroit Tigers, New York Mets, and San Diego Padres. In the 1968 World Series, Lolich emerged from Denny McLain's shadow to become the MVP of the Series by winning three games and hitting a home run. In his sixteen-year career, he recorded 217 wins, a 3.44 ERA, 2,832 strike outs, and 3,639 innings. Since retiring from baseball, Lolich operates a business in Lake Orion, Michigan.

INSIDE SPORTS MAGAZINE®

WORLD SERIES FACTBOOK

INSIDE SPORTS MAGAZINE®

WORLD SERIES FACTBOOK

GEORGE CANTOR

FOREWORD BY MICKEY LOLICH

VISIBLE INK PRESS

Detroit • New York • Toronto • London

Inside Sports World Series Factbook

Published by **Visible Ink Press™**
A division of Gale Research
835 Penobscot Building
Detroit, MI 48226-4094

Visible Ink Press™ is a trademark of Gale Research

Inside Sports Magazine ©1996, is a registered trademark of Inside Sports Inc.

Most Visible Ink Press™ books are available at special quantity discounts when purchased in bulk by corporations, organizations, or groups. Customized printings, special imprints, messages, and excerpts can be produced to meet your needs. For more information, contact the Special Markets Manager at the above address. Or call 1-800-776-6265.

Art Director: Michelle DiMercurio
Front cover photograph: *Inside Sports* magazine
Back cover photograph: A/P Wide World Photos, Inc.

Library of Congress Cataloging-in-Publication Data

Cantor, George, 1941–
Inside sports World Series factbook / by George Cantor ; foreword by Mickey Lolich.
p. cm.
Includes index.
ISBN 0-7876-0821-1
1. World Series (Baseball)—History. 2. World Series (Baseball)—Miscellanea. I. Title.
GV878.4.C36 1996
796.357'646—dc20 96-26849
CIP

Printed in the United States of America

10 9 8 7 6 5 4 3 2 1

Contents

The Greatest Event in Sports

by Mickey Lolich, 1968 World Series' MVP

I don't think I can tell you the details of a single game I pitched during the 1968 season. But I'll never forget a thing about the World Series. Every big out I had to get, the crowds, the noise. In my mind, it's like it all happened the day before yesterday.

That's what it means to be in the Series. I pitched in the majors for 16 years, but what people remember about me is what I did in one week of one October in my career. I don't think that a week has gone by since I opened my donut shop in Lake Orion, a city outside of Detroit, that someone doesn't stop in and want to shake my hand and tell me how great that Series was—not only from Detroit but from all over the country.

I guess I shouldn't be any surprised. When I was growing up in Portland, Oregon, there were no big league baseball teams within a thousand miles. We'd get the Game-of-the-Week on Saturday afternoons and that was about it. But during the World Series, those games would be coming in on the TV for a solid week. Everybody would be watching. Out in Oregon the games started at about 10 o'clock in the morning, so you'd have to figure out how you were going to talk your way out of going to school in order to see them.

It was the Yankees every year back then, of course. Since I was a left-hander, my hero was Whitey Ford. Every time there was a big game, there he was on the mound for the Yanks. I used to watch him and try to think of what it would be like, standing out there, with 60,000 people in the stands, pitching in the biggest game of the year. I never dreamed it would actually happen. When I signed a minor league contract that was the biggest thing that ever happened to me. My goal was to do well and maybe get a shot at making the major leagues. Pitching in a Series, that was beyond the beyond.

Mickey Lolich smacks his first career home run in the third inning of Game 2 of the 1968 World Series. Lolich and the Tigers won the game 8-1 on the way to a seven-game victory over the Cardinals.

Years later, I beat Whitey at Yankee Stadium in an Opening Day game. The papers quoted him the next day, "I'm so sick and tired of guys who say that I was their hero coming up here and beating me." I had to laugh when I read that.

Reading this book brought back all those memories of what it was like watching Whitey pitch in the Series back in the '50s. I think that once you're out of the game you start to appreciate the historical aspects a little more than you did when you were a player. A lot of these facts that George Cantor writes about I never knew before. Other details I had forgotten—things I saw on television as a kid years ago. It was great to read about them again and remember.

Of course, it was the most fun reading about '68. There's a Louisville Slugger about three times normal size hanging over our display case in the front of my store. I put a label on it, noting that I hit my Series home run with it. I got so excited running that thing out in St. Louis that I missed first base my first time around and had to go back and touch it.

I can still see Willie Horton making the throw to get Lou Brock out, turning the Series around for us. . . . Bill Freehan blocking the plate. . . . Al Kaline getting the hit that brought us back in game five. . . . And the fans in Detroit going absolutely crazy. All those great memories.

My wife, Joyce, says I slept like a baby before the seventh game. I was more concerned with getting tickets for my friends and relatives, and making sure my dad and uncle had seats on the team plane going home that night. I knew that I was going up against Bob Gibson, who was supposed to be the best pitcher in the world. I figured, all I could do was go out there and whatever happened would happen. Maybe if I had known how that game would have effected my life all these years later, I would have been a lot more nervous about it.

I'm proud to have a place in the record books. I'm happy that so many people still remember the three games I won that year and that it brought them happiness. The Series is still the greatest event in sports. When you read this book you'll remember why.

Introduction

Miss Macholl did not often sneak radios into Latin class, but this was different. This was the seventh game of the 1955 World Series and Johnny Podres was trying to stifle the Yankees. Even in a high school in Detroit, every mind was on the struggle taking place in Yankee Stadium.

No Latin was learned that day. And when the final out was made, Miss Macholl had to rush around the room, frantically trying to shush our cheers so the administrators wouldn't be tipped off to our clandestine transmission.

Every autumn of my youth is, in fact, marked by a similar recollection; something about the World Series that lodged in my mind and stuck there forevermore.

Carl Erskine setting the strikeout record against the Yanks. Willie Mays, cap flying off, dashing into the deepest centerfield in baseball to snag the drive by Vic Wertz. The almost comic scrutiny of the ball for a telltale smudge of polish from Nippy Jones' spikes. Bill Mazeroski's shot over the leftfield wall at Forbes Field.

I never left my living room; it's as if I saw it all.

I didn't actually see my first Series game in 1966. Covering it as a baseball writer, I was seated in the auxiliary pressbox at Dodger Stadium. What this meant is that I had a wooden board in front of me for my typewriter and sat in a grandstand seat behind home plate. On one side was a badly hung-over writer from Pittsburgh. On the other was the legendary Jimmy Cannon, who talked nonstop and very fast.

The game itself wasn't much. But I was thrilled beyond words to witness it, to be a part of this event, even with the groans and gab coming from either side of me. I would also get the chance to cover the matchless Bob Gibson overpowering Boston in 1967, the miracle of the 1969 Mets, and the Blue Jays carrying the championship off the Canada for the first time in 1992.

Most memorably, I watched Gibson and Mickey Lolich hook up in 1968 for the most excruciating pitching duel I'd ever seen. The Tigers were the team of my childhood, as well as the team I covered as a writer. When Jim Northrup's drive cleared the head of Curt Flood for the winning hit, it took all my journalistic professionalism to restrain myself from leaping to my feet and jumping up and down. My heart did that for me.

The Series brings out the child in all of us. Or it should.

They play these games at night now and I don't know how many little boys and girls will grow up with memories like these. Baseball has marked its most precious moments: Adults Only. It's a mistake that will haunt it in generations to come.

Still, there is magic in these memories. It was fun reliving the games I saw, fascinating to go back into the archives and read contemporary accounts of games and events that have passed into legend. I really can't call it a labor of love, because it wasn't labor at all. Just the sense of joy that a wonderful game can bring.

George Cantor
June 6, 1996

I see great things in baseball. It's our game. The American game. It will repair our losses and be a blessing to us.

—Walt Whitman

1903

Boston (AL) 5
Pittsburgh (NL) 3

After Deacon Phillippe pitched his third straight victory in game four, jubilant Pittsburgh fans marched him around the field on their shoulders. But that was the Pirates' last parade. Behind the pitching of Big Bill Dinneen, Boston came back to win four straight and take the first World Series, a best of nine match-up.

The Preview:

The two-year squabble between the established National League and the cocky American League was finally patched up. The Americans had raided the older franchises continuously, unmercifully stripping the National teams of one star after another to gain credibility for the new league. The furious National owners tried unsuccessfully to block their rivals in court. A $2,400 salary cap initially frustrated efforts to hold on to their stars, but the concept of higher pay seemed alien to many of the owners.

The peace agreement, signed early in 1903, was an almost total victory for the American League. Most big-name players who had jumped to the new league were allowed to remain with their current teams. In addition, the move of the Baltimore franchise to New York City was upheld, on the condition that the American League not move a team into Pittsburgh. A few National League teams, most notably the New York Giants, were furious. But the era of player raids was over, and the two leagues could tend to the business of playing ball.

The Boston Pilgrims, who would become the Red Sox in 1907, had done better than most in the raids. Concentrating on their local rivals, the National League Beaneaters (the future Braves), winners of consecutive pennants in 1897–98, the

Boston's Huntington Avenue Grounds, site of the first modern World Series game.

Pilgrims picked them clean. They took star third baseman Jimmie Collins and made him their manager. They also grabbed slugging outfielders Buck Freeman and Chick Stahl, as well as a sturdy young pitcher, Bill Dinneen. From the St. Louis club they added catcher Lou Criger and the celebrated Cy Young, greatest pitcher of the era. While Young was young no more, he still had enough stuff to win over 30 games in each of his first two seasons with Boston and was 28-9 this year.

For Pittsburgh, this was the third consecutive pennant. The Pirates had lost two starting pitchers, Jack Chesbro and Jess Tannehill, in the raids. Otherwise, Pirates' owner Barney Dreyfuss had done a good job of keeping his stars happy. (Ironically, Pittsburgh had won its nickname during an earlier period of inter-league warfare when it was accused of "pirating" a player.) Even without the two lost pitchers, this staff was good enough to throw six consecutive shutouts, starting the Pirates on a 15-game June win streak that broke open the pennant race. Phillippe and Sam Leever each won 25, while left-hander Ed Doheny chipped in with 16.

Shortstop Honus Wagner (.355) won his second of eight batting titles. At 29, he was regarded as the greatest player in the game. Leftfielder Fred Clarke was just 30 but already in his seventh season as a manager. His inspirational leadership and combative style of play were credited with holding the Pirates together during the raids. These two were backed by the marvelous leadoff hitter, Ginger Beaumont (.341), and feisty third baseman Tommy Leach (.298), both of whom stood less than five foot seven.

Pittsburgh's deep pitching and the experience of playing together as a unit for three straight pennants gave the Pirates an edge. As Pilgrims fans needled Pittsburgh players in their Boston hotel lobby before the opener, Wagner retorted that Young was overaged and "we'd run him out of the National League." Injuries to Wagner and Leever were regarded as only mildly troublesome. Still, this was the first competition between the leagues. No one really knew what to expect.

The Turning Point: Game Seven, First Inning

With the Series tied at three wins apiece, Pittsburgh owner Dreyfuss decrees a day off between games six and seven. He insists it is too cold to play. What he really wants, however, is a bigger gate for a Saturday game and an added day of rest for his tiring star pitcher, Charles "Deacon" Phillippe, who pitched three complete games in four days.

He gets his big crowd. The throng of more than 17,000 overflows the grandstand. Boston's Jimmie Collins and Chick Stahl immediately take advantage of the shrunken playing surface by slamming two ground rule triples off Phillippe into the standing room crowd in the first inning for a 2-0 lead. Boston goes on to hit a Series record five triples in the game. Moreover, Phillippe's arm is not restored. Instead, it is his 36-year-old opponent, Cy Young, who benefits from the extra day of rest. Hammered in the first game, the ageless Young comes back to win his second game in the Series, 7-3. That gives the Pilgrims the Series lead and sets the stage for Dinneen to wrap it up back in Boston.

The Managers:

Collins had been the spark of the great Boston National teams of the 1890s. A gifted fielder, he was especially adept at charging bunts, a major offensive weapon of the era. He led the team in RBIs for both of its pennant-winning years and anchored the greatest defensive infield of its time. His hitting tailed off when he was asked to take on managerial duties with the Pilgrims. But he brought with him the "scientific" brand of strategic baseball for which the Beaneaters were famous.

Clarke was named manager at Louisville in 1897 by Dreyfuss, a German-born brewing magnate who then owned the

Colonels. Despite three straight ninth-place finishes, the owner took Clarke with him when he moved to Pittsburgh in 1900 and combined his team with the existing franchise there. A fierce competitor as a player, Clarke inspired his teams by example and never finished out of the first division in his first 14 seasons as manager of the Pirates.

The Heroes:

FACT:
Pitcher Big Bill Dineen establishes a strikeout record (28) that stands for 61 years.

"Big Bill" Dineen ran a grocery store in Syracuse but he was definitely second banana to the great Young on Boston's pitching staff. Regarded as little better than a journeyman, Dinneen lost eight more games than he'd won in his previous five seasons in the majors. But a 21-12 record in 1903 built his confidence. When Young faltered in the Series opener, 7-3, it was Dinneen who propped up the Pilgrims. He shut out the Pirates in game two, 3-0. After a loss, he evened the Series by beating them again in the critical sixth game, holding Pittsburgh scoreless until Boston had built up a six-run lead. He would go on to close it out by pitching his second shutout, at Boston, 3-0, in game eight. His record of 28 strikeouts would stand for 61 years.

Phillippe was valiant in defeat. Exhausted at the end and standing virtually alone for the Pirates, he started five of the eight contests and pitched complete games every time out. He remains the only man ever to win three games for a losing Series team.

Freddy Parent, Boston's tiny shortstop, was a dynamo on defense in this error-filled Series, outplaying the great Wagner. He also banged out three of the Pilgrims' record 16 triples and led all players with 11 runs produced.

The Surprises:

Ed Doheny was known as a hard drinker who could become irascible. In his two seasons with Pittsburgh, the left-hander had gone 32-12 and shored up a staff depleted by the loss of two starters. As the season wore on, Clarke found the 28-year-old Doheny's behavior increasingly erratic and dangerously out of control. By September it became apparent that he could not be used in the Series. On October 13, the day the Series ended, Doheny went berserk in his home outside Boston and attacked a faith healer with a cast-iron footrest. He was committed to an insane asylum and never played baseball again.

Sam Leever was ineffective as the second and sixth game starter because of shoulder problems. A rifle had recoiled on the schoolteacher from Goshen, Ohio, while he was trap shooting late in the season. Doheny's absence and Leever's injury forced Phillippe to take on the burden of extra starts and were critical factors in Pittsburgh's collapse in the last four games.

Honus Wagner, trying to play over a leg injury, suffered through a miserable Series. He hit only .222 and made six errors. The entire left side of Pittsburgh's infield melted, with third baseman Tommy Leach committing four more errors. His wild throw let in three runs in the 6-3 loss in game six.

The Aftermath:

Phillippe was not the same pitcher after his Series marathon, dropping to only 10 wins in 1904. Wagner and Clarke were injured for much of the year and the Pirates fell to fourth place, 19 games behind the winning Giants

Young, supposedly reaching the end of the line, would go on for another eight years and win 133 more games. More than a century after his career began, Young is still regarded as the paragon of pitching, as evidenced by the annual award named in his honor that goes to the top pitcher in both leagues. His 511 career wins appears to be a record beyond approach. However, he would never pitch in another World Series.

Dinneen went on to win 23 games in 1904, but his effectiveness tailed off quickly after that. At his retirement in 1909, his career stats showed four more losses than wins. He went on to a long career as an American League umpire, noted as one of the few willing to stand up to the temper tantrums of Babe Ruth. At his death in 1955, he was nationally eulogized as the hero of the first Series.

Notes:

Boston's secret weapon was the Royal Rooters, a group of fanatic loyalists led by a bar-owner named "Nuf Ced" McGreevey. He won his nickname by settling all baseball arguments with that terse phrase. The Rooters constantly serenaded their heroes with a song called "Tessie," a tune that Leach later confessed "drove us crazy."

The first World Series home run was hit by Pittsburgh outfielder Jimmy Sebring in the seventh inning of game one. Boston's Patsy Dougherty came back with two homers in game two. There would not be another hit in the Series for 23 games, until Joe Tinker connected for the Cubs in 1908.

FACT:
The first World Series home run was hit by Pittsburgh outfielder Jimmy Sebring in game one. After two homers by Boston's Patsy Dougherty in game two, there wouldn't be another Series round-tripper until 1908.

The Series almost was called off because of a player strike. The Pilgrims' contracts expired on September 30 and they threatened to go home unless given most of the game receipts. A compromise was reached, but they wound up with a smaller share of the swag than the losing Pirates, a scandal that resulted in Boston team officials being forced to quit.

Line Scores:

Game One—October 1

Pit—401 100 100—7	Bos—000 000 201—3
Phillippe W	Young L

Game Two—October 2

Pit—000 000 000—0	Bos—200 001 00X—3
Leever L, Veil (2)	Dinneen W

Game Three—October 3

Pit—012 000 010—4	Bos— 000 100 010—2
Phillippe W	Hughes L, Young (3)

Game Four—October 6

Bos—000 010 003—4	Pit—100 010 30X—5
Dineen L	Phillippe W

Game Five—October 7

Bos—000 006 410—11	Pit—000 000 020—2
Young W	Kennedy L, Thompson (8)

Game Six—October 8

Bos—003 020 100—6	Pit—000 000 300—3
Dinneen W	Leever L

Game Seven—October 10

Bos—200 202 010—7	Pit—000 101 001—3
Young W	Phillippe L

Game Eight—October 13

Pit—000 000 000—0	Bos—000 201 00X—3
Phillippe L	Dinneen W

1904

No Games Today

The New York Giants were still seething over the year-old agreement that ended the period of warfare between the two leagues. Owner John T. Brush felt he had been sold out. The National League permitted the Americans to put a franchise in his territory, taking money out of his pockets. Moreover, his manager, John McGraw, bore a grudge toward American League President Ban Johnson. McGraw felt that he had been treated unfairly during his term as manager of the league's Baltimore team. Now, as if to rub it in, that was the very franchise that had been transferred to New York and became the Highlanders.

The Giants broke open the National League race by midsummer. Led by two 30-game winners, Christy Mathewson and Joe McGinnity, New York coasted in, 13 games in front. Even in August, Brush had indicated that he was not bound by the agreement between the leagues and would not meet the American League champions in a playoff. This was regarded as bluster in most baseball circles.

In the American League, the race was very close, going to the final weekend before a decision. League President Johnson, recognizing the importance of a strong team in New York, had engineered a deal that sent outfielder Patsy Dougherty from defending champion Boston to the Highlanders. The Pilgrims received very little in return and their fans were outraged. But the main force in New York was Jack Chesbro,

FACT:
New York Giants' owner John T. Brush, responsible for the cancellation of the 1904 Series, was depicted in a New York newspaper cartoon as a rat scurrying down a hole while Boston manager Jimmie Collins asks him to play ball.

John McGraw, manager of the NL champion Giants, refused to validate the three-year-old American League by playing their champion, Boston, effectively canceling that year's World Series.

raided from the Pirates two years before. Armed with a devastating spitball, Chesbro won 41 games, still the league record. In the season's next-to-last game, however, Chesbro's wild pitch over his catcher's head in the ninth inning gave Boston the pennant-clinching run.

With the country primed for the second World Series, Brush astounded everyone by sticking to his guns and refusing to allow his Giants to play. Some historians believe he had painted himself into a corner. Brush believed the Highlanders would win the American League pennant and he had no intention of allowing them to build credibility by playing his established New York team. When Boston emerged as the winner, Brush still refused to back down.

McGraw added that there was no need to play Boston because everyone knew "the American League was a minor league." This seemed to ignore Boston, but McGraw was not always a great one for logic.

Pittsburgh owner Barney Dreyfuss, among others, was outraged by Brush's decision. He ostentatiously declared that he would live up to the Pilgrims' defeat of Pittsburgh in the 1903 Series and scheduled a post-season series with his fourth-place counterparts in Cleveland. The New York press ridiculed Brush, with one cartoon depicting him as a rat scurrying down a hole while Boston manager Jimmie Collins asks him to come out and play ball.

All for naught. The games stayed cancelled and 1904 remains the Series that might have been.

1905

New York (NL) 4
Philadelphia (AL) 1

Christy Mathewson throws three shutouts, Joe McGinnity adds a fourth and the Giants win the Series where the hitters forgot to show up. Philadelphia's lone victory is also a whitewash, by Chief Bender. It is a pitchers' apotheosis, unlikely ever to be matched.

The Preview

The Giants came under so much abuse for refusing to play the Series in 1904 that owner John T. Brush not only apologized but took the lead in drawing up rules that formalized the annual championship between the leagues. From now on it would be a best-of-seven series. Both leagues noted how interest and attendance had waned for the eighth game in 1903 and decided they might be going to the well too often.

> **FACT:**
> Giants' star Turkey Donlin was legendary for late night escapades and amazing recuperative powers. When night baseball was introduced decades later he remarked, "how can they take away a man's nights like that?"

As anticipated, New York repeated as National League champs, cruising 9 games in front of Pittsburgh. Manager John McGraw had put together a fast, powerful team that played the intimidation game to perfection. They battled and bullied the rest of the league, becoming the most hated team in the game. Police protection was standard for them on the road and reporters joked that they should receive combat pay for covering the Giants. The swaggering Turkey Mike Donlin, whose late night escapades were legendary but whose recuperative powers enabled him to hit .356, typified the Giants style. (In later years, when night

New York's Christy Mathewson threw a record three shutouts in the 1905 Series, no doubt making manager McGraw glad he softened his stance on postseason play. All five games were won by shutout.

baseball was introduced, the long-retired Donlin groused: "How can they take away a man's nights like that.") Shortstop Bad Bill Dahlen, whom McGraw had urged Brush to trade for as the key to the pennant, anchored the infield. Catcher Roger Bresnahan was regarded as the best in the game at his position.

Joe McGinnity and Red Ames each were 20-game winners. Above them all was Mathewson. He went 31-8 during the year and his 1.27 earned run average was a fair indication of his dominance.

The A's weren't quite as well-rounded. There wasn't a .300 hitter among them, although first-baseman Harry Davis led the league with 83 runs batted in. The American League generally was down in hitting, with Cleveland's Elmer Flick the leader with a weak .306 average. That set a low mark for batting champs that would stand for 63 years. The A's did have the league's best offense, but still they scored 163 fewer runs than the Giants. They had to fight off Chicago for most of September and won the pennant by just 2 games.

Their pitching, however, seemed to match up well. Eddie Plank and Andy Coakley were 20-game winners and going against the great Mathewson was the incredible Rube Waddell. The hardest-throwing pitcher of the era, Waddell had gone 26-11 and led his league with a 1.48 earned run average. The Giants were favorites, but baseball fans looked forward to a memorable pitching confrontation.

Turning Point: Game Four, Eighth Inning.

The A's have already lost twice to Mathewson. They have beaten McGinnity once and in this game he is in and out of trouble, trying to protect a 1-0 lead.

Finally, in the eighth a leadoff walk to Bris Lord (appropriately nicknamed "The Human Eyeball") and a single by Lave Cross put the tying run on third with two out. Socks Seybold, a dependable .270 hitter through the season, comes to the plate. But McGinnity, calling on the reserves of strength that gave him the nickname of "Iron Man," reaches back and strikes him out.

The Giants hang on for the 1-0 win and Mathewson finishes off Philadelphia with his third shutout the following day.

The Managers:

John McGraw would recall the 1905 Giants as his favorite team. Even more than the Baltimore Orioles he had played for in the 1890s, they suited his personality, scrapping for every advantage, every edge. McGraw fought with everybody and expected his players to do the same. He even picked a fight with Pittsburgh's owner Barney Dreyfuss in 1905 and was fined and suspended by the league. Baseball was war to McGraw. He dressed his team in black broadcloth for this Series to reflect its disposition.

By contrast, Connie Mack was always the gentleman. The lean New Englander, soft-spoken and unexcitable, was also one of the best judges of talent the game has ever produced. Addressing his players by their Christian names (Rube Waddell was known to him alone as George), he expected his teams to win by out-thinking their opponents. A lack of desire or mental errors were regarded by him as inexcusable.

This was the first of three Series meetings between these managers, the two top winners in the history of the game.

FACT:
Baseball was war to Giants' manager John McGraw. He dressed his team in black broadcloth for this Series to reflect its disposition.

The Heroes:

Almost one century afterwards, it is hard to comprehend the impact that Christy Mathewson had on professional sports. There had been college men before him who made their mark, and baseball was not entirely dominated by illiterate roughnecks. But the former Bucknell star quickly established himself as the greatest pitcher in the game and, moreover, a paragon of comportment.

This was a time when many Protestant ministers preached the doctrine of "muscular Christianity." The manly man who lived his faith and excelled in physical activity was the model of the age. Mathewson was its very image. Many Americans who had disdained professional sports as gutter entertainment played by lower-class Irish and German immigrants were drawn to baseball by the appeal of the tall, blue-eyed, gentlemanly Mathewson.

Sportswriters were quick to embellish the image. Matty, as he was universally known, did smoke and was a moderate drinker. He also knew his way around a poker table. But he refused to play ball on Sunday and before anyone ever had heard of a sports role model he seemed conscious of the responsibility of being in the public eye and admired by children.

While the rest of the Giants were thoroughly despised around the National League, Mathewson was cheered everywhere. In turn his teammates looked up to him. "We would do anything for that guy," declared Chief Meyers, who caught him later in his career. "He never had a harsh word for anyone. If you made an error behind him, he just patted you on the shoulder and told you that we'd get 'em next time." His chief weapons were a screwball (which he called a fadeaway curve), almost perfect control and an exceptionally retentive memory for pitches that had resulted in hits.

Mathewson's three shutouts in this Series brought him to the pinnacle of national fame. While the World Series was not yet anything like the mega-event it would become, rating only a few paragraphs each day in newspapers outside the competing cities, Matty at 25 was the idol of New York. Then as now that counted for a lot.

Iron Man McGinnity, the only other New York starter in the series, was still in his prime at 34 years of age. A tireless worker, he won his nickname by frequently pitching both games in double headers. He had racked up more than 400 innings in each of the previous two campaigns and in his seven years in the majors had never won fewer than 21 games. His 21-15 record in 1905 was not his best, but the submariner was still a formidable opponent, as evidenced by his fourth game shutout.

Roger Bresnahan was one of the few batting stars in this Series. He hit .313 and was in the middle of New York's infrequent rallies. One of the few catchers fast enough to bat leadoff, Bresnahan also was credited with inventing shin guards. He was best known as a masterful handler of pitchers. In later years, McGraw praised him as typifying the sort of smart, aggressive ballplayer he admired. He is one of the members of the Hall of Fame whose credentials are called into question by a cursory glance at his career stats. But the universal admiration in which he was held by his contemporaries indicates that he was a player one had to see to appreciate.

The Zeroes:

Just as in 1903, the critical difference in this Series may have been an eccentric left-hander who wasn't there. This time it was Philadelphia's ace, Rube Waddell, who missed the call. And it was the sort of ridiculous incident that marked most of his career that was the cause. He declared himself sartorially offended when his teammate, Andy Coakley, showed up in a straw boater on September 1, after the summer season was over. Waddell tried to remove the hat forcibly on a railway platform and while wrestling with Coakley he injured his pitching shoulder. The injury did not heal in time for the Series.

Waddell was one of the oddest figures ever to rise to stardom in the game. He was almost the antithesis of Mathewson; a heavy drinker, rowdy, profane, a man who loved chasing fire engines as much as pitching, whose roommate once insisted on a clause in his contract that prohibited Waddell from eating crackers in bed.

Nevertheless, the man could throw a baseball through a wall. He had set the season strikeout record in 1904 with 349 and was the most feared pitcher in the sport. But in this Series he turned up missing and while he may not have been enough to turn the tide his absence left the A's on the beach.

The Aftermath:

The proud McGraw ordered the words "World Champions" imprinted on the front of his team's uniforms in 1906. But the glow faded quickly. Mathewson came down with a dangerous case of diphtheria and as the season went on one key player after another went out with injuries. Even full health for all might not have been enough to catch the Cubs, who won a record 116 games. McGraw, recognizing a formidable opponent, immediately started to rebuild with younger players.

Mack did the same. His A's dropped all the way to fourth, as some of the older stars he had raided from the National League began to tail off. While both teams contended for pennants within another season, it took the A's five years and the Giants six before they got into another Series.

Notes:

Philadelphia's .161 team batting average set a mark for Series futility that stood for 61 years, until the Los Angeles Dodgers were shut out three times in 1966 and hit .142.

The A's only win was notched by Chief Bender, whom Mack described as the best clutch pitcher he ever saw. Bender's mark of 6 Series wins is exceeded only by Bob Gibson among those who did not play for the Yankees.

In Mathewson's three shutouts he walked just one man and only eight fly balls were hit to the outfield.

Line Scores

Game One, October 9

N.Y.—000 020 001—3
Mathewson W

Phil—000 000 000—0
Plank L

Game Two, October 10

Phil—001 000 020—3
Bender W

N.Y.—000 000 000—0
McGinnity L, Ames (9)

Game Three, October 12

N.Y.—200 050 002—9
Mathewson W

Phil—000 000 000—0
Coakley L

Game Four, October 13

Phil—000 000 000—0	N.Y.—000 100 00X—1
Plank L	McGinnity W

Game Five, October 14

Phil—000 000 000—0	N.Y.—000 010 01X—2
Mathewson W	Bender L

1906

Chicago (AL) 4
Chicago (NL) 2

In the first Series ever played between teams from the same city, the White Sox pull off one of the biggest upsets in sports history. The Cubs, winners of a record 116 games, were toppled by a bunch of batters so ineffectual that they have come down through the decades known as The Hitless Wonders.

The Preview:

Cubs manager Frank Chance said that his biggest job was to persuade his team that the Series wasn't going to be "a walkover." The Cubs had shredded all opposition, winning the pennant by 20 games over the Giants. It would be another two years before New York journalist Franklin Pierce Adams would pen the immortal quatrain that began: "These are the saddest of possible words, Tinker to Evers to Chance." But the Cubs' infield, with the addition of former minstrel-show performer Harry Steinfeldt at third, already was the best in the game.

Shortstop Joe Tinker came to Chicago in 1902 and lantern-jawed Johnny Evers joined him at second base late in that season. Although the two didn't speak to each other for several years, they played together flawlessly. Chance was installed at first base in 1903 and became manager two seasons later. The trio, inseparable in baseball lore, entered baseball's Hall of Fame as a unit in 1946. Shrewd trades added Steinfeldt, outfielder Jimmy Sheckard and the stub-handed Indiana coal miner, Mordecai Brown. He lost one finger and part of another in a childhood accident and has gone down in history as "Three-Finger" Brown. But he was always called "Miner" by his admiring teammates. That was the nucleus of a team that would win four pennants in five years.

"Big Ed" Walsh led the underdog "Hitless Wonder" White Sox over the crosstown Cubs by notching two victories, striking out 17 batters in 15 innings of work. His Series ERA was a stingy 1.20.

The White Sox, on the other hand, won with smoke and mirrors. They missed the pennant by 2 games in 1905 while compiling a team batting average of just .237. While that was 18 points lower than the first-place A's, they scored only four fewer runs than the pennant winners. Moreover, their pitching staff led the league with a miniscule 1.99 earned run average. Sportswriters began referring to them even then as the Hitless Wonders. All they did right was win.

That team looked like a powerhouse compared to the 1906 edition. The team average of .230 was dead last in the American League, a full 49 points behind the mark of third-place Cleveland, which also had a lower team ERA. But the White Sox put together a 19-game winning streak in August and broke ahead of their pursuers. Stumbling in September, they recovered in time to lurch home 3 games ahead of New York. Twenty-nine of their 93 victories were by one run.

It was a team of resourceful veterans. Shortstop George Davis had been an outstanding star with the Giants in the 1890s, arguably the best player not yet voted into Cooperstown. The presciently-named Fielder Jones was a defensive genius in centerfield and a brilliant field leader. Frank Isbell, bald as a cue ball, was equally at home at second or first base and hit as dependably as anyone on this squad of over-achievers.

The team's core was its pitching staff. It was anchored by the handsome Big Ed Walsh, a man described as having "the body of Adonis and the grace of a wheelbarrow." One observer called the spitballer "the only man I ever saw who could strut while standing still." Behind him were left-handers Doc White and Nick Altrock. Altrock would go on to a long career as a baseball clown at Washington's home games, but at this time he was a formidable 21-game winner.

The Cubs' staff was just as tough, however, and their superior hitting seemed to make this Series just as Chance had described, a walkover. In Chicago, the Cubs were two to one betting favorites as the Series began. Even their staunchest fans didn't really believe the Sox had a prayer. In the previous fall's intra-city exhibition series between the teams, the Cubs had won four of five. That was regarded as a likely outcome for this far more important set, too. Nevertheless, the city came to a standstill for six October days as the Series switched back and forth between the Sox' park on the South Side and the West Side, which was then the home of the Cubs.

FACT:
White Sox ace Big Ed Walsh was described as having the body of Adonis and the grace of a wheelbarrow, and another observer called him "the only man I ever saw who could strut while standing still."

Turning Point: Game Five, Fourth Inning.

With the Series tied at two wins apiece, it seems that the mighty Cubs are about to take control. They rip Ed Walsh, the Sox' top pitcher, who had shut them out two days before, for three runs in the first inning. But the Sox will not go away. They tie the game in the third, driving out Cubs starter Ed Reulbach.

Reliever Jack Pfiester opens the White Sox fourth by walking Walsh. With one out, player-manager Jones singles. That brings up Frank Isbell, who already had roped two doubles in the game. Isbell promptly lines a third into the right-center alley, bringing in the lead run.

Isbell's hit opens the gates. The supposedly weak-hitting Sox go on to an 8-6 triumph, with Isbell smashing a record fourth double in the 6th. They lay another eight spot on the shocked Cubs the next day and wrap up the Series.

The Managers:

Fielder Jones replaced Nixey Callahan as manager of the White Sox 40 games into the 1904 season. For the next three seasons, Chicago had the best overall record in the American League. Jones drove them to third, second and finally first place finishes. Faced with the arduous chore of trying to manage the team while playing centerfield, his hitting dropped off. A consistent .300 hitter with three previous pennant winners in Brooklyn and Chicago, Jones hit only .230 in 1906. But baseball men regarded the 32-year old Jones highly for his ability to squeeze every run out of his lightweights.

Frank Chance arrived in Chicago on the recommendation of Cubs outfielder Bill Lange. Both were Californians, and since that part of the country was still regarded as a far, mysterious land, ballclubs often relied on shaky scouting reports to sign players. So when Chance declared himself a catcher it took the Cubs three years to determine that he was not. Not until he was installed at first base in 1903 did his true abilities and leadership qualities begin to show. He was named manager in 1905 and quickly won the nickname "The Peerless Leader" (although his players settled for the more prosaic "Husk"). He was 29 and at the peak of his form, having led the National League in runs and stolen bases.

The Heroes:

In an upset of this magnitude, it is axiomatic that the winners must find help from unexpected quarters. The Sox' came from George Rohe. A deservedly obscure utility infielder, Rohe found himself starting at third base when Lee Tannehill had to be shifted to shortstop to replace the injured Davis. All Rohe did was rock the Cubs with triples that helped win the first and third games. The first triple led to the first run of the Series, a lead Altrock would protect in a 2-1 victory. In game three, Rohe's two-out, bases loaded triple knocked in all the runs in Walsh's 3-0 victory. Rohe stayed in the lineup even when Davis returned, and he banged out five more hits in the final two games, finishing the Series with a .333 average. Four of the Sox' supposedly puny hitters finished over .300, although the team average was only .198.

As in the previous year, this Series also featured sustained pitching brilliance. Ed Reulbach gave up just one hit in game two (it came in the seventh inning), a performance that would not be matched until another Cub, Claude Passeau, did it in 1945. Then Walsh and Brown pitched consecutive two-hitters in games three and four. At that point, the Sox had a grand total of 11 hits and still were tied at two games apiece in the Series.

FACT:
Cubs' pitcher Ed Reulbach pitched a one-hitter in game two, a feat that would not be matched until 1945.

Isbell's feat of hitting four doubles in one game, his only extra base hits in the Series, has never been equalled.

The Zeroes:

Cubs rightfielder Jimmy Sheckard was a former teammate of Jones in Brooklyn. The Sox manager must have remembered something, because his staff sat down Sheckard without a hit in 21 times at bat. Since Sheckard batted second and was counted on to set up the middle of the batting order, the Cubs' offense never got untracked.

Joining him in the shutout circle was Sox catcher Billy Sullivan, who also went zero for 21. But Sullivan had been more Hitless than any of the other Wonders, batting just .214 during the season. He was not nearly the cog that Sheckard was supposed to be; so his drought was much less damaging.

Brown also came out of the Series deeply disappointed. Although his two-hitter in game four evened things up, he was the loser of both the opener and closer. Afterwards, Brown said that his arm hadn't felt strong in the final month, but he thought he'd be able to tough it out. He couldn't get through the second inning of game six, though, and gave up six insurmountable runs.

The Aftermath:

To a bitterly disappointed Chance, the outcome confirmed what he had feared most. His Cubs had coasted for the last month of the season and were not mentally prepared to take on a team that had fought to the last weekend. Moreover, he had not detected the weariness in Brown's right arm. He determined that he would never make those mistakes again.

The White Sox went on to contend for two more seasons, despite Altrock's arm going dead the next year. But the strain of trying to win without an offense was too much, and it would be 11 years before they returned to the Series, with a team built around its hitters. Rohe, because of his brilliant Series, was made the regular third-baseman for 1907. He hit .213, was released and never played in the major leagues again.

Notes:

Altrock's opening game win for the Sox was the first by a left-hander in World Series history.

Anticipating the more famous rhyme by a couple of years, Sox fans chanted: "Tinker, Evers, Chance and Brown. They don't play ball when the Sox come 'round."

League officials were so concerned about rowdiness in this all-Chicago Series that they cracked down on base coaches. Part of their job in those years was to arouse crowd response against the opposition and umpires. But National League President Harry Pulliam issued a directive barring such behavior and castigated those who engaged in it as "fourflushers."

Line Scores:

Game One, October 9
Chi (AL)—000 011 000—2
Altrock W
Chi (NL)—000 001 000—1
Brown L

Game Two, October 10
Chi (NL)—031 001 020—7
Reulbach W
Chi (AL)—000 010 000—1
White L, Owen (4)

Game Three, October 11
Chi (AL) 000 003 000—3
Walsh W
Chi (NL)—000 000 000—0
Pfiester L

Game Four, October 12
Chi (NL)—000 000 100—1
Brown W
Chi (AL)—000 000 000—0
Altrock L

Game Five, October 13
Chi (AL)—102 401 000—8
Walsh W, White (7) Sv.
Chi (NL)—300 102 000—6
Reulbach, Pfiester (3) L, Overall (4)

Game Six, October 14
Chi (NL)—100 010 001—3
Brown L, Overall (2)
Chi (AL)—340 000 01X—8
White W

1907

Chicago (NL) 4
Detroit (AL) 0, 1 tie

The Cubs, still stinging from the previous year's upset by the White Sox, roll right over Detroit, a good hitting team with major deficiencies on defense. Frank Chance conceives a game plan that emphasizes running at every opportunity and juggles his pitching rotation brilliantly to stop the Tigers' hitters.

The Preview:

While exhibiting the good grace of a sporting loser, Chance seethed inside over the loss of 1906. Much of it he blamed on himself. Once more, his Cubs had overwhelmed the rest of the National League, beating out Pittsburgh by 17 games. Every one of their five starters had an earned run average below 2.00. The staff mark of 1.73 has never been matched.

In later years, Chance said it was the work of his middle infielders, Joe Tinker and Johnny Evers, that should be credited for such pitching excellence. While their double play totals were low by modern standards because of the different style of play, Tinker and Evers closed off the middle to Chicago's opponents. In addition, catcher Johnny Kling had the strongest throwing arm in the league.

Not a single Cub batter hit .300, with Chance coming the closest at .293. But this was an era when teams won with great defense and none could compare with Chicago's.

Detroit, a lackluster franchise for most of its short history, suddenly came alive with its new manager, Hughie Jennings, and its brilliant young star, Ty Cobb. The 20-year-old Cobb led the league in hitting at .350 and in almost every other measure of offensive prowess or behavior. His combative style on the field and his readiness to swing at anyone who crossed him already

Jack Pfiester, an emergency starter in Game 2, stopped the Tigers 3-1, allowing Miner Brown a chance to get healthy enough to pitch a shutout in the deciding game.

marked him as the most disliked player in the game. Many years later, his teammates would recall how veteran Detroit players had hazed the young Georgian mercilessly, even going so far as to saw his bats apart when he got too many hits. His already edgy personality went into the red zone full time after this treatment.

Complementing Cobb was the more even-dispositioned Sam Crawford, who finished second in hitting. A powerful batter and outstanding fielder, still the all-time career leader in triples, Crawford was the league's most accomplished centerfielder. As a thinking ballplayer he also was Cobb's match. But Detroit's infield was shaky and catcher Boss Schmidt a large question. In fact, White Sox catcher Billy Sullivan, one of the top defensive backstops in the league, predicted before the opener that this position was where the Cubs could destroy the Tigers.

While Detroit's rotation featured three 20-game winners, including the veteran Wild Bill Donovan, who was 25-4, it could not compare in quality or depth with Chicago's. In addition, the Tigers had not clinched the pennant until the final weekend, going through a grueling race with the White Sox and A's. For all these reasons, the Cubs were strong favorites to win.

Turning Point: Game One, Ninth Inning.

Those who predict that Chicago's pitching and defense will squelch the Tigers have a good case going. Orvie Overall makes a 1-0 lead stand up, as catcher Kling picks two runners off third and guns down another attempting to steal.

Detroit finally breaks through in the eighth, as Crawford doubles in two and then forces an error with alert base-running to set up a third run. Donovan starts the ninth inning cruising with a 3-1 lead.

A single, hit batsman and error cut the margin to 3-2, with the tying run on third. With two outs, weak-hitting Del Howard is sent up to hit for Tinker. Donovan works the count to 2-2 and then breaks off a low curveball. Howard swings and misses—but Schmidt can't hold on to it. The ball rolls away and Harry Steinfeldt races in to tie the game, 3-3.

Schmidt says later that Howard foul-tipped the ball. No one else sees it quite that way, though. After the passed ball (which in those days was charged as an error to the catcher) no more runs are scored. The game is called because of darkness after 12 innings.

Chicago, given a reprieve, doesn't allow the Tigers another chance. The Cubs go on to stifle Detroit, allowing the Tigers only three runs in the next four games and sweeping the Series.

The Managers:

Chance always regarded this Series as the pinnacle of his career. Visitors to his California home commented on how the 1907 trophy dominated the display area. He refused to allow a repeat of the mistake he felt had been made the previous year, allowing his club to relax with a runaway lead in the pennant race. One Chicago official said afterwards that the Series was won in the railroad cars in the season's last week. Chance went over the Tigers' lineup repeatedly with his players and laid down the plan by which they could beat them.

Hughie Jennings had been the shortstop on the old Baltimore Orioles, the friend and teammate of John McGraw. A red-haired scrapper, Jennings brought the legendary aggressiveness of his old ballclub to Detroit. Fate decreed that the perfect vessel for this attitude already was there in Cobb. Jennings, 38, became an enormous favorite in Detroit. His cry of "Ee-Yah" from the third base coaching box to incite a rally was imitated around the city, and he turned the Tigers into the league's most formidable scoring machine.

FACT:

Tigers' manager Hughie Jennings was a fan favorite. His cries of "Ee-Yah" to help incite rallies was widely imitated around Detroit.

The Heroes:

Jimmy Slagle carried many nicknames around with him in his career. Rabbit, Shorty, The Human Mosquito. Lots of names for such a little man. But it was on Slagle's shoulders that Chicago's strategy rested. As the leadoff man, his job was to get on base and start to run. Slagle did it so well that he established a record that stood for 60 years. His six stolen bases in one Series was finally swiped by Lou Brock in 1967, although it took Brock two more games than the five Slagle played.

FACT:
Cubs' leadoff man Jimmy Slaggle, also known as Rabbit, Shorty, and The Human Mosquito, stole six bases in this Series—a record that would stand for 60 years before being swiped by Lou Brock.

Slagle's baserunning keyed the Cubs, who stole 16 bases in the Series. On the other hand, Kling allowed Detroit only 6 steals and stopped Cobb totally cold. "All that talk of what Cobb was going to do made us sick," said Slagle afterwards. Evers also took a dig at the Tigers, saying that they "lost heart when they found they couldn't run and did not play up to the teaching of Jennings."

Most Chicago fans expected Miner Brown to start game two. But Chance remembered his other mistake from the previous year, in which he failed to see signs of weariness in his star pitcher. Brown had picked up a cold in his shoulder and Chance, instead, started the left-hander, Jack Pfiester. He had led the league in earned run average at 1.15, but Chance was still roundly criticized for passing up Brown. Pfiester came through with a 3-1 victory, stopping Cobb and Crawford with one hit between them, and the Cubs were rolling. When Brown was finally ready to pitch he threw a 2-0 shutout in the final game.

The Zeroes:

Cobb hit only .200 in the Series and was never a factor. Cubs fans jeered at the inferiority of American League pitching, the only possible explanation they could come up with for his dominance during the season.

The Series began in Chicago with great excitement, but by the time of the wrapup in Detroit Tiger fans deserted the team. Only 7,370 turned out for the final game, and worse was to come in 1908. Detroit had been regarded as the weakest franchise in the league and Ban Johnson had been on the verge of moving it to Pittsburgh when the agreement between the leagues disallowed such a switch in 1903. Cobb stirred things up, but as the *Spalding Baseball Guide* noted, "the heart of Michigan had not throbbed with its accustomed vigor."

The worst fears about catcher Schmidt had been realized, but Jennings insisted that Schmidt was his man, benching him only

Hughie Jennings had hoped to play his old Baltimore teammate, John McGraw, manager of the Giants. Instead, he had to be content with telegrams from McGraw and their former manager, Ned Hanlon, urging Jennings to right the scale of justice and avenge the pennant that the Cubs had "stolen" from the Giants.

The Heroes:

"I was a pretty fair shortstop," Joe Tinker would say in later years, "unless you compare me with Honus Wagner. Then we all were tramps. He was beyond everyone." Tinker definitely was more champ than tramp in 1908. He played flawlessly in the Series, never making an error (astonishing for a shortstop of that era) and turning in several defensive gems in the opening game that kept the Cubs in it. Moreover, his home run in the eighth inning of game two broke open a scoreless duel between Overall and Wild Bill Donovan. It was the first homer in a Series since 1903. That big hit followed a triple off Mathewson that put the Cubs in front in the season-ending makeup game. Tinker was known for his ability to hit Mathewson, a knack unmatched by anyone else in the game. While never a great hitter, Tinker could hit with power. He led the Cubs in RBIs during the season and in the Series, as well.

Overall was incensed when Chance lifted him from the opening game in the eighth while he was protecting a 5-4 lead in relief. But the manager brought him back the next day as the starter. A mollified Overall won 6-1 and then closed out the Series with a three-hit shutout in game five. A strapping six-footer at a time when most players were shorter, the former University of California star had the ability to dominate games. Almost one-quarter of his starts with the Cubs from 1907 to 1909 were shutouts. Arm problems ended his career at age 29, two years after his Series triumph.

This was also Cobb's shining moment in Series play. He hit .368 and had four hits in Detroit's win in game three. Moreover, the base running skills that drove opponents to distraction were also on display. In game one, he suckered centerfielder Hofman into throwing behind him at second and sped on to third to set up a run. He then forced the usually steady Evers into a throwing error by unexpectedly going for an extra base, keying another rally. In game three, he singled, stole second and third and was finally put out when a delayed steal of home failed. Although hitless in the last two games, Cobb gave the National League its first—and only—glimpse of the force he was on the field. "That young man isn't reckless as we were told," said National League President Harry Pulliam. "He's one of the wonders of baseball."

The Zeroes:

According to Detroit lore, Boss Schmidt was a very popular man among the Tigers because he had beaten the daylights out of Cobb back in 1906. Nonetheless, the former coal miner from Arkansas once more was incapable of containing the Cubs. They stole 15 more bases to go along with 16 the previous year, still the two highest totals ever run up in a five-game Series. The humiliation of Schmidt was completed with his one-for-14 performance at the plate.

> **FACT:**
> Game 5 took only one hour and 25 minutes to play.

The failure of their catcher was compounded for the Tigers by the absence of their brilliant young shortstop, Donie Bush. He had sparked the pennant run with his play but joined the team too late to qualify for the Series roster. Instead, the Tigers had to fall back on veteran Charlie O'Leary, a journeyman on defense and a nullity at bat. Again, the Tigers infield could not measure up to the Cubs.

Once more, Detroit fans deserted their team, too. New majority owner Frank Navin had erected temporary bleachers, anticipating turnaway crowds. They never showed up. One Detroit paper blamed overenthusiastic reports of sellouts (in the rival paper, of course) for the disappointing crowd of less than 11,000 in game one. By game five, with the Cubs firmly in command, the attendance shrank to 6,210, the all-time low for a Series contest. In later years, Detroit would earn a reputation as an extremely supportive baseball town. But the front-runners predominated in 1908.

The Aftermath:

After this Series, Jennings went about changing his entire infield. By the mid-point of 1909, all four starters were gone and an entirely new group brought in. With Cobb and Crawford still the best two hitters in the league, the manager felt he could win if only he could find some infielders who could catch grounders.

> **FACT:**
> Cubs win! Cubs win! Cubs win! It's been almost 90 years now since that phrase was applied to a World Series victor.

This was the ultimate for the Cubs. As of this writing almost 90 years later, the second consecutive championship would be their last—the longest famine in American sports history.

The Cubs' ownership ran into financial problems. It decided to cut corners by standing tough to the salary demands of catcher Johnny

Kling, the best at his position in the game. So the aggrieved Kling sat out the entire 1909 season, and the Cubs finished second.

Notes:

Although Wild Bill Donovan lost both of his starts, he did attain a landmark of sorts. In the second inning of game five, he became the first pitcher ever to steal a base in the Series.

Besides being played before the smallest crowd in Series history, game five was also the fastest. It took only one hour and 25 minutes.

This was the first Series in which four umpires were used. Two of them, however, just sat in the stands, ready to go in case anything happened to the two men who worked the game.

Line Scores:

Game One, October 10

Chi (NL)—004 000 105—10	Det (AL)—100 000 320—6
Reulbach, Overall (7), Brown W (8)	Killian, Summers L (3)

Game Two, October 11

Det (AL)—000 000 001—1	Chi (NL)—000 000 06X—6
Donovan L	Overall W

Game Three, October 12

Det (AL)—100 005 020—8	Chi (NL)—000 300 000—3
Mullin W	Pfiester L, Reulbach (9)

Game Four, October 13

Chi (NL)—002 000 001—3	Det (AL)—000 000 000—0
Brown W	Summers L, Winter (9)

Game Five, October 14

Chi (NL)—100 010 000—2	Det (AL)—000 000 000—0
Overall W	Donovan L

1909

Pittsburgh (NL) 4
Detroit (AL) 3

This time Detroit forced the Series all the way to its first full-term run. But the end result was the same—a third straight loss for the Tigers. The teams alternated wins, the first time this sequence ever occurred. But the difference was Pittsburgh's Babe Adams. Although he was just a spot starter, twists of fate involving illness to another pitcher and a mid-season suicide put Adams in a critical role. The 27-year-old rookie delivered with three wins.

The Preview:

To the baseball world, this Series was the great confrontation between lovable Honus Wagner ("The Flying Dutchman") and vicious Ty Cobb ("The Georgia Peach"). The greatest stars of their time, the two men were total contrasts in personalities. The easy-going Wagner was universally admired as a man who played the game hard but fair. At 35, he won his fourth straight batting title (.339) and was still regarded with awe as a shortstop. At a time when most middle infielders were quick and small, Wagner was a 200-pounder who moved with astonishing speed. His hands were so large that stones and chunks of turf would often be thrown to first along with the ball, as he scooped up everything in reach. His peers, in recalling this era years later, ranked him without question as the greatest player in the game.

FACT:
The Pirates stole 18 bases in the Series—an all-time record—led by Honus Wagner with 6.

Cobb was now 22 and already the winner of three batting titles. If there had been such a thing as a Triple Crown, Cobb would have won it in 1909. He led the league in average (.377) and homers, but RBI's were not yet recognized as an official statistic. Stats aside, his greatest

Babe Adams, a spot-starting 27-year-old rookie, beat the Tigers three times in the 1909 Series, throwing a shutout in the final game for good measure.

strength was the mental game. He played it better than anyone before or since. To Cobb, baseball was psychological warfare, and the man who succeeded in intimidating his opponent would win. The style endeared him to Detroit fans, and made him among the most hated men in America everywhere else, including his own clubhouse.

There was more than these two men, of course. Since the Pirates' run of three straight pennants in 1901–03, manager Fred Clarke remade the team while staying competitive every year. Tommy Leach was still there, although he now played the outfield instead of third. And the old horses, Deacon Phillippe and Sam Leever, were effective as spot starters. Key new players were rookie second baseman Dots Miller, outfielder Owen Wilson and the dependable Moon Gibson, who caught 150 games during the season, an extraordinary feat by a catcher even today.

The pitching staff rested on Howie Camnitz (25-6) and Vic Willis (23-11), with a broad assortment of other starters available at Clarke's call. This team broke the three-year grip Chicago had on the pennant. But it took 110 wins to do it, because the Cubs, even in a second-place year, still had enough to win 104.

The Tigers were back for the third straight time, but the faces were new. Rookie Donie Bush, who had been ineligible the previous year, was now a fixture at short, and the scrappy George Moriarty, whose temperament fit right in with Cobb and Jennings, was at third. An aggressive baserunner, Moriarty was famed for his conviction that when a runner got to third base it was his responsiblity to score in any way possible. His steals of home were legendary. An inspirational tract drawn from his ethos, "Don't Die on Third," was widely disseminated at sales meetings and among church groups. It made Moriarty a national figure.

In mid-season, Detroit traded away the colorful second baseman Germany Schaefer to get the smooth fielding Jim Delahanty. Finally, the Tigers obtained another defensive standout, first baseman Tom Jones, from St Louis, and the makeover was complete. George Mullin (29-8) was the top winner in the league, and though Wild Bill Donovan was starting to fade this still looked like a deeper Detroit pitching staff. The Series was rated about even, but national sentiment strongly favored Pittsburgh and Wagner.

The Turning Point: Game Six, Ninth Inning.

The Series has been rough, sometimes even brutal, sparked by the rivalry between Wagner and Cobb. Now it spills over into something like mortal combat. With Detroit holding a 5-3 lead and trying to send the Series to a seventh game, Pittsburgh comes up for its final turn at bat in the top of the inning.

The Pirates jump on Mullin with two singles, and then Wilson puts down a sacrifice bunt. Catcher Charlie Schmidt grabs it, his throw to first arriving at the same instant as Wilson. The runner crashes into first-baseman Jones, knocking him unconscious. As the ball rolls away, a run scores and the other runners move to third and second.

The teams hurl threats at each other over the fallen Jones and after a 10-minute delay he is carried from the field to the hospital. Sam Crawford comes in from the outfield to play first base, and the next ball is hit to him. Despite the coach's warning, Bill Abstein tries to score from third. Crawford fires a perfect throw and Schmidt tags him out. But Abstein spikes the catcher and the two men get up swinging. Umpires again have to separate the teams.

FACT:

In one rough inning, Pirate baserunners knock the Tigers' first baseman unconscious and draw blood in spikings of the catcher and third baseman. Bloodied lips and stepped-on toes are also prevalent in this Series.

Now there is one out, with the tying run, Wilson, on second. A pinch hitter strikes out as Wilson takes off for third. The throw has him out, but he, too, comes in spikes high and Moriarty goes down with blood oozing through his stockings. He has to be helped from the field, snarling curses at the Pirates. The Tigers hold on, 5-4, but the carnage has taken a toll. Half of Detroit's infield is hurt and a lot of the starch gone out of the Tigers.

When the teams come back to play the seventh game after a day off, Detroit still seems dazed. Adams beats them easily, 8-0, to win the Series.

The Managers:

Clarke was now 37 and getting close to the end as a player but he still had enough left to play in all 152 games and bat a respectable .287, while leading the league with 80 walks. He was also as irascible as ever. After playing a sinking line drive single into a triple in one game, he came back to the bench and bawled out his team for not getting on him the way they would any other player who made such a mistake. His three-run homer broke a late-inning tie and won game five.

Jennings was just three years older than Clarke but his playing days were long behind him. Instead, he tutored Bush on the mysteries of shortstop and hoped that, for once, his team's aggressiveness would compensate for its ongoing weakness at catcher.

The Heroes:

Howie Camnitz had quinsy, a severe throat inflammation and swelling. It left Pittsburgh's top winner in a weakened condition and presented a major problem for Clarke: Which of his other pitchers had a chance to stop Detroit's sluggers?

Before the opener, the new National League president, John Heydler, paid him a visit. Heydler had replaced Harry Pulliam in mid season. New York still had not forgiven Pulliam for making the Giants replay the Merkle game with the Cubs in 1908, and the abuse he took in that city was appalling. Finally, unable to stand any more, he went into his New York Athletic Club room and put a bullet through his head.

Heydler, a former Washington resident, went home for a visit late in the season and saw a mediocre Senators' pitcher, Dolly Gray, stop Detroit. Gray pitched much like Pittsburgh's Adams, although with inferior stuff. So Heydler suggested that Clarke use Adams. He had gone 12-3 during the season with a fine 1.11 ERA, so the gamble wasn't all that great. He stopped Detroit in the opener, 4-1, and came back to win again, 8-4, in game five. Then with everything on the line, he pitched a six-hit shutout in the historic seventh game.

This Series marked the peak of Wagner's career. He outhit Cobb by a convincing margin, keying Pittsburgh's third game win with three hits and three stolen bases and then breaking open the final game with a two-run triple. There was also the famous incident in which Cobb called out his intention to steal second only to have Wagner split his lip open when he tagged him in the mouth. Cobb denied it ever happened and the story does seem to be a later invention. Maybe it falls under the heading of wishful thinking.

The Zeroes:

Poor Charlie Schmidt. Once more, the opposition ran wild on him in the Series. This time it was a record 18 steals for the Pirates, led by Wagner's six. This finally ended his days as a regular catcher. The following season he was replaced as the starter by Oscar Stanage and three years later was out of the majors. Oddly enough, there were few recriminations in Detroit about his three sorry Series. Years later, he was rehired by the team as a special coach. And 37 years after his death, the ballclub donated funds in 1969 to place a stone on his previously unmarked grave in Arkansas.

This was also not a good Series for Abstein. The 24-year old Pittsburgh first baseman, in his only season as a regular, struck out 10 times in 26 at bats, committed five errors and made several baserunning mistakes. The Tigers goaded him into further miscues, riding him mercilessly, which is why he chose to spike Schmidt in the sixth game. He was traded in the off season and gone from the majors the following year.

It was also a sad farewell for Donovan. A valiant performer in earlier defeats, he won the second game with a strong 7-2 effort. But the weather turned cold for the seventh game and his aging right arm could never get loose. In three innings, he walked six men, hit another, and forced in two runs with bases-loaded walks. He was Wild Bill, indeed, although he came back with two more strong seasons with Detroit before the arm finally gave out.

The Aftermath:

This was the last Series for both Wagner and Cobb. While adding top players such as Max Carey and Wilbur Cooper, the Pirates still went into a steady decline, with both Wagner and Clarke passing from the scene. There was still one more batting title left in Wagner, but his days as the National League's dominant player were coming to a close.

Adams, however, went on to a fine career in Pittsburgh, the only member of the 1909 champions who was still there when they won again in 1925. At the age of 43, a babe no more, he was put into the fourth game of the Series to pitch the last inning for sentiment's sake. The Pirates, down three games to one, never lost again after Adams' appearance, winning three straight games and the Series.

Cobb and the Tigers never were quite able to measure up to the great Philadelphia and Boston teams that won the next seven American League pennants. While hitting was never a problem in Detroit, the Tigers always found themselves short on pitchers, a lack that would keep them out of the Series for the next 25 years. That was a long time to live with their record of three straight losses.

Notes:

This was Pittsburgh's initial season in Forbes Field, first of the new wave of ballparks that were built during the following decade. Attendance records were shattered, with game two topping the 30,000 mark for the first time in Series history. Even listless Detroit managed to sell out three of the four games there.

There was no provision for playing a seventh game, since the situation had never arisen before. So the owners simply tossed a coin and Detroit's Frank Navin won. It was decided to take a day off before playing it, even though the previous game was also in Detroit.

Moriarty got revenge for his sixth-game spiking by stepping on Pittsburgh's third baseman, Bobby Byrne, when he tried to steal third in the first inning of game seven. But both players soon were forced from the game by their wounds.

Line Scores:

Game One, October 8

Det (AL)—100 000 000—1
Mullin L

Pitt (NL)—000 121 00X—4
Adams W

Game Two, October 9

Det (AL)—023 020 000—7
Donovan W

Pitt (NL)—200 000 000—2
Camnitz L, Willis (3)

Game Three, October 11

Pitt (NL)—510 000 002—8
Maddox W

Det (AL)—000 000 402—6
Summer L, Willet (1), Works (8)

Game Four, October 12

Pitt (NL)—000 000 000—0	Det (AL)—020 300 00X—5
Leifield L, Phillippe (5)	Mullin W

Game Five, October 13

Det (AL)—100 002 010—4	Pitt (NL)—111 000 41X—8
Summers L, Willett (8)	Adams W

Game Six, October 14

Pitt (NL)—300 000 001—4	Det (AL)—100 211 00X—5
Willis L, Camnitz (6), Phillippe (7)	Mullin W

Game Seven, October 16

Pitt (NL)—020 203 010—8	Det (AL)—000 000 000—0
Adams W	Donovan L, Mullin (4)

1910

Philadelphia (AL) 4
Chicago (NL) 1

After a one-year lapse, the Cubs returned to the Series, expecting to pick up right where they left off in battering Detroit. But a young, aggressive Philadelphia squad ran the Chicago veterans right off the field behind the pitching of 30-game winner Jack Coombs. It marked the start of another of the great early baseball dynasties.

The Preview:

The core of the Cubs remained unchanged since 1906. The team averaged 106 wins a season since that time, the best five-year mark in history. There was the same rock solid infield; the dependable outfield of Wildfire Schulte, Jimmy Sheckard and Solly Hofman; the great catcher, Johnny Kling, back after sitting out a year in a contract dispute; and the pitching of Miner Brown, Orval Overall and Ed Reulbach. They terrorized the National League with a blend of finesse and rowdiness and established themselves as one of the greatest teams in the game's annals.

But age was slowly creeping up on them. Both Overall and Reulbach tailed off noticeably in 1910 and only the pitching of rookie Leonard "King" Cole (20-4) kept the staff on track. Schulte turned into a decent power hitter, leading the league with an impressive 10 home runs, and Hofman hit .325. But a late-season injury took the soul out of the Cubs.

Johnny Evers, the perfect blend of quick intelligence and nastiness, was the force that drove Chicago. As a fighter who would never hesitate to give up his 125-pound body to win a game, he was the ideal complement to manager Frank Chance. But he did it once too often this year and broke a leg sliding home. The injury forced Chance to break up his famed infield

Chief Bender, who won one game and lost one, was overshadowed by Jack Coombs in the 1910 Series despite a 1.93 ERA. Bender would star in the postseason a year later.

combination and place young Heinie Zimmerman at second. He was a good hitter who later would become a batting star, but he wasn't nearly the presence that Evers was and he lacked the intangible rapport with shortstop Joe Tinker, a sense that enabled one man to know what the other was doing without even a look.

Philadelphia was hurting, too. Starting leftfielder Rube Oldring, a .308 hitter, also broke his leg. The great lefthander Eddie Plank (16-10) was down with arm problems. But even Plank, a future Hall of Famer, was not as essential to his team as was Evers to the Cubs.

FACT:
A's manager Connie Mack never made a substitution in this Series; the same nine who started each game were the same nine who finished.

Coombs, something of a journeyman in his first four years, suddenly went 30-9 in 1910, pitching 13 shutouts and becoming the league's dominant pitcher. A star at Colby College, Coombs brought the sort of analytical intelligence to pitching that Connie Mack admired in Plank and his other great veteran, Chief Bender (23-5).

Mack shrewdly blended young stars, such as second baseman Eddie Collins and third baseman Frank Baker, with a crew of veterans, many of them members of his 1905 champions. Most baseball observers felt the young A's were untested, even though they had run away from the rest of the league by 14 1/2 games. The Cubs had been through the fire so many times it seemed that they could handle anything Philadelphia threw at them.

The Turning Point: Game Three, Third Inning.

The A's come out the box roaring, beating Chicago easily in the first two games, 4-1 and 9-3, behind Bender and Coombs. Now the Series has moved to Chicago and the injury to Plank starts to tell. Mack goes with Coombs again on just one day of rest.

This time Chicago jumps on him, scoring three runs in the first two innings. But the A's match them, hammering Reulbach for three of their own and keeping the game tied 3-3. Chance, convinced that Reulbach is not going to right himself, brings in Harry McIntyre to start the third. He pitched well in five innings of relief in game one. This time, however, Philadelphia has him solved.

With one out, Collins beats out a hit and Baker brings him home with a booming triple to right, making it 4-3 for the A's. An unnerved McIntyre hits Harry Davis with a pitch. That brings Danny Murphy to bat. Murphy, a Philadelphia native and local favorite, was the starting second baseman on the 1905 team.

When Collins came up, Mack put him in rightfield, a move that was deeply resented by many fans. Murphy had come back with a .300 season, though, and was among the league's top sluggers. This time he sends one of McIntyre's pitches into the rightfield bleachers for a three-run homer and a 7-3 Philadelphia lead.

Chance, sensing that it is slipping away, goes into a tirade, insisting the hit should have been a ground rule double. He is thrown out of the game. The beating continues as the A's go on to win 12-5. After an extra-inning loss in the fourth game, they wrap it up behind Coombs in five.

The Managers:

For Chance, this was the last time at center stage. Like most great playing managers, his effectiveness as a leader seemed dependent on his inspirational example on the field. He was now 33 years old and played in just 87 games during the season. It was his last year as the regular first baseman, and the Cubs deteriorated when he moved permanently to the bench.

Mack, the consummate bench manager, watched in quiet satisfaction as the team he had crafted reached maturity. He knew it was just the beginning. More talent was in the pipeline and at 48 he was settling into the peak years of his career.

The Heroes:

Coombs was only 27 when the season began but it was starting to look as though his career has passed him by. He joined the A's right out of college, pitching a shutout in his first start. A few weeks later, he went all the way in a 24-inning marathon and his arm never seemed to come back. In his first four years with Philadelphia, his record was only 37-35.

He never stopped tinkering with his pitches, though, and in 1910 he developed a sharper curveball and better velocity. Mack also found that more work made him more effective. He had been reluctant to use him too much because of the events of his rookie year. But Coombs won three complete games in just six days in the Series and the A's rode his right arm to the championship.

Collins joined the ballclub the same year as Coombs, although he had to play under the name of Sullivan. He was the quarterback of Columbia University's football team and would have lost his eligibility if it were known that he played professional baseball. The name change was an accepted practice in those years, but the school found out anyhow. Nonetheless, Columbia still named him manager of the baseball team in his senior year. Collins returned to the A's under his own name in 1907. Within three years, he trailed only the great Nap Lajoie as the league's top second baseman and was the catalyst of the infield that would replace the Cubs' as the greatest in the game.

Three-quarters of the legendary "$100,000 Infield" already was in place by 1910, with Collins, Baker and shortstop Jack Barry. It would be complete in two more years when Stuffy McInnis joined the team at first base. But the Cubs couldn't begin to handle even $50,000 of that infield, Collins and Baker. The two of them banged out 18 hits in the five games and hit .419.

Murphy, almost forgotten today, capped off his long career in Philadelphia with nine runs-batted-in. He joined the A's in 1902 and stayed for 12 years, endearing himself to Mack by taking his move from second base to the outfield in stride. He hit .288 for his career and was a remarkably consistent and durable performer. He was a role-player at best but understood his place in Mack's system.

FACT:
Second baseman Eddie Collins and third baseman Frank "Home Run" Baker, who formed half of the legendary "$100,000 Infield" in 1912, bang out 18 hits in this five game Series and collectively hit .419.

The Zeroes:

Zimmerman played adequately at second base but no one could replace Evers. One writer described Zimmerman's defensive skills as "playing baseball by ear." The driving intelligence that spurred the team was missing.

This was also a sad farewell for three longtime Cubs stars. Third baseman Harry Steinfeldt and catcher Kling were stopped cold on offense, hitting a combined three-for-33. In addition, Steinfeldt commited four errors and the reliable Kling could not stop Collins, who stole four bases on him. Both players were traded to Boston in the off season.

Overall, the pitching star of the 1908 Series lasted only three innings in his game-one start and never appeared again. He returned home to California after the season and retired; a brief comeback in 1913 was unsuccessful.

The Aftermath:

This was just the beginning for the A's, who would win two more championships in the next three years. By 1914, Mack would have five future Hall-of-Famers on the team and several others who were regarded as among the best players of their times.

The Cubs were headed in the other direction. While finishing second in 1911, Evers suffered what was later described as a nervous breakdown and missed most of the season. Through as a player, Chance started feuding with the owner and left after the 1912 season. Brown had just one more good season left in him. By 1918, when the Cubs returned to the Series, not a single player from this team remained.

Notes:

This was the Series inaugural for Shibe Park. The home of the A's and later the Phillies for 60 years opened in 1909. This was also the first Series in which four umpires were on the field.

One of the more incredible statistics in this Series was that Mack never made a single substitution. The nine players who started every game were the same nine who finished. Mack later criticized himself for not pinch-hitting for catcher Ira Thomas in the tight fourth game. Thomas hit into a double play and the Cubs came back to win for the only time in the Series. Mack explained that he hadn't wanted to hurt his catcher's feelings.

Coombs not only won three as a pitcher, his .385 batting average was higher than any player on the Cubs. The A's hit .316 as a team against a staff that ranked first in the league.

Line Scores:

Game One, October 17

Chi (NL)—000 000 001—1
Overall L, McIntyre (4)

Phil (AL)—021 000 01X—4
Bender W

Game Two, October 18

Chi (NL)—100 000 101—3
Brown L, Ritchie (7)

Phil (AL)—002 010 60X—9
Coombs W

Game Three, October 20

Phil (AL)—125 000 400—12
Coombs W
Pfiester (3)

Chi (NL)—120 000 020—5
Reulbach, McIntyre L (3),

Game Four, October 22

Phil (AL)—001 200 000 0—3
Bender L

Chi (NL)—100 100 001 1—4
Cole, Brown W (9)

Game Five, October 23

Phil (AL)—100 010 050—7
Coombs W

Chi (NL)—010 000 010—2
Brown L

1911

Philadelphia (AL) 4
New York (NL) 2

This was the Series in which the words "home run" entered the national consciousness as never before. Philadelphia's Frank Baker hit two of them to help the A's win the championship, earning himself a nickname that would last the rest of his life.

The Preview:

The Giants were the fastest team ever assembled. They stole a record 347 bases, with nine players in double figures, led by Josh Devore's 61. It was also a team talented enough to lead the league in hitting, but their strategy was to run the opposition to distraction.

The only holdovers from the 1905 champions were on the pitching staff—Red Ames, Hooks Wiltse and the great Christy Mathewson. Now 31 and a longtime national icon, Mathewson was probably the single most popular player in baseball. His 26-13 season was actually a fairly average campaign for him, but for the fifth straight year his earned run average was under 2.00. He was joined by Rube Marquard (24-7) who had come to the Giants as a much heralded teenager and shown little in his first three seasons. Now 22, he had become a fit ally for Mathewson. The two dominated the league's pitching stats for the season.

The rest of the lineup, while devoid of superstars, was made up of players in the John McGraw mold—tough, smart and combative. Buck Herzog, whom McGraw hated on a personal basis, was brought back from exile in Boston midway through the season and made the regular third baseman. McGraw felt he was the final piece that he needed to win. He'd forgive anything if a player could win for him.

The defending champion A's were, if anything, stronger. They had added Stuffy McInnis at first base, rounding out the $100,000 infield, and he hit .321. That was only the fourth best mark on the team, behind Eddie Collins (.365), Baker (.334) and Danny Murphy (.329). So when McInnis went down with an injury and had to be replaced by veteran Harry Davis (.197) it was serious, but far from crippling.

Jack Coombs had come back with 29 wins and Eddie Plank was 22-8, matching up well with New York's two star pitchers. With the Series back in New York City after six years (an absence that would not be exceeded for 80 years) excitement for these games was at a new high. Newspapers from the South and West sent representatives to cover the Series for the first time ever. The Giants were the closest thing in 1911 to America's team, and New York was the country's media capital before anyone knew what a media capital was. Reports of these games were transmitted to a wider audience than ever before.

FACT:
For the first time, newspapers from the South and West sent representatives to cover the Series. The Giants are the closest thing to "America's team."

The Turning Point: Game Three, Ninth Inning.

As Christy Mathewson leaves the mound after the top of the eighth, the big crowd in the Polo Grounds rises in spontaneous tribute. He already has beaten the A's in the first game, 2-1, although giving up his first run in 28 innings of Series work. After Marquard loses game two, Matty has the A's stopped again, 1-0, going into the ninth.

Because of the unusual interest in this Series, the New York papers assigned ghostwriters to the major stars. They were supposed to interview their player and write a brief column reflecting his views after each game. In game two, Marquard lost 3-1 when he gave up a two-run homer to Baker in the sixth. Mathewson's ghost accused Marquard of not following orders and pitching Baker wrong. The criticism stung and Philadelphia fans taunted Marquard with cries of "Homer" everytime he stuck his head out of the dugout in the next game.

Mathewson starts the ninth by getting the dangerous Collins on a grounder. Then it is Baker's turn. Incredibly, the lean 25-year-old pulls the ball into the cozy rightfield seats. Another home run, tying the game 1-1. The crowd sits back in shocked silence, but the Giants are furious. Fred Snodgrass intentionally spikes Baker on a play at third in the 10th inning, ripping his pants leg open. McGraw directs an unending stream of invective at him, as if he had commited blasphemy by hitting Mathewson so hard.

John McGraw had his Giants wear black uniforms for good luck, to no avail. Connie Mack's A's won in six games, setting up the third and final McGraw-Mack matchup in 1913, which Mack also won.

The game stays tied into the 11th, when three singles (including one by Baker) and two New York errors bring in two runs. Coombs, who pitched hitless ball from the third inning on, gives up a double and a run in the New York half of the inning, but the A's hold on, 3-2. Baker's second homer turns the Series around and makes him "Home Run" Baker all the way into Cooperstown.

The Managers

Far from mellowing with the years, McGraw had grown more irascible. He even got into a fistfight with Boston coach Dan McGann, a former Giant. He baited umpires, opponents, even his own players. Trying to recapture some additional nastiness, he dressed his players in the black uniforms they had worn when they had beaten the A's in 1905.

Mack remained the unflappable manipulator of talent. He even showed a rare sentimental side by allowing his injured young first baseman, McInnis, to come in for the last play of the final game. This victory, over a team he felt had humiliated him six years before, was among the sweetest of his long career.

The Heroes:

It wasn't a complete surprise that Baker emerged as a slugging star. He had, after all, led the league in home runs in 1911 with a total of 11. This had been a big hitters' year, with two players—Ty Cobb and Joe Jackson—batting over .400. In addition, Wildfire Schulte set a 20th-century record with 21 home runs in the National League. Still, baseball remained a game played for one run at a time, populated by men who slid hard, ran fast and regarded home runs disdainfully as a brainless way to score. Baker would hit 39 homers between 1911 and 1914 leading the league in every season. In another decade, that would become little more than four months work for Babe Ruth.

Baker was a taciturn individual, an independent-minded man from rural Maryland. When he disliked Connie Mack's contract offer in 1915, he simply sat out the season and then was traded to New York. He also decided to stay home in 1920, the year his wife died. He never was the same hitter after taking the first season off, however, and in four more World Series he would hit just one more home run.

This was also a triumphant series for Philadelphia's catchers, Ira Thomas and Jack Lapp. They held the Giants to a total of four stolen bases and at no time did New York's trumpeted running game become a factor.

Bender, regarded by Mack as the most dependable of his pitchers, kept alive his streak of winning in three straight Series. He pitched complete game wins in the fourth and sixth games, going on just one day of rest to wrap up the championship.

The Zeroes:

It was a washout of a Series for New York rightfielder Red Murray, the team's second leading run-producer in the season. He went 0-for-21.

Devore, the Giants' top base-stealing threat, never had much of a chance to run. He hit .167 and struck out eight times.

Herzog, the man McGraw had hand-picked as his third baseman, made three errors in game three, the last one setting up the winning run in the 11th inning.

The weatherman was also a dud. The Series was delayed for seven days between games three and four by incessant rain in Philadelphia. It remains the longest weather delay in history.

FACT:
The Series was delayed seven days by incessant rain in Philadelphia, the longest weather delay in history.

The Aftermath:

The teams had to wait two seasons for a rematch. While the Giants won again in 1912 on the same formula of speed and pitching, the A's were toppled by a young Boston team and fell to third place. But Mack was already bringing a corps of young replacements to the majors, preparing the way for a tougher run in 1913.

Notes:

The Polo Grounds grandstand burned down on the night of April 14 and the Giants played most of the season in the park of their hated inter-league rivals, the Highlanders. The ballpark was rebuilt by the end of the summer and the crowd of 38,281 at game one established a new Series record.

Giants catcher Chief Meyers was convinced for the rest of his life that somehow A's coach and first baseman Harry Davis was stealing their signs. Everytime a Giant threw a fastball, Davis would yell "It's all right." In desperation, Meyers caught the last few games without signs.

The Series matched the two best Native American ballplayers of the time. Meyers was a full-blooded California Mission Indian, who was educated at Dartmouth. Bender, who was one-quarter Chippewa, attended Carlisle Indian School and Dickinson College.

Line Scores:

Game One, October 14

Phil (AL)—010 000 000—1
Bender L

NY (NL)—000 100 100—2
Mathewson W

Game Two, October 16

NY (NL)—010 000 000—1
Marquard L, Crandall (8)

Phil (AL)—100 002 00X—3
Plank W

Game Three, October 17

Phil (AL)—000 000 001 02—3
Coombs W

NY (NL)—001 000 000 01—2
Mathewson L

Game Four, October 24

NY (NL)—200 000 000—2
Mathewson L, Wiltse (8)

Phil (AL)—000 310 00X—4
Bender W

Game Five, October 25

Phil (AL)—003 000 000 0—3
Coombs, Plank L (10)

NY (NL)—000 000 102 1—4
Marquard, Ames (4), Crandall W (8)

Game Six, October 26

NY (NL)—100 000 001—2
Ames L, Wiltse (5), Marquard (8)

Phil (AL)—001 401 70X—13
Bender W

1912

Boston (AL) 4
New York (NL) 3, 1 tie

With Christy Mathewson needing just three more outs to seal the championship for the Giants, pinch hitter Clyde Engle lifts a routine fly ball to centerfield. What happened in the next few minutes has passed into legend—analyzed, reviewed and debated ever since. It made this one of the most memorable World Series ever played and the greatest of the dead ball era.

The Preview:

The Giants were back and they were nastier than ever. This time around they had hitting to match their speed. While Chief Meyers and Larry Doyle were among the batting leaders in the National League, Fred Merkle and Red Murray hit for power. Although stealing slightly fewer bases than the record-breaking 1911 team, the Giants scored 67 more runs and won four more games.

Their outstanding pitching was stronger, too. Mathewson had one more superb year, with a 23-12 record. Rube Marquard became a national figure, running up a stunning 19-game winning streak at the start of the season. Afterwards, he was only 7-11 (26-11 overall), but Marquard's record, which still stands, helped the Giants build a cushion over the still-formidable Pirates and Cubs and coast in. In addition, New York brought up Jeff Tesreau, a 6-foot-3 right-hander from Missouri, who rounded out the rotation with a 16-7 mark.

This was a year for long winning streaks. There were two 16-game pitching skeins in the American League. Walter Johnson had one. The other was put together by Boston's Smoky Joe Wood. The 23-year-old had improved steadily in his three previous seasons, but no one had anticipated a year like this. Wood went 34-5, pitched 10 shutouts and was acclaimed the fastest pitcher in the game. "There's no man alive who can throw harder than Smoky Joe Wood," Johnson himself declared that year. He was so overpowering that McGraw refused to match Mathewson against him in game one, holding him out instead an extra day.

The Red Sox had also assembled the game's finest outfield: Tris Speaker in center, flanked by Harry Hooper and Duffy Lewis. They were called the greatest defensive combination ever. All had exceptional range and arms, but Speaker was described by his contemporaries as the greatest centerfielder ever. Moreover, he hit .383, while Lewis drove in 109 runs.

FACT:
Red Sox Series hero, pitcher Smoky Joe Wood, entered professional baseball in Kansas on a team called The Bloomer Girls; half of the players were men in drag. Ever versatile, Wood later appeared in the 1920 Series with Cleveland as an outfielder.

Boston's infield was serviceable, with former University of Vermont star Larry Gardner its anchor at third base. But the pitching was shaky behind Wood, and the Sox couldn't begin to run with the Giants. New York came in as decisive favorites.

The Turning Point: Game Eight, Tenth Inning.

There had never been a Series like this. Not only is it the second to reach full term, it goes beyond, to eight games because game two ended in an 11-inning, 6-6 tie. Three others were decided by one run. And now, incredibly, the finale goes to extra innings with the championship on the line.

Mathewson clings to a 1-0 lead into the seventh inning. Boston's Hooper had saved the game in the fifth, bracing himself against the rightfield barrier and throwing himself halfway into the seats to take a home run away from Doyle. Then in the seventh a pop fly single and two-out double by pinch hitter Olaf Henriksen ties the game. Rookie Hugh Bedient pitches heroically for Boston, but in the eighth Wood comes in. Boston will ride its star the rest of the way, win or lose. Wood already has pitched in three games, looking a little shaky at times but winning two and striking out 19.

As the game enters the tenth inning, the tension at Fenway Park is indescribable. Murray reaches Wood for a one-out double and then Merkle lines a single to center. Speaker, famed for playing the shallowest centerfield in history, comes charging in, trying to make a play on Murray who is dashing for the plate. The flawless Speaker fumbles the ball for an error, Boston's fifth of the game, and Mathewson has a 2-1 lead.

"Smokey" Joe Wood won three games for Boston in the 1912 World Series, after a regular season in which he won 34 games, 10 of them shutouts.

Then it's Boston's turn. Engle lifts a towering fly ball to center and New York's Fred Snodgrass, rated an excellent outfielder, drops it. The newspapers would call the two-base error "Snodgrass' $30,000 muff," because that was the difference between the winning and losing team's share of the Series revenue. For the rest of his life, Snodgrass indignantly denied being the goat of this Series and John McGraw, the most unforgiving of managers, agreed. He said that the error was a mechanical mistake and those are unavoidable. It was what happened next that enraged McGraw.

Snodgrass makes a partial redemption with a running catch over his head of Hooper's long drive, with Engle taking third. Mathewson, pitching too carefully, walks Steve Yerkes, putting the winning run on base. It also brings to bat the man McGraw fears most. During a post-season exhibition series between the teams two years before, McGraw was astonished at Speaker's talents and called him the equal of Ty Cobb as a player. Now here he is with the championship on the line.

The noise is deafening as Speaker lifts a harmless pop foul down the first base line. Observers say that it could have been caught by first baseman Merkle, catcher Meyers or even Mathewson. Speaker said he heard Matty call for Meyers to take it, but it is too far up the line for him to reach. Merkle, who could make the catch easily, stands frozen, only reacting when it is too late. The ball falls harmlessly and Speaker is still alive. He then lines a single to right, tying the score and sending Yerkes to third. There Gardner picks him up with a long sacrifice fly and Boston wins the game and the Series.

FACT:
The Series is decided in extra innings in an extra game on a muffed fly ball and a muffed pop up.

The Managers:

This was the most galling of losses for McGraw. He had watched his Giants battle back from a 3-1 deficit in games with his hand-picked collection of players. He was three outs from victory with his most trusted pitcher in the game. To lose once more was almost intolerable. Moreover, a change in ownership would soon restrict the degree of control McGraw had enjoyed with the team. He would win six more pennants, but seemed to become a more distant and bitter man after 1912.

Boston's Jake Stahl was almost the temperamental opposite. He had played briefly with his older brother, Chick, on the 1903 Red Sox champions after a college career at Illinois. He then was traded and returned to Boston five years later. Upon marrying a banker's daughter he retired from the game in 1910 at the age of 31. New ownership convinced him to return as manager in 1912. Stahl's ambivalence towards the game was traceable to the death of his brother, who killed himself by drinking carbolic acid while Boston's manager in 1907. Jake stayed on the job less than two years and seemed almost relieved to return to the bank for good when he was fired in mid-season of 1913.

The Heroes:

This was the pinnacle of Smoky Joe Wood's career. He entered professional baseball in Kansas in the unlikeliest of manners, playing on a team called The Bloomer Girls, half of whom were men in drag. After his spectacular 1912 season, however, it was all downhill. He hurt his thumb during the next spring training and then permanently damaged his shoulder when he tried to pitch again too soon. Even so, he led the league in earned run average in 1915 before deciding the pain was too great to go on. He ended his career as an outfielder. Although he never again pitched in the Series, he played four games in rightfield for the world champion Cleveland Indians in 1920 before becoming baseball coach at Yale.

This was also the brightest flame of Bedient's career. He had capped an 18-9 rookie year by winning Boston's other Series game and pitching strongly in three others. But his production slowly declined, he jumped to the Federal League and by 1916 was out of the major leagues for good.

Buck Herzog and Red Murray came back with brilliant Series after being shackled in 1911. They got big hits in the New York victories in games three and six, and Herzog's 12 hits and .400 batting average led both sides. It was an especially sweet comeback for Murray, who had gone hitless the previous year. His first hit this time knocked in two runs in game one.

The Zeroes:

Snodgrass never lived down his muffed fly ball in the 10th, even though McGraw gave him a $1,000 raise the following season. Interviewed more than 50 years later, he sighed over the fact that whenever he was introduced to someone the response would be, "Oh yes, you're the guy who dropped that fly ball, aren't you?" Nevertheless, "if I had the chance I'd gladly do it all over again, every bit of it," he said.

Being involved in a mistake of such magnitude might have destroyed another man. But Merkle had already been through the worst with his 1908 baserunning blunder. So his fielding hesitance this time was more of the same. He went on to play in three more World Series and was a starting first baseman for another eight years.

The Aftermath:

Giants owner John T. Brush, McGraw's close friend, died of a heart attack while traveling to California in November. His son-in-law inherited the ballclub and McGraw found himself frozen out of key personnel decisions. Trades were made without his consultation and, while they worked out well, McGraw was infuriated. While the core of the team remained the same, a rot had set in, nevertheless.

With Wood's arm injured, the Red Sox were never a serious threat in 1913. But within two seasons, a completely rebuilt pitching staff, featuring a young left hander named Ruth, brought Boston back to the top.

Notes:

This was the first season for Fenway Park and just as Pittsburgh's Forbes Field did in 1909 it had the chance to host the Series. It has remained fairly unchanged through the years, aside from the levelling of a terrace that ascended 10 feet in front of the leftfield wall.

The crowd at the decisive eighth game was a disappointing 17,000—a bit more than half of capacity. A mix-up in seats for Boston's Royal Rooters in game seven had almost resulted in a riot and many of the team's biggest supporters boycotted the next game in protest.

Olaf Henriksen, who tied game eight with a single off Mathewson, was an early pinch hitting specialist. He stayed with Boston seven years in that capacity, but this was the only Series hit he ever made. While his nickname was "Swede," he was actually born in Denmark.

Line Scores:

Game One, October 8

Bos (AL)—000 001 300—4
Wood W

N.Y.(NL)—002 000 001—2
Tesreau L, Crandall (8)

Game Two, October 9

N.Y.(NL)—010 100 030 10—3
Mathewson

Bos (AL)—300 010 010 10—3
Collins, Hall (8), Bedient (11)

Game Three, October 10

N.Y.(NL)—010 010 000—2
Marquard W

Bos (AL)—000 000 001—1
O'Brien, Bedient (9)

Game Four, October 11

Bos (AL)—010 100 001—3
Wood W

N.Y.(NL)—000 000 100—1
Tesreau L, Ames (8)

Game Five, October 12

N.Y.(NL)—000 000 100—1
Mathewson L

Bos (AL)—002 000 00X—2
Bedient W

Game Six, October 14

Bos (AL)—020 000 000—2
O'Brien L, Collins (2)

N.Y.(NL)—500 000 000—5
Marquard W

Game Seven, October 15

N.Y.(NL)—610 002 101—11
Tesreau W

Bos (AL)—010 000 210—4
Wood L, Hall (2)

Game Eight, October 16

N.Y.(NL)—001 000 000 1—2
Mathewson L

Bos (AL)—000 000 100 2—3
Bedient, Wood (8) W

1913

Philadelphia (AL) 4
New York (NL) 1

In an almost perfunctory Series following the high drama of the previous year, the A's easily dispatch New York. A crippled Giants team is simply no match for the young, powerful group from Philadelphia.

The Preview:

This was once again a Giants team that counted on speed and pitching. With that formula it easily won its third consecutive pennant, with a 12 1/2 game bulge over the Philadelphia Phillies. The three top starters were all 20-game winners, Christy Mathewson leading the way at 25-11. It was his 11th straight season with over 20 victories, and he also led the league in earned run average.

However, the Giants were no longer the run-scoring machine of former years. There was little power in the lineup and third baseman Buck Herzog was down with an injury for half the season. The Giants did come up with a new leftfielder, George Burns, who would develop into one of the club's greatest leadoff hitters. But this team was so weak that Burns batted cleanup.

The A's, in contrast, seemed rejuvenated by their season away from the top. Pressed harder than expected by Washington, they still won the pennant by 6 1/2 games. Their $100,000 infield played like a million bucks, with Frank Baker leading the league in home runs and RBIs and Eddie Collins hitting .345. In addition, the A's brought up a young catcher, Wally Schang, who strengthened that problem position. Bullet Joe Bush joined the veteran starting rotation, still anchored by Chief Bender (21-10)

Frank "Home Run" Baker led the A's with a .450 average, and led all Series sluggers with seven RBI. He also hit his third career Series homer.

and Eddie Plank (18-10). Philadelphia was the big favorite, and deservedly so.

Turning Point: Game Four, Fourth Inning.

The ageless Mathewson still had enough to stop the A's in game two, evening the Series with a brilliant, 10-inning, 3-0 win. Philadelphia came back behind Bush to win game three easily. John McGraw's only chance to slow the Philadelphia express is rookie Al Demaree. He had been a strong fourth starter at 13-4, but now he must face the relentless Bender, even though the A's veteran is pitching on just two days rest.

Demaree holds them to a narrow 1-0 lead after three—the run scoring after yet another critical error by the luckless Fred Merkle. In the fourth, the gates open. After singles by Amos Strunk and Jack Barry, Schang makes it 3-0 with the third hit of the inning. The A's catcher goes around to third on a passed ball and Bender tops a roller to first base. Poor Merkle makes his second error of the game, as Schang scores for a 4-0 lead. The

A's get two more in the fifth, and although The Chief weakens in the late innings he has enough of a margin to coast in. Even Mathewson cannot save the Giants in game five and they go out meekly, 3-1, once again on a two-hit gem by Plank.

The Managers:

John McGraw was bitterly disappointed for the third straight year. His team was forced to play over injuries to Merkle and Fred Snodgrass. At one point, he even started centerfielder Snodgrass at first base to substitute for the even more severely injured Merkle. McGraw, who accepted no excuses, regarded injuries as part of the game, an obstacle good teams overcome. But they were too much for his already outmanned Giants.

FACT:
Fred Merkle, famous for a baserunning blunder in the '08 Series and implicated in the muffed pop up in the 1912 Series, makes two errors in one game and a misjudgement in another that contribute to Giants losses. He would play on five Series-losing teams.

A third championship in four years was the summit for Connie Mack. He thoroughly enjoyed beating McGraw and was a master at deploying his superior talent. All of his pitchers threw complete games, Baker and Collins both hit over .400 and this Series passed like a cool breeze.

The Heroes:

Baker and Collins combined for 17 hits, or more than half the total collected by the entire Giants team. What they did in the first game, a 6-4 Philadelphia win, was typical. In the fourth, off Rube Marquard, Collins tripled and Baker singled him home. In the fifth, Collins walked and Baker pounded yet another Series home run. In the eighth, with the Philadelphia lead cut to a run, Collins beat out a bunt, Baker singled him to third, and he was scored on a hit by Stuffy McInnis. The Giants had no idea how to stop them.

Substitute catcher Larry McLean, forced into action by still another New York injury, to Chief Meyers, hit .500 and did a creditable job of holding Philadelphia's running game in check. But no other Giant was an offensive threat—except for Mathewson, who batted .600.

This was the last hurrah for Matty, who was again let down by lack of support in the field. His record of five World Series wins has been broken. But his 1.15 Series earned run average, established against the top lineups of the opposing league in over 100 innings of work, stands as a beacon. His four shutouts and 10 complete games are also records.

The Zeroes:

Marquard and Tesreau were battered in their appearances, giving up a combined 14 runs in 17 innings. New York had no one besides Mathewson who could begin to stop the A's. Herzog, the previous year's hitting star, was held to one for 19 (0.53), with no RBIs.

The dark cloud that hovered above the head of Merkle was still raining on him this year. His two errors helped Philadelphia win game four. The next day he let a critical run score when he tried to tag out the batter on a bunt instead of throwing to the plate to get the runner coming in from third. In Merkle's career he would play in five World Series and lose every one of them. No kidding.

FACT:
Christy Mathewson, playing in his last Series, sets career Series records for wins (5, since broken), shutouts (4), and complete games (10); his lifetime Series ERA is 1.15, covering over 100 innings.

The Aftermath:

During the season McGraw had managed to get himself embroiled in a feud with Brooklyn owner Charles Ebbets and also had a falling out with his coach, Wilbert Robinson, a longtime friend from their days with the Baltimore Orioles. An amiable, rotund chap who came to be known as Uncle Robbie, the former catcher resigned at the end of the season and crossed the East River to become manager in Brooklyn. Many historians trace the origins of the long and bitter rivalry between the Giants and Dodgers to this move.

It was also a significant post-season for Mack. The A's manager received a lucrative offer to move to New York and lead the Highlanders as an American League rival to McGraw. Mack was tempted but went to Philadelphia owner Ben Shibe to discuss it. Mack was already a 25 percent owner of the club. Shibe raised it to 50 percent, giving Mack total authority over all matters relating to the playing field. It would enable him to stay on for another 37 years, through good and horrible years, to establish the all-time record for managerial wins.

While Mack was solidifying control, McGraw was losing his. During the off season, while McGraw was out of the country on a barnstorming tour, the Giants traded Herzog to Cincinnati for outfielder Bob Bescher. The manager was outraged. Even though he would have approved the deal anyhow, because

Herzog was made manager of the Reds and Bescher was the sort of fast outfielder he liked, McGraw could not bear the fact that it was done without his seal of approval.

Notes:

For the second time in four years, Mack played the entire Series without making a single substitution. He started three pitchers and nine position players (catcher Jack Lapp played one game) and everyone in the lineup went the whole game.

This was the only Series appearance for Eddie Grant. The Harvard graduate got into two games as a pinch runner and pinch hitter. Five Octobers later, on another field, he would become the only major leaguer to die in World War I, killed in the Argonne offensive.

This marked the third time the A's and Giants had met in nine years. It would be another 76 years before the franchises played each other again—in a series delayed by an earthquake—and by then they were located across San Francisco Bay from one another.

Line Scores:

Game One, October 7

Phi (AL)—000 320 010—6
Bender W

N.Y.(NL)—001 030 000—4
Marquard L, Crandall (6), Tesreau (8)

Game Two, October 8

N.Y.(NL)—000 000 000 3—3
Mathewson W

Phi (AL)—000 000 000 0—0
Plank L

Game Three, October 9

Phi (AL)—320 000 210—8
Bush W

N.Y.(NL)—000 010 100—2
Tesreau L, Crandall (7)

Game Four, October 10

N.Y.(NL)—000 000 320—5
Demaree L, Marquard (5)

Phi (AL)—010 320 00X—6
Bender W

Game Five, October 11

Phi (AL)—102 000 000—3
Plank W

N.Y.(NL)—000 010 000—1
Mathewson L

1914

Boston (NL) 4
Philadelphia (AL) 0

All these decades later, their achievement is no less shocking. They are still called "The Miracle Braves." They were regarded as flukes, an average team that got hot at the right time. The experts said that if anyone had a chance to sweep this World Series it was surely the lordly A's. But that's not what happened.

The Preview:

The basic facts are part of the game's lore. A 4-18 start, still in last place on July 19, and then a mad rush that left every other team bobbing in their wake within 48 days. The Braves finished the season with a 60-16 streak, winning the pennant easily, with a 10 1/2 game bulge over the Giants. There had never been anything quite like it.

The Braves had been a mediocre, fifth-place team in 1913. Aside from a brash rookie shortstop, Rabbit Maranville, they didn't seem to have much talent. Some youngsters were coming up from the top farm club in Buffalo, where the owners also plucked manager George Stallings. During the off-season, the team acquired the great Johnny Evers from Chicago. But he was 33, seemingly worn down by his years of all-out combat on the field and one unsuccessful season as manager of the Cubs. He would bring experience and some sass to this young team. That didn't seem to be nearly enough.

As the team foundered, Stallings began making moves. He traded with Brooklyn for third baseman Red Smith. From St. Louis he acquired outfielders Possum Whitted and Ted Cather. All of them added punch to his weak lineup. Stallings put in inexperienced Hank Gowdy as his starting catcher. Most significantly, he

The "Miracle" Braves of 1914 were in last place as late as July 19. After an amazing stretch run, they stunned the country by not only beating the heavily-favored A's, but by sweeping them in four games.

decided to stick with a three-man pitching rotation: Dick Rudolph, Bill James and Lefty Tyler. The trio was unbeatable as summer wore on, and the Braves started to roll.

Still, the opposition was Philadelphia, champions in three of the last four seasons. The A's were as deep and talented as ever. Eddie Collins and Frank Baker remained among the top hitters in the league. Connie Mack could choose among seven starters who had won 10 games or more. But Mack was concerned about attitude, fearing that his veterans took the Braves too lightly, much as they had been underestimated by the Cubs in 1910. One Boston sportswriter, however, asked by a friend to bet $500 on the Braves at two-to-one odds, tucked the money in a drawer, instead. He thought he was doing his pal a favor. The Braves had no chance.

The Turning Point: Game Three, Tenth Inning

The Series already has stunned the baseball world. The Braves win the first two games in Philadelphia, hammering the great Chief Bender in the opener and squeezing past Eddie Plank, 1-0, in game two. Now the A's know they have a fight on their hands. Although the Series has moved to Fenway Park (loaned by the Red Sox for the occasion), the A's are still dangerous. National sentiment has swung behind Boston, but there is still a sense that Philadelphia can rise up at any time and blow them away. That time seems to be now. Tyler and Joe Bush duel through nine innings with a 2-2 tie. But Tyler is tiring. A bases loaded single by Baker brings in two Philadelphia runs in the 10th and the A's look ready to take command.

The leadoff hitter in Boston's half of the inning is Gowdy. He already had done inordinate damage. A .243 hitter during the season, he doubled and tripled off Bender in game one. His double off Bush in the second rung up Boston's first run in this game. This time he slams Bush's pitch over the head of centerfielder Jimmy Walsh. It bounces into the seats and is ruled a home run.

FACT:
A's ace Chief Bender fails to pitch a complete game for the first time in 10 Series starts.

Now the Braves trail only 4-3, and Bush is shaken. He walks Herbie Moran and Evers singles him to third. Joe Connolly brings him in with a sacrifice fly and the game is tied once more. The A's have allowed Boston to get away. They would not get another chance to stop them.

Gowdy comes up again in the 12th and belts a leadoff double. After an intentional pass, Moran puts down a bunt. Bush, trying for the play at third, throws the ball into leftfield and the Braves win again, 5-4. The fourth game is merely a mopping-up exercise. The A's are a beaten team.

The Manager:

For Stallings, this Series is the end of a long, tiring trip. Once a medical student, he left school to try for a big league career but only managed to get into seven games. He became a manager in 1897, with indifferent success. The Highlanders let him go in 1910 after a fifth-place finish and he had caught on with Buffalo. He was now 46. A Southerner when few men from that part of the country were accepted as managers, he wore a pince nez as he sat on the bench in a dark suit. He also hated to lose. He cut a player in Buffalo for whistling after a defeat, bristled at any suggestion that his Braves were not a quality team and did not hesitate to play mind games.

In his fifth World Series, Mack now had the concerns of a 50 percent owner of the A's to go along with his other problems. Attendance had fallen off despite another pennant and the new Federal League was offering big contracts to his players. He wondered whether the prospects of big money were distracting the A's. Stallings didn't help by deliberately manufacturing a feud with him over workout times and threatening to punch him in the nose—a bizarre threat to make against the gentlemanly Mack.

The Heroes:

FACT:
Boston catcher Hank Gowdy, a .243 hitter during the season, bats .545 during the Series as the Braves' hitting hero.

Heroes didn't come more unlikely than Gowdy. The redhead from Ohio had arrived in the majors as a first baseman. His first manager, John McGraw, was unimpressed and sent him off to the Braves. After three years of bouncing up and down from the minors and learning how to catch, he became a regular. None of this serves as an explanation of how he hit .545 in this Series, with a slugging average of 1.273. These are numbers on a plateau that only Babe Ruth and Lou Gehrig would reach in another era. There were reports at the time that the A's pitchers held the Braves in such disdain that they refused to go over the scouting reports. Gowdy's brilliant Series did not carry over. He hit only .247 the next year and not much more, subsequently. Later in his career, after McGraw brought him back to the Giants, Gowdy did become a strong hitter, but this Series remains an anomaly.

This was also one of the finest hours for Evers, in his last season as a regular. Although he had feuded with his former Cubs' partner at shortstop, Joe Tinker, he was invaluable in speeding the development of Maranville, who would also go to the Hall of Fame. He hit .438 in this Series and knocked in the winning runs in the final game.

For Rudolph and James, the Series was a summit they would never reach again. During the season, Rudolph had gone 27-10 and James was 26-7. Each won two more in the Series; James pitched a two-hit shutout and won in relief, and Rudolph defeated Bender in the opener, then closed out the sweep in the fourth game. Rudolph, a balding, 27-year-old New Yorker, had spent several years in the minors and his record going into this season was 14-14. While he remained a starter with Boston for five more seasons, the 29 games he won in 1914 represented almost one-quarter of his career total. For James, 22, the fall was much faster. He dropped to 5-4 in 1915, then pitched just one more game in the majors.

The Zeroes:

This was a sad farewell for the stars of Philadelphia. Baker and Collins, who had ravaged National League pitching in three previous Series, were held to a combined .231 average. Nonetheless, they did far better than the rest of the team, which hit .172.

Bender, Philadelphia's greatest clutch pitcher, was treated especially disrespectfully by Boston. He was shelled from the mound in the sixth inning of the first game, the only time in his career he failed to pitch a complete game in the Series.

The Aftermath:

The miracle wore off quickly in Boston. The trio of Rudolph, Tyler and James, who won 69 games in 1914, totalled 35 the next year. Within three seasons, the Braves were back in the second division. Stallings, known ever after as The Miracle Man, remained as manager through 1920, but the magic touch was gone.

The changes in Philadelphia, however, were quick and shocking. An angry Mack deliberately dismantled his ballclub. He sold Collins to Chicago and released Bender, Plank and Jack Coombs. Baker decided to sit out 1915 and never played another game for the A's. The changes dropped Philadelphia all the way to last place, losing 109 games. The club would not win again for 15 years, until Mack could build another powerhouse. Some baseball historians feel that Mack thought he could still win with the young players he was bringing along and realized he could not hold onto his stars with the big contracts being offered by the Federal League. Whatever the reason, the A's were history. It was a process that would be repeated with two other championship franchises in the next six years.

Notes:

The success of the Braves inspired the construction of a new Braves Field, which opened in August, 1915. The first World Series there, however, was hosted by the Red Sox, as the Braves returned the favor and loaned the American League team their stadium. It would be another 33 years before the Braves played for a championship in their home park.

It was James Gaffney, one of the Boston owners, who gave the team its enduring nickname. He was a New York contractor who was closely tied in with the Tammany Hall political machine. The symbol of Tammany was an Indian, so his ballclub became the Braves. It followed the franchise to Milwaukee and Atlanta and was responsible for the infamous "tomahawk chop" of the 1990s.

Gowdy was a hero off the field, too. He made headlines in 1918 as the first major leaguer to enlist in the armed forces when America entered World War I.

Line Scores:

Game One, October 9

Bos (NL)—020 013 010—7
Rudolph W

Phi (AL)—010 000 000—1
Bender L, Wyckoff (6)

Game Two, October 10

Bos (NL)—000 000 001—1
James W

Phi (AL)—000 000 000—0
Plank L

Game Three, October 12

Phi (AL)—100 100 000 200—4
Bush L

Bos (NL)—010 100 000 201—5
Tyler, James (11) W

Game Four, October 13

Phi (AL)—000 010 000—1
Shawkey (L), Pennock (6)

Bos (NL)—000 120 00X—3
Rudolph W

1915

Boston (AL) 4
Philadelphia (NL) 1

The Red Sox won four consecutive one-run games, including three by the same 2-1 score. Superior defense and much deeper pitching were the difference, far too much for the power-hitting of the Phillies and the pitching of the great Grover Cleveland Alexander to overcome.

The Preview:

In just three seasons, the Red Sox rebuilt their entire pitching staff. Smoky Joe Wood was still around, but he could help out only part-time because of a chronically sore shoulder. (He appeared often enough, though, to win the league's ERA title at 1.49, with a 14-5 record). Wood's injury was hardly noticed because right behind him were Rube Foster (20-8), Ernie Shore (19-8), Dutch Leonard (14-7) and rookie left hander Babe Ruth, whose 18-6 mark was the top winning percentage in the league.

Boston took advantage of Connie Mack's fire sale in Philadelphia, picking up Jack Barry in mid season and starting him at second base. Shortstop Deacon Scott, a woefully weak hitter (.201), was nonetheless a sure and steady hand in the field. Back at the same old stand in the outfield were the incomparable triumvirate of Tris Speaker, Harry Hooper and Duffy Lewis. Still, the Red Sox were pushed to the limit in the pennant race. Although they won 101 games, Detroit was right on their heels with 100. It was the first time a team had reached triple figures in victories and still failed to win a pennant.

The Phillies, by contrast, set a record for the lowest winning percentage by a pennant

FACT:
Red Sox pitcher Rube Foster pitched a 3-hitter in game two and drove in the winning run in the top of the ninth.

Red Sox outfielders (l to r) Duffy Lewis, Tris Speaker, and Harry Hooper. Lewis made a game-saving catch in Game 3 and had clutch hits in Games 3, 4, and 5. Hooper had two homers in Game 5.

winner at 90-62. No one could have predicted they would come anywhere close to that. The Phils were hurt as badly as any team by the raids of the Federal League. After a strong second-place finish in 1913, they lost the middle of their infield, as well as 27-game winner Tom Seaton. Plunging to sixth in 1914, they traded star outfielder Sherry Magee, the league's RBI champ. They also started 1915 with a rookie shortstop, not usually a formula for success, even if he was future Hall-of-Famer Dave Bancroft.

Their assets included the greatest home-run hitter baseball had ever known. Gavvy Cravath hit a record 24 during this season, the third straight year he led the league. In four years with the Phillies, he slammed 73 home runs, a slugging record that baseball experts predicted would never be broken. First baseman Fred Luderus was the team's top hitter at .315.

The Phillies also had Alexander. He went 31-10, the first of three consecutive 30-win seasons, and led the league in almost every significant pitching category. The 28-year-old Nebraskan was just coming into his prime. That he pitched in tiny Baker Bowl, the best hitters' park in the game, made his achievements even more remarkable. Excellent control, an amazing memory for hitters' weaknesses and the most deceptively relaxed delivery in the game were his weapons.

Boston feared Alexander but felt it could easily handle any of the other Philadelphia pitchers. Erskine Mayer (21-15) had slumped late in the season and Eppa Rixey (11-12) was not yet the pitcher who would make the Hall of Fame.

Turning Point: Game Three, Third Inning.

Alexander, as tough as predicted, stops the Red Sox, 3-1, in the opener. But Foster comes back with a three-hitter in game two and even drives in the winning run in a 2-1 Boston win. Now Alexander's number is up again and he is facing Leonard.

The previous year, the Red Sox allowed the Braves to use more capacious Fenway Park for the Series. Now, with the new, even larger Braves Field opened, the National League team returns the favor. The third game attendance of 42,300 is a new Series record. But Braves Field has some other features, too.

Speaker, not used to the play of light and shadow in the park, loses the first fly ball of the game in the sun. It falls for a double. Leonard pitches over that mistake. But in the third he is in trouble again. A hit and an error put two runners on. Bancroft's single gives the Phils a 1-0 lead, with two runners in scoring position. This is what Boston dreads, for Alexander is unbeatable if he gets a big lead.

Dode Paskert lifts a dangerous pop fly to short right, but Barry, running with his back to the infield, manages to grab the ball, whirl and hold the runner at third. This brings up the dangerous Cravath. He pounds Leonard's delivery to deep leftfield.

In the Baker Bowl, the drive is a certain home run. If the game had been played in Fenway, Cravath's hit would have given Philadelphia a 4-0 lead. But Braves Field has the deepest dimensions in the majors—396 feet down the leftfield line, 375 to right and 550 feet to dead center. Ty Cobb, upon seeing the place, swore "there isn't a player alive who can hit the ball out of here." In later years, the fences were moved in. But in 1915, Lewis has all the room he needs. Racing frantically for the fence, the Boston leftfielder catches the ball in full stride for the out. The threat is over.

Leonard sets down the next 20 hitters in a row, and Boston manages to eke out two runs, the winner coming in on a two-out single by Lewis in the ninth. Alexander's defeat wipes out the last hope for the Phillies. If the Braves had not been so generous with their ballpark, it might have been a different Series.

The Managers:

He may have been a college star at Holy Cross, but Bill Carrigan earned his nickname of "Rough." As Boston's catcher for six seasons and after taking over as manager from Jake Stahl midway through 1913, Carrigan was known as a man who tolerated little foolishness. The team was split when he was named manager, with several stars still backing Stahl. Carrigan won some over, bullied others into line and slowly molded the Red Sox into a championship team. At 31, he was no longer the regular catcher but he still played occasionally.

The man in the other dugout was also a catcher, although Pat Moran had retired as a player. The backup to Johnny Kling on the great Cubs teams, Moran came to Philadelphia in 1910 and was made a coach. Promoted to manager before this season began, he set out to do a selling job on the defeatist Phillies, who hadn't won anything in their entire National League history, dating back to 1883. Moran knew the personnel, and he quickly got rid of complacent older players, announced that strict new rules would be enforced and worked tirelessly with his pitchers. They took over first place in mid-July and won by 7 games.

The Heroes:

Speaker was the leader and unquestioned star of the Red Sox, but this Series belonged to his outfield partners, Lewis and Hooper. The two Californians were personally scouted and signed by former team owner Harry I. Taylor. He had married into a prominent San Francisco family and on his frequent trips to the West Coast he looked for baseball talent. By 1910 they had joined Speaker to form what is still regarded as the finest defensive outfield ever assembled.

Lewis delivered critical hits in the last three games in a row. He beat Alexander in game three with a ninth inning single. The next day he doubled in the winner. And, in the closer, his two-run homer off Rixey tied the game in the eighth. Cobb, covering the Series for a new syndicate, called it the greatest World Series performance ever. Lewis hit .444 for the Series.

Hooper almost matched him. Only a .235 hitter during the season, he was a perfect leadoff man, drawing 89 walks and trailing only Speaker in runs scored. In the Series he elevated his game. He scored decisive runs in the second and third games and hit two homers in the closer. His blast in the ninth was Boston's winning margin.

Luderus contributed the only semblance of an offense the Phillies had. The first baseman hit .438 and knocked in six of his team's 10 total runs. The Phillies hit a pathetic .182 in the five games, but without Luderus it would have been .152.

The Zeroes:

Out of hitter-friendly Baker Bowl, Cravath turned out to be just another long fly ball hitter. He got only two hits in the Series (both for extra bases, however) and in a bizarre bit of strategy was called on to bunt with the bases loaded and none out in the final game. He hit into a double play. The play was argued about in Philadelphia for decades afterwards.

Philadelphia management, trying to squeeze a few extra admissions into their tiny ballpark, put up temporary bleachers in centerfield. That backfired badly. All three Boston home runs in game five landed there, Hooper's Series winner on the bounce.

While Ruth was ready and eager to pitch, Carrigan never used him. He said later that he was looking for the right spot and had the Series gone one more game he would have matched his young lefty against Alexander. The Babe did get his first Series at bat, though, as a pinch hitter against Alexander. He pulled a grounder to first. His heroics would have to wait one more year.

The Aftermath:

The Red Sox went home in a jubilant mood. But the Federal League folded during the off season and with the competition out of the way, several stars were given massive pay cuts. Among them was Speaker. That touched off a feud with ownership that would soon turn Boston upside down.

For the Phillies, it was fun while it lasted. They remained contenders for a few years, but didn't return to the Series for 35 long seasons. Moreover, Alexander's opening game victory remained the franchise's sole World Series win until 1980.

Notes:

This was the first Series attended by a President. Woodrow Wilson went to game two in Philadelphia and threw out the first pitch.

Phillies outfielder Possum Whitted used up a career full of luck over these two seasons. In 1914 he had been traded to the Braves in time to become a part of the Miracle. In the off season, he was then moved to Philadelphia and rode the underdog into the Series again. He never played for another winner in his 11-year career.

FACT:

This was the first Series attended by a President, as Woodrow Wilson threw out the first pitch in game two.

Boston's Jack Barry, on the other hand, cashed his fifth Series check in six years. His winnings totalled $14,781, a record of affluence that left teammates aghast. His luck ran out next season. Although on the team, he went down with a leg injury in August and missed the entire Series.

Line Scores:

Game One, October 8

Bos (AL)—000 000 010—1
Shore L

Phi (NL)—000 100 02X—3
Alexander W

Game Two, October 9

Bos (AL)—100 000 001—2
Foster W

Phi (NL)—000 010 000—1
Mayer L

Game Three, October 11

Phi (NL)—001 000 000—1
Alexander L

Bos (AL)—000 100 001—2
Leonard W

Game Four, October 12

Phi (NL)—000 000 010—1
Chalmers L

Bos (AL)—001 001 00X—2
Shore W

Game Five, October 13

Bos (AL)—011 000 021—5
Foster W

Phi (NL)—200 200 000—4
Mayer, Rixey (3) L

1916

Boston (AL) 4
Brooklyn (NL) 1

Another romp for the Red Sox, featuring the emergence of Babe Ruth as a national figure and the failure of Brooklyn's odd strategy of trying to beat Boston with left handers.

The Preview:

For Boston fans, the news was a complete shock. They had been aware of acrimony between star centerfielder Tris Speaker and team management over a 50 percent salary cut, but he had come to spring training and played in exhibition games. Surely, it was being worked out. A few days before the season opener, however, Speaker was traded to Cleveland for a pair of little known youngsters and replaced by journeyman Tilly Walker. Boston's hopes for a repeat championship seemed destroyed.

The league was also stronger. At the end, only 14 1/2 games separated first place from seventh, one of the tightest finishes on record. Almost every team but the hapless A's, who set a record by losing 117 times, had a turn in first place. Boston turned it on in late summer, and even without Speaker they cruised home two games ahead of Chicago.

With Speaker gone, only third baseman Larry Gardner (.308) gave Boston any semblance of offense. But their defense was again superb, anchored by shortstop Deacon Scott, acknowledged as the best glove man in the game. It was their pitching staff, however, that was clearly superior to all. Ruth was 23-12 in his second year in the majors, trailing only Walter Johnson in wins and leading the league in ERA. Behind him came Carl Mays (19-13), Dutch Leonard (18-12), Eddie Shore (15-10) and Rube Foster (14-7).

Boston's Larry Gardner (sliding) produced six RBI from only three hits in five Series games.

For the third straight season, an unexpected winner emerged from the National League. The Robins, unlike their two immediate predecessors, hadn't suddenly shot up from the second division. They finished third in 1915. Still, no one had expected this club, composed of patched up ex-Giants, youngsters and star outfielder Zack Wheat, to accomplish much.

Manager Wilbert Robinson, a former Giants coach, brought over catcher Chief Meyers and pitcher Rube Marquard, and acquired the ill-starred Fred Merkle late in the year. The team was pressed by the Phillies and Braves most of the way, and in the final weeks the rebuilt Giants came on with a rush, winning a record 26 straight games in September. The season ended on a bizarre note, with John McGraw leaving his club in Brooklyn and accusing the players of giving up. That prompted a demand for a league investigation by Phillies manager Pat Moran. But nothing beyond McGraw's boundless rancor towards Brooklyn was ever uncovered.

Jeff Pfeffer (25-11) was the Robins' top winner, followed by Larry Cheney (18-12). They were right-handers, and Robinson got it into his head that the way to beat Boston was by throwing lefties at them. So he reached deeper into his rotation and came up with Marquard (13-6) and Sherry Smith (14-10). Maybe

Robinson figured desperate measures were needed, because the Sox were prohibitive favorites.

The Turning Point: Game Two, 14th Inning.

Robinson's southpaw strategy has limited success. Marquard is hammered in the first game, although a late Brooklyn rally makes it close, 6-5. In the second, Smith hooks up with Ruth in one of the greatest Series duels in history.

A single by Hy Myers in the first inning takes a bad hop over Walker's head and goes for an inside-the-park home run to give the Robins a 1-0 lead. The weak-hitting Scott then leads-off the Boston third with a triple, and comes in to tie the game when Ruth's hard grounder is bobbled by second baseman George Cutshaw.

FACT:
Babe Ruth pitches all 14 innings in Boston's game two win.

That's how it stays, inning after inning. Brooklyn threatens in the eighth, but Mike Mowrey is cut down by Scott when he tries to score from third on a grounder. In the last of the ninth, Boston's Hal Janvrin is thrown out at the plate by Myers from centerfield on a one-out fly ball.

In the 10th, Scott overruns third and is tagged out by shortstop Ivy Olson. In the 13th, Duffy Lewis makes a long running catch of Smith's pop fly with two out and a runner at second.

Ruth gets the Robins in the 14th, then Dick Hoblitzell leads off for Boston with his fourth walk of the game. After a sacrifice, the Sox resort to a simple expedient. The left-handed Gardner has gone zero for five against Smith, so Boston sends up pinch hitter Del Gainor, a right-handed first baseman. Robinson, whose entire strategy is based on matching lefty against lefty, refuses to make a move, and Gainor lines the winning single over third base.

The 2-1 loss puts Brooklyn in an inescapable hole and despite a third-game win by veteran Jack Coombs, the Robins' wings are clipped. But Ruth is on his way to setting a Series record for consecutive shutout innings. This entire 14-inning marathon, incidentally, was played in two hours and 32 minutes.

The Managers:

Just as Boston was getting over the loss of Speaker, manager Bill Carrigan announced in mid-summer that win or lose this was his last season. Like his predecessor, Jake Stahl, he planned to retire and take a banking job. It didn't seem credible that at 32, with a shot at consecutive championships, Carrigan could be serious. But even team owner Joe Lannin was growing weary of the game's financial demands. Like Carrigan, he was making plans to move on, too.

No such thoughts crossed the mind of Brooklyn's roly-poly Robinson. An amiable, good-natured man, he kept a loose hand on the tiller and allowed his veterans to do things their way. When the talent supply ran thin in later years this managerial style created the Daffiness Boys of the 20s, classically inept ballclubs whose forte was the comically unexpected. But the 53-year old Robinson was still surrounded by quality in 1916.

The Heroes:

Once again, Duffy Lewis and Harry Hooper emerged to spark the Sox. The two outfielders hit well above their season averages, combining for a .342 mark. On defense, Hooper cut off critical Brooklyn rallies in the first two games by throwing out baserunners from rightfield. Lewis provided extra base punch with two doubles and a triple.

Gardner, Boston's top hitter during the season and the main reason Brooklyn went with left-handed starters, was held fairly well in check. But when he broke loose, he was murder. He only had three hits, but drove in six runs, and his three-run homer in game four was the winning margin.

Scott turned in a succession of big plays in the field, including a stop and throw from deep in the hole in the ninth inning to end game one. It came after the Robins had scored four runs to trim Boston's lead to 6-5 with the bases loaded.

Boston's pitching staff was again superb, holding Brooklyn to a .200 team average. Shore won both of his starts, while Foster, who had performed brilliantly in 1915, managed to appear only once for three shutout innings.

Brooklyn's lone hitting star was rightfielder Casey Stengel, who led all batters with a .364 mark. Stengel, who was then 26, already was a confidante of Robinson's; Chief Meyers recalled years later that many members of the Robins felt that Casey was actually planning strategy with the manager's approval.

FACT:
With two out and the bases loaded in the top of the ninth, Red Sox shortstop Deacon Scott saves game one by fielding a grounder deep in the hole and throwing out Jake Daubert at first.

The Zeroes:

Brooklyn's shortstop Ivy Olson was heckled consistently by the Red Sox, who delighted in reminding him of his defensive problems when he played for Cleveland. The shaken shortstop made four errors, including two on the same play that helped Boston to its lead in game five.

Veteran Rube Marquard was the key to Robinson's left-hander strategy. But he gave up nine runs in his two starts and never was a factor for Brooklyn.

Brooklyn owner Charlie Ebbetts raised the price of grandstand tickets to his home games to $5, for which he was attacked in the press and on the streets. Ebbetts replied that his park was only half as big as Braves Field, again the venue for Boston's home games, and he needed to equalize the receipts.

The Aftermath:

Both teams went sour in 1917, with Brooklyn going into free fall and finishing seventh. Aside from Marquard, its entire pitching staff collapsed and no one aside from Wheat had a decent year at bat. Within another year, the Robins had started on a quick rebuilding job.

Boston didn't slide as far, finishing second, 9 games out of first. But veteran Jack Barry was an inadequate replacement for Carrigan, who made good on his plans to retire to Maine. More ominously, Lannin sold the club a few months after the Series to a group headed by New York theater producer Harry Frazee. The move would have enormous repurcussions on the Boston franchise and the history of baseball.

Notes:

When Jack Coombs hung on to win game three for Brooklyn it marked the first time a pitcher had earned Series victories in both the American and National Leagues. Coombs won four times for the 1910-11 A's.

Carl Mays' save of Shore's first game win was the first in the Series in 10 years. Then two games later Jeff Pfeffer did it for Brooklyn.

The Series marked the farewell of Brooklyn's Nap Rucker, the team's top winner in a long run of second division finishes. The sentimental Robinson gave his 10-year veteran a chance to mop up in game four and he pitched two shutout innings.

Line Scores:

Game One, October 7

Bkn (NL)—000 100 004—5
Marquard L, Pfeffer (8)

Bos (AL)—001 010 31X—6
Shore W, Mays (9) SV

Game Two, October 9

Bkn (NL)—100 000 000 000 00—1
Smith L

Bos (AL)—001 000 000 000 01—2
Ruth W

Game Three, October 10

Bos (AL)—000 002 100—3
Mays L, Foster (6)

Bkn (NL)—001 120 00X—4
Coombs W, Pfeffer (7) SV

Game Four, October 11

Bos (AL)—030 110 100—6
Leonard W

Brk (NL)—200 000 000—2
Marquard L, Cheney (5), Rucker (8)

Game Five, October 12

Bkn (NL)—010 000 000—1
Pfeffer L, Dell (8)

Bos (AL)—012 010 00X—4
Shore W

1917

Chicago (AL) 4
New York (NL) 2

In an unexceptional Series, the heavily favored White Sox did exactly what they were supposed to do and rolled over the Giants. Red Faber won three times for the winners.

The Preview:

Chicago's penny-pinching management went on an uncharacteristic talent hunt in 1914 and within three years they brought back a pennant. From Philadelphia, they bought Eddie Collins in 1914 for the staggering sum of $50,000. Next season, they snared the great slugger, Shoeless Joe Jackson, from Cleveland. They returned to the same well for first baseman Chick Gandil. With these veterans added to a steady supply of young talent from the minors, the White Sox just missed the pennant in 1916. By the start of the next season they were regarded as the best team in baseball.

Eddie Cicotte, throwing his famed "shine ball," a mystery substance that seemed to defy chemical analysis, went 28-12, with Lefty Williams chipping in 17 wins to Faber's 16. Even with mediocre years from Jackson and Collins, the Chicago attack was the best in the league. Centerfielder Hap Felsch had turned into a genuine threat, with a .308 average and 102 RBIs. Catcher Ray Schalk was a brilliant defensive backstop and skilled handler of pitchers. It seemed like a team capable of dominating for years.

The Giants, on the other hand, had no great stars. They did enough things right, though, to win easily in a weak National League field. This may have been the high point of John McGraw's managerial genius. The 1915 team had collapsed on him, not only dropping out of the first division for his first time in New York but all the way to last place. Trading and patching for

Chicago's Red Faber, in his only World Series, won three games in four tries. Injuries kept him out of the 1919 Series, where his presence might have had a similarly positive impact.

all he was worth, McGraw got the team back to fourth the following year, even running off a 26-game winning streak down the stretch. In 1917, he was rolling again.

Jeff Tesreau remained from his great pitching staffs of the past, but the big winners were left-handers Ferdie Schupp and Slim Sallee. Schupp had shown much promise and little control until 1916, when he suddenly harnessed his talent and compiled a staggering 0.90 ERA (although not pitching enough innings to qualify for the title). He came back this year with a 21-7 record, and Sallee, a longtime star for the Cardinals, went 18-7. New York had plucked off the Federal League's biggest star, outfielder Benny Kauff, and he had his best year at .308. From the Cubs came Heinie Zimmerman, who led the league in RBIs while struggling with the challenges of playing the hot corner.

McGraw made one miscalculation. In his eagerness to get Buck Herzog back from Cincinnati he traded young Edd Roush, who went on to a Hall of Fame career with the Reds. Nonetheless, the Giants were on top again and McGraw had put them there.

Turning Point: Game Six, Fourth Inning.

The Giants have put up a decent fight, trailing three games to two as the Series returns to the Polo Grounds. They have blanked Chicago twice here (games three and four). But Faber, who already has won once as a starter (game two) and once as a reliever (game five), is on the mound again for the Sox. Opposing him is Rube Benton, another acquisition from Cincinnati. The left-hander beat Cicotte 2-0 in game three, and Schupp, another lefty, did likewise to the White Sox in the fourth game; these are the first two shutouts pitched by left handers in Series history. McGraw, in fact, has topped his old associate, Wilbert Robinson, in the Brooklyn strategy of the previous year. Every single Series game for the Giants is started by a left-hander. McGraw is hoping for one more strong outing from Benton, with Schupp waiting to start a seventh game.

FACT:
The Giants' Rube Benton and Ferdie Schupp become the first lefthanders to throw Series shutouts, in games three and four, respectively.

It doesn't work out, and the Giants come unraveled. Zimmerman starts it with a high throw to first on Collins' roller to open the fourth. Rightfielder Dave Robertson drops Jackson's fly ball (McGraw has terrible luck through the years with his defense) and Collins scoots to third. Now the dangerous Felsch comes to bat. He bounces one right back to Benton. Collins breaks prematurely for the plate and when the pitcher throws to Zimmerman at third base, the runner is hung up. But as Zimmerman moves down the line, the rest of the Giants pull a fade. Catcher Bill Rariden has moved towards Collins and first baseman Walter Holke fails to react to the situation, leaving home uncovered. With a quick pivot, Collins bolts past Rariden and sets off for the plate with the startled Zimmerman in futile pursuit. Collins easily beats him across for the run. Gandil then singles in two more for a 3-0 lead that Chicago will not lose.

Zimmerman is castigated for his "bonehead" move, but McGraw defends his third baseman, saying that Rariden and Holke had made the mental mistakes. "Who was I supposed to throw the ball to, (Home plate umpire) Bill Klem?" Zimmerman later remarked.

The Managers:

McGraw was now 44 years old but had lost none of his zest for combat. During a spring barnstorming tour he tried to pick a fight with Ty Cobb and so enraged the Detroit star that he left his own team to continue working out elsewhere. He punched out an umpire in June and when he was suspended, McGraw accused the owner of the Phillies, his top adversary in the pennant race, of running the league. When he tried to repudiate the statement, the Baseball Writers of America demanded a hearing and McGraw was fined $1,000. He kept the kettle merrily bubbling, setting his Giants at war with the rest of the world.

Chicago's Clarence Rowland never played a game in the majors and was hired, surprisingly, right off the Dubuque farm club in 1915. He had won a lasting nickname as a "Schoolboy" in that town when trying to score from second in a pair of trousers that gradually slid down to his ankles en route. From then on, he was known as "Pants." An inoffensive sort, he was more at home in the front office than the dugout and later became a minor league executive.

FACT:
Chicago manager Clarence "Pants" Rowland earned his nickname as a schoolboy when his trousers fell down as he tried to score from second.

The Stars:

Faber didn't reach the big leagues until he was 26, coming up from Dubuque one year before Rowland. The spitballer made the most of his chance. While Cicotte was the team's top winner, Faber was a solid number two starter. They were the only two Chicago pitchers capable of stopping the Giants. Cicotte won the opener, while Faber took game two, picked up a win in relief in game five and then closed it out in the 4-2 finale. It turned out to be his only Series appearance. Arm problems took him out of the tarnished Series of 1919 and while he stayed with Chicago another 14 years, the White Sox were rarely out of the second division.

Collins had tailed off to a rather ordinary .289 average during the season, the first time in eight years he hit below .300. But he perked up, as was his wont with the A's, for the Series. He led the Sox with a .409 average and played errorless ball at second base.

Dave Robertson, the National League home run champ with 12, had an outstanding Series at bat, with 11 hits and a .500 average. Benny Kauff was held in check, though, except for game four, which he pretty much won by himself with two home runs to back Schupp's shutout pitching.

The Zeroes:

Along with his fielding woes, Zimmerman had a terrible time at bat. He hit only .120 without a single RBI. The self-styled "Zim the Great" could never live down his alleged blooper in the sixth game and was out of baseball in just two more seasons.

It was also a bad Series for Sallee, who proved to be the weak link in McGraw's parade of lefties. The Sox hammered him for 13 hits and 8 runs in his second of two starts, both of which he lost.

The Aftermath:

The Giants were still a few players short of being a consistent contender. Within four years they would pour into the Polo Grounds to create a New York dynasty. McGraw slid back to second for the next three years and bided his time.

Faber and Jackson went off to join the military for World War I in 1918 and the White Sox fell all the way to sixth. That cost Rowland his job, but as things worked out he may have been lucky.

Notes:

This marked the only World Series for a great athlete from other arenas, Olympics and football star Jim Thorpe. McGraw had signed the Native-American hero right after his 1912 triumph in Stockholm. Thorpe never quite solved big league pitching. He was listed as the starting rightfielder in game five, but when the Giants rallied in the top of the first and the Sox changed pitchers, Robertson batted for him. Thorpe never actually got into the field or to bat. But his name is in the box score.

Faber endured one of the more embarrasing incidents of his career in game two when he tried to steal third. Unfortunately, the base already was occupied by his teammate Buck Weaver.

This was the first Series in which one of the teams did not have a single player on its roster who went to the Hall of Fame. Thorpe made football's Hall, but otherwise the Giants were empty.

Line Scores:

Game One, October 6

N.Y. (NL)—000 010 000—1
Sallee L

Chi. (AL)—001 100 00X—2
Cicotte W

Game Two, October 7

N.Y. (NL)—020 000 000—2
Schupp, Anderson (2) L, Perritt (4), Tesreau (8)

Chi. (AL)—020 500 000—7
Faber W

Game Three, October 10

Chi. (AL)—000 000 000—0
Cicotte L

N.Y. (NL)—000 200 00X—2
Benton W

Game Four, October 11

Chi (AL)—000 000 000—0
Faber L, Danforth (8)

N.Y.(NL)—000 110 12X—5
Schupp W

Game Five, October 13

N.Y.(NL)—200 200 100—5
Sallee L, Perritt (8)

Chi (AL)—001 001 33X—8
Russell, Cicotte (1), Williams (7), Faber (8) W

Game Six, October 15

Chi (AL)—000 300 001—4
Faber W

N.Y.(NL)—000 020 000—2
Benton L, Perritt (6)

1918

Boston (AL) 4
Chicago (NL) 2

Almost cancelled by war and then threatened by a players' strike, this turned out to be a most forgettable round of games. Many top stars were in the military and for the only time in history the October Classic was played entirely in September. Babe Ruth and cohorts were the victors in a sloppy, mediocre Series.

The Preview:

It was only three weeks before the shortened wartime schedule ended on Labor Day that permission to hold a Series came through. Under a "Work or Fight" directive, the government had ordered all able-bodied men to either serve in war plants or the military—and that included baseball players. Washington permitted a 130-game schedule for morale purposes. After that, baseball was to pitch in and help beat the Kaiser, too. But in mid August, Gary Herrmann, chairman of the game's governing board, the National Commission, got clearance for a full-length Series, though with only one travel break in the middle.

The Cubs went into the season with high hopes. After an inglorious fifth-place finish in 1917, they swung a stunning deal for Grover Alexander, paying the Phillies $60,000 for a pitcher who had won 30 games three times in a row. But when America entered the war, Alexander was drafted. That still left the Cubs with a rotation of Hippo Vaughn (22-10), Lefty Tyler (19-9) and Claude Hendrix (19-7), more than enough to carry away the pennant in a weakened league.

Rookie shortstop Charlie Hollocher came up to hit .316 and lead the league in total bases. Chicago also got decent production from veteran outfielder Les Mann and the unfortunate first baseman Fred Merkle. They went into the Series as favorites.

Hippo Vaughn, 22-10 for the Cubs in the 1918 regular season, pitched three complete games, allowing a total of three runs . . . and took two losses for his efforts.

The Boston team was more of a cut-and-paste job. The war had taken star leftfielder Duffy Lewis and pitchers Ernie Shore and Herb Pennock. Even manager Jack Barry had gone into the service. But new owner Harry Frazee was in the chips and helped Connie Mack clean out the last of his A's stars—first baseman Stuffy McInnis, outfielder Amos Strunk, catcher Wally Schang and pitcher Bullet Joe Bush. They helped push the Red Sox to a 3 1/2 game winning margin over Cleveland.

The war had other, more far-reaching results. Because of Lewis' absence in leftfield, new manager Ed Barrow decided to experiment. He started Babe Ruth there on days he did not pitch. Ruth went 13-7 as a pitcher, but led the league in home runs with 11. More than half of the hits in his .300 average went for extra bases. This received much attention.

The Sox also had submariner Carl Mays (21-13), the defensive brilliance of shortstop Deacon Scott and rightfielder Harry Hooper. Sad Sam Jones, a throw-in from Cleveland in the 1915 deal for Tris Speaker, suddenly blossomed into a 16-5 pitcher. Even with the last four games of the Series scheduled to be played in Boston, however, the Sox were decided underdogs.

The Turning Point: Game Four, Fourth Inning.

For the third straight year, a National League team decides the way to a championship is through its lefties. Chicago starts only left handers Vaughn and Tyler for the entire six games of the Series. The Cubs figure this strategy will keep Ruth on the bench. Manager Fred Mitchell fears Ruth more than any other Boston batter and knows that the right-handed starter in leftfield is only a journeyman minor leaguer, George Whiteman, brought up as a wartime fill-in.

Even with Ruth sitting it out—aside from pitching a 1-0 shutout in the opener—Boston wins two out of three in Chicago. Now the Series is back at Fenway Park and Tyler, who stopped the Sox in game two, is pitching against Ruth. The teams are scoreless after three, but Tyler walks Dave Shean and Whiteman in the fourth. This brings up Ruth, batting seventh as a pitcher in Barrow's lineup.

For all his vaunted power, until now Ruth is hitless in 10 World Series at bats. But this time he crushes a full-count Tyler delivery. The ball finds the right-center gap for a triple, and Boston has a 2-0 lead. Tyler is virtually unhittable the rest of the way. Although the Cubs rally to tie the game in the eighth, they have to

FACT:
Babe Ruth's first Series record is a 29 2/3 inning scoreless streak. He begins his Series career hitting like a pitcher, taking 11 at bats to get a hit.

pinch hit for Tyler during the rally. Reliever Phil Douglas promptly blows the game in the bottom of the inning when he makes a wild throw on a bunt and allows the eventual winning run to score.

Ruth's blast gives Boston the edge and an insurmountable 3-1 lead in games. As a pitcher, he also extends his string of scoreless innings, started in 1916, to 29 2/3. That breaks the record set by Christy Mathewson in 1905 and 1910.

The Managers:

Both men were making their only Series appearance as managers, although Barrow would go on to head the front office of the New York Yankees in the 1920s as they established their dynasty. Barrow had come to this job after serving as president of the International League. At 50, he was now better suited to executive posts than field managing, but was still tough enough to handle a free spirit like Ruth.

Mitchell had earned a reputation as George Stallings' top assistant with the Braves. A former pitcher, albeit not a terribly distinguished one, he was given credit for shaping the 1914 staff into a championship unit. He acquired Lefty Tyler from that Boston team and under Mitchell's coaching, Tyler had his best season in the majors. Mitchell had also coached at Harvard and was respected as a keen baseball analyst.

The Heroes:

George Whiteman had two brief trials in the majors, once with the Red Sox in 1907 and with the Highlanders six years later. They amounted to a grand total of 43 times at bat. But with the war taking many regulars (although not nearly as many as World War II in the next generation), Boston called up the 35-year-old outfielder from its Toronto farm team. He did a fair job, hitting .266 for the season. But when Chicago's lefties kept Babe Ruth on the bench, he had to start all six Series games and bat cleanup. He responded by hitting .250 and figured in decisive rallies in every Boston win. Since the Red Sox scored just 8 runs in their four wins, that didn't amount to a lot. But Whiteman's key contribution was noted by every observer of the Series. Those were also the last six games he ever would play in the majors.

This was the peak of Carl Mays' career. He won two complete games for Boston, including a three-hitter in the 2-1 closer, while giving up just 2 runs. Hippo Vaughn was almost as brilliant for Chicago. He pitched three complete games and gave up just 3 runs; still, he lost twice.

FACT:
Cubs' pitcher Hippo Vaughn pitched 3 complete games and gave up only 3 runs; still, his record was 1-2.

The entire Boston defense was extraordinary, committing only one error in 53 innings: a dropped fly ball by Whiteman that did not figure in the scoring.

The Zeroes:

As far as the financial end went, the Series was a washout. With American troops engaged in heavy fighting in France, interest in baseball's championship was at its lowest point in years. The Cubs had moved into the new Wrigley Field in 1916, but optimistically scheduled their Series home games in the more capacious Comiskey Park. They couldn't sell even half the seats. The Red Sox, who had played the Series at Braves Field in 1915 and 1916, stayed home this time but also were let down at the gate.

To make things worse, it was arranged for the first four finishers in each league to share in the receipts. This was a new setup, and because interest in the games was so low the owners had dared not raise ticket prices. Much less money had to be split among many more hands. The result was a winner's share of $1,103—not even one-third of what it was the year before.

So, before game five in Boston, the players announced a strike and refused to play unless a monetary readjustment was made. Despite pleading from officials and the mayor of Boston, the players remained unmoved. It took a tearful, intoxicated speech from American League President Ban Johnson to get the game played. Fans were so offended that only 15,238 showed up for the Series finale.

Chicago rightfielder Max Flack suffered artistically as well as financially. In the game four loss, he broke up two budding rallies by getting picked off base. Then, in game six, he let in the winning runs by mangling Whiteman's line drive to him with two runners on in the third inning.

The Aftermath:

This was the twilight moment of greatness for the Boston franchise. After winning four championships in seven years, the team was destroyed by owner Harry Frazee to cover his financial losses on Broadway. Within two years, most of his top stars had been sold. The bulk of them, including Ruth, went to the Yankees and were the foundation of the first New York championship era. As of this writing, the Red Sox have never won the Series again.

The Cubs, too, went into a slide. They hit bottom in 1925, finishing last for the first time in their history. Looking for answers, the club hired minor league manager Joe McCarthy and the slow climb back to first began.

Notes:

Wrigley Field had been built for Chicago's Federal League franchise. When the league folded the Cubs snapped it up. Because of the switch of home games to Comiskey Park, the first Series in Wrigley's cozy confines wasn't held until 1929.

The U.S. Navy did its part to boost morale for the Series, granting a furlough to Boston third baseman Fred Thomas so he could play. His contribution was minimal, just a .125 average, but the gesture was appreciated.

Boston's 9 runs scored and .186 team batting average still stand as Series lows for a winning team.

Line Scores:

Game One, September 5

Bos (AL)—000 100 000—1
Ruth W

Chi (NL)—000 000 000—0
Vaughn L

Game Two, September 6

Bos (AL)—000 000 001—1
Bush L

Chi (NL)—030 000 00X—3
Tyler W

Game Three, September 7

Bos (AL)—000 200 000—2
Mays W

Chi (NL)—000 010 000—1
Vaughn L

Game Four, September 9

Chi (NL)—000 000 020—2
Tyler, Doughlas (8) L

Bos (AL)—000 200 01X—3
Ruth W, Bush (9) SV

Game Five, September 10

Chi (NL)—001 000 020—3
Vaughn W

Bos (AL)—000 000 000—0
Jones L

Game Six, September 11

Chi (NL)—000 100 000—1
Tyler L, Hendrix (8)

Bos (AL)—002 000 00X—2
Mays W

1919

Cincinnati (NL) 5
Chicago (AL) 3

The last World Series of the dead ball era almost put baseball in its grave. As many as eight members of the Chicago White Sox may have accepted money to throw games to the underdog Reds. They ended up being banned from the game for life, and an aura of mystery and betrayal still hangs over the memory of this Series.

The Preview:

After a run of rather lackluster Series, the country was hoping for better things this time around. The pace of life was accelerating in postwar America. A whiff of sin, a jazz chord, a frantic rush to good times began to permeate life in the big cities. Baseball was touched by the same sense of change. Irresistible sentiment was growing to liven up the game—to juice up the ball for more home runs and to take away the pitchers' ability to apply juice of a different nature—the spitball.

The game was still on a semi-wartime footing in 1919, with the season shortened to 140 games. As a compensating factor, it was agreed to make this a best five-of-nine Series, the first time that was tried since 1903.

The White Sox seemed clearly superior. The champions of 1917 were back at full strength and more. Eddie Collins had rebounded from two sub-par years to hit .319, and Shoeless Joe Jackson had come back from the war for his best year in Chicago, posting a .351 average

FACT:
Among the "eight men out"—accused of throwing the World Series—Shoeless Joe Jackson batted .375 and tied a Series record with 12 hits, and the eight combined for a .247 average (including 1 for 13 by pitchers Cicotte and Williams), while the rest of the team hit .186.

Eddie Cicotte, the key man in the Black Sox plan to throw the Series, hit the first batter in Game 1, signaling the gamblers that the fix was on. He lost two games in the Series.

and 96 runs batted in. Buck Weaver was now regarded as the top third baseman in the game and Hap Felsch was a consistent, powerful hitter and an exceptional centerfielder.

Red Faber, the hero of 1917, had developed arm problems and could not pitch in the Series. But Eddie Cicotte (29-7) and Lefty Williams (23-11) were the top two starters in the league, and behind them was Dickie Kerr, who had checked in at 13-7 as a rookie.

Cincinnati had slowly built itself up from the league doormat. Edd Roush, stolen from the Giants three years before, won his second batting title at .321 and played a flawless centerfield. Another ex-Giant, third baseman Heinie Groh, with his famous bottle bat, was the team's other offensive leader, at .310.

The Reds' strength was their pitching. Slim Sallee, yet a third acquisition from New York, had gone 21-7. Right in back of him were Hod Eller (20-9) and Dutch Ruether (19-6). Cincinnati won the pennant by 9 games over their benefactors from New York, while Chicago had to fight off a strong challenge from Cleveland and won by only 3 1/2 games. However, the American League was regarded as much stronger and the White Sox were heavy favorites.

Or were they? In the days before the Series, money started coming in on the Reds. A few insiders thought that was peculiar and had suspicions, especially since the reputations of some of the White Sox were less than savory. There had been whispers of a payoff to the Tigers in 1917 in the final, pennant-clinching series of the season. Nothing had ever been proven, but the stories persisted. Now with the sudden surge of East Coast money on Cincinnati, suspicions were raised as the odds lowered.

Turning Point: Game One, First Inning.

The signal has been worked out in advance. If the fix is in, starter Cicotte plunks Cincinnati's leadoff man in the ribs with his first pitch. Cicotte obliges and the fate of this Series is sealed. The Reds go on to win the opener 9-1 and then beat Williams 4-2 to send the Series back to Chicago with a two-game lead.

There are already deep suspicions among the press and in the dugouts. Chicago manager Kid Gleason knows something is wrong but thinks his players are just apathetic, taking the Reds too lightly. And when the Sox win game three at Comiskey Park, there is a sigh of relief. Now things will go as planned. But the Reds win the next two on consecutive three-hit shutouts and everyone knows it is hopeless.

FACT:

The signal has been worked out in advance. If the fix is in, White Sox pitcher Ed Cicotte will hit the first batter with his first pitch.

Cincinnati closes it out in eight games. The Series goes down as an inexplicable upset, but one with an unmistakable stench around it.

The Managers:

For William J. "Kid" Gleason this pennant was the culmination of a long career. Chicago's 52-year-old manager broke in as a pitcher with the Phillies in 1888, then became a second baseman, including one season with the legendary Orioles. He retired in 1907, coached since then and finally was given his chance to manage, with the best team in baseball on the field.

This Cincinnati team had been put together primarily by Christy Mathewson, who was named manager in 1916. But he had gone off to war late in 1918 and while serving in a chemical weapons unit in France was accidentally gassed. Still gravely ill (the incident would lead to his death five years later), Mathewson had to be replaced with Pat Moran. The former catcher repeated his achievement with the Phillies of 1915, bringing his team in first in his first year as manager.

The Heroes:

Dickie Kerr's performance in this Series won him a permanent place in the gallery of lost causes. Backed by players who had agreed to lose, he still won two games, including a three-hit shutout in game three and an extra-inning 5-4 win in game six. He won the second time even with three errors behind him by co-conspirators Swede Risberg and Hap Felsch (although Jackson threw out a runner at the plate and the winning run was produced on hits by Jackson, Weaver and Chick Gandil.)

To show how deceptive statistics can be, Jackson led all hitters with a .375 average and tied a record with 12 hits. Some historians even insist that the White Sox agreed to throw only the first two games and were playing all out the rest of the way. Investigators have pored over the play-by-play for decades, trying to spot exactly where the fixers might have let up. All that can be pointed to with assurance is this: Williams lost three times, a single-Series record. And Cicotte lost twice, including a 2-0 decision in game four in which both runs scored on his errors.

Hod Eller set a record by striking out six consecutive Chicago hitters in his fifth game shutout. Three of them were ostensibly trying, too.

The Zeroes:

Despite Jay Gatsby's assertion in F. Scott Fitzgerald's novel ("Why that's the man who fixed the World Series, old sport"), the work was probably accomplished by several syndicates based in New York and Philadelphia. Arnold Rothstein, aided by former boxing champ Abe Attell, made some of the contacts, and so did ex-pitcher Sleepy Bill Burns. The players were promised as much as $100,000, but never received more than a fraction of that sum. While a few gamblers made fortunes on the fix, others, who thought the entire team was in on it, let their winnings roll over in game three and were wiped out in Kerr's shutout.

The Aftermath:

It took a year for the story to come out. By then, first baseman Chick Gandil, the key go-between in the fix, had announced his retirement (despite a .290 season in 1919) and was playing in an outlaw league in the West. As elements of the story began to leak out from the gamblers, Cicotte broke down and confessed. The others were quickly implicated—Williams, Jackson, Felsch, shortstop Swede Risberg, utility man Fred McMullin. Weaver was also named, although he went to his grave protesting his innocence. No hard proof of a payoff or even advance knowledge of the fix was ever attached to him. Nonetheless, he shared the fate of the others.

None of the Black Sox were indicted by a grand jury. Public opinion was solidly against them, however, and Judge Kennesaw Mountain Landis, the newly named baseball commissioner, moved assertively to ban them for life. While some criticized Landis for going too fast, baseball was under the gun and needed to show its stern new face immediately.

With the heart of the team ripped away, Chicago plunged to the lower depths for years to come. It would be 40 seasons before the White Sox won another pennant. So, for the third time in seven years, a dominant franchise had been destroyed in the American League. The Yankees were poised to fill the vacuum.

Many of the Reds were convinced that they had won an honest, hard-fought Series. Roush, while suspecting something was amiss, nonetheless protested for years that Cincinnati would have won anyhow. The Reds remained a contending team throughout the 1920s but never quite measured up to the power of the Giants. They wouldn't return to the Series for 20 years.

Notes:

While this was Cincinnati's first pennant, the city's winning tradition went back further than any other. Surviving members of the 1869 Red Stockings, the first professional team in the sport, who won 56 games and tied one, attended the Series opener on their 50th anniversary.

The winner's share in this crooked Series was $5,207 a man, the largest in history and the equivalent of a season's salary for most players.

Combined Series batting average for the eight banned White Sox: .247. For the rest of the team: .186.

Line Scores:

Game One, October 1

Chi (AL)—010 000 000—1	Cin (NL)—100 500 21X—9
Cicotte L, Wilkinson (4), Lowdermilk (8)	Ruether W

Game Two, October 2

Chi (AL)—000 000 200—2	Cin (NL)—000 301 00X—4
Williams L	Sallee W

Game Three, October 3

Cin (NL)—000 000 000—0	Chi (AL)—020 100 000—3
Fisher L, Luque (8)	Kerr W

Game Four, October 4

Cin (NL)—000 020 000—2	Chi (AL)—000 000 000—0
Ring W	Cicotte L

Game Five, October 6

Cin (NL)—000 004 001—5	Chi (AL)—000 000 000—0
Eller W	Williams L, Mayer (9)

Game Six, October 7

Chi (AL)—000 013 000 1—5	Cin (NL)—002 200 000 0—4
Kerr W	Ruether, Ring (6) L

Game Seven, October 8

Chi (AL)—101 020 000—4	Cin (NL)—000 001 000—1
Cicotte W	Sallee L, Fisher (5), Luque (6)

Game Eight, October 9

Cin (NL)—410 013 010—10	Chi (AL)—001 000 040—5
Eller W	Williams L, James (1), Wilkinson (6)

1920

Cleveland (AL) 5
Brooklyn (NL) 2

The first World Series of the Jazz Age opened just a few days after the worst scandal in baseball history was uncovered. The deceit of the Black Sox had come to light in the last week of September. Fortunately, Cleveland's first championship had enough big moments to help blot out some of the stains.

The Preview:

When Tris Speaker was traded to Cleveland before the 1916 season, the centerfielder refused to report unless he was given a percentage of the purchase price. Actually, he didn't want to show up at all. The franchise had a bad reputation as a demoralized organization that didn't want to spend the money to win.

With Speaker in the lineup, the Indians began a steady ascent to the top of the league. They finished .500 in his first season, and within two years were challenging for the pennant. A stream of young talent joined the team, led by infielders Ray Chapman and Billy Wambsganss, catcher Steve O'Neill, and pitchers Stan Coveleski and Jim Bagby. At Speaker's behest, Cleveland traded for his old Boston teammate, third baseman Larry Gardner. Coming along as a throw-in was young outfielder Charlie Jamieson, who would quickly develop into a fine leadoff hitter.

By 1920, these elements melded into a team that outlasted Chicago and New York in a fierce three-way battle. Speaker had struggled after being named manager early in 1919, but he wore the burden lightly this season. He hit .388, joining six other Indians' regulars over the .300 mark in the brave new world of the lively ball. Bagby had a career year with a 31-12 record, but Speaker still regarded Coveleski (24-14) as his most reliable starter.

Cleveland's Bill Wambsganss completed the first, and so far only, unassisted triple play in Series history. He did not fare as well at the bat, however, hitting a paltry .154 in seven games.

In August, however, it almost came undone. During a critical series with the Yankees, shortstop Chapman was beaned by Carl Mays and died the following morning. Speaker, faced with a daunting test of his leadership, pulled the team together after the tragedy. Moreover, the player called up as a replacement was Joe Sewell, who would become a Hall of Fame shortstop. Under unrelenting pressure, the rookie hit .329 down the stretch. The White Sox, with the previous year's Series fix about to be made public, faded, and Cleveland coasted home with a two-game edge.

Brooklyn was another in a succession of National League surprises. A fifth place team in 1919, it developed the deepest pitching staff in the league. Led by young spitballer Burleigh Grimes (23-11), the Robins also held over Jeff Pfeffer, Rube Marquard and Sherry Smith from the pennant winners of 1916.

But their hitters could not compete with the home run circus in the American League, where Babe Ruth's total of 54 was more than all but one major league team could manage. The Robins still had a dead ball style of attack, with Zack Wheat topping it out at a .328 average and 9 homers. Hy Myers added a little help

(.304, 80 RBIs), but this was a team built on defense. They were decided underdogs going into the Series, which again was a best five of nine.

The Turning Point: Game Five, First Inning

The Robins stun Cleveland by taking two out of three at Ebbets Field, a shutout by Grimes and a three-hitter by Smith. Coveleski evens things up with a 5-1 win at League Park. With the next three also scheduled in Cleveland, game five is decisive.

FACT:
In game five, the first grand slam in Series history is hit by Cleveland outfielder Elmer Smith, and Cleveland's Jim Bagby becomes the first pitcher to hit a Series homer.

Cleveland sends out its big winner, Bagby, while Brooklyn comes back with Grimes. The spitballer is pitching with a full three days rest, but it quickly becomes apparent that he is off. Jamieson and Wambsganss open with singles, and Grimes falls down trying to make a play on Speaker's sacrifice bunt, loading the bases.

This brings up rightfielder Elmer Smith, 29 years old and on his second go-round with the Indians. While no Ruth, he led the team with 12 home runs and knocked in 103. But he hadn't hit the ball out of the infield in four tries against Grimes in game two. This time he drives a rising liner that easily clears the rightfield fence. The first Series of the lively ball era, appropriately, features the first Series grand slam home run. The 4-0 lead is more than enough for Bagby and, in fact, Cleveland never trails again for the rest of the Series.

As important as Smith's hit was, however, it is almost forgotten because of what happens four innings later. Cleveland's lead has grown to 7-0, but Brooklyn shows signs of life in the fifth. Singles by Pete Kilduff and Otto Miller put two on and bring relief pitcher Clarence Mitchell to bat. A converted first-baseman, Mitchell is a fairly good hitter and would finish his long career with a .252 average. So he hits for himself.

Mitchell scorches one towards rightfield and both runners break on the hit. But second baseman Wambsganss spears the ball with a flying leap. His momentum carries him right across second base to double off Kilduff. As he wheels around, there is Miller, stopped a few feet from the bag, waiting to be tagged. In photographs, it appears Miller is stunned, not quite believing what he has just seen. Wambsganss, too, later recalled the dead silence in the few seconds after the play, as the crowd of 26,884 realizes what has happened. By the time he reaches the dugout, they are standing, cheering wildly for one of the greatest moments they will ever witness—the only unassisted triple play in Series history.

The grand slam and triple play crush the Robins. They score only one more run in the entire Series and the Indians sweep all four games at home to close it out.

FACT:
Cleveland second baseman Billy Wambsganss turns an unassisted triple play in game five—the only one in Series history.

The Managers:

Speaker was 31 when he was named manager of the Indians. He only accepted the job on the go-ahead of his predecessor, Lee Fohl, and his average quickly dipped to .296, the only time he hit below .300 aside from his first and last full seasons. He was back in stride in 1920, reaching personal highs in most offensive categories and playing his usual unmatchable centerfield. He was the last playing-manager to lead a team into the Series from the outfield.

Wilbert Robinson was now 57, an avuncular figure who increasingly was falling out of touch with the game. Highly popular in Brooklyn, he stayed on for another 11 years, but rarely did the team emerge from its second division hole.

The Heroes:

Stan Coveleski had come out of Pennsylvania's hard coal country for a brief trial with the A's in 1912. This was in the middle of Philadelphia's championship run and he couldn't break into that staff. He developed a spitter while in the minors, came back with Cleveland in 1916 and was one of the league's top winners for a decade. His 214 career wins are less than many pitchers who have not been voted into Cooperstown. But Coveleski's three victories in the 1920 Series seemed to provide the impetus for his election in 1969. He pitched three complete games and allowed the Robins just two runs.

The moment of glory was brief for Wambsganss (who sometimes did typesetters a favor and played under the name of Wamby). A Cleveland native, he had come to the majors as a shortstop, moving to second to make room for Ray Chapman. Never more than a so-so hitter, he jokingly complained that he played 13 years in the majors and was remembered only for one play. He stayed with Cleveland three more years, then was traded to Boston.

Smith's sojourn was even shorter. Another local boy (he came from nearby Sandusky), he boosted his home run total to 16 the following year but then preceded Wambsganss on the shuttle to Boston.

The Zeroes:

Part of the reason Kilduff and Miller got themselves tripled off base in Wambsganss' historic play was that they were so unaccustomed to being there. In this Series, they went four- for-35 combined.

This was also a rather inglorious final Series for Rube Marquard, who had grown up in Cleveland. He lost his only start and then was charged with scalping tickets before the seventh game. Marquard claimed it was all a cruel misunderstanding, but a disgusted Robinson took him out of the rotation and, instead, pitched Grimes again on one day's rest. He lost to Coveleski, 3-0.

The Aftermath:

It would be two decades before either of these teams returned to the Series. Even the addition of Dazzy Vance couldn't shore up Brooklyn's aging pitching staff, and the team also developed a fatal inconsistency on defense. After challenging for the pennant in 1924, the Brooks settled back into a long run in the vicinity of sixth place.

Under Speaker, the Indians continued to be one of the top hitting teams in the game throughout the 1920s. But Bagby faded and only George Uhle came up to help Coveleski as a starter. The Indians, too, were a second division team for many years.

Notes:

In addition to hitting into a triple play, Clarence Mitchell came up three innings later and banged into a double play. That made five outs in two at bats.

Leon Cadore was a 15-game winner for Brooklyn during the season but couldn't get past the second inning in his only Series start. Many commentators noted that he never seemed to be the same pitcher after going the entire route in a famed 26-inning scoreless duel with Joe Oeschger earlier in the year.

With the spitball soon to be made illegal except by those pitchers already in organized baseball, the seventh game match-up of Grimes and Coveleski was the last in which two such specialists started against each other in the Series.

FACT:
Brooklyn's Clarence Mitchell, who hit into the triple play by Wambsganss, hit into a double play in his next at bat.

Line Scores:

Game One, Oct 5

Cle (AL)—020 100 000—3
Coveleski W

Bkn (NL)—000 000 100—1
Marquard L, Mamaux (7), Cadore (9)

Game Two, October 6

Cle (AL)—000 000 000—0
Bagby L, Uhle (7)

Bkn (NL)—101 010 00X—3
Grimes W

Game Three, October 7

Cle (AL)—000 100 000—1
Caldwell L, Mails (1), Uhle (8)

Bkn (NL)—200 000 00X—2
Smith W

Game Four, October 9

Bkn (NL)—000 100 000—1
Cadore L, Mamaux (2), Marquard (3), Pfeffer (6)

Cle (NL)—202 001 00X—5
Coveleski W

Game Five, October 10

Bkn (NL)—000 000 001—1
Grimes L, Mitchell (4)

Cle (AL)—400 310 00X—8
Bagby W

Game Six, October 11

Bkn (NL)—000 000 000—0
Smith L

Cle (AL)— 000 001 00X—1
Mails W

Game Seven, October 12

Bkn (NL)—000 000 000—0
Grimes L, Mamaux (8)

Cle (AL)—000 110 10X—3
Coveleski W

1921

New York (NL) 5
New York (AL) 3

An injured elbow took Babe Ruth out of the final three games and the Giants won all of them to take the first in a long succession of Subway Series. It was also the last of the nine-game World Series, with the National Leaguers coming from two down to win.

The Preview:

This was more than a World Series to John McGraw. This was a vendetta, a vindication of his career and his game against the tenants in his ballpark and the man who was rewriting the rules. The Giants were completely made-over from the 1917 pennant-winners, with centerfielder George Burns the only remaining starter. The minors had supplied three future Hall of Famers—Frank Frisch, Ross Youngs and George Kelly. McGraw skilfully extracted four key players from the lowly Phillies, shortstop Dave Bancroft, second baseman Johnny Rawlings and outfielders Irish Meusel and Casey Stengel. His pitching staff was also patchwork, with several veterans acquired in trades. The two top starters, Art Nehf (20-10) and Jess Barnes (15-9), had been spirited away from the Braves.

It was, by far, the top run-producing team in the league. Like most McGraw outfits it ran well, and as a nod to the new power game Kelly led the league in home runs with 23. It was a stat McGraw would just as soon have ignored. He did not care for the changes coming over baseball. The old running game, the sacrifice and stolen base, the tight pitching duel, all were slowly fading away. Like most of the men who had grown up in the dead ball style, McGraw railed against the changes. He thought they were brainless, unchallenging, resulting in the sort of baseball any boob could play.

New York's Jess Barnes won two games in relief of ineffective starter Fred Toney, hitting .444 in the process. He struck out 18 in his two appearances, 10 in Game 6.

The fact that the man who played it best, Babe Ruth, was with the Yankees, the team McGraw detested above all others, made it even worse. McGraw had regarded the American League team as enemy number one ever since he arrived in New York. He had, in fact, announced his refusal to play the 1904 World Series on the supposition that they would be his opponent. Now they shared his ballpark and, worse yet, had the biggest gate attraction in the game, a national hero. The Giants were in danger of becoming strangers in their own stadium.

Since coming to New York in 1920, Ruth had put together two seasons that rewrote the record books. He had set records in home runs, slugging percentage, extra base hits, and RBIs. In just two years he hit 113 home runs. The entire league hit 98 in 1918. There had never been a sports figure like him. He was starting a climb to a level of celebrity never attained by any other athlete, a symbol of the Roaring '20s. McGraw hated all of it.

The Yankees were in the midst of stripping the bones of the Boston franchise. Besides Ruth, they acquired catcher Wally Schang and pitchers Carl Mays and Waite Hoyt. More would follow soon. The Yankees paid a reported $100,000 for Ruth and also picked up a second mortgage on Fenway Park in the deal.

Then they hired Boston's former manager, Ed Barrow, to run their front office. He became the principal architect of the Yankee dynasty.

This was a hitter's era and New York's .300 team average was only fourth best in the league. But no 20th-century team had yet approached their mark of 948 runs scored. Along with the firepower was the deepest pitching staff in the league, anchored by Mays (27-9), Hoyt (19-13) and Bob Shawkey (18-12). Bob Meusel, younger brother of the Giants' leftfielder, was a distant runner-up to Ruth in homers with 24, while the infield defense was solid.

The Yankees were expected to win, and the Series began with thousands of empty seats for the opener. Fans had been scared off by media reports of a sellout. But what galled McGraw more than anything was that in his ballpark, in a game in which the Giants were designated the home team, the crowd cheered for the Yankees.

FACT:
The Yankees paid Boston a reported $100,000 for Ruth (and picked up a second mortgage on Fenway Park). The Red Sox haven't won a World Series since these sales to their rivals.

Turning Point: Game Three, Third Inning.

The Giants have been stopped twice, shut out by submariner Mays in game one and then blanked on a two-hitter by Hoyt the next day. And now in game three, it is happening again. Starter Fred Toney is shelled from the game in the third, as the Yankees score four times and run off to a 4-0 lead behind Shawkey.

Jess Barnes is called in and stops the rally. The 29-year-old Oklahoman is not much of a hitter. But the game is young and McGraw, hoping to get a few more innings out of him, allows him to bat for himself leading off the home half of the inning. Barnes surprises everyone with a single. The hit seems to shake Shawkey to the point of collapse. With one out Bancroft also singles. Then Shawkey walks Frisch, Youngs and Kelly in a row, forcing in two runs and putting the Giants right back in the game. By the time reliever John Quinn can stop the bleeding, two more runs have scored and the game is tied.

With Barnes holding off the big Yankee sluggers, the Giants slowly draw a bead on Quinn. In the seventh, they strike. Before the inning is over they score 8 runs, the biggest inning yet in Series history. Emil "Irish" Meusel delivers the big hit, a bases-loaded double. The Giants win easily and go on to take five of the next six games, the first team ever to lose the first two and then win the Series.

The Managers:

For McGraw, this was Series number five. He had lost four in a row, which still stands as a managerial record. The losses were a jarring reminder of the better talent in what he always regarded as the inferior league. He was now 48, a fixture in New York and just as feisty as ever. Early in the year, he was involved in a fight involving two actors, one of whom wound up with a broken jaw. McGraw was popularly supposed to have been the miscreant, although nothing was ever proven.

While sportswriters referred to the 5-7 McGraw as "Little Napoleon," his 5-6 counterpart in the Yankee dugout, Miller Huggins, was dubbed "The Mighty Mite." It underlined the difference in temperament. It was a constant struggle for the mild, thoughtful Huggins to keep his ballclub, led by the roistering Ruth, under control. A former infielder whose greatest talent was drawing walks, Huggins had managed the Cardinals for five years with mixed results. American League President Ban Johnson personally recommended him for the critical job of breathing life into the New York franchise. Hired in 1918, he won more games each year, topping it off with the pennant in 1921.

The Heroes:

Barnes followed his effort in game three with an encore in game six. Toney, the starter, was again batted from the game, this time in the first inning. With three runs across, Barnes was called in once more. He went the rest of the way, striking out 10, while the Giants rallied for an 8-5 win. He was also in the middle of the winning rally with a single off Shawkey in the fourth. Barnes, whose younger brother, Virgil, also would pitch for the Giants, was the first pitcher ever to win two games in relief in a Series. He also hit .444.

The Barnes brothers would never get to play together in the Series. But the Meusels faced each other three years in a row as star outfielders on opposing sides. Bob, three years the younger at 25, had come up to the Yanks in 1920 and quickly took over rightfield. A slugger with a strong throwing arm, he was at the core of the Murderers Row teams. Irish had kicked around for three years with the terrible Phillies before McGraw rescued him midway through 1921. He became the top run-producer in the Giants lineup. The Meusels finished their major league careers with a one-point difference in lifetime average, Irish at .310 and

Bob at .309. This Series, however, belonged to Irish. His seven RBIs led both sides, and clutch extra base hits keyed decisive rallies in four Giants victories.

This was also a brilliant Series for the 22-year-old Hoyt, who had grown up in Brooklyn and was affectionately called "Schoolboy" by New York fans. He pitched one shutout, beat the Giants 3-1 in game five and then lost 1-0 in the finale on an error by shortstop Roger Peckinpaugh. He didn't give up an earned run in 27 innings.

The Zeroes:

When Ruth was able to play, he contributed enough to lead the Yankees in hitting at .313. But he was not the force that he had been in the regular season. After a ninth-inning home run in the game four loss, he was not a factor at all. With an already swollen elbow, he mustered only a bunt single while striking out three times the next day. That finished his Series except for an unsuccesful pinch hitting appearance in the ninth inning of the final game. While not a failure, he turned up missing at the wrong time.

Shawkey was a major disappointment, blowing a four-run lead in game three by walking three men in a row and then losing game six with ineffective relief work.

The Aftermath:

Neither team stayed with a pat hand. Instead, they made major changes in the off-season. For the Giants, it was farewell to Burns, a McGraw favorite, who was traded to Cincinnati for Heinie Groh. He was the final member of the scrappy bunch who had helped win four previous pennants. But McGraw never let sentiment get in the way of winning.

Meanwhile, the Yankees continued to desecrate the corpses of the Boston and Philadelphia franchises—adding four more starters from those two clubs at minimal cost and ensuring a pennant repeat.

Notes:

While the 1906 Series also matched intracity opponents, the games were played in two different ballparks. This was the first time the entire Series was played in one place. The teams took turns being the home team at the Polo Grounds.

This was the last hurrah for Phil Douglas, who won two games as a starter for the Giants. Late in 1922, he was barred from the

> **FACT:**
> This is the first Series played entirely in one ballpark—the Polo Grounds, home to both the Yankees and the Giants.

game without appeal by Commissioner Landis for allegedly asking an opposing team for money in return for tanking the rest of the season.

Line Scores:

Game One, October 5

NY (AL)—100 011 000—3	NY (NL)—000 000 000—0
Mays W	Douglas L, Barnes (9)

Game Two, October 6

NY (NL)—000 000 000—0	NY (AL)—000 100 02X—3
Nehf L	Hoyt W

Game Three, October 7

NY (AL)—004 000 010—5	NY (NL)—004 000 81X—13
Shawkey, Quinn (3) L, Collins (7), Rogers (7)	Toney, Barnes (3) W

Game Four, October 9

NY (NL)—000 000 031—4	NY (AL)—000 010 001—2
Douglas W	Mays L

Game Five, October 10

NY (AL)—001 200 000—3	NY (NL)—100 000 000—1
Hoyt W	Nehf L

Game Six, October 11

NY (NL)—030 401 000—8	NY (AL)—320 000 000—5
Toney, Barnes (1) W	Harper, Shawkey (2) L, Piercy 9

Game Seven, October 12

NY (AL)—010 000 000—1	NY (NL)—000 100 10X—2
Mays L	Douglas W

Game Eight, October 13

NY (NL) 100 000 000—1	NY (AL)—000 000 000—0
Nehf W	Hoyt L

1922

New York (NL) 4
New York (AL) 1, 1 Tie

Same two teams, same result. Only this time the Giants were far more efficient, taking just five games to dispatch the Yankees. One of the games was suspended and ended in a draw. Babe Ruth was shackled while the Giants riddled the Yanks' pitchers.

The Preview:

After his first Series victory in 16 years John McGraw was in no mood to relax. He went about making his strong Giant team even better. The big move was picking up Heinie Groh from Cincinnati. McGraw let him go in 1913 when he was loaded with veteran infielders and had regretted it ever since. Groh grew into a regular .300 hitter using a distinctive bat with a bottle-shaped barrel; he was also a top defensive third baseman. McGraw had coveted him for the 1921 season, but his desires were too apparent and he was reprimanded for tampering by the league. This time he wrapped up outfielder George Burns in a trade package and got his man.

That freed up Frank Frisch to move over to second, a position that better suited his speed. McGraw had veteran Casey Stengel on hand to fill Burns' vacated slot and he responded with his finest year, hitting .368. In fact, every regular except Groh batted over .300 on this team, and it breezed to the pennant by 7 games over the Reds.

Pitching was a bit troublesome behind Art Nehf (19-13). Early in the season McGraw picked up Jack Scott, a veteran who was considering retirement until his North Carolina tobacco barn burned down. Needing an income, Scott joined the Giants and went 8-2. McGraw also wheedled Hugh McQuillan from the

Heinie Groh of the Giants led all Series hitters in 1922 with a .474 average and nine hits. His four runs scored tied him with teammate Dave Bancroft for the lead in that category.

hapless Braves, giving his staff the necessary depth. Most commentators thought this was the best Giants team ever.

The Yankees, meanwhile, kept loading up with stars from less favored franchises. From the A's came centerfielder Whitey Witt. The Red Sox continued their grand giveaway with third baseman Joe Dugan, shortstop Deacon Scott and pitchers Joe Bush and Sad Sam Jones. Bush was especially brilliant, with a 26-7 record, and Bob Shawkey bounced back from a miserable World Series to go 20-12.

Ruth, however, missed 44 games with a variety of ailments and suspensions as the power struggle between the Sultan of Swat and manager Miller Huggins intensified. He dropped to third in the league in home runs (35) and failed to drive in 100 runs (narrowly missing with 99). The Yankees were pressed all the way by the St. Louis Browns, who had assembled the greatest team in that woeful franchise's history and missed the pennant by just one game.

This year it was the Yanks who were perceived as being outgunned on offense, and the Giants entered the Series as strong favorites to repeat.

Turning Point: Game Two, Eighth Inning.

The Giants win the opener, erupting with four straight singles off Bush in the eighth to score three times and take a 3-2 decision. Now they are in danger of blowing a late lead themselves. They stake Jess Barnes, pitching hero of 1921, to a 3-0 lead in the first inning. But the Yanks chip away, with a run in the first and another in the fourth.

Finally, in the eighth, the Yankees' big guns start to fire. Ruth slams a double to the leftfield wall. After a long fly out to center, Bob Meusel drives him home with a double up the left-center alley. Here, at last, is the celebrated Yankee power. But it is the last vestige of it that their sluggers will display.

FACT:
For the second straight year, Art Nehf pitches a complete game, Series-clinching win—the only time this has ever been accomplished.

This game ends in a controversial 3-3 tie. Ruth, Wally Pipp and Meusel all swing for the fences in the 10th and final inning, but none of them can get the ball out of the infield. For the rest of the Series, the heart of the Yankees batting order bats .212, with Ruth entirely hitless. Scott, McQuillan and Nehf handle them easily and the Giants sweep to three straight wins. This eighth inning outburst turned out be the final fizzle for the Yanks.

The Managers:

McGraw reigned as the king of New York, a man who had adapted succesfully to a new style of play he didn't altogether trust. He had assembled a powerful collection of hitters who seemed capable of dominating the National League for years.

Huggins was having problems. He had hired a detective during the season in an attempt to keep his rowdy team in line, as the Yankees kept threatening to dissolve in chaos. Co-owner Tillinghast Huston, a tough engineer who had made a fortune in Cuba, sympathized with Ruth more than the manager and pushed constantly to get Huggins out. In the end it was Huston who sold his part of the club to brewing millionaire Jacob Ruppert, and Huggins remained secure.

The Heroes:

Frisch and Groh tormented the Yankees throughout the short Series. They combined for a .473 average and were constantly on base ahead of cleanup hitter Irish Meusel. He led all hitters with seven RBIs for the second season in a row.

Scott also tortured New York, using his assortment of off-speed pitches in a four-hit, game three shutout, 3-0.

The least likely star was Bill Cunningham, a second-year player who platooned in centerfield with Stengel. Casey went down with a leg injury in game two, and Cunningham got the job full time against the Yanks' strong right-handed staff. He practically saved the Series in game four. In the first inning, with two men aboard, he raced almost to the clubhouse in deepest center to haul in a drive by Ruth. It was highly unlikely that the 32-year-old Stengel could have reached the ball. When the next hitter, Pipp, drove a hit to right-center, Cunningham threw him out at second as he tried for a double. The two plays cut off a potentially huge inning for the Yanks. They settled for two runs, a lead the Giants overcame in the 4-3 win. In the final game, a 5-3 win, Cunningham knocked in the first two runs with a single off Bush.

FACT:
Ruth finished the Series with a horrendous .118 average. He would never again hit below .300 in October.

The Zeroes:

Ruth finished the Series with an horrendous .118 average, his worst as a full-time player. He would never again hit below .300 in October.

The greatest debate in this Series was the decision of the umpires to suspend game two as a 3-3 tie after 10 innings. The game was long, taking two hours and 40 minutes. But there was still ample daylight to play by in this era before artificial illumination. Over the years, a legend developed that the sun was still high in the sky when the umpires called it. Most contemporary observers agreed it was light enough to complete, at most, another inning. There was a near riot at the stadium, as infuriated customers demanded the game be played to a conclusion. Commissioner Landis supported the decision but blistered the umpiring crew privately. He then announced all revenues from the game would be donated to charity.

The Aftermath:

A well-pleased McGraw made only minor adjustments to his Giants, fine-tuning the two-time champions with a modest infusion of youth. But the Yankees, deeply disappointed, put together the final pieces of the championship puzzle. They snared one final star from the Red Sox, and, on the far side of the Harlem

River, finished a stadium of their own, known as the House that Ruth Built.

Notes:

One of the lesser Yankees supplied most of the team's power in this Series. Second baseman Aaron Ward, who had cranked out just seven homers all year, connected for two in the Series. That represented the sum total of Yankee home runs.

Ward also had the distinction of making the only error for the Yankees, matching the Series team record set by the 1918 Red Sox.

Little-used sub Lee King drove in the winning run of the Series in game five with a two-out bloop single in the eighth. It was his only time at bat ever in a Series and his last time up in his major league career.

FACT:
Little-used sub Lee King drove in the Series-winning run in game five—his only at bat ever in a Series and the last time he batted in his career.

Line Scores:

Game One, October 4
NY (AL)—000 001 100—2 NY (NL)—000 000 03X—3
Bush L, Hoyt (8) Nehf, Ryan (8) W

Game Two, October 5
NY (NL)—300 000 000 0—3 NY (AL)—100 100 010 0—3
Barnes Shawkey

Game Three, October 6
NY (AL)—000 000 000—0 NY (NL)—002 000 10X—3
Hoyt L, Jones (8) Scott W

Game Four, October 7
NY (NL)—000 040 000—4 NY (AL)—200 000 100—3
McQuillan W Mays L, Jones (9)

Game Five, October 8
NY (AL)—100 010 100—3 NY (NL)—020 000 03X—5
Bush L Nehf W

1923

New York (AL) 4
New York (NL) 2

For the only time in baseball history, the same two teams met a third straight year for the championship. But now it was the Yankees' turn to shine. Their big hitters, muffled for two years by Giants pitching, finally broke loose in a stadium of their own.

The Preview:

The last two pieces of the Yankees' puzzle arrived in April. The first was Herb Pennock. The 29-year old left hander had soldiered on in Boston while all the other stars on the roster were sold and traded around him. He was among the last to go. A curve-ball artist with precise control, Pennock needed all the forbearance of his Quaker heritage to survive in Boston. His record had fallen to 10-17 in 1922 and he was seriously considering retiring to his fox farm in Pennsylvania. The trade to the Yankees was a career-saving move.

The other key addition was Yankee Stadium. The new park, where the team opened the 1923 season, had been forced upon the ballclub by the Giants. The National League team was tired of their tenants stealing the glory at the Polo Grounds and brusquely informed them their lease would not be renewed. In an act of revenge, Jacob Ruppert, the owner of the Yanks, assembled a land parcel in the Bronx, just a short walk across the Harlem River bridge. Despite predictions that fans would not follow the Yanks out of Manhattan, the huge stadium was sold out on opening day and for many afternoons thereafter.

FACT:
This was the first Series held in Yankee Stadium, "the house that Ruth built." A record crowd of 62,817 attended Game five.

Brothers Irish (left) and Bob Meusel faced each other in three straight World Series, 1921–1923. In those Series, they combined for 41 hits, 3 of them homers.

Tailored to accommodate Babe Ruth, Yankee Stadium was a place in which left-handed pitchers had an enormous advantage. While rightfield was cozy and close, the leftfield power alley went on forever. With their four top starters all right-handers, the search for a quality lefty was imperative. Pennock was the answer. He went 19-6 in his first season, joining Sam Jones (21-8), Joe Bush (19-15) and Waite Hoyt (17-9) in the team's deepest rotation ever. New York's pitching carried the team to an easy 16-game pennant margin over Detroit.

Ruth rebounded from a so-so campaign to hit .393 and lead the league in homers (41) and RBIs (131). No one else in the lineup approached those figures, although Wally Pipp had 108 RBIs.

The Giants, meanwhile, brought up some of their rising stars. When shortstop Dave Bancroft went down with pneumonia, young Travis Jackson moved into the slot and the team never missed a beat. Another rookie, Jimmy O'Connell, split time with Casey Stengel in center, although Stengel had another good year at .339. Frank Frisch, Irish Meusel and George Kelly all finished with more than 100 RBIs, while Ross Youngs led in runs scored. From top to bottom it was the best lineup in baseball.

The pitching, however, had thinned. Jack Scott and Rosy Ryan, with 16 wins apiece, led the staff. Art Nehf dropped to 13-10, but rookie Jack Bentley picked up some of the slack with a 13-8 mark. For all of the attention focused on Ruth and company, it was the Yankees pitching that looked to be the difference between these teams.

Turning Point: Game Six, Eighth Inning.

The Yankees have the ability to strike so quickly that the previous two games are as good as over by the second inning. After Nehf fashions a brilliant six-hitter, 1-0, in game three, the Giants lead the Series two games to one. They have won both games at Yankee Stadium and John McGraw, whose hatred of the Yanks is boundless, is the cheeriest man in the city.

In game four, the Yanks strike for six runs in the second against Scott, their tormentor from the previous year. They cruise behind Bob Shawkey to an 8-4 win. The next day, they rip Bentley for seven runs in the first two innings and get an easy 8-1 win. Now the Giants are one game from elimination and McGraw stakes everything on Nehf.

The left-hander pitched complete game wins to close out the previous two Series, the only man in history ever to do that. But his tough shutout effort two days before leaves him exhausted. Still, he goes up against Pennock in a courageous effort to stave off defeat. The Yankee starter is not sharp and going into the eighth the Giants lead 4-1. Ruth homers in the first, but Nehf recovers and does not give up a hit after the second inning. Then, so quickly that McGraw cannot react, it all collapses.

With one out, Wally Schang singles and weak-hitting Deacon Scott sends him to third with another single. With Pennock due up, the Yanks go to their bench and send up reserve catcher Fred Hoffmann. An erratic batter, sometimes effective against lefties, Hoffmann only has to stand there. A visibly exhausted Nehf misses the plate four times and the walk loads the bases.

With the left-handed Whitey Witt due up, manager Miller Huggins pulls a surprise and sends pitcher Joe Bush to hit for him. Bush was a solid .274 hitter during the season, but McGraw feels that even a tiring Nehf can handle him. It is a bad miscalculation. Nehf has nothing left and again cannot put the ball anywhere near the plate. Bush, too, walks on four pitches, forcing in a run and cutting the Giants lead to 4-2.

McGraw finally brings in Ryan, but he can't find the plate, either. He walks Joe Dugan on four pitches. Giant pitchers now have delivered 12 balls in a row and their lead has shriveled to one run.

The crowd is screaming as Ruth walks to the plate. But Ryan comes back to strike him out on a bad pitch. Two out, still a 4-3 Giants lead and lingering hope that maybe they can get out of the inning. But Bob Meusel lashes a single to center. Two runs score, one more follows on a throwing error, and the Yankees have scored five times in their final big inning of the season to take a 6-4 lead. The game ends that way and the Yanks have their first championship.

The Managers:

Two straight wins over his greatest rival would be enough to satisfy most men. But the previous Series victories were merely an appetizer for McGraw. He wanted the entire feast, an obliteration of the Yankees, beating them one more time in front of their own fans in their own stadium. Even though Cincinnati furnished surprisingly tough competition in the pennant race, the ultimate triumph over the Yankees was what this season was about for McGraw.

Huggins was hoping to avoid matching McGraw's distinction of managing three consecutive Series losers. Under fire for his team's previous two failures and his run-ins with Ruth, Huggins turned in his most skillful managing job this year, coasting to the pennant and then bringing the team up for a peak performance against the Giants.

The Heroes:

While he had been a pitching star in two previous Series, this was the first time Ruth's full presence as a hitter was felt in

October. His three home runs were all hit with the bases empty, but they rattled the Giant pitchers. He wound up walking eight times and also scored eight runs, while amassing a slugging percentage of 1,000. He was, at last, the central presence in the Yankee lineup.

Aaron Ward, who had surprised everyone with his uncharacteristic long ball power the previous year, came back to lead both sides with 10 hits and a .417 average. And he hit another home run, too.

FACT:
This was the first Series held in Yankee Stadium, "the house that Ruth built." A record crowd of 62,817 attended Game five.

This was the biggest Series Stengel would have as a player. His ninth-inning, inside-the-park home run into the left-center cavern at Yankee Stadium won the opener, 5-4. Descriptions of the 33-year-old Stengel laboring desperately around the bases to score have passed into the game's comic tradition. He then came back two days later and won the third game, 1-0, with a homer in the seventh—a more conventional shot into the seats. He matched Ward with a .417 average and led the Giants with 4 RBIs.

The Zeroes:

Aside from Nehf, the Giants starters were cuffed around mercilessly. None of them made it past the fourth inning. Sensing, perhaps, that he was in trouble, McGraw chose to go with the little-used Mule Watson in the first game, but he couldn't get past the second inning. Nehf performed heroically, but when he stumbled in game six, McGraw had no one to pick up the pieces.

Bancroft recovered from his illness but sealed his fate with the Giants by going just two-for-24 in the Series.

The Aftermath:

When the Braves came to McGraw in the off season and sought a deal for Bancroft, with the view of making him manager, the Giants jumped at the chance. The shortstop was shipped out with Stengel for outfielder Billy Southworth. Jackson was then installed as the regular shortstop in 1924, as McGraw continued to keep his champions young and won an unprecedented fourth straight pennant. Stengel, however, would have to wait 26 years to get back to the Series, when he would be wearing pinstripes as manager of the Yankees.

Nehf had averaged 269 innings pitched in his previous four years with the Giants, but he never quite bounced back from his exertions in this Series. While only 31, Nehf never again pitched more than 176 innings in a season.

The Yankees had every reasonable expectation of a return trip to the Series, too. But in 1924 they were overtaken by a chronic tail-ender and collapsed altogether the following year. That only laid the foundation, however, for the construction of the most powerful baseball team ever.

Notes:

All three games at Yankee Stadium set new Series attendance records. The mark of 47,373, at Braves Field in 1916, fell in the opener, as 55,307 showed up. By the fifth game of the Series, the third held in the Bronx, that number was up to 62,817.

Needless to add, the winning player's share of $6,143 was also the largest in history.

Despite the fact that Yankee Stadium was constructed as a home run playpen for Ruth, the slugger hit all three of his Series homers at the Polo Grounds. Of the three home runs that were hit at Yankee Stadium, two were inside the park.

Line Scores:

Game One, October 10

NY (NL)—004 000 001—5
Watson, Ryan (3) W

NY (AL)—120 000 100—4
Hoyt, Shawkey (3) L

Game Two, October 11

NY (AL)—010 210 000—4
Pennock W

NY (NL)—010 001 000—2
McQuillan L, Bentley (4)

Game Three, October 12

NY (NL)—000 000 100—1
Nehf W

NY (AL)—000 000 000—0
Jones L, Bush (9)

Game Four, October 13

NY (AL)—061 100 000—8
Shawkey W, Pennock (8) SV

NY (NL)—000 000 031—4
Scott L, Ryan (2), McQuillan (2), Jonnard (8), V. Barnes (9)

Game Five, October 14

NY (NL)—010 000 000—1
Bentley L, Scott (2), V. Barnes (4), Jonnard (8)

NY (AL)—340 100 00X—8
Bush W

Game Six, October 15

NY (AL)—100 000 050—6
Pennock W, Jones (8) SV

NY (NL)—100 111 000—4
Nehf L, Ryan (8)

1924

Washington (AL) 4
New York (NL) 3

In what many call the greatest World Series ever played, the teams struggled for 12 innings of the seventh game to decide the championship. Walter Johnson held off the Giants valiantly in relief, but the real hero may have been the groundskeeper at Griffith Stadium.

The Preview:

The country was pulling for the Senators but betting on the Giants. In an enormous outpouring of sentiment, everyone was rooting for Walter Johnson. He was now 36 years old and had appeared to be well past his prime. The overpowering Johnson, who had won more than 20 games 10 years in a row and whose ERA had never been as high as 2.00 for nine of them, had faded. In his place was a pitcher whose aging arm hadn't adjusted to the lively ball. He had twice lost more games than he won since 1920. While the strikeout pitch was still there occasionally, his season totals had been steadily declining for eight years.

Everyone understood the irony. In the years that Johnson was unhittable, he pitched for a mediocre team, a consistent second-division outfit that inspired the saying, "Washington—first in war, first in peace and last in the American League." Now that new ownership finally was developing the talent to win, Johnson's skills had diminished. But in 1924, The Big Train pulled back into the depot. At 23-7, he was again the top pitcher in the league. Behind him now were players like Goose Goslin, leading the league with 129 RBIs. Sam Rice and Joe Judge also came in among the league's top hitters. The infield defense, especially on the left side, with Ossie Bluege and Roger Peckinpaugh, was the best around.

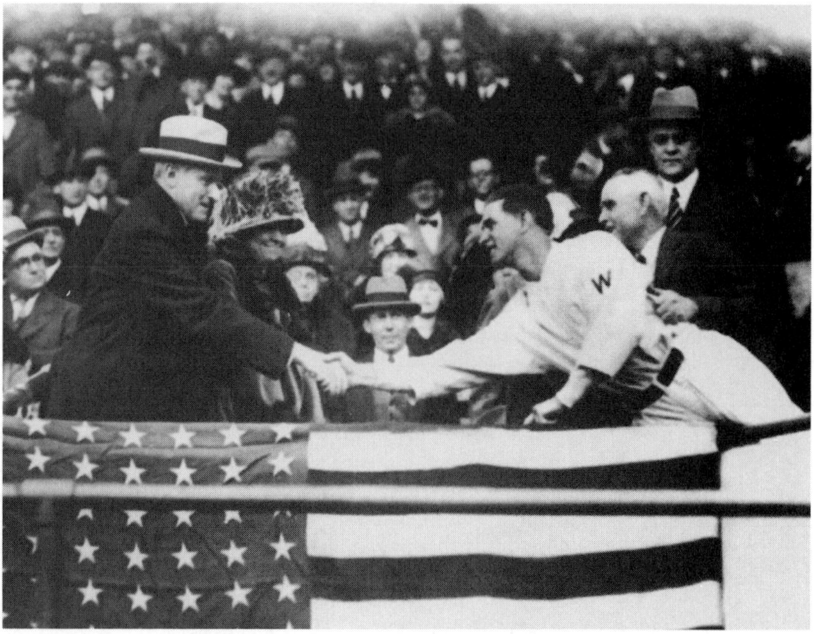

Bucky Harris, Washington's player-manager, led all Series hitters with seven RBI and 11 hits. He also hit two home runs and set a record as the youngest man to manage in the World Series at 27 years old.

The Senators had struggled throughout the summer with the Yankees, sparked by Babe Ruth on the way to his only batting championship. At the end, however, Johnson put together a 13-game winning streak. He was assisted by Curly Ogden, who won eight in a row down the stretch after being picked up from the A's.

The Giants were just as formidable as ever. Their lineup was loaded with power, with George Kelly driving in 136 runs and Ross Youngs batting .356. Travis Jackson, the young shortstop, joined the .300 circle. Two newcomers also improved as the season progressed—Hack Wilson in centerfield and Bill Terry, who platooned with Kelly at first base. Seven members of this team's lineup would go on to the Hall of Fame.

However, New York did not overpower the rest of the league. Brooklyn pushed them right to the wire, losing by just 1 1/2 games, and right behind them was Pittsburgh. The Giant pitching did not measure up. Virgil Barnes and Jack Bentley were 16-game winners, but after them it was a struggle. The bullpen's 21 saves were more than twice as many as any other team in this era before relief specialists. Manager John McGraw had to juggle his staff as never before. Still, New York's long Series experience and lineup of sluggers made the Giants clear favorites.

The Turning Point: Game Seven, Eighth Inning.

Never has been there a roller coaster ride like this. Johnson goes 12 innings in the opener, only to lose 4-3. He loses again in game five, 6-2, as the teams keep trading victories. Washington comes home trailing three games to two, and the capital watches in suspense as Tom Zachary outduels Art Nehf, 2-1, in game six. The Series is going the full seven for only the third time in history.

Young manager Bucky Harris has a plan for the deciding game. Terry is killing the Senators, hitting .500 for the first six games. He and 18-year old Fred Lindstrom, rushed into action when third baseman Heinie Groh goes down with a leg injury, are keeping New York in the Series. But Terry is a platoon player. McGraw does not start him against left-handers. If Washington can get him out of the lineup early, Harris figures his chances will improve immeasurably.

So he calls on right-hander Ogden, who had not yet pitched in the Series, to start the big game. He strikes out one man, walks the next and Harris suddenly motions for George Mogridge, a left-hander, to come in. Mogridge is rested and ready to go the rest of the way. He retires Terry twice, striking him out in the fourth. In the sixth inning, with New York trailing 1-0, the Giants pinch hit for Terry. But they rally for three runs and take a lead into the eighth. It appears that the loss of Terry will not hurt them.

Barnes weakens, however, and loads the bases with one out. Earl McNeely flies weakly to left and the runners hold. It is still 3-1, with player-manager Harris coming to bat. Harris drove in Washington's only run with a homer in the fourth. This time he sends what look like a routine, rally-ending grounder to Lindstrom. But just before it reaches him, the ball takes a strange bounce and scoots into leftfield. Two runs score and the game is tied. Lindstrom disgustedly goes over the dirt with his spikes, trying to find the pebble that did the damage.

Just as the noise from the tying hit subsides, it builds once more, this time into a deafening roar. Johnson is coming in to pitch the ninth. Already a two-time loser, he has been written off for the rest of the Series. Now he is back on just one day of rest and the Washington crowd greets him with a frenzied ovation.

Frank Frisch triples with one out, but Johnson pitches out of trouble immediately. He strikes out George Kelly on three pitches and gets Irish Meusel, batting where the dangerous Terry would have been, on a grounder. New York puts runners on in every inning, but Johnson holds them off, striking out five. McGraw,

Washington's Walter Johnson waited 18 years to get into a World Series, and had center stage once he got there. He won Game 7 with four innings of shutout relief, after losses in his two starts.

meanwhile, empties his bullpen as Washington also threatens constantly. Johnson, in fact, backs centerfielder Wilson all the way to the stands in the 10th, just missing a Series-ending home run.

The Washington 12th begins with Bentley on the mound. After an easy out, catcher Muddy Ruel hits a pop foul. Hank Gowdy, the hero of the 1914 Series and New York's starting catcher this time, goes off in pursuit. He drops his mask before making the catch, but instead of hurling it off to the side, as all catchers are taught, he drops it right in front of him. He steps on it, kicks it forward, steps on it again, and, as he stumbles, Gowdy drops the ball. Now it is as if everyone in the park knows that something big is coming from that blunder. Ruel immediately doubles, and Johnson, an excellent hitter, bats for himself. He grounds to short but Ruel, feinting a run to third, confuses Jackson, who boots the ball.

McNeely now carries the Washington hopes. The rookie was brought up from the minors in mid-season. He reported with a throwing hand so sore he couldn't even raise it to shake hands with owner Clark Griffith, who was furious over being sold damaged goods. But McNeely recovered to hit .330 as a platoon outfielder.

This time he hits a grounder to third, almost to the same spot where Harris had hit his four innings before. Lindstrom sets himself to field it. Incredibly, just as in the eighth, the ball hits something in the dirt and bounces high over the third-baseman's head. Ruel races in to score and the Senators are champions.

The Managers:

For McGraw, this was the ninth trip to the Series, more, by far, than any other manager. It hadn't been an easy season. Outfielder Jimmy O'Connell was banned from the game for offering a bribe to a Phillies player to "go easy" on the Giants in a late-season Series. Also implicated was McGraw's assistant, Cozy Dolan, supposed by the players to be a spy for the manager. O'Connell named several of the top Giants' stars as part of the scheme, but he had no evidence and no action was taken against them. McGraw hired Dolan a lawyer, to no avail. American League President Ban Johnson called for suspending the World Series, but was ignored. McGraw, however, seemed perceptibly mellower.

Harris, at the other extreme, was in his first season as manager. He was called "The Boy Wonder." The 27-year-old second baseman, in his fifth year with Washington, was stunned when Griffith chose him to be a playing manager. He addressed his team before the season, saying: "Boys, just play the way you can and make me a great manager." Harris would go on to a managerial career that spanned four decades and put him in the

Hall of Fame. But this year it seemed that a boy was being sent out to do a manager's job.

The Heroes:

Take your pick. This was a Series that abounded in great performances. Several players rose well above their season stats to play at the peak of their abilities and beyond.

Harris not only managed well, he led both teams with 7 RBIs and 11 hits. Under the greatest pressure imaginable, he knocked in five consecutive Washington runs; the first three in the seventh game and the only two the team scored in the 2-1 game-six win. The two homers he hit exactly doubled his output for the season. It was the most remarkable exhibition of leadership by example in Series history.

Lindstrom, who had played in just 52 games before being rushed from the wings to start, performed brilliantly. His 10 hits matched the great Frank Frisch's total for New York and he played errorless ball. McGraw installed him as the regular third baseman the following season at the age of 19.

While Johnson got most of the notice, it was left-handers Zachary and Mogridge, along with reliever Fred "Firpo" Marberry, who kept Washington alive. The three of them either won or saved all of the Senators' other wins, as the staff combined for a 2.15 ERA against the mighty Giants.

Ultimately, however, this was Johnson's Series. A consummate gentleman in an era that favored roughnecks, he was admired as much for his comportment as his skill. Ty Cobb confessed later that he took advantage of Johnson repeatedly by crowding the plate as he did against no other pitcher. Johnson was so fearful of hitting someone with his fastball that he always worked outside on Cobb. A complete athlete who hit well enough to have been a position player, Johnson capped his career with this Series performance.

The Zeroes:

McGraw had gritted his teeth through a 2-for-24 Series by shortstop Dave Bancroft the previous year. This time he had to watch his replacement, Jackson, go for 2 for 27 and commit three errors.

Washington's Ruel endured an 0-for-18 start. However, he broke out of it just in time. His first hit of the Series keyed the tying rally in the eighth inning of the last game and he scored the winning run after doubling in the 12th.

FACT:
Washington's catcher, Harold "Muddy" Ruel, broke out of an 0-18 slump with key hits in the eighth and twelfth innings of the deciding game.

It was also a rough introduction to the Series for Hack Wilson. He struck out nine times in 30 at bats.

The Aftermath:

On the train pulling out of Washington on the evening of the seventh game, McGraw was in a contemplative mood as he spoke to reporters. "I've had enough glory for a lifetime," he said, "but look at those people out there. It's the greatest day Washington has ever known in baseball and you can't mind losing if it touches off a celebration like this." It would be the last time McGraw figured in a Series. While his Giants remained competitive, they didn't return until 1933, one year after he resigned. Four months after the Giants' won that championship, he died at the age of 60.

> **FACT:**
> This was the 9th and last Series for the Giants' legendary manager John "Little Napoleon" McGraw, who finished with 3 champions and 6 runners-up.

Harris, however, set off eagerly to strengthen his championship team. The Senators picked up two quality starters in the off-season and prepared to repeat as pennant winners for the only time in their history.

Notes:

While Ogden remained with Washington in 1925, he didn't get into another Series game. So his record remains an October oddity—one start, one-third of an inning pitched, no hits allowed.

The Series almost turned on a leg injury to shortstop Peckinpaugh. It forced Washington to play its outstanding defensive third baseman, Bluege, at an unfamiliar position, where he made three errors. One of them let in a run in the decisive game. Moreover, his replacement at third, Ralph Miller, made two boots, and never played in the Majors again.

Line Scores:

Game One, October 4

NY (NL)—010 100 000 002—4
Nehf W

Was (AL)—001 000 001 001—3
Johnson L

Game Two, October 5

NY (NL)—000 000 102—3
Bentley L

Was (AL)—200 010 001—4
Zachary, Marberry (9) W

Game Three, October 6

Was (AL)—000 200 110—4 Marberry L, Russell (4), Martina (7), Speece (8)	NY (NL)—021 101 01X—6 McQuillan, Ryan (4) W, Jonnard (9), Watson (9) SV

Game Four, October 7

Was (AL)—003 020 020—7 Mogridge W, Marberry (8) SV	NY (NL)—100 001 011—4 Barnes L, Baldwin (6), Dean (8)

Game Five, October 8

Was (AL)—000 100 010—2 Johnson L	NY (NL)—001 020 03X—6 Bentley W, McQuillan (8) SV

Game Six, October 9

NY (NL)—100 000 000—1 Nehf L, Ryan (8)	Was (AL)—000 020 00X—2 Zachary W

Game Seven, October 10

NY (NL)—000 003 000 000—3 Barnes, Nehf (8), McQuillan (9), Bentley (11) L	Was (AL)—000 100 020 001—4 Ogden, Mogridge (1), Marberry (6), Johnson (9) W

1925

Pittsburgh (NL) 4
Washington (AL) 3

Playing in their first Series in 16 years, the underdog Pirates became the first team ever to come back from a 3-1 deficit in a seven-game set. Pebbles helped win the previous year's Series for the Senators but mud lost it for them this time.

The Preview:

Washington had been the surprise of 1924. This time they weren't sneaking up on anyone. If anything, they were even stronger—easy winners of the pennant by 8 1/2 games over Philadelphia.

Owner Clark Griffith had acquired two top pitchers to help back up Walter Johnson. From Cleveland came Stan Coveleski. The hero of the 1920 Series was now 35 and had been placed on waivers by the cost-conscious Indians. He went 20-5 and led the league in earned run average. The Senators picked off Dutch Ruether by the same route. He had been a disappointment during Brooklyn's pennant run the previous year, but he turned it around to go 18-7 for the Nats. With Johnson having another fine season at 20-7, the Washington staff was the deepest in the league.

The team's offensive strength was outfielders Sam Rice (.350) and Goose Goslin (.334, with 113 RBIs). It also was tops in stolen bases, while shortstop Roger Peckinpaugh had no peer on defense. He was awarded the forerunner of the Most Valuable Player award for the year. Moon Harris, picked up early in the season, was a consistent .300 hitter whose sad adventures afield had kept him from a regular job in the majors. With Washington he was platooned at first and the outfield and hit .313.

The Pirates had built an offense that was even stronger. Every starter aside from second baseman Eddie Moore hit over

Washington outfielder Sam Rice, whose controversial catch in Game 3 was the subject of debate until his death, when a letter he left confirmed that he had caught the ball. Rice led both teams with 12 hits.

.300, and Moore finished at .298. Young stars Kiki Cuyler (.357) and Pie Traynor (.320) keyed the batting order, while veteran Max Carey, in his 15th year with the club, had his greatest season at the age of 35. He hit .343 and was still fast enough to lead the majors in steals with 46. The Pirates also picked up Stuffy McInnis, three times a champion with the A's and Red Sox. As an occasional starter he hit .368. Equally important, he knew how to win.

When Pittsburgh finished third the previous year, owner Barney Dreyfuss was convinced his team was too soft. He felt that two of his regulars, Charlie Grimm and Rabbit Maranville, were having far too much fun to win. So he packaged them with 20-game winner Arlie Cooper to the Cubs. It was a gamble and a highly unpopular trade in Pittsburgh. In return, the Pirates received a good-hitting infielder, George Grantham, and a younger pitcher in Vic Aldridge. It seemed to toughen the team. The Pirates had five starters with more than 15 wins, led by Spec Meadows at 19-10. It was a staff without a dominant pitcher, but it was more than adequate for a team with Pittsburgh's firepower. Nonetheless, the Pirates were the underdogs entering the Series.

Turning Point: Game Seven, Seventh Inning.

For the second straight year it comes down to seven games, with Johnson holding the hopes of Washington. But the point is reached by two vastly different scenarios. In 1924, Johnson was hit hard and beaten twice in two previous starts, coming on to get the ultimate victory in relief. This year he overpowers the Pirates. He beats them 4-1 with 10 strikeouts in the opener, then tosses a 4-0 shutout in game four before an adoring home crowd.

While trying to stretch a hit into a double in game four, Johnson suffers a charley horse. The leg injury seems to bother him only slightly, but three days later, when he takes the mound again, it has stiffened badly. A rainout gives him a full three days of rest, but it is cold and overcast as game seven begins.

Washington drives a disorganized Aldridge from the game in the first inning, as he walks three and throws two wild pitches. Johnson has a 4-0 lead before throwing a pitch, and the Series seems to be all his. But it is apparent that he cannot throw with his usual force because of the sore leg. Then, in the third it begins to rain.

By the fifth, weather conditions are the worst in Series history. The downpour is constant and the outfielders are only dim figures in the haze. Groundskeepers continually scatter sawdust around the pitcher's mound and basepaths. Players are slipping all over sodden Forbes Field. But Commissioner Landis refuses to consider a postponement. It is October 15, the Series has been going for a week and, in his opinion, it's time to get it over with. In the 1990s, when the Series doesn't even begin until late October, that viewpoint seems almost quaint. Landis directed that the game must go on.

In addition to his bad leg, Johnson is slipping on the mucky mound when he comes down on his follow-through. He is in deep distress and the Pirates start teeing off on him in the third, scoring three times. Washington makes it 6-3, but back to back Pirate doubles in the fifth close it to 6-4. Then, in the seventh, everything falls apart.

Johnson has given up 10 hits and is visibly exhausted. Almost the entire Washington staff is ready to work the last three innings. But manager Bucky Harris doesn't make the move. Pittsburgh's first hitter, Moore, pops up. Peckinpaugh, back-pedaling in the slosh, drops the ball. It is his seventh error in the Series, an almost unbelievable defensive collapse by a top shortstop. Given that life, Carey slashes his third double of the game, and now it is 6-5. Then, with two outs, Traynor finds the right center alley. The tying run scores on the triple and the Pirates are even.

Peckinpaugh, desperately seeking atonement for his fielding lapses, gets the first hit off reliever Remy Kremer in the Washington eighth, a homer into the leftfield seats. Surely, with the Senators in the lead, Johnson will come out of the game. But out he trudges for the eighth. It's as if the teams are taking part in some Teutonic tragedy, which must be played out in darkness and mist. Johnson gets the first two hitters. Then Earl Smith doubles and Carson Bigbee lines another double over Goslin's head. The game is tied again, 7-7. Johnson has now given up 14 hits and has nothing left. But he continues on through the downpour. After a walk, Carey sends a grounder to Peckinpaugh. His throw to second for the forceout is high, for his eighth error. Cuyler then sends a slicing drive into the rightfield corner. At first, it is ruled a home run, then revised to a ground rule double. No one clearly saw where the ball landed in the darkness. But two runs are in, the Senators go down in the ninth, and Pittsburgh wins, 9-7.

The Managers:

Bucky Harris received a telegram from American League President Ban Johnson after the seventh game. "You have thrown away a championship for mawkish sentiment," it said. The manager could never satisfactorily explain why he kept Johnson in the game. None of his other pitchers had been especially effective, but Johnson, who would be 38 in three weeks, was a spent force. Harris was only in his second year as a manager; he heard the second-guessing for the remainder of his 29-year career. He wouldn't return to the Series until 1947.

Bill McKechnie had taken over the helm of the Pirates in 1922 and the team won more games each season. The 1925 race, in which he had beaten the hated John McGraw by 8 1/2 games, endeared him deeply to owner Dreyfuss. A hometown product and former Pirates third baseman, McKechnie had won an early reputation as an astute baseball mind. He was now a rather elderly 39 with a sober mien that won him the nickname of "Deacon." While not highly popular among his players, he got them to win.

FACT:
"You have thrown away a championship for mawkish sentiment," read a telegram from American League President Ban Johnson to Washington manager Bucky Harris, following the seventh game.

The Heroes:

Max Carey had waited a long time to get into a Series and Pittsburgh's longest-serving veteran wasn't going to let the chance pass unnoticed. His three doubles off Johnson in the seventh game kept bringing the Pirates back into it. He also scored the winning run in game five. Overall, he hit .458, and his three steals were more than the entire Washington team could manage.

Moon Harris was his counterpart with Washington. At 34, his career had seemed over on many occasions. Given this chance, he hit .400, slugged three homers and just missed a fourth when his two-out, ninth-inning drive in game six hit high off a temporary screen in dead center for a double. Had it cleared, it would have tied the game.

FACT:
The most controversial out in Series history occurs in the eighth inning of game three when the Senators' Sam Rice dives over the centerfield fence to catch a ball, disappears, then emerges moments later with the ball in his glove. A brouhaha ensued, but the umpire stuck with his "out" call. In 1994, twenty years after Rice died and according to his will, a note was opened that revealed whether or not he had actually caught the ball.

Remy Kremer had pitched in obscurity for years in the Pacific Coast League and didn't reach the majors until he was 31. In his abbreviated career, he twice led the league in ERA and twice won 20 games. In this Series, he shored up an erratic Pittsburgh staff, went all the way to win the sixth game, then came back with four innings of one-hit relief to win game seven.

Sam Rice led everyone with 12 hits, but it was his catch in game three that was best remembered. On an eighth-inning drive by Earl Smith, the Washington centerfielder flung himself over a low barrier at the temporary seats built for the Series. Rice seemed to make the catch, but disappeared into the seats for several seconds before re-emerging, waving the ball. The umpire signalled a putout and the Pirates raged. A home run would have tied the game. Instead, Washington held on, 4-3. Since Pittsburgh eventually won the Series, Rice's catch became only a footnote, but he would never say whether or not he actually caught the ball. "The umps said I did," was his sole contribution to the debate. At his death in 1974 he left instructions that 20 years later a note he wrote about the play should be opened. In 1994 the letter was opened. It contained a declaration that Rice had, indeed, caught the ball.

The Zeroes:

The collapse of Peckinpaugh was among the most inexplicable events in Series history. He had been an outstanding fielder in a 13-year career with New York and Washington. While his range had diminished through age, he was still regarded as a sure-handed, steady shortstop. His eight errors led to six unearned runs and contributed directly to two Washington losses.

Besides his managing problems in the seventh game, it was also a struggle at bat for Bucky Harris. He went only 2-for-23 in his last Series as a player.

The Aftermath:

Both teams suffered immediate letdowns. Age finally caught up with Washington's pitchers. Johnson never had another winning season and both he and Coveleski were gone within two years. Peckinpaugh's days as a regular shortstop were also over and in 1928 he was named manager at Cleveland. Johnson took over from Harris in Washington one year later.

The Pirates split wide open in 1926, with former manager Fred Clarke, who served as McKechnie's assistant on the bench, in the middle of it. He made disparaging remarks about the declining skills of Carey, who asked his teammates for a secret ballot on whether Clarke should be asked to leave the bench. Carey lost and was immediately released, along with two allies—Bigbee and longtime Pittsburgh favorite Babe Adams, who had won the 1909 Series for Clarke. At the end of the season, both McKechnie and Clarke quit.

Notes:

Echoes of past World Series sounded throughout the first two games. The bitter opponents of 1909, Honus Wagner and Ty Cobb, still active as player-manager of the Tigers, were introduced before game one and given a thunderous tribute.

That night, word of Christy Mathewson's death from lung disease was received. There was a solemn procession to the centerfield flagpole before game two, led by John McGraw and Judge Landis, as both teams lined up and a band played "Nearer My God to Thee."

Stuffy McInnis came off the bench to start the last three games at first base on the advice of McGraw. He told McKechnie that he remembered McInnis as a formidable opponent with the A's. But since McInnis was injured in 1911 and hit only .118 in 1913, maybe McGraw was thinking of someone else.

Line Scores:

Game One, October 7

Was (AL)—010 020 001—4	Pit (NL)—000 010 000—1
Johnson W	Meadows L, Morrison (9)

Game Two, October 8

Was (AL)—010 000 001—2
Coveleski L

Pit (NL)—000 100 02X—3
Aldridge W

Game Three, October 10

Pit (NL)—010 101 000—3
Kremer L

Was (AL)—001 001 20X—4
Ferguson W, Marberry (8) SV

Game Four, October 11

Pit (NL)—000 000 000—0
Yde L, Morrison (3), Adams (8)

Was (AL)—004 000 00X—4
Johnson W

Game Five, October 12

Pit (NL)—002 000 211—6
Aldridge W

Was (AL)—100 100 100—3
Coveleski L, Ballou (7), Zachary (8), Marberry (9)

Game Six, October 13

Was (AL)—110 000 000—2
Ferguson L, Ballou (8)

Pit (NL)—002 010 00X—3
Kremer W

Game Seven, October 15

Was (AL)—400 200 010—7
Johnson L

Pit (NL)—003 010 23X—9
Aldridge, Morrison (1), Kremer (4) W, Oldham (9) SV

1926

St. Louis (NL) 4
New York (AL) 3

For the third straight year, the Series ended with one of the game's all-time great pitchers performing in a cauldron of hysteria. Grover Alexander locked the door on the Yankees in a legendary finish to give St. Louis its first championship.

The Preview:

The Cardinals, perennial National League doormats, had made slow, methodical progress after Branch Rickey was named manager in 1919. But the team seemed to hit a plateau, and when it fell all the way back to sixth in 1924, owner Sam Breadon pulled the plug. He moved the scholarly Rickey to the front office at the start of 1925 and promoted his star second baseman, Rogers Hornsby, to manager.

Hornsby was the most feared hitter in the league. He topped .400 three times in four years (and hit .397 in a fifth) and led the league in batting six straight seasons. A man who freely admitted that he had no life outside of baseball, Hornsby expected no less a degree of dedication from those around him. Doomed to disappointment in that regard, it made him less than a successful manager. But in 1926, his ballclub caught lightning.

The Cards came out of spring training with a competitive team. Hornsby and first baseman Jim Bottomley were proven sluggers, and there were some promising players after them. Bob O'Farrell solidified the catching and defensive whiz Tommy Thevenow, called up from the minors as shortstop at Hornsby's demand, closed down the middle. As spring progressed St. Louis pulled off two deals that turned the team into contenders.

First, Billy Southworth was picked up from the Giants. He had not worked out as a centerfielder in New York, and McGraw

The Cardinals' Tommy Thevenow was an unlikely Series hero. A .256 hitter during the season, his first and last as a regular, he hit .417 in the Series, with a game-winning bases-loaded single in the finale.

needed to fill that position. The Cards' Heinie Mueller seemed like a good fit to him. In St. Louis Southworth could switch to rightfield. He hit .317 in the number-two slot in the lineup.

A few weeks later came Grover Alexander. He was now 39, the oldest pitcher in the league. When he challenged the authority of Cubs' rookie manager, Joe McCarthy, whom Alexander scornfully described as a man who had never played an inning in the majors, he was placed on waivers. He had a reputation as a drunk and a hard case, but Breadon picked him up after four other teams had passed on him. Alexander went 9-7 and seemed to get tougher as the pennant race wore on.

The race developed into a four-team dogfight, with St. Louis taking the lead in early September. Because of the peculiarities of the schedule, it spent the entire season after Labor Day on the road. Even with this handicap, the Cards staggered home in front, although their 89-65 record was the lowest pennant-winning percentage up to that time in league history.

The Yankees, meanwhile, rebounded from a horrendous year in which the club had plunged to seventh place. That year had seen Babe Ruth laid up with what was described as a bellyache, but it was actually venereal disease. The team was remade from the three-time winners of the early '20s. Lou Gehrig had taken over at first, while rookies Tony Lazzeri and Mark Koenig were the middle infielders. Earle Combs was now a fixture in center. The team was younger, even more dangerous on offense, and was not yet in its prime.

The pitching staff, however, was still anchored by veterans Waite Hoyt (16-12) and Herb Pennock (23-11), while Urban Shocker, picked up from the Browns, was a solid 19-11. But it was still The Babe's ballclub. With 47 homers and 145 RBIs, he remained beyond comparison the greatest force in the game. Hornsby was determined that he would not allow Ruth to beat the Cardinals, but his team was not given much of a chance against the Yanks.

Turning Point: Game 7, 7th Inning.

Again it comes down to the waning moments of the seventh game—the Series tied at three wins apiece, the championship now an endurance contest. The Cards had come back to Yankee Stadium needing to sweep both games to win the title. Alexander took care of game six, as Cardinal batters made his job easy with a 10-2 hammering of Bob Shawkey. The deciding game is a far more delicate affair.

St. Louis goes out to a 3-1 lead in the fourth on two New York errors and a two-run single by Thevenow. Veteran catcher Hank Severeid gets one back in the sixth on a double that scores Joe Dugan. Now the Cards' Jess Haines has just a one-run cushion. Hornsby is confident that the knuckleballer can hold on. He was 13-4 during the season and excelled in the tight ones.

Earle Combs starts the New York seventh with a single and is bunted to second. This sets up an obvious intentional pass for Ruth, the tenth time he has walked in the Series. He pounded the Cards for three home runs in game four and crashed one into the bleachers in the third inning of this one. Hornsby will not give in to the slugger.

Haines gets Bob Meusel on a forceout at second but seems to struggle against Gehrig. He finally walks him to load the bases and Hornsby goes over to confer with his pitcher. Haines holds up his right hand. A blister has broken where the knuckler is released and blood is streaming down the pitcher's finger. Haines cannot continue. Hornsby motions to his bullpen and Alexander slowly trudges to the mound.

FACT:
Babe Ruth hit a Series record 3 home runs in one game, a feat he would duplicate in the 1928 Series. Another Yankee would match it in 1977. Ruth also walked 11 times.

Many observers remark later on how long it took him to make the walk in. According to legend, Alexander is badly hung over. A vigorous celebration of his victory the previous day has left him barely in condition to stand, let alone pitch. Both Alexander and Hornsby vehemently denied this. They insist that he had a few drinks the night before but when he entered the game "he was as clear-eyed as I was," Hornsby says, "and I never drink."

Standing at bat now is Lazzeri. The rookie had driven in 114 runs, second only to Ruth during the season. He also struck out 96 times, tops in the league. Alexander starts him off with a nasty curve on the outside corner, "a classic pitch to watch," in Hornsby's words. Then the pitcher comes back inside and Lazzeri swings. He is in front of the pitch, but the crowd rises in anticipation as it heads towards the leftfield line. Alexander said it landed 10 feet foul, but to Hornsby it looked more like two feet. When everyone resumed breathing, Alexander fired once more, over the outside corner, and Lazzeri went down swinging. The threat was over; Alexander finished with two innings of hitless relief and St. Louis was champion of baseball.

The Managers:

While Hornsby had hit .403 in his first season as manager, this pennant race got to him. Under the pressure, his average dipped 86 points, the only time he would hit below .360 during the 1920s. It was also the last time he would manage for an entire season and finish higher than the second division. His cranky, dictatorial methods cost him a last chance to return to the Series. The Cubs fired him in 1932 after 97 games and then won the pennant under the cheerier Charlie Grimm.

Coincidentally, it was Miller Huggins who managed the Cards when Hornsby arrived, and it was he who installed him as a regular second baseman. The Yankees' Series record was now 1-3 and the usual rumblings of discontent with Huggins were heard throughout New York.

The Heroes:

This was the culmination of Alexander's career. Eleven years after his unsuccesful debut in the Series with the Phillies he had returned triumphantly. While Flint Rhem was the nominal ace of the staff, with a 20-7 record, it was the veteran Alexander whom Hornsby chose to bring the Cards home.

Thevenow was no more than a .247 hitter during his 15-year career. This was to be his only season as a regular shortstop with the Cards. But his .417 average topped all the sluggers in this Series, and in the games St. Louis won he hit .500. His two-out, bases loaded single in the fourth inning of game seven was the winning margin of the Series.

Ruth ended up walking a record 11 times. He got only six hits, but four of them were homers.

It was also an outstanding Series for Pennock, who outdueled Willie Sherdel twice in memorable battles and did his best to hold the Cards in with three innings of scoreless relief in the seventh game.

The Zeroes:

Years later, when Alexander bumped into Lazzeri in San Francisco, the old pitcher told him, "I sure am getting tired of striking you out." Both men spent the rest of their lives retelling the story of their confrontation. While Lazzeri and Mark Koenig would make up for it in subsequent years, the two rookies both suffered through subpar Series. They hit a combined .155, while Koenig's four errors hurt the Yankees repeatedly.

It was also a lackluster Series for future Hall-of-Famer Chick Hafey. The Cards leftfielder hit only .185, struck out seven times and put his own centerfielder, Taylor Douthit, out of commission for the last three games when he collided with him while going for a fly ball.

The Aftermath:

For the Yanks, this was merely a learning experience. They were about to be molded into what most baseball historians still regard as the greatest team of all time.

The Cardinals were set to replace the Giants as the pre-eminent franchise in the National League. They would win nine pennants in the next 21 years. But first their owner pulled off one of the most shocking trades ever made, nearly tearing apart his new champions by sending Hornsby to the Giants in exchange for Frank Frisch. In the long run, it was a great deal. But it stunned St. Louis. Breadon had to disconnect his telephone as furious Cardinals fans threatened him with great bodily harm and newspapers outdid themselves in attacking him. Hornsby had been on the outs with the owner for several months, and Breadon promised himself that no matter what happened during the season, the manager was out. It was a scenario that would be eerily repeated after another Cardinals championship in 1964.

Notes:

Sportsman's Park was owned by the St. Louis Browns, with the Cardinals as tenants. Anticipating that they would be making the pennant run, Browns management almost doubled its seating capacity for 1926, to 33,000. It was the Cards, however, who raked in the chips, a Series winner's share of $5,585.

Another single-game attendance record was set in game two at Yankee Stadium, as 63,600 turned out. But for the second year in a row, the seventh game was played in dank and cold conditions. Only 38,000 fans showed up for the showdown.

The Series had one of the strangest conclusions of any ever played. With the Yanks trailing 3-2 and two out in the ninth, Ruth walked for the 11th time. To the shock of all, he then tried to steal second base, and was thrown out easily by Bob O'Farrell. Needless to say, it is the only Series ever to end in that fashion.

FACT:
This was the only Series to end with a runner caught trying to steal. He represented the tying run.

Line Scores:

Game One, October 2

SL (NL)—100 000 000—1
Sherdel L, Haines (8)

NY (AL)—100 001 00X—2
Pennock W

Game Two, October 3

SL (NL)—002 000 301—6
Alexander W

NY (AL)—020 000 000—2
Shocker L, Shawkey (8), Jones (9)

Game Three, October 5

NY (AL)—000 000 000—0
Ruether L, Shawkey (5), Thomas (8)

SL (NL)—000 310 00X—4
Haines W

Game Four, October 6

NY (AL)—101 142 100—10
Hoyt W

SL (NL)—100 300 001—5
Rhem, Reinhart L (5), Bell (5), Hallahan (8), Keen (9)

Game Five, October 7

NY (AL)—001 000 001 1—3
Pennock W

SL (NL)—000 100 100 0—2
Sherdel L

Game Six, October 9

SL (NL)—300 010 501—10
Alexander W

NY (AL)—000 100 100—2
Shawkey L, Shocker (7), Thomas (8)

Game Seven, October 10

SL (NL)—000 300 000—3
Haines W, Alexander (7) SV

NY (NL)—001 001 000—2
Hoyt L, Pennock 7

1927

New York (AL) 4
Pittsburgh (NL) 0

It was a quiet execution for Murderers Row. For the second time in Series history, one team was eliminated in four straight games. The result was expected but the Pirates still put up a decent battle against overwhelming forces.

> **FACT:**
> Even all these years later, the 1927 Yankees are the measure of baseball excellence. It was a team without a flaw. Power. Speed. Defense. Pitching. The team had it all.

The Preview:

Even before the season was over they were being acclaimed as the greatest team in history. Even all these years later, the 1927 Yankees are the measure of baseball excellence. It was a team without a flaw. Power. Speed. Defense. Pitching. The Yankees had it all.

This was the year that Babe Ruth hit 60 homers, but wasn't voted the Most Valuable Player. That award went to Lou Gehrig, who drove in 175 runs on 47 home runs and actually had more total bases than The Babe. Gehrig had emerged as a great hitter, taking his place beside Ruth as the most devastating hitting combination the game has ever known.

There was more. Tony Lazzeri finished third in homers with a modest 18, but also had 102 RBIs. Earle Combs hit .356 and finished right behind Ruth and Gehrig in runs scored. The closest thing to a soft spot in the lineup was third baseman Joe Dugan, who hit .269 and swore that he was once fined for stalling a rally by only getting a single.

As usual, Waite Hoyt (22-7) and Herb Pennock (19-8) anchored the pitching staff. This year they were joined by 30-year-old rookie Wilcy Moore, who won 13 games in relief, saved 13 more and finished with a 19-7 record. Moore threw a heavy

Babe Ruth (l) and Lou Gehrig (r) led the Yankees' mauling of the sacrificial-lamb Pirates, collecting 11 of New York's 19 RBI on six extra-base hits—two doubles and two triples by Gehrig and two Ruth homers.

sinker and for one season, at least, it was almost unhittable. Moore only started 12 games and writers liked to claim years later that he was the first true relief pitcher. That isn't quite accurate. The Senators began using Firpo Marberry in that sort of role in 1924 and the following year all of his 55 appearance were out of the bullpen. But Moore did it in New York and that always makes a difference.

The Yanks led from opening day to the finish and won the pennant by 19 games over Philadelphia. The team they were meeting in the Series, however, was not quite ready to roll over. The legend goes that when the Pirates saw the Yanks take batting practice, blasting ball after ball into the distant rightfield seats at Forbes Field, they were beaten before the first game began. That seems to be a later invention. The Pittsburgh lineup had three future Hall of Famers of its own: third baseman Pie Traynor and the Waner brothers, Paul and Lloyd, in the outfield. A fourth inhabitant of Cooperstown, Kiki Cuyler, hero of the 1925 Series, sat on the bench for the entire Series because of a feud with his manager.

Pittsburgh had won the pennant without him, fighting off the Cardinals by 1 1/2 games. And it may be that Cuyler would have made no difference against the Yankees. Still, this is one of the odder episodes in the history of player-manager relations. Manager Donie Bush had moved Cuyler into the number two slot in the batting order in an effort to shake him out of a batting slump. But Cuyler hated hitting second. He didn't feel comfortable there and did not regard himself as a good opposite field hitter, a prerequisite for the hit-and-run plays a number-two hitter is often called on to make. Bush refused to back down and was joined by an indignant owner, Barney Dreyfuss. Cuyler was benched in July and never played again. Claude Barnhart was inserted in the lineup instead, and while he hit .319 he was sorely lacking in speed and defense.

Paul Waner hit a league-leading .380; his little brother, in his rookie year, set a record with 198 singles, while hitting .355. Both Traynor and shortstop Glenn Wright knocked in over 100 runs. While the Pirates couldn't play long ball with New York, this was an excellent offensive team.

It also had the league's ERA champ in Remy Kremer (19-8), along with Carmen Hill (22-11), suddenly a winner 12 years after he first broke in, and Specs Meadows (19-10). On paper it was not a mismatch at all. But not many bet that way.

Turning Point: Game Two, Seventh Inning.

After three straight Series of towering drama, it is a bit hard to locate a precise point at which this set turns, especially since the Yanks never trail by more than 1-0, and that for just two innings. New York, for all its power, hits only two home runs, both by Ruth, and the team batting average of .279 is well off the season mark.

They win the first game, but it is a 5-4 struggle with clutch relief work by Moore saving it for Hoyt. Pittsburgh must win the second game at Forbes Field to have any chance of extending the Series. The Yanks jump off to a 3-1 lead against Vic Aldridge. But in the seventh, the Pirates look as if they may break through on surprise starter George Pipgras, who was only 10-3 during the season.

George Grantham leads off with a drive that caroms off the rightfield wall, but Ruth, playing it perfectly in the corner, holds the leadoff man to a double. It is almost forgotten what a graceful fielder Ruth was. In the old movies, which usually show only his home run trot, he appears to be almost ungainly. Like Ruth, part of the strength of this Yankees team was its defensive excellence as well as its power.

With the runner at second instead of third, the infield can set itself at normal depth without worrying about giving up a run. So shortstop Mark Koenig is in easy position to toss out Moon Harris on a grounder, while holding Grantham at second. Johnny Gooch then sends a soft liner towards right, but Lazzeri sprints back and makes a leaping grab of the ball, then flips it in one motion to Koenig to double the runner off the bag.

The threat is over and the New York defense has stifled Pittsburgh's last chance. The Yanks erupt for three in the eighth to win the game, 6-2, and take the Series home to New York where they can finish off the sweep.

The Managers:

This was only Bush's second test as a big league manager. He had lasted one year in Washington, fired in favor of Bucky Harris after the 1923 season. He returned to his hometown of Indianapolis and was named president of a minor league team. When Pittsburgh called in 1927 Bush was ready. Unfortunately, his feud with Cuyler clouded an impressive season and he lasted only two more years with the Pirates. In his final two years as a manager, with the White Sox and the 1933 Reds, he finished dead last.

This was the season that cinched Miller Huggins' reputation. His handling of this collection of stars and the efficient way they dispatched all opposition finally won him the respect of the New York media and fans. At 48, he was at the pinnacle. But the clock already has started to wind down on him.

The Heroes:

In the 1926 Series, the Cardinals walked Ruth 11 times. Bush chose to pitch to him, possibly because Gehrig had grown into a threat almost as formidable behind him in the batting order. Ruth hit .400, led both teams with 7 RBIs and walked just twice. He and Gehrig knocked in 12 of New York's 20 runs-batted-in.

Mark Koenig also made up for his weak 1926 performance by hitting .500 and fielding flawlessly.

While the Waner brothers, the Big Poison and Little Poison of Pirate lore, found themselves outgunned, it was no fault of theirs. They were amazed when their tiny hometown of Harrah, Oklahoma, held a welcoming parade for them after the Series, despite the sweep. Most townsfolk had bet the Waners would hit higher than the Ruth-Gehrig combination, and they had come through on that score. The brothers hit .367, while the Yankee sluggers batted .357. Oddly enough, Lloyd, who set a record for singles during the season, led the Pirates in Series extra base hits with two.

Pennock pitched one of the Series masterpieces. Until Traynor singled with one out in the eighth in the third game, the New York veteran had a perfect game. He eventually gave up three hits in the 8-1 win.

The Zeroes:

Cuyler's replacement in the outfield, Barnhart, hit a respectable .313 and led the team with 4 RBIs. Still, it was a slower, more easily defensed Pittsburgh team without him. The Pirates did not steal a single base in the Series, while Cuyler, who played only half a year, led the team with 20.

The catching combination of Earl Smith and Gooch combined for 73 RBIs during the season. In the Series, they went 0-for-13.

The Aftermath:

Owner Barney Dreyfuss was infuriated by the sweep, saying there was no excuse for one pennant winner to lose four straight to another. There was no forgiveness for Cuyler, either. He was sent to the Cubs for infielder Sparky Adams shortly after the Series, then went on to help Chicago win two pennants. Paul Waner said that he often wondered as years went by how good Pittsburgh might have been with an outfield of Cuyler and the Waners. The Pirates would not win another pennant for 33 years.

While the Yankees may have reached their peak, they were a long way from being knocked off the mountain. Illness took Shocker out of the pitching rotation, but the 1928 version of Murderers Row was the same thunderous bunch.

Notes:

For the second straight season, the Series ended on a strange play. Pittsburgh reliever John Miljus loaded the bases with none out in the ninth and the score tied, 3-3. He then struck out Gehrig and Bob Meusel. But with one strike on Lazzeri, he threw the ball over the catcher's head and the winning run scored on the wild pitch.

The Pirates had been so impressed with the way Moon Harris hammered them in the 1925 Series with Washington that they picked him up from the Senators at the start of the season. He hit .326 as the regular first baseman, but this time the October magic was missing. He hit only .200 against the Yanks and lasted just one more season in the majors.

FACT:
The Series ended in the bottom of the ninth, game four, when the winning run crossed the plate on a wild pitch.

Line Scores:

Game One, October 5

NY (AL)—103 010 000—5
Hoyt W, Moore (8) SV

Pit (NL)—101 010 010—4
Kremer L, Miljus (6)

Game Two, October 6

NY (AL)—003 000 030—6
Pipgras W

Pit (NL)—100 000 010—2
Aldridge L, Cvengros (8), Dawson (9)

Game Three, October 7

Pit (NL)—000 000 010—1
Meadows L, Cvengros (7)

NY (AL)—200 000 60X—8
Pennock W

Game Four, October 8

Pit (NL)—100 000 200—3
Hill, Miljus (7) L

NY (AL)—100 020 001—4
Moore W

1928

New York (AL) 4
St Louis (NL) 0

This was payback time for the 1926 Series and it was brutal. New York not only swept the Cards, they clobbered them. The closest game was decided by three runs and the Yanks outscored St Louis by 27-10.

The Preview:

It took a year for the Cardinals to shake off the shock of Rogers Hornsby's stunning departure following the 1926 championship. It turned into a lingering malady, as the National League had to help the franchise buy out Hornsby's stock in the ballclub in order for the trade to go through. That took several months. His replacement, Frank Frisch, eventually mollified the fans by playing well. Catcher Bob O'Farrell, who did not want the job, was named manager. He had to deal with arm problems throughout the year and the added burden was too much for him. Shortstop Tommy Thevenow suffered a broken ankle, and was never again the same player. Still, the team had lost the pennant by just 1 1/2 games and was primed for another run.

Volatile owner Sam Breadon decided that O'Farrell was not the one to lead the team, despite his near miss. Instead, he named Bill McKechnie, who had come over as a coach in 1927 after quitting as manager at Pittsburgh. The unencumbered O'Farrell still couldn't throw, but the Cards swung a deal to get Jimmie Wilson, a great defensive receiver, from the Phillies.

The shortstop problem was solved when veteran Rabbit Maranville was brought up from the minors. One of baseball's merriest pranksters, he had been exiled to AAA ball after annoying one team too many. At 37, he was still an outstanding shortstop and the Cards installed him as their starter.

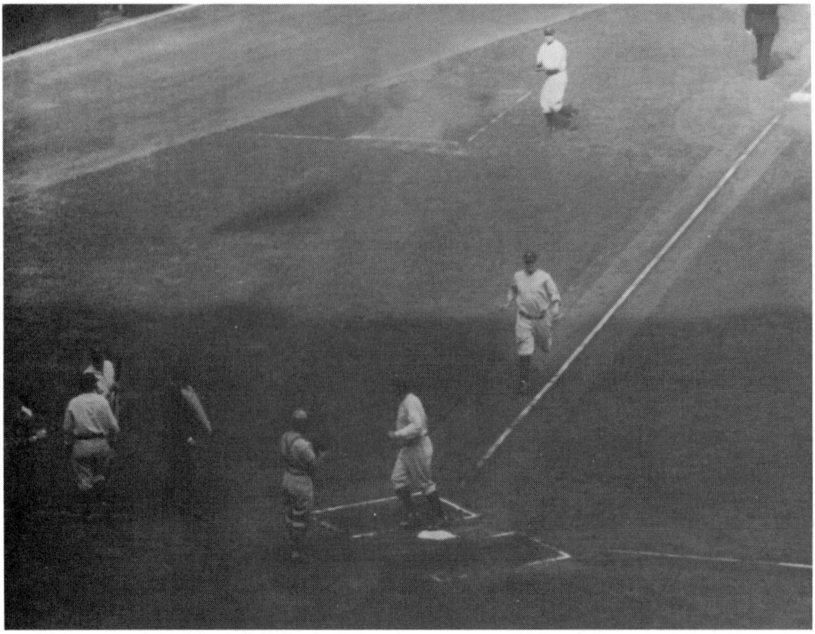

Babe Ruth crosses the plate on a Lou Gehrig home run, a common occurrence in the 1928 Series. Gehrig had four homers and nine RBI, while Ruth contributed three homers and four RBI. They combined to hit .592.

Jim Bottomley led the league in homers (31) and RBIs (136), while Chick Hafey's .337 average was high on the team. Frisch slipped a bit, by his standards, hitting an even .300, but his defensive play and speed made up for it.

Both Willie Sherdel (21-10) and Jess Haines (20-8) were back from the '26 champs, while Grover Alexander kept rolling along at 41 with a 16-9 record.

Moreover, the Yanks had declined somewhat. While Babe Ruth and Lou Gehrig mauled the opposition, their supporting cast was showing some wear. The sluggers had tied for the lead in RBIs with 142 and Ruth slammed 54 homers, the fourth time he exceeded 50. But the Series would begin with centerfielder Earle Combs and third baseman Joe Dugan both injured. Herb Pennock (17-6), a brilliant performer in the previous two Series, had a sore arm, and so did second baseman Tony Lazzeri, who could barely throw. Even Ruth was hobbled by a bad leg.

The crippled Yanks had faded badly down the stretch and were almost caught by Philadelphia, winning by just 2 1/2 games. They were down to two reliable starters, George Pipgras (24-13) and Waite Hoyt (23-7). The Cardinals had every reason to expect a competitive Series, in which they stood a good chance of winning.

Turning Point: Game Two, First Inning.

Hoyt stops the Cards easily in the opener, giving up three hits in a 4-1 win. But now it's Alexander's turn, and St. Louis is confident that the hero of '26 can stymie the Yankees again and take a split back to Sportsman's Park.

But it doesn't happen. Cedric Durst, filling in for Combs, leads off with a single and, with one out, Ruth walks on four pitches. Gehrig then drives a tremendous shot into the right-field seats and before the crowd is even settled the Yanks are off to a 3-0 lead.

The Cards actually struggle back against Pipgras to tie the game in the second. But the New York onslaught continues. Durst drives in another run in the home half of the inning and the Yanks are in front again, 4-3. Then Alexander is shelled from the game in the third when three more Yankees cross the plate.

And that's that. The Cardinals now know they have no one capable of holding New York. Gehrig's shot, one of four he hit in the Series, serves notice of that. It is to be a New York cakewalk all the way.

The Managers:

McKechnie, who is just one year older than Alexander, has his second winner in three years with two different clubs. No manager had ever produced pennants so quickly after switching teams. However, Breadon is mortified by the Series sweep and is already looking for a replacement.

For Miller Huggins, this sixth Series is his final one. He has conquered his critics but within a year he will be diagnosed with cancer and will die just five days later. The passing of Huggins ends the first great era of Yankee dominance.

The Heroes:

This was strictly a Ruth and Gehrig production. The numbers they put up in this Series were mindboggling. Gehrig hit .545, drove in 9 runs and slammed 4 homers. Ruth, meanwhile, hit at a .625 clip, knocked in 4 runs and swatted 3 homers, all of them coming in the last game. The Yankees may have been lame and the rest of the team only hit .196, but Ruth and Gehrig were able to get it done alone.

Hoyt's two complete game wins gave him 6 for his career, tying him with Chief Bender of the A's.

FACT:
This was strictly a Ruth and Gehrig production: Gehrig hit .545, drove in 9 runs, and slammed 4 homers, while Ruth hit .625, knocked in 4 runs, and swatted 3 homers.

Tom Zachary, picked up from Washington late in the season, was pressed into emergency action because of Pennock's sore arm. The left-hander was only 9-12 during the season. He had won twice in 1924, and picked up his third Series victory with a complete game, 7-3 win in game three.

The Zeroes:

Alexander looked to be every one of his 41 years in this Series. Besides his terrible game two start he was belted again in relief in the last game and finished with an earned run average of 19.80.

The two critical St. Louis acquisitions during the season were catcher Jimmie Wilson and outfielder George Harper, who came over from the Giants and hit .305. During the Series, the two newcomers combined for a .100 average, going 2-for-20.

The Aftermath:

It didn't take Breadon long to broom McKechnie. With the team in fourth place next June, he switched managers, sending McKechnie to the Rochester AAA team and bringing Billy Southworth to the majors. By the end of the season, he'd seen enough of Southworth and fired him, only to bring him back 11 years later to become his most succesful manager.

This was the last hurrah for several of New York's starters. Mark Koenig, Joe Dugan and Bob Meusel would all lose their jobs within the next year as the Yanks entered a rebuilding period to prepare for even greater success. They would find the manager to take them there on the following year's National League champs.

Notes:

Because of the injury to Lazzeri's throwing arm, the Yankees had to substitute for him in the late innings. His replacement infuriated the Cards with his heckling. It was an art form that the sub, Leo "The Lip" Durocher, would develop to perfection in later years.

There were a pair of future stars on the benches in both dugouts. Bill Dickey, who would take over as New York's regular catcher next year, never got into a game. The Cards used Pepper Martin as a pinch runner. Three years later, while still technically a rookie, he would turn in one of the greatest Series performances ever.

FACT:
Injured Yankee second baseman Tony Lazzeri was replaced in the late innings by a player whose heckling infuriated the Cardinals. It was an art form Leo "The Lip" Durocher would perfect.

Ruth's 10 hits in a four-game set was a record, one of 19 individual Series marks he held at the end of this season.

Line Scores:

Game One, October 4

SL (NL)—000 000 100—1
Sherdel L, S. Johnson (8)

NY (AL)—100 200 01X—4
Hoyt W

Game Two, October 5

SL (NL)—030 000 000—3
Alexander L, Mitchell (3)

NY (AL)—314 000 10X—9
Pipgras W

Game Three, October 7

NY (AL)—010 203 100—7
Zachary W

SL (NL)—200 010 000—3
Haines L, S. Johnson (7), Rhem (8)

Game Four, October 9

NY (AL)—000 100 420—7
Hoyt W

SL (NL)—001 100 001—3
Sherdel L, Alexander (7)

1929

Philadelphia (AL) 4
Chicago (NL) 1

A first game shock and a fourth game sunburst took the A's to a surprisingly easy victory over the Cubs. Only a win in game three saved the National League from the ignominy of being swept three years in a row.

The Preview:

It took Connie Mack 15 agonizing years to get back to the top. After breaking up his 1914 pennant winners, he watched his A's plunge to the bottom of the league like a shipwreck. Only in 1925, as the nucleus of his future champions settled into place, did Philadelphia finally crawl out of the second division.

That was the year the battery of Lefty Grove and Mickey Cochrane, two of the most intense competitors in baseball history, arrived. They joined second-year man Al Simmons, who was starting a streak of 11 consecutive years in which he'd knock in more than 100 runs. Jimmie Dykes was also on hand, although still shuttling between second and third base. But this group could not break the stranglehold of the Yankees on first place. Mack tried bringing in great names from the past—Ty Cobb, Tris Speaker, Zack Wheat, even Eddie Collins from his former champions. They got the A's closer, but that was all. They almost caught the Yankees in 1928, only to fall 2 1/2 games short.

This time there was no stopping them. Jimmie Foxx (.354) was installed at first base and teamed with Simmons (.365) to become the league's most potent batting combination from the right side. Only the Babe Ruth—Lou Gehrig lefty duo outdid them. Bing Miller, a former member of the A's who was traded and then reacquired, checked in at .335, just ahead of Cochrane's .331.

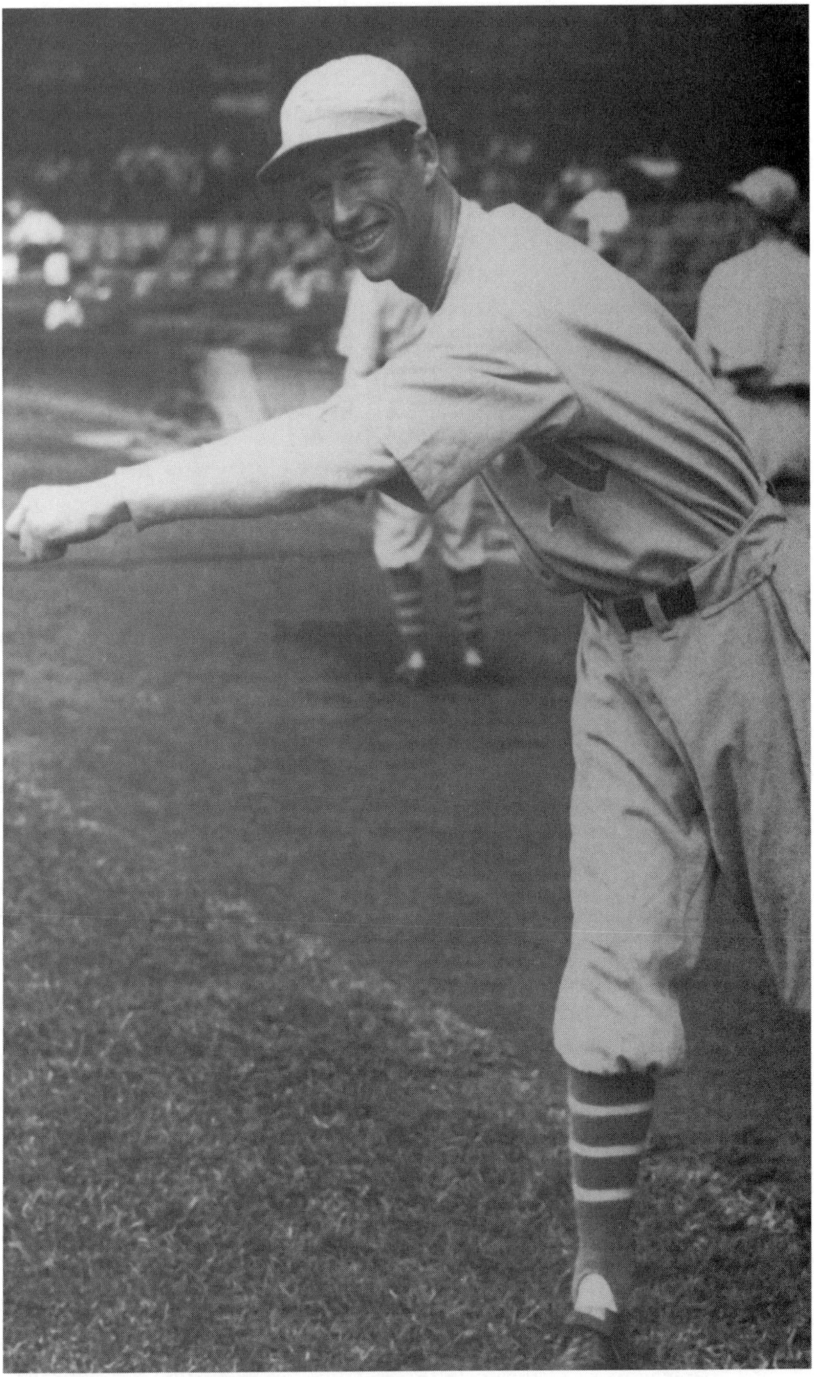

Lefty Grove, after a dominant 20-6 regular season, pitched out of the bullpen for Connie Mack, saving two games with six shutout innings.

Grove was 20-6 and in this golden age of hitting he was the only pitcher in either league with an earned run average below 3.00. That was a fair indication of his dominance. Backing him up were the capable George Earnshaw (24-8) and Rube Walberg (18-11). Mack cannily refused to say which one would start the opener.

That was a problem. Because as strong as Philadelphia's lineup was, the Cubs predominantly right-handed attack was even tougher. The combo of Hack Wilson and Rogers Hornsby drove in an incredible 308 runs and hit 79 homers. The rotund Wilson had sparkled since coming over from the Giants in 1926, leading the league in homers three years and topping it in RBIs this time. Named for his physical resemblance to the wrestler Hackenschmidt, Wilson was an outfielder of uncertain skills. The only thing that gave him more trouble than a high fly was a highball. As the title of his biography phrased it: His hands were always wet. Nonetheless, he was a terrific force at bat.

After being traded by the Cardinals, Hornsby went to New York, where he feuded with John McGraw, and then to the Braves, where he couldn't get along with anybody. His hitting didn't suffer, but those teams could hardly wait to get rid of him. In Chicago, however, he found a home, hitting .380 and scoring a league-high 156 runs. That wasn't all. The Cubs also had Kiki Cuyler, another fugitive from a rancorous former employer. Benched for the 1927 Series in Pittsburgh, he thrived at Wrigley Field. Cuyler hit .360 and led the league with 43 stolen bases. And then there was Riggs Stephenson, who had been cut loose by Cleveland. Always a terrific hitter, he was a disastrous second baseman. With the Cubs, though, he moved out of harm's way, to left field, and hit .362.

This was such an efficient run machine that it survived even the loss of Hall of Fame catcher Gabby Hartnett, who went down with an arm injury. Zack Taylor was picked up from the Braves in mid season and stabilized that position. The Cubs had no pitcher as overpowering as Grove, but Pat Malone (22-10), Charlie Root (19-6) and Guy Bush (18-7) were the best three starters in the league. This was a team that figured to restore much of the National League's battered prestige.

Turning Point: Game Four, Seventh Inning.

The exciting Series is not turning out as expected. The A's take two in Chicago, but then Bush comes back in game three to win a 3-1 decision at Shibe Park, the first National League win after 10 straight losses.

In game four, the Cubs maul 45-year-old veteran Jack Quinn, the second surprise starter Mack sprung on Chicago in the Series. By the seventh it is 8-0 behind the dependable Root. The Cubs will have evened the Series with their top winner, Malone, ready to pitch the fifth game. Things are looking as bright as the sunny autumn weather for the Cubs.

Even a leadoff homer by Simmons doesn't stir the crowd. Foxx singles and then Bing Miller lifts a fly to center. The day before, Stephenson had reported problems seeing the ball during batting practice because of the late afternoon sun. His warning apparently went unheeded. Wilson loses sight of Miller's pop fly and it falls safely. Two more singles make it 8-3 and now the crowd is aroused. Pinch hitter George Burns pops out, but one more single and the score is 8-4. The big lead has been cut in half.

Veteran Art Nehf, star of two Series with the Giants, comes in to pitch and Mule Haas sends a hard liner directly at Wilson. The centerfielder comes running in, then stops short and again holds his hands up helplessly. He loses the ball in the sun for a second time. By the time he recovers, Haas has come all the way around for a three-run homer. It is now, shockingly, 8-7. As Dykes watches the ball bounce past Wilson, he slaps the player next to him hard on the back, sending him sprawling. To his horror, he sees the man on the ground is Mack. He rushes up to apologize but Mack is grinning. "That's all right, James," he says. "Everything is all right now."

Nehf walks Cochrane and Sheriff Blake comes in for Chicago. But the A's aren't through. Simmons and Foxx both single again, tying the score. Miller is hit by a pitch and Chicago now must bring in tomorrow's starter, Malone, to stop the rally. But the back-slapping Dykes rifles a double off the leftfield wall, bringing home two more Philadelphia runs. The A's have scored 10 times in the inning, the biggest comeback in Series history.

Grove, designated as a Series relief pitcher by Mack, comes in and blows the Cubs away for the last two innings. The A's walk off with a 10-8 win. There is still one more game to play but everyone knows the Series is over. No team can recover from an inning like this.

FACT:
The biggest comback in Series history occurs in the seventh inning of game four, as the A's score 10 runs and erase an 8-0 deficit; they win 10-8.

The Managers:

This was Connie Mack at the very height of his wizardry. His astonishing choice of Howard Ehmke as his first game starter, his moving of Grove to the bullpen—these were two of the most daring bits of strategy in Series history. Anyone other than Mack might not have dared to try them. He was now 67 years old and a beloved institution in Philadelphia. It had been 24 years since he first managed in a Series, a record for longevity no other manager has matched. And he wasn't done yet.

Joe McCarthy had grown up in Philadelphia rooting for Mack's teams. He never made it out of the minors as a player. Phil Wrigley plucked him out of Louisville to take over his lackluster Cubs in 1926. Under McCarthy they improved each year before making the breakthrough to the Series. He was responsible for bringing most of the team's key players to Chicago, and once he got them there he knew how to keep the many strange personalities in line. His success did not go unnoticed, especially by the men who ran the Yankees. However, they felt sure that Wrigley would never let him go.

FACT:
In one of the most daring moves in Series history, Connie Mack, who managed 53 years and in 8 Series, selects seldom used Howard Ehmke as his first game starter and moves the great Lefty Grove to the bullpen. Ehmke sets a Series record by striking out 13 and Grove saves 2 games. Ehmke, 35, was considered washed up and only pitched 3 more games in his career, while Grove had just completed the third of seven straight twenty-win seasons.

The Heroes:

Ehmke was 35 years old and considered long washed up when Mack called him into his office two weeks before the season ended. He had once been a top starter for second division teams in Detroit and Boston. Ehmke expected this meeting was called to tell him that he had been cut. He quickly began pleading his case, telling Mack, "I still have one more good game left in this arm." That was what the manager wanted to hear. He had no intention of cutting Ehmke, but wanted him to leave the team to scout the Cubs. He had a hunch that Ehmke's repertoire of off-speed curves might hold off the Chicago power hitters for a few innings. It would also enable Mack to move Grove to the bullpen, where he would be an overpowering presence.

Mack didn't announce his starter for the opener until the teams took the field. He was so secretive that even Ehmke wondered if he had understood him right at their meeting. He then pitched the game of his life, a tough 3-1 win in which he set a Series record by striking out 13. Only when the A's scored twice in the ninth did Ehmke have any breathing room. He ended the game with a flourish, striking out Chuck Tolson with the tying run on base. Mack called this performance the greatest thrill he ever had in baseball. It was also the last game Ehmke would win in the majors.

Grove also did just what he was told. He saved two games in relief and pitched six shutout innings.

Haas only finished with five hits. One of them was the three-run homer that brought the A's back into game four, and another was a two-run homer in the ninth that tied the final game. Miller ended the Series a few moments later with a two-out single that scored Simmons with the winning run.

The Zeroes:

Hack Wilson, oddly enough, led all hitters in this Series at .471, but he didn't drive in a single run and his fielding miscues set up the record 10-run rally in game four.

This was also a terrible Series for Hornsby, who struck out eight times in 21 times at bat and hit only .238. The Cubs set a record by striking out 50 times in the five games.

The Aftermath:

For the third time in four years, the manager of the National League team did not survive the next season. Phil Wrigley was so upset by the performance of his Cubs that he decided to put McCarthy on a short leash. When the team was mathematically eliminated from the 1930 race, he replaced him with Hornsby, who had missed most of the season with injuries. The Cubs hadn't missed him as a player. They scored even more runs than the 1929 edition, but still finished second behind St. Louis.

The A's were just getting started, however. With the same line-up and rotation of pitchers, they breezed to a second straight pennant.

Notes:

This Series ended a few days before the stock market crash. That accounts for the tumultuous reception given to President Herbert Hoover, who attended game three in Philadelphia. Newspapers called it the most affectionate ballpark greeting for a chief executive in memory.

Earnshaw got credit for the second game win although he only pitched 4 2/3 innings. Under present scoring rules, the victory would have been awarded to Grove. Oddly enough, the record books credit Grove with a save, although that statistic was unknown under 1929 scoring rules.

The opening day crowd at Wrigley Field went over 50,000, or about 10,000 above the park's present capacity. Temporary bleachers were built in centerfield. Wider seats installed in a 1937 remodeling of the park cut its capacity. In Philadelphia, however, owners of apartment houses beyond the rightfield wall erected wildcat stands, on which the ballclub didn't make a dime.

Line Scores:

Game One, October 8

Phi (AL)—000 000 102—3
Ehmke W

Chi (NL)—000 000 001—1
Root L, Bush (8)

Game Two, October 9

Phi (AL)—003 300 120—9
Earnshaw W, Grove (5) SV

Chi (NL)—000 030 000—3
Malone L, Blake (4), Carlson (5), Nehf (9)

Game Three, October 11

Chi (NL)—000 003 000—3
Bush W

Phi (AL)—000 010 000—1
Earnshaw L

Game Four, October 12

Chi (NL)—000 205 100—8
Root, Nehf (7), Blake (7) L, Malone (7), Carlson (8)

Phi (AL)—000 000 (10)0X—10
Quinn, Walberg (6), Rommel (7) W, Grove (8) SV.

Game Five, October 13

Chi (NL)—000 200 000—2
Malone L

Phi (AL)—000 000 003—3
Ehmke, Walberg (4) W

1930

Philadelphia (AL) 4
St. Louis (NL) 2

In a season dominated by hitters, the superior pitching of the A's prevailed. Using what amounted to a two-man staff, Philadelphia kept the Cards in check and the American League won its fourth consecutive Series.

The Preview:

There has never been a year quite like it. Hitting records fell like trees in a cyclone. Bill Terry hit .401, and Hack Wilson drove in 190 runs. The batting average for the entire National League was .303. One pitcher, Pittsburgh's Remy Kremer, won 20 games with an ERA of over 5.00. It was the most incredible offensive outburst in the game's history.

Every single regular in the St. Louis lineup hit over .300—and it was only the third best-hitting team in the league. There were no Cardinal league leaders, although rookie George Watkins hit .373. Frank Frisch recorded a personal high of 114 RBIs, to go along with a .346 average, and Chick Hafey chipped in with a .336 mark.

The core of the team was the same as the 1928 pennant winners. The left side of the infield had changed, with Charlie Gelbert, a college football star at tiny Lebanon Valley, at shortstop, and Sparky Adams, who was obtained from Pittsburgh, moved from second base to third. The Cards also were forced to keep backup catcher Gus Mancuso when Judge Landis ruled that he had been optioned to the minors too many times. It was a fortunate decision. When Jimmie Wilson went down with injuries, the rookie stepped in and hit .366.

It was the pitching that was a bit of a problem. Aside from Wild Bill Hallahan (15-9), no pitcher won more than 15. And

Philadelphia outfielder Al Simmons led all hitters with a .364 Series average and eight hits. He also tied teammate Mickey Cochrane with two homers while driving in four runs in six games.

Hallahan was on the unpredictable side. True to his nickname, control problems had held back his development and returned often enough for him to lead the league in walks. But the Cards pulled off a major deal early in the season by prying veteran Burleigh Grimes from the Braves. The 37-year-old spitballer went 13-6 after the trade and assumed the role of the staff's stopper.

Philadelphia was almost a match for the Cardinals in hitting. Despite holding out for most of spring training, Al Simmons stepped right in and hit .381 with 165 RBIs. Jimmie Foxx, the next batter in the lineup, added 156 runs batted in, and his 37 homers trailed only the redoubtable Babe Ruth and Lou Gehrig. There were also big years for Mickey Cochrane (.357) and Bing Miller (100 RBIs).

But the critical difference was pitching. In Lefty Grove, the A's had the best in the game. Not only was he 28-5, his 2.54 ERA was more than two runs below the league average. No one was even a close second. And just to round things out, he also saved 9 games in relief. Right behind him was George Earnshaw (22-13). Rube Walberg, the other starter, had tailed off to 13-12, but with Grove ready to start three times, the A's felt they would have no major problems with St. Louis. Connie Mack was a firm believer in the adage that good pitching stops good hitting. He was about to put that to the test.

The Turning Point: Game Five, Ninth Inning.

The A's do just about as they like with St. Louis in the first two games, with Grove and Earnshaw stopping their hitters and the Philadelphia sluggers crackling with extra base power.

When the Series moves to St. Louis, things change in a hurry. Hallahan and the 37-year-old knuckleballer Jess Haines stymie the A's, defeating Grove in the process. Suddenly, the Series is tied, with Earnshaw and Grimes going at each other in a pivotal fifth game.

The two men duel grimly, 0-0, for seven innings. St. Louis can't get anyone beyond second and Grimes turns away each of Philadelphia's mild threats. In the 8th, Mule Haas beats out a bunt and steals second. Joe Boley's infield hit sends him to third. With the chance at a breakthrough, Mack has to pinch hit for Earnshaw. Grimes walks Jim Moore to load the bases. Then he gets a forceout at the plate from Max Bishop and a harmless grounder from Jimmie Dykes. The threat is over, it's still 0-0 and Earnshaw is out of the game. But Grove is in. Working on no days of rest, he disposes of St. Louis easily in the home half of the inning.

Grimes, pitching too carefully, walks Cochrane to start the ninth. Simmons lifts an easy fly out and Foxx, a slugger whose home-run distances rival those of the mighty Babe, comes to bat. Double X was discovered by his fellow Maryland native, Home Run Baker. The former A's star signed him to a minor league contract and then sold him to Mack. In a tight situation in game one, the 22-year-old Foxx recalls that Grimes had outsmarted him. He went to his mouth, but then threw him a hard curve. Totally fooled, Foxx struck out with two runners on.

FACT:
Of the 52 innings in this six-game Series, the A's Lefty Grove and George Earnshaw pitched 44 of them, giving up only 5 runs and 28 hits; each won 2 games.

Mack warns him to be ready this time. Again Grimes seems to wet the ball for the spitter, but when the curve comes Foxx is right on it. The ball rockets deep into the leftfield bleachers as the Philadelphia runners circle the bases in almost complete silence. One of the great duels in Series history is over. With the lead regained, the A's return home and wrap it up easily, 7-1, in the sixth game.

The Managers:

Connie Mack continued to use his pitchers masterfully. Of the 52 innings in this Series, Grove and Earnshaw pitched 44 of them. They started all but one game, with Earnshaw working the deciding win on one day's rest. No one could squeeze more out of a pitching staff than the lean old man in the business suit on the Philadelphia bench.

For the Cardinals, this was their third different manager in five Series. Owner Sam Breadon had demoted his 1928 manager, Bill McKechnie, to the minors the following year, then decided to bring him back when he didn't like his replacement, either. A disgusted McKechnie accepted an offer with the Braves in 1930, so pitching coach Gabby Street was promoted to manager. A tough old catcher who had teamed with Walter Johnson in Washington, Street was called "Old Sarge" because of his rank in World War I. The 1930 Cards won a four-team battle in which just 6 games separated them all at the end. In a showdown series with Brooklyn, pitcher Flint Rhem turned up lame with a story of being kidnaped by gamblers and forced to drink bootleg whisky, and couldn't start against the Dodgers. It took a tough manager to survive that.

The Heroes:

The A's won with power. Of their 35 total hits, 18 went for extra bases. Every hit in their first and sixth game wins was a double, triple or home run. Simmons led the way with a .364 average and two homers, while Dykes made every one of his four hits an extra base job and topped both teams with 5 RBIs.

Earnshaw, while usually overshadowed by Grove, was a tireless pitcher in the midst of a run of three straight 20-win years. He worked 296 innings during the season and topped that off with three Series starts in which he gave up just two runs.

Grove, finally getting a chance to start after being used only in relief in 1929, won twice, although in one of those, in the fifth game, he came out of the bullpen.

The Zeroes:

The big Cardinal bats went almost totally silent in this Series. Jim Bottomley was 1 for 22 and struck out nine times. Centerfielder Taylor Douthit was almost as futile at 2 for 24. In fact, Grimes, with 2 hits, equalled or surpassed three of the regulars. It was the second straight year that Philadelphia's pitching had stopped a supposedly overpowering attack.

No one abducted Rhem during the Series, although the 29-year-old right-hander may have wished they had. He was driven out in the fourth inning after giving up 6 runs in his only start. In four World Series with the Cards, Rhem never won a game.

The Aftermath:

For once, Breadon did not make any abrupt changes after the Series. Street returned as manager and most of the regular players came back as well. But two rookies were called in for 1931. One of them was pitcher Paul Derringer, the other a wild, young outfielder named Pepper Martin.

The A's also played a pat hand. Mack dearly wanted a third straight championship, a prize that had eluded him after his consecutive wins in 1910-11, and also proved beyond the grasp of John McGraw in 1923. Mack felt the third title would mark his team as the greatest of all time.

Notes:

This was Frisch's sixth Series in 10 years and his double in the second game established a new career record for hits, with 43. He would go on to play in two more and wind up with 58 hits, a mark exceeded, eventually, only by Yogi Berra and Mickey Mantle, who played in many more Series than Frisch. He is, in fact, one of only two non-Yankees in the top nine on the career hit list; the other is Pee Wee Reese.

FACT:
The Cards' Frank Frisch established a new Series career hit record with 43; he wound up with 58, third all time behind Yogi Berra and Mickey Mantle.

The Depression was well underway but it didn't affect attendance. The fourth game crowd of 39,946 at Sportsmans Park was the largest ever to see a ballgame in St. Louis.

An exception to the Cards lethargy at the plate was Hafey. Of his six hits, five were doubles, setting a mark that still stands for a six-game Series.

Line Scores:

Game One, October 1

SL (NL)—002 000 000—2	Phi (AL)—010 101 11X—5
Grimes L	Grove W

Game Two, October 2

SL (NL)—010 000 000—1	Phi (AL)—202 200 00X—6
Rhem L, Lindsey (4), Johnson (7)	Earnshaw W

Game Three, October 4

Phi (AL)—000 000 000—0	SL (NL)—000 110 21X—5
Walberg L, Shores (5), Quinn (7)	Hallahan W

Game Four, October 5

Phi (AL)—100 000 000—1	SL (NL)—001 200 00X—3
Grove L	Haines W

Game Five, October 6

Phi (AL)—000 000 002—2	SL (NL)—000 000 000—0
Earnshaw, Grove (8) W	Grimes L

Game Six, October 8

SL (NL)—000 000 001—1	Phi (AL)—201 211 00X—7
Hallahan L, Johnson (3), Lindsey (6), Bell (8)	Earnshaw W

1931

St Louis (NL) 4
Philadelphia (AL) 3

The Philadelphia dream of three straight championships was shredded by a human buzzsaw named Pepper Martin. Running wild against the greatest catcher in the game and hitting every pitcher on the A's staff, the rookie carried his team to the National League's first triumph in five years.

The Preview:

The three previous St. Louis pennants had been won with sweat and anguish. They were closely contested affairs, with three and sometimes four teams bunched together at the end. Not this time. The Cards breezed home by 13 games and were the first team since the 1913 Giants to win more than 100 games in the National League.

They had the batting champ in Chick Hafey (.349). Outside of him, however, the Cards did not figure high in individual stats. Frank Frisch was voted Most Valuable Player with his .311 average and usual outstanding defensive work at second base. It was essentially the same group as the 1930 team, although it scored almost 200 fewer runs. Jim Bottomley was hurt much of the year, but still managed to hit .348, and most other regulars were down significantly from their 1930 outputs. The big addition was centerfielder Pepper Martin, whose spirited play forced a trade of veteran Taylor Douthit. Martin had reported for spring training with a three-day stubble of beard after being arrested in Georgia for hooking a ride on a freight train. This was, after all, the Depression. Installed as a regular, he hit an even .300, and his dirt-on-the-face style of play endeared him to the St. Louis fans, known as the rowdiest in the league. It was the debut of the Gas House Gang style.

St. Louis's "Pepper" Martin (scoring) sparked the Cardinals' Series victory with a home run in Game 5 and 12 hits (for a .500 average), as well as five steals, five RBI, five runs, and four doubles.

The biggest improvement, though, was the pitching staff. Bill Hallahan topped the league's pitchers at 19-9, leading as well in both walks and strikeouts. Ageless Burleigh Grimes, now on hand for an entire season, went 17-9, while rookie Paul Derringer was 18-8.

The A's had Lefty Grove, who was in a league of his own. The A's star put together one of the greatest years of any pitcher after the dead ball era. With a 31-4 record and a miniscule earned run average of 2.06, he was at the peak of his skills, unquestionably the dominant pitcher of his era. He was joined, as usual, by the tireless George Earnshaw (21-7), one of the great pressure performers, and a rebounding Rube Walberg (20-12).

Al Simmons won his second straight batting title at .390, and while Jimmie Foxx slipped a bit in average (.291), he still knocked in 120 runs. Mickey Cochrane, the soul of the team, was indisputably the greatest catcher in the game; some would say the best in history. A relentless competitor and clutch hitter, he refused to allow the A's to lose.

Philadelphia won 107 games and easily outdistanced the rest of the league for the third straight year. There seemed to be no slowing them, and the A's entered the Series as heavy favorites.

Turning Point: Game Five, Sixth Inning.

"What is that Martin hitting," an exasperated Connie Mack asks Earnshaw at one point in the Series. "Every damn thing I throw up there," replies his pitcher. After getting three hits in an opening loss, Martin scores both runs in a 2-0 St. Louis win, stealing second twice after singles to set up the scores. In game three, he collects two more hits, doubling off the scoreboard to help beat the formidable Grove. In game four he has the only two hits the Cards get off Earnshaw in their loss.

Now it is the fifth game and the Series is tied. The A's must win to take a lead back to St. Louis for the last two games. Mack, as he often does in such situations, turns to one who has been there before. Waite Hoyt, picked up in mid-season from Detroit and a veteran of six Series with the Yankees, is asked to come in and hold the Cardinals and Martin.

For five innings he does a creditable job. The Cards cling to a 1-0 lead behind Hallahan. The lefty had walked seven men in his second-game shutout, but this time he has control to go along with his stuff and the A's are helpless. Hoyt holds Martin to a bunt single, although Martin does back Simmons to the leftfield wall in his other time at bat.

With one out in the sixth, Frisch doubles down the third base line. Martin, who played the first five games batting in the sixth slot, has been elevated to cleanup for this one. He comes up now and drives Hoyt's pitch into the upper deck of the leftfield pavilion for a home run. The St. Louis lead is now 3-0, more than enough of a margin for Hallahan.

Martin is not through, however. He bats once more in the eighth, with a runner on second, and slashes a single off Rube Walberg, driving in another run. It is his 12th hit of the Series. Immediately afterwards he is thrown out for the first time while trying to steal by Cochrane. That was the last hit for Martin, although he still has one more steal in him to torment the A's during a seventh game rally. The advantage he has given the Cards is more than the A's can overcome. St. Louis dethrones them as champions.

The Managers:

This was the final walk in the sun for Mack. As financial pressures mount during the Depression, he is forced to sell off his stars one-by-one to hold the franchise together. Just as it happened 17 years before, the A's again fall to the bottom of the league. This time they do not re-emerge in Mack's lifetime.

This was also the last Series in the much shorter career of Street. The team, with four pennants in six years, was about to enter a period of change, and the impatient Sam Breadon was not one to stick with his manager under those conditions.

The Heroes:

Eventually, other players would surpass Martin's total of 12 hits in a Series, but no one would anyone combine such clutch hitting and base running until another Cardinal, Lou Brock, did it three decades later. Martin signed up for a vaudeville tour after the Series turned him into a national figure. He quit halfway through the tour and went back home to Oklahoma to be plain old Pepper. The fun was just beginning for him in St. Louis, though, as a kindred spirit named Dean was about to join the team.

FACT:
The Cardinals' Bill Hallahan was brilliant in his two starts, winning both and allowing only one run in 18 innings. He also came in and got the final out of the seventh game with the tying run on base.

Hallahan was brilliant in his two starts, allowing just one run to a team that was reputed to eat left handers for breakfast. He also came in and got the final out of the seventh game with the tying run perched on first. Grimes, who won the other two for St. Louis, was almost as tough, outwitting the A's with his relic of a spitball and shadow of a curve.

For the second straight year, Mack handed the paddle to Grove and Earnshaw and rode the rapids with them. The two men had pitched 44 of the 52 innings of the 1930 Series. This time they combined for 50 out of 61 innings and a 2.16 ERA.

The Zeroes:

This was an experience unlike any in his career for Cochrane. A fierce competitor and an outstanding receiver, he was regarded by his peers as the best there was. Martin's five steals against him were irritating, and Cochrane was so distracted that he hit only .160 with no extra base hits. It was a low point in his brilliant career.

It was also a disappointment for the rookie Derringer, who was clubbed out by the A's in both his starts. He would go on to lose four straight Series assignments during his career before turning it around in 1940 and clinching that championship for Cincinnati with two wins.

FACT:
In this Series, Grove and Earnshaw pitch 50 out of 61 innings and combine for a 2.16 ERA.

The Aftermath:

The clock ticked loudly in the background for the A's. Attendance had fallen off sharply as the Depression took hold in Philadelphia and the club could no longer afford the salaries its big stars were paid. Mack would manage to hold it together for one more season before he was forced to break up his team. The emergency sale brought a pennant to Detroit and restored Boston to contention after years in the second division. But it doomed the A's to a barren era that would last through 41 years and two franchise switches.

Changes also came quickly for the Cards. They dropped all the way to seventh as age caught up to the veterans who had won four pennants in six seasons. Despite his performance in the Series, Grimes was peddled to the Cubs and never had another winning year. By the end of 1932, Bottomley and Hafey were gone and Gelbert had to be replaced after discharging a shotgun into his leg in a hunting accident. But an even rowdier version of the Cards was about to take shape as the fabled Gas House Gang hit St. Louis.

Notes:

Sportsmans Park was only half full for the deciding seventh game. While a Series high of 39,401 watched the A's blowout in game six, the count dropped to a puny 20,805 the next day.

Game two almost ended in a brawl when the plate umpire ruled that catcher Jimmie Wilson had trapped a two-out third strike on Jim Moore. Wilson, thinking the game was over, snapped a triumphant toss to the third baseman while the alert Moore ran safely to first. Since that loaded the bases with St. Louis clinging to a 2-0 lead, the Cards went bonkers. But Bottomley got them out of trouble by making a tumbling catch of Max Bishop's pop foul into the A's bullpen.

Line Scores:

Game One, October 1

Phi (AL)—004 000 200—6
Grove W

SL (NL)—200 000 000—2
Derringer L, Johnson (8)

Game Two, October 2

Phi (AL)—000 000 000—0
Earnshaw L

SL (NL)—010 000 10X—2
Hallahan W

Game Three, October 5

SL (NL)—020 200 001—5
Grimes W

Phi (AL)—000 000 002—2
Grove L, Mahaffey (9)

Game Four, October 6

SL (NL)—000 000 000—0
Johnson L, Lindsey (6), Derringer (8)

Phi (NL)—100 002 00X—3
Earnshaw W

Game Five, October 7

SL (NL)—100 002 011—5
Hallahan W

Phi (AL)—000 000 100—1
Hoyt L, Walberg (7), Rommel (9)

Game Six, October 9

Phi (AL)—000 040 400—8
Grove W

SL (NL)—000 001 000—1
Derringer L, Johnson (5), Lindsey (7), Rhem (9)

Game Seven, October 10

Phi (AL)—000 000 002—2
Earnshaw L, Walberg (8)

SL (NL)—202 000 00X—4
Grimes W, Hallahan (9) SV

1932

New York (AL) 4
Chicago (NL) 0

In a Series that was more like an avalanche, the Yankees destroyed the Cubs. In terms of scoring margin, it was the greatest mismatch in Series history, but thanks to Babe Ruth it still provided one of the game's indelible moments—at least in legend.

The Preview:

After three years of looking up at the A's, the Yanks were back. This was to be a transition team, composed in equal parts of stars from the '20s and the players who would lead New York to an era of even greater domination. Babe Ruth was now 37 and perceptibly slower in the field. He moved, in his own phrase, "like the baselines run uphill." Still, he was a terror at bat. He led this team with 41 homers, trailing only Jimmie Foxx in the league, and batted .341. His old partner Lou Gehrig also put up big numbers—34 homers, 151 RBIs and an average of .349.

Other holdovers from the previous decade were Tony Lazzeri and Earle Combs, both with seasons over .300. Catcher Bill Dickey and leftfielder Ben Chapman, who had never played with a winner before, were new contributors to an offense that scored over 1,000 runs and left Philadelphia flailing 13 games in its wake. The Yanks lineup also included Hall of Famer Joe Sewell, brought over from Cleveland and moved to third base.

George Pipgras remained as a starter from the former champions and the ageless Herb Pennock occasionally showed off his endless assortment of curves. But the staff was now keyed by Lefty Gomez (24-7) and Red Ruffing (18-7), the two pitchers who would carry New York through the 30s.

The Cubs had come through a typically brutal National League race, fighting off the Pirates by 4 games and fighting

Babe Ruth watches his last Series homer leave the park in 1932. This was the infamous "called shot" homer that has been the subject of much debate and conjecture over the years.

among themselves for half a season. Rogers Hornsby, a humorless disciplinarian as a manager, was let out in late summer with the team in second place and nearing open revolt. Later in life, Hornsby was a patient teacher of youngsters in Chicago sandlot clinics, but he could never grasp why major league ballplayers could not do the things that came so effortlessly to him. His replacement was amiable first baseman Charlie Grimm, cut loose by Pittsburgh years before because the management was convinced that such a cheerful guy could never be a winner. The Cubs, relieved at Hornsby's departure, rallied around Grimm.

This was not a great team by any measure. Riggs Stephenson was its biggest threat, with 85 RBIs and a .324 average—figures dwarfed by the New York heroes. Rookie Billy Herman came through with a good year at second base, at .314. But Kiki Cuyler and Gabby Hartnett were both down from former seasons, and overall the Cubs were no better than fourth in the league offensive stats.

Pitching was the team's strength. Lon Warneke, in just his second season, went 22-7 and led the league with a 2.37 earned run average. He was assisted by holdovers from the 1929 staff—Guy Bush (19-11) and Charlie Root (15-10). But the year had been a struggle for Pat Malone (15-17), and Burleigh Grimes, obtained from St. Louis after his great performance in the 1931 Series, had reached the end at 6-11.

Shortstop Mark Koenig, the Yankees' starter in the '20s, was a key acquisition. Cut loose by Detroit after the 1931 season, Koenig was playing in the Pacific Coast League when the Cubs found him. He hit .353 and played brilliant shortstop in place of the injured Billy Jurges. But Chicago voted him only half a share of the Series swag. His old pals on the Yanks were furious at this slight and determined to remind the Cubs about it at every opportunity.

Turning Point: Game Three, Fifth Inning.

The Yanks mauled Chicago in the first two games in New York by scores of 12-6 and 5-2. Now the Series was back at Wrigley Field, and if the Cubs were going to make any kind of move, this was the time.

It is a nasty set of games, with the teams riding each other endlessly over the Koenig issue and anything else that comes up. A healthy Jurges goes back to shortstop in game two and Koenig sits in embarrassed silence on the Cubs bench as his old teammates heap abuse on his current colleagues.

New York starts off the third game as if determined to remove all doubts quickly. Ruth smashes a three-run shot before Root can get a man out in the first. The Cubs struggle back against Pipgras and by the fifth the game is knotted, 4-4. The only hit Root gives up after the first is a homer by Gehrig in the third.

Sewell starts off the Yankee fifth with an infield out and Ruth settles in to hit. He missed a try for a shoestring catch the previous inning on a drive by Jurges. The ball fell in for a double and Jurges then came around with the tying run. The Cubs let him know about it, while the Yanks are in full cry back at them.

Now comes the part at which history and myth part ways. On a two-strike pitch from Root, Ruth hits a tremendous clout into the centerfield bleachers. It is the last home run he would ever hit in the Series and is clearly the turning point of this game. It becomes famous in baseball lore as the "called shot." According to the story, Ruth held up one finger at each strike. After the second pitch, he motions to the bleachers, indicating where the next ball would land. Then he hits it right there.

> **FACT:**
> After the second pitch, Ruth motions to the bleachers, indicating where the next ball would land. Then he hits it right there.

The problem is the a lack of any contemporary corroboration to this story. Chicago baseball writer Jerome Holtzman spent years tracking down the origins of the story and concluded that almost certainly it was a later invention. No news reports on the game included it. H.G. Salsinger, of the *Detroit News,* considered the most astute baseball observer of his time, starts his game story by writing: "The Ruth, crushed to earth, rose again." Nowhere in his description of the key home run is there a mention of Ruth calling the shot. Veteran players claim that if Ruth had tried to show up the hot-tempered Root in such a manner, the following pitch would have been directed at the vicinity of his ear.

Still, the story has been repeated so often that a dozen years later Ruth himself was convinced it happened. In a newspaper article, he called it his greatest day in baseball and began the description by saying: "Nobody but a blankety-blank fool would have done what I did that day."

Gehrig followed the mythic blast with another home run, giving the Yanks a 6-4 lead and finishing Root's work for the day. The Yanks go on to win, 7-5, then crush the Cubs 13-6 to polish off the Series. The Babe has prevailed once more.

The Managers:

This was a grim sort of revenge for Joe McCarthy. He had been fired by the Cubs in 1930 when he failed to repeat as a winner, despite almost universal acclaim as the best young manager in the game. The Yankees snapped him up immediately and within two years he had them back on top. McCarthy is now 45, and his best days are still ahead.

Grimm bore the distinction of being the first manager to win a pennant after being named a mid-season replacement. His nickname, Jolly Cholly, said it all. A delightful man, still an active player at 34, he believed in letting his players play, on and off the field. He would go on to win two more pennants for the Cubs and establish the foundation of the great Milwaukee Braves teams of the 50s. Ironically, he would also end up on the wrong end of a pennant-winning manageral switch in just six more years.

FACT:
The Yankees sweep their third straight Series (1927, 1928, 1932). Gherig and Ruth combined for 40 hits, 14 homers, and 38 RBIs in those 12 games.

The Heroes:

For a third World Series, this was simply a case of Ruth and Gehrig annihilating the opposition. The "called shot," fictitious though it may be, gets Ruth most of the attention when this Series is considered. He batted a "mere" .333, though, and his two homers in game three were the only ones he hit.

Gehrig, however, was unstoppable. He hit .529, drove in 8 runs and slugged 3 home runs. In the last three Yankee appearances in the Series—1927, 1928 and 1932—Gehrig went 19 for 41, with 7 homers and 21 RBIs. Over the same period, Ruth was 21 for 46, with 7 homers and 17 RBIs. Is there any wonder the Yankees swept 12 consecutive Series games?

This was also a successful debut for Gomez, who would go on to win six Series games without a loss—the best career percentage ever. Gomez at this time is 23 and a 20-game winner in both of his full big league seasons. He is securely established as Pennock's successor, the left-hander who must be a big part of any effective Yankee team. Gomez stopped the Cubs in game two, 5-2, while striking out 8.

The Zeroes:

Chicago's staff ERA was 9.26, which sums up everything you need to know about this Series. Warneke managed to make it through a complete game, but every other Chicago starter had an ERA in double figures. The Cubs were especially unprepared to face a team featuring Ruth and Gehrig because their only left-hander was Jakie May, who pitched relief. May had no more luck that his right-handed confreres, giving up 7 runs in less than 5 innings.

Pipgras did his part as a pitcher, getting the credit for New York's third game victory. In a more dubious achievement, he broke a Series record with his offensive efforts, striking out five times at the hands of four different pitchers.

The Aftermath:

The Cubs were halfway into an odd cycle that would see them win a pennant every three years between 1929 and 1938. After getting smeared in this Series, they faded back to a competitive third place, 6 games off the pennant pace of the Giants. But a group of younger talent already was in the pipeline, and right on schedule, in 1935, the Cubs were back on top again.

The return to the summit also was brief for the Yankees. Ruth and Combs were starting to fade. Before New York could develop its next crop of superstars, the Yanks had to be content running second to Washington and a talented Detroit team. But when New York got it together again in 1936, it went off on a tear like baseball had never seen.

Notes:

When Pennock came in to save New York victories in games three and four it established a record for longevity. He had first appeared in the Series in 1914, as a young reliever for the A's during the sweep by Boston. The 18-year span between his first and final Series appearances is still a record for pitchers.

This was the worst year of the Depression and it was reflected in the New York crowds. Yankee Stadium was one-third empty for the Series opener, with just 41,459 in the park. Observers reported that it was the cheap seats in the bleachers that were almost bare. Nonetheless, there were full houses in both games at Wrigley Field.

Line Scores:

Game One, September 28

Chi (NL)—200 000 220—6
Bush L, Grimes (6), Smith (8)

NY (AL)—000 305 31X—12
Ruffing W

Game Two, September 29

Chi (NL)—101 000 000—2
Warneke L

NY (AL)—202 010 00X—5
Gomez W

Game Three, October 1

NY (AL)—301 020 001—7
Pipgras W, Pennock (9) SV

Chi (NL)—102 100 001—5
Root L, Malone (5), May (8), Tinning (9)

Game Four, October 2

NY (AL)—102 002 404—13
Allen, Moore (1) W, Pennock (7) SV

Chi (NL)—400 001 001—6
Bush, Warneke (1), May (4) L, Tinning (7), Grimes (9)

1933

New York (NL) 4
Washington (AL) 1

The Giants used pitching to win their first pennant in nine years, and it proved strong enough to stifle the Senators, too. Carl Hubbell baffled Washington twice in the National League's most impressive showing in the Series in a decade.

The Preview:

Many sportswriters derided this Giants team as the '30s equivalent of the Hitless Wonders. That was overstating the case. The entire league had fallen off 37 points since establishing a record .303 average in 1930. Hitting was in a down cycle—occasioned, in part, by the arrival of young pitchers such as Carl Hubbell, Dizzy Dean and Lon Warneke. Bill Terry, who hit over .400 in 1930, was only a .322 hitter this year. Leading the Giants by a wide margin, it was also the fourth best mark in the league.

Even with all the hitting, New York had finished third in 1930. Now it was back on top thanks to pitching and defense. Second baseman Hugh Critz and shortshop Blondy Ryan shored up the middle of the infield. With Hall of Famer Travis Jackson unable to play, Ryan became a critical component of the team, even though he hit just .238. His telegram to the Giants as he was about to rejoin them after an injury became a rallying cry. "Can't lose," it read. "I'm on my way." Ryan was heckled the rest of the season for his hubris, but the Giants did keep winning.

Mel Ott, recognized as the top power hitter in the league, drove in 103 runs, while Jo-Jo Moore, in leftfield, was a .292 hitter. The Giants had some bench strength, too. They added Lefty O'Doul from the Brooklyn roster and the 36-year-old slugger still had enough pop in his bat to hit .306. When third baseman Johnny Vergez went down with appendicitis, the team called up

Cliff Bolton, a reserve catcher, pinch-hits in the eleventh inning of Game 4 with the bases loaded. Bolton's double play grounder ended the game and Washington's hopes of winning the Series.

Chuck Dressen from the minors. The 35-year-old infielder would begin his long managerial career next season, but he was still able to help the Giants through this stretch run. While not playing in the Series, Dressen had some valuable scouting information, as we shall see.

But it was the royal combination of King Carl Hubbell and Prince Hal Schumacher who carried the Giants. His deadly screwball had taken Hubbell to the top of the game's pitchers, with a 23-12 record and league-leading 1.66 earned run average. Schumacher was 19-12, while Freddy Fitzsimmons, at 16-11, rounded out the best starting three in the league.

There was a sense of *deja vu* about the Series. Just as when these teams met in 1924, the Senators were led by a young manager who was also a star infielder. At 26, Joe Cronin was even a year younger than his boy wonder predecessor, Bucky Harris, had been when he got the job. Seemingly indifferent to the added responsibilities, he drove in 118 runs, hit .309 and led the league's shortstops in fielding.

The Nats had reacquired Goose Goslin, a hero of the 1924 team, from the St. Louis Browns, and Ossie Bluege remained where he was in that memorable year, starting at third base.

Washington's lineup looked to be far tougher than the Giants', paced by leftfielder Heinie Manush (.336), who led the league in hits, and first baseman Joe Kuhel (.322), a defensive rock.

While there was no one quite as dazzling as Hubbell, the Senators still had the league's top winner in General Crowder (24-15), and right behind him was Earl Whitehill (22-8), long the ace of a thin Detroit staff. Also coming over from the Browns in the Goslin deal was Lefty Stewart (15-6) to round out the rotation. Because of its pitching the National League team found itself as the slight favorite for the first time in many years.

FACT:
Carl Hubbell pitched two shutouts, giving up just 13 hits and fanning 15 in 20 innings. This was the season he had set a record by pitching 46 consecutive scoreless innings. The next season he would strike out 5 straight Hall of Famers in the second All Star Game.

Turning Point: Game Four, 11th Inning.

Hubbell, as expected, stops the Senators cold, 4-2, in game one, with both Washington runs unearned. The surprise comes when Schumacher does the same in the next game, a 6-1 romp. As the Series moves to Washington, Whitehill gets the Nats on the board with a 4-0 blanking.

Now it is Hubbell's turn again against Monte Weaver. Lightly used during the season (but a 22-game winner the previous year), Weaver holds off the Giants, except for Terry's 4th-inning homer. Hubbell makes the 1-0 lead stand up, getting the first 10 men he faces.

Then the Senators lose their top hitter. Outraged over a close call at first base in the 6th, Manush puts up a prolonged argument before returning to the dugout. When he goes out to leftfield at the start of the 7th, umpire Moran informs the Senators that he has been ejected from the game for bumping him. Manush has to be pulled off Moran and the Senators run over to complain directly to Commissioner Landis, who backs up his umpire. Most observers felt, however, that the ump had blown both the call and the claim of contact.

Nonetheless, the Nats tie it that inning when Hubbell fumbles a bunt and catcher Luke Sewell lines a two-out single. Washington has yet to score an earned run off Hubbell, but it has forced him into extra innings.

In the 11th, Jackson, who is starting at third and supposedly cannot run at all, stuns the Washington infield by dropping a leadoff bunt. After a sacrifice, Ryan ("Can't lose. I'm on my way") drives him home with a single. It is now 2-1. Washington has one more crack at Hubbell, though.

A single, a bunt that refuses to roll foul, a sacrifice and an intentional pass to Sewell load the bases with one out. The pitcher's slot is next and everyone in the park expects to see Cronin bring in the great veteran Sam Rice to pinch hit. Now just a sub, the 43-year old Rice can still run. He hit .294 during the year and has the savvy to handle this situation. Instead, Cronin sends up Cliff Bolton, with just 83 times at bat in his entire big league career.

A reserve catcher, Bolton hit .410 in limited action this season. Dressen, recalling him from the minors, gets word to Terry that Bolton is as slow as they come. "Get him to hit it on the ground and it's a sure double play," Dressen says. Hubbell follows orders, Bolton slaps a shot to Ryan and the Giants pull off the game-ending twin killing.

Ott's 10th inning homer to win next day is merely a mopping-up exercise. The double play on Bolton is the true end of this Series.

The Managers:

Bill Terry had taken over from John McGraw in 1932. Growing ever more irascible with age, the 59-year-old McGraw was losing control of the team. Many of the younger players, led by Fred Lindstrom, chafed under his restrictive rules and a full fledged revolt was threatened. Confronted with this, McGraw decided to retire, and the ownership, in a surprise, named Terry as his successor. Lindstrom, who thought the job would devolve to him, asked for and received a trade. The hitting star of the Giants, Terry quickly established a rapport with the other unhappy players. With little of McGraw's media flair, however, he was never a popular manager with the fans.

This was the first Series since 1906 in which playing managers opposed each other. Cronin was the best shortstop in the American League and his appointment following the 1932 season was also a major surprise. He replaced the revered Walter Johnson, who had won an average of 93 games in the previous three seasons but couldn't seem to get to the next level. As a manager, Cronin became known as a hunch player. Connie Mack remarked that he hated managing against him because of his unpredictability. For one year, at least, it paid off.

FACT:
This is the first Series since 1906 in which playing managers oppose each other.

The Heroes:

It was during this season, as he set what was then a league record of 46 consecutive shutout innings, that Hubbell first began to be called "The Meal Ticket." He was discovered in the Texas League in 1928, after the Tigers sent him to the minors because they didn't trust his screwball. But he mastered it and became one of the top control pitchers in the game. Between 1933 and 1937, he won more than 21 games every year and rose to his greatest fame after striking out five consecutive American Leaguers in the 1934 All Star Game. His two victories in this Series were his first appearances on the national stage.

Ott had arrived in New York two years before Hubbell as a 17-year-old. He hit .383 in a brief test and the intrigued McGraw installed him as his regular rightfielder. By the age of 20 he had smashed 42 home runs in a season. Ott would go on to lead the league in homers six times. In this Series, he hit a two-run homer on his first time at bat to provide the winning margin in the first game. Then he won the finale with a home run in his last time at bat. He also led both sides with a .389 average.

This was also a fine finish to the long career of Dolf Luque. The 43-year-old Cuban right-hander, who had pitched for the Reds back in the 1919 Series, got credit for the fifth game win in this one with four innings of shutout relief.

The Zeroes:

The Giants squelched Washington's top two hitters, Kuhel and Manush. The two of them were a combined 5-for-38, with no extra base hits.

It was also a disappointing Series for Goslin. He had an atypically low number of RBIs during the season, with just 64. He also got in Cronin's doghouse for failing to execute a sacrifice against Hubbell in the fourth game, a move that could have led to the winning run since Cronin followed with a pop fly single. It made Goslin susceptible to trade offers from Detroit, which got him into the Series for the next two years.

Crowder was also ineffective, giving up 9 runs in 16 innings and losing twice. Like Goslin, he would go on to the pennant party with the Tigers in 1934.

The Aftermath:

The glow was brief for the Senators. Their pitching collapsed in 1934, injuries took down Kuhel and Sewell, and even the arrival of Cecil Travis to take over at third base couldn't save them from a slide to seventh place. It would be 32 years, and a franchise switch to Minnesota, before their next pennant.

The Giants also slipped a bit, losing the pennant by two games. An intemperate remark by Terry in spring training was part of the trouble. When a reporter asked him, half-seriously, about the prospects of the Dodgers, Terry replied: "Is Brooklyn still in the league?" The Dodgers remembered and took great joy in knocking the Giants out of the race in September. But the Giants would be back on top in another two years, after a remake of their infield.

Notes:

Even the return of the Giants to the Series couldn't revive fan interest during the Depression. Crowds were below 30,000 for all three games in Washington and more than 10,000 seats were empty at the Polo Grounds for game two. The winning player's share of $4,257 was the lowest in 13 years.

O'Doul, in his only Series appearance, made his one time at bat count. His pinch hit single knocked in the lead runs in game two. Washed up as a pitching prospect at 26, he made himself an outfielder in the Pacific Coast League. McGraw brought him back to the majors five years later, and in his golden years O'Doul twice led the National League in hitting and carried a .349 lifetime average. He retired after 1934 to become a fulltime restraunteur in his native San Francisco.

Line Scores:

Game One, October 3

Was (AL)—000 100 001—2
Stewart L, Russell (3), Thomas (8)

NY (NL)—202 000 00X—4
Hubbell W

Game Two, October 4

Was (AL)—001 000 000—1
Crowder L, Thomas (6), McColl (7)

NY (NL)—000 006 00X—6
Schumacher W

Game Three, October 5

NY (NL)—000 000 000—0
Fitzsimmons L, Bell (8)

Was (AL)—210 000 10X—4
Whitehill W

Game Four, October 6

NY (NL)—000 100 000 01—2
Hubbell W

Was (AL)—000 000 100 00—1
Weaver L, Russell (11)

Game Five, October 7

NY (NL)—020 001 000 1—4
Schumacher, Luque (6) W

Was (AL)—000 003 000 0—3
Crowder, Russell (6) L

1934

St. Louis (NL) 4
Detroit (AL) 3

In a Series that finally reawakened the nation's imagination, the rowdy Gas House Gang defeated the Tigers in a furious battle that ended in a riot. Detroit slugged it out with the Cards but, in the end, had no one to compare with the Brothers Dean.

The Preview:

Leo Durocher was credited with the name. While talking to New York sportswriters during the season, he was asked which American League team the Cardinals could be compared with. "They wouldn't allow us in the American League," retorted Durocher. "They'd say we're just a bunch of gas house players." The label stuck and the hell-for-leather style of these cowboys in spikes seemed to strike a chord with Depression-Era America.

There was Pepper Martin, still running like the wild horse of the 1931 Series. There was Durocher, the combative shortstop, brought over from Cincinnati after Charlie Gelbart's hunting accident left the position open for the Cards. There was Ripper Collins, the league's home run champ and an apt running mate to the other free spirits on the team. There was Frank Frisch, who learned his baseball at the side of John McGraw and passed on that legacy to the players he now managed.

Mostly there was Dizzy Dean. He had come out of Arkansas with a scalding fast ball and enormous ego and led the league in strikeouts all three years he was in it. "If you can do it, it ain't braggin'," he said, and Dean kept doing it better each season. After 18 and 20 wins, he went all the way to 30-7 in 1934. At 23, he was the first National League pitcher to win that many since the end of the dead ball era and quickly became a national celebrity. He was joined by his younger brother, Paul, who was

Dizzy Dean, the St. Louis ace with 30 regular season victories, combined with his brother Paul to shut down the Tigers, both winning two games. Diz contributed a clutch run-scoring single in Game 6.

19-11 in his rookie year. Although he was quickly nicknamed Daffy, his personality was actually the polar opposite of his elder brother. With all that Dizzy had to say there were few words left over for Paul.

The Cardinals won out when the Giants collapsed down the stretch. Nonetheless, they led the league in most hitting stats, with leftfielder Joe "Ducky" Medwick batting .319 and the catching combination of Spud Davis and Bill DeLancey knocking in 105 runs. The pitching was thin behind the Deans, but Dizzy told everyone not to worry about that. "Me an' Paul will win four," he said.

Detroit was no walkover. The Tigers had won their first pennant in 25 years behind the power of the G Men: Hank Greenberg, Charlie Gehringer and Goose Goslin. They had all knocked in over 100 runs, as did shortstop Billy Rogell. In fact, the infield was nicknamed The Battalion of Death, so devastating was its hitting. Not quite as catchy as the Gas House Gang, but it got the message across. Greenberg, just getting established as one of the game's great sluggers, drove in 139 runs, while Gehringer, the best second baseman in baseball, led the team with a .356 average. Goslin, considered over the hill in Washington at 33, rebounded with a .305 season.

The Tigers brought up Lynwood Rowe at the end of the 1933 season. This year, the 24-year-old righthander, who was known as Schoolboy, reeled off a 16-game winning streak on the way to a 24-8 season. During a network radio broadcast in the middle of the streak he had sent a message to his girlfriend back in Arkansas: "How'm I doin', Edna?" Bench jockeys rode him unmercifully, shrieking the phrase at Rowe in a girlish falsetto for the rest of the season. But few could hit him. The Tigers also had Tommy Bridges (22-11), submariner Eldon Auker (15-7) and General Crowder, who joined them from Washington for the stretch run and went 5-1.

FACT:
The Tigers' Schoolboy Rowe was taunted endlessly with "How'm I doin', Edna?"—rendered in a girlish falsetto.

The soul of this team was its manager, Mickey Cochrane. He was purchased from cash-strapped Connie Mack for $100,000 after the 1933 season by Detroit owner Frank J. Navin. Navin didn't have the money, either, but borrowed it from his partner, industrialist Walter O. Briggs, who would soon take over the club. With his fiery field leadership, Cochrane transformed the Tigers from a placid, young team into a raging group of warriors. They were suitable opponents for the Gas Housers.

Turning Point: Game Six, Seventh Inning.

By the end of three games, the Deans are halfway home on their boast. Each of them wins his first start as the Cards take a 2-1 Series lead. Then the Tigers clobber the St. Louis staff, 10-4, in game four and achieve the unthinkable by beating Diz, 3-1, the next day. The Series is going back to Detroit with the Tigers needing just one game to close it out.

First they have to beat Paul. Cochrane has his ace, Rowe, ready to work on four days rest. He stopped St. Louis, 3-2, in a 12-inning classic in game two, retiring 22 consecutive hitters at one point. However, it becomes apparent that this game will be a struggle. There are reports that Rowe showed up with a swollen right hand but insisted on pitching anyhow.

Medwick singles home a run in the first, and the Tigers quickly get it back. In the fifth, hits by Durocher and Martin and a throwing error by Goslin give the Cards a 3-1 lead. Again the Tigers claw their way to a tie against Paul Dean, with Greenberg's two out single knotting it up in the sixth.

Rowe has sharp control but his pitches are not moving with their usual break. The seventh, however, looks easy. The bottom of the order is up and Rowe easily disposes of Ernie Orsatti. That brings up Durocher, a hitter so weak that New York writers called him "The All-American Out." But he uncorks a drive out of Jo-Jo White's reach in center and cruises in for a double. That brings up Dean, a decent .241 hitter during the season. Frisch waves off any thought of a sacrifice and lets his pitcher swing. Dean lines a single to right, Durocher scores, and the Cards have a 4-3 lead in front of a stunned Navin Field.

The Tigers cannot break through again. Durocher throws a runner out at the plate on a grounder in the seventh and Collins makes a corkscrew catch on Greenberg's pop foul to end the eighth with two runners on. The Cards win and they also know that Dizzy is ready to close it out the next day. He does, by an 11-0 thumping. But Durocher, the weakest hitter on the Gas House Gang, is the one who undoes Detroit.

The Managers:

McGraw and Mack opposed each other three times in the Series. Now it is their apprentices, men whom they had trained for the role of leadership. Frisch came out of the New York City sandlots and Fordham University to join the Giants as a 20-year-old. He had been the spark on four pennant winners and was one of McGraw's favorites, although that didn't stop the manager from trading him when he had the chance to get Rogers Hornsby. The trade backfired on New York, though, and McGraw badly wanted to get Frisch back as his own replacement. But Cardinals owner Sam Breadon had his own plans for Frisch. He soured on Gabby Street in 1933, claiming the manager went too easy on the veterans of his 1931 champions. So he replaced him with the hard-driving Frisch and watched the Gas House Gang coalesce around him.

Black Mike Cochrane, a scowling Irishman, had come out of Boston to join the A's in 1925. He was now only 30, and as tough a catcher as ever strapped on a mask. His peers regarded him as the best there ever was at that position and stood in awe of his flaming will to win. Mack wanted to sell him and Lefty Grove as a package, but the Tigers were convinced the pitcher was past his prime (Grove would win another 105 games for Boston). Cochrane was a perfect fit in Detroit, a manager who captured the heart of this tough industrial city like no other in history. The street behind the leftfield wall of old Tiger Stadium was named for him after his death.

The Heroes:

No brother act had ever played a World Series like this one. The Deans were the stuff of American legend, a frontier myth come to rollicking life. There was a nasty edge to some of the Gas House frivolity. Anti-Semitic slurs were tossed at Greenberg throughout the Series and Dizzy Dean repeatedly referred to Detroit's Jewish first-baseman as "Moe." But it was a less sensitive era and at heart the country seemed to sense that Dizzy didn't mean anything by it. The Deans' combined Series record of 4-1 with 28 strikeouts was all the pitching St. Louis needed. This was the Series in which Dean, put in as a pinch runner to spark the team in game four, was knocked unconscious by a relay to first by Rogell. He was taken to the hospital for an examination that produced the immortal headline: "X-Rays of Dean's Head Show Nothing."

No fewer than three Cards wound up with 11 hits. Martin added to his total of 12 from 1931, and was joined by Medwick and Collins.

Gehringer matched their total for Detroit. One of the most consistent ballplayers the game has ever seen, he was called the Mechanical Man because he rarely made a mistake in the field and had little to say about it afterwards. "He's in a rut," according to the famous Lefty Gomez description. "He hits .333 on Opening Day and he's still hitting .333 when the season ends."

The Zeroes:

It was a vexing Series all around for Detroit third baseman Marv Owen. A .317 hitter during the season, he went just 2 for 29 and then had the added indignity of getting spiked by Medwick in the incident that touched off a seventh game riot.

The Detroit fans had backed the Tigers ardently and as the Cards cruised to their 11-0 crushing of the hometown team in the seventh game, the crowd of 40,000 was desperately unhappy. During a 6th inning rally, Medwick slid into third and slashed Owen, who then belted the runner with the ball. The two players started fighting and had to be pulled apart. With the score 9-0, Medwick went out to leftfield and the Detroit fans began pelting him with everything from overripe produce to bottles. After 20 minutes of this barrage—and how the spectators managed to get all the stuff into the ballpark remains a mystery—Commissioner Landis ordered that Medwick be replaced. The Cards protested but Landis was adamant, stating it was the only way the game could be finished. So the Detroit fans, who had failed to show

FACT:
Detroit fans began pelting Cardinal left-fielder Ducky Medwick with everything from overripe produce to bottles. After 20 minutes of this barrage, Commissioner Landis ordered Medwick to be replaced.

up at the 1907 and 1908 Series, went to the other extreme this time and embarrased themselves again.

The Aftermath:

The Gas House came down in a hurry. Despite great performances by the Deans and Medwick, the Cards slipped to second in 1935. Then Paul Dean hurt his arm and they went to third. Then Dizzy ruined his arm trying to return too soon after a foot injury, and that was all she wrote. It took eight years for St. Louis to get to the top again, but when they did the Cards stayed for a while.

Detroit came back with the same lineup in 1935 and with no Deans in their way swept to the first championship in the franchise's history.

Notes:

The Tigers started this Series with a bad case of the jitters. They made five errors in the first three innings of game one, including two by Owen and one by the usually unflappable Gehringer. That helped St. Louis build a two-run lead for Dizzy Dean, which was ample.

While he pitched just one and one-third innings, Dazzy Vance, the longtime Brooklyn star, did manage to get into one game for the Cards, the only taste of the Series in his career.

As an index of economic recovery, the winner's share of $5,390 was the highest since the last pre-Depression year of 1929.

Line Scores:

Game One, October 3

SL (NL)—021 014 000—8
D. Dean W

Det (AL)—001 001 010—3
Crowder L, Marberry (6), Hogsett (6)

Game Two, October 4

SL (NL)—011 000 000 000—2
Hallahan, Walker (9) L

Det (AL)—000 100 001 001—3
Rowe W

Game Three, October 5

Det (AL)—000 000 001—1
Bridges L, Hogsett (5)

SL (NL)—110 020 00X—4
P. Dean W

Game Four, October 6

Det (AL)—003 100 150—10
Auker W

SL (NL)—011 200 000—4
Carleton, Vance (3), Walker (5) L, Haines (8), Mooney (9)

Game Five, October 7

Det (AL)—010 002 000—3
Bridges W

SL (NL)—000 000 100—1
D. Dean L, Carleton (9)

Game Six, October 8

SL (NL)—100 020 100—4
P. Dean W

Det (AL)—001 002 000—3
Rowe L

Game Seven, October 9

SL (NL)—007 002 200—11
D. Dean W

Det (AL)—000 000 000—0
Auker L, Rowe (3), Hogsett (3), Bridges (3), Marberry (8), Crowder (9)

1935

Detroit (AL) 4
Chicago (NL) 2

The Tigers finally break through for a championship. With their top slugger unable to play because of a broken hand, they still have enough to hold off the Cubs and set off the Motor City on a night of wild revelry.

The Preview:

The Cubs were sticking to their triennial schedule. Once every three years they popped up in the Series and 1935 was again their turn. Winning an even 100 games, they came in 4 games ahead of the Cardinals.

It was an odd assortment of the old and new in Chicago. Fred Lindstrom, the star third baseman of the Giants for several years, returned to his hometown as a centerfielder. Chuck Klein, who had been a hitting terror with the Phillies early in the decade, also was on hand—although his .293 average and 21 homers were a far cry from the numbers he once posted. A new generation of Cub stars were at the infield corners. Hometown hero Phil Cavaretta replaced manager Charlie Grimm at first. And the team's best third baseman in a generation, Stan Hack, hit a solid .311.

Holdovers from the 1932 winners were the foundation of this team, though. Catcher Gabby Hartnett hit .344 with 91 RBIs and second baseman Billy Herman, best at the position in the league, was right behind him at .341. Lon Warneke, another veteran from the former pennant winners, was 20-13 and Charlie Root, in his third Series with the Cubs, still had enough vim to go 15-8.

Bill Lee, in only his second season, became the team's top starter, at 20-6, and left-hander Larry French, who had come over

Detroit's "Mechanical Man," Charlie Gehringer (covering second base) turned in a typically stellar performance in the 1935 Series, batting .375 on nine hits, with four runs scored, another four batted in, and three doubles in six games.

from Pittsburgh, went 17-10. This was regarded as a solid, if unspectacular ballclub, good enough to lead the league both in batting and earned runs. It finished with a rush, too, constructing a 21-game winning streak to break open the race in September.

The Tigers were a powerhouse. Hank Greenberg crashed 36 homers and drove in 170 runs, leading the American League in both categories, while hitting .328. That was just two points behind Charlie Gehringer, who drove in 108 runs, which was just one less than Goose Goslin. A few players had come down from their high statistical plateaus of 1934 and Detroit was pressed fairly hard by the Yankees, who lost by just 3 games. There was power throughout the lineup.

The pitching staff was again anchored by Tommy Bridges (21-10) and Schoolboy Rowe (19-13). General Crowder was on hand for the entire season this time and worked up a 16-10 record, and there was also Eldon Auker, at 18-7.

Moreover, there was the sense that this was their time. Both teams had lost four World Series in a row, a fact duly noted by the newspapers. The only two championships the Cubs won had, in fact, come at the expense of Detroit. After the riotous, frustrating Series of 1934, the Tigers were determined that this one would not get away.

Turning Point: Game Six, Ninth Inning.

The Series has become a survival contest. Warneke pitches brilliantly, winning both of Chicago's games. But while working on the sixth inning of a shutout in game five, he feels something give in his right shoulder. Hartnett sees it at once and motions to the bench for Grimm to take the pitcher out. Warneke protests, but is forced to leave, and with him goes the Cubs one reliable starter.

In Detroit's view this only evens things up. Greenberg went down after game two, breaking his hand in a collision with Hartnett at the plate. The Tigers still win two of the next three, but runs are proving hard to come by with their cleanup hitter gone.

Game six between these wounded ballclubs matches Bridges and French. The Detroit right-hander, who throws one of the best curveballs in the game, has beaten the Cubs once. But Grimm is convinced that without Greenberg the Tigers are vulnerable to left-handed pitching. Both pitchers struggle. Herman's fifth-inning homer gives the Cubs a 3-2 lead, but a two-out single by Marv Owen, fighting a slump for the second consecutive Series, ties it in the sixth.

They go into the ninth at 3-3. That appears to be a temporary condition when Hack leads off with a triple over Gee Walker's head in center. Almost anything now will get the lead run home. Chicago's number eight batter, shortstop Billy Jurges, is the weak link on offense this season, hitting just .241. After him comes the pitcher and Grimm already has said that he has no one to come in behind French.

The manager allows Jurges to bat and he goes down swinging futilely on three pitches. French follows him to the plate. He hit exactly 100 points lower than Jurges and he, too, cannot get Hack in. He bounces right back to Bridges who holds the runner on third. Finally, leadoff hitter Augie Galan sends a long fly to left, but at this point it is just the third out. Bridges is out of the threat and the Tigers are coming to bat with a chance to win the Series.

A ripple of anticipation begins to build. With one out, Mickey Cochrane singles off Herman's glove. Gehringer then smashes a drive down the first base line, but Cavaretta makes a spectacular stab for the out, with Cochrane going to second. That leaves it to Goslin. He sends a looping liner to right. As the ball falls in and Cochrane races home, Navin Field erupts in joy. The city celebrates madly throughout the night, as if Goslin's blow has heralded the end of the Depression and the start of great times forevermore.

The Managers:

This was Cochrane's fifth Series in seven years as a player and manager. He had caught just 100 games this year, the fewest total in his career. His inspirational skills as a manager seemed to feed off his performance on the field. At 32, he was starting to wear down but there seemed to be several peak years still ahead of him.

The affable Grimm had decided to retire as a player at the end of the previous season to make room for Cavaretta. He was now 37, played a mean left-handed banjo and made the Cubs a happy place to play.

The Heroes:

This was the Tigers time to build Bridges over troubled waters. The right-hander's two complete game victories were the margin in a Series that was closer than expected. Bridges had led the league in strikeouts, with a modest 163, and was in the midst of a three-year run of 20-win seasons. He had been overshadowed by the exploits of Rowe during Detroit's two pennant-winning years. His gutty performance to close out the Cubs in the sixth game brought him out to center stage.

Before his injury, Warneke also pitched brilliantly. He had 20 wins in three of his four major league seasons and while he never reached that level again, he remained a consistent winner with the Cubs and Cardinals.

With Greenberg down for Detroit, someone had to step up and fill his role. That turned out to be one of the quieter Tigers, Pete Fox. The rightfielder often was lost in the pizzazz of the stars that surrounded him, although putting together a .321 season. He led all hitters in the Series at .385 after Cochrane elevated him to the fifth position in the batting order.

The Zeroes:

His hand injury was a crushing blow to Greenberg, who had only one hit in the Series, Detroit's only homer. Worse yet was the performance of the men who replaced him. Owen was moved to first base, and shuttled in to start at third was little-used sub Flea Clifton. Owen suffered through his second sub-par Series in a row, going just 2 for 20, while Clifton was collared in 16 at bats.

It was not an auspicious return to the Series for Lindstrom, who had been right in the middle of things as a teenager in 1924.

This time he hit just .200. When called in from the outfield to play third once more in game three, his 11th inning error led to the unearned run that won the game for Detroit.

The Aftermath:

Greenberg's hand did not heal properly and the first baseman had to sit out virtually the entire 1936 season. The Tigers could not get untracked and fell steadily behind the rejuvenated Yankees. Cochrane, unable to control his emotions as manager, left the team in June after suffering what was later called a nervous breakdown. The following year, his playing career ended after he was beaned by the Yankees' Bump Hadley. Unable to function as a bench manager, he left the game. Moreover, longtime owner Frank Navin had died in a horseback riding accident one month after attaining his long-sought championship. Control of the Tigers passed to Walter O. Briggs, a man with the resources to permanently turn Detroit into one of the league's stronger franchises.

FACT:
The Series began with a stream of abusive heckling from both benches. It got so bad that at the beginning of game three, Commissioner Landis ordered managers and umpires to have it stopped.

The Cubs went into their three-year siesta, finishing second to the Giants for the next two seasons. But the core of this team had one more turn at the big prize coming to it.

Notes:

The Cubs were under the impression that the Tigers had knuckled under the verbal intimidation of the Gas Housers in 1934. So the Series began with a stream of abusive heckling from both benches. It got so bad that Commissioner Landis called in both managers and umpire George Moriarty, the old Detroit third baseman, before game three and told them it had to stop. It did.

Ten years later, when the Cubs returned to Detroit for the 1945 Series, Hack reportedly went immediately to look at the playing field. When asked why, he replied: "I wanted to see if I was still waiting to score on third."

FACT:
"I wanted to see if I was still waiting to score from third"—Hack, explaining why he immediately went to look at the playing field upon arriving in Detroit ten years after the 1935 World Series.

This was the Series in which famous prizefight manager, Joe Jacobs, attending a bitterly cold first game in Detroit, offered his often-quoted regret: "I shoulda' stood in bed."

Line Scores:

Game One, October 2

Chi (NL)—200 000 001—3	Det (AL)—000 000 000—0
Warneke W	Rowe L

Game Two, October 3

Chi (NL)—000 010 200—3	Det (AL)—400 300 10X—8
Root L, Henshaw (1), Kowalik (4)	Bridges W

Game Three, October 4

Det (AL)—000 001 040 01—6	Chi (NL)—020 010 002 00—5
Auker, Hogsett (7), Rowe (8) W	Lee, Warneke (8), French (10) L

Game Four, October 5

Det (AL)—001 001 000—2	Chi (NL)—010 000 000—1
Crowder W	Carleton L, Root (8)

Game Five, October 6

Det (AL)—000 000 001—1	Chi (NL)—002 000 10X—3
Rowe L	Warneke W, Lee (7) SV

Game Six, October 7

Chi (NL)—001 020 000—3	Det (AL)—100 101 001—4
French L	Bridges W

1936

New York (AL) 4
New York (NL) 2

The Yankees finally lost a Series game. This was so upsetting that they immediately went out and broke a single-game scoring record and then trampled the Giants in six, in a less than stirring renewal of the Subway Series.

The Preview:

The veteran Giants stars left over from the John McGraw era—Bill Terry and Travis Jackson—were hobbled and reaching the end. Hal Schumacher, the number-two starter on the pitching staff, lost more games than he won. Only one hitter reached double figures in home runs.

Somehow, out of this hodge-podge the Giants managed to eke out a pennant. This team bore slight resemblance to the fierce lineups of the '20s. Mel Ott, with a league-leading 33 home runs and 135 RBIs, was the lone offensive threat. Dick Bartell, in his second year after coming over from the Phils, contributed stability at shortstop. Burgess Whitehead, whose chief claim to fame was that he was Phi Beta Kappa at North Carolina, turned into a solid second baseman upon arriving from the Cards. Otherwise, there were some good players having decent years, but barely a superstar in the bunch.

On the other hand, Carl Hubbell had his greatest season, leading the league with 26 wins and a 2.31 ERA. Down the stretch he was unbeatable, putting together a 16-game streak that was still alive when the season ended. Behind him, though, there was not much. The Giants did not figure to be a threat to the Yankees.

And the Yanks were very much back in business. After winning just once in seven years, they were hungry. They had run

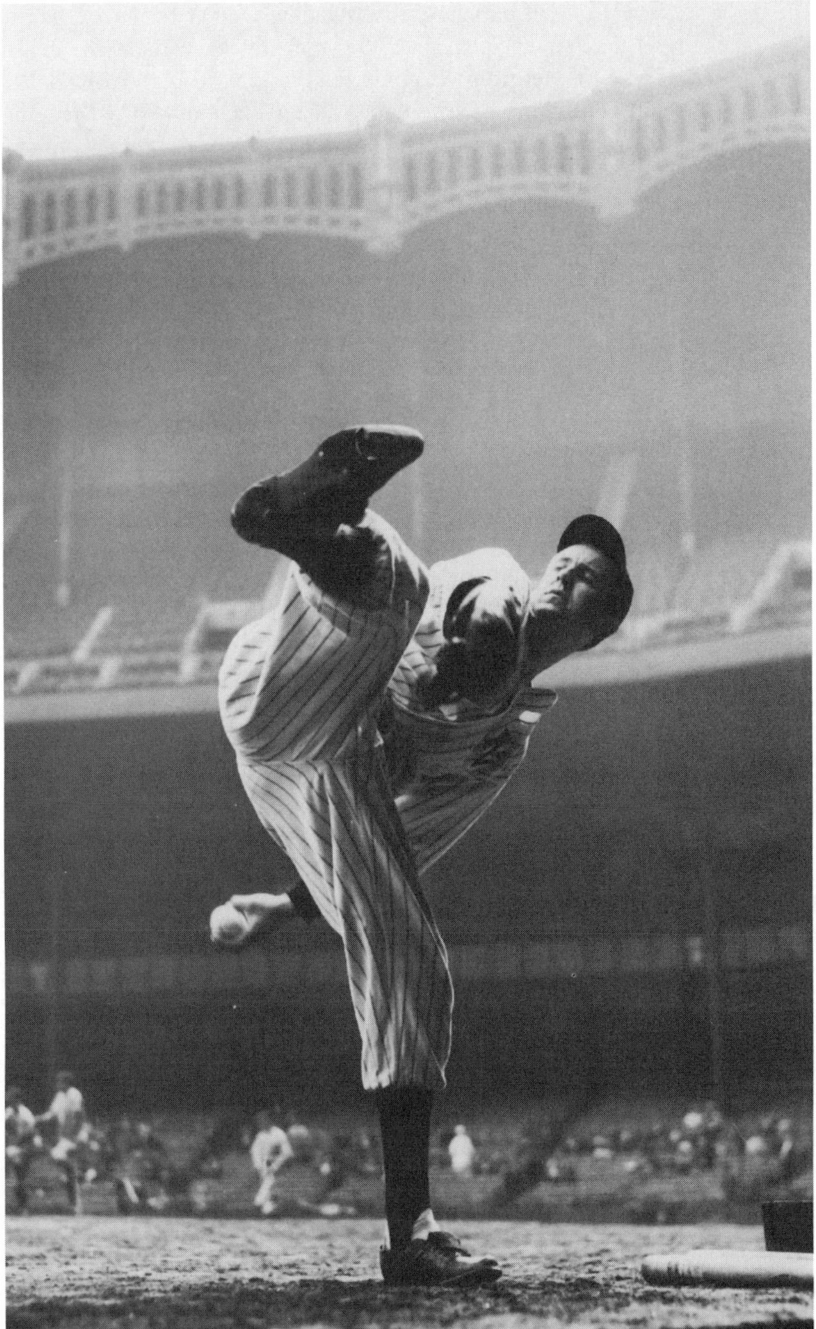

"Lefty" Gomez won two games in two tries for the Yanks in the 1936 Series, despite a 4.70 ERA. His proudest moments came at the plate, where he had two hits, three RBI, and a run scored.

away from all pursuers, outdistancing Detroit by 19 1/2 games and clinching the pennant by September 9, the earliest date in history. Lou Gehrig's 49 homers were tops in baseball and Bill Dickey had his best year, with a .362 average and 107 RBIs.

The real news, though, was the arrival of Joe DiMaggio. The rookie from San Francisco quickly settled into Babe Ruth's former spot, right in front of Gehrig, in the Yankee batting order. In a year of heavy offense in the league, he did not figure high in any individual stats—although a .323 average, 29 homers and 125 RBIs did get noticed. He also redefined the art of playing centerfield, giving the Yanks the best outfield play in their history.

Tony Lazzeri and rightfielder George Selkirk also drove in more than 100 runs for this offensive machine that churned out 1,065 runs—or an average of almost 7 a game.

This made things fairly simple for a staff led by Red Ruffing (20-12) and Monte Pearson (19-7), who had come over in an off-season trade with Cleveland. Even a subpar season for Lefty Gomez (13-7) couldn't halt this machine, which had no discernible weaknesses. The Giants looked to be so much fresh meat.

Turning Point: Game Four, Third Inning.

Hubbell shocks the country in the opener, holding the Yankees to one run in a 6-1 Giants romp on a drizzly afternoon. The Polo Grounds is a muddy swamp next day and the game is called off. When the Yankees return to action, they are an aroused team. They slaughter the Giants, 18-4, the worst beating in Series history. Then they go to the other extreme and take a 2-1 win behind Bump Hadley.

Now it is Hubbell's turn again, and because of the postponement he is pitching on an extra day of rest. This is the Giants' big chance and a record World Series crowd of 66,669 has jammed Yankee Stadium to see it.

This is not the Hubbell of the first game, though. The Yanks go ahead 1-0 in the second when Selkirk drives in a run after a Jackson error. Then in the third, the Yanks strike again on a Frank Crosetti double and a single by Red Rolfe. Hubbell manages to get DiMaggio on a pop foul, but now it is Gehrig's turn. The veteran first baseman, always at his best in the Series, has been hitless against Hubbell and is batting only .250 for the Series. In another of his defining moments, however, he sends Hubbell's delivery into the rightfield seats for a two-run homer.

That gives the Yankees a 4-0 lead and Pearson makes it stand up the rest of the way. Even Schumacher's courageous 10-inning effort to win the next day can only delay the inevitable.

With Hubbell's loss, the Giants' tank is empty. The Yanks administer the final blow in game six, scoring seven times in the 9th inning to obliterate the Giants, 13-5. Gehrig's blast started them on the road to oblivion.

The Managers:

This was Terry's final year as a player. He still hit .310, his lowest mark in 10 years, but was slowed by a steady succession of injuries to his 37-year-old body. He got through the Series, even after Gehrig's smash off his leg left him limping through the last three games. After this, he was strictly a bench manager, but made the adjustment in fine fashion in 1937.

Joe McCarthy had methodically assembled the team he wanted. A great scouting system in California had turned up DiMaggio, Crosetti and Gomez. The farm system was primed to start producing top talent that would sustain the Yankee dynasty for almost 30 years. As good as the teams of the '20s had been, baseball had really seen nothing yet.

> **FACT:**
> It is the mark of great teams that heroes emerge from the most unexpected places. Jake Powell burns the Giants repeatedly, hitting .455 and tying a record for a six-game Series by scoring 8 runs.

The Heroes:

It is the mark of great teams that heroes emerge from the most unexpected places. No one was less expected than Jake Powell. The 28-year-old outfielder came over from Washington in a mid-season trade for Ben Chapman, a player who was not a McCarthy favorite. Powell had shown some promise as a rookie with the Senators and perked up after the trade to hit .299 this season. He ranked far down on the list of Yankee threats and hit seventh in the order. In this Series, however, he burned the Giants repeatedly, hitting .455 and tying a record for a six-game set by scoring 8 runs.

Lazzeri may have batted eighth in the Yankee lineup but he was the most formidable eight hitter in the game's history. The lowest batter among the New York regulars at .287, he nonetheless drove in 109 runs. His grand-slam homer in the third inning of game two capped a 7-run explosion that turned the game into a riot.

Schumacher performed valiantly in game five. Pitching over three errors and six walks, he managed to hold off the Yanks just long enough for the Giants to get a 10-inning, 5-4 win. He also struck out 10.

> **FACT:**
> The Yankees' 18-4 romp over the Giants in game two is the worst beating in Series history.

The Zeroes:

The Giants bullpen was thoroughly mauled. Aside from Slick Castleman, who contributed 4 effective innings in game six, the rest of the Giants relievers worked a combined 9 innings and gave up 21 runs.

This was no fun for Whitehead, either. The Giants second baseman went 1 for 21. It was also an inglorious finish to Jackson's career. His bad legs relegating him permanently to third base, he was only a shadow of his old self. He hit .190, made three errors in the field and never played in the majors again.

The Aftermath:

The Giants managed to pull the pieces together for another pennant run in 1937. A few astute trades and the arrival of rookie Cliff Melton to give Hubbell a hand got them through.

The Yankees, while a touch less overpowering, were still the best ballclub on the planet by a very wide margin. They swept into the Series again with minimal problems.

Notes:

The Series provided some of Gomez's proudest moments. A notoriously poor hitter, with a .147 lifetime average, he nonetheless participated gleefully in the carnage inflicted on the Giants pitching. He had two hits and three runs batted in and in the victorious clubhouse he preferred to talk more about that than his two wins.

Mark Koenig, who had stirred such a row when he was short-changed by the Cubs in 1932, turned up again in this Series to play his old Yankee teammates. He was a utility infielder for the Giants and got to bat three times as a replacement for Whitehead. This time, however, it was quiet and also his final games in the majors.

Line Scores:

Game One, September 30

NY (AL)—001 000 000—1
Ruffing L

NY (NL)—000 011 04X—6
Hubbell W

Game Two, October 2

NY (AL)—207 001 206—18
Gomez W

NY (NL)—010 300 000—4
Schumacher L, Smith (3), Coffman (3), Gabler (5), Gumbert (9)

Game Three, October 3

NY (NL)—000 010 000—1
Fitzsimmons L

NY (AL)—010 000 01X—2
Hadley W, Malone (9) SV

Game Four, October 4

NY (NL)—000 100 010—2
Hubbell L, Gabler (8)

NY (AL)—013 000 01X—5
Pearson W

Game Five, October 5

NY (NL)—300 001 000 1—5
Schumacher W

NY (AL)—011 002 000 0—4
Ruffing, Malone (7) L

Game Six, October 6

NY (AL)—021 200 017—13
Gomez W, Murphy (7) SV

NY (NL)—200 010 110—5
Fitzsimmons L, Castleman (4), Coffman (9), Gumbert (9)

1937

New York (AL) 4
New York (NL) 1

Haven't we heard this song before? In a Series rematch the Yankees pound merrily upon the Giants, with only Carl Hubbell getting in the way of a sweep. It is done with such dull efficiency that fans were walking out on the games in one of the more boring Series in history.

The Preview:

When Bill Terry came out of spring training with what he described as "the best infield we've had in years," many of the writers thought he was hallucinating. The team's big names were just memories now. Dick Bartell and Burgess Whitehead were back to play the middle from the 1936 team. Lou Chiozza was obtained from the Phils to replace the retired Travis Jackson at third. Taking Terry's spot at first was Johnny McCarthy. This was not a quartet to send imaginations soaring.

Mel Ott remained the only real offensive threat. He hit 31 homers and drove in 95 runs while winning the Most Valuable Player award. The catching was also in capable hands, with Gus Mancuso and Harry Danning splitting the assignment and driving in 90 between them. Centerfielder Hank Leiber had to sit out most of the year after getting beaned by Bob Feller in a spring exhibition. Wally Berger came over from the Braves, though, and the veteran slugger supplied some badly needed power, with 12 homers in 59 games.

Hubbell was as good as ever with a 22-8 record. He finished the 1936 season with a 16-game win streak and then won eight in a row at the start of this year. Some enthusiasts claimed that added up to 24 and constituted a new record. But Hubbell would have none of that. He pointed out that the streak actually had

New York's Tony Lazzeri, in his last Series, led both teams with a .400 average and scored the winning run in the finale.

ended at 17 when the Yankees beat him in the fourth game of the previous year's Series. Joining him was the rookie mountain man from North Carolina, Cliff Melton, who stood six-foot-five, went 20-9 and saved seven more. Hal Schumacher (13-12) was still the third man in the rotation. Veteran Fred Fitzsimmons was dealt to Brooklyn in mid-season, another of the handful of John McGraw's old boys who had remained.

The Yankees were fully as awesome as ever. Joe DiMaggio was even more compelling a player as a sophomore, leading the league with 46 homers (his career high) and driving in 167. It was just like old times, with Gehrig, hitting right behind him, blasting 37 homers and driving in 159. Bill Dickey also had another big year, with 29 homers and 133 RBIs. In most other positions, though, the Yanks declined from 1936. Tony Lazzeri was coming to the end of his career, and by mid-season the hero of the previous Series, Jake Powell, was riding the bench, replaced by Myril Hoag and rookie Tommy Henrich.

Lefty Gomez led the league in most pitching stats, compiling a 21-11 record with a 2.33 ERA. Right beside him was Red Ruffing at 20-7. There was a sharp fall-off after that, but Johnny

Murphy, with a delivery so easy and comfortable that he was called "Grandma," developed into a bullpen ace, with a 13-4 record and 10 saves. The Yanks romped home 13 games in front of Detroit and didn't figure to stop until the Giants were stomped.

Turning Point: Game One, Sixth Inning.

The Giants' only hope is Hubbell and everyone knows it. He won the opener in 1936, giving the Giants a brief Series spark and it is believed that he, at the least, might be able to slow the Yanks again.

And so he does . . . for five innings. The Giants put together singles by McCarthy and Jimmy Ripple to score off Gomez, and as the game develops it appears that is all Hubbell will get from his teammates.

Evil omens encircle the sixth when the notoriously weak-hitting Gomez leads off with a walk. Frank Crosetti, least dangerous of the Yankee regulars, follows with a single. Now the business end of the batting order is coming up. But as Red Rolfe backs off a pitch he had squared around to bunt, catcher Mancuso rifles the ball down to second, trapping Gomez well off the bag. Bartell, however, drops the throw for an error. Gomez gets back safely and then comes the tidal wave.

Rolfe singles, DiMaggio singles in two runs, Gehrig walks and Dickey singles in another, making it 3-1. When George Selkirk's single drives in two more, Hubbell is gone and so is any lingering doubt about who will control this Series. Gomez cruises to a 6-1 win. Ruffing and Monte Pearson do likewise in games two and three, the Giants managing no more than a single run in both games.

With Hubbell pitching again in game four, the Giants finally snap out of it, pounding Bump Hadley and successors for a six-run outburst in the second and sending their ace to a 7-3 win. But that just salvages a little pride. Gomez closes it out next day and once more the Yankees reign supreme.

The Managers:

Bill Terry's icy exterior began to lose him points with the Giants. After Leiber was knocked unconscious by Feller, for example, and complained of headaches for weeks afterwards, Terry kept him in the lineup. Doctors finally ordered further tests and only then was Leiber placed on the disabled list. Leiber never forgave the manager and didn't really recover as a hitter until traded to the Cubs. While sharing the tough outlook of his mentor, John McGraw, Terry had little of that manager's personal charm or magnetism.

Joe McCarthy, at 50, was also a rather austere individual, but was accorded a whole-hearted respect. He was also surrounded by the best talent in the game, with more arriving every season, which made the respect easier to command.

The Heroes:

This was the apotheosis of Gomez's career. A friendly, affable man, he was largely the creation of the New York newspapers, which would similarly turn Yogi Berra into a folk hero a generation later. Some of the best minds in the writing business created the lines credited to Gomez and he became the walking embodiment of the baseball proposition that all left-handers are half mad. In this Series, the Giants found him wholly unhittable, scoring just 3 runs off him in 18 innings, as he beat them twice.

This was also the parting salvo for the 33-year-old Lazzeri. He had started his World Series career with a famous strikeout in 1926. He ended it by leading both sides with a .400 average. He also scored the winning run of the final game after tripling.

FACT:
Yankee second-baseman Tony Lazzeri started his Series career with a famous strikeout in 1926 and ends it by leading both teams with a .400 average. He scores the winning run of the final game after tripling.

Giants leadoff man Jo-Jo Moore did what he could to get his team jump-started with a Series-leading 9 hits; but there was no one behind him to pick him up.

The Zeroes:

Crosetti, who replaced Leo Durocher in the New York media as the archetype of the non-hitting shortstop, was just 1-for-21 in the Series. But his lone hit set up the winning rally off Hubbell in game one.

Slick Castleman was the only Giant relief pitcher who pitched well in 1936 and was fairly effective in his 11-6 record this season. He was also a favorite of Terry, who saw a lot of potential in the 24-year-old right-hander. But an arm injury sidelined him for the Series and hampered him for the rest of his brief career, during which he won just 5 more games.

The Aftermath:

There was a subtle shift in the baseball establishment after this season. The Giants' feeble performance discouraged many of their fans. The team slowly tumbled to the second division in the coming seasons and attendance fell, too, at the Polo Grounds.

Meanwhile, a revolution was underway in Brooklyn. With the coming of Durocher in 1939, the lowly Dodgers were transformed into contenders and then into a dynasty to challenge the Yankees. Within a decade they had become the pre-eminent National League team in New York, with historic consequences for baseball and the city.

The Yankees grew stronger each season. The loss of a great veteran like Lazzeri was quickly compensated for by the arrival of talented rookie, Joe Gordon. And so it went down the lineup, as the team prepared to make history by advancing on a third straight championship.

FACT:
The Yankees play errorless ball, the first time in Series history that had been done.

Notes:

Commentators noted that this Series attracted scant national attention. The rematch between such unevenly matched teams was a turnoff outside New York. Even in the city, attendance was far below capacity in both stadiums and crowds began leaving several of the games in the seventh inning.

The Yankees were in such control that they played absolutely errorless baseball, the first time in Series history that had been done.

Giants reliever Dick Coffman suffered one of life's more embarrasing moments in the first game. He came in to pitch only to learn that Terry had actually called for another right-hander, Harry Gumbert, who also was warming up. Coffman had to turn around and go all the way back to the bullpen. He got his chance just one batter later, though, and walked two men to force in a run.

Line Scores:

Game One, October 6

NY (NL)—000 010 000—1
Hubbell L, Gumbert (6), Coffman (6), Smith (8)

NY (AL)—000 007 01X—8
Gomez W

Game Two, October 7

NY (NL)—100 000 000—1
Melton L, Gumbert (5), Coffman (6)

NY (AL)—000 024 20X—8
Ruffing W

Game Three, October 8

NY (AL)—012 110 000—5
Pearson W, Murphy (9) SV

NY (NL)—000 000 100—1
Schumacher L, Melton (7), Brennan (9)

Game Four, October 9

NY (AL)—101 000 001—3
Hadley L, Andrews (2), Wicker (8)

NY (NL)—060 000 10X—7
Hubbell W

Game Five, October 10

NY (AL)—011 002 000—4
Gomez W

NY (NL)—002 000 000—2
Melton L, Smith (6), Brennan (8)

1938

New York (AL) 4
Chicago (NL) 0

Back came the Cubs for their regular three-year drubbing by the American League. For the Yanks, this made three straight championships and a string of six Series in which they lost just three games. "Break up the Yankees" became more than a joke among observers who felt their superiority was destroying the game.

The Preview:

The Cubs appeared to be a badly confused organization in 1938. They obtained Tony Lazzeri from the Yankees during the winter, then discovered, as if shocked, that they didn't have a position for him to play. Then they gave up $185,000 and three young players for Dizzy Dean, whose arm was so dead that he could barely reach the plate on some days.

Charlie Grimm, promoted to manager in 1932 to calm a club angered by the dictatorial Rogers Hornsby, was now discerned as too easy-going and his players undisciplined. Grimm resigned in July and was replaced by longtime star catcher Gabby Hartnett, who felt he had a mandate to get tough. But his biggest contribution was a ninth-inning homer in the late September gloom (the "Homer in the Gloaming") that beat Pittsburgh and put the Cubs in first place to stay.

They won a paltry 89 games and most of the Cubs went through rather ordinary years. Both Hartnett and star second baseman Billy Herman lagged along in the .270s. The closest thing to a power hitter was the old Gas House Gang first baseman, Rip Collins, who hit only 13 homers. Stan Hack sparkled as the leadoff hitter with a .320 average and American League retread Carl Reynolds helped in the outfield after being salvaged

Chicago's Wrigley Field, site of years of World Series disappointment since the Cubs' last championship in 1908. The litany continued in 1938, as the Cubbies were swept by the mighty Yankees.

from the minors. Lazzeri only got to bat 120 times as a part-time shortstop.

Bill Lee led the league with a 22-9 record and 2.66 ERA, and behind him was Clay Bryant, at 19-11. After that, the Cubs were reduced to occasional starters, such as Charlie Root (8-7) and even Dean, who managed to fool enough hitters with his slow stuff to go 7-1 in 10 starts.

The Yanks didn't have to bother fooling anyone. They just beat their brains out. Joe DiMaggio was again splendid, with 32 homers and 140 RBIs to accompany his .324 average. At 31, Bill Dickey was the game's premier catcher and he chipped in with 115 RBIs. It was true that Lou Gehrig was finally starting to slow down visibly. Although his season would have satisfied most players (29 homers, 114 RBIs, .295) it was substantially below his standards. At times, he looked as if he were struggling, but still he managed to stay in the lineup and extend his consecutive game streak to 2,102.

Joe Gordon replaced Lazzeri without missing a beat, with 25 homers and 97 RBIs, while Tommy Henrich moved into rightfield and knocked in 91 more. It was a lineup of terrifying consistency.

This was Red Ruffing's turn to lead the pitching staff and he ran up a solid 21-7 record. Lefty Gomez was 18-12 and the under-rated Monte Pearson finished at 16-7. No other threesome of starters in the league came close. In all regards, it was a team without a weakness.

Turning Point: Game Two, Eighth Inning.

The Wrigley Field crowd sits transfixed for seven innings, watching one of the great displays of pitching courage in Series history. His fastball only a memory but his heart undiminished by time, Dizzy Dean is holding off the Yankees. They swing at his motion. He has nothing left, but New York hasn't figured it out yet.

The Yanks took the first game, 3-1, with Ruffing outdueling Lee in a surprisingly tight match. With Yankee Stadium looming ahead for the next three games, the Cubs must win now if they hope to extend the Series beyond the minimum.

Reserve outfielder Joe Marty, making his first start, knocks in three runs with a sacrifice fly and a two-run double off Gomez. That hit comes in the third, and since then Dean clings to a 3-2 lead. Even the two New York runs are flukes. Hack and shortstop Billy Jurges collide in the 2nd while going for a grounder to the left side. Both men lay stunned on the infield dirt as the ball rolls to a stop in short leftfield. Two runs score, with Gehrig coming in all the way from first. That is all the offense New York can muster and it gives Dean only the slimmest of margins to work with.

He has retired 11 in a row going into the 8th. Even when George Selkirk leads off with a single, Dean comes back to get Gordon and pinch hitter Myril Hoag on easy outs. Now there is only weak-hitting Frank Crosetti to contend with to get out of the inning. Dean reaches a 3-2 count on him, then Crosetti fouls off five in a row. Dean decides to try and outguess him and sneak in a low fastball. But Crosetti is on it and the ball lands in the left-field bleachers, as the hopes of 42,000 rush out of Wrigley Field.

DiMaggio seals it with another two-run shot in the 9th and a beaten, but not defeated, Dean leaves the game to a standing ovation. The Yanks win 6-3 and take the Series to New York, where the end comes as quickly as the rules allow.

The Managers:

Hartnett proved an antidote to Grimm's free-and-easy style. But after the successful 1938 season, his tougher approach began to wear thin with the Cubs. After two full seasons, as his value as a player was just about finished, he was traded to the Giants.

Joe McCarthy now had the Grail that had escaped Connie Mack and John McGraw, the elusive third straight championship. Only Mack had won more times in the Series, and McCarthy was just one behind him with 4. That gap would close very quickly.

The Heroes:

Ruffing came to New York in 1930, after losing 96 games in little more than five seasons for the hapless Red Sox. He would become the Yanks' most dependable starter for the next decade, four times a 20-game winner. Moreover, he would hit over .300 six times, almost an unfair advantage considering the power in the rest of the New York lineup. Ruffing's career mark of 7-2 was one of the best in Series history and this year saw him at peak form. He pitched two complete games and beat the Cubs twice in typical fashion, bearing down when he had to in the tight 3-1 opener and then relaxing in the easy 8-3 finale.

FACT:
Joe McCarthy captured the Grail that had escaped Connie Mack and John McGraw, the elusive third straight championship.

There had always been a rough edge, a cockiness to Dean that some regarded as offensive. But his heroic performance in this Series, which won him ovations even at Yankee Stadium when he appeared in a game, solidified his stature among the public. This was his last Series but he parlayed his colorful reputation into a successful career as a broadcaster in St. Louis and on network television.

The light-hitting Crosetti had only four hits in the Series but they were good for six RBIs, tops on both sides.

This was Joe Marty's brief fling with fame. He finished the Series as a .500 hitter, but by the final game the Yanks caught on that among those things he could not hit were curveballs. He was traded to the Phillies the following season and was out of the majors in two more years.

The Zeroes:

Hartnett was so disgusted with his own performance that he benched himself after the third game. He also sat down veteran outfielder Carl Reynolds, who was hitless in 11 at bats. Hartnett's replacement, Ken O'Dea, hit a two-run homer in the finale, but it was futile in the Yankee landslide.

While Phil Cavaretta was one of Chicago's top hitters at .462—after going through his worst year in the majors at .239—he came under

FACT:
Despite Dizzy Dean's rough edges, his heroic performance in the 1938 Series won him ovations at Yankee Stadium.

severe media criticism for throwing to the wrong base and setting up New York's winning rally in game two. Hartnett benched him the next day, although he wouldn't say if that was because a left-hander was pitching or because of the mental error.

The Aftermath:

This was the final Series for the core of the Chicago team that had won four pennants in 10 years. By 1940, the Cubs were an aging second division club and their big names were on their way out. The franchise emerged briefly from its funk to sneak off with a wartime pennant before plunging into the longest drought in baseball history.

The Yankees went into 1939 with a new slugger on the way up and one of their greatest players on the way out. But the end result would be just the same.

Notes:

Brawls were rare in the Series, but both benches emptied after Selkirk was knocked down by Larry French in the eighth inning of game three. The pitch followed a Dickey home run. French insisted that Yankee coaches were stealing their signs and relaying them to the hitters. When Selkirk got a tight fastball while looking for a curve, the trouble began. But no one was ejected and the melee was more milling than fighting.

It was an empty feeling for Charlie Grimm. Not only did he see his ballclub sweep to the pennant after his resignation, but the players he had managed for more than half the season voted him no share in the Series money.

Line Scores:

Game One, October 5

NY (AL)—020 001 000—3
Ruffing W

Chi (NL)—001 000 000—1
Lee L, Russell (9)

Game Two, October 6

NY (AL)—020 000 022—6
Gomez W, Murphy (8) SV

Chi (NL)—102 000 000—3
Dean L, French (9)

Game Three, October 8

Chi (NL)—000 010 010—2
Bryant L, Russell (6), French (7)

NY (AL)—000 022 01X—5
Pearson W

Game Four, October 9

Chi (NL)—000 100 020—3
Lee L, Root (4), Page (7), French (8), Carleton (8), Dean (8)

NY (AL)—030 001 04X—8
Ruffing W

1939

New York (AL) 4
Cincinnati (NL) 0

A brand new opponent simply meant fresh meat for the Yankees. The result was the same, a four-game sweep, although New York had to exert itself a bit more than usual, with two of the contests not decided until the last time at bat.

The Preview:

Another season, another runaway. The Yanks cruised to a fourth straight pennant, 17 games ahead of the Red Sox. Joe DiMaggio led the league in hitting at .381 and drove in 126 runs. Joining him in triple digit figures were Joe Gordon, George Selkirk and Bill Dickey. So consistent were these Yankees that over the course of the season they scored exactly one more run than they had in 1938.

This was also the season that the Iron Horse broke down. Lou Gehrig, weakened by the disease that would kill him in two more years, left the lineup in the spring. His departure resulted in a revolving situation at first base that would last almost 20 years. Moving into the number three spot in the New York batting order was rookie Charlie Keller. With a physique that earned him the nickname King Kong (which he detested), the former University of Maryland star hit .334—seven points higher than another top rookie; Boston's Ted Williams.

Red Ruffing duplicated his mark of the previous year at 21-7. But there was an unaccustomed dropoff after him. The Yanks had six different pitchers who won no more than 13 and no less than 10 games. It was a measure of Joe McCarthy's genius that he extracted the maximum out of each of them. It also made for an extremely busy year for Johnny Murphy, who saved 19

Yankees rookie Charlie Keller slides into third with a triple in Game 1. He would eventually score the winning run on a Bill Dickey single. For the Series, Keller hit .438 with three homers, six RBI, and eight runs.

games as a relief specialist, a role that was becoming increasingly common in baseball.

Winning was all quite new and wonderful for the Reds. It was their first pennant in 20 years. The team almost went broke during the Depression. Only the installation of lights in 1935, enabling Cincinnati to become the first franchise to play night games, saved the team. The move was widely criticized at the time, but many teams followed suit in a few years. Of course, the World Series would be played only during the day, as usual.

The Reds had bumbled along deep in the second division since the mid 1920s. But there were stirrings in 1938. That's when Bill McKechnie, a two-time winner, was brought over from Boston to take over as manager. The fences were also brought in—or rather the plate was moved out—by about 15 feet. Crosley Field, one of the toughest home run parks in the majors, suddenly became the domicile of sluggers. First baseman Frank McCormick knocked in 128 runs to lead the league while hitting .332. Ernie Lombardi, a catching stalwart and fan favorite, added 20 homers, and Ival Goodman hit .323. But the key addition was third baseman Bill Werber. Obtained in a waiver deal with the A's, he shored up a perennial weak spot for the Reds, leading the league in most defensive stats and hitting .289.

Cincinnati put this pennant away with pitching. The combination of Paul Derringer and Bucky Walters won 52 games—more than any other team's top three starters. Walters, a converted infielder, came over from the Phillies the year before at McKechnie's behest, and in his first full season as a starter went 27-11 with a league-leading 2.29 ERA. The veteran Derringer was 25-7. Oddly enough, Johnny Vander Meer, who had astonished baseball by pitching consecutive no-hit games in 1938, could not get untracked and was never a factor in the race, finishing 5-9. But Junior Thompson, a rookie who worked as a swing man out of the bullpen, checked in at 13-5.

McKechnie thought he had a team that could stay with New York and pitching that might be good enough to beat them. But his was decidedly a minority opinion.

Turning Point: Game One, Ninth Inning.

The Yankees tantalize before they destroy. It is part of their mystique. The opener, matching the two aces, Ruffing and Derringer, regarded as the two top right-handers in baseball, proves that. It is a great battle, with each pitcher showing complete command and precise control.

Cincinnati manages to get a run in the 4th when Goodman walks, steals second and comes home on McCormick's single. But the Yanks tie it in the 5th in the most annoying way possible. With one out, Gordon singles and Babe Dahlgren, the first-baseman who took over for Gehrig, slams a double down the third base line. Veteran leftfielder Wally Berger runs the ball down and then makes a fundamental mistake, throwing behind the lead runner to second base. Gordon, seeing where the throw is going, just keeps coming, rounding third and scoring easily, to tie the game.

Some commentators tried to excuse Berger, saying that this was a planned decoy play and second baseman Lonnie Frey was out of position. He was supposed to grab the ball behind second and throw immediately to the plate. But the consensus is that Berger blew it, a mistake compounded when two pop flies end the inning.

After that upheaval, neither team can get even a base runner into the 9th. But with one out in the New York half of the inning, King Kong connects. His drive up the right center gap barely eludes the grasp of Goodman, who gets a glove on it, but it falls for a triple. That brings up DiMaggio, who is quickly given an intentional pass. This leaves McKechnie two options. He can issue another walk and hope for a double play from Selkirk. Or, he can pitch to Dickey.

He chooses the latter course. The manager explains later that Selkirk is an excellent low ball hitter and he doesn't want to force Derringer to keep the ball down on him. Dickey ends all ruminations with a single over second, bringing in Keller with the winning run.

With that, the Yankee snowball is rolling and it doesn't stop until the Reds are mowed under in yet another Series sweep.

FACT:
Manager Bill McKechnie wins three pennants with three different teams, a feat that wouldn't be matched until Dick Williams pulled it off between 1967 and 1984.

The Managers:

It is the third pennant with three different teams for McKechnie, a feat that wouldn't be matched until Dick Williams pulled it off between 1967 and 1984. It took McKechnie 14 years to complete his trifecta, starting with the 1925 Pirates and then the 1928 Cardinals. Afterwards, he spent eight years with the Boston Bees, and some commentators feel that his two first-division finishes with that sorry outfit may have been his most impressive managerial achievement. It took him just two years to take the Reds to the top. Now 53, McKechnie was regarded as a master handler of men, recognizing who needed a kind word and who required a swift kick and administering either remedy with equanimity.

His technique was much like McCarthy's, who now had won an unprecedented 5 championships. McCarthy was one year younger than McKechnie and in 14 big league seasons he never finished out of the first division. In the previous 11 years, with the Cubs and Yankees, his teams finished either first or second. It was the longest run of managerial success in the game's history.

The Heroes:

While McKechnie felt he had good scouting reports on most of the Yankees, he was a little worried about Keller. The rookie played only 111 games and the book on him was sketchy. McKechnie's fears were well-founded. The rest of the Yankees hit only .174, but Keller destroyed the Reds with a .438 average and three homers. Of his seven hits, five went for extra bases. His triple set up the winning run in the opener, he slammed two

two-run homers in the 7-3 third game win and then topped it off with another home run and some slam-bang base running that knocked Lombardi cold in the finale.

Monte Pearson was a tough Series performer throughout his career with New York. Just 12-5 during the season, Pearson now was working in his last championship. He made the most of it, blanking the Reds on two hits in the 4-0 second game. He had given up just one baserunner until Lombardi broke up the no-hitter with one out in the eighth.

FACT:
Rookie Charlie Keller destroyed the Reds with a .438 average and three homers. Of his seven hits, five went for extra bases.

The Zeroes:

Two of Cincinnati's starters, Berger and Frey, were a combined 0-for-32, putting an enormous crimp in the Reds attack.

Poor Lombardi was ridiculed by the New York press for what was described as his "swoon" in the 10th inning of the last game. With two runners on and the score tied, DiMaggio lined a single to right. The hit scored Frank Crosetti with the go-ahead run, and when Goodman bobbled the ball in right, Keller kept right on coming from first. The throw and the runner got to Lombardi simultaneously. The catcher was knocked flat and the ball dribbled out of his mitt, coming to rest just a few feet away from him. DiMaggio continued to run and also scored as Lombardi lay helpless. The catcher later explained that in the collision with Keller he had been hit in the groin. In excruciating pain, he was unable to move. The run that scored was totally meaningless and yet Lombardi, undeservedly, was made the Series goat.

The real blunder of the game was made by shortstop Billy Myers. He botched a perfect double play by dropping the throw on the pivot and set up a two-run Yankee rally in the ninth that tied the score.

The Aftermath:

Some teams were destroyed after going through the Yankee grinder in a Series. The experience seemed to toughen the Reds. They went on to a repeat trip, winning 100 games in an uncustomarily easy National League race.

What happened in the American League was even more than uncustomary. It was unthinkable. The Yankees lost. Time claimed some of their perennial stars before their replacements were ready and New York toppled all the way to two games off the pennant.

Notes:

One of the wildest of all wild pitches was uncorked by Thompson in game three. He walked Dickey on the errant pitch in the first and by the time Lombardi could chase the ball down the New York catcher, not the swiftest of runners, had made it all the way to third base.

The Reds were held without an extra base hit until McCormick doubled in the second inning of the last game. They then added two more doubles and a triple by Myers. They were the first team since the 1927 Pirates, also swept in four by the Yanks, to fail to hit a home run in the Series.

Line Scores:

Game One, October 4

Cin (NL)—000 100 000—1
Derringer L

NY (AL)—000 010 001—2
Ruffing W

Game Two, October 5

Cin (NL)—000 000 000—0
Walters L

NY (AL)—003 100 00X—4
Pearson W

Game Three, October 7

NY (AL)—202 030 000—7
Gomez, Hadley (2) W

Cin (NL)—120 000 000—3
Thompson L, Girssom (5), Moore (7)

Game Four, October 8

NY (AL)—000 000 202 3—7
Hildebrand, Sundra (5), Murphy (7) W

Cin (NL)—000 000 310 0—4
Derringer, Walters (8) L

1940

Cincinnati (NL) 4
Detroit (AL) 3

The most competitive Series in years demonstrates once again that consistent pitching usually makes the difference in a short set of games. The Tigers just could not match up with Cincinnati's deeper staff. Compelling human drama, however, gave this Series a special flavor.

The Preview:

Cincinnati refused to stand pat after being swept in 1939 and its formidable pitching staff was made even tougher. The three top starters again turned in exceptional seasons. Bucky Walters led the league in ERA for the second straight year, at 2.48, and posted a 22-10 record. Paul Derringer joined him with a fine 20-12 mark and Junior Thompson improved slightly to 16-9. This year, it didn't end with those three.

Veteran Jim Turner was obtained from Boston and went 14-7, while Joe Beggs, plucked from the Yankee system, turned into the league's top reliever, with a 12-3 record and 7 saves. The acquisitions were especially fortunate because Johnny Vander Meer again was a disappointment and was sent to the minors in mid-season to try and regain his form. He was recalled in time to pitch the pennant clincher, however. This was far and away the best staff in either league, and it enabled the Reds to romp home, 12 games ahead of Brooklyn.

The hitting, however, tailed off. Frank McCormick again was the largest threat, with 127 RBIs and a .309 average. Rookie outfielder Mike McCormick (no relation) was a pleasant surprise, filling the troublesome leftfield spot for the Reds during most of the season and batting .300. Catcher Ernie Lombardi also came back with a solid year at .319 and 74 RBIs.

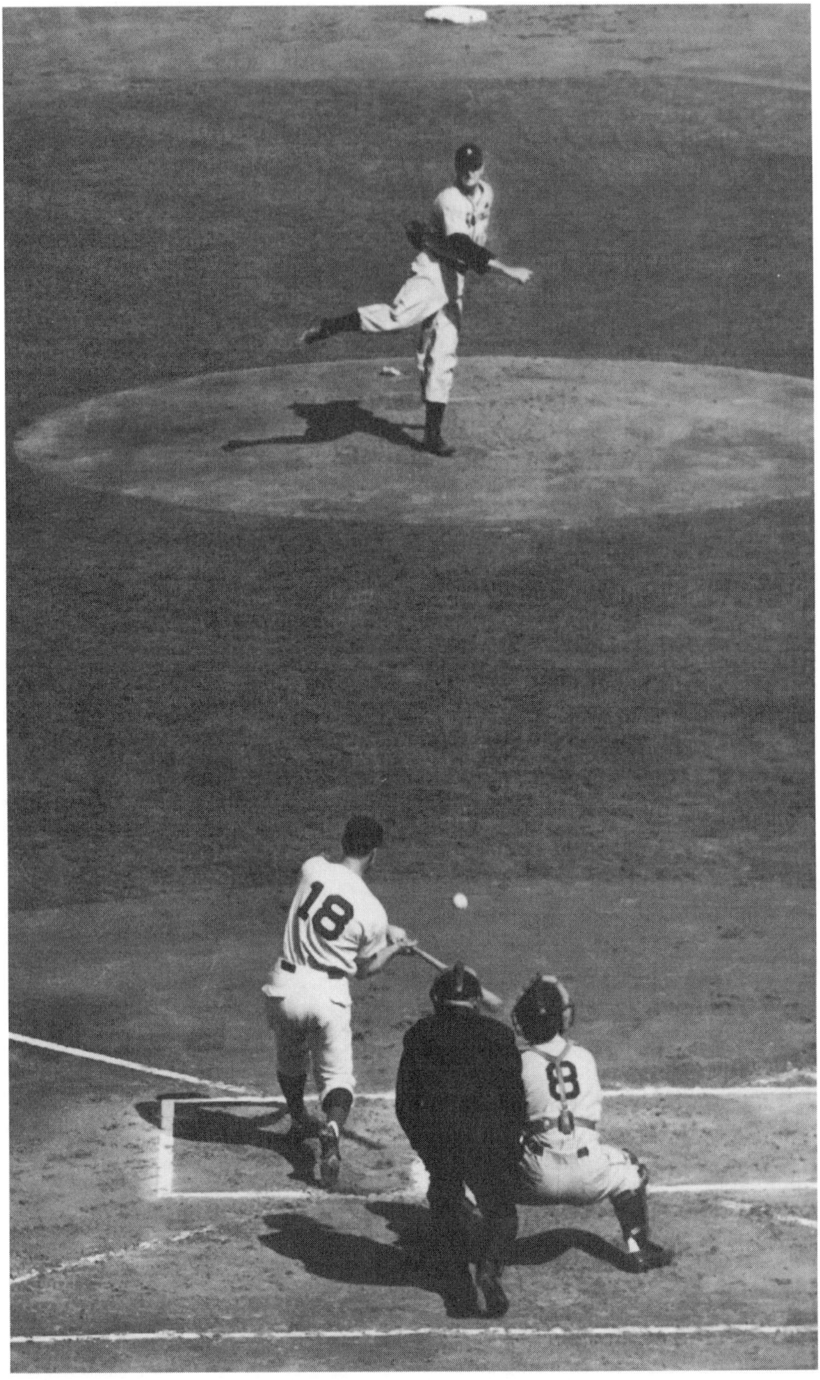

Bobo Newsom (pitching), who won two games with a 1.38 ERA in Detroit's seven-game loss, pitched a shutout in Game 5, despite the death of his visiting father the night before.

Catching, one of the team's strongest points, suddenly turned into a void. Backup catcher Willard Hershberger committed suicide in August in a Boston hotel room. The 29-year-old Californian had been hitting .309 and was highly regarded by the Reds. But among his emotional problems, a string of bad games during a tightening race had plunged him into despondency, with tragic results. Starting catcher Lombardi sprained his ankle in September and had to go on the injured list. That left only bullpen coach Jimmie Wilson, who had not caught on a regular basis since 1936. The 40-year-old Wilson gamely strapped on the chest protector for the last 16 games of the year and prepared to start against the Tigers, too. It seemed to be a major weakness in the Cincinnati lineup.

FACT:
Bullpen coach Jimmy Wilson, who had not caught on a regular basis since 1936, gamely strapped on the chest protector for the last 16 games of the year, and prepared to start against the Tigers. In the Series, he caught six of the seven games, hit .353 and did not allow a stolen base.

Detroit had to battle to the last weekend to win a bitter pennant race with Cleveland by one game, with the Yankees just one game in back of the Indians. Tiger fans had hung out baby clothes to heckle the Indians. Cleveland players had complained about the harsh regime of their manager, Ossie Vitt, and were quickly labelled "cry babies." In return, the Tigers were showered with fresh produce in Cleveland. Obscure rookie Floyd Giebell finally outpitched Cleveland's star Bob Feller to clinch the flag.

This was a strong Detroit team. Hank Greenberg, playing leftfield, led the league in homers (41) and RBIs (150) while hitting .340. He was moved from first base by the need to find a position for Rudy York, who chipped in 33 homers and 134 RBIs. Charlie Gehringer was on the downside of his great career, but still was capable of a .313 season. And second year man Barney McCosky slashed out 200 hits on the way to a .340 season.

Tommy Bridges (12-9) and Schoolboy Rowe (16-3) were holdovers from the championship team of 1935. But the main attraction was Bobo Newsom, an amiable hulk of a man who looked as if he had just ambled in from riding a boxcar. A journeyman performer for some awful second division teams, Newsom joined Detroit in 1939 and blossomed into a 20-game winner. This year he went 21-5, a mark exceeded only by Feller.

The Tigers were narrowly favored in the Series simply because of the apparent superiority of the American League. It had won five straight.

Turning Point: Game Seven, Seventh Inning.

For the first time in six years, the Series is going the full route and the matchup is a classic. Derringer, a loser of four previous World Series starts, had won the fourth game and now has the chance to erase the memory of earlier frustrations. Opposing him is Newsom. The 33-year-old right-hander already has won twice. He pitches his soul out in game five, blanking the Reds after his father, who had come up from South Carolina to watch his son perform at his proudest moment, died of a heart attack. The poignant sight of this somewhat comic figure, doing what he did best to honor his father's memory, captures the nation's sentiment.

FACT:

After his father died of heart attack, Newsom pitches his soul out in game five, blanking the Reds. The poignant sight of this somewhat comic figure, doing what he did best to honor his father's memory, captures the nation's sentiment.

Newsom is going on just one day of rest, but he is masterful in this deciding contest. Detroit scratches out a run in the third when third baseman Bill Werber's throwing error scores Billy Sullivan. Detroit's only other threat is thwarted by shortstop Billy Myers, who goes behind second base to snare Pinky Higgins' smash up the middle in the 6th and turns it into a forceout with two runners on.

Newsom has shut down the Reds for 16 consecutive innings going into the 7th. But Frank McCormick, held without an extra base hit so far, leads off with a double to the leftfield wall. That brings up Jimmy Ripple, a mid-season pickup from Brooklyn, who moved into a starter's job for the Series. Detroit expects a bunt and Newsom challenges him with a fastball. Instead, Ripple sends a liner to deep right. Bruce Campbell races to the wall and leaps, but the ball just clears his glove. It hits the wall and lands right at Campbell's feet.

McCormick, thinking the ball would be caught, holds up at second. By the time he reaches third the ball is in the hands of relay man Dick Bartell, who has one of the best throwing arms on the team. But his back is to the infield and he can't hear the shouts to throw to the plate. Instead of being an easy out, McCormick comes home unchallenged with the tying run and Ripple is perched on second.

After a walk and a sacrifice, the Tigers, expecting a hit and run, order three pitchouts to the weak-hitting Myers. That puts Newsom in a hole and he has to come in with a pitch. Myers drives a long fly ball to center, Ripple scores easily, and with him comes the final margin of the Series.

The Managers:

Bill McKechnie achieved the distinction of becoming the first manager ever to win championships with two different franchises. The mark has been equalled three times since, but never surpassed. He continued to manage the Reds for six more seasons, never finishing higher than second, before calling it a career and retiring to raise dogs, which some friends said he loved even more than baseball.

One commentator described the opposing managers in this Series as "the triumph of Casper Milquetoast." Detroit's Del Baker, a longtime coach with the team, was thrust into the job when Mickey Cochrane quit in 1938. A substitute catcher for the Tigers for three seasons, this was the mild-mannered Baker's only fling at leading a big league club. For one season, at least, he made the right moves. He was let go after 1942 when the team fell to fifth place.

The Heroes:

This was the shining hour for Newsom. A good-natured bear of a man, he could never remember anyone's name and so called them all "Bobo." In return, the tag was applied to him, although teammates usually referred to him as "Buck." In his long career, which didn't end until he was 46, he led the league in losses four times, pitched for eight different teams and had the distinction of being traded to Washington on four separate occasions. Never again would he win more than 14 games in a season, but he came within an inch of pitching the Tigers to a Series practically by himself, and established a lasting reputation for heart.

It was an extraordinary Series for Wilson, as well. He caught six of the seven games, hit .353 and did not allow a stolen base. They were the last big league games he ever played. The Cubs were so impressed by his performance that they hired him as the manager, strictly on the bench, for the 1941 season.

They weren't quite as flamboyant as the Dean brothers in 1934 against Detroit, but once more all four victories against the Tigers were accumulated by the opposition's two top starters. Derringer won the big one, but Walters was even more impressive, holding Detroit's big sluggers to just three runs in two complete games.

The Zeroes:

Rowe battled back from severe arm problems and was no longer the hard thrower he had been in 1934–35. But in limited duty he had the top winning percentage in the league. In his Series starts, however, he couldn't make it out of the fourth inning in one and was blasted out in the first in the other.

While Cincinnati's emergency catcher shone in the Series, Detroit's two regulars had big problems. The combination of Sullivan and Birdie Tebbetts, who had hit for a .300 average in shared service during the season, went 2 for 24.

The Aftermath:

Ironically for the Reds, just as Vander Meer regained his effectiveness, Derringer and Thompson lost theirs. McCormick and Lombardi, the two big power hitters during the pennant years, also tailed off quickly. The Reds would not seriously challenge again for two decades.

Detroit became the first team affected by the gathering war clouds when Greenberg enlisted in the Army in 1941. That time also saw the decline of Gehringer and the total collapse of their pitching. His absence sends the Tigers spiraling to fifth place. They would wait until Hank came marching home again before winning once more.

Notes:

This marked the eighth time in which a Series had gone the full route of seven games. On seven of those occasions, including this one, the attendance for the deciding game was lower than it had been for game six. The lone exception was in Detroit in 1909.

Those who had witnessed other Series celebrations, however, reported that Cincinnati's topped all the previous ones. Downtown was thronged with merry-makers until dawn and even beyond as the city hailed its first championship in 21 years.

Until the second inning of the seventh game this had been the only Series in which there were no stolen bases. Finally, a steal was pulled off by the least likely candidate on the field—Jimmie Wilson, the Reds' 40-year-old catcher.

Line Scores:

Game One, October 2

Det (AL)—050 020 000—7
Newsom W

Cin (NL)—000 100 010—2
Derringer L, Moore (2), Riddle (9)

Game Two, October 3

Det (AL)—200 001 000—3
Rowe L, Gorsica (4)

Cin (NL)—022 100 00X—5
Walters W

Game Three, October 4

Cin (NL)—100 000 012—4
Turner L, Moore (7), Beggs (8)

Det (AL)—000 100 42X—7
Bridges W

Game Four, October 5

Cin (NL)—201 100 010—5
Derringer W

Det (AL)—001 001 000—2
Trout L, Smith (3), McKain (7)

Game Five, October 6

Cin (NL)—000 000 000—0
Thompson L, Moore (4), Vander Meer (5), Hutchings (8)

Det (AL)—003 400 01X—8
Newsom W

Game Six, October 7

Det (AL)—000 000 000—0
Rowe L, Gorsica (1), Hutchinson (8)

Cin (NL)—200 001 01X—4
Walters W

Game Seven, October 8

Det (AL)—001 000 000—1
Newsom L

Cin (NL)—000 000 20X—2
Derringer W

1941

New York (AL) 4
Brooklyn (NL) 1

It wasn't the usual Yankee blowout. The games were close and hinged on breaks that could have turned either way. Still, the result was yet another Yankee championship in the first meeting between teams who would become familiar October rivals.

The Preview:

The warm, joyful celebration that a winning baseball team brings to a community returned to Brooklyn in 1941. This season was the birth of the popular image of the Dodgers. The Sym-Phoney band. The cowbells. The balloons. The wild adulation of "Dem Bums." All of it moved to a central role in baseball, as Brooklyn celebrated its first pennant in 21 years.

The Dodgers had been a long-running joke. They were tail-enders who accumulated some of the most eccentric individuals in the game. Baseballs hit them on the head. Three of them wound up on a base at the same time. "Overconfidence may cost the Dodgers sixth place," was a gag line of the '30s. They were sneered at by their hated rivals, the Giants, and totally ignored by the lordly Yankees, who inhabited a different universe.

By the late '30s, the owners had heard enough laughter. They hired Larry McPhail from Cincinnati, where he had turned another tail-ender into a contender as general manager. After pulling a trade for Leo Durocher, McPhail named him player-manager in 1939. Durocher's pugnacious attitude, in which other teams were evil and umpires their appointed agents, translated itself to his team. He moved the Dodgers to third and then to second in his first two seasons, battling everyone they could find along the way.

They traded for established stars: Joe Medwick from the Cards, Billy Herman from the Cubs and Dolf Camilli from the

Brooklyn catcher Mickey Owen runs for the ball after the third strike on Tommy Henrich eludes him in the ninth inning of Game 4. Henrich made it to first, keeping alive a rally that would eventually sink the Dodgers.

Phils. They picked up a sore-armed castoff in the minors and installed Dixie Walker as "the people's cherce" in rightfield. All of them responded to the new surroundings with big years. Camilli led the league in homers (34) and RBIs (120), while Medwick's .318 was the league's third best batting average. The top mark in that category went to Pete Reiser at .343. The 22-year-old centerfielder, playing in his first full season, was the brightest young star in the game. His range in the outfield was limitless, he could run, and he hit with power. No one doubted that he would become the Joe DiMaggio of the '40s.

Durocher replaced himself at shortstop with Pee Wee Reese. In his second season, the youngster hit only .229 but gave Brooklyn its best defense at that position in a generation.

The Dodgers pitching staff was a thing of shreds and patches. Whit Wyatt, a fringe performer on three American League teams, was rescued from the minors and went 22-10. Also brought back from AAA oblivion was Hugh Casey, who alternated between starting and relieving and went 14-11. The Phillies, a perennial contributor of promising young players to contending teams, coughed up Kirby Higbe, and his 22-9 record was the best in the league. The Dodgers beat off a challenge from St. Louis and won by 2 1/2 games.

They went up against a New York team that had reloaded and was highly irritated at being deprived of their accustomed seat at the Series table in 1940. If Reiser was the new DiMaggio, the original was at the height of his career. This was the season of the 56-game consecutive hitting streak, when the nation was fixated on DiMaggio's pursuit of the record. He finished with a .357 average, drove in a league-leading 125 runs and won every American League award in sight—this despite the .406 year of Ted Williams with second-place Boston.

Charlie Keller was right in back of DiMaggio with 122 RBIs, and both he and Tommy Henrich joined the centerfielder in hitting more than 30 home runs. The Yanks also sported a new shortstop. Rookie Phil Rizzuto hit .307 and with Joe Gordon formed the top double-play combination in the game.

This was not a vintage year on the pitching staff, though. Both Red Ruffing and Lefty Gomez were still in the rotation, but they were aging and ailing. They had to be spot-started and won just 15 games each. That, however, was high on the staff. Manager Joe McCarthy, as in 1939, had to juggle several fairly decent pitchers, but no stars, to get the team through. Johnny Murphy again was a busy man in the bullpen, with 15 saves and an 8-3 record. But it was Marius Russo who turned into the workhorse with a 14-10 record. When Gomez, the other left-handed starter, came up with a sore shoulder before the Series, Russo became a critical element in New York's plans.

The Turning Point: Game Four, Ninth Inning.

The first three contests are all decided by one run, with Casey twice being called in to quell tight situations. He steps into a 0-0 eighth-inning tie in game three after starter Fred Fitzsimmons is forced out by a liner off his leg. But Casey surrenders two runs and Russo makes them stand up in a 2-1 Yankee win.

Now the Dodgers have come back from a 3-0 deficit in game four, and behind Casey's tough relief pitching they are about to tie the Series. Reiser thrills the Ebbets Field sellout crowd by giving the Brooks a 4-3 lead with a two-run homer over the rightfield scoreboard in the fifth. Casey, who came on during the top half of that inning, shuts down the Yanks on two singles into the ninth.

He quickly retires Johnny Sturm and Red Rolfe, to bring Henrich to the plate. The count goes to 3-2 and Casey breaks off a nasty pitch that breaks into the ground. Henrich swings and misses and the Dodgers win, apparently. But as the crowd starts to scream, the cry of triumph freezes in their throats. The ball has bounced past catcher Mickey Owen and rolls to the backstop. Police came out on the field at the start of the inning to control the victory celebration and as Owen turns to pursue the ball he has to dodge cops clustered behind the plate. By the time he retrieves the ball, Henrich reaches first easily.

Henrich says the pitch was well out of the strike zone and was ball four if he could have held up his swing. Some observers thought Casey had loaded one up and thrown a spitter, so sharply down did the pitch break. Owen, too overcome to speak in the clubhouse, only shakes his head in anguish. The Yankees are alive and what happens next becomes a waking nightmare in Brooklyn.

DiMaggio singles and then Keller rifles a double off the rightfield wall to give the Yanks a 5-4 lead. After a walk, Gordon pads the margin to 7-4 with another double. In an instant, the Dodgers go from tying the Series to being sunk in an impossible 3-1 hole. The game becomes legendary as an illustration of the awful things that occur when the Yankees are given the tiniest breathing room. They close it all out the next day, 3-1, over token resistance.

FACT:
In an instant, the Dodgers go from tying the Series to being sunk in an impossible 3-1 hole. The game becomes legendary as an illustration of the awful things that occur when the Yankees are given the tiniest breathing room.

The Managers:

The sneering, pugnacious demeanor that Durocher brought to the game as a player was multiplied by a factor of ten as a manager. Baseball was more war than sport to him. It was a struggle in which anything went, from baiting the opposition with the most scurrilous words imaginable to badgering umpires incessantly. He was a hero in Brooklyn, and detested everywhere else. He willed the Dodgers to a pennant.

The calm, controlled Joe McCarthy simply got the best from the tools available to him. Many of the tools were formidable, but he prided himself in being able to coax the maximum effort out of more ordinary players. In a short Series, especially, McCarthy had the ability to find the unexpected star, like Joe Gordon, who makes the difference.

The Heroes:

There are those analysts who claim that playing for the Yankees hurt a performer's chances at getting to Cooperstown.

The reasoning is that so many New York superstars already are there that one must match a higher standard than those held up for players on other teams. Joe Gordon is one of the prime examples. His career stats match up against any contemporary second baseman, and he was a defensive whiz. Playing in a park unfriendly to right-handed hitters, he still put up impressive power numbers. Yet he languishes, without much serious consideration, outside the Hall. This was Gordon's best of five Series with the Yankees. He hit .500, was on base 14 times in 21 plate appearances and drove home decisive runs in the first and last games.

FACT:
This was Joe Gordon's best of five Series with the Yankees. He hit .500, was on base 14 times in 21 plate appearances and drove home decisive runs in the first and last games.

New York's thin pitching staff came through under pressure. McCarthy used five different starters against Brooklyn. Ruffing, Russo and Ernie Bonham, who pitched the closer, all had complete game wins. The Dodgers were held to a wan .182 average.

Fred Fitzsimmons started three Series games for the Giants in the '30s and lost every one of them. While he only pitched 13 times during the season, Durocher made him a surprise game three starter. Fitzsimmons was magnificent, shutting out the Yanks on four hits in a 0-0 duel with Russo. But then the other pitcher lined a shot off his leg for the last out of the seventh and Fitzsimmons could not come out for the next inning. Brooklyn lost the game despite a valiant final effect by the 40-year-old veteran.

The Zeroes:

It was a dud of a Series for Brooklyn's hitters. Only Reiser showed any signs of life, hitting the Dodgers' only homer and getting three extra base hits. But even he batted just .200.

Owen could never live down the muffed third strike in game four, although most observers agree that the ball Henrich whiffed on was uncatchable. The 25-year-old receiver, whose defensive skills were highly regarded, went on to a 13-year career in the majors, but he never made it back to the Series and never heard the end of his one trip there.

The Aftermath:

Durocher regarded this Series as just dumb Yankee luck and a learning experience for his team. His 1942 team was even tougher, picking up veterans Arky Vaughan for third base and pitcher Larry French. It won 104 games. But Brooklyn was overtaken in September by a torrid Cardinal stretch drive and the Dodgers never returned to the Series with Durocher as manager.

The Yankees went into 1942 with their third first baseman in four years after Gehrig had played every game there for over 14 seasons, and some young blood on the pitching staff. They were unstoppable, as usual.

Notes:

Interest in the Dodgers was running so high in the borough with New York's largest Jewish population that Commissioner Landis was asked to postpone the start of the Series for a day. It was scheduled to begin on Yom Kippur. But the first game went on as planned, and Yankee Stadium set a new Series attendance record at 68,540.

There was also serious thought given to switching Brooklyn's home games from the smallest park in the National League to the Polo Grounds. This had been done fairly often in cities with two ballparks during the World War I years. But Ebbets Field was regarded as such an intrinsic part of the Dodgers' character that the idea was never carried out.

Even the dignified DiMaggio bristled at the Dodgers. After a Wyatt fastball knocked him back from the plate in the fifth game, he yelled to the pitcher on the way to the dugout and both benches emptied. DiMaggio had fruit tossed at him when he took his position in Ebbets Field, a first for one of the most admired players of his time.

Line Scores:

Game One, October 1

Brk (NL)—000 010 100—2
Davis L, Casey (6), Allen (7)

NY (AL)—010 101 00X—3
Ruffing W

Game Two, October 2

Brk (NL)—000 021 000—3
Wyatt W

NY (AL)—011 000 000—2
Chandler L, Murphy (6)

Game Three, October 4

NY (AL)—000 000 020—2
Russo W

Brk (NL)—000 000 010—1
Fitzsimmons, Casey (8) L, French (8), Allen (9)

Game Four, October 5

NY (AL)—100 200 004—7
Donald, Breuer (5), Murphy (8) W

Brk (NL)—000 220 000—4
Higbe, French (4), Allen (5), Casey (5) L

Game Five, October 6

NY (AL)—020 010 000—3
Bonham W

Brk (NL)—001 000 000—1
Wyatt L

1942

St. Louis (NL) 4
New York (AL) 1

Shocking would be an understatement to describe this Series. The Yankees hadn't been humbled like this in 20 years. This young Cardinal team ran over the astonished Yankees as most of the country rejoiced.

The Preview:

The Yankees not only won eight of the previous 15 Series, their record in those games was 32-4, with five Series ending in sweeps. Only once had they been forced to go as far as a sixth game. There had never been this sort of total dominance before.

The 1942 edition was in the classic Yankee image. There was power; Charlie Keller had 26 homers and Joe DiMaggio 21, and both of them had more than 100 RBIs, as did second baseman Joe Gordon, who went through his best season at bat with a .322 average. DiMaggio had a subpar year by his exalted standards, slipping to a .305 average and not leading the league in anything. Moreover, rightfielder Tommy Henrich was gone to the Army, the first of the Yankees taken by demands of the war. New York had to patch up by acquiring journeyman Roy Cullenbine from the Senators. He turned around and hit .364 down the stretch, so that didn't look like a big problem, either. It wasn't quite the run machine of the late '30s, but it scored enough to win 103 games.

Moreover, the pitching had come back. Ernie Bonham, who closed out the previous year's Series, assumed the leadership role, going 21-5 with six shutouts. This time he was capably assisted by Spud Chandler (16-5) and the tireless Red Ruffing (14-7), who was 38 but still going strong. In addition, rookie Hank Borowy went 15-4, giving New York its deepest rotation in years.

George "Whitey" Kurowski's four hits accounted for five RBI, which was enough to lead the Cardinals. He hit a game-winning two-run homer in the ninth inning of the final game.

The Cards caught fire in August, going 43-9 in the last weeks of the season and blowing away a 10-game Brooklyn lead after Labor Day. It was the youngest team ever to win a National League pennant, with just one regular over the age of 30. It also had a distinctly regional flavor. The scouting system set up by Branch Rickey concentrated on the South, and the Cards were able to pluck outstanding prospects from the area. This was still a time when the South was regarded as a region far different than the rest of America. The common background gave the team a cohesiveness.

There were a few players from other parts, though. The top rookies, Stan Musial and Whitey Kurowski, were a pair of Polish-American kids from Pennsylvania. Musial hit .315 and trailed only Enos Slaughter for team honors in most batting stats. Slaughter hit .318 with 13 homers and 98 RBIs, marks well below those of New York's big hitters.

This was a team that relied on defense. Marty Marion, regarded as an anomaly at shortstop because of his 6-2 height, was nicknamed "Octopus" by the Cards because his long arms seemed to swoop up every ground ball. St. Louis claimed centerfielder Terry Moore was the equal of the great DiMaggio as a defensive player.

Its pitching staff compiled an ERA of 2.55, lowest in the National League since the end of the dead ball era. Mort Cooper was its leader, with a 22-7 record and 1.78 earned run average, both league-leading figures. Rookie John Beazley had a 21-6 mark. Behind them was an assortment of youngsters who were spot-started. The most critical from a strategic standpoint was left-hander Ernie White. A 17-game winner the previous year, he was bothered by injuries and went only 7-5. But the Yankees were supposed to be vulnerable to left-handers and the Cardinals had plans for him. Nonetheless, the Yankees were prohibitive favorites to win their ninth straight Series with little strain.

Turning Point: Game Three, Third Inning.

The Cards display a disturbing sort of resilience. Trailing 7-0 in the opener, they drive out Ruffing and shake the Yankees with a four-run rally in the ninth, which doesn't end until the tying run is on base with Musial at bat. Then in game two, the Cards shake off a game-tying three-run homer by Keller in the eighth, the sort of late hit that buckled other teams in the past. This time the Cards merely score another run in the bottom of the inning and even the Series.

Now it is back to Yankee Stadium, with a record crowd of 69,123 on hand to watch Chandler start against White. For two innings the teams are scoreless. Kurowski walks to open the third and Marion shortens up to bunt, an unusual play with the pitcher coming to bat next. Marion gets the sacrifice down moving the runner to second. But the Yankees charge the umpires and argue that the ball had actually hit Marion's bat twice, making it a foul. After several minutes of debate, the umpires reverse the call and Marion is made to bat again.

The Cards are outraged. There it is again. When you play the Yankees everything is against you. A successful play has been taken away from them and the Yanks have another shot at retiring Marion with no advance. The shortstop bunts again, but this time the ball rolls dead along the third base line and he beats it out. Instead of one out and a runner at second, the Cards have none out and two on. The big protest has backfired on the Yankees. White also bunts the runners along and when Gordon goes for a play at first on a grounder for the second out, the run scores.

As it turns out, that's the only run White needs. His shutout is the first against New York since Jess Haines did it in 1926, the last time New York lost a Series. It isn't an easy job. Moore has to race into the well of left-center to make a dazzling stab of DiMaggio's liner with a man on in the sixth. Then in the seventh, Slaughter leaps against the rightfield barrier to take a certain home run away from Keller.

Slaughter singles home an insurance run in the ninth and the Yanks lose 2-0 and are behind in the Series. It is far from over but the Cards have shown they will not be cowed by bad breaks. They will not lose again in the Series.

The Managers:

Billy Southworth was given one shot at managing the Cardinals in 1929. But owner Sam Breadon found him wanting. His tough, disciplined approach offended the players who used to be his teammates and the Cards refused to respond. Eleven years later, Breadon hired him back. But this was a relaxed, wiser Southworth. He was more counselor than martinet and the young St. Louis team went all out for him. He was also a starter on the 1926 Cards, the last team to win a Series from New York.

Joe McCarthy, unchallenged as the best manager in the game, had not tasted October defeat in 13 years, when he was with the Cubs. He accepted it graciously and immediately turned to the task of getting his war-depleted Yankees ready to exact their revenge.

The Heroes:

Beazley is the archetype of the player whose career will always remain a question mark because of the war. He came out of Tennessee with a live arm and a refusal to be intimidated. The 24-year-old rookie emerged from the bullpen in mid-season to go 15-3 as a starter and pace the Cards' late-season run. He pitched two complete games in the Series, stopping the Yanks in the fifth game to close them out, and was the man of the moment. But he went into the military right after the Series and when he emerged in 1946 he was never the same pitcher. He won just nine games the rest of his career. Southworth tried to find a place for him after moving to the Braves, but Beazley never got the magic back.

FACT:
Slaughter turned in the two defensive gems of the Series. In game three, his leaping catch against the rightfield wall took a game-tying homer away from Keller. In game two, he cut down pinch runner Tuck Stainback, the tying run, as he tried to go from first to third on a single in the ninth.

Kurowski had only four hits in the Series but he made them count, driving in five runs to lead the Cards. His two-run homer off Ruffing in the ninth inning of game five was the final margin of victory. He had contracted a bone disease after a childhood accident and lost most of the ulna in his right arm. The injury rendered him 4-F for the draft but did not interfere with his throwing.

Slaughter turned in the two defensive gems of the Series. In game three, his leaping catch against the rightfield wall took a game-tying homer away from Keller. In game two, he cut down pinch runner Tuck Stainback, the tying run, as he tried to go from first to third on a single in the ninth. The Yankees had been told to run on Slaughter because his arm was strong but inaccurate. This throw altered their thinking and saved the game for Beazley.

The Zeroes:

While Cooper turned in the lowest ERA in the National League in nine years, he was no mystery to the Yanks. He gave up 10 runs in 13 innings in his two starts and blew a 6-1 lead in game four, which nearly got the Yanks back in the Series.

Yankee first baseman Buddy Hassett drove a foul ball off his wrist in the first inning of game three and was out for the rest of the Series. Not only was he hitting .333, the injury forced McCarthy to move Gerry Priddy to first base, a position he had played just 11 times during the season. Priddy hit only .100 the rest of the way.

It was also a tough Series for Gordon, who had been unstoppable in 1941. This time he was 2 for 21 and struck out seven times.

FACT:
Cooper turned in the lowest ERA in the National League in nine years. He gave up 10 runs in 13 innings in his two starts and blew a 6-1 lead in game four, which nearly got the Yanks back in the Series.

The Aftermath:

This Series was the end of an era, a golden age that stretched from the introduction of the live ball in 1920 to the loss of top players to the draft in World War II. It was a time dominated by big hitters whose names still mark the record books and by the emergence of the Yankees as the game's greatest franchise. Although the country had been at war for 10 months when this Series began, the game still was lightly affected. Not until 1943 did the real wartime era begin with the best players off fighting for democracy. At war's end, social and economic changes would transform baseball into a different—and in most regards better—game. But it would never be the same.

Notes:

On successive days, Yankee Stadium set Series attendance records, with a crowd of 69,902 watching the fourth game. Writers noted that about half of the big crowds seemed to be cheering for the Cardinals. It appeared that New York, just like everyplace else, was growing bored with Yankee dominance.

The Cards were known for their speed and Braves' manager Casey Stengel described them as "more like a track team than a ballclub." They stole no bases in the Series, but their aggressiveness on the bases, especially Slaughter's, forced the unflappable Yankees into five throwing errors.

Line Scores:

Game One, September 30

NY (AL)—000 110 032—7
Ruffing W, Chandler (9) SV

SL (NL)—000 000 004—4
Cooper L, Gumbert (8), Lanier (9)

Game Two, October 1

NY (AL)—000 000 030—3
Bonham L

SL (NL)—200 000 11X—4
Beazley W

Game Three, October 3

SL (NL)—001 000 001—2
White W

NY (AL)—000 000 000—0
Chandler L, Breuer (9), Turner (9)

Game Four, October 4

SL (NL)—000 600 201—9
Cooper, Gumbert (6), Pollet (6), Lanier (7) W

NY (AL)—100 005 000—6
Borowy, Donald (4) L, Bonham (7)

Game Five, October 5

SL (NL)—000 101 002—4
Beazley W

NY (AL)—100 100 000—2
Ruffing L

1943

New York (AL) 4
St. Louis (NL) 1

Once stung, the Yankees were aroused. They spanked the Cardinals in five games in a return match. The country seemed to turn to this Series as a relief from the war, but the two teams, who had lost many of their biggest names to the military, responded with lackluster baseball.

The Preview:

These were easy pennant races for both teams. The Yankees won by 13 1/2 games and the Cards by 18. The larger struggle was trying to field a consistent ballcub with so many players off to the war.

From one Series to the next the Cards had lost two of their regular outfielders—Enos Slaughter and Terry Moore—as well as second baseman Jimmy Brown and pitchers John Beazley and Howie Pollet. But Stan Musial, in his second full season, burst out to become the league's top hitter. He led in average (.357) and hits (220) as well as pacing the Cards in homers (13) and RBIs (81). Catcher Walker Cooper had a big year with a .318 average and 81 RBIs, and he held together a constantly changing cast of pitchers. A trade with the Phillies brought Danny Litwhiler to fill one of the outfield holes, and Harry Walker, Dixie's younger brother, came up from AAA to hit .294 as the centerfielder.

St. Louis pitching once again dominated the league. Led by Mort Cooper (21-8) and Max Lanier (15-7), the staff went through an assortment of starters as the draft and injuries took a toll. Pollet was leading the league in ERA when he departed. But another young lefthander, Alpha Brazle, went 8-2 with a 1.53 ERA as his replacement.

Walker (left) and Mort Cooper, brothers and batterymates for the 1943 Cardinals. Both played well in the Series, even after learning of their father's death after Game 2. Walker hit .294 while Mort won one of two decisions.

The Yankees were left with a yawning gap in center where Joe DiMaggio was wont to roam. They were also missing Phil Rizzuto, Buddy Hassett and Red Ruffing, while Red Rolfe had retired to coach college baseball.

Charlie Keller was still around, though, and he was good for 31 homers, while Bill Dickey, reduced to part-time duties as a catcher, still was spry enough to hit .351. The Yanks plugged their first base hole with a grateful refugee from the Phillies, Nick Etten, who led the team with 107 RBIs. Their dependable minor league system coughed up third baseman Billy Johnson, who drove in 94 more while hitting .280. No other regular hit that high. Johnny Lindell, a converted pitcher, was inserted in DiMaggio's spot in center, but hit only .245.

That left it to the pitchers to get things done. Spud Chandler responded with a 20-4 season and league-leading 1.64 ERA. He was abetted by Ernie Bonham (15-8, 2.27) and Hank Borowy (14-9, 2.82). Johnny Murphy, who had redefined the role of the bullpen stopper, contributed 12 wins and eight saves. It was far from prime Yankee material, but the oddsmakers still made them the favorites against the previous year's champs.

Turning Point: Game Three, Eighth Inning.

For most of the first three games, the script is the same as 1942. The Yanks win the opener behind Chandler, 4-2. Then Cooper, held out of the first game because of ineffectiveness against New York the previous year, stops the Yanks 4-3. He and his brother, Walker, are playing one day after learning of their father's death back in Missouri.

The previous Series had turned in game three when left-hander Ernie White shut out New York. This time, another lefty, Brazle, is doing almost as well. Through seven innings, he nurses a 2-1 lead, with the only New York run scoring on a fumbled grounder by Whitey Kurowski at third.

Lindell starts the eighth with a single and hurries into second when Walker bobbles the ball in center. It is the third St. Louis error of the game and the seventh of the Series. Number eight is coming right up. When pinch hitter Snuffy Stirnweiss bunts, Cards first baseman Ray Sanders picks up the ball and whips it to third, well ahead of Lindell. But the New York runner comes crashing into Kurowski and knocks the ball out of his hand for an error.

In 1942 it was St. Louis who had been the aggressive team, forcing the Yankees into several mistakes with their speed on the bases. The Yankees decided that they would not be pushed around like that again. Veteran observers said they had not seen a Yankee team play with so much feistiness in many years. The Yanks keep applying the pressure, too. On a fly ball to left, Stirnweiss tags and takes off for second, daring Litwhiler to make a play on him so Lindell can score from third.

Southworth now makes the critical decision of the game. Instead of pitching to the weak-hitting Frank Crosetti, he orders him walked and instead goes after the rookie Johnson, who abruptly clears the bases with a triple up the left-center alley, putting New York into a 4-2 lead. The Yankees score twice more before the inning is through. A patented, late Yankee rally turns the game around and the reeling Cards go back to St. Louis. They drop two more before they even know what hit them.

The Managers:

Southworth showed an uncharacteristic edginess in this Series. After being beaten by seldom-used Marius Russo in game four he snapped at reporters and then closed the St. Louis clubhouse to the press before the next game. Frustrated at seeing his team's aggressiveness being thrown back in their faces, he could not get the Cards turned around. This Series was the most irritating of his career.

Joe McCarthy, however, seemed to enjoy watching his Yankees get down in the dirt to scrap with St. Louis. When Lindell was criticized for rough play because of his slide into Kurowski in game three, McCarthy snapped: "This isn't a pink tea party." It was a satisfying seventh championship and, as it turned out, his last one.

FACT:
Russo, only a 5-10 pitcher during the season, was the surprise choice for game four. Not only did he stop the Cards on one unearned run, he also scored the winner after doubling in the eighth.

The Heroes:

Two veterans of the great Yankee teams of the 30s, Crosetti and Dickey, enjoyed a last turn in the spotlight. Crosetti, who only started at shortstop because Rizzuto went off to war, responded with a fine effort. He knocked in the winning run in game four and was a factor in both of the team's two-run rallies in game one. He finished the Series hitting .278. That matched Dickey's mark. He led everyone with four RBIs, including the winning two-run shot off Cooper that put away the closing game.

Chandler was nearly untouchable, allowing just two runs in two complete game wins to cap his finest season. The Georgian had not reached the majors until he was 30 and now, six years later, the clock is ticking loudly for him. He misses the next two seasons to the war, but still comes back for one more 20-victory year before his arm gives out.

Russo, only a 5-10 pitcher during the season, was the surprise choice for game four. Not only did he stop the Cards on one unearned run, he also scored the winner after doubling in the eighth.

Mort Cooper gave his all in winning the Cards only game the day after his father's death. Reminiscent of the Bobo Newsom scenario in the 1940 Series, the Cooper brothers declared that "Dad would have wanted us to play" and formed the battery that beat the Yanks, 4-3, in game two.

The Zeroes:

The St. Louis defense turned to putty, commiting 10 errors in just five games and placing constant pressure on the Cardinal pitchers. The blame was evenly spread, with four different players making two errors apiece.

It was a fairly punchless performance for the top St. Louis hitter. Musial was held with no extra base hits, no RBIs and was virtually a non-factor.

The Aftermath:

The Cards still had enough manpower left in 1944 to breeze to a third consecutive pennant. It was a team even more powerful than the 1943 edition and with a more consistent pitching staff.

The war caught up to the Yankees, though. Their denuded roster was not up to another run and the team fell back to third place, six games off the pace set by the Browns. It was New York's most distant finish in 10 years.

Notes:

Travel restrictions were in effect for the Series. The first three games were played in New York and, no matter how long it lasted, all the others were scheduled for St. Louis. As it turned out that meant just two.

Another attendance record was smashed at Yankee Stadium, when 69,990 turned out for game three. The Series also had the largest radio audience in history, for it was the first to be beamed to U.S. troops overseas.

FACT:
Another attendance record was smashed at Yankee Stadium, when 69,990 turned out for game three. The Series also had the largest radio audience in history. It was the first to be beamed to U.S. troops overseas.

Line Scores:

Game One, October 5
SL (NL)—010 010 000—2
Lanier L, Brecheen (8)
NY (AL)—000 202 00X—4
Chandler W

Game Two, October 6
SL (NL)—001 300 000—4
Cooper W
NY (AL)—000 100 002—3
Bonham L, Murphy (9)

Game Three, October 7
SL (NL)—000 200 000—2
Brazle L, Krist (8), Brecheen (8)
NY (AL)—000 001 05X—6
Borowy W, Murphy (9)

Game Four, October 10
NY (AL)—000 100 010—2
Russo W
SL (NL)—000 000 100—1
Lanier, Brecheen (8) L

Game Five, October 11
NY (AL)—000 002 000—2
Chandler W
SL (NL)—000 000 000—0
Cooper, Lanier (8), Dickson (9)

1944

St. Louis (NL) 4
St. Louis (AL) 2

It took a world war for the Browns to win their first pennant. They then gave the team that shared their ballpark a surprisingly tough Series before succumbing. For this forlorn franchise, though, it was a short and solitary walk in the sun.

The Preview:

The Browns burst totally unexpected out of the American League depths. A decent team in the 1920s, they had fallen into the nether regions in the next decade and could not get out. Between 1930 and 1941, they never finished higher than sixth and averaged about 200,000 in annual attendance. Meanwhile, the Cardinals were bringing home pennants and championships to St. Louis. It was a hopelessly unequal struggle, and whenever the Browns did come up with a decent player they were forced to sell or trade him to keep paying the bills.

But the team changed ownership in 1936, and Bill DeWitt, a protege of Branch Rickey with the Cardinals, was hired as president. He began the long, tedious job of building this hopeless organization into a winner. By 1942, he had lifted the Browns to third place. It was, to be sure, a distant third—18 1/2 games behind the Yankees—but it was the club's highest finish in the standings since 1928.

The team fell back to sixth in 1943, but DeWitt had a plan. Seeing the way things were going, he managed to assemble the deepest pool of 4-F athletes in the game. Some were young, some were old, and one who came in later, Pete Gray, had only one arm. But in 1944 they broke through. It took a four-game sweep against the Yankees on the last weekend of the season, but the Browns beat out Detroit by one game.

"Whitey" Kurowski (left) congratulates Mort Cooper on his victory in Game 5. Cooper had pitched out of a bases loaded jam in the sixth inning, striking out two of the Browns' top hitters. His Series ERA was 1.12.

The team's star was shortstop Junior Stephens, one of only two hitters in this wartime American League season to hit 20 or more homers. He also knocked in 109 runs to lead everyone, while hitting .293. The rest of the infield was pretty good, too. First baseman George McQuinn added 72 RBIs, while third baseman Mark Christman had 83. Veteran Mike Kreevich (.301) and second-year man Al Zarilla (.299) were the best in the outfield. The two catchers didn't hit much, but considering that Ray Hayworth was 40 and Gus Mancuso 38, it was a triumph just getting them to crouch.

The strength was in the pitching. Nels Potter, who had been kicking around with undistinguished results for years, had his best season at 19-7. Jack Kramer, a product of the farm system who also had shown little, went 17-13. George Caster, a two-time league-leader in losses with the A's, which seemed to make him prime material for the Browns, blossomed into a decent reliever, with 12 saves and a 2.44 ERA.

The Cards contrived to preserve the core of their pennant-winning lineup and coasted home by 14 1/2 games. Since the third place team in the National League had won more games than the Browns, the Cardinals weren't terribly concerned about this Series.

Stan "The Man" Musial was again their driving force, with a .347 average and 94 RBIs. Shortstop Marty Marion was voted the league's Most Valuable Player for his outstanding defensive work. Johnny Hopp, who never could find a position with earlier Card teams, was now assigned full time to centerfield and responded with a blazing .336 season. The two catchers, Walker Cooper and Ken O'Dea, drove in 109 runs between them.

The team also maintained its superiority in pitching. Mort Cooper was a 20-game winner for the third straight year, coming in at 22-7. In back of him were left-handers Max Lanier (17-12) and Harry Brecheen (16-5). The big addition was another gem from the apparently inexhaustible lode in the Cardinal system, Ted Wilks. With his 17-4 record, the team was able to survive the mid-season drafting of George Munger (11-3 with a 1.34 ERA at the time) without missing a beat.

Turning Point: Game Five, Sixth Inning.

Expecting a pleasant outing, the Cardinals find themselves fighting for their lives. The Browns win game one behind the tough pitching of Denny Galehouse, a desperation choice since he was the only starter not used in the pennant-clinching series in New York. Only a brilliant relief effort by the Cards Blix Donnelly holds the Browns off in game two, and then the Browns hammer Wilks in the third game behind Kramer's 10-strikeout pitching. The Cards pull even again behind Brecheen in game four. With the Series tied, Galehouse is baffling them once more. Cooper, who lost the first game, is also airtight, and the game goes into the sixth at 0-0.

The Cards threaten repeatedly, but Galehouse, who has put together just one winning season in his nine-year career, turns them away every time. However, with two out in the sixth, Ray Sanders gives him no chance to recover. The first baseman, who was discovered playing softball in St. Louis, puts one over the rightfield pavilion and the Cards, at last, provide their ace a 1-0 edge.

FACT: Cooper simply blows Zarilla and Christman away. Neither one takes the bat from their shoulders and they are both called out on strikes. That is the Browns' last gasp. The Cards wrap it up next day and the Browns' only chance at a championship in the entire 52 years of their existence is gone.

The Browns, who are this game's designated home team, will not go quietly. Kreevich opens their half of the inning with a single. After a force-out, Stephens also singles, sending the runner to third. Cooper pitches carefully to McQuinn, the hottest hitter in the Series, and walks him to load the bases. Almost any sort of batted ball can now tie the game and the Browns have two of their top hitters, Zarilla and Christman, coming up.

Cooper simply blows them away. Neither one takes the bat from their shoulders and they are both called out on strikes, unforgivable lapses in this critical situation. That is the Browns' last gasp. Danny Litwhiler slugs another homer in the eighth to make it 2-0 and Cooper finishes with a flourish, striking out the side in the ninth. The Cards wrap it up the next day and the Browns' only chance at a championship in the entire 52 years of their existence is gone.

The Managers:

Most observers were astonished that Luke Sewell would want to leave a secure coaching job in Cleveland to take over the hapless Browns. The 43-year-old Sewell, a starter on the 1933 Washington team and a knowledgeable catcher for many years, had a reputation as a handler of pitchers. This was the most pressing need for the Browns, and Sewell, who came aboard in the spring of 1941, got results. His performance this season was hailed as little less than miraculous by a country caught up in the triumph of a perennial underdog.

Billy Southworth was now 51 and had put together the best three-year run of any National League team since the Cubs of 1906-08. He won 316 games and three straight pennants. With a fabulously well-stocked farm system, there seemed to be no slowdown in sight for the Cardinals. It appeared to be an organization as solid as the Yankees, and one destined to be their top rivals for years to come.

The Heroes:

McQuinn was typical of the players DeWitt had gathered to build the Browns. He came to the majors with Cincinnati as a 27-year-old rookie but was quickly supplanted by Frank McCormick. Joining the Browns two years later, he settled in as a consistent slugger and excellent defensive first baseman. His .438 average and five RBIs, including a two-run homer that beat Cooper in game one, led both teams.

Donnelly, a 30-year-old rookie who was used mainly in long relief, pulled the Cards back from the brink in game two. The Browns had driven out Lanier to tie the game and were threatening to take a two-game lead in the Series. Donnelly came in to strike out the side in the eighth with the lead run on second. Then he held the Browns off into the 11th, throwing out a runner at third in that inning on an attempted sacrifice with none out. The Cards pulled it out in the bottom of the inning to give him the win.

This was also an outstanding Series for Cards second baseman Emil Verban. The weakest hitter in the lineup during the season, at .257, Verban batted .412 in the Series. He was infuriated when

Browns management assigned his wife a seat behind a post for their home games at Sportsman's Park.

The Zeroes:

Just as the Cards had kicked away the 1943 Series by committing 10 errors, the Browns went and did likewise. The same numbers of miscues resulted in seven of the Cards' 16 total runs. Bobbles by Potter, second baseman Don Gutteridge and Stephens were responsible for the losing margin in two games. Middle infielders Gutteridge and Stephens made six errors between them.

FACT:
Ten errors by the Browns resulted in seven of the Cards' 16 total runs. Bobbles by Potter, second baseman Don Gutteridge and Stephens were responsible for the losing margin in two games. Middle infielders Gutteridge and Stephens made six errors between them.

It was also not a good Series at third base for Christman. He went 2-for-22 and struck out six times.

Sig Jakucki had his moment when he pitched the pennant-clinching game against the Yanks. But the redoubtable Jakucki, who had spent the previous seven years in the minors, and at 35 was the epitome of the wartime player, could not make it past the fourth in his only Series start.

The Aftermath:

When the Series ended the Browns had only nine years left to their existence. They dropped to third place in 1945 and when the 1-A's came back from the war the Browns quickly slipped to their usual haunts at the bottom of the standings. Finally, when even the marketing genius of Bill Veeck couldn't draw crowds to see such wonders as a midget batter, the team moved to Baltimore and became the Orioles, with much better results.

The Cards slipped to second in 1945. The loss of Musial and both Coopers, Walker to the military and Mort by forcing a trade, was too much to overcome. By the margin of three games they missed becoming the first team ever to win five straight pennants—since they rose to the top again in 1946. But Southworth, upon receiving a "once in a lifetime" financial offer from the Braves, asked to be released from his contract after the 1945 season.

Notes:

The teams established a pair of records for futility. In just the sort of performance that gave wartime baseball its sorry reputation, they combined for 92 strikeouts. That surpassed in six games the old mark of 87 which had taken the A's and Cards seven games to achieve in 1931.

This was also the first Series in which there was not a single stolen base. None was even attempted.

With wartime travel restrictions in effect, this turned out to be the perfect Series. All six games were played in Sportsman's Park, only the third time in history one ballpark hosted an entire Series. The Polo Grounds was the other such venue in the 1921–22 Series between the Giants and Yankees.

Line Scores:

Game One, October 4

SL (AL)—000 200 000—2
Galehouse W

SL (NL)—000 000 001—1
Cooper L, Donnely (8)

Game Two, October 5

SL (AL)—000 000 200 00—2
Potter, Muncrief (7) L

SL (NL)—001 100 000 01—3
Lanier, Donnely (8) W

Game Three, October 6

SL (NL)—100 000 100—2
Wilks L, Schmidt (3), Jurisich (7), Byerly (7)

SL (AL)—004 000 20X—6
Kramer W

Game Four, October 7

SL (NL)—202 001 000—5
Brecheen W

SL (AL)—000 000 010—1
Jakucki L, Hollingsworth (4), Shirley (8)

Game Five, October 8

SL (NL)—000 001 010—2
Cooper W

SL (AL)—000 000 000—0
Galehouse L

Game Six, October 9

SL (AL)—010 000 000—1
Potter L, Muncrief (4), Kramer (7)

SL (NL)—000 300 00X—3
Lanier W, Wilks (6) SV

1945

Detroit (AL) 4
Chicago (NL) 3

In a Series that has come down in baseball lore as the worst ever played, the Tigers outlasted their old foes from Chicago. While artistically imperfect, the games seemed to satisfy fans in both cities, who filled the parks for all seven games in a postwar celebration.

The Preview:

The two remaining holdovers from Chicago's 1935 pennant-winners were key elements in this combination of the draft-proof and infirm. First baseman Phil Cavaretta, in his 11th big league season and still only 29 years old, had a career year. He led the league in hitting at .355 and also drove in 97 runs. Across the infield was Stan Hack, still plugging away at 35. He hit .323, played a stalwart defensive game and still managed to steal 12 bases.

Bill Nicholson, who had become the first player ever to lead the National League in homers and RBIs for two straight years, in 1943–44, tailed off. He hit just 13 home runs and sank to a .243 average. But Andy Pafko took up the slack, knocking in 110 runs on a .298 average.

The Cubs won the pennant on pitching, though. Hank Wyse, who had come up from the minors as a wartime replacement, had his finest season at 22-10. Two veterans whose prewar credentials were beyond reproach also chipped in with effective years. Claude Passeau, a Cub since 1940, went 17-9 and Paul Derringer, who had pitched on previous winners in St. Louis and Cincinnati, had a 16-11 year.

The key acquisition was made in July when the Yankees, inexplicably, put Hank Borowy on waivers. The 29-year-old right-hander had been one of New York's top pitchers for the

Hank Greenberg (left) of the Tigers and Phil Cavaretta provided offensive fireworks in the Series. Cavaretta hit .423 while Greenberg, after returning from the war earlier in the season, hit .304 with five extra base hits.

previous three years, a critical element on their 1942–43 pennant-winners. The Yankees claimed that he had started fading in the late innings. Nonetheless, he was still their most effective starter, with a 10-5 record. The Cubs had passed on a chance to get Mort Cooper earlier in the year, but after Borowy slipped past every American League team (all of whom complained bitterly about it afterwards) the Cubs grabbed him for $100,000. He then pitched Chicago through the stretch with an 11-2 record, for a 21-7 mark overall. He was also recognized as the league's earned run leader—although under current eligibility rules the honor, instead, would have gone to his teammate, Passeau.

Detroit also had another major returnee from the 1935 Series: Hank Greenberg was released from military duty and rejoined the team in early summer. He drove in 60 runs in 78 games, including a pennant-winning grand slam on the last day of the season. The rest of the Tigers' power was supplied by first-baseman Rudy York, a holdover from the 1940 team, who drove in 87 runs. Outfielder Roy Cullenbine, picked up from Cleveland in April, tied York with 18 homers and had 93 RBIs. Its spark-plug, however, was second baseman Eddie Mayo. A minor league journeyman, he joined Detroit in 1944 and one year later, at the age of 35, got his payoff. His .285 average and excellent defense made him the team's most valuable player.

The overpowering pitching of Hal Newhouser put the Tigers over the top. The left-hander dominated every statistic, with a 25-9 record and 1.81 ERA. His 212 strikeouts were 83 more than anyone else in the league. While he bore the stigma of being a wartime player for decades afterwards, his performance remains impressive, even making allowances for the lower caliber of the competition.

Behind him were Dizzy Trout (18-15) and also Al Benton (13-8), who shifted between starting and relief for most of the season and put together his finest year. The staff got an enormous boost in the last week of the season when Virgil Trucks, a 16-game winner in 1943, was released from the Navy and permitted to join the team in time for the Series. (Normal Series eligibility rules were waived to allow returning servicemen to play.) Still, the Tigers had won just 88 games and the Cubs were regarded as narrow favorites.

Turning Point: Game Seven, First Inning.

The Series is a victim of hyped expectations. With the war over for two months, everyone is eager for a return to normal times, including a return of the stars to major league lineups. But only a handful are back for this Series. So, all the frustration over the mediocrity of the game for the last three seasons seems to focus on these games. The caliber of play, while no better than the previous two Series, is certainly no worse.

The teams take turns punching each other out for six games. Detroit is shut out twice, once in the opener by Borowy and the other time on a one-hitter by Passeau. Trout and Trucks respond with strong efforts for Detroit in games two and four. While Newhouser is not the same pitcher he was during the season, he has enough to put Chicago away in game five and give the Tigers a 3-2 lead in games.

It is the wild sixth game, won by Chicago 8-7 in 12 innings, that probably wins this Series its dreadful reputation. It is an error-filled slugfest, highlighted by Detroit's Chuck Hostetler falling down as he rounds third with what would have been the winning run. Chicago finally wins it when Hack's line drive hit takes a bad hop over Greenberg's head in left and rolls for a double. Greenberg is given an error, but the call is later reversed when it is pointed out that he never had a chance to touch the ball.

FACT:
The wild sixth game is an error-filled slugfest, highlighted by Detroit's Chuck Hostetler falling down as he rounds third with what would have been the winning run.

Game seven matches the aces, Borowy and Newhouser. A one-day delay is declared to prepare for the deciding contest (although games four through seven were all played in Chicago because of travel restrictions.) The Cubs' staff is exhausted. Everyone was thrown into the 12-inning battle and Borowy pitched four shutout innings of relief. Newhouser, on the other hand, will work with two full days of rest.

The point becomes academic very quickly. It is obvious that Borowy has nothing left and the Tigers pounce on him. Three straight singles in the first make it 1-0 and drive him from the game. The Cubs bring in Derringer, who stopped Detroit twice in 1940. But he is now a week short of his 39th birthday and this will be his last game in the majors. He, too, is a spent force. He manages to get two outs with no further damage while loading the bases. Then he walks Jimmy Outlaw to force in a second run.

This brings up catcher Paul Richards. He is just 2 for 15 in the Series but is an automatic starter whenever Newhouser pitches. The pitcher credits Richards for his success and regards him as a genius, a reputation that will follow him into a succesful managerial career with Baltimore and the White Sox. This time he measures Derringer and drives the ball into the leftfield corner. The double clears the bases and Newhouser has a 5-0 lead. Those runs are more than he'll need as the disappointed Wrigley crowd watches the Tigers ease home with a 9-3 victory and the Series. In the end, the addition of Trucks to Detroit's staff for two Series starts gives the Tigers just enough depth to outlast the Cubs.

The Managers:

Charlie Grimm was in his second go-round with the Cubs. Kicked up to the radio booth in 1938 because he was regarded as too easy-going, he was brought back to the dugout in 1944 after a succession of second-division finishes. The team responded to his light touch to give him his third pennant with the Cubs.

Another amiable oldtimer sat on the Detroit bench. Steve O'Neill, longtime catching star in Cleveland, was regarded as a knowledgable, albeit unexciting, baseball man. He was hired in 1943 with instructions to get at the untapped potential in Newhouser. O'Neill brought in Richards, who had spent the last seven years in the minors, and turned the young lefthander, who was then 22, over to him. The mentoring program paid quick dividends and in two years O'Neill had his winner.

The Heroes:

Cavaretta took his batting championship stroke right into the Series, cranking out 11 hits for a .423 average. A remarkably consistent player who was with the Cubs for 20 years, he was another performer labeled a wartime player, and his accomplishments were unfairly belittled. Still, he started a World Series as a 19-year-old and hit .293 for a career.

Passeau had been a winner for the Cubs ever since they rescued him from the Phillies. He won 113 games in the next six and a half seasons, while averaging more than 30 starts. There was no suspense about his one-hitter, since York slashed his single cleanly into leftfield in the second inning. The Tigers had just one other baserunner, on a walk in the sixth, and he was immediately wiped out in a double play.

FACT:
It was a grand return for Greenberg, who hit .304 with five of his seven hits going for extra bases. He had three doubles in game five, a game-winning homer in game two, and an eighth inning blast in game six to send that contest into extra innings.

It was a grand return for Greenberg, who hit .304 with five of his seven hits going for extra bases. All three doubles came in Detroit's 8-4 win in game five, with one of them getting lost in the vines on the leftfield wall. His three-run homer off Wyse was the margin of victory in game two and his other shot, in the eighth inning of game six, sent that contest into extra innings.

The Zeroes:

Derringer had started 30 games and won 16, both of them high totals for him since he was with the Reds in 1940. But Chicago writers had criticized him for what they regarded as indifference. He was passed over as a starter in the Series and after two lackluster relief jobs he decided to call it quits, with 223 wins in his dossier.

Another hero of Series past was also treated rather rudely. Tommy Bridges, who had thwarted the Cubs in 1935, rejoined the Tigers from the service in September. But the 38-year old Bridges was hit hard in his only appearance, and after nine ineffective outings in 1946 he, too, called it a career.

York was fairly much neutralized by the Cubs. The Detroit first baseman was held to a .179 average and convinced the Tigers to unload him over the winter and move Greenberg back to first base.

The Aftermath:

When the 1-A's came marching home in 1946, the pennant equation in both leagues was thoroughly scrambled. The Cubs fell back to a distant third and then slowly slipped from sight completely. It was the start of the longest pennant drought in baseball history. At this writing, it is 50 years and counting, easily eclipsing the former record of 43 years by the St. Louis Browns. Ironically, the Browns had ended their winless streak one year before the Cubs started theirs.

The Tigers retained a solid core of players that kept them in contention for several years. Greenberg, however, despite leading the league in home runs and RBIs in 1946, was sold to Pittsburgh. Newhouser proved that he could beat the real players, too, but developed arm problems after 1946 that limited his effectiveness for the rest of his career. It would be 23 years before Detroit would reach the Series again.

Notes:

Clyde McCullough, who got into the ninth inning of the final game as a pinch hitter, became the only player ever to appear in a Series without being in a single game with the club during the season. He had been the Cubs regular catcher from 1941–43 and was thus eligible for the military waiver.

One of the primary complaints about the 12-inning sixth game was its outrageous length. It took three hours and 28 minutes, a situation exacerbated by the fact that Wrigley Field had no lights. In another four decades, a three and a half hour Series game was regarded as about par.

The Tigers were masters of the big inning. They were shut out in 35 of the first 37 innings of the Series and still managed to win two games by bunching all their scoring in two four-run rallies.

Line Scores:

Game One, October 3

Chi (NL)—403 000 200—9
Borowy W

Det (AL)—000 000 000—0
Newhouser L, Benton (3), Tobin (5), Mueller (8)

Game Two, October 4

Chi (NL)—000 100 000—1
Wyse L, Erickson (7)

Det (AL)—000 040 00X—4
Trucks W

Game Three, October 5

Chi (NL)—000 200 100—3
Passeau W

Det (AL)—000 000 000—0
Overmire L, Benton (7)

Game Four, October 6

Det (AL)—000 400 000—4
Trout W

Chi (NL)—000 001 000—1
Prim L, Derringer (4), Vandenberg (6), Erickson (8)

Game Five, October 7

Det (AL)—001 004 102—8
Newhouser W

Chi (NL)—001 000 201—4
Borowy L, Vandenberg (6), Chipman (6), Derringer (7), Erickson (9)

Game Six, October 8

Det (AL)—010 000 240 000—7
Trucks, Caster (5), Bridges (6), Benton (7), Trout (8) L

Chi (NL)—000 041 200 001—8
Passeau, Wyse (7), Prim (8), Borowy (9) W

Game Seven, October 10

Det (AL)—510 000 120—9
Newhouser W

Chi (NL)—100 100 010—3
Borowy L, Derringer (1), Vandenberg (2), Erickson (6), Passeau (8), Wyse (9)

1946

St. Louis (NL) 4
Boston (AL) 3

A classic confrontation of speed against power resulted in another victory for the quicker feet. Enos Slaughter's were the quickest of them all when he raced home from first on what appeared to be a single and scored the deciding run.

The Preview:

Both teams entered spring training with a sense of ecstacy, surrounded by the sort of talent that hadn't been seen in years. The boys were back and the country looked forward to this pennant race with keen anticipation.

For the Cardinals, it was almost an embarrassment of riches. The team had won two pennants in the war years and now had more talent than it had open positions. Four members of the wartime teams followed their manager, Billy Southworth, to the Boston Braves. That still left so many top players for the Cards that they were picked almost unanimously for their fourth pennant in five years.

In the reshuffling, Stan Musial wound up at first base and observed the move by winning his second batting title (.365) and driving in 103 runs. Enos Slaughter came back from three years in the service and led the league in RBIs with 130 while hitting .300. Wartime holdovers Marty Marion and Whitey Kurowski gave St. Louis the best left side of any infield in the game. And young Red Schoendienst came in from the outfield, his position during his rookie year in 1945, to assume his place as one of the best second basemen.

There were some problems. The Cards had sold off Walker Cooper, and the two young catchers asked to replace him—Joe Garagiola and Del Rice—were not quite up to the job. They

Enos Slaughter slides home safely with the winning run in Game 7 after his "mad dash" beat a stunned Johnny Pesky's throw. Slaughter scored from first base when Pesky hesitated before making the relay throw home.

drove in just 34 runs between them. Terry Moore also was not the same player upon his return, which left problems in the outfield. Moreover, John Beazley, hero of the 1942 Series, came back with a sore arm and didn't throw well all season. That still left Howie Pollet (21-10), Murray Dickson (15-6) and Harry Brecheen, whose break-even 15-15 record was belied by a 2.49 ERA, fifth best in the league.

The Cards dominated every team statistic but were pressed to the limit by the Dodgers. St. Louis won only after sweeping a two-out-of-three playoff, the first in baseball history.

The Red Sox had no such problems. They cruised in 12 games ahead of the Tigers for their first pennant in 28 years. The team was loaded with big hitters, led by Ted Williams. Leading the league in no major stat, he was runner up in all three of the Triple Crown categories (.342, 38 homers, 123 RBIs) and astonished the baseball world by pulverizing the top National League pitchers in the All Star Game. His massive home run off Rip Sewell's blooper ball was the talk of the country.

Bobby Doerr drove in 116 runs, and Dom DiMaggio played an incomparable centerfield, while hitting .316. There were, however, some defensive problems in the infield. While shortstop

Johnny Pesky (.335) hit line drives almost everytime he swung his bat, showing no effects from his three years in the service, he was, at best, adequate in the field. The Sox had traded their wartime shortstop, Eddie Lake, to Detroit to get first baseman Rudy York. It added yet another big bat to the Boston lineup, as York knocked in 119 runs. He was once described, however, as being "part Indian, part first baseman," and his defense reflected that.

Pitching had been Boston's weakness in a run of disappointing finishes in the '30s and early '40s. But this time Boo Ferriss (25-6) and Tex Hughson (20-11) led an unusually deep staff. Behind them was Mickey Harris, a left-hander who went 17-9, and Joe Dobson, at 13-7. Boston hadn't enjoyed such quality at the top and depth in the middle since its great staffs of the World War I era. The Red Sox chafed at the delay caused by the National League playoffs and tried to keep sharp with some exhibition games against a team of American League all stars. The Sox entered the Series believing the Cardinals were mentally exhausted. They expected a championship.

Turning Point: Game Seven, Eighth Inning.

As it turns out, the playoff only fueled the Cards' competitive fires. They trade wins with Boston through the first six games. Moreover, they wax the Red Sox, 12-3, in the fourth game at Fenway Park, where Boston is supposed to be unbeatable. For the third time in Series history, the Cardinals return to St. Louis trailing three games to two and needing a sweep at home. Having escaped from Fenway alive, they are confident about getting it done.

They take the sixth game behind Brecheen, 4-1. It is his second win of the Series and he has given up just one run to a team that devours lefties like carrot sticks. But Boston has rested its ace, Ferriss. Manager Joe Cronin deliberately held him out of the sixth game to give him a full five days of rest. He shut out the Cards in game three and the loser of that game, Dickson, is all that stands between Boston and the championship.

Both teams score early on sacrifice flies. In the fifth it is Dickson himself who delivers the killing shot to Ferriss. His double drives home the lead run, then he scores himself on Schoendienst's single. Dickson makes the 3-1 lead stand up into the eighth. Then Boston suddenly strikes. Pinch hitters Rip Russell and George Metkovich bang out a single and a double, and the Sox have the tying run on second with none out.

Manager Eddie Dyer has already notified Brecheen that he may have to go in on one day's rest and the left-hander is ready. He quickly disposes of Wally Moses and Pesky, but DiMaggio drives a double off the rightfield wall. As he races for second, however, he twists his ankle and cannot continue. Williams ends the inning with a pop foul, and although the game is tied Boston's outfield defense has suffered a mortal blow.

St. Louis, too, takes a hit before the inning is over. Garagiola, a major surprise as a hitter in the Series, is forced from the game when a foul tip splits his finger. That injury looks even bigger after Slaughter leads off with a single. Failing in a sacrifice attempt, Rice, batting in Garigiola's spot, goes down on a short fly ball. That brings up Harry Walker, who had been the most reliable Cardinal hitter.

FACT:
Would Slaughter have dared to run if DiMaggio were still in center? Could Pesky have caught him with a quicker throw? The questions are debated endlessly.

He lines reliever Bob Klinger's delivery over Pesky's head, towards the left center gap. Leon Culberson, filling in for DiMaggio, cuts the ball off, but Slaughter is running with contact and doesn't even slow down as he reaches third. Culberson's throw comes in to Pesky, who hesitates to check on Slaughter's whereabouts before throwing. The instant is all that Slaughter needs to score, on a play reminiscent of Cincinnati's wining run in the 1940 Series.

Would Slaughter have dared to run if DiMaggio were still in center? Could Pesky have caught him with a quicker throw? The questions are debated endlessly. Walker is credited with a double on what most observers agree was actually a single. The run stands up as the winner. Brecheen survives two leadoff singles in the ninth to put the game away and become the first pitcher to win three in a Series since Stan Coveleski in 1920.

The Managers:

When Billy Southworth asked permission to accept an offer from the Braves, St. Louis owner Sam Breadon knew immediately whom he wanted as a replacement. Eddie Dyer had been with the organization since 1922, as a pitcher, coach, farm director and minor league manager. At 45, he retired to enter private business in Houston, but his family convinced him to take Breadon's offer and manage in the majors for the first time. Entering the job under intense pressure, with anything less than a pennant considered a failure, Dyer came through.

His opponent, Joe Cronin, had also won a pennant as a freshman manager. That was 13 years ago, in Washington. Traded to Boston two years later (even though he was owner Clark Griffith's son-in-law), Cronin was immediately named manager and turned the Red Sox into perennial bridesmaids. The restless Boston press decided that nothing less than a pennant would do for 1946, so Cronin also was under the gun to bring one home with this collection of stars.

The Heroes:

In only his fourth full year in the majors, the late-blooming Brecheen had celebrated his 32nd birthday the day before his third Series win. Armed with a screwball, excellent control and a feline grace that won him the nickname "The Cat," Brecheen now was recognized as one of the top left-handers in the game. In two years, he would lead the league in ERA, strikeouts and shutouts. But this was unquestionably his finest hour. While Dyer did not risk pitching him in that tomb of southpaws, Fenway Park, he stopped the Red Sox on one run in 20 innings in St. Louis.

The Cards catching, so weak during the season, became a strength in the Series. The combination of Garagiola and Rice hit .360. The 20-year-old Garagiola would go on to parley the resulting name recognition and a quick wit into a broadcasting career that led to the heights of network television.

York was one of the few Boston sluggers who lived up to expectations. His 10th inning homer off Pollet won the first game, and his three-run shot over the Fenway netting in the first inning of game three provided Ferriss with his winning margin.

Even in the 1940s, Slaughter was regarded as a throwback, an echo of the Pepper Martin-Gas House Gang era. The two men played together with the Cards for three seasons and much of Martin's run-'em-into-the-ground style seemed to rub off on the younger man. So much the soul of the Cardinals that he would weep when finally traded, Slaughter and his mad dash to the plate became the symbol of this Series.

The Zeroes:

His only time on the big stage turned into a major bust for Williams. The Cards employed an exaggerated form of the shift utilized by Cleveland's Lou Boudreau, stacking the infield on the right side and forcing the pull-hitting Williams to try and go the opposite way. In some of the games, St. Louis even placed third baseman Kurowski at second, but Williams did manage to beat that when he dropped a successful bunt. Otherwise, the greatest batter of his era hit just .200 with no extra base hits and one

FACT:
His only time on the big stage turned into a major bust for Williams. The greatest batter of his era hit just .200 with no extra base hits and one RBI.

RBI. During the exhibitions arranged to keep the Red Sox sharp before the Series, Williams had been hit on the elbow by a pitch and sat out the rest of those games. Some Red Sox officials felt that he was not fully recovered from that injury, but Williams never offered that as an excuse.

The one hitter who rivalled Williams during these years was Musial. He, too, had a subpar Series. But while hitting just .222, four of his six hits went for doubles and he drove in four runs. Still, he was not a central figure in the Cardinals win and the anticipated confrontation between the two sluggers was a disappointment.

The Aftermath:

The builder of the trail-blazing St. Louis farm system, Branch Rickey, left the club after the 1942 Series to become president of the Dodgers. His goal was to reconstruct the Brooklyn chain along the St. Louis lines and place it on the same competitive level. The 1946 playoff marked the point at which the fortunes of the two franchises intersected. The Cards had won nine pennants in 21 years, but starting in 1947 the Dodgers would take 10 pennants in 20 years. Illness to Musial and a decline in the pitching staff set the Cards back in 1947 and the replacement talent from the minors dried up. It would be 18 years before they won again.

The future would be even more maddening for Boston. The most powerful team in baseball would lose two pennants on the season's final day, in 1948 and 1949, and then go into a long, steady decline. The Sox would have to wait 21 years before they won again and were reunited with the Cardinals in the Series.

Notes:

With enthusiasm for the game reaching unparalleled heights in postwar America and attendance records falling in many cities, this Series ended up in two of the smallest ballparks in the majors. While every game was a sellout, the biggest crowd was a mere 36,218 at the opener in St. Louis. So the winner's share was just $3,742, the smallest total since the last time the Red Sox were in it, in 1918.

It was an injury to Pollet, the Cards' top left-hander during the season, that opened the way for Brecheen's heroics. Pollet had pulled a back muscle late in the season, then pitched a playoff win and all 10 innings of the Series opener with the injury taped. But he couldn't get past the first inning when he tried to start game five, and the Cards had no one left but Brecheen to stop Boston.

Line Scores:

Game One, October 6

Bos (AL)—010 000 001 1—3
Hughson, Johnson (9) W

SL (NL)—000 001 010 0—2
Pollet L

Game Two, October 7

Bos (AL)—000 000 000—0
Harris L, Dobson (8)

SL (NL)—001 020 00X—3
Brecheen W

Game Three, October 9

SL (NL)—000 000 000—0
Dickson L, Wilks (8)

Bos (AL)—300 000 01X—4
Ferriss W

Game Four, October 10

SL (NL)—033 010 104—12
Munger W

Bos (AL)—000 100 020—3
Hughson L, Bagby (3), Zuber (6), Brown (8), Ryba (9), Dreisewerd (9)

Game Five, October 11

SL (NL)—010 000 002—3
Pollet, Brazle (1) L, Beazley (8)

Bos (AL)—110 001 30X—6
Dobson W

Game Six, October 13

Bos (AL)—000 000 100—1
Harris L, Hughson (3), Johnson (8)

SL (NL)—003 000 01X—4
Brecheen W

Game Seven, October 15

Bos (AL)—100 000 020—3
Ferriss, Dobson (5), Klinger (8) L, Johnson (8)

SL (NL)—010 020 01X—4
Dickson, Brecheen (8) W

1947

New York (AL) 4
Brooklyn (NL) 3

In one of the classic Series, the Yankees are pushed to the full seven games for the first time in 21 years. The Dodgers' effort falls short, but they give the game two of its most indelible moments.

The Preview:

Things have changed in New York. Joe McCarthy is gone as manager of the Yankees after winning seven championships, more than any other man in history. New ownership, led by Larry McPhail, brought over from Brooklyn in 1945 to take over as team president, was not to McCarthy's liking. Attendance broke all records, lights were installed at Yankee Stadium, and a private club was added for season ticket holders. But the Yankees finished fourth in 1945, and when they were slow out of the blocks the following year, McCarthy resigned, irritated with what he perceived as interference from the front office. Bill Dickey and Johnny Neun finished out the year, with the Yanks coming in a confused 17 games off the pace, the first time they lagged by double digits since 1931.

In 1947 Bucky Harris, who had not managed in three years and not won anything in 22, was named to lead the team. The Yanks swung two trades to strengthen their infield and pitching. Joe DiMaggio bounced back from a subpar season. Rookies Yogi Berra and Spec Shea arrived. And just like that they were back on top, beating Detroit by an easy 12 games.

The biggest deal sent veteran second baseman Joe Gordon to Cleveland. In return, the Yanks obtained pitcher Allie Reynolds. The trade was made on the recommendation of DiMaggio, who was unable to get around on Reynolds' fast ball and felt lesser

Yankees players try to reach the safety of the clubhouse as joyous fans celebrate New York's seven-game victory over the Dodgers. The Series featured a near no-hitter by Bill Bevens and the postseason debut of Jackie Robinson.

mortals might be having the same problem. Reynolds went 19-8 to lead the Yankees, with the 26-year-old Shea right behind at 14-5. The other key pitcher was reliever Joe Page, who came out of the bullpen throwing flames. He went 14-8 and saved 17 more. Rookie Vic Raschi (7-2), veteran Spud Chandler (9-5) and a veteran's veteran, 40-year-old Bobo Newsom (7-5), rounded out the staff. Another starter, Bill Bevens, was just 7-13 and not expected to be heard from in the Series.

The Gordon trade resulted in Snuffy Stirnweiss moving to second base, while Billy Johnson reclaimed the starting role at third. He had performed brilliantly as a rookie in 1943 and finally regained his prewar form to drive in 95 runs and hit .285. The major power was supplied by DiMaggio, who raised his average 25 points, to .315, while knocking in 97 runs. Tommy Henrich led the team with 98 RBIs. The other big additions were Berra, who switched between outfield and catching and hit .280, and veteran first baseman George McQuinn, a hero of the 1944 Series with the Browns, who had a comeback season at .304 with 80 RBIs.

If change improved the Yankees, it electrified the Dodgers. Leo Durocher was suspended from the team for a year during spring training by Commissioner A.B. "Happy" Chandler on the grounds of consorting with known gamblers. The Dodgers were furious because Durocher, in reality, had cut off contacts with those dubious pals. They suspected McPhail was behind the charges, in which even irreproachable team president Branch Rickey was named. Rickey turned to a trusted old friend, Burt Shotton, who hadn't managed in 13 years and was living in Florida retirement, to replace Durocher for the season.

The mild Shotton not only stepped into a pennant race but a major social confrontation, too. This was the year that Rickey chose to end segregation in baseball. Jackie Robinson was brought up to play first base for the Dodgers, and all hell broke loose. The Cardinals threatened to strike rather than play against him. The Phillies taunted him viciously and almost instigated a riot. Even some of his own teammates wanted him gone. But the team leader, shortstop Harold "Pee Wee" Reese, a native of Kentucky, stood firmly by Robinson and through force of character drew the team together. Robinson, enduring the abuse with superhuman restraint, also removed the doubts by hitting .297 and becoming a base-running force, combining aggressive speed and intelligence.

Veteran Dixie Walker, one of the most vocal in opposition to Robinson, led the team's hitting attack with 94 RBIs. The sensation of the 1941 team, Pete Reiser, returned from a run of injuries to bat .309. Two second-year players also played critical roles, with outfielder Carl Furillo hitting .295 and catcher Bruce Edwards, a major surprise, at .295 with 80 RBIs.

Twenty-one-year-old Ralph Branca was the strength of the staff with a 21-12 record. Behind him was Joe Hatten (17-8) and reliever Hugh Casey (10-4, 18 saves). The pitching scared no one. The Dodgers, in fact, excelled in no single area. But they beat out the Cards by five games and seemed to have swiped that team's fabled pugnacity as well. Still, no one was picking against the Yanks.

Turning Point: Game Seven, Second Inning.

Brooklyn refuses to buckle. Hammered in the first two games, they come back to outlast the Yankees in two slugfests. The Dodgers win another with a ninth-inning rally that breaks up a no-hit try by Bevens, just the sort of comeback the Yankees used so often to crush other opponents. Sandwiched in among the Dodger victories, Shea wins game five for New York. So it all comes down to one more at Yankee Stadium, with Shea starting for the third time. His opponent is Tom Gregg, an unimpressive 4-5 during the season. He pitched seven strong relief innings to hold the Yanks close in the comeback against Bevens, but even without that encouragement, he is all the Dodgers have left. The staff is exhausted after being pummelled by the big Yankee hitters.

The Dodgers know they must play aggressively to win. In the first they go a bit overboard, as Yankee catcher Aaron Robinson cuts down two runners on attempted steals. Shea, meanwhile, working on just one day of rest, is obviously struggling. Gene Hermanski triples in the second and Edwards quickly cashes him in with a single. When Furillo follows with a third straight hit, another single, Bucky Harris wastes no time. He calls for Bevens, the almost-hero of game four. This time there is no wait for a hit. Mike Jorgensen immediately drills a double to right, scoring Edwards and sending Furillo to third. The Dodgers are up 2-0 and looking to break it open.

Gregg is up next. He is not a bad hitter, with a .265 average during the season. He sends one to the left side and Furillo takes off for home. Phil Rizzuto, playing like a little buzzsaw in this Series, never hesitates. He whips a throw to Robinson and the third run of the inning, instead, is cut down at the plate. Bevens then settles down and gets Eddie Stanky on a pop up.

The Brooklyn threat is over and so is its chance. For the rest of the game, Bevens and Page will hold them to two harmless singles. No Dodger will get past first base. Meanwhile, the Yankees zero in on Gregg. They get one back in the second, then go ahead in the fourth on two-out hits by Rizzuto, pinch hitter Bobby Brown and Henrich. Then they steadily pull away in the middle innings for an easy 5-2 Series-clinching win. Bevens had won lasting fame for coming within an out of a no-hitter in this Series, but his clutch performance in this game is what actually turned it for the Yanks.

The Managers:

Both were surprise choices to manage contending clubs, but Shotton was probably the bigger upset. Called in under the most trying of conditions, the former outfielder for the Browns and Cardinals was 62. He had been Rickey's Sunday manager in St. Louis, running the team while his devout boss took the sabbath off. He also managed some dreadful Phillies teams for six seasons, finishing out of the second division just once. But he had worked as a scout for years and was regarded as a top judge of young talent. Moreover, he could get along

> **FACT:**
> Bevens had won lasting fame for coming within an out of a no-hitter in this Series, but his clutch performance in game 7 is what actually turned it for the Yanks.

with all comers. Rickey respected his judgment and felt his mild demeanor was ideal for this stressed out Brooklyn team.

It had been a long time since Harris was a Boy Wonder, the Series-winning rookie manager with the Senators in 1924. He was still just 50, but with 20 years of managing behind him seemed far older than that. He had worked steadily, with the Tigers, Red Sox and a second term with Washington. But Harris rarely finished above .500. Let go by the seventh-place Phillies in 1943, he had been out of the dugouts ever since. For one season, however, he recaptured the magic and brought the Yankees back to the title.

The Heroes:

There had been a few shots at Series no-nos before. Ed Reulbach, in 1906, and Claude Passeau, in 1945, had fashioned one-hitters. In 1927, Herb Pennock carried a perfect game into the eighth. But Bevens came within a pitch of a no-hitter in this fourth game. He had already walked 8 men and given up a run when he entered the ninth inning with a 2-1 lead. A one-out walk to Furillo and a stolen base by pinch runner Al Gionfriddo put the tying run on second. Harris ordered an intentional pass to Reiser, a questionable bit of strategy since it placed the winning run on base. Pinch hitter Cookie Lavagetto then lined a double off the rightfield wall, both runners scored, and Bevens lost everything. The 30-year-old right-hander was in his fourth, and by far his poorest, season with the Yankees. He redeemed himself in this Series by cutting off the Dodgers in the seventh game, but he couldn't make the squad in 1948 and never pitched in the majors again.

Gionfriddo was another whose one moment of fame came in this Series. His twisting stab of DiMaggio's long drive to the centerfield bullpen stopped a Yankee rally in the 6th game and helped Brooklyn hold on to an 8-6 win. Lavagetto's hit and Gionfriddo's catch both attained a certain immortality because of broadcaster Red Barber's unforgettable calls, which have been replayed thousands of times over the years. Barber's cry of "Oh, doctor" after the catch has become a part of the game's audio lore. Gionfriddo, a utility man who got into just 37 games for Brooklyn during the season, never again played in the majors.

Casey, in a stalwart showing, appeared in six of the games for Brooklyn, won two of

FACT:
Gionfriddo was another whose one moment of fame came in this Series. His twisting stab of DiMaggio's long drive to the centerfield bullpen stopped a Yankee rally in the 6th game and helped Brooklyn hold on to an 8-6 win. Gionfriddo, a utility man who got into just 37 games for Brooklyn during the season, never again played in the majors.

them and allowed just one run in better than 10 innings of work. Page, with a save in the first game and five innings of one-hit relief to get the win in the finale, emerged as the New York pitching star.

The Yankees combed Brooklyn pitching for an average of 10 hits a game. Most productive of the New York hitters was outfielder Johnny Lindell, who batted an even .500 and paced both sides with seven RBIs.

Rizzuto was, by far, New York's most valuable player, not only because of a .308 batting average but because of his flawless handling of every play in the field. Reese almost matched him, hitting .304 and making just one error. The two rivals gave the Series some of the finest shortstop play in its history.

The Zeroes:

Brooklyn's starters were much worse than anticipated. None of them could get through the fifth inning of any game. Harry Taylor could not get a single out in game four and Rex Barney, who went farther than any other starter, walked nine men in his four and two-thirds innings.

Lavagetto, whose big double broke Bevens' spell and won game four, didn't get another hit in the Series, going 0-for-6. It was also his final hit because he, too, never played in another big league game.

The Aftermath:

Both teams fell back to third place in 1948, but they were only retooling for bigger things to come. The Yanks fired Harris after missing the pennant by two and one-half games. His replacement, Casey Stengel, regarded as an utter failure in previous managerial assignments, was greeted with howls of disbelief. But with bench strength deeper than any team in history and a pitching staff that was machinelike in its efficiency, the Yanks would begin their run of five straight championships.

Change came even faster in Brooklyn. With the team unable to get above .500, the prodigal Durocher quit in July and shockingly announced he was taking over the hated Giants. Shotton had to be called in to replace him again. After a lapse of a year the Dodgers were winners once more in 1949, poised to become baseball's perennial second greatest team for most of the '50s.

Notes:

It was a phenomenal Series for pinch hitters. Besides Lavagetto's big poke, Berra delivered the first pinch hit home run in Series history in game three. Bobby Brown was called on four times and was perfect—two doubles, a single and a walk.

The attendance marks continued to fall at Yankee Stadium. A record game one turnout lasted just six days, until 74,065 people showed up for game six.

This was the second time in history that three straight Series went seven games—the other being 1924–26. From the start of Series play until 1940 only eight went to a seven-game decision. That mark would be equalled in just 14 seasons, between 1945 and 1958.

Line Scores:

Game One, September 30

Bkn (NL)—100 001 100—3
Branca L, Behrman (5), Casey (7)

NY (AL)—000 050 00X—5
Shea W, Page (6) SV

Game Two, October 1

Bkn (NL)—001 100 001—3
Lombardi L, Gregg (5), Behrman (7), Barney (7)

NY (AL)—101 121 40X—10
Reynolds W

Game Three, October 2

NY (AL)—002 221 100—8
Newsom L, Raschi (2), Drews (3), Chandler (5), Page (7)

Bkn (NL)—061 200 00X—9
Hatten, Branca (5), Casey (7) W

Game Four, October 3

NY (AL)—100 100 000—2
Bevens L

Bkn (NL)—000 010 002—3
Taylor, Gregg (1), Behrman (8), Casey (9) W

Game Five, October 4

NY (AL)—000 110 000—2
Shea W

Bkn (NL)—000 001 000—1
Barney L, Hatten (5), Behrman (7), Casey (8)

Game Six, October 5

Bkn (NL)—202 004 000—8
Lombardi, Branca (3) W, Hatten (6), Casey (9) SV

NY (AL)—004 100 001—6
Reynolds, Drews (3), Page (5) L, Newsom (6), Raschi (7), Wensloff (8)

Game Seven, October 7

Bkn (NL)—020 000 000—2
Gregg L, Behrman (4), Hatten (6), Barney (6), Casey (7)

NY (AL)—010 201 10X—5
Shea, Bevens (2), Page (5) W

1948

Cleveland (AL) 4
Boston (NL) 2

Two long-deprived franchises finally made it back to the Series, but it turned out to be a rather wan meeting. The Indians, emotionally exhausted by one of the great pennant races in American League history, still had enough power and pitching to easily handle the banged-up Braves.

The Preview:

It had been 34 years for the Braves, the longest wait for a pennant in the National League. There was no Miracle, as with their predecessors of 1914. This time it was just a slow, steady accretion of talent after the arrival of Billy Southworth as manager two years before.

Southworth inherited a small core of skill that included outfielder Tommy Holmes, catcher Phil Masi and two outstanding pitchers, Warren Spahn and John Sain. In two years, Southworth discarded virtually everybody else to put together his winner.

The key acquisition was third baseman Bob Elliott, filched from Pittsburgh as the price for the fading Billy Herman, whom the Pirates wanted as their manager. Elliott immediately became the rock of the Boston lineup with two straight 100-RBI years. Not a home run threat in Pittsburgh's capacious park, he knocked out 45 in two seasons at Braves Field.

The other big addition for 1948 was veteran slugger Jeff Heath, whom they acquired from Cleveland. The 33-year-old leftfielder hit .319 and drove in 76 runs to trail only Elliott in both stats. Holmes led the team with a .325 average, while rookie shortstop Alvin Dark, a football star at Louisiana State, proved he knew a bit about baseball, too, with a .322 season.

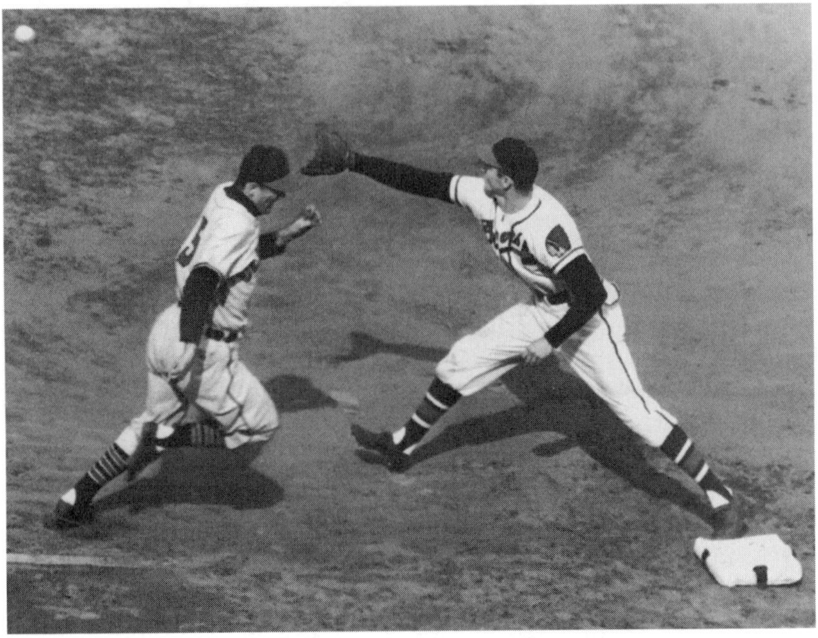

Lou Boudreau, Cleveland's player-manager, is thrown out as Earl Torgeson stretches for the throw. Boudreau had four doubles in six games while leading the Indians past the Braves.

This was the team that inspired the rhyme defining its pitching success as "Spahn and Sain and prayer for rain." Sain, the tall, curve-baller from Arkansas, had his finest season at 24-15. Spahn tailed off a bit from his 21-game standard of the previous year, but still finished at 15-12. Behind them was a void, with Vern Bickford (11-5) and Bill Voiselle (13-13) the only glimmers of light.

The Braves were not a great offensive team but led the league in hitting. They had no depth in their rotation but led the league in ERA. They won the pennant by 6 1/2 games over the Cards, so they had to be doing something right. But when Heath broke his ankle in a meaningless game in the season's last week, it seemed to take away whatever chance they had.

Cleveland, by contrast, was a team with overpowering strengths. After a wait of 28 seasons, the Indians had put together the best infield since the Tigers of the mid-'30s. Joe Gordon, Ken Keltner and manager Lou Boudreau all knocked in more than 100 runs, while Gordon and Keltner hit over 30 homers apiece. First baseman Eddie Robinson was only a bit behind with 83 RBIs. The outfield featured the slashing line-drive hitter Dale Mitchell (.336) and rookie slugger Larry Doby, the first African-American star in the league. He was signed out of the Negro leagues the previous year, given an inconclusive trial as an infielder and then handed a starting job. He repaid the confidence by finishing at .301.

The soul of the team was Boudreau. The 31-year-old shortstop, in his seventh year as a playing manager, was a man on fire. An inspirational leader, a brilliant strategist and a flawless defender, he exceeded all previous levels he had reached in the majors. His .355 average, 106 RBIs and 18 homers were all personal highs. He as much as willed the Indians to the pennant in an incredible three-team run to the wire with Boston and New York. In the playoff victory over Boston, the only one in league history before divisional play, he hit two home runs and went 4 for 4. The season was the apogee of his Hall of Fame career.

Bob Feller had yet to reach his 30th birthday, but had been the league's dominant pitcher for a decade. His right arm was no longer the weapon it once was. He struggled in the early months and actually heard boos in Cleveland, but finished with a rush when it was needed in September to go 19-15. This season, unlike so many before, he had help. Converted outfielder Bob Lemon was now a full-time pitcher and he went 20-14. The surprise of the staff was a lanky rookie, left-handed knuckleballer Gene Bearden. He truly came out of nowhere, compiling a 20-7 mark and pitching the critical playoff game in Fenway Park, even though the place was known as death on lefties.

This season was also a personal triumph for team president Bill Veeck. The greatest promoter the game had ever seen, Veeck was willing to do anything, from circuses to fireworks to giveaways to holding a special salute to a fan ("Good Old Joe Early Night"), to get bodies into the massive 80,000-seat lakefront stadium. His shenanigans broke every attendance record, brought enthusiasm for baseball to levels thought unattainable and, incidentally, fielded a winner. He also was hated by every other executive in the game.

FACT:
When the high point of the first three games of the Series is a pickoff play, you know you've got a snoozer on your hands. The blown umpiring call on the pick off attempt at second by Feller helps give game one to the Braves, 1-0.

Turning Point: Game Four, Seventh Inning.

When the high point of the first three games of the Series is a pickoff play, you know you've got a snoozer on your hands. The blown umpiring call on the pickoff attempt at second by Feller helps give game one to the Braves, 1-0. Boston can get only one run in the next two games off Lemon and Bearden and the Indians, while not setting the woods on fire with their hitting, hold the Series lead.

In game four, though, the Braves get a chance to draw even. They have the pitching advantage. Sain, who outdueled Feller in the opener, is accustomed to going on short rest and will pitch again. Cleveland comes back with Steve Gromek. The 28-year-old right-hander started just 9 times during the season, but Boudreau feels that Feller requires the extra day of rest. So the seldom-used Gromek gets the call.

For six innings, he answers with aplomb. Before an enormous Cleveland crowd that sets a new attendance record for any baseball game, he shuts out the Braves on four hits. The Indians build a 2-0 lead on a double by Boudreau and a Doby home run. Outside of those key hits, though, Sain stays out of trouble and, in fact, seems to be getting stronger.

Marv Rickert opens the seventh with a home run, the first for the Braves. Indeed, it is only their third run of the Series. Mike McCormick follows with a single and suddenly things are serious. The Cleveland bullpen is up and Gromek is walking on the edge. This is Boston's chance. Instead, Gromek slaps down the Braves, easily disposing of Eddie Stanky, Masi and Sain. Boston gets just one more hit and Gromek goes the distance to get the 2-1 decision.

The Braves finally come out of their slump and rake Feller in game five. But Lemon and Bearden combine to close it out in six and bring Cleveland its second championship in history. Gromek's performance sealed Boston's fate.

The Managers:

Southworth is now officially anointed as a genius. The 55-year-old manager was brought over to do a job with a hopeless franchise. In one year, he got them into the first division for the first time since 1934, and in three years he put them in the Series. He irritated some players with his inability to remember names, and a few others were put off by his constant platooning, but his resuscitation of the Braves goes down as one of the great managerial accomplishments.

Boudreau inherited the manager's job in 1942, just as a fairly competitive Cleveland lineup was about to be torn apart by the war. He got the Indians back to fourth place in 1947 and felt sure he could win this year. There had been speculation that Boudreau, who was playing on weakened ankles, might be traded to St. Louis for Vern Stephens. Instead, Veeck signed him to a two-year contract. He gathered many of the club's veteran stars into his confidence, drawing on their knowledge for advice, and used Gordon, three years his senior, as an assistant manager. He drove Ted Williams to distraction with the radical infield shift he devised against him and was regarded as without a peer at positioning his fielders. He would manage 16 years in all with indifferent success. This season was all his.

The Heroes:

Bearden finished up his dream season just the way a fantasy is supposed to end. He blanked the Braves on five hits in game three, and when Lemon started going sour with a 4-1 lead in the eighth inning of the sixth game, Bearden came in to get the last five outs of the Series. His final totals: 10 2/3 innings, no runs, one win, one save! He had been obtained in an obscure minor league deal with the Yankees. The price was Sherman Lollar, who would develop into an outstanding catcher with the White Sox. But for this season, there were no doubts about who got the better of that trade.

> **FACT:**
> Bearden finished up his dream just the way a fantasy is supposed to end. His final totals: 10 2/3 innings, no runs, one win, one save!

Both pitching staffs compiled shiny stats, as the Indians were held to a .199 team average and the Braves scored 11 of their 17 total runs in one game. Lemon emerged as the leading performer overall with two wins.

Sain pitched two complete games, did not walk a single hitter and allowed just two runs. But the Braves scored just two runs for him and he only got a 1-1 record out of it.

Boudreau banged out four doubles in these games. Surprisingly, Cleveland's most consistent hitter was catcher Jim Hegan. An outstanding receiver of one of the best pitching staffs ever assembled, Hegan was never much of a hitting threat in his career, but he led everyone in this run-starved Series with five RBIs.

The Zeroes:

This was the biggest disappointment of Feller's long career. After losing a tough 1-0 game in the opener, he came out with nothing in game five, giving up seven runs into the seventh inning and taking a second loss. Although he was also a member of the 1954 Indians, he never got into a Series game that year. His career ended without the prize of a Series win.

Much of the blame for that rested with umpire Bill Stewart. The Indians worked the timed pickoff at second base better than any team in baseball. In fact, Lemon would pull it off in game two with Boudreau. Stewart, a National Leaguer, wasn't ready for it and, to all appearances, blew the call on the eighth inning pickoff of Masi in the opener. Boudreau had to be physically restrained from going after the umpire and Feller and Gordon were beside themselves. Commissioner Chandler backed up the ump, but when Cleveland officials asked to see the film of the play they were told that the official photographer somehow had missed it. Other film did exist, however, and it seemed to bear out the Indians. When Masi scored right afterwards on Holmes' single, Feller's best chance of winning was gone.

The Aftermath:

Veeck was never sold on Boudreau's abilities as a manager. When the team slipped to third in 1949 and then to fourth (although just six games off the pace), he sent off the longtime Cleveland hero to Boston and brought in Al Lopez as manager. While loaded with talent, the Indians were constantly frustrated by Yankee teams that won five consecutive pennants. They couldn't break past them until 1954.

The Braves decline was swift. They dropped to fourth in 1949 and the players voted to give Southworth only half a share of Series receipts, a decision reversed by the Comissioner. Boston finished fourth twice more and Southworth was replaced by Holmes. When they fell all the way to seventh in 1952, the fans stopped coming. That prompted the first big league franchise switch in 50 years. Just five seasons after their long wait for a pennant had ended, the Braves were gone to Milwaukee.

Notes:

Because of a mixup on VIP reservations for the first game in Cleveland, a crowd of "only" 70,000 showed up. A furious Veeck got things straightened out in a hurry, and for Gromek's win in game four a throng of 81,897, largest ever to see any baseball game, was on hand. That mark lasted one day. A total of 86,288, drawn by Feller's pursuit of his Series win, turned out for game five.

The Series was also marked by the first appearance of a black pitcher. It happened to be one of the greatest pitchers in history, the immortal Satchel Paige. His age was somewhere between 45 and 55 but he still had some oomph behind his pitches. Paige joined the Indians in mid-season, partially as a publicity ploy by Veeck, but he helped the Indians, going 6-1. He was brought in to pitch to two men in game five, retired them both, and also managed to balk. It was his only Series appearance.

Line Scores:

Game One, October 6

Cle (AL)—000 000 000—0
Feller L

Bos (NL)—000 000 01X—1
Sain W

Game Two, October 7

Cle (AL)—000 210 001—4
Lemon W

Bos (NL)—100 000 000—1
Spahn L, Barrett (5), Potter (8)

Game Three, October 8

Bos (NL)—000 000 000—0
Bickford L, Voiselle (4), Barrett (8)

Cle (AL)—001 100 00X—2
Bearden W

Game Four, October 9

Bos (NL)—000 000 100—1
Sain L

Cle (AL)—101 000 000—2
Gromek W

Game Five, October 10

Bos (NL)—301 001 600—11
Potter, Spahn (4) W

Cle (AL)—100 400 000—5
Feller L, Klieman (7), Christopher (7), Paige (7), Muncrief (8)

Game Six, October 11

Cle (AL)—001 002 010—4
Lemon W, Bearden (8) SV

Bos (NL)—000 100 020—3
Voiselle L, Spahn (8)

1949

New York (AL) 4
Brooklyn (NL) 1

After playing the Yankees so tightly two years before, the Dodgers were confident that this would be their breakthrough season. Instead, New York broke them down in just five games, with two ninth-inning rallies doing most of the damage.

The Preview:

It had been a spell of uncharacteristic confusion at Yankee Stadium. Larry MacPhail inexplicably quit as team president right after the 1947 Series. He was replaced by farm director George Weiss, who then fired Bucky Harris immediately following the 1948 season in which New York had missed the pennant by a mere 2 1/2 games. Even near misses were unacceptable to the Yankees.

More perplexing yet was Weiss's choice as the new manager. Casey Stengel was regarded as the class clown, a comic figure from the depths of the second division. He was certainly not an heir to the great tradition of Miller Huggins and Joe McCarthy. The New York media was indignant over the treatment of Harris and gave Stengel a contemptuous, hostile reception.

Things immediately got worse. Joe DiMaggio suffered a heel injury during spring training and it was announced that he would be out for almost the entire first half of the season. An aging Tommy Henrich already had been pulled in to play first base, which meant that Stengel had to constantly shift outfield combinations to keep things together until DiMaggio's return.

Somehow it all worked. Rookie Jerry Coleman was installed at second base, hit .275 and teamed well with veteran Phil Rizzuto. The little shortstop was the team's strength, playing in

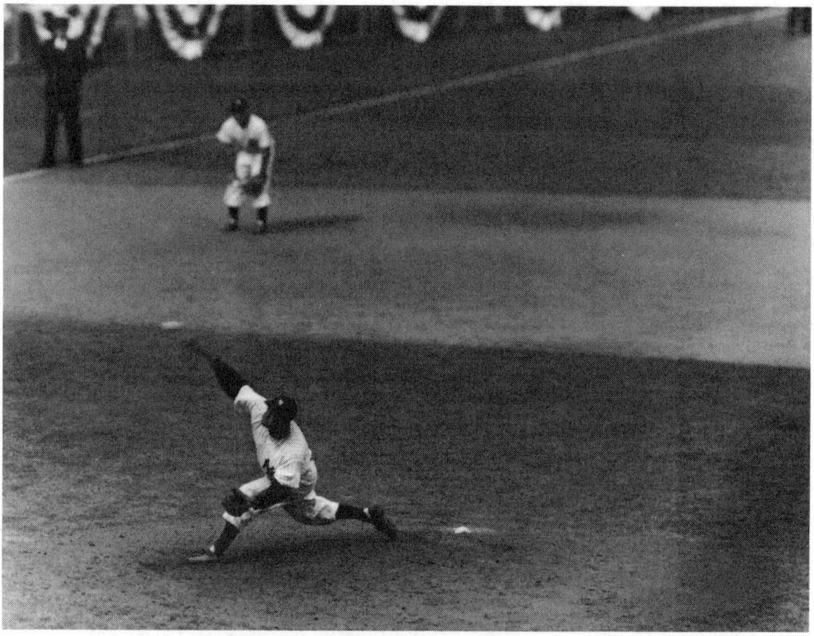

Allie Reynolds provided a win, a save, and 14 strikeouts to New York's five game effort over the Dodgers. In 12⅓ innings of work, he did not allow an earned run.

every game but one and stabilizing the entire defense. Yogi Berra was made the starting catcher and responded with 20 homers and 91 RBIs, while Henrich led the regulars with a .287 average and 85 RBIs. The Yanks stayed close, and when a rested DiMaggio returned he carried the ballclub, finishing with a .346 mark and providing the spark for overtaking Boston on the final weekend to win the pennant.

The pitching was solid all the way. The four-man rotation of Vic Raschi (21-10), Allie Reynolds (17-6), Ed Lopat (15-10) and Tommy Byrne (15-7) made the New York staff far deeper than any other. Moreover, Joe Page had his finest year, winning 13 and saving 27 more. No other reliever in either league saved more than 10 games. He stood alone as a closer before that term or that concept had come into common use.

The Dodgers also went down to the last day before closing it out, edging the Cards by one game. All the elements of the great Brooklyn teams of the next decade were now in place. Joining the holdovers from 1947 were Gil Hodges, Duke Snider and Roy Campanella, all power hitters with great defensive skills. Jackie Robinson had developed into a superstar, leading the league with a .342 average and driving in 124 runs. Carl Furillo also knocked in more than 100 runs, while hitting .322. Pee Wee Reese drove in 73 more and was rivaled only by Rizzuto as a shortstop. On top of all this, Brooklyn was fast, with its 117 stolen bases almost twice as many as any other team in the game.

The Dodgers swung a great trade with Pittsburgh after the 1947 season, unloading the aging Dixie Walker and getting a great defensive third baseman, Billy Cox, and a solid starting pitcher, Preacher Roe. The left-hander went 15-6 during the season, teaming with rookie right-hander Don Newcombe (17-8) to give Brooklyn a tough tandem. But behind them, quality tailed off quickly, which was a problem in the short Series format. Still, most writers picked the Series as even money and predicted it would go the full length.

Turning Point: Game Three, Ninth Inning.

For two games and eight innings, the Series confounds the experts. The sluggers are shackled. Reynolds tops Newcombe, 1-0 in the opener, with Henrich winning it on a ninth-inning homer. Then Roe beats Raschi by the same score in game two.

Now the starting pitchers are Byrne and Ralph Branca, and entering the ninth it is yet another tight duel, a 1-1 deadlock. Page comes in when Byrne suddenly loses his control in the fourth and escapes from a one-out, bases-loaded fix by getting Luis Olmo and Snider on easy outs. Since then he has given up just one hit, but Branca has allowed only two. Byrne's single in the third after a walk to Cliff Mapes (the first one allowed by the Dodgers in the Series) sets up New York's only run.

Branca quickly disposes of the dangerous Henrich and DiMaggio around a walk to Berra in the ninth. But Bobby Brown singles sharply for New York's third hit and Branca then walks Gene Woodling. Mapes is scheduled up, but instead the Yanks call for Johnny Mize. They obtained the veteran National League star in late August for late help down the stretch, a pattern that Yankee teams would follow for the next 10 years to the ongoing dismay of their pursuers. A four-time home run champ and .300 hitter for nine of his 10 seasons in the majors, Mize's productivity had slipped with the Giants and Leo Durocher was happy to unload him.

He singled in his first Series pinch hitting assignment the day before. Now he measures Branca, works him to a 2-2 count then slams a low fastball high off the rightfield wall. Two runs score as the lumbering Mize holds at first. Coleman adds another run with a single off reliever Jack Banta for a 4-1 lead. As it turns out, New York needs that last score, too, as both Olmo and Campanella homer off Page in the ninth before he can close it by striking out Bruce Edwards. The Dodgers will not seriously challenge the rest of the way. While Mize's role in the pennant race was peripheral, he turns the Series around.

The Managers:

Burt Shotton won the pennant in 1947, then stepped aside when Durocher returned from his suspension the next year. When the Dodgers stumbled and Durocher jumped to the Giants, Shotton was called in again. The team rallied under him and actually got into first place for a few days in 1948. In charge right from the start this year, he brought them in once more, taking full advantage of the combination of speed and power that made the Brooklyn starting lineup the best in the game.

Stengel was 58 when he was named manager of the Yanks. He had been out of the majors for five years. As the leader of atrocious teams in Boston and Brooklyn during the late '30s and early '40s, he was dismissed as a wisecracking nonentity, a public relations figure intended to mollify the press with wit and disguise the absence of any playing talent. He never finished higher than fifth. The announcement of his appointment with the Yankees was greeted with a mixture of disbelief and outrage. Five consecutive world championships later, Stengel would grow into a folk hero. But in 1949 he was very much a man under the gun.

FACT:
The announcement of Stengel's appointment as manager of the Yankees was greeted with a mixture of disbelief and outrage. During the late '30s and early '40s, he was dismissed as a wisecracking nonentity without any playing talent. Five consecutive world championships later, Stengel would grow into a folk hero.

The Heroes:

They called Reynolds the Superchief, alluding to his Creek heritage as well as to the crack Santa Fe passenger train that ran across his native Oklahoma. Behind his back, though, the nickname wasn't as complimentary. Then they called him The Vanishing American, because the word was that he looked for help in the late innings and couldn't finish close games. He had only four complete games in 1949, at a time when starting pitchers were expected to go the distance. In this Series, Reynolds put that reputation to rest. His tense 1-0 win in game one, followed by three plus innings of relief in game four, in which he set down 10 straight men and struck out five of them, did the trick.

Bobby Brown settled the Series virtually by himself in the last two games. He went five for seven, with a double and two triples, and drove in five runs in those contests, both won by New

York. For the Series, the future president of the American League batted .500, and his five RBIs topped both sides.

This was Henrich's last season as a regular with the Yankees and never was the 36-year-old slugger's nickname, Old Reliable, more apt. His leadoff ninth-inning homer off Newcombe in game one, after the Dodger pitcher had given up just four hits and struck out 11, got the Yankees off to a jump start.

The Zeroes:

DiMaggio had nothing left after the incredible pennant race he had been through. The heel injury, followed by a bout with pneumonia, sapped the strength of the 34-year-old superstar and he went 2-for-18. Stengel, however, realized the emotional factor of having DiMaggio play and kept him in the lineup.

The gag line on Rex Barney was that he would be the greatest pitcher in the world if the strike zone were high and outside. A tremendously hard thrower, the 24-year-old Barney walked 10 during six innings of work in the 1947 Series. This time he started once and walked 6 in 2 2/3 innings. He never could harness his control and this was his final Series.

The Aftermath:

The Yanks were just getting started and with essentially the same cast in 1950 they beat out Detroit in another closely run race.

Brooklyn again had to go to the last game of the season for a decision, but this time the Whiz Kids from Philadelphia edged them out. Shotton was fired immediately, as the Dodgers assumed the attitude of the Yankees. With the talent on hand, it was inexcusable not to win.

Notes:

This was the first Series carried on national television, as all three networks beamed the games to their affiliates. It also was the first to feature theater showings. A Brooklyn movie house sold out all 4,000 seats and showed the games on the big screen.

Roe split a finger on his throwing hand during his game two shutout and was sidelined the rest of the way. It was the final, fatal blow to Brooklyn's skimpy staff.

The Dodgers had threatened to run at will on Berra, whose throwing arm was questionable. But Reese got their only stolen base, in the eighth inning of the scoreless first game.

FACT:
This was the first Series carried on national television and the first to feature theater showings. A Brooklyn movie house sold out all 4,000 seats and showed the games on the big screen.

Line Scores:

Game One, October 5

Bkn (NL)—000 000 000—0
Newcombe L

NY (AL)—000 000 001—1
Reynolds W

Game Two, October 6

Bkn (NL)—010 000 000—1
Roe W

NY (AL)—000 000 000—0
Raschi L, Page (9)

Game Three, October 7

NY (AL)—001 000 003—4
Byrne, Page (4) W

Bkn (NL)—000 100 002—3
Branca L, Banta (9)

Game Four, October 8

NY (AL)—000 330 000—6
Lopat W, Reynolds (6) SV

Bkn (NL)—000 004 000—4
Newcombe L, Hatten (4), Erskine (6), Banta (9)

Game Five, October 9

NY (AL)—203 113 000—10
Raschi W, Page (7) SV

Bkn (NL)—001 001 400—6
Barney L, Banta (3), Erskine (6), Hatten (6), Palica (7), Minner (9)

1950

New York (AL) 4
Philadelphia (NL) 0

It seemed just like old times as the Yanks barely worked up a sweat polishing off an upstart National League opponent in four straight. The Phillies got decent pitching but little else, except a bad case of stage fright.

The Preview:

When the Braves won their first pennant in 34 seasons in 1948, the distinction of the longest wait went to the Phillies. But the famine ended at 35 years in 1950 with a group of players so young that they became known forevermore as the Whiz Kids.

Philadelphia had climbed to a giddy third place finish in 1949, their highest since 1917. Most analysts were inclined to dismiss that as a fluke, and picked the Phils well back in the pack for the following season. But they broke fast and until mid-September were not seriously challenged. Then they woke up, saw where they were, and came down with vertigo. The Whizzes snapped out of it just in time to fend off the oncharging Dodgers, with Dick Sisler hitting a three-run homer in the 10th inning to beat them in the final game.

Sisler, son of Hall-of-Famer George Sisler, was a factor all year. He had his best season, playing leftfield and hitting .296 with 83 RBIs. The big power, though, came from hometown hero Del Ennis, whose 126 RBIs led the league, along with 31 homers and a .311 batting mark. Third baseman Willie Jones and shortstop Granny Hamner combined for 170 RBIs and gave the Phils solid defensive work on the infield's left side.

FACT:
The big power came from hometown hero Del Ennis, whose 126 RBIs led the league, along with 31 homers and a .311 batting mark.

Granny Hamner typifies the Phillies' frustration in the 1950 Series, as he's thrown out at home. Philadelphia's "Whiz Kids," inexperienced and shorthanded, were overmatched by the seasoned and healthy Yankees, succumbing quickly in a sweep.

The big news, however, was the comeback of Eddie Waitkus. The first baseman's story was the basis for Bernard Malamud's novel, *The Natural.* Critically wounded in the chest by a deranged female admirer in Chicago after the Cubs traded him to Philadelphia in 1949, he was not expected to play ball again. He came back with a .284 season and was on the field for every game.

Robin Roberts, signed out of Michigan State University, became one of the league's top winners (20-11) at 23. Another local talent, Curt Simmons, backed him up with a 17-8 season. The big surprise, however, was reliever Jim Konstanty. The 33-year-old right-hander had been kicking around for several years with scant success. But he developed a palm ball in the off season, an off-speed curve that dropped sharply at the last minute. With the new pitch, he suddenly became a world-beater, with a 16-7 record and 22 saves in 74 appearances out of the bullpen.

Just before the Series, however, Simmons' National Guard unit was activated and he was gone. So was pitcher Bubba Church, hit in the face with a line drive in the final week. In addition, catcher Andy Seminick was limping with a painful ankle injury, later diagnosed as a bone chip. Philadelphia was in far from prime shape.

That was unfortunate because this Yankee team was loaded, as dangerous as some of their great units of the past. Yogi Berra emerged as the league's best-hitting catcher, with a .322 average and 124 RBIs. While Joe DiMaggio struggled for much of the year, as usual he came on at the end to finish at .301 with 32 homers and 122 RBIs. The real spark came from Phil Rizzuto. The shortstop had a Most Valuable Player year, batting .324 with scintillating defensive work while answering the bell for every game.

There was also a big year from Hank Bauer, moving into a regular role with a .320 average. John Mize settled in as a utility player and slammed 25 home runs in just 274 times at bat. Although he had slowed down greatly, one can trot when the ball goes into the seats.

Once again, New York's four-man rotation was the best in the game. Vic Raschi (21-8), Ed Lopat (18-8), Allie Reynolds (16-12) and Tommy Byrne (15-9) all worked over 200 innings and gave the Yankees the sort of depth other teams only dreamed of. To augment those four, rookie Whitey Ford arrived in late summer to go 9-1 down the stretch, which was almost unfair. In a year dominated by hitters, his 2.81 ERA would have led the league by a wide margin if he had worked more innings. The Yanks were pressed by Detroit until late September and eased in by just three games, but no one seriously thought the Phils could challenge them.

The Turning Point: Game Two, Tenth Inning.

For the third straight year, the Series opener ends 1-0. Raschi gives up just 2 hits and outduels Konstanty, a desperation choice, in his first start of the season. He pitches well enough to win, but a fourth-inning double by Bobby Brown followed by two long fly balls gives the Yanks all they need.

Roberts, who pitched the pennant-clinching game, now takes the ball in game two, knowing that the Phils must even things before the Series moves to Yankee Stadium. He, too, ends up in a tight game, this time against Reynolds. The Yanks get a run in the second on a walk and singles by Reynolds and Gene Woodling. The Phils finally score their first Series run in the fifth, on singles by Mike Goliat and Waitkus and a fly ball by Richie Ashburn.

There it stays through nine innings. Roberts is in frequent trouble, but the Yanks leave 11 men on base and can't break through on him. Reynolds also struggles, giving up four doubles and a triple, but the Phils, too, cannot cash in on any of their chances.

The game moves into the 10th with DiMaggio leading off. He is 0 for 6 in the Series, and over the last two years has been only 2 for 24. Always an imposing figure, DiMaggio does not always come off at his best in the championship round. His final career average in Series games will be more than 50 points below his regular lifetime mark of .325. Although this is his 9th Series, he has not been the key player in any of them. But on a 2-1 pitch from Roberts, he follows an inside slider down and drives it deep into the leftfield pavilion of Shibe Park. Reynolds makes the blow stand up in the bottom half, and the Yanks have a 2-1 win and a two-game advantage to take back to New York. The Yankee Clipper snips off Philadelphia's last hope.

The Managers:

Stengel was still not taken seriously by the New York media. He is described as a "pushbutton manager," with so much talent that he merely has to plug players into the right holes. His platooning also irritates several Yankees who feel that they should be in the lineup every day. Stengel lets it all roll off his back and keeps on winning.

Eddie Sawyer was a manager more in the Joe McCarthy mold. He never played in the majors and made his managerial reputation in the Eastern League. Moreover, he was an erudite individual, teaching biology during the off season at Ithaca College. He was the surprise choice to take over the Phils in mid-1948. Using many of the players he had worked with in the minors, he brought the city of Philadelphia its first Series in 19 years.

The Heroes:

The whole Yankee pitching staff gave up just three earned runs in 37 innings, an ERA of 0.73. Reynolds was once again outstanding, with a win and a save. His string of shutout innings, going back to 1949, was snapped at 16, but it was the only run he had allowed in the last two Series.

It was also the first of many triumphant moments for Ford, who would go on to become the winningest Series pitcher ever. He had the Phils shut out with a 5-0 lead and two outs in the ninth of the last game when Woodling let a fly ball get away from him for a two-run error. Stengel trudged out to the mound and after a lengthy consultation waved Reynolds in to finish the game. The booing at Yankee Stadium was thunderous.

FACT:
Reynolds's string of shutout innings, going back to 1949, was snapped at 16, but it was the only run he had allowed in the last two Series.

Konstanty was valiant in defeat, working in three of the four games. That included a seven-inning relief stint in the last game when starter Bob Miller was knocked out in the first. The Yanks finally caught up to him when the exhausted Konstanty gave up three runs in the sixth.

The Zeroes:

As if the lack of hitting wasn't enough of a handicap, the Phillies defense deserted them in the third game. With the team clinging to a 2-1 lead, Hamner muffed a two-out, bases loaded grounder in the eighth to permit the tying run to score. Then in the ninth, sub second baseman Jimmy Bloodworth couldn't reach two moderately difficult grounders. Both were generously scored as singles. Jerry Coleman then ended it all with a line drive single.

The most critical loss was the absence of Simmons. When the Korean War broke out in June, the Phillies quickly placed him in a National Guard unit to avoid the draft, thinking that they would lose him only for two weeks each summer. Instead, he missed the Series and the entire 1951 season. While the Korean conflict was not nearly as disruptive to everyday life as World War II, many of the game's top players missed a season or two in the early '50s.

The Aftermath:

With Simmons gone and Konstanty a mere mortal once more, the Phillies were no match for the rest of the top teams in 1951. With the exception of Ashburn, every regular's production declined and the erstwhile Whiz Kids joined the ranks of the Was. They fell to fifth and didn't seriously challenge again for the rest of the decade.

The Yanks, however, survived the loss of Ford to the Army and the decline of the mighty DiMaggio. Far from the best team on paper, they took their third straight pennant going away.

Notes:

Tommy Henrich, a hero of the 1949 Series, was taken off the eligibility list just before the opener. It became apparent that the succession of injuries he'd suffered during the season were too much to overcome. He never played again.

Henrich's place on the roster was taken by John Hopp. The Pittsburgh first baseman was actually leading the National League in hitting when the Yanks picked him up in August for the stretch run. (Stan Musial, eventually, overtook him and saved the league the embarrassment of having its batting champ playing for the opposition.) Put in as a defensive replacement for Mize in game one, Hopp immediately saved it by robbing Ashburn of an apparent double in the ninth with a stab of his shot down the line.

Line Scores:

Game One, October 4

NY (AL)—000 100 000—1
Raschi W

Phi (NL)—000 000 000—0
Konstanty L, Meyer (9)

Game Two, October 5

NY (AL)—010 000 000 1—2
Reynolds W

Phi (NL)—000 010 000 0—1
Roberts L

Game Three, October 6

Phi (NL)—000 001 100—2
Heintzelman, Konstanty (8), Meyer (9) L

NY (AL)—001 000 011—3
Lopat, Ferrick (9) W

Game Four, October 7

Phi (NL)—000 000 002—2
Miller L, Konstanty (1), Roberts (8)

NY (AL)—200 003 00X—5
Ford W, Reynolds (9) SV

1951

New York (AL) 4
New York (NL) 2

The Giants, pumped up by their implausible triumph in the most famous pennant race in history, started off as if they meant to run the Yankees right off the field. In the end, depth and experience were too much to overcome, and the Giants became the third straight Yankee Series victim.

The Preview:

There had never been a race quite like it. America watched transfixed as the Giants concluded the greatest comeback in baseball history; from 13 1/2 games down in mid-August to Bobby Thomson's three-run homer in the ninth to beat the Dodgers in the playoff. With television beaming the incredible moment with an immediacy never felt before, the Giants became America's team on the spot.

Leo Durocher had come over from Brooklyn in 1948 to take over a second division team of big, slow sluggers, still run by men who had grown up under John McGraw. He promised to transform the Giants into "my kind of team" and immediately began unloading the power hitters to get younger, faster players who could pick up and throw the ball. From the Braves came the middle infield combination of Alvin Dark and Eddie Stanky. From the Negro leagues came third baseman Hank Thompson and outfielder Monte Irvin. From the Cards came pitcher Jim Hearn, and from banishment for jumping to the outlaw Mexican League came Sal Maglie, "The Barber," a pitcher with a disposition fully as nasty as his manager's.

By 1950 the Giants finished third, just five games off the pace. Durocher thought he had an excellent chance in 1951 against the favored Dodgers. Irvin was a dependable slugger,

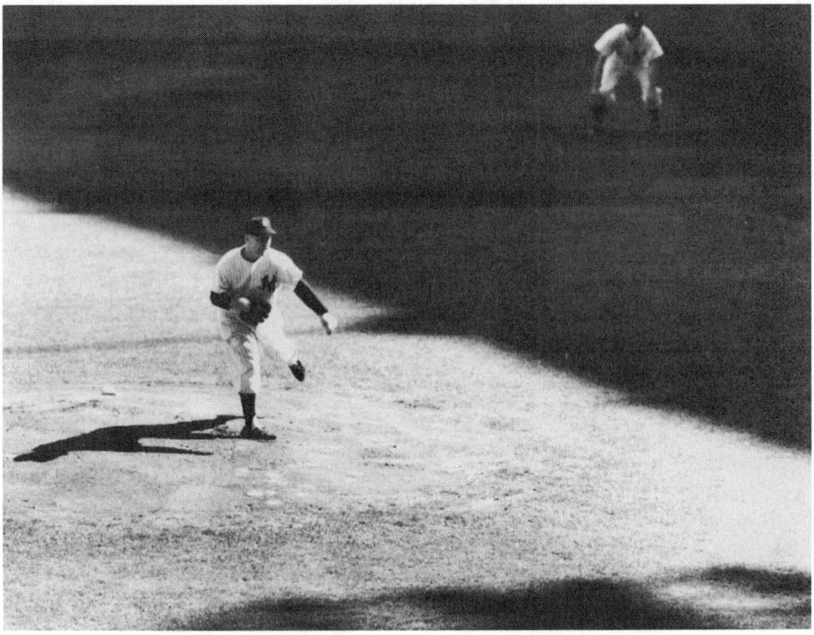

The Yankees' Eddie Lopat dominated the Giants, posting two complete game victories with an ERA of 0.50. The Series was considered somewhat anti-climactic after the Giants' epic pennant chase and three-game playoff victory.

leading the league with 121 RBIs, and right behind him was Bobby Thomson. The outfielder was converted into a third baseman in mid-season when Hank Thompson went down with injuries, and he responded with 32 homers and 101 RBIs. Dark had a steady .303 year and was Durocher's field leader. Whitey Lockman also made the move from outfield to infield, although not without protests. Still, he adjusted to playing first base and turned in a .282 season.

The biggest move, however, came in May when 19-year-old sensation Willie Mays was brought up from the minors. Durocher nurtured the youngster and watched him blossom into the most exciting player in the game, the greatest of his generation. Overcoming a terrible start, Mays finished at .274 with 20 homers and played a centerfield that already was being compared to Joe DiMaggio and Tris Speaker in their primes.

Maglie was the top pitcher in the league, at 23-6, and beside him was Larry Jansen, at 23-11. Hearn rounded out the starting three at 17-9. The Giants did not win by accident. The accident was an 11-game losing streak in April that necessitated their wild stretch run. They were a worthy opponent for the Yankees.

The champs, although winning the pennant by five over Cleveland, were not quite the overpowering crew of 1950. Most of their big hitters tailed off, although Yogi Berra was voted MVP for his .294 average and team-leading 88 RBIs. DiMaggio was now only a shadow of himself, slowed up and in and out of the lineup. He finished at .263, although still second on the team with 71 RBIs.

The farm system, however, was producing big time once more. Joe Collins shored up the defense at first base and hit a solid .286. Gil McDougald caught Casey Stengel's eye in spring training and the manager did everything he could to juggle his infield combinations and make room for him. Alternating between second and third, McDougald hit .306 and was named Rookie of the Year.

The other new arrival was Mickey Mantle. He appeared at spring training in a blaze of trumpets as DiMaggio's heir. Stengel felt he wasn't quite ready, and Mantle was sent back to AAA ball. He returned in mid-summer and finished with 13 homers and 65 RBIs in just 96 games.

The pitching rotation was narrowed down to three when Whitey Ford was drafted and an ineffective Tommy Byrne was peddled to the Browns. But Vic Raschi (21-10), Eddie Lopat (21-9) and Allie Reynolds (17-8 with seven saves) were at their peaks, and rookie Tom Morgan popped up from the minors in late summer to go 9-3 down the stretch. In addition, the Yanks made their usual last-minute pickup of a National League star, snaring Johnny Sain from the Braves to bolster their bullpen.

Turning Point: Game Five, Third Inning.

For three games the Giants show no sign of losing their momentum. They win the opener, driving Reynolds from the mound as Irvin gets four hits and tops it off by stealing home. Lopat slows them up in game two, 3-1, but next day they hammer Raschi. Stanky kicks the ball out of Phil Rizzuto's hand on a play at second and it lights a fire under the Giants. They stage a five-run rally, enough for their second win. But that was the last salvo.

The implacable Reynolds comes back in game four to out-pitch Maglie, 6-2. Now the Series is tied and it is Lopat against Jansen before an expectant Polo Grounds throng. The Giants don't disappoint them, as Dark's aggressive base running forces an error by Gene Woodling in the first and gives them a 1-0 lead.

Jansen starts to wobble in the third. With one out, he walks Woodling and Rizzuto. Berra hits into a forceout, but DiMaggio, whose two-run homer was the winning margin in game four, lines a run-scoring single to left. An error by Irvin on the play moves the runners up a base and the Giants decide to walk the veteran Johnny Mize, a danger they know well, to deal with the unknown rookie, McDougald. He takes one ball and sends the next pitch deep into the leftfield pavilion. It is the third grand slam homer in Series history.

The slam makes it 5-1 Yankees and the Giants never recover. They lose the game 13-1 and the Yankees close them out next day. Later, they blame a storm that caused a one-day rain delay between games three and four. They said it cooled them off when they were at their hottest. But it was the Yankee depth more than the weather that decided this Series.

The Managers:

Stengel plays his entire roster, switching players in and out of the lineup constantly. Only his two bullpen catchers see no action as he consistently keeps one step ahead of his adversary in his batting and defensive matchups. A few holdouts still insist that it is simply dumb luck, but Stengel is finally acknowledged by most as a master of the game.

Durocher does what he can with a lineup feeling the loss of outfielder Don Mueller, who was injured during the winning rally in the playoffs. With three Giants playing out of position, defensive lapses are inevitable and all of Durocher's well-advertised brilliance cannot overcome them.

The Heroes:

This was Lopat's Series. The left-hander, who became Whitey Ford's mentor, could not throw hard. His precise control and ability to change speeds and location constantly on his limited assortment of pitches kept the Giants off stride throughout the Series. Stengel was reluctant to start him in game five, since the Polo Grounds was known as death on curveballing lefties. The fences were so short that even a fooled batter's bloop to the wrong field could fall for a homer. But he pitched his second of two complete games there and gave up just two runs for the Series.

Irvin was superb for the losers, slamming out 11 hits for a .458 average and stealing the only two bases of the Series. He was assisted by Dark, who had 10 hits, played errorless ball and slammed a big three-run homer in the opener.

While Hank Bauer's hitting was not a factor, the rightfielder saved the Series with a fine sliding catch on a sinking liner in the ninth inning of the last game. With the Yankees holding on to a 4-1 lead, reliever Bob Kuzava was brought in with the bases loaded and none out. Irvin and Thomson sent out two long fly balls that brought in two runs. Pinch hitter Sal Yvars then slashed a sinking drive to right. Had it fallen in, the game was tied. But Bauer's catch at his knees ended the game and the Series.

The Zeroes:

This first confrontation between Mays and Mantle was a disappointment for both. Mays batted only .182 and in the fourth game hit into three double plays off Reynolds. It was even worse for Mantle. Playing rightfield in game two, he stepped into a drainage hole at Yankee Stadium, injuring his knee and taking him out of the Series. The injury bothered him for the rest of his career and in the minds of many longtime Yankee observers kept him from achieving the maximum his talents allowed.

FACT:
This first confrontation between Mays and Mantle was a disappointment for both. Mays batted only .182 and in the fourth game hit into three double plays off Reynolds. It was even worse for Mantle. Playing rightfield in game two, he stepped into a drainage hole at Yankee Stadium, injuring his knee and taking him out of the Series.

All of Durocher's position-shifting caught up with him. For some reason, when Hank Thompson came off the injured list he was sent out to rightfield to replace the injured Mueller, while Bobby Thomson, usually an outfielder, stayed at third. Each player made two errors in the Series and so did Lockman, the converted outfielder at first base. The Giants made a total of 10 errors.

The Aftermath:

Mays went to the draft, Irvin broke his leg, Stanky became the manager of the Cardinals. It was all too much for the Giants to overcome and they fell back to 4 1/2 games behind the Dodgers.

The Yankees had to fight off a determined Cleveland challenge, overcome the loss of Jerry Coleman in the draft and the retirement of DiMaggio. No problem. They were back for the fourth straight time in 1952.

Notes:

The Yanks pulled off a record 10 double plays, constantly thwarting Giants efforts to get back into the Series. Part of the reason for the high number was the fact that Yankee pitchers walked 25 men, led by Reynolds' 11. The total of 51 walks by both teams was another Series mark.

FACT:
Yankee pitchers walked 25 men, led by Reynolds' 11. The total of 51 walks by both teams was another Series mark.

McDougald's grand slam was the first in the Series since 1936, when Tony Lazzeri, who also played second base for the Yankees, hit one, also against the Giants.

Line Scores:

Game One, October 4

NY (NL)—200 003 000—5
Koslo W

NY (AL)—010 000 000—1
Reynolds L, Hogue (7), Morgan (8)

Game Two, October 5

NY (NL)—000 000 100—1
Jansen L, Spencer (7)

NY (AL)—110 000 01X—3
Lopat W

Game Three, October 6

NY (AL)—000 000 011—2
Raschi L, Hogue (5), Ostrowski (7)

NY (NL)—010 050 00X—6
Hearn W, Jones (8) SV

Game Four, October 8

NY (AL)—010 120 020—6
Reynolds W

NY (NL)—100 000 001—2
Maglie L, Jones (6), Kennedy (9)

Game Five, October 9

NY (AL)—005 202 400—13
Lopat W

NY (NL)—100 000 000—1
Jansen L, Kennedy (4), Spencer (6), Corwin (7), Konikowski (9)

Game Six, October 10

NY (NL)—000 010 002—3
Koslo L, Hearn (7), Jansen (8)

NY (AL)—100 003 00X—4
Raschi W, Sain (7), Kuzava (9) SV

1952

New York (AL) 4
Brooklyn (NL) 3

In their third meeting in six years, the Dodgers had their old adversaries hanging on the ropes. They couldn't deliver the final blow, however, and the Yanks escaped to win their fourth straight championship.

The Preview:

The Dodgers entered the Series with the best team in franchise history. Their infield was the strongest in baseball. The outfield was superb. Their catcher was quite possibly the toughest in the game. And yet the Yankees were 3-to-5 favorites to win.

Part of that was because they were the Yankees. But the Dodgers also lacked respect from the oddsmakers because of a problem with their pitching. There wasn't much of it. No team had ever gone into a Series without a starter who had won, at least, 15 games. Tops with Brooklyn was Carl Erskine, at 14-6, and behind him was a void.

Don Newcombe was lost to the draft. Preacher Roe had faded to 11 wins. Ralph Branca, a key starter on the last two pennant winners, was no longer a factor. He never recovered from giving up Bobby Thomson's homer in the 1951 playoffs, won just 4 games and was gone from Brooklyn completely in another year.

Only the unexpected emergence of Joe Black saved the Dodgers. The hard-throwing, 28-year-old rookie had been kicking around for years in the Negro League and Cuba. He was sent into the Brooklyn bullpen and went 14-3 as a reliever, with 15 saves. The closer he got to the Series, the more manager Charlie Dressen began to think that Black was the answer to the larger problem. With the pennant wrapped up, he experimented by starting him in two games against Boston. He went the distance to

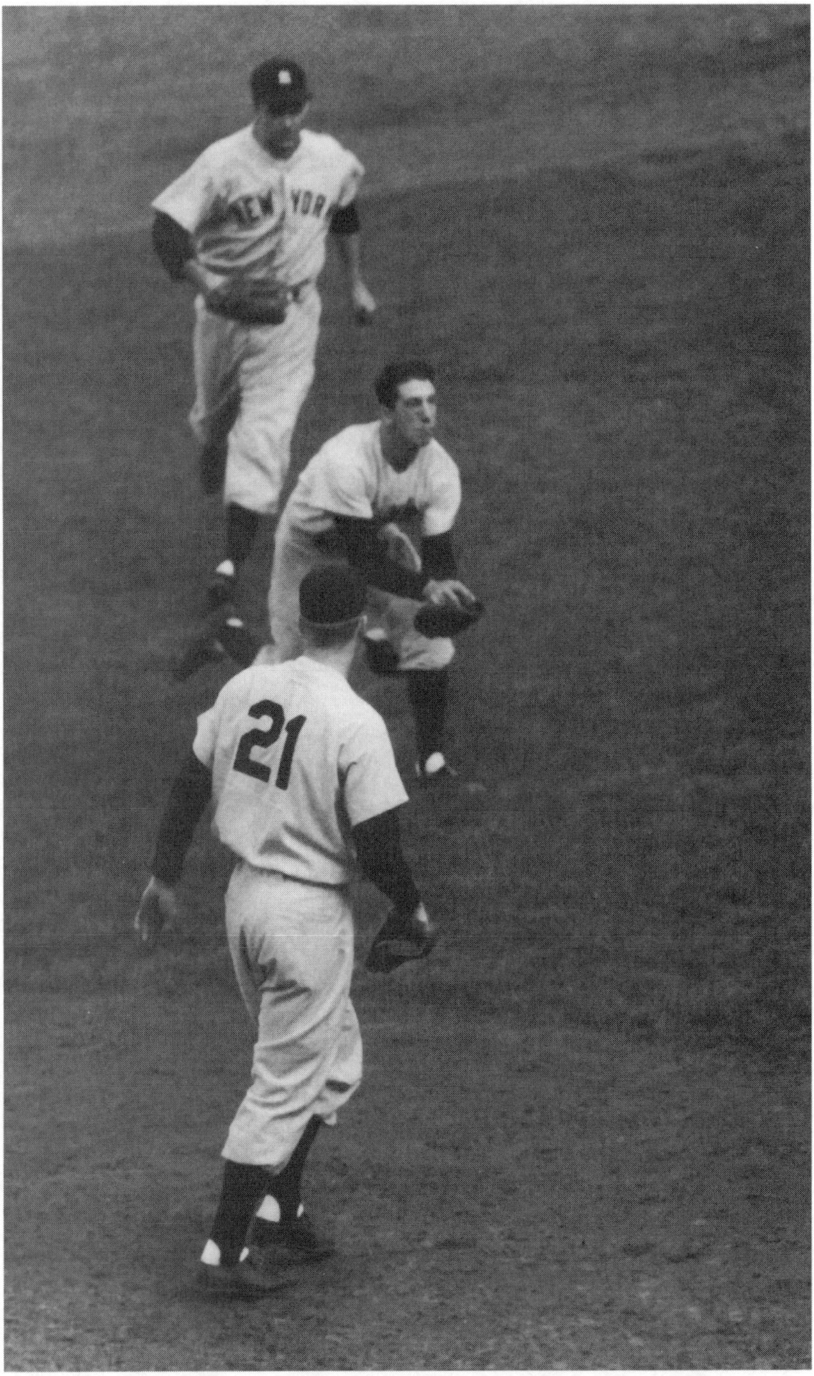

Second baseman Billy Martin (center) makes a Series-saving catch on Jackie Robinson's infield pop-up in the seventh inning of Game 7. Martin also contributed five hits and four RBI.

win one and although he was batted out in the other, Dressen had seen enough to be convinced that Black was his missing starter.

While Brooklyn led the league in most batting stats, the hitters actually tailed off from their big 1951 years. Gil Hodges paced the team with 32 homers and 102 RBIs. The most consistent threats were Jackie Robinson, at .308, and Duke Snider, who hit .303 with 92 RBIs. Roy Campanella was also a major contributor with 97 RBIs and 22 homers.

The Yankees did not have that kind of explosiveness throughout their lineup. Yogi Berra was again the team leader, with 30 homers and 98 RBIs. Mickey Mantle, in his first full season, hit .311 with 23 home runs, many of them of extraordinary length. But Jerry Coleman was gone to the Army and rookie Billy Martin, a Casey Stengel favorite, had to be rushed in as a replacement. He hit a weak .267. Gil McDougald also dropped off significantly from his great rookie year and Johnny Mize was reduced to a few spot starts and pinch hitting.

Even in pitching the Yankees were not what they had been. Stronger than the Dodgers, to be sure, but by their own high standards considerably weaker. Allie Reynolds had his greatest year, going 20-8 and leading the league with 160 strikeouts and a 2.06 ERA. Vic Raschi was 16-6. But Eddie Lopat dropped to 10 wins and Stengel had to scramble to coax anything more out of a rather ordinary staff. Johnny Sain, splitting his time between starting and relieving, became a factor with an 11-6 record and seven saves, while Bob Kuzava, who had saved the final victory in 1951, also worked as a swing man and went 8-8.

Turning Point: Game Seven, Seventh Inning.

Aside from their 1942 upset loss to St. Louis, the Yanks have seldom felt this kind of pressure. Even when Brooklyn forced them to seven games in 1947, they always seemed in control, just waiting to close it out. This time they are fighting for their lives. The Dodgers take a 3-2 lead back to Ebbets Field and need only one of the final two games to finally win a championship.

They fall short in game six, 3-2, but accomplish something almost as important. The Yanks are forced to use Reynolds in relief to save the game for Raschi. New York must go into the deciding game with its two top pitchers exhausted.

The Dodgers come back with Black for the third time. He repaid Dressen's confidence by stopping the Yanks 4-2 in the opener. He is almost as strong in a 2-0 loss to Reynolds in game four. The Yankees send out Lopat, who was hit hard in a 5-3 loss in game three. The Dodgers, in fact, hit all lefties hard. Only one has beaten them all year. The club is so loaded with right-handed power it seldom even sees left-handed pitching. Stengel regards this as an edge. The unfamiliar might beat them. On the other hand, there is little else he can do but hope for the best. The 34-year-old Lopat has the wile if not the speed to win.

For three innings, the two pitchers exchange zeroes. But in the fourth they both start to weaken. The Yanks break through on a double by Phil Rizzuto and a single by Mize, a starter once more when the going gets tough. Brooklyn drives out Lopat on a single by Snider and consecutive bunt singles by Robinson and, improbably, the slow-moving Campanella. The bases are loaded with none out and Ebbets Field is in an uproar as Reynolds, weary but game, is summoned. He has pitched 10 shutout innings in the last three days and, with nothing to hold back for, he is willing to try again.

FACT:
The Dodgers hit all lefties hard. Only one has beaten them all year. The club is so loaded with right-handed power it seldom even sees left-handed pitching. Stengel regards this as an edge. The unfamiliar might beat them.

He gets the side out, but the tying run scores on a long fly by Hodges. The Yanks shoot ahead again in the fifth on a Woodling homer. Reynolds, obviously dead tired, cannot hold off the Dodgers. A double by Billy Cox and Pee Wee Reese's single to left make it 2-2. In the sixth, Mantle smashes a tremendous home run over the rightfield scoreboard to make it 3-2 and finish off Black. With Roe on the mound in the seventh, he knocks in yet another run with a single.

Reynolds, however, can go no further than the 6th. Raschi, the previous day's starter, has to come in to work the 7th. He, too, is going on nerve alone. The Dodgers quickly load the bases on him with one out on two walks and a single by Cox. This brings up Snider, who already has driven in eight runs as Brooklyn's top hitter. The Yanks send for Kuzava, their top left-handed reliever. For the second year in a row, this obscure 29-year-old journeyman is being called on to save the Series.

He gets Snider on a pop foul. The next hitter is Robinson and everyone expects that Stengel will come back with a right-hander to face him. But the manager likes the way Kuzava is throwing, and, instead, he stays in. Once more he induces a simple pop up, but this one quickly leaves the realm of the routine. The three Dodger runners are tearing around the bases, the crowd is screaming—and no one is moving towards the ball. First baseman Joe Collins says later that he is blinded by the late afternoon glare. The left side of the infield is pulled too deep and Berra is slow to react. The ball starts its descent as Martin, the only

Yankee with a chance at it, dashes madly toward the center of the infield. The only thought going through his mind is to grab the ball in his bare hand so that when he is hit by another fielder, as he was sure he would be, the ball wouldn't roll out of his glove. He grabs the ball on the dead run with no one near him, and with that catch the Dodgers are done. Kuzava allows just one runner, on an error, in the last two innings and the Yanks are 4-2 winners.

The Managers:

The last time Stengel and Dressen faced each other, fifth place was at stake. It was 1936 and both were handling dreadful teams, Stengel in Brooklyn and Dressen with Cincinnati. Both endured long exiles from the majors and, ironically, it was the same job that brought them back. Stengel led the Oakland Oaks to the Pacific Coast League pennant before getting the call to the Yanks in 1949. He was now 62 and rumors swirled throughout this Series that he would announce his retirement, win or lose, when it was over.

Dressen, eight years his junior, was finally getting his big chance and was making the most of it. He had taken over from Stengel in Oakland, won there, and followed him to the majors two years later. Stengel was already famous for his assaults on the English language, but Dressen spoke an equally impenetrable argot, which involved whistles, hand signals and slang terms known only to Dressen. He was not shy about proclaiming his genius as a strategist, either. "Hold 'em close," was his rallying cry, "and I'll think of something."

The Stars:

Reynolds was now 37 and still as hard a thrower as there was in the game. His reputation for fading in the clutch long forgotten, he was never better than in this Series. He shut out the Dodgers in a game the Yankees had to win, saved game six two days later and then, working with no rest, came back to pick up another win in the last game with three innings of relief. He was acclaimed as the top money pitcher in the game.

This was the Series in which the 26-year-old Snider emerged as a superstar. Already recognized as a good hitter, he erupted for four homers and set a Series record with 24 total bases. He drove in the winning runs in the first and fifth games and accounted for both Brooklyn runs with two homers in the 3-2 game six loss. After this Series, he played on a higher plateau, with at least 40 home runs in each of the next five years. He became a true rival to Mantle and Willie Mays as the top centerfielder in New York City.

This was also Mantle's moment to assume the leadership of the Yankees. He topped the team with 10 hits and his home runs were the margin of difference in the critical sixth and seventh games. The shot over the scoreboard in the seventh game was noted at the time as the first "tape measure" home run, a term popularized by media coverage of Mantle, in a Series.

For the 39-year-old Mize, who was supposed to be announcing his retirement, this Series was a tonic. Inserted back in the starting lineup, he slammed out homers in three consecutive games, a Series record. Mize added a double, led the Yanks with six RBIs and hit .400.

FACT:
Mantle topped the Yankees with 10 hits and his home runs were the difference in the critical sixth and seventh games.

The Zeroes:

The opposing first basemen never made it into the hit column. Joe Collins, who was counted on by the Yankees more for defense than power, was hitless in 12 at bats. His slump gave Mize the chance to play again.

Hodges fared even worse. The big first baseman tied a record by being held 0-for-21. The best-liked player on the Dodgers and a dependable clutch hitter, Hodges suffered through a nightmare. The fans sent him carloads of good luck charms. The Brooklyn clergy led prayers for him. In the last two games, he was given standing ovations to encourage him. Nothing worked. His slump was the critical difference in the Series.

The Aftermath:

While the result was a crushing disappointment to the Dodgers, they were so deep in talent that they bounced back stronger than ever in 1953. Black faded away, but Carl Erskine turned into a 20-game winner, and several of the big hitters put together career years.

The Yankees now stood on the brink of history. They had tied the record of their 1936–39 predecessors in pinstripes, and could hardly wait to go for five straight championships. Both Stengel and Mize abandoned retirement plans and announced that they would return. So would Whitey Ford, out of the Army and ready to pick up where he had left off in 1950.

FACT:
Despite good luck charms from fans, prayers by Brooklyn clergy, and standing ovations, Hodges tied a record by being held 0-for-21. His slump was the critical difference in the Series.

Notes:

The combined total of 16 home runs shattered a Series record. In fact, the old mark of

12, set in 1925, fell in the sixth game. The Yankees hit at least one in all seven games.

Kuzava was only the second pitcher in history to be on the mound at the end of two consecutive Series. Art Nehf did it by pitching complete game wins for the Giants against the Yanks in 1921–22. Thirty years later, Kuzava accomplished the feat by way of the bullpen.

For all the power hitting that went on, the two teams combined for a mere .215 batting average. The Yankees' mark of .216 was the lowest ever recorded by a winning Series team.

Line Scores:

Game One, October 1

NY (AL)—001 000 010—2
Reynolds L, Scarborough (8)

Bkn (NL)—010 002 01X—4
Black W

Game Two, October 2

NY (AL)—000 115 000—7
Raschi W

Bkn (NL)—001 000 000—1
Erskine L, Loes (6), Lehman (8)

Game Three, October 3

Bkn (NL)—001 010 012—5
Roe W

NY (AL)—010 000 011—3
Lopat L, Gorman (9)

Game Four, October 4

Bkn (NL)—000 000 000—0
Black L, Rutherford (8)

NY (AL)—000 100 01X—2
Reynolds W

Game Five, October 5

Bkn (NL)—010 030 100 01—6
Erskine W

NY (AL)—000 050 000 00—5
Blackwell, Sain (6) L

Game Six, October 6

NY (AL)—000 000 210—3
Raschi W, Reynolds (8) SV

Bkn (NL)—000 001 010—2
Loes L, Roe (9)

Game Seven, October 7

NY (AL)—000 111 100—4
Lopat, Reynolds (4) W,
Raschi (7), Kuzava (7) SV

Bkn (NL)—000 110 000—2
Black L, Roe (6), Erskine (8)

1953

New York (AL) 4
Brooklyn (NL) 2

Galvanized by an unlikely hero, the Yankees rode to an unexpectedly easy fifth straight championship. Billy Martin rapped out a record-tying 12 hits, including the winner in the sixth game.

The Preview:

Now it was personal. Their previous three seasons had ended in frustration and defeat in the final game of the year. Their last four trips to the Series had ended with a crash against the immovable Yankees. No team had more talent than Brooklyn. They ripped apart the National League in 1953, winning a franchise record 105 games and cruising home 13 games ahead of the newly transplanted Milwaukee Braves. Infuriated by their near-miss of 1952, they were on a mission, coming back to dump the Yankees once and for all.

For Pee Wee Reese, who had suffered through all four Series defeats, for Jackie Robinson and Carl Furillo who had been through it three times, this was payback time. Furillo had led the league in hitting with a .344 mark, 97 points higher than his dreadful 1952 campaign. Robinson switched positions to make room for rookie leadoff man Jim Gilliam and the veteran thrived. Shifting between leftfield and third, he hit .329 and knocked in 95 runs. Duke Snider finally became the power hitter the Dodgers had expected, belting out 42 homers, driving in 126 and hitting .336. Roy Campanella had a career season, leading the league in RBIs with 142, smashing 41 homers and hitting .312. Gil Hodges was right there with the others, rebounding from his awful Series with 31 homers, 122 RBIs and a .302 average.

Mickey Mantle watches his third inning grand slam leave the yard in Game 5. Up to this point, the injury-plagued Mantle had been having a terrible Series, but his blast led the way to another Yankee championship.

Not a team in baseball even came close to numbers like these. There wasn't a weak spot in the lineup, and the Brooklyn total of 955 runs was more than 150 beyond any other team in the game. The pitching, which had been doleful the previous year, also rebounded. Carl Erskine, always about to break out with a big year, went 20-6. The terrible-tempered Russ Meyer, who led the majors in broken clubhouse implements after a loss, had few reasons to get destructive during a 15-5 season. Joe Black came down with arm problems and was never a factor. But Clem Labine picked up the slack with an 11-6 mark and 7 saves as a reliever. The Dodgers still missed Don Newcombe, in the second year of his Army hitch, but the staff had depth and a genuine stopper in Erskine.

Instead of fading, the Yankees won 99 games, the most during their five-year run. They put the pennant away in mid-season with an 18-game winning streak and finished 8 1/2 in front of Cleveland. While figuring in no major stats, the Yankees had rare consistency. Eight of their nine starters were in double figures in homers. Yogi Berra was the most productive with 108 RBIs, but right behind him was Mickey Mantle at 92. Gene Woodling and Hank Bauer, shuttled in and out of the lineup in Casey Stengel's platoon rotation, had amazingly similar seasons: For Woodling, a .306 average with 10 homers and 58 RBIs; for Bauer, .304, 10 homers and 57 RBIs. Consistency.

Billy Martin, now the full-time second baseman, hit only .257 but showed surprising power with 15 homers and 75 RBIs. Gil McDougald, finding a permanent home at third, contributed 83 RBIs.

The pitching showed the same trait. Whitey Ford was back and went 18-6. His tutor, Eddie Lopat, led the league in ERA at 2.42 and posted a 16-4 mark. But the most valuable men in Stengel's rotation were the old horses, Allie Reynolds and Johnny Sain. He asked them both to continually alternate between starting and relieving, the most difficult adjustment a pitcher must make. Sain wound up pitching the second most innings on the team, behind Ford, and posting a 14-7 record with 9 saves. Reynolds was right behind, at 13-7 and 13 saves, but he injured his back in a freak accident when the team bus hit a bridge abutment in Philadelphia. It seemed to affect both his durability and velocity. Nonetheless, the Yankees looked ready to meet the Brooklyn challenge.

Turning Point: Game Five, Third Inning.

It is a curious Series. Homers are flying every which way and the record total set only the previous year is broken. Top pitchers are clubbed out in an inning, then come back a few days later and look like world-beaters. Mantle is so ineffective that a disgusted Stengel bats him leadoff in one game, while New York's top production comes from Martin. Stengel, always quick to adjust to a hot hitter, moves him to sixth in the batting order by the fourth game.

Both teams defend their home turf, winning two apiece to forge a tie in games. Erskine, clobbered in the opener, comes back to set a strikeout record, nailing 14 in a 3-2 win in game three. By game five, however, both sides have gone through their top starters and the pitching choices are tinged with desperation.

For Brooklyn, the choice is a rookie-left-hander, Johnny Podres. He was 9-4 during the season and seemed to be coming on at the end. Still, this is a tough situation for a kid five days past his 21st birthday. When Woodling leads off the game with a homer, it seems that Charlie Dressen's choice is very unfortunate.

His opponent is Jim McDonald, one of the Yankees' lesser lights at 9-7. He started just 18 times during the season and nothing in his career indicates that he is up to an assignment like this. He is rocked for three hits in the second as Brooklyn ties the game, and only a great throw by Woodling to the plate cuts down Hodges with the lead run.

The New York third starts innocuously, with a walk to Rizzuto followed by a bunt and an infield out. Joe Collins sends a hard grounder right at Hodges, which should end the inning. But the dependable first baseman boots it for an error, and the Yanks are back in front, 2-1. Podres cannot recover. He hits Bauer, walks Berra and Mantle limps to the plate.

The Yankee centerfielder is bothered by a leg injury that dates back to the 1951 Series. He missed 27 games during the season because of it and is still slowed up noticeably. Erskine struck him out four times in game three and he seems uncertain of himself, taking far too many good pitches. Hitting leadoff in game four he strikes out twice more but singles in his last time at bat. Stengel takes this as a good sign and restores him to his usual fifth spot in the order.

He grounded out weakly against Podres in the second. Dressen, concerned at his young pitcher's stability, had Meyer warming up since the first inning. He decides it is time to send for him. Meyer, noting the number of pitches Mantle is taking, decides to get ahead of him with a fast ball on the plate. When last seen, the ball was disappearing into the upper deck in leftfield for a grand slam, the fourth in Series history.

Mantle's hit is only New York's second of the game, but it gives the Yanks a 5-1 lead. While the Dodgers bang out 14 hits and rally furiously in the late innings, they cannot catch up, losing 11-7. That sends the Series back to New York with the Yanks needing just one to win. They seldom falter in such a situation and don't this time. Even a two-run, game-tying homer by Furillo in the 9th can't stave off the inevitable. Martin ends it with a one-out single off Labine in the New York half of the inning. But while Martin takes Series hitting honors, the hobbled Mantle's slam turns it around.

FACT:
When he brought the Yankees into Ebbets Field in 1952, Stengel took Mantle to show him how to play caroms off the centerfield wall. "He couldn't figure out how I knew about that," Stengel chuckled later. "It never dawned on him that this old coot had played that wall for years."

The Managers:

The man who arrived at Yankee Stadium five years before as a clown and failure had joined the sport's pantheon. No one ever won five in a row before, not in any sport. Stengel had prevailed over injuries, the draft and initial distrust by players and media. When he brought the Yankees into Ebbets Field in 1952, he took Mantle to show him how to play caroms off the centerfield wall. "He couldn't figure out how I knew about that," Stengel chuckled later. "It never dawned on him that this old coot had played that wall for years." At a time when retirement looks very good to most people, Stengel was just getting warmed up, redeeming a life of missed hopes.

For Dressen, however, the big prize was elusive. Nonetheless, he felt that he had proved his mettle with two straight pennants and the narrowest of misses. He wanted, at least, a commitment to security with the Dodgers. It was a fatal miscalculation.

The Heroes:

Martin is a special favorite of Stengel's. The Italian kid from California is a throwback to the players Casey knew in his youth, willing to make up for a shortage of talent by hard work and aggressiveness. A minor talent among all the stars on the Yankees, Martin wills himself into a starting job, turning himself into a serviceable second baseman and a dangerous clutch hitter. Still, no one expected this sort of Series. He gets the Yanks off with a three-run triple off Erskine in the first inning of game one. His seventh-inning homer off Preacher Roe in game two ties a game in which the big hitters had been thwarted. He triples again in game four, homers in game five. And with one out in the ninth and the winning run on second, he singles in the sixth game to end the Series. He finishes with 8 RBIs and a .500 average.

Erskine couldn't get the job done in either the first or last games, but in game three he was heroic. With his curveball darting to perfection, he struck out 14 hitters, breaking Howard Ehmke's record from 1929. The game was tight all the way with Brooklyn only pulling it out in the eighth on a Campanella homer off Vic Raschi. Erskine, who would become the central figure in a famous baseball routine by Brooklyn-born comic Phil Foster (in which he is known as "Oiskine"), gets pinch hitter Johnny Mize in the ninth for the record.

The Dodger hitters were as tough as advertised. Brooklyn hit .300 as a team, the first time that level was reached since the Yankees did it in 1936, and the first time it had been done by a losing team. Five different Brooklyn players end up with eight hits.

FACT:
Erskine couldn't get the job done in either the first or last games, but in game three he was heroic. With his curveball darting to perfection, he struck out 14 hitters, breaking Howard Ehmke's record from 1929.

The Zeroes:

Joe Black, Brooklyn's top pitcher in the 1952 Series, was reduced to one ineffective inning this time. In later years, he blamed

Dressen for trying to change his delivery and getting him to work with pitches he couldn't master. But he was a one-year wonder and was dealt away by the Dodgers two years later.

Bob Kuzava was called upon once more to save a game for the Yanks. It wasn't the closing game of the Series this time, and he didn't come through. He did halt a four-run Brooklyn rally in the eighth inning of the fifth game by striking out pinch hitter Dick Williams. But in the ninth, a homer by Gilliam and a single by Snider led Stengel to bring in Reynolds to get the last outs and the save. Kuzava was traded the following year and never appeared in another Series, but left an impressive career line: three appearances, one run, two saves.

The Aftermath:

Dressen presented the Dodgers with an ultimatum after the Series, demanding a two-year contract and even getting his wife into the act through the press. The Dodgers responded by dumping him and hiring unknown minor league manager Walt Alston. The Dodgers then fell back to second place in 1954.

The Yanks went on to win 103 games, however, their highest total in 12 years. But Cleveland set a league record and won 111, breaking the New York run at five championships.

Notes:

With a new television contract factored into the equation, the winning player's share was up to $8,281, by far the biggest ever.

It was the first time in 18 years, since Goose Goslin's sixth-game single in 1935, that the Series ended on a base hit.

The combined total of 17 homers broke the record set the previous year by one. And it had taken the teams a full seven games to establish that one. Furillo got the record-breaker in dramatic fashion, a two-run game-tying shot off Reynolds in the ninth inning of game six.

Line Scores:

Game One, September 30

Brk (NL)—000 013 100—5
Erskine, Hughes (2),
Labine (6) L, Wade (7)

NY (AL)—400 010 13X—9
Reynolds, Sain (6) W

Game Two, October 1

Brk (NL)—000 200 000—2
Roe L

NY (AL)—100 000 12X—4
Lopat W

Game Three, October 2

NY (AL)—000 010 010—2
Raschi L

Bkn (NL)—000 011 01X—3
Erskine W

Game Four, October 3

NY (AL)—000 020 001—3
Ford L, Gorman (2), Sain (5), Shallock (7)

Bkn (NL)—300 102 10X—7
Loes W, Labine (9) SV

Game Five, October 4

NY (AL)—105 000 311—11
McDonald W, Kuzava (8), Reynolds (9) SV

Bkn (NL)—010 010 041—7
Podres L, Meyer (3), Wade (8), Black (9)

Game Six, October 5

Bkn (NL)—000 001 002—3
Erskine, Milliken (5), Labine (7) L

NY (AL)—210 000 001—4
Ford, Reynolds (8) W

1954

New York (NL) 4
Cleveland (AL) 0

In an upset that shocked everyone but the Giants, the Cleveland Indians, winners of 111 games, were swept in four. The pinch hitting of Dusty Rhodes and one unforgettable catch by Willie Mays knocked the fight out of the Indians.

The Preview:

The witch is dead. The Yankees have finally been laid to rest. Cleveland swept a Labor Day double header from them to break open the race and then coasted in by 8 games. The last team to win a pennant before the New York run of five straight titles became the one to break the streak, as well.

There were a few holdovers from the 1948 squad. Larry Doby, now a seasoned slugger, led the league in homers with 32 and RBIs with 126 while hitting .272 and playing an exemplary centerfield. Jim Hegan, still the best defensive catcher in the league, handled the extraordinary pitching staff. Bob Lemon was the leader of Cleveland's great collection of pitchers, going 23-7. Bob Feller, now 35 and rapid no more, still got in 19 starts and went 13-3.

Otherwise, the cast had changed. The Indians had a batting champion in second baseman Bobby Avila, who hit .341. Another power hitter was set at third in Al Rosen, with 24 homers and 102 RBIs. First baseman Vic Wertz, a mid-season pickup from Baltimore, regained his stroke in Cleveland and added 14 homers.

The Indians' strength was their pitchers. Early Wynn, who had been acquired in 1949 as insurance for a pennant repeat, finally caught a winner and matched Lemon's victory total, at 23-11. Mike Garcia led the league in ERA at 2.64 and went 19-8. Art

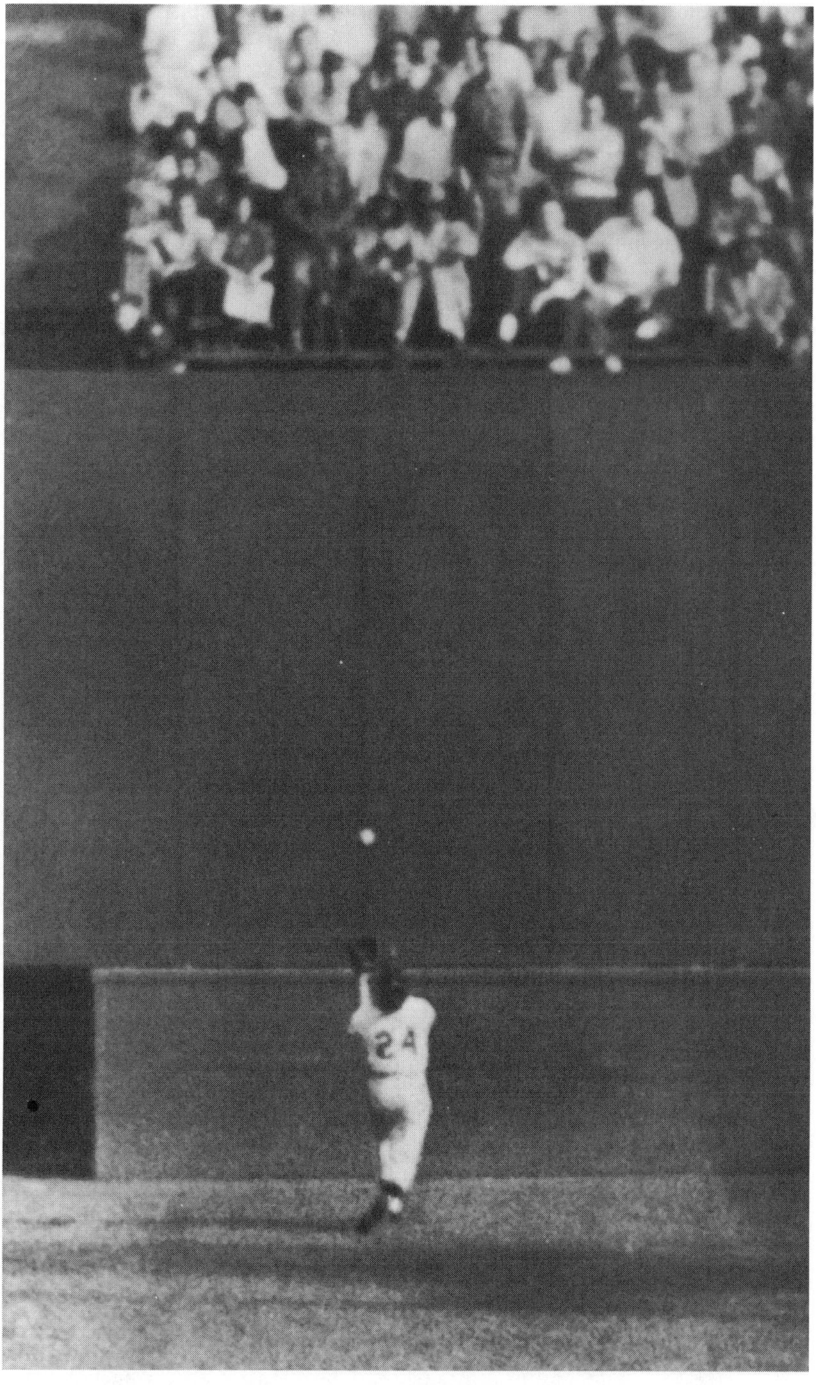

Willie Mays makes "The Catch" of Vic Wertz's eighth-inning drive into the deepest center field in baseball in Game 1. Along with Dusty Rhodes' pinch-hitting heroics, the play keyed New York's sweep of the heavily-favored Indians.

Houtteman came over from Detroit and compiled a 15-7 mark. Then there was the bullpen. In Ray Narleski and Don Mossi, the Indians had put together a deadly righty-lefty combination of closers, the first such tandem the game had seen. They saved 20 games between them, and in case they were otherwise occupied there was veteran Hal Newhouser, who saved seven more. Commentators called it the greatest pitching staff ever assembled, and on that basis alone installed Cleveland as the Series favorite.

The Giants, a weak fifth-place outfit in 1953, had been recharged by the return of Willie Mays from the service. When he left after the 1951 season, he was still a promising, but unpolished kid. He came back a superstar. His .345 average led the league and he also pounded 41 homers and 110 RBIs. His defensive work, in the cavernous centerfield of the Polo Grounds, was unlike anything in Giants history. There was no ball he could not get to, no play he could not make. His breezy personality turned him into a media darling, the most popular ballplayer in the country.

There were lots more behind him. Rightfielder Don Mueller, whose injury had sorely cost the Giants in the 1951 Series, finished runner-up to Mays in hitting at .342. Hank Thompson, back at third base, belted 26 homers with 86 RBIs. It was also a big year for the field leader, shortstop Alvin Dark, the finest hit-and-run man in the game. As New York's number two batter, he hit .293 with 20 home runs.

The pitching, however, was nowhere close to Cleveland's level. Johnny Antonelli, a bonus signee with the Braves who never seemed to reach his potential there, was acquired for ex-hero Bobby Thomson. Antonelli went 21-7 with a league-leading 2.30 ERA. After that, it was slim. Ruben Gomez went 17-9, but was not Leo Durocher's favorite choice as a clutch pitcher, while veteran Sal Maglie slid to 14-6. The bullpen was a strength. Marv Grissom, a 36-year-old right-hander who had been kicking around for years, having broken in with the Giants in 1946, suddenly turned into a stopper. He saved 19 games and went 10-7. He was assisted by knuckleballer Hoyt Wilhelm, who was 12-4 with 7 saves. Wilhelm already was 31, in only the third season of his big league career. No one could have guessed that he would go on, effortlessly tossing his dancing knuckler, for another 18 years and set a record for most appearances by a pitcher.

Turning Point: First Game, Eighth Inning.

The game summarizes Cleveland's experience in this Series. They get chances, cannot take advantage and then are beaten by the unbelievable. The opener matches Lemon and

Maglie, two pitchers who know about Series pressure. Both respond to the situation.

Cleveland breaks through in the first. After a hit batsman and a single, Wertz tags a tremendous drive off the rightfield wall. It would have been a home run in Cleveland but in the Polo Grounds it caroms into the vast spaces in right-center and he settles for a two-run triple.

That lead survives only into the third, though. Whitey Lockman and Dark start the inning with singles and one run scores on a forceout. Thompson then picks up the second run on a single and the game is tied 2-2.

Both sides threaten for the next several innings, but they are turned away. Wertz slams two more singles and twice moves into scoring position but the Indians cannot solve Maglie to get him in. Then in the 8th, Maglie shows sign of strain. He walks Doby to start the inning and Rosen slashes a single off Dark's bare, outstretched hand. Doby stops at second and up comes Wertz, who has blasted Maglie all day.

Durocher calls in Don Liddle, the best left-hander available to him and the logical choice to face the left-hand hitting Wertz. But the slugger unloads, getting everything behind his swing, and the ball departs for the farthest reaches of the park. When he hits it, Wertz doesn't doubt for a moment that it is in the stands. The Giants leap from their dugout seats, hoping Mays will be able to run it down for a double and hold Cleveland to only one run. It is 475 feet to dead center, the longest distance in baseball. Mays turns at contact and sprints full tilt towards the wall. At the last possible instant, he reaches out his glove and catches the ball over his shoulder, back to the plate.

In no other ballpark would such a catch be possible and there is probably no other player who could have made it. Everyone who sees it knows that they have witnessed a remarkable moment, one of the greatest plays in Series history. But the Giants are still not out of the inning. Doby has the presence of mind to tag up and reaches third with the go-ahead run.

Having seen enough of Liddle, Durocher motions for his main stopper, Grissom. Dale Mitchell, another Cleveland holdover from 1948, draws a pinch hit walk to load the bases. But then Dave Pope, another pinch hitter, is called out on strikes, and the weak-hitting Hegan flies out to end the threat.

FACT:
In one of the greatest plays in Series history, Mays turns at contact and sprints full tilt towards the wall. At the last possible instant, he reaches out his glove and catches the ball over his shoulder, back to the plate.

The Indians don't know it but they are cooked. They mount one more threat in the 10th, when Wertz leads off with his fourth hit of the game, a double that again would have been a homer in Cleveland. But Grissom foils the Indians with the lead run standing on third.

Then, with one out in the last of the 10th, Mays walks and steals second. Thompson is intentionally passed to bring Monte Irvin to bat. Durocher, always a hunch-player, lifts the veteran and, instead, sends up left-hand hitting Dusty Rhodes. He pops up down the rightfield line. But in the peculiar geography of the Polo Grounds, that is dangerous ground, only 258 feet to the stands. The harmless fly ball drifts into the first row of seats to become a three-run homer, as Lemon throws his glove 20 feet in the air in disgust.

The Giants win the opener, 5-2. Cleveland never recovers from Mays' catch and Rhodes' cheap homer and before they know what hit them the Series is over.

The Managers:

On his third visit to the Series, Durocher finally gets away with his first win. He is now 49 and a national celebrity. Married to a movie star, he talks of a career in films and hangs out with a show business crowd. There are those who suspect the fires that had driven him before are banked, the demons that once had led him to warn about what happens to nice guys—they finish last—had been exorcised. His time is running out in New York.

Al Lopez is the temperamental opposite, a phlegmatic, easy-going individual, father-confessor rather than demon. He held the record for games caught in the National League for many years, but never once in his 19-year career did he play for a winner. Known as a masterful handler of pitchers, Lopez was the top choice to succeed Lou Boudreau as manager of the Indians in 1951. In his first nine years, he never finished lower than second and he never will manage a losing team over a full season. But Lopez will never win the top prize, either.

The Heroes:

The original Dusty Rhodes probably was a pitcher for the 1893 Louisville team. Since that time, everyone who reached the majors with the name of Rhodes or Rhoads is automatically tagged Dusty. With James LaMar Rhodes, from rural Alabama, it may have fit. The 27-year-old utilityman, in his third season with the Giants, was a figure right out of the game's lore. He was the obscure bench-sitter whose great moment arrives. Rhodes was known as a pull-hitter who could take advantage of the Polo

Grounds short rightfield. During the 1954 season, he hit 15 homers and drove in 50 runs in just 164 times at bat. Projected over a full season, those are Ruthian numbers. But there were no full seasons for Rhodes because of his inadequacies as a fielder and runner. Still, he hit .333 as a pinch hitter, so there was no big surprise in Durocher sending for him to end the first game with his 10th inning homer. But he wasn't through. Next day, his pinch hit homer off Wynn broke open a one-run game and gave the Giants their final 3-1 margin. Finally, in game three, he pinch hit in the third inning and got a bases loaded single, driving in New York's first two runs in a 6-2 win. Three at-bats, three hits, six RBIs. Cleveland had no answer for that.

FACT:
James LaMar Rhodes, an obscure bench-sitter whose great moment arrived in the 1954 Series, came through in three games with three at-bats, three hits, six RBIs.

Wertz followed up his big first game as Cleveland's only substantial threat throughout the Series. He finished at .500, with half of his eight hits going for extra bases.

Antonelli was at his best. He went all the way in the second game to beat Wynn, then came back to get the final five outs of the finale, striking out Wertz and Wally Westlake, the tying runs in the 8th, with two men on.

The Zeroes:

Feller did not get a call in the Series. The big Cleveland crowd at the finale pleaded with Lopez to get him into the game, but the manager refused. He explained that it would have been demeaning to the great pitcher to be put in to mop up. Cleveland trailed at one point in the game 7-0 before rallying to cut the margin to 7-4. But the Indians closed with Mossi and Garcia.

Cleveland's power was completely cut off by the Giants. Doby and Rosen did not drive in a run and went a combined 5-for-28. Aside from Wertz, the rest of the lineup hit .149. The two shortstops, George Strickland and Sam Dente, were altogether hitless in 12 at bats.

The Indians' starters—Lemon, Wynn and Garcia—were also rudely treated. Supposedly the team's greatest strength, the three of them gave up 18 runs in 25 1/3 innings.

The Aftermath:

The Giants turned ordinary again very quickly. Even a 51-homer year by Mays could not prevent their fall to a distant third and Durocher's departure as manager. This was to be their final pennant in New York and the last Series at the Polo Grounds.

Cleveland remained a constant threat under Lopez but never again could the Indians break through against the Yankees. In fact, it took 41 long years before they won anything again. The franchise slipped back to become a perennial non-challenger for three decades, before finally assembling another winner in 1995.

Notes:

With a fat new television contract and games in the two biggest stadiums in either league, revenues from the Series soared to an unprecedented $11,118 per man for the Giants. In these years, when the average salary was less than twice that amount, it was a huge bonanza.

Cleveland's 111 wins set an American League record, but the Indians suffered the same Series fate as the National League record-holders. The 1906 Cubs won 116 times and fell to the White Sox in six.

Line Scores:

Game One, September 29

Cle (AL)—200 000 000 0—2
Lemon L

NY (NL)—002 000 000 3—5
Maglie, Liddle (8), Grissom (8) W

Game Two, September 30

Cle (AL)—100 000 000—1
Wynn L, Mossi (8)

NY (NL)—000 020 10X—3
Antonelli W

Game Three, October 1

NY (NL)—103 011 000—6
Gomez W, Wilhelm (8) SV

Cle (AL)—000 000 110—2
Garcia L, Houtteman (4), Narleski (6), Mossi (9)

Game Four, October 2

NY (NL)—021 040 000—7
Liddle W, Wilhelm (7), Antonelli (8) SV

Cle (AL)—000 030 100—4
Lemon L, Newhouser (5), Narleski (5), Mossi (6), Garcia (8)

1955

Brooklyn (NL) 4
New York (AL) 3

Dodgers Dood It” read the headlines. Euphoria, late in coming, at last arrived in Brooklyn. The franchise won its first championship in history. The fact that it came at the expense of the detested Yankees made it all the grander. There would never be another moment to match it.

The Preview:

It looked like the same old story. The Dodgers had the toughest lineup in baseball. Power, experience, defensive skill. No team could match them. As usual they led the league in runs and in batting, bashing the opposition into pulp, winning by 13 1/2 games.

Now, for a change, there was pitching. Not great quality, but deep enough to make this a different kind of Dodger team. Don Newcombe had recovered his prewar form after a bad comeback year and went 20-5. After him, Brooklyn came at you with numbers. The Dodgers got some starts out of Carl Erskine (11-8), Billy Loes (10-4) and a few more out of young Johnny Podres (9-10). Then, late in the season, they brought up two young flashes who provided a finishing kick. Roger Craig went 5-3 and Don Bessent, pitching mostly in relief, put up an 8-1 record with 3 saves. The bullpen mainstay was Clem Labine, who pitched 60 times and won 13 games (second only to Newcombe) while saving 11 more. It was a staff that could survive a long Series.

About the hitting there was never a doubt. The middle of the lineup—Duke Snider, Roy Campanella, Gil Hodges—was as deadly as ever. Snider hit 42 homers and led the league with 136 RBIs. Campanella topped the team with a .318 average and 107 RBIs, while Hodges also passed the century mark with 102 RBIs.

Sandy Amoros, installed in left field an inning earlier, stretches to snag Yogi Berra's liner in the sixth inning of Game 7. The relay throw doubled up Gil McDougald at second base, killing a Yankee rally.

Jackie Robinson was now at third base but was starting to fade. His .256 average was the lowest of his career. He still had the speed to steal 12 bases, and his will to win was the driving force of the Dodgers.

The Yankees, however, had muscled up. Mickey Mantle's 37 homers led the American League and Yogi Berra turned in another typical season, 32 homers and 107 RBIs. They added a big-hitting first baseman in Moose Skowron (.319) who split time with Joe Collins. Between them they drove in 106 runs. Billy Martin was back from the Army, and in 20 late season games hit .300.

New York also overhauled its pitching staff. The three starters who had led them to five straight pennants were gone. To replace them, the Yankees swung a huge trade with Baltimore, giving up several top prospects for two quality pitchers—Bob Turley and Don Larsen. Turley moved right into the rotation and went 17-13. In addition, they reacquired Tommy Byrne. Traded away in 1951, he came back with his finest season, a 16-5 mark. Whitey Ford, now the anchor of the staff, led the league in wins in compiling an 18-7 record.

Mantle's chronic leg problems started acting up again in September, however, and it became apparent that the Yankees could not count on him for the Series. Rookie Elston Howard was moved into the lineup to play leftfield. A .290 hitter, Howard would not hurt them at the plate. But Mantle's absence damaged New York on defense and made the Yankees a far more vulnerable team.

Turning Point: Game Seven, Sixth Inning.

For the first six games home field wins. The Yanks take the first two at Yankee Stadium and then Brooklyn turns around to sweep three at Ebbets Field. Podres looks especially sharp in game three there, going the distance in an 8-3 win. Once back in New York, though, the redoubtable Ford, who was held out of the rotation in the tiny Brooklyn ballpark, stops the Dodgers cold in game six, 5-1, on a four-hitter. Now for the third time in these confrontations, it goes to seven games.

The Yanks have Byrne, who won game two at the Stadium. The Dodgers come back with Podres. The previous two times a Yankee-Dodger Series went seven, the deciding game see-sawed back and forth early before the Yankees took control in the middle innings.

Accordingly, Brooklyn breaks ahead. A Campanella double and Hodges' single in the fourth put the Dodgers up, 1-0. Sure enough, Berra answers in the Yankee half with a leadoff double. This time, though, the scenario changes. New York cannot score him, as Podres gets out three tough right-handed hitters in a row.

In the top of the sixth, the Dodgers strike again. A single by Pee Wee Reese, a dropped throw by Skowron on a bunt and a walk to Carl Furillo load the bases with one out. Bob Grim comes out of the pen to face Hodges, who drives in his second run of the 2-0 game with a long sacrifice fly. During the rally, manager Walter Alston pinch hits for his second baseman, Don Zimmer. So Jim Gilliam has to be called in from leftfield to play second, while Sandy Amoros is sent into the game to left. In a few moments, that switch will decide the Series.

Martin leads off the Yankee sixth with a walk and Gil McDougald beats out a bunt, only the fourth hit off Podres. Now the Dodger bullpen is up, and Berra, the most dangerous man in the New York lineup, comes to bat. Alston knows that this is the last man Podres can face. Berra swings late and lifts a twisting fly down the leftfield line. Amoros, pulled over into the left-center alley, as Berra is a dead pull-hitter, races desperately

FACT:
Amoros, pulled over into the left-center alley, as Berra is a dead pull-hitter, races desperately across the field, his glove fully outstretched before him. A few strides from the foul line he makes a running grab of the ball.

across the field, his glove fully outstretched before him. A few strides from the foul line he makes a running grab of the ball. It is a catch that would have been impossible for Gilliam, a right-handed thrower.

Amoros recovers his balance and alertly fires the ball to Reese, who relays it to Hodges. McDougald, the tying run, was sure the ball would drop in and makes the turn at second. Reese's relay doubles him up easily. A revived Podres gets Hank Bauer to end the inning with a ground out.

Podres isn't quite home yet. The Yanks put two on in the 8th and he must again face Berra; he gets Yogi on a short fly ball, and then strikes out Bauer. In the 9th, the Yanks go down in order and pandemonium reigns in Brooklyn. For the second year in a row, the Series turns on an incredible catch in the outfield.

The Managers:

Stengel has tasted enough success to be philosophical. He knew that his banged-up team had given everything they could. Mantle was injured and Phil Rizzuto was not the Scooter of former years. He blamed himself for ordering his hitters to take too many pitches from Podres because he felt he could tire out the young left-hander. The Yanks did not have the guns this time in losing the second Series in their last 15 tries.

For Alston, in his second season in the majors, this was almost unreal. He still lived in the same part of rural Ohio in which he had been born, 43 years before. His entire big league experience had been one time at bat with the 1936 Cardinals, in which he struck out. As self-effacing as Dressen was bombastic, he was an odd fit for Brooklyn. But it was the start of a 23-year managing career in which he won more championships than any National League manager in history.

The Heroes:

The year had been disappointing for Podres. In his third season with the Dodgers, the 23-year-old left-hander from upstate New York was supposed to break through and take a place next to Newcombe on the Brooklyn staff. Instead, he had struggled to finish 9-10 and could complete only five games. With a changeup that was already admired as one of the best, he seemed right on the verge of putting his game together. He did, and just in time. This was the first year in which *Sport Magazine* awarded a Corvette to the outstanding player in the Series and Podres drove away in it.

Snider again went on an extra-base explosion. He hit four homers, drove in eight runs and hit .320. His three-run shot over the rightfield screen broke open a one-run game and gave Brooklyn an 8-5 win in game four. He hit two more the next day, the margin of victory in the 5-3 win. He was the first player ever to hit 4 home runs in two different Series.

Ford assumed his position as Chairman of the Board, the man the Yankees wanted out there in the big games. He won the opener and then gave New York its chance with a brilliant four-hitter in game six.

FACT:
Snider again went on an extra-base explosion. He hit four homers, drove in eight runs and hit .320. He was the first player ever to hit 4 home runs in two different Series.

The Zeroes:

It was a bitter experience for Mantle. For the second straight Series, his leg injuries frustrated him, making it impossible for him to run or swing with his customary stride. He only got into parts of 3 games, hit .200, but still managed to swat one home run.

It also was not the best showcase for Robinson. He stole home in the first game, a dramatic dash that cut the Yankees' lead to one run in the 8th inning and almost got Berra ejected from the game because of his protests. (Photographs of the play seemed to indicate that Berra had a strong case.) But he hit only .182 and for the triumphant seventh game he was on the bench.

The Aftermath:

"The trouble with the Yankees," said former pitching star Waite Hoyt after the Series, "is that they don't have enough Yankees." The tremendous bench strength that defined the old New York teams was gone and the injury to Mantle exposed the fact that the talent was thinner than before. Rizzuto retired a few weeks into the 1956 season, cutting the last tie with the prewar Yankee teams. But New York had many years to go before the dynasty would end and this Series was just a glitch.

At the peak of their triumph, the Dodgers, too, were contemplating change. Team owner Walter O'Malley was complaining that Ebbets Field was too small and outmoded. He scheduled several home games in Jersey City and began making demands for a tax abatement to build a new ballpark. But no one seriously believed that anything would come of it. Nothing could possibly take the bloom from this moment in Brooklyn.

Notes:

Snider almost fell victim to the same sort of injury that sidelined Mantle. He stepped in a Yankee Stadium drainage hole in the third inning of game six and had to come out. But he had merely bothered an old high school injury and was back in the lineup the next day.

Newcombe was hammered for six runs in the opener and was not seen again. The Dodgers, instead, went to the rookie Craig in game five and then to seldom-used Karl Spooner, who gave up 5 runs in the first inning of game six and never pitched in the majors again. The tag of being unable to win the big games would haunt Newcombe for the rest of his career.

Line Scores:

Game One, September 28

Bkn (NL)—021 000 020—5
Newcombe L, Bessent (6), Labine (8)

NY (AL)—021 102 00X—6
Ford W, Grim (9) SV

Game Two, September 29

Bkn (NL)—000 110 000—2
Loes L, Bessent (4), Spooner (5), Labine (8)

NY (AL)—000 400 00X—4
Byrne W

Game Three, September 30

NY (AL)—020 000 100—3
Turley L, Morgan (2), Kucks (5), Sturdivant (7)

Bkn (NL)—220 200 20X—8
Podres W

Game Four, October 1

NY (AL)—110 102 000—5
Larsen L, Kucks (5), Coleman (6), Morgan (7), Sturdivant (8)

Bkn (NL)—001 330 10X—8
Erskine, Bessent (4), Labine (5) W

Game Five, October 2

NY (AL)—000 100 110—3
Grim L, Turley (7)

Bkn (NL)—021 010 01X—5
Craig W, Labine (7) SV

Game Six, October 3

Bkn (NL)—000 100 000—1
Spooner L, Meyer (1), Roebuck (7)

NY (AL)—500 000 00X—5
Ford W

Game Seven, October 4

Bkn (NL)—000 101 000—2
Podres W

NY (AL)—000 000 000—0
Byrne L, Grim (6), Turley (8)

1956

New York (AL) 4
Brooklyn (NL) 3

For the first four games, the Series followed the same script as in 1955. The home team won. Then in game five something totally unprecedented and astonishing landed on the Dodgers. Perfection. Afterwards, Brooklyn could never get untracked and the Yankees were champions again.

The Preview:

The Yankees made several adjustments after the shock of 1955. Gil McDougald, who had started and played capably all over the infield, became the regular shortstop. While added defensive responsibilities are supposed to bother most players, he hit .311, the best mark since his rookie year. Bill Skowron was installed as the fulltime first baseman and responded with a .308 season and 90 RBIs. Yogi Berra again was the most dependable of cleanup hitters, with 30 homers and 105 RBIs.

This was also the year that Mickey Mantle became the player the Yankees had dreamed of. Healthy at last, running free, he won the Triple Crown with stats right out of the game's golden age. He hit .353, became the first Yankee since Babe Ruth to clear 50 homers (with 52) and drove in 130 runs. He was in a league by himself, and the Yankees romped in by nine games.

Whitey Ford was on cruise control, going 19-6 and leading the league with a 2.47 ERA. This year the supporting cast got younger. A pair of second-year players gave Ford plenty of help. Johnny Kucks, a 23-year-old from across the river in Hoboken, went 18-9, and 26-year-old Tom Sturdivant was 16-8. In addition, Don Larsen, who was something of a throw-in amid all the bodies in the Bob Turley deal, began experimenting with a no-windup delivery late in the year. It seemed to help his concentration and he went 11-5.

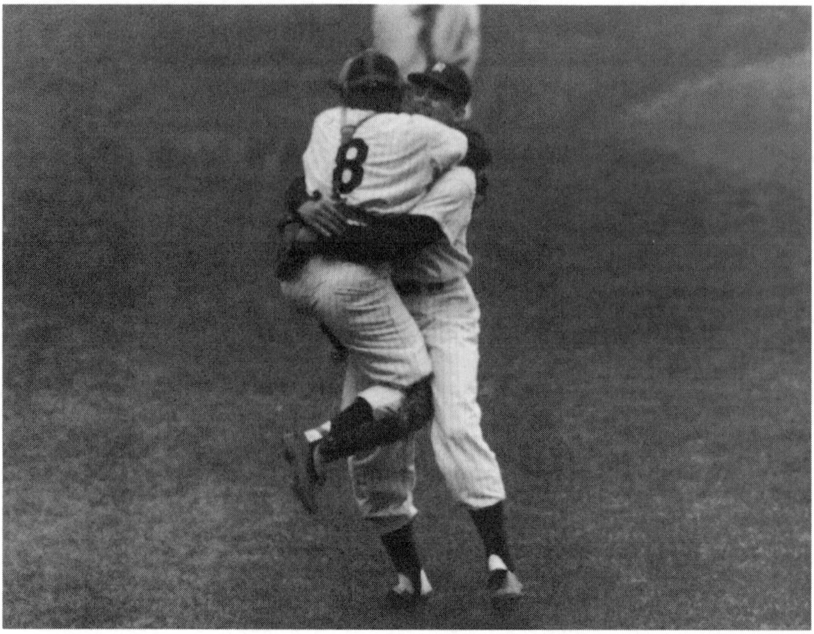

Don Larsen (right) catches Yogi Berra for the celebratory hug after Larsen's perfect game in Game 5. Larsen's gem, the first perfect game in the majors since 1922, followed a disastrous two-inning stint in Game 2.

The Dodgers, meanwhile, were in a struggle for their lives. The Braves pursued them right down to the final weekend and Brooklyn won out by one game, with Cincinnati just a game behind Milwaukee. This edition was not nearly in the class of previous Dodger teams. Snider had another good year, with 43 homers and 101 RBIs, although his average slipped to .292. But Roy Campanella slid to .219 with just 73 RBIs, while Gil Hodges struggled at .265, although coming through with 87 RBIs. Jackie Robinson was now a fill-in, alternating between leftfield and third base. Pee Wee Reese and Carl Furillo, the old campaigners, continued to play well as regulars.

Don Newcombe was the league's dominant pitcher, with a 27-7 record, 18 complete games and a 3.06 ERA, a commendable mark in tiny Ebbets Field. But there was the usual shortage of talent behind him. John Podres was gone to the Army. Carl Erskine struggled at 13-11 and Roger Craig, in his second year, was 12-11. Clem Labine again got plenty of work in relief, with a 10-6 record and 10 saves. The man who saved the Dodgers was their former hated adversary from the Giants, Sal Maglie.

The Barber had been cut loose by New York the previous year, picked up by Cleveland and then dumped again after a bad start in 1956. The Dodgers signed him and Maglie returned to life, revived by the pennant race. He went 13-5 and pitched three wins in the last ten days, including a no-hitter. With Maglie and Newcombe, the Dodgers felt they had a good chance to repeat.

Turning Point: Game Five, Ninth Inning.

If anyone had guessed during warmups which pitcher might be dealing in perfection in this game, the money would have been on Maglie. The 39-year-old veteran with the assassin's demeanor—his pitches cut so close that he was nicknamed "The Barber"—had baffled New York in the opener, outpitching Ford in a 6-3 game. The Yankees felt that he didn't throw nearly as hard as when they had seen him in 1951. But they hadn't faced a smarter pitcher all year. He simply did not make mistakes in the strike zone.

The Dodgers had wiped out a 6-0 New York lead in game two to go two up in the Series, only to see the Yankees draw even behind Ford and Sturdivant in the Stadium. To avoid going back to Brooklyn a game behind, they have to beat Larsen. That doesn't seem like an impossible task. It was Larsen who blew the big lead in game two, driven for cover in the second inning. But he comes out with a live, hopping fast ball in this one, striking out Jim Gilliam and Reese in the first. Reese takes a called third strike on a full count, the only time a Dodger will get to a three-ball count on Larsen all day.

Robinson smashes one off the glove of third baseman Andy Carey to start the second, but McDougald grabs the carom and throws him out. The catlike Robinson of former years would have easily beaten out the hit. The tension starts to build in the fourth. Neither pitcher had allowed a hit, but in the home half of the inning Mantle curls a drive just inside the rightfield foul pole. It is 1-0, Yankees.

In the fifth, Hodges drills one deep into the left center alley, but Mantle outruns it and makes a one-handed, backhanded catch to save the no-hitter. Sandy Amoros then pounds one right down the rightfield line and into the stands. Umpire Ed Runge waves it foul at the last second and another crisis is passed. The Yanks then score another in the sixth on singles by Carey and Hank Bauer to make it 2-0.

Now there are three innings to go and even the Dodger fans are starting to pull for Larsen, because what they are watching is impossible. Bill Bevens of the Yankees had come the closest, taking a no-hitter to two outs in the ninth in 1947 before losing the game. But he was all over the place in that game, walking 10

Dodgers before the hit. There had not been a perfect game in the majors since 1922. Larsen is closing in on one.

Robinson steps out of the batter's box in the eighth, saying there is something in his eye. The crowd starts to boo over this attempt to rattle Larsen. Robinson grins and then bounces one right back to the pitcher. "I didn't care about a perfect anything," he says later. "I was still trying to win the game."

FACT:
"I thought it was outside, but what's the difference," says Mitchell. "I couldn't hit the strikes he threw me anyhow."

Hodges, next up, lines a low dart but Carey grabs it at third on his shoetops. Amoros flies out and now there are three outs to go. There is no sound in the ballpark. Ford, ordered to the bullpen by Casey Stengel just in case, stops throwing to watch the drama.

Furillo goes to a 1-2 count, fouls off two pitches and flies to right. Campanella fouls a pitch then grounds to second. Veteran American Leaguer Dale Mitchell, who has hit against Larsen often, is sent up to bat for Maglie. The air is vibrating. Mitchell takes a ball, then a called strike and misses for strike two. Another pitch and he fouls it off. One more, the 97th of the game, and Mitchell takes it. Umpire Babe Pinelli waves strike three. "I thought it was outside, but what's the difference," says Mitchell. "I couldn't hit the strikes he threw me anyhow."

Berra leaps into Larsen's arms as the Yankees pour out of the dugout in a bellowing mass. They are now up 3-2 in the Series. The Dodgers will score only one more run on seven hits the rest of the way. That is enough to win game six, 1-0, but in the clincher the Yanks smash Newcombe and romp home behind Kucks, 9-0. Larsen's perfect game demoralizes the Dodgers. The Yanks win the last Series these two teams ever will play connected by the subways of New York.

FACT:
Larsen's perfect game demoralizes the Dodgers. The Yanks win the last Series these two teams ever will play connected by the subways of New York.

The Managers:

Casey Stengel's image has subtly changed. He is still known as a brutalizer of the language and a figure of rare comic potential. But now he is also the percentage player who will suddenly be hit by inspiration, do something against the book and, invariably, have it pay off. The Yankee media write about him as if he possesses a sight denied to ordinary mortals; an ability to look down his bench and immediately see who is ready to get a pinch hit. Stengel loves the role.

Alston still has not been certified as a genius. His Series record, after all, is merely 1-1. That will have to wait another three years, at the far end of the continent, when he brings to a championship a team dismissed as an empty shell.

The Heroes:

During spring training, Larsen had been involved in an accident. At 5 a.m., without any warning a utility pole had jumped in front of his car, wrecking it. Stengel was deeply annoyed, but the inability to follow rules was a part of Larsen's makeup. It was one of the reasons the Orioles were ready to deal him to the Yankees and it was why he had been unable to reach his potential. After the perfect game, his no-windup delivery was copied by dozens of pitchers. They overlooked the fact that part of the reason it worked for Larsen was because of the pitcher's size—6-4 and 215 pounds. He didn't need a windup to get his body behind the pitch. Larsen would continue with the Yankees for another three years, and even wound up pitching against them in the 1962 Series. But this season's 11 wins represented a personal high, and he would win a total of just 41 more regular season games.

Labine had started several games early in his career with the Dodgers. Of his 62 appearances this year, only three had been starts. The 30-year-old veteran had been used lightly in the Series, though, and was handed the intimidating task of facing New York the day after Larsen's game. He responded with a 10-inning shutout. The Dodgers scored their only run off Turley when Enos Slaughter, unfamiliar with the late autumn glare in Yankee Stadium's leftfield, let a Robinson liner get over his head for a game-winning hit. Labine's effort enabled the Dodgers to go to the seventh game.

This was Berra's finest Series, as the squat catcher drove in a record 10 runs, with 3 homers, while batting .360. His consecutive two-run homers off Newcombe in the seventh game gave the Yankees a 4-0 lead and all the runs they would need. He also had a grand-slam in a losing cause in game two.

FACT:
This was Berra's finest Series, as the squat catcher drove in a record 10 runs, with 3 homers, while batting .360. His consecutive two-run homers off Newcombe in the seventh game gave the Yankees a 4-0 lead and all the runs they would need.

The Zeroes:

The Dodgers scored 6 runs in one inning in the second game, and then one run in 28 innings over the last three. This stunning reversal by a team that practically defined the power game in the '50s gave Brooklyn no chance. The

Dodgers had hit 23 homers in their last 3 Series. This time they had 3—and none after Snider's three-run shot in the second inning of game two.

Most inept of Brooklyn's hitters was one of the previous year's heroes, Amoros, who was 1 for 19. Jim Gilliam went a feeble 2 for 24.

Despite his 27 wins, Newcombe could not get past the fourth in either of his two starts. He lost them both, gave up 11 runs and 4 homers—three of them by Berra. His performance seemed to sap his confidence. He was traded by the Dodgers in 1958, never pitched in another Series and ended up with a career record of 0-4 in the fall games.

The Aftermath:

The Yanks go rolling merrily along, bring up Tony Kubek, their shortstop of the future and Rookie of the Year in 1957, and swing a trade of prospects to Kansas City for pitching depth. They again had an easy time winning the pennant, despite injuries to Mantle and Ford.

For the Dodgers, change was swift and stunning. They traded Robinson to the Giants in the off-season, and he retired rather than accept exile to his hated opponents. Pee Wee Reese, Campanella and Newcombe were fading. Even the arrival of young pitchers Don Drysdale and Sandy Koufax couldn't arrest the slide to third place. Moreover, the battle between owner Walter O'Malley and Parks Commissioner Robert Moses over a new stadium had passed the point of civility. O'Malley announced that he was moving to Los Angeles and taking the Dodgers with him to California. A stunned New York City watched in disbelief as an era ended in 1957, and baseball's brave new world of big money and small heart was first unveiled.

Notes:

The last Series game ever played in Ebbets Field ended appropriately, on a Jackie Robinson strikeout. For Brooklyn fans, his trade to the Giants was an eerie foreshadowing of the terrible reality that was yet to come, almost a day of civic mourning.

Almost unnoticed in the carnage of game seven was a grand slam homer by Skowron. Hit in the seventh, it accounted for the final runs in the 9-0 slaughter. It was the first time two slams had been hit in the same Series.

Several newsmen noted that they saw spectators at Larsen's perfect game leaving Yankee Stadium in the eighth inning so they could beat the traffic.

Line Scores:

Game One, October 3

NY (AL)—200 100 000—3
Ford L, Kucks (4), Morgan (6), Turley (8)

Bkn (NL)—023 100 00X—6
Maglie W

Game Two, October 5

NY (AL)—150 100 001—8
Larsen, Kucks (2), Byrne (2), Sturdivant (3), Morgan (3) L, Turley (5), McDermott (6)

Bkn (NL)—061 220 02X—13
Newcombe, Roebuck (2), Bessent (3) W

Game Three, October 6

Bkn (NL)—010 001 100—3
Craig L, Labine (7)

NY (AL)—010 003 01X—5
Ford W

Game Four, October 7

Bkn (NL)—000 100 001—2
Erskine L, Roebuck (5), Drysdale (7)

NY (AL)—100 201 20X—6
Sturdivant W

Game Five, October 8

Bkn (NL)—000 000 000—0
Maglie L

NY (AL)—000 101 00X—2
Larsen W

Game Six, October 9

NY (AL)—000 000 000 0—0
Turley L

Bkn (NL)—000 000 000 1—1
Labine W

Game Seven, October 10

NY (AL)—202 100 400—9
Kucks W

Bkn (NL)—000 000 000—0
Newcombe L, Bessent (4), Craig (7), Roebuck (7), Erskine (9)

1957

Milwaukee (NL) 4
New York (AL) 3

The fabled arrogance of the Yankees caught up with them. After a run of eight Series in which they had to travel no further afield than Philadelphia, they arrived in the Midwest and were appalled. Friendly people were holding up signs of welcome. "Bush," snarled the Yankees, and the country rejoiced as the Braves put them away behind three wins by Lew Burdette.

The Preview:

The bedraggled Boston Braves arrived in Milwaukee in 1953 and were immediately swept up in an outpouring of civic pride and love unlike any other franchise in the majors. They drew 2 million people a year. Going to see the Braves became a Wisconsin ritual. The team responded by turning into contenders and, in the fifth year in their new home, broke through to win the pennant.

Enthusiasm helped, of course, but the Braves also had put together a team of tremendous talent. Warren Spahn, the lone holdover from the last Boston winners, was the game's premier pitcher, a savvy craftsman who outwitted most hitters. At 36, he seemed ageless and was in the midst of a run of eight 20-win seasons in nine years. In 1957, he went 21-11, most wins in the league. He also led in complete games and was second in innings pitched. Supplementing Spahn were two right-handers, Bob Buhl (18-7) and Lew Burdette (17-9), while Don McMahon was the bullpen stopper.

The Braves also bristled with power. Rightfielder Henry Aaron, who had won a batting title the previous year, had the first of eight 40-plus home run seasons in his career. He led the league with 44 and also drove in a top figure of 132. Eddie Mathews, the

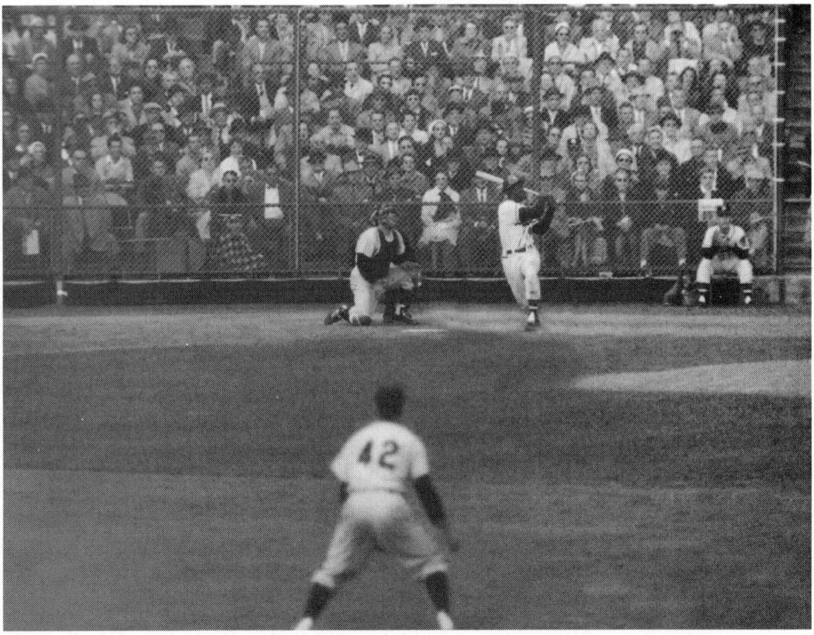

Hank Aaron hits one of his three Series homers. Aaron led all hitters in batting average (.393), hits (11), RBI (7), and homers to complement Lew Burdette's three Series victories.

left-handed complement to Aaron, hit 32 homers and drove in 94 as the regular third baseman. They were also stocked with veterans who had won before. Second baseman Red Schoendienst, picked up in mid-season from the Giants, hit .310, and Andy Pafko, who had played on winners in Chicago and Brooklyn, was a solid bench player. Young Wes Covington, in his second season, socked 21 homers in limited action. Bob Hazle, called up from the minors in August, filled in for injured Billy Bruton and won the nickname Hurricane for his .403 performance down the stretch.

The main addition for the Yankees was rookie Tony Kubek, a Milwaukee native. Switching between short, third and then centerfield when Mickey Mantle was hurt, he hit .297 and was named Rookie of the Year. The main subtraction was Billy Martin. When a group of top New York players got into an unseemly brawl in a nightclub, the Yankees decided that Martin, the least of the stars involved, would have to go. Despite his popularity with Stengel, he was exiled to Kansas City within a few days. His departure gave Kubek and another rookie, Bobby Richardson, the chance to play.

Mantle, although injured, had another superb season, batting .365 with 34 homers and 94 RBIs. The other big hitter was Bill

Skowron, who drove in 88 runs on a .304 average. Yogi Berra had slowed somewhat, with numbers down to 24 homers and 82 RBIs. But it was still a lineup strong enough to lead the league in scoring and batting.

The problem was in the pitching. Ford had arm problems, threw only 129 innings and went 11-5. Tom Sturdivant inherited the lead role on the staff and came through with a 16-6 mark. The most valuable pickup was left-hander Bobby Shantz, a veteran of many dreadul teams with the A's, who went 11-5 and led the league with a 2.45 ERA. Bob Turley was a commendable 13-6 and Bob Grim, now a fulltime reliever, saved 19 games and won 12 more. This was not a vintage Yankee staff, but three of the top four ERAs in the league belonged to its members. At any rate, it was supposed to be good enough to beat the Braves. With Bruton, one of the game's top defensive centerfielders, out of the Series, and Aaron forced to play out of position, no one gave Milwaukee much of a chance.

Turning Point: Game Four, Tenth Inning.

It appears the Yankees haven't lost the touch. Ford wins the opener at the Stadium with an easy five-hitter, 3-1. Burdette, surprisingly, stops them in game two, defeating Shantz, 4-2. When the games move to Milwaukee, the Yanks clobber the Braves before the hometown fans, 12-3, with Kubek rubbing it in by marking his homecoming with two home runs.

In game four, it gets even worse. The Braves build a 4-1 lead for Spahn, marked by Aaron's three run homer in the fourth. Spahn disposes of the first two hitters in the ninth. Then Berra and Gil McDougald poke singles to right and Elston Howard comes to the plate. Skowron is down with a back injury suffered in game one and Howard, who played just 2 games at first base in his entire career, is pressed in as an emergency replacement. That appears to be a prescient move as he shocks the crowd into silence with a three-run homer off Spahn to tie the score, 4-4.

The game goes into the tenth and again Spahn has troubles with two out. Kubek singles and Hank Bauer blasts a triple off the rightfield fence to cash him in. Now the Yanks have a lead for reliever Tommy Byrne, who has retired four Braves without incident, to protect. He can build their advantage in games to a fairly hopeless 3-1.

The Braves are down in bench strength and the best available pinch hitter for Spahn is Vernal "Nippy" Jones. A 32-year-old sub first baseman, he had played with the Cards for several seasons and was used briefly in the 1946 Series. But he hasn't even played in the majors in five years. An injury to regular first baseman Joe Adcock resulted in Jones' callup and because of Bruton's injury he is retained on the Series eligibility list. He batted just 79 times during the season and hit .266.

Tommy Byrne throws a low inside pitch that skips past Berra. Plate umpire Augie Donatelli calls it a ball. But Jones quickly grabs the ball as its rebounds from the backstop and shows Donatelli a black smudge on the surface. It is shoe polish, he says. The umpire examines it carefully and agrees. Jones is waved to first as a hit batsman and the Braves have life. Milwaukee clubhouse man, Charles Blossfield, explains later that he uses polish rather than saddle soap to give the spikes a lustrous shine. Blossfield becomes the unsung hero of the Series.

The New York closer, Grim, comes into the game and Milwaukee sacrifices the runner into tying position. Johnny Logan sends a screeching double into the leftfield corner and the game is tied once more, 5-5. It brings Mathews to the plate with Aaron on deck. Picking his poison, Stengel chooses to pitch to Mathews. He responds with a two-run homer to end the game, 7-5, and pull the Braves into a tie.

The shoe-polish affair turns the Series around. Burdette outduels Ford the next day, 1-0, and after Turley stops them in game six, the Braves call on Burdette again for the closer. Working on two days' rest, he gets his second straight shutout, 5-0, and Bushville wins its championship.

The Managers:

They booed Stengel in Milwaukee. He had refused to pose for pictures with the welcoming committee when the Yankee train arrived and it seemed all a part of that storied New York arrogance. He was second-guessed for pitching to Mathews on the winning homer in game four. He was second-guessed for playing Kubek at third, where he made a costly throwing error in game seven. He shrugged it off. But losing his second Series in three years did make Stengel uncharacteristically grumpy. "I hear that Burdette is supposed to be a funny guy," he said after losing to the Milwaukee pitcher for the third time. "Well, he ain't looked funny to me yet."

Like Stengel, Fred Haney had bounced around for a long time with little respect. He had been a decent third baseman with the Tigers in the 1920s, then was plagued with the manager's job on two horrific teams—the Browns of 1939–41 and the Pirates of 1953–55. He finished last four times. Still, when the Braves decided to let Charlie Grimm go in early 1956, it was Haney they brought in. He drove them to a near-miss second place and one year later won it all. He was now 59, still not secure in the job, and had come under severe criticism for his decision to stick with the faltering Spahn in game four. "If the Braves hadn't come back, it would have meant the end of Haney's career," wrote one national commentator. But they did, and it wasn't.

FACT:
The Series was the first national showcase for Aaron. He responded with 3 homers, 7 RBIs and a .393 average—tops for both teams in all categories.

The Heroes:

Burdette hadn't made much of an impression when he was on the Yankee roster in 1950. "Casey always called me 'Hey, you,'" he said later. He was sent to the Braves in the trade for Johnny Sain the following year. While Sain worked out well in New York, Burdette became one of the Braves top starters, a winner of 179 games for them in 11-plus seasons. He threw a screwball and several varieties of curves, one of which bore a distinct resemblance to a spitball. The Yankees complained repeatedly about it and were convinced that somehow catcher Del Crandall was loading it up for Burdette. But after being shut out for 26 straight innings in his three wins, the Yankees still had no clue.

The Series was the first national showcase for Aaron. He responded with 3 homers, 7 RBIs and a .393 average—tops for both teams in all categories.

While Mathews wasn't as consistent, his homer won the fourth game and his two-run double provided Burdette with the winning margin in the seventh. In addition, he beat out an ordinary grounder to Jerry Coleman at second to start the winning rally off Ford in game five and closed the Series with his stab of Skowron's smash down the line with the bases loaded in the ninth in game seven.

The Zeroes:

Another Series, another injury for Mantle. This time it was a wrenched shoulder. He was 1 for 9 in the last four games and couldn't start in games five and six. Once again his absence was a critical factor in New York's loss.

So was Skowron's back problem, suffered when he tried to move a window air conditioner. A hulking, muscular man, Skowron was tormented throughout his career by nagging injuries. He took the collar in 4 at bats.

Schoendienst also had to leave the Series with a leg strain in game five. His replacement, Felix Mantilla, went 0 for 10.

The Aftermath:

His Series success turned Burdette into a 20-game winner for the first time and the Braves were easy repeaters in 1958. Hurricane Hazle had blown himself out, though, was traded to Detroit in mid-season and was out of baseball by year's end. After the shoe polish game, Nippy Jones never came to bat in the majors again. But every team in both leagues adopted the use of black polish from that time on.

The Yanks also repeated, almost off-handedly. They won by 10 games over Chicago, but with their lowest win total in 12 years. It was a team that seemed to accomplish more than the sum of its parts and most observers felt the end of the dynasty was at hand.

FACT:
The Braves' victory marked the first time the world championship had rested outside of New York City since 1948. The wild civic celebration in Milwaukee brought 750,000 people into the streets, most of them waving banners that paid tribute to "Bushville."

Notes:

The Braves' victory marked the first time the world championship had rested outside of New York City since 1948. The wild civic celebration in Milwaukee brought 750,000 people into the streets, most of them waving banners that paid tribute to "Bushville."

The tides turn quickly. The previous year's hero, Don Larsen, started the deciding game against Burdette and was shelled out in the third inning. Johnny Kucks who had pitched the win in game seven in 1956 appeared in just two-thirds of an inning in relief this year.

Line Scores:

Game One, October 2

Mil (NL)—000 000 100—1
Spahn L, Johnson (6), McMahon (7)

NY (AL)—000 012 00X—3
Ford W

Game Two, October 3

Mil (NL)—011 200 000—4
Burdette W

NY (AL)—011 000 000—2
Shantz L, Ditmar (4), Grim (8)

Game Three, October 5

NY (AL)—302 200 500—12
Turley, Larsen (2) W

Mil (NL)—010 020 000—3
Buhl L, Pizzaro (1), Conley (3), Johnson (5), Trowbridge (7), McMahon (8)

Game Four, October 6

NY (AL)—100 000 003 1—5	Mil (NL)—000 400 000 3—7
Sturdivant, Shantz (5), Kucks (8), Byrne (8), Grim (10) L	Spahn W

Game Five, October 7

NY (AL)—000 000 000—0	Mil (NL)—000 001 00X—1
Ford L, Turley (8)	Burdette W

Game Six, October 9

Mil (NL)—000 010 100—2	NY (AL)—002 000 10X—3
Buhl, Johnson (3) L, McMahon (8)	Turley W

Game Seven, October 10

Mil (NL)—004 000 010—5	NY (AL)—000 000 000—0
Burdette W	Larsen L, Shantz (3), Ditmar (4), Sturdivant (6), Byrne (8)

1958

New York (AL) 4
Milwaukee (NL) 3

Just as it appeared the Braves were about to beat the Yankees twice in a row, and in emphatic fashion, New York found its rudder. Bob Turley took the Yankees on his helm, winning two of the last three games and saving the other. It was only the second time a team had come back from a 3-1 deficit to win the Series.

The Preview:

The Braves won the pennant by exactly the same margin as the year before, 8 games. Little had changed in Milwaukee. Henry Aaron had another year of superlatives, hitting .326 with 30 homers and 95 RBIs. Eddie Mathews and Red Schoendienst both tailed off a little, but centerfielder Billy Bruton was healthy again and hit .280, while catcher Del Crandall put together his best season, with 18 homers and 63 RBIs. Moreover, Wes Covington was a force in leftfield. Limited to just 90 games by injuries, he still hit 24 homers, and his 74 RBIs were just three fewer than Mathews'.

Lew Burdette's performance in the previous Series transformed him into a national figure. He followed up with a 20-10 season, his best in the majors. Warren Spahn had a year of typical excellence, at 22-11. The two men also topped the league in innings pitched. In former years the story of the Braves had been "Spahn, Sain and pray for rain." Now it was "Spahn, Burdette and hope for wet." Arm problems limited Bob Buhl to just 11 appearances and Bob Rush, obtained from the Cubs, was only 10-6. The Braves got some innings out of a group of younger pitchers, but

FACT:
In 1958 the story of the Braves was "Spahn, Burdette and hope for wet."

relied almost totally on their big two, which could be a fatal flaw in the Series.

The Yankees also had their problems with pitching. This was the year Bob Turley finally had the season that was expected of him when he came over from the Orioles. His 21-7 record was the best in the league, as were his 19 complete games. Whitey Ford improved slightly to 14-7, and his miniscule ERA of 2.01 was also the league best. No other Yankee pitcher won in double digits, though. In fact the team's top weapon was reliever Ryne Duren. He came into the game squinting through Coke bottle glasses, terrifyingly wild, one of the most intimidating pitchers who ever lived. He saved 20 games for the Yanks and, somehow, always managed to throw strikes when it mattered.

FACT:
The Yankee's top weapon was reliever Ryne Duren. Squinting through Coke bottle glasses, he saved 20 games for the Yanks and, somehow, always managed to throw strikes when it mattered.

Mickey Mantle slipped a bit from his Olympian standards of the previous two seasons. He hit only .304, but his 42 homers were high in the league and he also drove in 97. Moreover, he was healthy and in the lineup for 150 games, the most important consideration of all. As usual, Yogi Berra was productive with 22 homers and 90 RBIs. Norm Siebern, in his second season, moved into leftfield as a regular and hit .300 and Tony Kubek was solid as the regular shortstop. Otherwise, the cast was pretty much the same. Elston Howard, alternating between catcher and leftfield in a platoon arrangement, was increasingly hard to keep out of the lineup, hitting .314.

For the first time in many years, though, the Yankees were not the oddsmakers' darlings going into the Series. The Braves, it seemed, had enough weapons to fight them off for a second year.

Turning Point: Game Six, 10th Inning.

Four games into the Series and the Yanks are on the brink of elimination. Spahn beats them twice: a 10-inning thriller, 4-3, in the opener, and then a two-hit shutout, 3-0, in game three. Burdette adds another win, although lacking the panache of 1957. He goes the distance, but is touched for all the runs in a rather easy 13-5 game two. The Braves batter Turley, though, with a seven-run first inning. Only Don Larsen can stem the tide, teaming with Duren for a 4-0 blanking in game three.

Then Burdette finally stumbles. Trailing just 1-0 to Turley in the sixth inning of game five, he blows up. Six Yankees score to hand Burdette his first loss after four straight Series wins. Still,

"Bullet" Bob Turley, who had come to the Yankees with fellow Series hero Don Larsen, came up with two clutch wins and a save, collecting 13 strikeouts, as the Yankees added another championship to their vast collection.

the Series returns to Milwaukee for game six, with the Braves needing just one win to put it away.

The Yanks are desperate. They must use their only reliable starter, Ford, on two days' rest after he had pitched seven innings in losing to Spahn in game four. Through his career he is never noted for durability. But Casey Stengel has little choice. He doesn't announce his decision until just before game time, though, as rain wipes out batting practice.

Milwaukee, however, decides to counter with its own ace, Spahn, who also is going on two days' rest. It is a decision that puzzles many commentators. Spahn is 39 and already has worked 19 pressure-filled innings. Moreover, with a game in hand, the Braves can afford to gamble, perhaps with Rush, coming back with a fully rested Spahn, and Burdette waiting in relief, for game seven.

Spahn is quickly touched for a first-inning homer by Hank Bauer, his fourth of the Series. The Braves get it back immediately when Aaron's single drives in a run. And in the second they look ready to break it open. Ford, who is obviously not in form, gives up three straight singles, to Covington, Andy Pafko and Spahn. That brings in a run. When a walk to Schoendienst loads the bases, Stengel can go no farther and calls in Art Ditmar. A spot starter who was just 9-8 during the year, Ditmar had not been used at all in the Series. He must come in now with the game almost out of hand.

Johnny Logan drills a shot to Howard in fairly deep left. The 37-year-old Pafko was not a burner, even when young, but he is sent in by third base coach Billy Herman. Howard cuts him down on a perfect throw to Berra and the rally is over with Milwaukee gaining just a 2-1 advantage.

Ditmar continues to hold off the Braves until the Yanks can break through for the tying run in the sixth, on singles by Mantle and Howard and a sacrifice fly by Berra. Duren then takes over in the 7th and mows Milwaukee down, giving up just one hit, striking out seven and forcing the game into extra innings.

Spahn is visibly tired as the 10th inning begins and Gil McDougald rocks him with a leadoff homer. Still, he stays in and gives up two more singles, to Howard and Berra. Finally, Don McMahon relieves him, only to give up another single to Bill Skowron for a 4-2 New York lead.

Duren, too, is running out of steam. He gets two outs around a walk in the bottom of the 10th, but allows Logan to steal second when he takes a full windup. Aaron then singles him in and it is 4-3. Joe Adcock bounces another single through the middle and the full house goes wild as Aaron races to third. Duren is at the end, his fastball swollen to hittable size. Turley, who had pitched the full nine innings two days before, is called in. Left-hand batting Frank Torre is sent up to pinch hit against him and he lines one towards right. But Milwaukee's cheers die in the throats as McDougald, pulled deep into the hole at second base, grabs it for the out.

The Braves lose the gamble. Spahn is beaten, 4-3, and there will be a seventh game, which must be pitched by Burdette on short rest. Like Spahn, he cannot go the distance and the Yankees gain their revenge.

The Managers:

Reporters reaching Fidel Castro in Cuba after his takeover in 1959 said that one of the first things he asked them was, "Why did Fred Haney pitch Spahn in the sixth game?" It was an excellent question. For the second straight year, the Milwaukee manager miscalculated with his top pitcher at a critical time. In 1957 the Braves saved him by pulling it out with a three-run rally in the 10th; this time there was no such deliverance and Haney would hear the criticism for the rest of his career.

For Stengel this was vindication. He had noted that many of the Braves began acting a bit cocky after taking a 3-1 lead. He angrily drew his team's attention to it, with emotional results. "They got pretty smart, didn't they?" he said amid the jubilation of the winning clubhouse. It was Stengel's seventh championship, tying him with Joe McCarthy for a career record. But it would also be his last.

The Heroes:

Turley had come to the majors with the St. Louis Browns in 1954, hailed as a reborn Bob Feller. Although going just 2-6, he was more publicized than any other young pitcher in the game. Then he led the league in strikeouts the next year after the team moved to Baltimore. But the Orioles needed to rebuild massively to become a contender. When the Yankees offered a carload of prospects to get Turley and Don Larsen, the offer was accepted. Turley won 17 his first season in New York, but then seemed to regress. He won just 21 in his next two years and his control frequently went south on him. But this was the season it came together. With the Series hanging on every game, he was unbeatable. He struck out 10 in a five-hit 7-0 win in game five. He saved game six for Duren. Then, when Larsen faltered in the third inning of game seven, he gave up just 2 hits and 1 run the rest of the way as the Yanks rallied for 4 runs in the eighth and pulled out the game and the Series, 6-2. Skowron's three-run homer off Burdette put it away. That was it for Turley, though. Arm troubles assailed him the next year and he won just 26 more times the rest of his career.

Bauer had made a reputation as one of the game's toughest clutch performers. A Marine who had seen extensive combat in World War II, he was now 36 and reaching the end of the line in New York. Not known as a consistent power hitter, and hitting leadoff for most games, he surprised the Braves by hitting four homers and driving in eight, the highest on either side. He knocked in all the runs in New York's 4-0 win in game three.

Howard, whose defensive skills were supposed to be as a catcher, saved the Series with two big plays in leftfield. His sliding catch of Schoendienst's pop fly with a man on in the sixth inning of game five turned that one around. He doubled up the baserunner and the Yankees, who had led just 1-0, immediately rallied for six runs. Then in the second inning of game seven, he ended a dangerous Milwaukee rally by gunning down Pafko at the plate on a fly ball.

The Zeroes:

It was a complete turnaround for Burdette from 1957. He was touched up for two big rallies by the Yanks in his two losses, giving up 17 runs in just 22 innings.

The Braves used just six pitchers in the seven games, compared to 9 by the Yankees. Buhl and Gene Conley had sore arms and Haney did not trust the rest of his staff. The lack of support forced his overuse of Spahn and Burdette, with negative results.

Kubek also had a reversal of fortune from his triumphant return to his hometown in 1957. He was just 1-for-21 in the Series and made the only two errors committed by the New York infield.

The Aftermath:

Many of the weaknesses that the Yankees revealed during this season returned extensively in 1959. Age and infirmity began exacting their price, and the run of four straight pennants ended. The team dropped all the way to third, a shocking 4 games over .500. It was time to reload and the Yanks did, pulling off one of their best trades to obtain the hitter who would rejuvenate them, Roger Maris.

The Braves also had their problems. Schoendienst, the linchpin of the infield, went down with tuberculosis. That and the familiar lack of pitching depth enabled the Dodgers to catch them in the season's final week, then upset them, two straight, in a playoff. Haney was replaced immediately thereafter.

Notes:

It was a tough Series for Mathews, who struck out 11 times to set a record. But he had competition. Teammate Del Crandall fanned 10 times, which would also have been a new record for a 7-game Series. The Giants' George Kelly had struck out 10 times in 1921, but it took him 8 games to do it.

This was the first time that four straight Series had gone a full seven games. It was also the 10th straight year that one of the Series teams was from New York. Both strings would be broken in 1959. Coincidentally or not, it was also in 1959 that pro football began its rapid ascendance in terms of television audience and began to challenge baseball's long dominance in the critical New York market.

Line Scores:

Game One, October 1

NY (AL)—000 120 000 0—3	Mil (NL)—000 200 010 1—4
Ford, Duren (8) L	Spahn W

Game Two, October 2

NY (AL)—100 100 003—5	Mil (NL)—710 000 23X—13
Turley L, Maas (1), Kucks (1), Dickson (5), Monroe (8)	Burdette W

Game Three, October 4

Mil (NL)—000 000 000—0	NY (AL)—000 020 20X—4
Rush L, McMahon (7)	Larsen W, Duren (8) SV.

Game Four, October 5

Mil (NL)—000 001 110—3	NY (AL)—000 000 000—0
Spahn W	Ford L, Kucks (8), Dickson (9)

Game Five, October 6

Mil (NL)—000 000 000—0	NY (AL)—001 006 00X—7
Burdette L, Pizarro (6), Willey (8)	Turley W

Game Six, October 8

NY (AL)—100 001 000 2—4	Mil (NL)—110 000 000 1—3
Ford, Ditmar (2), Duren (6) W, Turley (10) SV	Spahn L, McMahon (10)

Game Seven, October 9

NY (AL)—020 000 040—6	Mil (NL)—100 001 000—2
Larsen, Turley (3) W	Burdette L, McMahon (9)

1959

Los Angeles (NL) 4
Chicago (AL) 2

The World Series arrived on the West Coast and the largest baseball crowds in history jammed the Los Angeles Coliseum to watch it. Behind the relief pitching of Larry Sherry, the Dodgers won the second championship in franchise history in just their second season in California.

The Preview:

The classic Dodgers of the early '50s were back in Brooklyn. Too many of the greats were gone and those who remained had slipped several notches. But enough remained to sneak up on Milwaukee, force a playoff and end the Braves' two-year lock on the pennant.

There was a familiar ring to the two top hitters. Duke Snider was still the main threat, with a .308 average and 88 RBIs, while Gil Hodges kept plugging along, with a team-high 25 homers and 80 RBIs. The new gun in town was Wally Moon. The outfielder had hit well since coming into the league with St. Louis. But after a subpar 1958 season, the Cards were willing to let him go. He rebounded in Los Angeles. His .302 average coupled with his Moon Shots, wrong field homers over the 250-foot leftfield screen at the Coliseum, made him a devastating weapon. It was also a big season for Charlie Neal, who had joined the club in Brooklyn as Pee Wee Reese's replacement at shortstop. He wasn't cut out to do that, but he settled in as a second baseman. This was his best season, hitting .287 with 83 RBIs.

Don Drysdale had arrived in Brooklyn as a teenager, but he attained star quality when the team moved to his California home. He topped the pitchers at 17-13. There was limited consistency after him. Johnny Podres, pitching in a tough park for

Gil Hodges smashes a game-winning homer in the eighth inning of Game 4, helping the Dodgers to a world title in their World Series debut as representatives of Los Angeles. In his last Series, Hodges hit .391.

lefties, went 14-9, and Roger Craig, another Brooklyn holdover, was a solid 11-5. He fell one inning short of qualifying for the ERA title, which he would have won easily at 2.06. Sandy Koufax received national attention by striking out 18 to tie the record in August. But he had yet to harness his talent with any certainty and was just 8-6 for the year.

The veteran Clem Labine was still regarded as the bullpen stopper. Twenty-four-year-old Larry Sherry arrived during the season and ran up a snappy 7-2 record as a swing man. He only had three saves, but Walter Alston liked his mental toughness. When Sherry pitched seven shutout innings to win the first playoff game at Milwaukee it caught his attention.

While the Dodgers' wait between pennants had been a short one, this Series ended a 40-year drought for the White Sox. The franchise was wrecked by the gambling scandal of the 1919 Series, and only in the '50s did it again become a serious contender. Their former general manager, the innovative Frank Lane, had restructured it for capacious Comiskey Park, emphasizing speed and defense. He promoted the team as The Go-Go Sox. Lane's nonstop dealing kept the team in flux, but by the end of the decade the Sox had assembled a solid core. Nelson Fox was the best second baseman in the league, a great hit and run man on a team that relied on manufacturing runs to win. He hit .306 and knocked in 70 runs on just 2 homers. The main power source was catcher Sherman Lollar, who led the team with 22 homers and 84 RBIs, besides being a top handler of pitchers. The man who put the Go in the Sox, though, was shortstop Luis Aparicio. An outstanding fielder, he teamed with Fox to give Chicago the best middle infield defense in the game. He also stole 56 bases, having led in that category all 4 of his years in the majors. He keyed the Chicago attack as the leadoff man. Longtime Cincinnati slugger Ted Kluszewski joined the team in August and became the starter at first base, hitting .297 down the stretch.

Thirty-nine-year-old Early Wynn seemed to shed the years when he rejoined his old manager, Al Lopez, in Chicago. He led the league with a 22-10 record and pitched more innings than anyone else, too. He even finished third in strikeouts. He was ably assisted by Bob Shaw, carelessly cut loose by Detroit, who developed a devastating slider and went 18-6. Veterans Billy Pierce and Dick Donovan rounded out the starting staff, but both lost more games than they won. Lopez leaned heavily on his relief combination of Gerry Staley and Turk Lown, who saved a combined 29 games and won 17 more.

The Sox, morever, were run by master promoter Bill Veeck. He brought fun and circuses to the South Side and every franchise attendance record was shattered. Chicago won the pennant by 5 games over Cleveland, the former home of Veeck, Lopez and Wynn. That made it an especially sweet season, and the odds favored Chicago to make it even sweeter in the Series.

Turning Point: Game Three, Eighth Inning.

The Sox are supposed to play in the tradition of the franchise's Hitless Wonders of 1906, but Chicago seems determined to bury that canard in this Series. They dismantle the Dodgers in the opener behind Wynn in an 11-0 laugher at jubilant Comiskey. They also jump ahead in game two, but the Dodgers rally behind Podres to carry a 4-2 lead into the seventh. Alston then surprises everyone by choosing Sherry to protect it.

It looks like a shaky decision, as the Sox close to within a run. But a great relay from Moon to shortstop Maury Wills gets the tying run at the plate in the eighth, and from there on Sherry handles the last five hitters for the save.

Now the Series is in California, and a six-inning scoreless duel is engaged by Drysdale and Donovan. The Dodgers finally break through when a single off the screen by Neal and walks to Hodges and Norm Larker load the bases with one out in the seventh. The Sox bring in Staley, and Alston responds with one of his veterans, Carl Furillo. The rifle-armed rightfielder, now 37, is strictly a utility player now but Alston hopes he can come through on memory. Furillo sends an easy hopper to the left side, but Aparicio has trouble seeing it. The bright glare and summer-like background of white shirts stops him for an instant. His hesitation gives the ball just enough room to bounce over his glove for a two-run single and a 2-0 Dodger lead.

The Sox quickly threaten to retaliate. Kluszewski leads off the eighth with a single and Lollar sends a fly to short left. Moon, too, is baffled by the background and can't get to the ball. It falls for a single. This brings Sherry into the game again. The Sox have seen him once and there is the danger they may have measured him. He doesn't help himself by hitting Billy Goodman on a two-strike count to load the bases. But Al Smith bangs into a double play, with a run scoring. Given that reprieve, Sherry gets the final out and then blows away Chicago in the ninth, striking out pinch hitter Norm Cash, Aparicio and Jim Landis.

It is now apparent that Sherry has Chicago's number. He comes in once more the next day in a tied game in the eighth and gets the win when Hodges homers off Staley. Then he closes it out in Chicago when he picks up for Podres in the fourth inning and shuts down the Sox on 5 2/3 innings of shutout relief. It is one of the great pitching performances in Series history. The bright California sun and the smoke from Sherry's hard one turn it around in game three.

The Managers:

This was the Series that convinced the media that Alston knew his stuff. Riding the hot hand with the untested Sherry was the sort of managerial trick that only the certified greats were supposed to handle. He blended a combination of tiring veterans and stars-to-be to steal this title. He was even able to get along with the ego of former Dodger manager Charlie Dressen as a coach.

Lopez had now finished first or second in every season in the majors. Moving to Chicago in 1957 he quickly elevated the Sox into the Yankees' top challengers and made the final breakthrough in three years. But again, with the top prize within his grasp, he is turned away empty. Although he will make other pennant runs, it is his last visit to the Series.

FACT:
Sherry had been regarded as just an average prospect in the rich Dodger farm system. But during the winter of 1958-59, he developed a slider while pitching in a Venezuelan league. The pitch turned him into the rage of California in this Series.

The Heroes:

Sherry had been regarded as just an average prospect in the rich Dodger farm system. But during the winter of 1958–59, he developed a slider while pitching in a Venezuelan league. The pitch turned him into the rage of California in this Series. Born with a weakness in his legs, he was forced to wear braces for much of his childhood. Now he stood at the peak of L.A. celebrity. While Sherry became a good reliever with the Dodgers and Detroit, and racked up 82 career saves, he never again was the sort of pitcher who controlled the 1959 Series.

It had been a long wait for Kluszewski and he took advantage of it. The muscular first-baseman, a former football star at Indiana, hit 3 homers and led both teams with 10 RBIs.

It was also a notable Series for Chuck Essegian, who once played football for Stanford. The utility man hit two pinch homers, the first time that had been done in the Series. The first one touched off the winning rally off Shaw in game two. Essegian became the second athlete to play in both the Rose Bowl and the World Series—the other being Jackie Jensen, of California and the 1950 Yankees.

The onetime center of the Brooklyn batting order—Snider, Hodges and Furillo—only saw limited duty. Hodges hit .391 and all three of them got hits that either won games or put Los Angeles into the lead. None of them ever played in another Series.

The Zeroes:

Wynn's right elbow stiffened in the eighth inning of his opening game shutout. He tried to start twice more and gave up nine runs in 13 innings, losing the closer.

Chicago's Go-Go went-went in this Series. Their 113 steals (a total that would be eclipsed by individual players in a few years) had made them the talk of the game and they were expected to run wild on young L.A. catcher John Roseboro. Instead, he nailed three of them in game three and the Sox stole only twice, a major handicap for their weak batting attack.

The Coliseum was castigated as the worst ballpark ever to host a Series. Lopez called it "a freak park," with its cavernous rightfield and "The Thing," the screen that sat just 250 feet away in left. So many routine flies caromed off the screen that games here were referred to as Screeno. "If I managed here," said Donovan, "I'd play eight men and an ape to climb the screen." It would be home for the Dodgers for just two more seasons, until the stadium at Chavez Ravine was completed.

FACT:
The Coliseum was castigated as the worst ballpark ever to host a Series. Lopez called it "a freak park," with its cavernous rightfield and "The Thing," the screen that sat just 250 feet away in left. So many routine flies caromed off the screen that games here were referred to as Screeno.

The Aftermath:

The old Dodgers finally slowed up in 1960 and the team fell to fourth. But within two years, a team built around the speed of Wills and the pitching of Drysdale and Koufax was storming the gates as the franchise once again dominated the league.

The White Sox thought they were answering their biggest problem in obtaining sluggers Roy Sievers and Gene Freese for the team in 1960. Instead, they slowed up the running attack and the pitching fell off sharply. Chicago dropped to third and has yet to win another pennant, thus joining its uptown rivals, the Cubs, as the two franchises that have been away from the Series for the longest time.

Notes:

Los Angeles made Series attendance records on three successive dates, with the game five turnout of 92,706 setting the mark that still stands. Unless another team decides to play in a football stadium, it is unlikely ever to be broken.

The payout of $11,231 exceeded the previous high, set in 1954 by Cleveland and New York, by $113 per man.

Line Scores:

Game One, October 1

LA (NL)—000 000 000—0
Craig L, Churn (3), Labine (4), Koufax (5), Klippstein (7)

Chi (AL)—207 200 00X—11
Wynn W, Staley (8)

Game Two, October 2

LA (NL)—000 010 300—4
Podres W, Sherry (7) SV

Chi (AL)—200 000 010—3
Shaw L, Lown (7)

Game Three, October 4

Chi (AL)—000 000 010—1
Donovan L, Staley (7)

LA (NL)—000 000 21X—3
Drysdale W, Sherry (8) SV

Game Four, October 5

Chi (AL)—000 000 400—4
Wynn, Lown (3), Pierce (4), Staley (7) L

LA (NL)—004 000 01X—5
Craig, Sherry (8) W

Game Five, October 6

Chi (AL)—000 100 000—1
Shaw W, Pierce (8), Donovan (8) SV

LA (NL)—000 000 000—0
Koufax L, Williams (8)

Game Six, October 8

LA (NL)—002 600 001—9
Podres, Sherry (4) W

Chi (AL)—000 300 000—3
Wynn L, Donovan (4), Lown (4), Staley (5), Pierce (8), Moore (9)

1960

Pittsburgh (NL) 4
New York (AL) 3

In the strangest Series ever played, the Yankees absolutely annihilated Pittsburgh in three games and outscored the Pirates by a two-to-one margin. But New York lost, improbably, when the seventh game turned on a bad hop and ended, for the first time in history, on a home run.

The Preview:

It had been a long haul for the Pirates. One of the league's premier franchises in the century's early years, they had not won a pennant in 33 seasons. They were a doormat through the '50s. Branch Rickey, who had rebuilt dormant teams in St. Louis and Brooklyn, came to Pittsburgh in the early '50s and tried to pump some life into the franchise. He traded away the team's handful of stars, concentrating on young players, but was replaced before his efforts started paying off.

One of his first successes, however, was an outfielder taken from the Brooklyn system, Roberto Clemente. He reached Pittsburgh in 1955 and after five seasons of finding the range burst out in 1960 as a top hitter. He finished at .314 with 94 RBIs. Dick Groat, a basketball star at Duke, returned to his hometown to become the starting shortstop. He won the batting title in 1960, at .325, and gave the Pirates field leadership. Another key ingredient was Bill Mazeroski, who had become the best defensive second baseman in the league and displayed occasional power.

The Pirates had no big power hitter, although first baseman Dick Stuart almost made up for his appalling deficiencies in the field with 23 homers. He shared the position with Rocky Nelson, and the two of them accounted for 118 RBIs. The Pirates also

Bobby Richardson pounded Pirate pitchers for a .367 average (on 11 hits), two doubles, two triples, one homer, a record 12 RBI, and the Series MVP award . . . all in a losing effort.

profited by the platooning of catchers Smokey Burgess and Hal Smith, which produced 84 RBIs and a .294 average.

Pitching was in the hands of two steady, right-handed starters. Vern Law (20-9) and Bob Friend (18-12) gave the staff stability, and behind them were Wilmer Mizell (13-5) and Harvey Haddix (11-10). The league's busiest reliever was Roy Face, who saved 24 games and won 10 more in 68 appearances. The Pirates won the pennant by seven games and were the popular favorites entering the Series, but they were facing a reconstituted Yankee team.

New York had swung a typical deal in the off-season, prying power hitter Roger Maris loose from Kansas City (which functioned as little more than a holding tank for New York's future stars and its castoffs). The Yankees gave up a gang of players to get him, the best of which was Norm Siebern. But the short rightfield in Yankee Stadium was made for Maris and he led the league with 112 RBIs on 39 homers, while being voted MVP. The A's finished last.

Mickey Mantle was the only American League hitter with more homers than Maris, hitting 40. Bill Skowron also had a productive season, topping the team with a .309 average on 91 RBIs. Yogi Berra was now a part-timer, but still dangerous, with 15 homers and 62 RBIs.

Once more, however, there was a shortage of consistent pitching. Art Ditmar, who had emerged from the shadows in the 1958 Series, had the best mark on the team at 15-9. But he overpowered no one and when his control was slightly off, his stays were short. Whitey Ford was only 12-9, his weakest season since coming to the majors. The old campaigner Bob Turley saw limited duty with a 9-3 year and the top man out of the bullpen was Bobby Shantz, with 11 saves. But he relied on guile and was hardly in the flame-thrower mode of his predecessor, Ryne Duren. Duren faded badly, however, as he struggled with alcoholism. It was a Yankee team with profound weaknesses, but was still the top-heavy favorite in the Series.

Turning Point: Seventh Game, Eighth Inning.

No one has seen anything quite like this Series. The Pirates keep getting stomped, losing by scores of 16-3, 10-0 and 12-0, the latter two are shutouts by Ford. Bobby Richardson, who drove in just 26 runs all season, is shattering the Series RBI mark with 12. And yet the Pirates force a seventh game. Law gives them two strong starts and Haddix another, and it is enough to tie the Series.

Law is going again in the seventh game at Forbes Field and Turley, who knows all about seventh game pressure and pitched strongly in the 16-3 explosion, will face him. It is soon apparent that Turley is not in a groove. Nelson hits a two-run homer in the first and Jim Stafford replaces the starter in the second. He gives up two more and Pittsburgh is off to a 4-0 lead.

The Yanks are only waiting to pounce. Skowron finally reaches Law for a homer in the fifth. Then, in the sixth, the tiring starter puts the first two men on base. Face, who has saved all three Pittsburgh wins, is called in to try and go the distance one more time. But he isn't up to it. A run-scoring single and then a three-run homer by Berra put the Yankees out in front, 5-4.

They seem to wrap it up against Face in the eighth, when two more come in on a walk, two singles and a Clete Boyer double. Shantz has shut down the Pirates on one hit since entering the game in the third, and the bullpen is ready as the Pirates come to bat. Pinch hitter Gino Cimoli stirs the crowd with a leadoff single.

Then comes one of those inexplicable events on which ballgames and careers suddenly turn. Bill Virdon sends a grounder to short. At first, it seems that Tony Kubek will field it and start a possible double play. But at the last instant the ball strikes a pebble and takes a sharp bounce up, catching Kubek in the throat. He goes down in agonizing pain, both runners are safe and the tying run is now at bat. It turns out to be the most significant bad hop since 1924, when two such erratic grounders tied and then won the Series for Washington. Kubek has to leave the game.

Groat follows with a third single. That does it for Shantz. Jim Coates, a 13-3 pitcher during the year and Stengel's top right-handed choice out of the pen, takes over. Coates gets the first two hitters he faces, but Clemente beats out a roller down the first-base line. Now it is 7-6 for the Yankees. Hal Smith, who usually plays only against left-handers, is the next hitter. His platoon partner, Burgess, already left the game while Shantz was in. Smith is another ex-Kansas City player, but he had somehow eluded the Yankee talent scouts. The 29-year-old catcher, in his first year with the Pirates, is almost about to become one of the biggest heroes in Series history. He belts Coates' delivery over the leftfield wall for a three-run homer, and Pittsburgh is back in front 9-7. As events play themselves out, Smith's dramatic drive becomes merely a footnote.

FACT:
Game seven featured the most significant bad hop since the 1924 Series; a dramatic bottom of the eighth home run that put the Pirates ahead 9-7; a two-run rally by the Yankees in the top of the ninth keyed by Mantle's alert baserunning; and Mazerowski's series-winning home run in the bottom of the ninth.

Friend cannot hold the Yankees in the ninth. Singles by Richardson and pinch hitter Dale Long put two runners on with the middle of the Yankee lineup coming up. The Pirates bring in Haddix to deal with it. He gets Maris, but Mantle sends a long RBI single to right center, and the tying run moves to third. Then comes another of this game's remarkable plays. Berra shoots a hard grounder to Nelson at first He steps on the bag and throws to second, hoping to complete the double play before the tying run comes in. But Mantle, sizing up the situation, feints toward second and quickly dives back safely to first; the force play was negated when Nelson retired the batter. The run scores unchallenged and it is now 9-9. Haddix gets the next out and the game goes to the last of the ninth.

Ralph Terry entered the game in the eighth to close that inning. The leadoff batter is Mazeroski. Terry's second pitch is a high fastball, and Mazeroski sends all of Pittsburgh into orbit with a home run over the leftfield wall. In one of the most dramatic conclusions of a seventh game, the Pirates prevail. But without the bad hop to Kubek, it could have been just another Yankee romp.

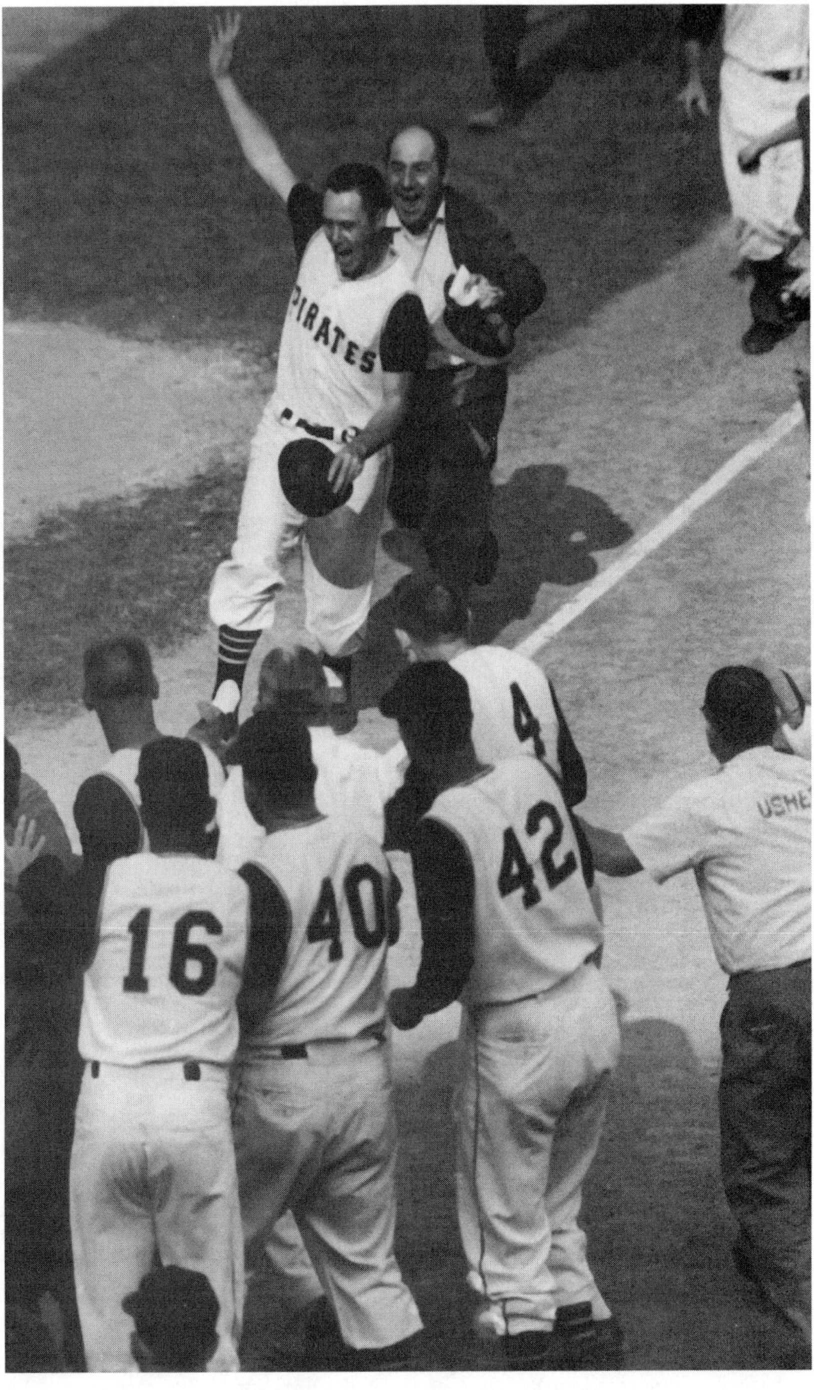

Bill Mazeroski rounds third and picks his way through jubilant fans toward home after his ninth-inning homer ends the Series and renders Richardson's heroics meaningless. This is the first time the Series is ended by a home run.

The Managers:

Danny Murtaugh had kicked around the majors during the 1940s as a second baseman with the Phillies and Pirates. The team's new general manager, Joe L. Brown (son of the famous comedian, Joe E., a big fan who made several movies with a baseball theme), got to know him then and as the Pirates struggled in the cellar late in 1957 called him up to the big team. Murtaugh actually got them to play over .500 the rest of the way and the next year brought them in an astonishing second. He was now 42, an enormously popular figure in Pittsburgh and regarded as a low-key operator who knows how to coax the most from limited talent.

The 70-year-old Stengel is operating under a win-or-else directive. The New York ownership suspects that he is too old for the job, that the game is passing him by. Younger players report in amusement that he sometimes takes cat naps on the bench and the coaches are effectively running the team. When New York falters in this peculiar Series, despite the obvious edge in personnel, the Yankees lower the ax. The protests over Stengel's dismissal are just as outraged as those that greeted his hiring 12 years before. But he is unemployed for just a year. The expansion New York Mets hire him in 1962 to preside over their inept collection of ballplayers in one of the most colorful episodes of baseball history in the big city.

The Heroes:

Mazeroski was in his fifth season with Pittsburgh. He would stay for 12 more, long enough to get into the 1971 Series as a utility man. He already was noted for his dependability, primarily as a defensive asset, but was not much more than a number eight hitter in the lineup. That never changed. Unlike some Series heroes who seem to gain momentum from their achievements before a national audience, Mazeroski went on just about as he was. He never hit more than 19 homers in a year, never hit higher than .283 and never faltered in the field. He actually was one of Pittsburgh's top hitters in the Series, with a .320 average and a team-high 5 RBIs. His earlier home run helped the Pirates break open a one-run game in their 6-4 win in the opener. But the one he hit in the closer made him a shining name in Pittsburgh.

There was nothing in Richardson's past that suggested this kind of Series explosion. He had gone hitless in two previous years as a sub and was 0 for 4 in the opener. But for the rest of the 1960 Series, the New York second baseman was 11 for 26. He hit a grand slam in game three and a record six RBIs for the game.

Although Richardson drove off with the top player award, he had plenty of rivals on the Yankees. Mantle shattered the old RBI record with 11. Skowron had 12 hits. Elston Howard hit .462. Ford pitched two complete game shutouts.

The Zeroes:

Pittsburgh's pitching was in shambles as the Series ended. Starters Friend and Mizell were battered for 14 runs in a combined 8 1/3 innings. Even Face, who managed to save 3 of the games, wound up with a 5.23 ERA. All 4 wins were accumulated by Law and Haddix, the only stable forces amid the carnage.

It was also a terrible comedown for Ditmar, New York's top winner during the season. He couldn't get past the second inning in either of his two starts.

Every Yankee regular hit over .300 for the Series, except for Maris and Gil McDougald, who was so embarrassed that he retired right afterwards. Also feeling poorly was third baseman Boyer. He started his first Series game in the opener, but Stengel pinch hit for him in the 2nd inning, before he could bat even once. Boyer didn't get another start until game six.

The Aftermath:

The Yankees were furious over this lapse. They felt the Series had been stolen from them by a vastly inferior team and the search for a scapegoat settled on Stengel. He was criticized for using Coates and Terry instead of Duren, who had pitched effectively in two earlier stints, when the final game was on the line. His choice of Ditmar rather than Ford in the opener was also questioned. Stengel was unceremoniously dumped and replaced by former bullpen catcher Ralph Houk, who won his first pennant right out of the chute.

An arm injury to Law and dreadful years by Friend and Mizell were more than Pittsburgh could overcome. The Pirates fell all the way back to sixth place in 1961 and made only one more meaningful challenge for the pennant during the '60s. It would take 11 years to assemble the parts for another winner.

Notes:

Pittsburgh's horrendous 7.11 team ERA was the worst compiled by any team since the 1932 Cubs. During their thrashing by the Yankees, in which they were swept, Cubs pitchers were scored upon at a rate of 9.26. The Yanks also shattered the old record for team

FACT:
Pittsburgh's horrendous 7.11 team ERA was the worst compiled by any team in the Series since the 1932 Cubs.

batting average. Their mark of .338 was 22 points higher than what the A's achieved against the Cubs in 1910.

Even with all the dramatics and pitching changes in the final game, total playing time was only two hours and 36 minutes.

Forbes Field had opened just in time for the 1909 Series. This was the last one that would be played there.

Line Scores:

Game One, October 5

NY (AL)—100 100 002—4
Ditmar L, Coates (1), Maas (5), Duren (7)

Pit (NL)—300 201 00X—6
Law W, Face (8) SV

Game Two, October 6

NY (AL)—002 127 301—16
Turley W, Shantz (9)

Pit (NL)—000 100 002—3
Friend L, Green (5), Labine (6), Witt (6), Gibbon (7), Cheney (9)

Game Three, October 8

Pit (NL)—000 000 000—0
Mizell L, Labine (1), Green (1), Witt (4), Cheney (6), Gibbon (8)

NY (AL)—600 400 00X—10
Ford W

Game Four, October 9

Pit (NL)—000 030 000—3
Law W, Face (7) SV

NY (AL)—000 100 100—2
Terry L, Shantz (7), Coates (8)

Game Five, October 10

Pit (NL)—031 000 001—5
Haddix W, Face (7) SV

NY (AL)—011 000 000—2
Ditmar L, Arroyo (2), Stafford (3), Duren (8)

Game Six, October 12

NY (AL)—015 002 220—-12
Ford W

Pit (NL)—000 000 000—0
Friend L, Cheney (3), Mizell (4), Green (6), Labine (6), Witt (9)

Game Seven, October 13

NY (AL)—000 014 022—9
Turley, Stafford (2), Shantz (3), Coates (8), Terry (9) L

Pit (NL)—220 000 051—10
Law, Face (6), Friend (9), Haddix (9) W

1961

New York (AL) 4
Cincinnati (NL) 1

For the first time in 11 years, the Yankees made hash out of a National League opponent. With Whitey Ford at the peak of his game and the lineup loaded with power, New York has very little problem with the Reds.

The Preview:

Just as Pittsburgh ended its 33-year pennant wait in 1960, the Reds, who were next in line at 21 years, came through this year. They had power-laden teams in the mid-'50s, but the Reds were chronically short of pitching. They hadn't had a 20-game winner in 14 years. Many times they had trouble finding a 13-game winner.

The Reds got back to the top by assembling their best pitching staff since the early '40s, and combining it with just enough hitting to get by. Joey Jay, a pickup from the Braves and the first Little Leaguer to make it to the bigs, led the team with a 21-10 mark. Behind him was Jim O'Toole, the top lefty on the staff, at 19-9. In addition, there was Bob Purkey, who had come over from Pittsburgh three years before, at 16-12. That was the best three-man rotation in the league and the Reds backed it up with a bullpen that saved 32 games. The righty-lefty combination of Jim Brosnan and Bill Henry got 16 apiece.

The top hitters were outfield partners Frank Robinson and Vada Pinson. A top star since setting a record for rookie home runs (38) five years before, Robinson had his best all-around season. He hit .323 with 37 homers and 124 RBIs, among the leaders in all categories. The speedy Pinson, in his third full year, was runner-up in hitting at .342 and added 87 RBIs. The infield corners, first baseman Gordy Coleman and third baseman Gene Freese, mirrored one another with 26 homers and 87 RBIs apiece.

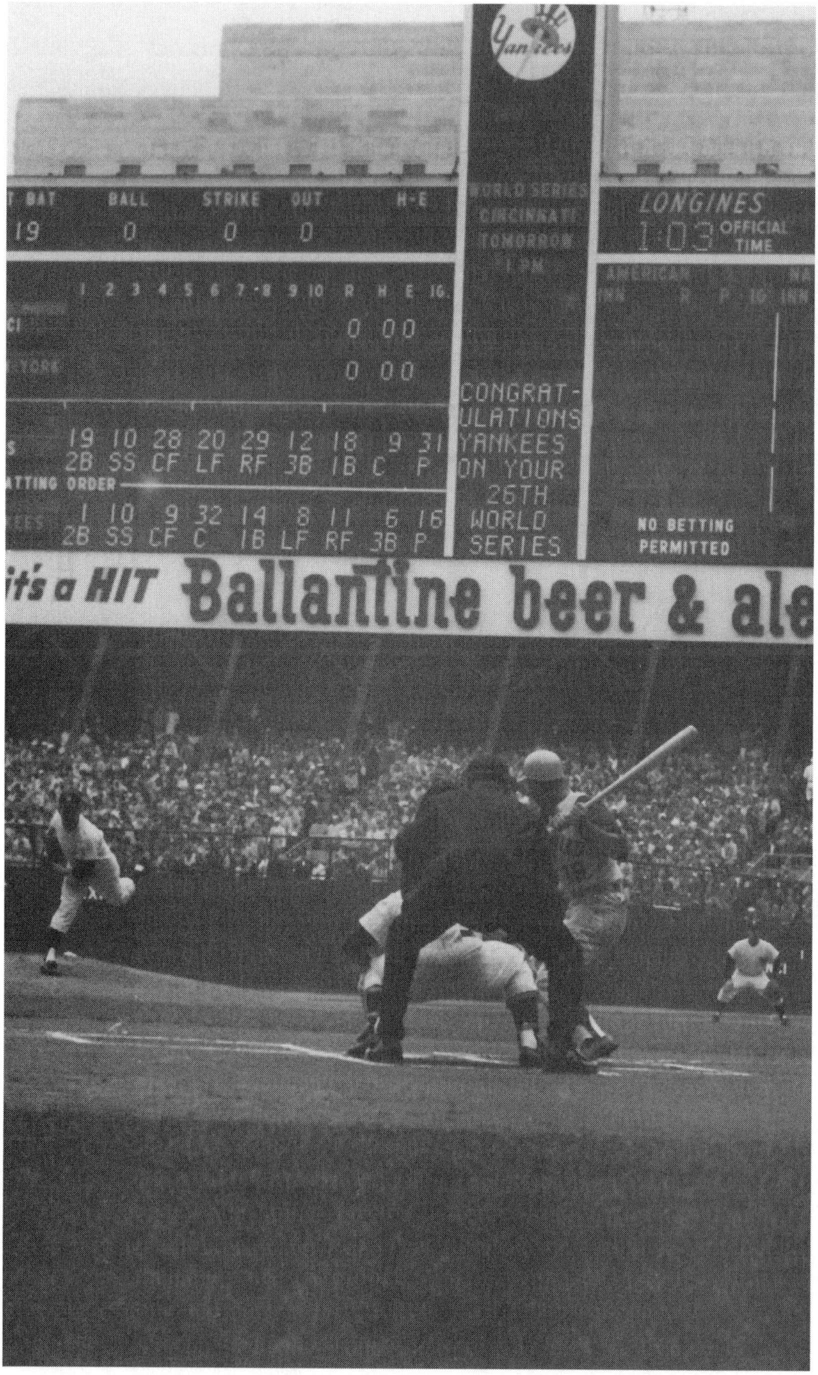

Whitey Ford delivers the first pitch of the 1961 World Series. Ford solidified his postseason dominance by breaking Babe Ruth's record for consecutive shutout innings with two shutout wins on a combined six hits (following two shutouts in 1960).

The outfield platoon of Wally Post and Gus Bell added 90 RBIs. But the key positions of shortstop and catcher were problem areas all season, not good news for a Series team.

This was the first expansion year in the American League, with new franchises created in Los Angeles and Washington. The resulting dilution of pitching depth made 1961 a hitter's holiday and no team took advantage of it more fully than the Yankees. They won 109 games, just one less than the fabled 1927 squad. They were, in fact, more murderous than the old Murderers Row, with a record 240 home runs. Almost half of them were hit by just two men. Roger Maris broke Babe Ruth's one-season mark with 61 (albeit in a schedule that was 8 games longer), and Mickey Mantle added 54. There had never been a one-two punch like this. The power didn't stop there. Bill Skowron hit 28. Yogi Berra, now permanantly assigned to leftfield, added 22, and catcher Elston Howard had 21 on a .348 average. Even sub Johnny Blanchard hit 21 in just 243 at bats.

The pitching staff featured Ford in his peak year, with a 25-4 record. More unusual, he also led the league in innings pitched. Behind him was Ralph Terry, recovered from giving up the winning homer in the previous Series, at 16-3. Bill Stafford, in his first full season, was 14-9. In addition, the Yanks had come up with a left-handed screwballer, Luis Arroyo. He had kicked around the National League with limited success for several years. But his big pitch made him almost unhittable, at least for this season, in relief. Arroyo went 15-5 and saved a league high 29 games. The Yanks put away the Tigers with a September spurt and won by eight games. But in the final weeks, Mantle went down with yet another leg injury and had surgery to remove an abcess. In former years, a Yankee team without Mantle usually ran into trouble. Still, they were prohibitive betting favorites.

Turning Point: Game Three, Ninth Inning.

The opener goes right according to script. Ford pitches a 2-hit shutout, his third straight in the Series, and the Yanks score on homers by Howard and Skowron to win 2-0. But Jay stops them in game two, 6-2, with the Yankee runs again coming by way of the home run, a two-run shot by Berra. Now the Series is back in Cincinnati and the Reds will have to contain the New York power in tiny Crosley Field.

Purkey does a great job of it. Even with Mantle in the lineup for the first time, the Yanks cannot do much with his knucklers. Purkey gives up just one hit in the first 6 innings, protecting a 1-0 lead garnered for him in the third: Elio Chacon, a sub second baseman, beats out a bunt, goes to second on a wild throw and scores on Robinson's two-out double.

In the seventh, though, Tony Kubek singles, moves up on a passed ball and scores on a bloop single by Berra. The Reds move right back out in front, though, on a double by John Edwards and a two-out single by Eddie Kasko. Purkey gets the first two outs in the eighth easily and Blanchard comes up as a pinch hitter. He has gone 0 for 5 in the Series, starting game two in place of the injured Mantle. This time he blasts one into the rightfield stands and just like that it is tied once more.

Arroyo comes in as the reliever and sits the Reds down in order to send the game into the ninth. Leading off against Purkey is Maris. The season has turned into a nightmare for the 27-year-old slugger. A media assault unlike anything ever seen in sports is unleashed on him in September as he chases The Babe for the home run record. His hair starts falling out. Usually a polite if quiet man, Maris, who grew up in North Dakota, far from crowds that were madding or otherwise, becomes surly and uncommunicative. He is hitless in 10 at bats in this Series and the national media scoffs at this pretender to the great Ruth's title. Purkey, behind 2-1 in the count, comes inside with a low fastball. Maris pulls it into the rightfield seats, to the stunned silence of the sell-out Cincinnati crowd.

It is Maris' only homer of the Series, one of just two hits he will get overall. But it is all Arroyo needs. He has to make a tough play, knocking down Bell's smash to the mound with a runner on second and two out, to close it out. The Yanks win 3-2 to take control of the Series. The Reds are thoroughly demoralized. They gave up just 12 hits in their two losses, but 4 of them were home runs and they make the difference. "You can't make a mistake against anybody," moaned reserve Dick Gernert after this game. The Yanks win the next two in routs and it is all over.

The Managers:

Ralph Houk is billed as a player's manager. It was an indirect slap at his predecessor, Casey Stengel, who presumably was unable to communicate well with men who were 45 years his junior. The Major, a tough veteran of World War II, spoke their language. A catcher who had the bad luck to come to the Yankees at the same time as Yogi Berra, Houk spent his entire career in the bullpen. He got to bat only 158 times in seven seasons, but cashed lots of World Series checks. This one was the sweetest.

Fred Hutchinson had been known as a terrible-tempered competitor when he pitched for the Tigers. It is said of

Hutchinson that after being taken out of a game, you could follow his trail to the clubhouse by the smashed lightbulbs in the dugout tunnel. He transferred much of that intense attitude to his ballclub and became an enormously popular figure in Cincinnati. This was his only winner, but the city still gives out an annual award named in his honor to a local sports figure.

The Heroes:

Ford also drew a bead on one of Babe Ruth's most enduring records. While Maris hit his 61 homers during the season, Ford pitched his 30 innings during the Series. The string of consecutive shutout innings broke the mark Ruth had established with the Red Sox in 1916 and 1918. Ford began the skein with two shutouts of Pittsburgh in 1960. He won this opener, 2-0, and in the third inning of game four broke the record. He had to leave in the sixth after injuring an ankle, but the Yanks already had a four-run lead, which they built on to win 7-0. His record of 32 innings was extended by 1 2/3 in 1962 before the Giants broke through on him with a squeeze bunt.

FACT:
In the same year Babe Ruth's season record of 60 homers was topped, Whitey Ford pitched 30 scoreless innings in the Series, a streak that surpassed the one Ruth established in the 1916 Series—a record that meant more to Ruth than all his hitting marks.

While hitting lots of homers, the Yankees actually considered themselves to be in a bit of a slump. They batted only .255 for the Series. The exception was Blanchard. The 28-year-old sub catcher had his best season. His .305 average was 50 points more than he ever hit again. A Yankee to his fingertips, he breaks down and cries when he is traded in 1965. This is his finest hour, as he bats .400, with homers in consecutive times at bat in the third and fifth games. His two-run shot in the first inning of the closer touched off a five-run rally that ended the contest early.

For the second year in a row, Bobby Richardson rose to another level in the Series. Just a .261 hitter during the season, and somewhat lost among the behemoths around him, the second baseman led everyone with 9 hits and hit .391.

FACT:
For the second year in a row, Bobby Richardson rose to another level in the Series. Just a .261 hitter during the season, he led the Series with 9 hits and batted .391.

The Zeroes:

It was a tribute to the depth and quality of this Yankee team that Mantle was hardly even missed. He got to bat just six times, got one hit, and caught just one fly ball. The injury took 54 homers out of the New York lineup, a devastating loss to most teams. It was barely a blip to the Yanks.

While none of the Reds had an especially good Series, it was as if Freese and Pinson hardly showed up. They were a combined 3-for-38. The power loss was especially acute in Pinson's case. He was the team's top running threat and the Reds could not steal a base in the Series. Moreover, he hit right ahead of Robinson and set him up for RBIs. But Pinson did not score a run in the Series.

The Aftermath:

While home run production dwindled somewhat and the pitching wasn't quite as deep, the Yankees still managed to build their current run to three straight pennants in 1962—the sixth time in franchise history New York had turned that trick.

The Reds, by some measures, were even stronger in 1962, winning five more games than the previous year's winners. But they fell back to third place, as expansion and its consequent hitting explosion reached the National League. They would not win again until a rebuilt machine propelled them to the pennant nine years later.

Notes:

The Yankees were so confident about wrapping up the Series that coach Frank Crosetti drove his car from New York to Cincinnati to get a head start on his homeward trip to California.

Ford was given a special day at Yankee Stadium in September and presented with a new car by appreciative fans. Then he won the Corvette as the most outstanding player in the Series. "Maybe I'll start a livery service," he said.

Ruth often remarked that the Series shutout record meant more to him than any of his hitting marks. But when Ford broke it at the end of the third inning of game five, Crosetti had to rescue the ball he used from Cincinnati pitcher O'Toole. The Yankees had just tossed it to the pitching mound, as they would at the end of any other inning.

Line Scores:

Game One, October 4

Cin (NL)—000 000 000—0	NY (AL)—000 101 00X—2
O'Toole L, Brosnan (8)	Ford W

Game Two, October 5

Cin (NL)—000 211 020—6	NY (AL)—000 200 000—2
Jay W	Terry L, Arroyo (8)

Game Three, October 7

NY (AL)—000 000 111—3	Cin (NL)—001 000 100—2
Stafford, Daley (7), Arroyo (8) W	Purkey L

Game Four, October 8

NY (AL)—000 112 300—7	Cin (NL)—000 000 000—0
Ford W, Coates (6) SV	O'Toole L, Brosnan (6), Henry (9)

Game Five, October 9

NY (AL)—510 502 000—13	Cin (NL)—003 020 000—5
Terry, Daley (3) W	Jay L, Maloney (1), Johnson (2), Henry (3), Jones (4), Purkey (5), Brosnan (7), Hunt (9)

1962

New York (AL) 4
San Francisco (NL) 3

Once the teams shared the same ballpark. Now they were a continent apart, playing in the first bicoastal World Series. After a three-day rain delay, the longest in 51 years, the Yankees concluded their fifth straight Series defeat of the Giants in a tough, well-played set of games. It was the first Series since 1909 in which the teams alternated wins throughout.

The Preview:

For San Francisco, the effort of reaching the Series was strain enough. Just as in the last two meetings between these teams, the Giants were coming off a grueling race with the Dodgers, and were involved in an emotional, tightly fought playoff that wasn't decided until a ninth-inning rally in the final game.

This was a powerful, talented San Francisco team. Although forced to play half the year without injured slugger Willie McCovey, there was more than enough talent to pick up the slack. Willie Mays showed the way with a league-leading 49 homers and was runner-up with 141 RBIs. Orlando Cepeda, who moved into McCovey's spot at first base and forced him to left-field when he returned, smashed 35 homers and 114 RBIs. Rightfielder Felipe Alou was the leading batter with a .316 average and he also hit for power, with 25 homers and 98 RBIs. When McCovey recovered, he joined the parade with 20 home runs in just 229 times at bat. Even considering that this was the first expansion year in the National League and pitching was spread thin, it was an impressive display. The Giants wound up with more homers than the mighty Yankees.

The pitching staff had been assembled out of spare parts from all directions. Jack Sanford, rookie of the year with the

Yankees pitcher Ralph Terry tosses his glove in celebration after Willie McCovey's line drive is caught at second base to preserve his shutout and seal New York's victory in Game 7. Terry had surrendered Bill Mazeroski's blast in 1960.

Phillies five years before, had his best season with a 24-7 mark. Billy O'Dell, who had never quite lived up to the early promise he had shown with the Orioles, was 19-14. Billy Pierce, long the top man on the White Sox staff, was considered over the hill when Chicago dealt him over the winter. He was 16-6 and pitched a shutout in the first playoff game. The fourth man in the rotation was future Hall of Famer Juan Marichal. In his third year with the team, the 24-year-old right-hander was 18-11. Consistency in the bullpen was a problem. The stopper was the diminutive Stu Miller, who bore the distinction of being the only man charged with a balk in an All Star game when the wind blew him off the mound. His endless assortment of off-speed curves were maddening to hit against. The gag was that one of his pitches was "so slow it almost turned around and went back." Nonetheless, he had 19 saves.

The Yankee power output dipped inevitably from its awesome 1961 totals. Roger Maris again topped the team with 33 homers and 100 RBIs, and was roundly criticized for falling short of the impossible standard he had set the previous year. Injuries limited Mickey Mantle to 123 games, the fewest since his rookie year. But he still hit 30 homers and his .321 average was the best on the team. Elston Howard came back with 21 homers and 91 RBIs, while Bill Skowron produced 23 homers and 80 RBIs. The major addition was rookie shortstop Tom Tresh. When Tony Kubek went down with injuries, Tresh moved from the outfield to play short, much as Kubek had done five years before. He showed unanticipated power with 20 homers and 93 RBIs, and when Kubek was able to play again Tresh returned to the outfield without missing a beat. Moreover, Bobby Richardson, who usually didn't hit his stride as a batter until the Series, did it for an entire season, with a .302 average.

The pitching was essentially in the hands of Ralph Terry (23-12) and Whitey Ford (17-8). It was the second big season in a row for the 26-year-old Terry. Nonetheless, he was still haunted by his home run pitch to Bill Mazeroski in the 1960 Series. For Ford it was just another year at the office. He was now 33, in the process of rewriting the Series record book, and had never experienced a losing season or one in which his ERA was higher than 3.21. Behind those two, the Yanks had problems. Bill Stafford was a so-so 14-9. Last year's stopper, Luis Arroyo, had lost the touch and the Yanks had to turn to Marshall Bridges, a fastballer more in the classic mold. He saved 18 while going 8-4.

Turning Point: Game Seven, Ninth Inning.

The Giants are far tougher opponents than the Yankees ever anticipated. Sanford shuts them out in game two and Pierce also goes the route to win game six. Ford, while getting his fifth straight Series victory in the opener, has a no-decision in game four. With the chance to put the Series away in the sixth game, he is shelled out in the fifth inning. That leaves Terry to start a seventh game, and only because of meteorological intervention. He wins game five in New York, 5-3, but when the Series moves back to San Francisco it is rained out for three straight days. With the travel day and the playing of game six, that makes five days in which Terry can gather his strength. But the same is true of his opponent. Sanford pitched a three-hitter in game two and went seven strong innings before Tresh beat him with a three-run homer in game five.

It is evident from the start that both pitchers are sharp for the deciding game. Through four uneventful innings it is 0-0. Then Sanford finds himself in terrible trouble. Singles by Skowron and Clete Boyer and a walk to Terry load the bases in the fifth with none out. Kubek sends a hard grounder to shortstop Jose Pagan. Since it is early in the game, the Giants correctly choose to convert the double play and allow the run to score. Richardson then pops out. The inning seemingly ends well for San Francisco, with the Yanks getting only one run out of a dangerous situation. As it turns out, that is all they need.

Terry has mowed down the first 17 men, with Sanford breaking the spell in the sixth with a single. Then in the seventh, the Giants show signs of life. Mays belts a tremendous drive to left but Tresh manages to grab it as he runs into the wall in the left-field corner. McCovey then blasts a triple over Mantle's head in dead center. But Terry regains control and strikes out Cepeda.

In the eighth the Yankees again load the bases with none out on singles by Tresh and Mantle and an error by Pagan. O'Dell comes in, and once more the bomb is defused. Maris forces one runner at the plate and Howard slaps a grounder to third for a double play. The Giants escape, but they still trail, 1-0.

Now they are down to the last three outs. Pinch hitter Matty Alou starts the 9th by lifting what appears to be a simple pop foul. But the Candlestick Park wind is kicking up and the ball keeps blowing away until it falls safely into the dugout. Alou then beats out a drag bunt. Terry, unfazed, fires the ball past Felipe Alou and Chuck Hiller, only his third and fourth strike-outs of the game. This brings up Mays. He has just 6 hits in the Series but the Yankees know he is at his most dangerous in this situation. And their worst fears are realized. He punches a line drive into the rightfield corner. Alou is running at contact, streaking towards third base with the tying run. The crowd is shrieking, anticipating a play at the plate. Maris fields the ball quickly and fires to Richardson. But as Alou reaches third, coach Whitey Lockman holds him up. Elston Howard insists later that if Alou had tried to score he would have been out easily. Doubts still persist.

McCovey is next up. Manager Ralph Houk walks to the mound, asking Terry if he wants to walk him and pitch to Cepeda. Terry decides to be careful and take his chances. He throws one pitch and McCovey smashes a liner towards right. But Richardson is stationed perfectly, and the drive dies in his glove. The game is over, 1-0, and the Yanks have held on for championship number 20. The decision to hold Alou at third dooms the Giants.

The Managers:

Alvin Dark was only in his second year of running the Giants, the team he starred for in the 1951 and 1954 Series. A pupil of Leo Durocher, his temperament was vastly different. A deeply religious man, the 40-year-old Dark was soft-spoken.

Sometimes, though, his inner fires flared up. After one loss he threw a clubhouse stool against the wall and required emergency stitches in his hand when it caught on the metal underside. He was also known for occasional, if non-profane, outbursts at players who were not putting out.

Houk was now the only manager ever to win championships in his first two years. In fact, at 43, his two titles match what only 11 other men in baseball had attained in their careers. But Houk already was considering other possibilities.

FACT:
Ralph Houk is the only manager to win championships in his first two years.

The Heroes:

Terry had become the main man on the Yankee staff. But he still could not put his experience of 1960 totally behind him. It was like a nagging irritation that kept popping unbidden into his mind. He had driven to Mexico for a vacation right after that Series only to be located and quizzed by local journalists about the pitch to Bill Mazeroski. This Series more than evened things out. After losing game two on a strong five-hit performance, he came back to outduel Sanford twice in excruciatingly tough games. His seventh-game, 1-0 achievement was one of the classic clutch Series performances.

Tresh carried his rookie performance right into the Series. He led the Yankees with a .321 average, saved the seventh game with a wall-defying catch in the leftfield corner and won the fifth game with a three-run shot off Sanford in the eighth.

FACT:
Tom Tresh carried his great rookie performance into the Series. He led the Yankees with a .321 average, saved the seventh game with a wall-defying catch in the leftfield corner and won the fifth game with a three-run shot in the eighth inning.

The Giants actually outscored, outhit and outpitched the Yankees on the stat sheet. Much of their punch came from the unexpected vicinity of the middle infield. Shortstop Pagan was the top hitter in the Series at .368, while second baseman Hiller smashed a grand-slam homer off the top Yankee reliever, Bridges, to win game four.

The Zeroes:

While Mantle was healthy enough to play all seven games, the Giants took him out of the action. He had his second straight poor Series, going 3 for 25 with no runs-batted-in.

Marichal's lone appearance in the only Series of his career was brief and inconclusive. He started game four against Ford and was ahead 2-0 when he had to leave in the fifth. He had injured his hand when trying to bunt in the top half of the inning.

As with the 1959 Series in Los Angeles, the California style of weather became a major influence on the games. Instead of glare from the sun, though, it was a Pacific monsoon that washed out the affair for three days and the San Francisco wind that turned every fly ball into an outfield adventure.

The Aftermath:

The Giants still packed more power than any other National League club in 1963. But despite their fine Series, both Pagan and Hiller collapsed at the plate. Pierce also hit the wall, dropping to 3-11. San Francisco finished third, 11 games off the pace, and fell into the role of perennial also-rans. It would be a 27-year wait, longest in franchise history, before the Giants were back in the Series.

The Yankees decided it was time to get younger. They brought up first baseman Joe Pepitone and two new pitchers, Jim Bouton and Al Downing. The result was an easy 10 1/2 game romp to a fourth straight flag, despite major injuries to both Mantle and Maris.

Notes:

In addition to the three-day weather delay between games five and six, there was another rainout in New York between the fourth and fifth games. In 1911, the Giants and A's had to wait a full week to play game three as the heavens emptied over Philadelphia. That Series didn't wrap up until October 26, a record for the pre-playoff era.

To try and stay sharp, the two teams boarded buses during the long delay and rode to Modesto, 90 miles east of San Francisco. The town with the closest dry field, it had once been the home of a Yankee Class C farm team. An overflow crowd estimated at 10,000 turned out for batting practice and cheered loudest for Mantle.

Ford's record streak of scoreless innings ended at 33 2/3 innings in game one. Mays and Jim Davenport singled in the second and with two outs, Pagan laid down a perfect squeeze bunt for the run. Ford's winning streak also ended at five when he threw a pickoff attempt into centerfield in the sixth game, enabling the Giants to launch a three-run rally. He never won again in the Series.

Game One, October 4	
NY (AL)—200 000 121—6 Ford W	SF (NL)—011 000 000—2 O'Dell L, Larsen (8), Miller (9)
Game Two, October 5	
NY (AL)—000 000 000—0 Terry L, Daley (8)	SF (NL)—100 000 10X—2 Sanford W
Game Three,m October 7	
SF (NL)—000 000 002—2 Pierce L, Larsen (7), Bolin (8)	NY (AL)—000 000 30X—3 Stafford W
Game Four, October 8	
SF (NL)—020 000 401—7 Marichal, Bolin (5), Larsen (6), O'Dell (7) SV	NY (AL)—000 002 001—3 Ford, Coates (7) L, Bridges (7)
Game Five, October 10	
SF (NL)—001 010 001—3 Sanford L, Miller (8)	NY (AL)—000 101 03X—5 Terry W
Game Six, October 15	
NY (AL)—000 010 010—2 Ford L, Coates (5), Bridges (8)	SF (NL)—000 320 00X—5 Pierce W
Game Seven, October 16	
NY (AL)—000 010 000—1 Terry W	SF (NL)—000 000 000—0 Sanford L, O'Dell (8)

1963

Los Angeles (NL) 4
New York (AL) 0

With a display of power pitching and game-breaking speed unlike anything seen in the Series in decades, the Dodgers humiliate their old antagonists by sweeping the Yankees. It is the first time New York had ever lost in four.

The Preview:

After six seasons on the left coast, only a handful of Dodgers were left from the old days in Brooklyn. They were Jim Gilliam, now the regular third baseman, and all three starting pitchers—Johnny Podres, Don Drysdale and Sandy Koufax. The team had been rebuilt in concept as well as personnel. Tiny Ebbets Field was now an apartment block in Flatbush, and the Dodgers cavorted in the open spaces of Chavez Ravine. Accordingly, they put together one of the fastest teams the majors had seen in years and brought the stolen base back into the offensive arsenal.

Shortstop Maury Wills had accomplished that transformation almost by himself. A switch hitter with no power whatsoever, Wills turned himself into a runner who routinely converted bunt singles into doubles, with a steal. In 1962, he shattered Ty Cobb's 20th-century record by swiping 104 bases, more than entire teams had stolen in recent decades. This year he toned it down a bit and stole only 40. Running alongside him was centerfielder Willie Davis, who may have even been faster but got on base less often. He stole 25. Even batting champion Tommy Davis (.326) stole 15 times, although his main role was the club's top RBI threat, with 88. What slight power the Dodgers mustered came from the bat of hulking Frank Howard, a former basketball star at Ohio State. The 6-7 leftfielder hit 28 homers, but managed to drive in just 64 runs.

Sandy Koufax (left) and catcher John Roseboro count up Koufax's record 15 strikeouts in Game 1. Koufax completely dominated the Yankees, allowing only three runs in two complete game victories and adding eight strikeouts in his second outing.

Pitching was a big part of the Dodger makeover. Always struggling to find quality pitchers in Brooklyn, the Dodgers hit the mother lode in Los Angeles. Koufax, signed as a hometown sensation back in Brooklyn, had struggled for years, trying to add control to his stunning array of weapons. In 1963 he did it and the results were astonishing. He went 25-5 with an ERA of 1.88, 11 shutouts and 306 strikeouts, all of them league-leading figures. Others may have thrown a bit harder, but no one had a curve that came in quite as fast or broke quite as sharply as Koufax's. Set up by the fastball, it broke down the best hitters and made the darkly handsome left-hander a pitching phenomenon.

But he had lots of help. Drysdale was 19-17 and Podres 14-12, while Ron Perranoski saved 21 games and won 16 more as the bullpen stopper. It was on pitching that L.A. won the pennant by 6 games.

The Yankees still featured the long ball, although in not nearly the giddy profusion of former years. Mickey Mantle was 31 and so banged up he could only get into 65 games. Roger Maris, too, was limited to 90 games and the two of them combined for just 38 homers. Elston Howard was now the top power source on the Yankees, with 28 homers and 85 RBIs on a .287 average. The big left-handed threat was rookie first baseman Joe Pepitone, with 27 homers and 89 RBIs, while Tom Tresh filled in for Mantle in centerfield most of the year and added 25 homers.

The pitching, however, was formidable. Whitey Ford put together one of his best years, with a 24-7 record. Rookie Jim Bouton, a free spirit who did not quite fit the Yankee mold, nonetheless was 21-7, while left-hander Al Downing, called up in mid-season, went 13-5. Ralph Terry slipped a bit to 17-15. But this was, far and away, the best starting rotation in the league. There was no intimidator coming out of the pen, though. Marshall Bridges, who had filled the role in 1962, was shot during an after hours spring training misunderstanding and was never a factor. Instead, Hal Reniff and Steve Hamilton combined for 23 saves as the bullpen committee.

Turning Point: Game One, Second Inning.

There comes a time when even the best teams know they are overmatched. That time comes early in this Series. Koufax had started a Series game in 1959 and acquitted himself well, going seven innings and giving up a run while taking the loss. But that was the old Koufax. The new, improved model is a whole different problem. While his exploits during the season are well known to the Yankees, they still feel he probably isn't anything they can't handle.

This concept dies quickly. In the first inning, Koufax strikes out Tony Kubek, Bobby Richardson and Tresh. In the second, the Dodgers erupt for four runs off Ford, with catcher Johnny Roseboro applying the finishing touch with a three-run homer. This sort of thing is not supposed to happen to Ford. Especially not in Yankee Stadium. Especially not by a left-handed hitter.

Koufax, however, is just getting the range. He mows down Mantle and Maris to start the second before Howard finally accomplishes something—a pop foul to Roseboro. There is more to come. By the end of the fourth 12 straight Yankees have gone down. Nine of them strike out and only one of them manages to hit a fair ball. This is not the sort of pitching anyone had ever seen before.

Even when Koufax begins to tire in the eighth and Tresh reaches him for a two-run homer, it is just a gesture. He finishes up by striking out Harry Bright to end the game. His 15 strikeouts establish a new Series record, erasing by one the mark set by Carl Erskine

FACT:

Sandy Koufax's 15 strikeouts in game one establish a new Series record. He became a national figure during this series with two complete game wins in which he struck out 23.

against the Yanks in 1953. More than that, it seems to knock the fight right out of the Yankees.

They score just two more runs in the next three days. Podres, Drysdale, then Koufax again shackle them. It is the most feeble performance by a Yankee team on record; a total of 4 runs, on a .171 team average. One look at Koufax was all it took.

The Managers:

Walter Alston has presided over the big change, converting the Dodgers from the power game to a team that wins on speed. Although he never changed teams, it was like he won with two different franchises, so profound was the alteration. There are still three pennants for him to win, but this may have been his finest hour.

The sweep cannot diminish Ralph Houk's achievement of three pennants in three years. But the chance at expanded opportunities beckons. He will move into a front office job after the Series.

The Heroes:

Koufax became a national figure during this Series. His two complete game wins, in which he struck out 23 men and gave up three runs, was one of the great performances in the game's history. He struck out more hitters in a four-game Series than anyone else had in 7. At this time, the only pitcher who ever had more strikeouts was Bill Dinneen of the 1903 Red Sox and he had eight games in which to do it. All three runs off Koufax scored on homers—one by Tresh and one by Mantle. Otherwise, the Yankees were unable to sustain any kind of rally against him.

This was a nice payback for Bill Skowron against his former team. He had been sent packing by the Yanks after 9 seasons and hit only .203 as a part-timer with the Dodgers. But he came alive in the Series, hitting .385 with a homer and 3 RBIs against the Yanks.

Overlooked in Koufax's heroics was an excellent performance by Drysdale. He stopped the Yanks on three hits in a 1-0, game-three duel with Bouton, the first Series game to be played at Dodger Stadium.

The Zeroes:

Mantle was again a non-factor. Although he played in all four games, the effects of his injury were still apparent. He went just 2 for 15.

In an effort to blame somebody for this storm of misfortune, the New York media fastened on Pepitone. The Yankee first baseman lost a throw from third baseman Clete Boyer in the seventh inning of the final game in a background of glare and white shirts. The ball hit his wrist, rolled all the way to the stands and Gilliam, the batter, wound up on third base. Willie Davis then scored him with a sacrifice fly. The error made a loser of Ford, even though he gave up just two hits in a great pitching duel with Koufax.

The Aftermath:

The Dodgers said all the right things: about how the Yankees could have broken out at any time and that they were just glad not to have to play them any more. But Alston hit the right note when he told his team not to be afraid of the pinstripes, because the Mets wore them, too. The Yanks were unmistakably in decline and while they were able to stave off collapse, barely, for one more year the end of baseball's longest dynasty was at hand.

The Dodgers lost Koufax in mid-summer of 1964 and went into a tailspin, sliding all the way to sixth place. Their scant offense declined even further, as only the two expansion teams at the bottom of the standings scored fewer runs. Koufax got healthy again in 1965 and so did Los Angeles.

Notes:

Koufax had to end the Series twice before it was officially over. With two outs in the ninth inning of game four, Howard hit a grounder to Wills who flipped over to Dick Tracewski for the game-ending force. Koufax went into a victory dance . . . but Tracewski dropped the ball. So he turned around and did it all over again, with Hector Lopez hitting the ball to Wills. This time it counted.

Koufax, an observant Jew, took off every autumn for the High Holy Days of Rosh Hashanah and Yom Kippur. After his opening win, several of the Yankee coaches, according to media reports, asked for almanacs to check if there were any more Jewish holidays coming up soon. There weren't.

After the sweep was over, Yankee co-owner Del Webb suggested that with jet travel in general use there really was no need for a travel day off, even between cities on opposite coasts. Of course, he had an ax to grind. Without a travel day, the Yankees would not have faced Koufax twice in four games. The last Series in which no travel day was scheduled was the

> **FACT:**
> Koufax took off every autumn for the High Holy Days of Rosh Hashanah and Yom Kippur. After his opening win, several of the Yankee coaches reportedly asked for almanacs to check if there were any more Jewish holidays coming up soon.

final Brooklyn-Yankee subway Series in 1956. But even in the New York-Cleveland Series of 1954 there was no day off. The figuring at the time was that none was needed since the two cities were just a short train ride apart. Since 1957, however, the travel day has remained on the Series schedule no matter how close the cities are, except when a rainout intervenes.

Line Scores:

Game One, October 2

LA (NL)—041 000 000—5
Koufax W

NY (AL)—000 000 020—2
Ford L, Williams (6), Hamilton (9)

Game Two, October 3

LA (NL)—200 100 010—4
Podres W, Perranoski (9) SV

NY (AL)—000 000 001—1
Downing L, Terry (6), Reniff (9)

Game Three, October 5

NY (AL)—000 000 000—0
Bouton L, Reniff (8)

LA (NL)—100 000 00X—1
Drysdale W

Game Four, October 6

NY (AL)—000 000 100—1
Ford L, Reniff (8)

LA (NL)—000 010 10X—2
Koufax W

1964

St. Louis (NL) 4
New York (AL) 3

The Yankees kept popping St. Louis with the sort of rallies that crunched their opponents in so many other Series. But the Cardinals wouldn't go away, and behind the record-breaking pitching of Bob Gibson they came back to win for the third time in five tries against New York.

The Preview:

The Yankees were back, reeling off their fifth straight pennant and their 14th in 16 years. But this one was a labor. Both Chicago and Baltimore grappled with them down the stretch and, finally, it took a harmonica to energize the team. When utility infielder Phil Linz started playing it on the team bus after a loss, rookie manager Yogi Berra blew up. He ripped such behavior as un-Yankeelike, contrary to the tradition of champions. His players got the message and eked out a one-game margin over the White Sox at the finish line.

A healthy Mickey Mantle was a big help. He only missed 19 games this season and his 35 homers and 111 RBIs led the team. Roger Maris was also back in form and added 26 homers, while Elston Howard drove in 84 runs to go along with his team-best .313 average. But Tony Kubek, Clete Boyer and Tom Tresh all fell off sharply, making it difficult. The Yanks were still near the top in homers and runs scored, but at a much lower level than previous seasons.

The three core starters held up, though. Whitey Ford, unbeatable as always, went 17-6. Second year men Jim Bouton (18-13) and Al Downing (13-8, with a league-leading 217 strikeouts) also followed through with good years. Down the stretch, Mel Stottlemyre arrived from AAA and, just as Ford had done 14

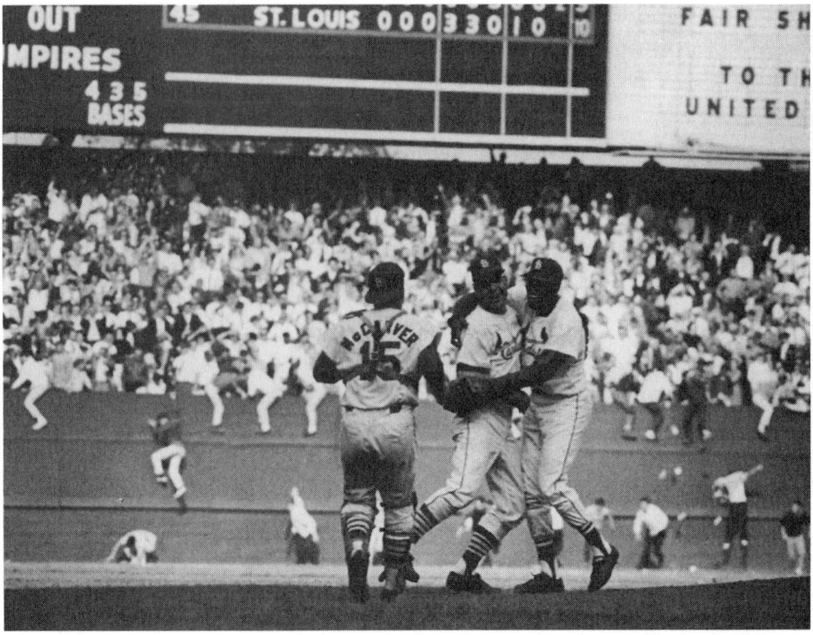

Tim McCarver (left), Ken Boyer (center), and Bob Gibson celebrate the Cardinals' first World Championship since 1946. McCarver delivered a tenth-inning home run to win Game 5. Gibson won two games in three starts with 31 strikeouts.

years before, brought the Yankees home. He had a 9-3 run in the last two months. Again, though, there was no consistent stopper out of the bullpen. It was a problem so acute that the team acquired veteran Pedro Ramos for the stretch drive, though he was ineligible for the Series.

The Cards, winning for the first time in 18 years, had struggled to the top on the last weekend of the season in the closest pennant race in history. At the end, four teams finished three games apart, as the Phillies, who seemed to have things easily in hand, lost their grip with a week to go. It was one of the worst collapses in the game's history.

St. Louis was led by a smart, veteran infield and a young, enthusiastic outfield. Longtime third baseman Ken Boyer (brother of the Yankees' Clete) had his best year, leading the league with 119 RBIs on 24 homers. Keeping pace with him was first baseman Bill White, moved by the Giants when that team wound up with too many good players at the same position. The future president of the National League hit 21 homers and 102 RBIs. At shortstop was Dick Groat, a winner with the Pirates 4 years before, who hit .295.

The top addition, however, was leftfielder Lou Brock. He came over in a little-noticed trade with the Cubs in June (although in retrospect it was noticed plenty and is considered one of the worst trades ever). He immediately caught fire and wound up hitting .348 in St. Louis, 97 points higher than his mark in Chicago, while stealing 43 bases.

Ray Sadecki, only 23 but in his fifth season with the Cards, led the staff at 20-11, and 35-year-old Curt Simmons went 18-9 in a big comeback year. The hot commodity, though, was 28-year-old Bob Gibson. He had his best season to date at 19-12 while striking out 245 hitters. He was still not widely known outside St. Louis. The National League was dominated by Sandy Koufax and Don Drysdale, who had both performed in the Series, and by Juan Marichal, with his high-kick motion. Gibson had not reached that level of performance and so went into this Series as an unknown quantity. That would change in a hurry.

Turning Point: Game Five, Tenth Inning.

The teams split a pair of blowouts in St. Louis and when the Series moves back to New York, the Yankees prepare to blow down the house of Cards. Mantle strikes in traditional fashion, leading off the last of the ninth with a game-winning homer off reliever Barney Schultz to win game three, 2-1. Then, nothing goes right. Instead of being intimidated, the Cards just keep on coming. Falling behind 3-0 after one inning of game four, they hold the Yankees at bay behind the pitching of ex-Dodger Roger Craig, until Boyer blasts a sixth-inning grand slam off Downing to win, 4-3.

That sets up a fifth game matchup between Gibson and Stottlemyre. The rookie outpitched him in game two, 8-3, when Gibson wobbled for two runs in the seventh and the bullpen gave up four more in the ninth. Still, he looked exceptionally fast, striking out five of the first six hitters he faced. Stottlemyre went the distance in that one.

In this game, Gibson has to fight out of trouble early. Two walks and a hit batter load the bases with one out in the New York second. But Gibson simply strikes out Clete Boyer and Stottlemyre and that settles that.

The Cards break through on Stottlemyre in the fifth. Gibson starts it with a single, a looping fly ball that just clears the glove of the back-pedaling Linz, filling in for the injured Tony Kubek at shortstop. Stottlemyre, a low ball pitcher who gets lots of ground-outs, gets a bouncer out of Curt Flood, but reliable Bobby Richardson fumbles it and there are two men on. Brock then bounces a single through the right side to score Gibson. When

White hits into a force play, barely beating the relay to first, Flood scores the second run.

After his close call in the second, Gibson is almost perfect. He gives up just two harmless singles, and by the ninth is working on a four-hit shutout with 11 strikeouts. But Groat opens the door for the Yankees by fumbling Mantle's leadoff grounder for an error. Howard strikes out, but Joe Pepitone sends a bullet back to the mound. The ball hits Gibson in the hip and bounces to the third base line. The pitcher races after it and manages to make an off-balance throw that nips Pepitone by a hair. The St. Louis trainer comes out to make sure Gibson is all right and he tries a few tosses to test the hip.

On the next pitch that counts, Tresh lines the ball over the 407-foot sign in right-center for a game-tying homer. New York has done it again. At the last possible moment, the Yankees jump up to take a certain win away from the opposition.

The game now goes into the 10th, the first extra-inning game in the Series since 1958. Pete Mikkelsen, New York's top reliever, retired the first five men he faced, but he opens the 10th with a walk to White. Ken Boyer then lays down a perfect sacrifice bunt. Neither Mikkelsen nor Pepitone can get to it and everyone is safe. When Groat also shortens up to bunt, Howard fires a pickoff throw to second. White is trapped far off the base. But when he breaks for third, Linz's throw is low and he slides in safely with a stolen base. Groat then hits a grounder to third, and White has to hold as Boyer is forced at second.

This brings up catcher Tim McCarver. He is St. Louis' hottest hitter, with an 8-for-17 Series, and Mikkelsen works on him carefully, hoping for a double play grounder. On a full count, his sinker comes in at belt level and McCarver blasts it six rows deep in the rightfield seats. The Cards recover from Tresh's blow to deliver a knockout of their own. Gibson makes the 5-2 lead stand up and the Series returns to St. Louis with the Cards needing just a split to wrap it up. Gibson delivers the win in game seven, 7-5.

FACT:
The Yogi Berra image created by the media, the comical little man with a knack for imbuing the English language with deeper meanings by malapropisms ("it's like *deja vu* all over again") is not quite accurate.

The Managers:

Rookie manager Yogi Berra is one of the best-known figures in baseball. A star on 13 Series teams, he has played in more of these games than anyone in history. He moved into the manager's seat when Ralph Houk went to the front office and did exactly what was expected of him, producing a winner right off the reel. But still there is dissatisfaction. The Berra image created by the media, the comical little man with a knack for imbuing the English language with deeper meaning by his malapropisms, is not quite accurate. He is far more serious than that and much less outgoing. He is trapped by the image and his bosses wonder if he really is the man they want representing the proud Yankees.

Johnny Keane is in his third full season with the Cards. A lifer in the minors, he improved the club in each of his years there. But there has been an upheaval in St. Louis. With the team lagging out of first place by double digit numbers in August, owner Gussie Busch fired general manager Bing Devine. The 52-year-old Keane was a close associate of Devine's and was certain that his neck was also on the block. At the time, he was absolutely right. Then the equation was upset entirely when the Cardinals confounded everyone and became World Champions.

The Heroes:

This was the year the country discovered Gibson, just as it had learned about Koufax a year before. The right-hander from Omaha, one of the best pure athletes in the game, had toured with the Harlem Globetrotters for a year. He came up with the Cards in 1959 and, gradually, learned to channel a deep rage of racial injustice that burned within him. This focused intensity made him one of the great clutch pitchers in the game's history. His performance in 1964 began a run of seven straight wins, establishing a new Series record. His 31 strikeouts also set a record for a Series, one exceeded only by Gibson himself in 1968.

McCarver continued his big hitting performance, compiling a .478 mark while catching all 7 games. He led the team with five RBIs.

Richardson, who always excelled in the Series, came up with his best effort of all. His 13 hits broke the record and he hit .406.

It was also a Series comeback of sorts for Mantle. After three sub-par performances in a row, he hit three homers and led both sides with six RBIs. His third homer was a dramatic, three-run shot off Gibson in game seven. It brought the Yankees back in a game they had trailed by 6 runs, although they eventually lost. It was also his last Series homer.

FACT:
Bob Gibson's performance began a record run of 7 straight wins, and his 31 strikeouts established a new Series record, which he exceeded in 1968.

The Zeroes:

While Gibson was starting to chalk up Series records, Ford was ending his run. Trying to pitch over a heel injury, he could start just one game and was knocked out in the sixth inning of the opener, his third straight Series loss. It made his final Series record 10-7, the most wins and the most losses of any pitcher. Despite problems in his last two Series, his lifetime ERA was 2.71—or 0.04 lower than his career ERA for the regular season.

The loss was the culminating shock for the Yankee dynasty. After dropping their first two Series, in 1921–22, New York was 20-6 in these games. It had not lost two in a row since the very first ones. In 1964 the crack in the Yankee foundation was too wide to ignore any longer.

The Aftermath:

The bitter brew in St. Louis was too far gone to save with a championship. Keane, fed up with his treatment by management, quit right after the Series. Then, shockingly, he signed to manage the team he had just defeated. But it would take more than a change of managers to save the Yankees. Entire volumes have been written about why the dynasty collapsed. The baseball draft equalized talent among teams. The Yankees were too slow to sign black and Hispanic stars. The big players wore out faster than a depleted farm system could replace them. In any event, the Yankees sank to sixth, eight games under .500 in 1965. With Houk called out of an administrative job to become manager again in 1966, they plunged all the way to last place. The dynasty was done.

A stunned Berra, who never saw the blow coming, rejoined his old boss Casey Stengel as a coach with the Mets after being fired. Eventually, he took over as manager there and also led that team to a pennant. The Cards named coach and former star second baseman, Red Schoendienst, as manager. After two disappointing seasons he turned it around to win two pennants in a row.

Notes:

McCarver, a future network broadcaster and a star of this Series, was one of several media figures to be associated with these teams. His understudy, Bob Uecker, who didn't play, also made it big as an announcer after retirement and even had his own sitcom for a few seasons. The injured Kubek came back for one more year then he, too, retired to become a network baseball analyst. Cardinal rightfielder Mike Shannon worked for several years as one of the St. Louis play-by-play announcers.

New York pitcher Jim Bouton won two games in the Series. But his arm would give out the following spring, an event that led him to bounce around and directed him towards a literary career. His best-selling book, *Ball Four,* was a sensation. It gave the first no-holds-barred look at what life with the Yankees and baseball in general was really like and the first distinctly unheroic portrait of Mantle. Bouton parlayed it into a sports anchor job on New York television and a few movie roles. He even rode the publicity into a short-lived comeback at 39 as a knuckleballer with Atlanta in 1978. Bouton went 1-3 in 5 games.

Line Scores:

Game One, October 7

NY (AL)—030 010 010—5
Ford L, Downing (6),
Sheldon (8), Mikkelsen (8)

SL (NL)—110 004 03X—9
Sadecki W, Schultz (7) SV

Game Two, October 8

NY (AL)—000 101 204—8
Stottlemyre W

SL (NL)—001 000 011—3
Gibson L, Schultz (9),
Richardson (9), Craig (9)

Game Three, October 10

SL (NL)—000 010 000—1
Simmons, Schultz (9) L

NY (AL)—010 000 001—2
Bouton W

Game Four, October 11

SL (NL)—000 004 000—4
Sadecki, Craig (1) W,
Taylor (6) SV

NY (AL)—300 000 000—3
Downing L, Mikkelsen (7),
Terry (8)

Game Five, October 12

SL (NL)—000 020 000 3—5
Gibson W

NY (AL)—000 000 002 0—2
Stottlemyre, Reniff (8),
Mikkelsen (8) L

Game Six , October 14

NY (AL)—000 012 050—8
Bouton W, Hamilton (9)

SL (NL)—100 000 011—3
Simmons L, Taylor (7),
Schulz (8), Richardson (8),
Humphreys (9)

Game Seven, October 15

NY (AL)—000 003 002—5
Stottlemyre L, Downing (5),
Sheldon (5), Hamilton (7),
Mikkelsen (8)

SL (NL)—000 330 10X—7
Gibson W

1965

Los Angeles (NL) 4
Minnesota (AL) 3

The Twins combined the proper blend of power and pitching and beat the best of the Dodgers staff in the first two games. They couldn't do it on the second time around, however, and behind overpowering pitching Los Angeles came back to win the Series.

The Preview:

In their fifth season after arriving in Minnesota as the wretched Washington Senators, the Twins ended the franchise's 32-year run of futility. In Washington's capacious Griffith Stadium, power hitters did not get far. Once in cozy Metropolitan Stadium, the Twins developed into the most expansive collection of home run hitters in the game.

They were paced by Harmon Killebrew. He played no position very well but always found a place to play simply because he hit the ball a very long distance. An enormously strong man, Killebrew had topped 40 home runs in five of the previous six years. Injuries hampered him in 1965, keeping him out of the lineup for a month and a half. Still, he managed to lead the team with 25 homers. Ordinarily, the loss of Killebrew would have stifled any chance for the Twins, but the club was bristling with hitters. Tony Oliva, at 25, won his second batting title in two years in the majors. He hit .321 and drove in 98, to lead the team. Other mashers were leftfielder Bob Allison (23 homers), first baseman Don Mincher (22) and centerfielder Jimmie Hall (20). The heart of the Twins was Zoilo Versalles. An inspirational leader, he played a dynamic shortstop, stole 27 bases and could also hit with power (19 homers) when the occasion demanded. In fact, his total of 76 extra base hits was high on the team. He was the league's MVP as the Twins beat out Chicago by seven games.

Bob Allison makes a sliding catch on Jim Lefebvre's curving line drive in the fifth inning of Game 2 to preserve a scoreless tie. Minnesota would eventually win the game behind Jim Kaat.

Top pitchers were the righty-lefty combination of Mudcat Grant (21-7) and Jim Kaat (18-11). Camilo Pascual no longer threw the hard stuff that had led the league in strikeouts for three straight years, but had enough left to go 9-3. Jim Perry rounded out the starters at 12-7. Al Worthington was the top man in the pen with 21 saves and 10 wins.

It had been a tougher row to hoe for the Dodgers, who lived and died with pitching. Sandy Koufax, recovered from his finger injury, led the league in everything—26-8 mark, 2.04 ERA and a modern record 382 strikeouts. Not since the prime of Bob Feller, or perhaps Lefty Grove, had there been a pitcher like this. Don Drysdale was almost as keen, at 23-12, and Claude Osteen was a tougher pitcher than his 15-15 record indicated. Ron Perranoski again was the closer, with 17 saves.

It was a terrible struggle to score runs, though. Only the last two teams in the standings scored less than Los Angeles. Maury Wills was again running amok on the bases with 94 steals, and his .286 average led the team. But two-time batting champ Tommy Davis broke his leg early in the year and could not play. Second baseman Jim LeFebvre was the closest thing to a power hitter, with 12 homers and 69 RBIs, and rightfielder Ron Fairly added 70 RBIs. Then up from the minors in mid-season came Lou Johnson—well-traveled, 30, a washout in two earlier trials with the Cubs and Braves. He seemed to fit right in with the scrappy style of the Dodgers, though. He hit 12 homers, stole 15 bases and developed a charisma that the Dodgers rallied around. Riding their pitching and Johnson's clutch hits, they edged the Giants by 2 games and entered the Series a slight favorite on the benefit of experience and pitching.

Turning Point: Game Three, First Inning.

The Twins shock everyone, including themselves, by ripping through Koufax and Drysdale in the first two games at Minnesota. Drysdale is pounded for 7 runs in less than 3 innings in the 8-2 opener. Then Koufax can't hold the Twins, either. Kaat outpitches him in the 5-1 second game, which is broken open late against the Los Angeles bullpen.

The Series moves back to Dodger Stadium and Osteen is all that stands between the Twins and a rout. The left-hander came over from Washington, the team that replaced the Twins in the capital, in an off-season deal for gigantic slugger Frank Howard. He only finished 9 of his 40 starts, but he gives Los Angeles a third consistent pitcher. Opposing him is Pascual. Long the star of the staff, shoulder surgery had slowed him down. He relies on craftiness, and at 31 is no longer in his prime.

The Twins start off as if they mean to take the Dodgers out early. Versalles opens the game with a double to the leftfield corner and goes to third on an infield out. Osteen gets Oliva on another grounder and Versalles has to hold. Osteen wisely decides to be extremely careful with Killebrew and ends up walking him. That brings up catcher Earl Battey. His power numbers have declined but he hit .297 this year and at 30 is still a tough out.

Osteen falls behind in the count 2-0. But on the next pitch, Killebrew breaks for second. Catcher Johnny Roseboro, not quite knowing what to make of this odd sight, looks Versalles back to third and then throws through to second. Versalles decides at this point to head for the plate on a delayed steal. Wills alertly fires the ball right back to Roseboro. Versalles is trapped in a rundown for the third out and Osteen is out of trouble. Manager Sam Mele explains later that Battey missed the hit-and-run sign.

The foul-up takes the Twins out of the inning and Osteen takes control of the game. Minnesota never gets another runner to third and the Dodgers catch up to Pascual in the fourth. Roseboro's bases loaded single to right brings in two runs and gives the Dodgers the lead. They gradually add to the margin and Osteen coasts in with a 4-0 win.

The victory is all Los Angeles needs to brake the Minnesota momentum. The Twins are stopped by Drysdale and Koufax in the next two games. They give up just two runs, strike out a total of 21 and the Dodgers end up sweeping at home. Although Minnesota finally catches up to Osteen in game six, it is too late. Koufax is primed for the deciding game and he is too much for any team. He hands the Twins their third shutout of the Series, 2-0, on a 3-hitter. The missed sign in game three means Minnesota misses the boat in this Series.

The Managers:

Only four teams ever lost the first two games of a Series and came back to win. Walter Alston has now managed two of them, the 1955 and 1965 Dodgers. Imperturbable in the worst of times and unexcitable in the best, Alston keeps the fragile Dodger vessel afloat for the second championship in three years and the fourth of his career.

Sam Mele was a competent if uninspiring outfielder for several American League teams in the '50s. He managed the same way. As the Twins foundered during their first season in Minnesota, he was brought in. He put them into contention the following year and, after a slight fall backwards in 1964, they broke through for him this year. But Mele remained uneasy. Owner Calvin Griffith liked the energetic qualities of coach Billy Martin, and it is rumored that whenever Mele falters Martin will step in. Still, Mele earned himself a little security with this pennant. Not until the spring of 1967 does Griffith can him and the irascible Martin doesn't take over until 1969.

The Heroes:

For the second time in three seasons, Koufax dominates the Series. He is undisturbed by his loss in game two. "I gave up 2 runs and my ERA for the season was 2.00," he says. "So what's the big deal?" He shows exactly how small a deal it is by blanking Minnesota for the next 18 innings, while striking out 20. The circulatory problem in his finger, however, is not something that can be corrected by surgery and Koufax knows that the condition, which leaves his hand numb, may shorten his career. He doesn't know how short that will be, though.

Lou Johnson continued to be the man on the spot right through the Series. He hit .400 in the 4 games Los Angeles won, and his home run off the foul pole against Kaat in game seven provided Koufax with the only run he needed.

Grant won 2 games for the Twins, stopping the Dodgers with his sinking curveball, taught to him by pitching coach Johnny Sain. Grant also became the first American League pitcher to hit a Series homer since Jim Bagby for Cleveland in 1920.

Fairly led a surprisingly robust Los Angeles offense. His marks of 11 hits, a .379 average and 6 RBIs led everyone and his two-run single in the sixth broke open a tight 3-2 Dodger lead in game four.

The Zeroes:

The Los Angeles left-handers stopped Minnesota's three top left-handed hitters completely. Oliva and Mincher hit a combined .163, while Hall played only in the games against Drsydale and went 1 for 7. That left the offensive burden on the shoulders of Killebrew and Versalles and they couldn't carry it all.

LeFebvre was Los Angeles' top hitter at .400 when he had to go to the sideline with a badly bruised heel after game three. Dick Tracewski was his replacement and went just 2 for 17.

FACT:
Bob Allison's sliding catch along the left-field line in game two was one of the best in Series history, ranking with those of Mays and Amaros.

The Aftermath:

Versalles and Grant returned to earth in 1966 and the Twins fell with them, dropping to second place. Allison also was sidelined most of the year and the string ran out on Pascual. The Twins would remain a force for several years, winning division titles in two of them. But not until 1987 did they return to the Series.

The Dodgers, meanwhile, became the first team to be confronted with the changing economic realities of the game. Koufax and Drysdale staged a combined contract holdout in 1966 that lasted through spring training. A $100,000 ceiling generally was accepted in the sport for the top stars. But the two pitchers, aware of how much they meant to the wealthy Dodgers, who were breaking attendance records in Los Angeles, demanded 50 percent more. They got it, too. And while it took the Dodgers a while to get organized, they won the pennant once more.

FACT:
Willie Davis's 3 stolen bases in game five tied a Series record set by Honus Wagner in 1909.

Notes:

Willie Davis tied Wills for the lead in stolen bases in the Series with 3. But Davis got all of his in the fifth game. His one-game performance tied a record set by Honus Wagner in 1909.

Observers called Allison's sliding catch along the leftfield line in game two one of the best in Series history. The game was scoreless at the time and the Dodgers had a runner on base. A hit would have given Koufax a lead. But Allison cut off the rally. While his catch looked huge at the time, events turned it into a footnote.

Koufax sat out the first game because it fell on Yom Kippur. That meant he had to work on just two days' rest to pitch a third time in the Series in game seven. It didn't seem to hurt him.

Line Scores:

Game One, October 6

LA (NL)—010 000 001—2	Min (AL)—016 001 00X—8
Drysdale L, Reed (3), Brewer (5), Perranoski (7)	Grant W

Game Two, October 7

LA (NL)—000 000 100—1	Min (AL)—000 002 12X—5
Koufax L, Perranoski (7), Miller (8)	Kaat W

Game Three, October 9

Min (AL)—000 000 000—0	LA (NL)—000 211 00X—4
Pascual L, Merritt (6), Klippstein (8)	Osteen W

Game Four, October 10

Min (AL)—000 101 000—2	LA (NL)—110 103 01X—7
Grant L, Worthington (6), Pleis (8)	Drysdale W

Game Five, October 11

Min (AL)—000 000 000—0	LA (NL)—202 100 20X—7
Kaat L, Boswell (3), Perry (6)	Koufax W

Game Six, October 13

LA (NL)—000 000 100—1	Min (AL)—000 203 00X—5
Osteen L, Reed (6), Miller (8)	Grant W

Game Seven, October 14

LA (NL)—000 200 000—2	Min (NL)—000 000 000—0
Koufax W	Kaat L, Worthington (4), Klippstein (6), Merritt (7), Perry (9)

1966

Baltimore (AL) 4
Los Angeles (NL) 0

Never has a World Series team stopped hitting so completely as the Dodgers of 1966. In one of the major shocks in the game's history, the Orioles swept the defending champions, shutting them out for 33 consecutive innings. The total Los Angeles output for the Series was 2 runs.

The Preview:

The Orioles won this pennant in the off-season. In one of the great steals of all time, they got Frank Robinson from Cincinnati in exchange for pitcher Milt Pappas and some lesser lights. Robinson had been the Reds' top hitter for the last 10 years and he was just 30. The Reds said he was "an old 30." Besides, he was rumored to be a pain in the clubhouse and Cincinnati figured they were just one starting pitcher away from challenging for the pennant.

The opposite was true in Baltimore. The Orioles had come to town in 1954 as a thing of shreds and patches, the erstwhile St. Louis Browns. Over the years they steadily improved, with a foundation built on pitching. By 1964 they had come within two games of a pennant, but they slid back the following year. They lacked a game-breaking power hitter in the middle of the lineup, someone who would improve the players around him by his very presence. Baltimore had the core. Brooks Robinson was the best third baseman in the game; some would say the best defensively who ever played the position. A tall man of almost uncanny quickness, he made breathtaking plays appear casual. At shortstop was the

> **FACT:**
> The Dodgers hit only .142 for the Series and scored only 2 runs.

Willie Davis picks up the ball after one of his record three errors in the fifth inning of Game 2. His woes extended to the batter's box, where he managed only one hit for a .063 average.

former White Sox star, Luis Aparicio. Teamed with Robinson, he gave Baltimore one of the great defensive infields in history. At first was Boog Powell, an amiable giant of a man who had yet to establish himself as a consistent hitter.

Enter Frank Robinson. He wins the Triple Crown, hitting .316 with 49 homers and 122 RBIs. Powell responded with 34 homers and 109 RBIs, while Brooks Robinson joined the fun by slamming 23 homers and driving in 100 runs. Suddenly, Baltimore had one of the most potent lineups in the game. There was also a tremendous defensive centerfielder, Paul Blair, and two rookies who filled vacancies at second and catcher, Davey Johnson and Andy Etchebarren.

Baltimore already had the best young pitching staff around. While there were no big winners—Jim Palmer was tops at 15-10—it was deep. Dave McNally (13-6), Steve Barber (10-5) and Wally Bunker (10-6) rounded out the rotation, and the oldest of them was 27. The bullpen was also deep and varied, running from junk pitcher Stu Miller (9-4, with 18 saves) to fireballing Moe Drabowsky (6-0 and 7 saves).

Still, the Dodgers had experience and they also had Sandy Koufax. The top player in two of the last three Series, he missed all of spring training in a contract dispute. He then went 27-9, again leading the league in both ERA (1.73) and strikeouts (317). As the Dodgers struggled in the final week, he topped things off by pitching the clincher on the last day. It was a tougher year for Don Drysdale, who had joined Koufax in the holdout. He was never quite himself and finished at just 13-16. Claude Osteen came back with another good season at 17-14 and rookie Don Sutton contributed a 12-12 year. The Dodgers, too, had enriched themselves at small cost in the off-season. They acquired reliever Phil Regan from Detroit and he became so efficient at picking up late wins and saves that he quickly won the nickname "The Vulture." He finished 14-1 with 21 saves.

Hitting was the same old sad tale. There was second baseman Jim LeFebvre, with 24 homers and 74 RBIs, tops on the club. Ron Fairly hit .288 and Lou Johnson, up for the entire season, added 17 homers and 73 RBIs. Tommy Davis slowly mended from his terrible leg injury and hit .313 but could not run and did not hit for much power, either. The Dodgers again were third from the bottom in runs. Moreover, Maury Wills was slowing up, swiping just 38 bases and failing to cover the ground in the field. Nonetheless, Los Angeles was the odds-on choice, and one local writer predicted the Dodgers would win it in three.

Turning Point: Game One, Third Inning.

Because Koufax had to bring the Dodgers home on the last Sunday of the year, it falls to Drysdale to open the Series. He still is not on his game. Before he gets the second out of the first inning, Frank Robinson clubs a two-run homer and Brooks Robinson adds one more for a 3-0 Baltimore lead.

Another scores off him in the second as the Dodger Stadium crowd looks on in sullen, disbelieving silence. Los Angeles has never lost a Series home game in this park and the fans do not like what they are seeing. The Dodgers start coming back on McNally in their half of the second. LeFebvre homers and Wes Parker doubles. He gets to third before Wills strikes out to leave him there. But the Dodgers are hitting McNally hard.

In the third McNally falls apart. With one out, he walks Johnson, Tommy Davis and LeFebvre to load the bases. The Orioles decide to send for Drabowsky. The tall, Polish-born right-hander never quite delivered on his early promise with the Cubs, and had shown little in subsequent stints with Milwaukee, Cincinnati and Kansas City. As a starter, he tends to run out of gas in the middle innings. But after being picked up in the winter draft, he is told to think nothing but long relief—to come in and throw hard sliders for as long as he can.

He immediately fans Parker, but then slips up and walks Jim Gilliam to force in a run, cutting the Baltimore lead to 4-2. The bases are still loaded and the dangerous John Roseboro is coming to bat. No one could possibly have guessed, but right here the Dodgers are already through for the Series. They will never score another run, and get only 15 more hits. Drabowsky gets Roseboro on a pop foul and Los Angeles settles in to one of the longest runs of hitting mediocrity ever seen in the championship.

Drabowsky goes on to strike out six in a row in the fourth and fifth, tying the record set by Cincinnati's Hod Eller in 1919 (against a team that presumably wasn't even trying, the Black Sox). He gives up one hit the rest of the way to get a 5-2 win. In the next three games, Palmer, Bunker and McNally each follow with shutouts—the final two by a 1-0 count. The Dodgers find themselves swept for the first time in their history and embarrassed by a performance that made the Hitless Wonders look like Murderers Row.

The Managers:

Walter Alston was now in his 13th season with the Dodgers and had seen too much to be overly distressed about this Series. "Were we tired?" he asked in response to a question after the fourth game. "The Orioles played the same number of games that we did. You never look too good when you get beat." He understood that when the hits don't come, there is very little you can do.

For Hank Bauer, in his third year as manager of the Orioles, it was satisfaction to be part of the first American League Series sweep that did not involve his former team, the Yankees. It was regarded as clever to describe the ex-Marine as having "a face like a clenched fist." The 44-year-old Bauer also had a hard-driving approach to the game, a style that did not quite fit in with the Orioles' personnel. They won on talent rather than aggressiveness and it took Bauer's replacement, Earl Weaver, to bring out their best.

FACT:
Moe Drabowsky goes on to strike out 6 in a row, tying the record set by Cincinnati's Hod Eller in the 1919 Series. Drabowski was known as a practical joker whose favorite prop was a rubber snake.

The Heroes:

Drabowsky was known as a practical joker whose favorite prop was a rubber snake. After being traded from Kansas City, he dialed the A's bullpen on his next trip into their park and, disguising his voice, ordered one of their pitchers to start throwing. He threw for five minutes until the Kansas City bench caught on and told him to sit down. The A's were not amused. The

Orioles picked Drabowsky up for the $25,000 waiver price after Brooks Robinson advised the front office that he could never get around on his hard stuff. His relief job in game one was the critical point of this Series.

Frank Robinson cemented his MVP year with home runs that won the first and fourth games. Both came off Drysdale, the kind of hard-throwing right-hander who, presumably, gave him trouble. This season, no one gave Robinson trouble.

The Zeroes:

Not only did Willie Davis fail to hit, his fielding lapses in game two were more than even Koufax could overcome. He dropped two fly balls in a row, losing them both in the Dodger Stadium glare. He followed up the second drop by picking up the naughty ball and throwing it past third base for his third error of the inning. Koufax stomped around the mound in silent fury and three unearned runs scored as the result of the mistakes. Next inning, when Davis caught a throw during the warmups, he was given a standing ovation. He went 1-for-16 in the Series, too.

The Series was also notable for the absence of Sutton, who would go on to be the Dodgers' top all-time winner. Alston had planned to use the rookie if Los Angeles took the lead in the Series. It was not to be and he had to wait another eight years to get his first Series start.

The Aftermath:

Koufax shocked the Dodgers shortly afterwards by announcing his retirement. The circulatory problem in his fingers was getting worse and he risked permanent paralysis if he continued to pitch. So, at the age of 30 he was finished. While his career was abbreviated, his peak seasons were so outstanding that he was an easy selection for Cooperstown five years later. His loss destroyed the Dodgers, though. A team with no hitting was now robbed of its best pitcher. Los Angeles plunged to eighth place in 1967 and didn't really return to contention for five years.

The Orioles also did a fast fade in 1967. Frank Robinson ran into injuries and all their bright young pitchers collapsed, with Palmer out for almost the whole year with arm problems. They finished a distant sixth. When they failed to rally at the start of 1968, Bauer was out and Weaver was in, to effect an immediate revival.

Notes:

The Dodgers' six errors in game two tied a Series record. They were also the only errors Los Angeles made.

The old record of 28 straight shutout innings had been inflicted upon the Philadelphia A's in 1905 by Christy Mathewson and Joe McGinnity of the Giants. The A's hit only .161 in that Series but the Dodgers managed to do even worse. Their mark for the four games was .142. The total of 2 runs was also a negative record; even the 1905 A's, although shut out 4 times, managed to score 3.

It was the first time an American League team other than the Yankees had won the Series in 18 years, since the 1948 Indians.

Line Scores:

Game One, October 5

Bal (AL)—310 100 000—5
McNally, Drabowsky (3) W

LA (NL)—011 000 000—2
Drysdale L, Moeller (3), Miller (5), Perranoski (8)

Game Two, October 6

Bal (AL)—000 310 020—6
Palmer W

LA (NL)—000 000 000—0
Koufax L, Perranoski (7), Regan (8), Brewer (9)

Game Three, October 8

LA (NL)—000 000 000—0
Osteen L, Regan (8)

Bal (AL)—000 010 00X—1
Bunker W

Game Four, October 9

LA (NL)—000 000 000—0
Drysdale L

Bal (AL)—000 100 000—1
McNally W

1967

St. Louis (NL) 4
Boston (AL) 3

The teams resumed their interrupted battle of 21 years before with yet another gripping seven-game set. But the inspired play of Lou Brock and Bob Gibson was more than the Red Sox could overcome.

The Preview:

It had been one of the most emotionally draining races in American League history. Four teams went into the final weekend with a chance to win and Boston came out with the pennant. The Sox clinched it in their clubhouse at Fenway Park while listening tensely to a radio transmission of Detroit's loss in the second game of a double-header. It concluded one of the more improbable climbs in history. Boston had finished ninth, 26 games off the pace in 1966, an uninspired and sparkless bunch.

The spark of 1967, Carl Yastrzemski, took the Red Sox on his back and carried them to a pennant. With one big hit after another in the final month, Yaz refused to let the team fold and he won a Triple Crown and MVP Award in the process, the second straight season the league had witnessed such a performance. Yastrzemski had stepped into the starting lineup in 1961 as heir to Ted Williams, an impossible burden to place on anyone. He won a batting title in his third season, but never could match the great man in power or stature. In 1967 he burst out with 44 homers and 121 RBIs, while leading the league at .326. He would never put up numbers like that again, but for one year Yaz was more than the Red Sox had dreamed.

His main assistance came from first baseman George Scott. In his second year, he hit .303 with 82 RBIs and showed a defensive

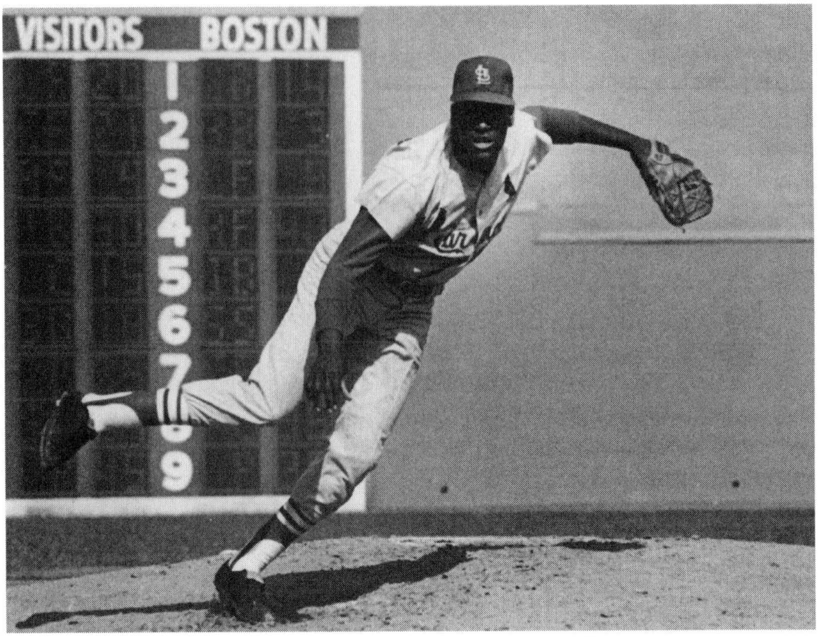

Bob Gibson won three complete games, striking out 26 while giving up only three runs. He also helped himself to a 3-0 lead with a home run in the fifth inning of Game 7.

flair, too. Young slugger Tony Conigliaro was injured in August, smashed in the face by a fastball, a terrible blow that not only ended his season but shortened his career. He was replaced by Ken Harrelson, made a free agent because of contract irregularities in Kansas City, a decision that foreshadowed the upheaval of the game's economic structure in the following decade. The Sox also acquired veteran Elston Howard from the Yankees for experience behind the plate in the stretch run.

Another key to Boston's sudden success was the performance of Jim Lonborg. The lanky Stanford graduate was in his third year with the team and it had been a struggle throughout. But in 1967 he learned to pitch inside, driving hitters off the plate and hitting 24 of them. It all clicked. He led the league with a 22-9 record and 246 strikeouts. Behind him there were problems, but curveballer Jose Santiago had come back from shoulder trouble to go 12-4 and was strong late in the season. Gary Bell (12-8) rounded out the rotation and John Wyatt, with 20 saves, was the top man in relief.

St. Louis, by contrast, had breezed to the pennant, winning by 10 1/2 games, and was well rested for the Series. Especially

Bob Gibson, who had missed two months of the season with a broken leg. As a result, his record was a mediocre 13-7, but his arm was a lot stronger than that. In his absence, the Cards patched together a staff of youngsters, who not only held on until Gibson returned but actually put distance between St. Louis and its pursuers. Dick Hughes, a rookie, led the way at 16-6 and Steve Carlton, who had started only 9 times the previous season, came back with a 14-9 year. The other starter was Nelly Briles, at 14-5.

The St. Louis offense was multi-faceted. First baseman Orlando Cepeda was the power source, with a league-leading 111 RBIs and 25 homers, a good total in the vast reaches of Busch Stadium. He also hit .325. Centerfielder Curt Flood led the team with a .335 average. The chief weapon was Lou Brock. He not only hit .299 with 21 homers, but his 52 steals set up the capable hitters behind him with lots of fastballs. Another addition was Roger Maris. The former Yankee slugger hit only 9 homers but was a steadying influence and a consistent performer and he was overjoyed to be out of the pressure cooker of New York.

Turning Point: Game Seven, Fifth Inning.

The headline in the Boston paper on the morning of the seventh game reads: "Lonborg and Champagne." It seems that the Sox will finally fill the cup after a wait of 49 years. Lonborg looks beyond the ken of the Cards. In game two, he throws a perfect game into the seventh, and a no-hitter through two outs in the eighth. He finishes with a one-hit, 5-0 win. Then in game five, with the Sox at the edge of extinction, he sends the Series back to Boston with a 3-hitter, winning a 3-1 duel with Carlton.

In the clincher he is up against Gibson, one of the greatest clutch pitchers the game has seen. He, too, is almost unhittable. He stops Boston, 2-1, in the opener, striking out 10. Then in game four, he weaves a five-hit shutout in the 6-0 Cardinal win.

Unknown Gary Waslewski, a desperate pitching choice for Boston, gave Lonborg and the Sox another chance in game six. He holds off the Cardinals long enough for Boston to rally late against the St. Louis bullpen and win 8-4. Now it comes down to the two stars for all the bread.

It is apparent, though, that Lonborg, on two days' rest, is struggling. In the third, Dal Maxvill, weakest of the St. Louis hitters, reaches the centerfield wall for a leadoff triple. He stays there as Lonborg gets past Gibson and the dangerous Brock, a .400 hitter in the Series. But Flood then cashes in the run with a single and Maris sends him to third with another single. Lonborg, trying to work inside on Cepeda, throws a wild pitch and the second run comes over.

If Gibson can be kept within hailing distance, Boston feels it has a chance. After walking the leadoff man in the first, Gibson cuts down 12 batters in a row, striking out 7 of them. Then in the fifth it all comes apart. Lonborg gets the pesky Maxvill, but Gibson, who prides himself on his hitting ability and has 12 homers in his career, parks one into the leftfield screen. The blow makes it 3-0. More than that, it indicates that Lonborg is done, but the Cards are not. Brock singles and then steals second and third to ride home on Maris's sacrifice fly. It is now a 4-0 lead. Even Boston's first hit, a triple by Scott, who continues on to score on a wild relay, can't put a dent in Gibson. Julian Javier's three-run shot off Lonborg in the sixth ices it. The Cards coast in with a 7-2 win on Gibson's third victory of the Series, a 3-hitter. Lonborg's valiant effort sails into the leftfield nets with Gibson's home run.

The Managers:

Dick Williams was a sub on the Brooklyn pennant winners of the early '50s and brought some of that scrappiness to a franchise that truly needed it. The Red Sox were derided as a country-club team, indulged by a benevolent owner, Tom Yawkey, who is only too happy to give his stars what they want, even if it undercuts his manager's authority. But the tough-talking Williams gets his group of prima donnas to produce and electrifies New England with this totally unanticipated pennant. It is the first of four he will win in a distinguished big league career.

Red Schoendienst helped beat Boston in 1946 as the Cards' second baseman and now he is back in the dugout to try again. A calm individual, he uses his cadre of experienced veterans, most of whom know how to win, to get the team through. He has lots of aces to play and manages to put them on the table at the right time.

FACT:

Lou Brock stole 7 bases, erasing the record of 6 that stood for 60 years. He hit .414, going 4 for 4 and scoring both runs in the opener, slugging a two-run homer to tie up game six, touching off one rally after another and driving the Red Sox crazy with his speed.

The Heroes:

It is almost impossible to choose between the top St. Louis performers, Gibson and Brock. For his second consecutive Series, Gibson has been a dominant pitcher. His 26 strikeouts are short of the record he had set in 1964. In his three victories, he was totally in control, his one lapse being a home run to his pitching opponent, Santiago, in the opener.

Brock was the true personification of the one-man gang. On the one hand, he stole

7 bases, running almost at will on Howard and the Boston pitchers, erasing Jimmy Slagle's record of six steals that had stood for 60 years. He also hit .414, going 4 for 4 and scoring both runs in the opener, slugging a two-run homer to bring the Cards back into a tie in game six, touching off one rally after another and driving the Red Sox crazy with his speed. It was the closest thing anyone had seen to Pepper Martin's team-wrecking performance in 1931.

The Series was also tremendously satisfying to Maris, who finished with 10 hits and led everyone with a .385 average. As the Cards celebrated wildly after the seventh game, a familiar scene to Maris, he simply sat quietly, a small smile on his face, watching the revelry around him.

Yastrzemski continued his clutch performance right through the Series. He hit .400 for Boston, drilled three homers, including two in Lonborg's one-hitter, and drove in five runs. When he was hit by a pitch on his first time up in St. Louis, one New England newspaper publisher editorialized on the front page that the offending pitcher, Briles, be suspended for the rest of the Series. That was the grip Yaz had on the faithful at the time.

The Zeroes:

Both teams had tremendous imbalances in hitting, with two or three players on either side carrying the attack. For St. Louis, Cepeda and Flood, two of the top hitters during the season, were a combined 8-for-57. The two additions to the Red Sox, Howard and Harrelson, went 3-for-31.

Hughes, the top Cardinal winner during the season, couldn't finish either of his starts, losing one and leaving early in the other. In game six, Yaz, Reggie Smith and Rico Petrocelli all homered off him in the fourth, the first time any pitcher ever gave up 3 homers in one inning in the Series. Hughes, a 29-year-old sinkerball specialist, had truly come out of nowhere and returned there almost as quickly. His entire major league experience prior to this year had been 6 games. Then in 1968 he started only 5 and went 2-2. He never returned to the majors.

The Aftermath:

Lonborg celebrated his great season with a skiing vacation over the winter. He fell, suffered severe leg injuries and was never the same pitcher again. The Red Sox could not make up for that loss, and their problems were

FACT:

The first 3-homer Series inning occurs when Carl Yastrzemski, Reggie Smith, and Rico Petrocelli all connect in the fourth inning of game six.

multiplied by wretched years for Scott and shortstop Petrocelli. Even another batting title by Yastrzemski (his .301 mark was the lowest winning figure in history) couldn't rescue Boston from a distant fourth-place finish.

The Cardinals, however, were back at the same old stand, with Gibson putting together one of the most overpowering seasons of any pitcher since the dead ball era. Despite an almost total lack of long ball power, St. Louis still won by a nine-game margin over the Giants.

Notes:

As the Cardinals bashed Boston's hopes in game seven, the perfect metaphor for the Red Sox season swirled to the heavens beyond the leftfield wall. A fire in an empty building sent smoke streaming across the skies, just as Boston's season was going up in flames, too.

St. Louis threw in eight pitchers in the sixth game in an effort to stem the Boston tide in the 8-4 Red Sox win. That was the most ever to appear in a single Series game. The 20 pitchers used by both teams in the Series also tied a record.

Line Scores:

Game One, October 4

SL (NL)—001 000 100—2
Gibson W

Bos (AL)—001 000 000—1
Santiago L, Wyatt (8)

Game Two, October 5

SL (NL)—000 000 000—0
Hughes L, Willis (6), Hoerner (7), Lamabe (7)

Bos (AL)—000 101 30X—5
Lonborg W

Game Three, October 7

Bos (AL)—000 001 100—2
Bell L, Waslewski (3), Stange (6), Osinski (8)

SL (NL)—120 001 01X—5
Briles W

Game Four, October 8

Bos (AL)—000 000 000—0
Santiago L, Bell (2), Stephenson (3), Morehead (5), Brett (8)

SL (NL)—402 000 00X—6
Gibson W

Game Five, October 9

Bos (AL)—001 000 002—3
Lonborg W

SL (NL)—000 000 001—1
Carlton L, Washburn (7), Willis (9), Lamabe (9)

Game Six, October 11

SL (NL)—002 000 200—4
Hughes, Willis (4), Briles (5), Lamabe (7) L, Hoerner (7), Jaster (7), Washburn (7), Woodeshick (8)

Bos (AL)—010 300 40X—8
Waslewski, Wyatt (6) W, Bell (8) SV

Game Seven, October 12

SL (NL)—002 023 000—7
Gibson W

Bos (AL)—000 010 010—2
Lonborg L, Santiago (7), Morehead (9), Osinski (9), Brett (9)

1968

Detroit (AL) 4
St. Louis (NL) 3

In a closely fought, memorable Series, the Tigers, behind the pitching of Mickey Lolich, broke Bob Gibson's seven-game winning streak. Detroit came back from a 3-1 deficit and upended the Cards on a misjudged liner that fell for a triple.

The Preview:

The Tigers felt that they had blown the 1967 pennant and broke from the gate this year as if they were a team on a mission. Never seriously challenged, they won by 12 games over Baltimore behind the astonishing pitching of Denny McLain. The 23-year-old right-hander was erratic the previous year, missing the last weeks of the close race with a foot injury incurred under mysterious circumstances. Detroit tried to trade him over the winter but could not connect on a deal. McLain, fitted out with contact lenses, then came back and went 31-6—the first big leaguer to win 30 since Dizzy Dean in 1934.

This was the year of the pitcher in baseball. Levels of fine pitching and rotten hitting that hadn't been approached since the dead ball era were commonplace. McLain's performance, and the drama gathering around him as he drew closer to 30 through August and September, was in a class by itself. His face leered from magazine covers all summer long. Cocky and abrasive, he did, indeed, seem like a TV-age version of Dizzy Dean, but he backed up his boasts with wins. In comparison, the other Detroit pitchers faded into the woodwork. Mickey Lolich struggled in mid-season but came up at the end to finish 17-9. Earl Wilson was 13-12. There was no main stopper in the bullpen. With McLain going every fourth day, there was no need of one.

Longtime Tiger star Al Kaline went down with a hand injury in May. In other years, that would have doomed Detroit, but the Tigers

Mickey Lolich, overshadowed by Denny McLain's 31 wins during the season, starred in the Series on the mound with three complete-game victories and a 1.67 ERA, and at bat with a homer, two RBI, and three hits.

were loaded with young outfielders. Willie Horton took over most of the hitting, with 36 homers and 85 RBIs to go with his .285 average. Jim Northrup led the team with 90 RBIs, which included 4 grand slams, two in the same game. A great defensive centerfielder, Mickey Stanley, rounded out the starters. Added to them was extraordinary pinch hitter Gates Brown, who hit .370 with a succession of game-winning, late-inning hits. First baseman Norm Cash and catcher Bill Freehan slammed 25 homers apiece, as Detroit was by far the most powerful club in the majors. But shortstop was a problem: The Tigers rotated three men in the position; none of them could hit and Tom Matchick, the top hitter at .203, couldn't field.

Manager Mayo Smith had another problem: Where was he going to play a healthy Kaline in the Series? The most popular player in Detroit, the veteran had finished strong at .287. After he had starred all these years, it was unthinkable to bench him. So the Tigers took one of the most bizarre gambles in Series history. Stanley, with a total experience of 9 games at the position, was named the starter at shortstop.

The Cardinals were favored anyhow. As good as McLain was, Gibson was frightening. He went 22-9, and his ERA of 1.12 was the lowest recorded by a starter in the live ball era. He pitched 13 shutouts, struck out 268 hitters and had games in which he threw like a perfect, impersonal machine. Moreover, Nelson Briles had developed into a tough pitcher, with a 19-11 record in his first full year as a starter. Behind them were Steve Carlton (13-11) and Ray Washburn (14-8).

Like everyone else in baseball, the St. Louis hitting declined drastically in 1968. Mike Shannon, the most consistent power hitter, had just 15 homers and 79 RBIs. Orlando Cepeda dipped to a .248 average and 73 RBIs, one of his worst seasons. Curt Flood still hit well, at .301, but Lou Brock tailed off to .279. His base running (62 steals), however, remained one of the top St. Louis weapons. The experience of the Cards and the proven pressure pitching of Gibson were enough to convince the oddsmakers. With an out-of-position shortstop facing them, too, St. Louis was the automatic choice.

Turning Point: Game Five, Fifth Inning.

Never has a Series turned as decisively and completely as this one. Until this point, it has been almost all St. Louis. Afterwards, it is a Tiger triumph. The Cards lead three games to one. Gibson has won twice, setting the strikeout record with 17 in the 4-0 opener and then breezing in as Detroit is humilated, 10-1, in game four.

Brock, for the second year in a row, is unstoppable. By the eighth inning of game four he already has equalled his own record of 7 steals, set the previous year. Detroit's Freehan is totally unable to control him. Moreover, Brock has gone 11-for-19 at bat, tormenting the Tigers with one big hit after another. McLain has been beaten twice and is complaining of a sore arm. It appears to be a wipeout for the Tigers, and when Cepeda starts this game with a three-run homer off Lolich in the first inning, the countdown seems like a formality.

Lolich beat St. Louis in game two, hitting the only homer of his major league career (and in his first Series at bat) in the process. But Briles now has a three-run cushion to close it out. The Tigers start coming back on him in the fourth. Stanley, who is playing an exemplary shortstop, leads off with a triple to the rightfield corner. Cash brings him in with a sacrifice fly, and then Horton rips another triple, to right-center. Northrup cashes him in with a single and it is only a 3-2 St. Louis lead.

Brock sets about to take care of this challenge himself. With one out in the fifth, he doubles off the wall in left center, his 11th hit of the Series. No one ever had made more than 9 hits in a five-game Series before, and it seems that he is about to make some more history. Julian Javier then singles to left and Brock takes off for the plate. Leftfielder Horton charges the ball well. Although not known for his arm, he uncorks a rocket to Freehan at the plate. Brock, believing he has the play beaten easily, comes in standing up, but Freehan, a former University of Michigan football star, has the plate blocked perfectly. The catcher knocks Brock's foot aside, less than an inch from the plate, wheels around and tags him as he tries to scramble back to home. Umpire Doug Harvey signals out and while the Cards protest vigorously, the decision stands. And the Cardinals are kaput.

Detroit rallies for three runs in the seventh, with Kaline getting the winning hit on a bases-loaded single. Lolich makes it stand up for a 5-3 victory, sending the Series back to St. Louis.

The Tigers then annihilate the Cards, 13-1, with a record tying, 10-run inning in game six, featuring yet another Northrup grand slam. That sets up a Lolich-Gibson showdown; each pitcher has won two games. After 6 innings of no runs and unbearable drama, Northrup hits a liner that Flood breaks in on. The ball carries over his head in deep center for a two-run triple. Lolich goes all the way in the 4-1 victory to conclude one of the great Series comebacks.

The Managers:

Mayo Smith was typical of the hail-fellow-well-met, hospitality room hanger-on who once abounded in baseball. He had managed the Phillies and Reds previously, the last job ending in 1959. Since then the 53-year-old Smith, a wartime player with the A's for one season, had been employed in various capacities, most often as an advance scout. A genial companion, he was nicknamed "America's Guest" and his selection as Detroit's manager in 1967 raised no great hopes. But he quickly made one good move, shifting a mediocre shortstop, Dick McAuliffe, who became an outstanding second baseman. He also seemed to have a gift for handling his collection of wild and crazy spirits on the Tigers.

Red Schoendienst was in his fourth year as manager of the Cards. He would stay for 8 more, the longest tenure of any manager in St. Louis history. And while he frequently had competitive teams, this would be his final winner.

The Heroes:

The 28-year-old Lolich had been the perennial number two man on Detroit's staff during his six years with the team. A hard-thrower, he ran into inexplicable mid-season slumps, often brought on by his annual two-week stint with the National Guard. For two years in a row,

FACT:
A hard thrower, Lolich ran into inexplicable mid-season slumps, often brought on by his annual two-week stint with the National Gaurd. A self-described "unlikely hero"—pot-bellied and jug-eared—his seventh game duel with Gibson, who had another phenomenal Series including a record-setting 17-strikeout perfomance in game one, was one of the top Series upsets ever.

Smith had to take him out of the rotation and send him to the bullpen to pull himself together. In 1967, his finishing kick almost pitched Detroit to a pennant. This year he gave them a championship. A self-described "unlikely hero," pot-bellied and jug-eared, Lolich stymied the Cardinals on the mound and also hit .250, with a home run and a single that touched off the winning rally in game five. His duel with Gibson in game seven was one of the top Series upsets ever.

Brock did everything in this Series but win it. His 13 hits tied Bobby Richardson's record of 1964 and his seven steals matched his own mark. Almost all his damage, however, was done by the midpoint of game five. When Lolich picked him off first in the sixth inning of game seven (followed a few moments later by a pickoff of Flood) the Series slowly slipped from St. Louis' grasp.

Gibson broke his own strikeout record with 35, including the record 17 in the opener. He finished with the same numbers as Lolich—three complete games, 27 innings, five runs. He was given a standing ovation when he walked to the bullpen to warm up before game seven, so sure were the Card fans of success. It didn't come, but it wasn't Gibson's fault.

Detroit's gamble to get Kaline in the lineup paid off big. The star rightfielder led the Tigers with 11 hits, hit .379 and drove in a Series-high 8 runs.

The Zeroes:

The usually dependable Flood made a classic fielding blunder. Northrup's seventh game line drive was hit like a bullet directly at him. It was apparent immediately that he could not pick up the ball in the white background. Just one step in was enough to allow the drive to clear him, although there were some who questioned whether he could have caught it anyhow.

Shortstop Dal Maxvill took the collar for the Series, going 0 for 22. Oddly enough, when most other hitters were taking a dive, 1968 had been the most productive season for the usually weak-hitting Maxvill. He finished at .253. But the slump that began in the Series dogged him through all of next season, as his average swooned to .175.

Freehan also went hitless in his first 16 at bats, before getting a single on his first time up in game six. He then drove in Northrup for Detroit's third run off Gibson in game seven. But his hitting problems, as well as his throwing problems against Brock in the early going, made the first half of the Series a flop for him.

The Aftermath:

The Tigers could not sustain success and finished 19 games behind the runaway Orioles in 1969. Moreover, in a continuation of the shortstop experiment Stanley hurt his throwing arm, which limited his effectiveness as an outfielder for the rest of his career. Smith did not survive two more seasons, getting canned late in 1970 and leaving with the bitter observation that "Detroit fans wouldn't know a ballplayer from a Japanese aviator." Nonetheless, a national group of expatriate Tiger fans call their organization, as a tribute to the manager, the Mayo Smith Society.

The Cards also hit a rocky road. They traded off Cepeda, Roger Maris retired and something happened to the team chemistry. They finished a poor fourth in 1969. Then the organization went for a major overhaul, shipping off several starters after that season. Among them was Flood. Rather than report to Philadelphia, however, he challenged baseball's reserve clause in the courts and won, opening the way to the huge free agent salaries that came into the game by the mid-'70s.

FACT:
Jose Feliciano's rock-soul rendition of the National Anthem before game four in Detroit enraged thousands of TV viewers, who flooded network switchboards in protest.

Notes:

This was the Series in which the National Anthem raised more of a furor than the games. Jose Feliciano's rock-soul rendition of the Anthem before game four in Detroit enraged thousands of TV viewers, who flooded network switchboards in protest. During the era of Vietnam War protests, Feliciano's singing was interpreted as a revolutionary act.

The final line on Stanley as a shortstop: 31 chances, two errors, Series lead in assists with 16. Neither of his errors resulted in a run, and by the end of the Series his appearance at short was accepted as a matter of course. "It was fun," he shrugged.

Detroit's 10-run third inning in game six tied the mark set by the A's in 1929. The difference, however, was that when Philadelphia exploded for 10, it was behind 8-0. Detroit already had the lead, 2-0.

Line Scores:

Game One, October 2

Det (AL)—000 000 000—0	SL(NL)—000 300 10X—4
McLain L, Dobson (6), McMahon (8)	Gibson W

Game Two, October 3

Det (AL)—011 003 102—8
Lolich W

SL(NL)—000 001 000—1
Briles L, Carlton (6), Willis (7), Hoerner (9)

Game Three, October 5

SL(NL)—000 040 300—7
Washburn W, Hoerner (6) SV

Det (AL)—002 010 000—3
Wilson L, Dobson (5), McMahon (6), Patterson (7), Hiller (8)

Game Four, October 6

SL(NL)—202 200 040—10
Gibson W

Det (AL)—000 100 000—1
McLain L, Sparma (3), Patterson (4), Lasher (6), Hiller (8), Dobson (8)

Game Five, October 7

SL(NL)—300 000 000—3
Briles, Hoerner (7) L, Willis (7)

Det (AL)—000 200 30X—5
Lolich W

Game Six, October 9

Det (AL)—02(10) 010 000—13
McLain W

SL(NL)—000000 000—1
Washburn L, Jaster (3), Willis (3), Hughes (3), Carlton (4), Granger (7), Nelson (9)

Game Seven, October 10

Det (AL)—000 000 301—4
Lolich W

SL(NL)—000 000 001—1
Gibson L

1969

New York (NL) 4
Baltimore (AL) 1

There are upsets, and then there are upsets. The Mets, baseball's longest running joke, shocked the country by winning a pennant, a playoff and then rolling over the Orioles, winners of 109 games, in this first year of divisional play.

The Preview:

The Mets were born in futility in 1962, in the first round of National League expansion. They dropped things. They fell down. They lost a lot—120 times in that first season. In their first eight years, they finished last 6 times and next to last, which was regarded as an enormous improvement, twice. "Can't anybody here play this game?" inquired a nonplussed Casey Stengel as he eyed the array of "talent" he was hired to manage in the first year. The New York media played along with the gag and turned the Mets into a synonym for inept fun, baseball's lovable losers, the antithesis of the lordly Yankees.

In 1969, something happened. Actually, it had started the year before, when the young pitching combination of Tom Seaver and Jerry Koosman won 35 games and made the Mets a serious team on the days they pitched. This year, Seaver was the league's best. He was 25-7 and won his last 11 straight as New York charged from back in the pack to overtake and demolish the front-running Cubs. Koosman was 17-9. The pair were joined by a third reliable starter, Gary Gentry, who was 13-12. It was a team loaded with pitching talent, including a young long reliever, Nolan Ryan, who was 6-3.

The hitting was still on the short side. Leftfielder Cleon Jones blossomed into a .340 hitter with 75 RBIs, and Tommie Agee gave the team outstanding play in centerfield, as well as

Donn Clendenon (far right) is congratulated by teammates after another of his three clutch homers in the Series. He led both teams with four RBI and hit .357 to lead the Mets over the stunned Orioles.

26 homers and 76 RBIs. Art Shamsky, in platoon duty, hit .300, and first baseman Donn Clendenon, a fine hitter in Pittsburgh for several years, was acquired in mid-season. He hit .252 and gave the Mets another player who could reach the seats, with 12 homers. Otherwise, this was a team of pesky hitters, none of whom hit very often. They surprised Atlanta in the playoffs, but few thought they would go any farther.

The Orioles simply blew teams away. Big hitters permeated their lineup. The biggest was Frank Robinson, with 32 homers, 100 RBIs and a .308 average. He was matched by Boog Powell, with 37 homers, 121 RBIs and a .304 mark. It had been a down year for Brooks Robinson as a hitter, with only a .234 average, but he still drove in 84 runs on 23 homers. In addition, players known for defense also turned into boomers. Centerfielder Paul Blair blasted 26 homers and knocked in 76 more, while shortstop Mark Belanger, regarded as a dead spot in the lineup, checked in with a .287 season. This was a team with no easy pieces.

The pitching was just as formidable. The Orioles had traded with Houston for Mike Cuellar, a left-handed screwballer. He had stitched together some decent years with a woebegone team but escaped notice. Once in Baltimore, he went 23-11. Two young veterans of the 1966 champions also were big winners, with Dave McNally going 20-7 and Jim Palmer at 16-4. The fourth man in the rotation, Tom Phoebus, was 14-7. Two stoppers out of the pen, Eddie Watt and Pete Richert, combined to save 28 games. Baltimore swept to a division title by 19 games, trounced Minnesota three straight in the playoffs and prepared to polish off the Mets for dessert.

Turning Point: Game Two, Ninth Inning.

On the surface, the Mets don't seem to lack for confidence. Rookie outfielder Rod Gaspar predicts a sweep after the playoffs. When informed of this, Brooks Robinson asks in sincere confusion: "Who's Rob Gaspar?" When told that he'd gotten the first name wrong, Robinson repeats the question. It doesn't appear that the Mets belong on the same field with Baltimore. The concept of winning four straight is silly.

FACT:
As one fan's sign reads: "If a man can walk on the moon, the Mets can win the Series."

Nonetheless, the New York media remind everyone that just nine months before, a similar underdog, the New York Jets, turned the football world on its ear by beating the mighty Baltimore Colts in the Super Bowl. Same two cities. It could happen again. Besides, as one fan's sign reads: "If a man can walk on the moon, the Mets can win the Series."

Baltimore almost casually beats Seaver, New York's best and hottest pitcher, in a 4-1 opener in Baltimore. Game two matches left-handers Koosman and McNally, and again the New York players seem overwhelmed at where they find themselves. Then in the 4th inning, a group of players' wives begin parading through the stands, holding up "Let's Go, Mets" signs and trying to stir the small scattering of New York fans. Coincidentally or not, Clendenon promptly hits a wrong-field homer to give them a 1-0 lead.

Koosman, meanwhile, cannot be touched. The Orioles have no hits until Blair opens the seventh with a single. Koosman then takes care of the two most threatening power hitters, Frank Robinson and Powell, on a fly ball and a pop up. But with two outs, Blair steals second and the reliable Brooks Robinson singles him in. The big Baltimore crowd lets out a sigh of relief. Everything is back on track. Now it is just a matter of time.

Into the ninth, though, it is still 1-1. McNally strikes out Clendenon, and Ron Swoboda is out on a grounder. When

Ed Charles singles, no one even squirms. The bottom of the Met lineup is weak. But catcher Jerry Grote sends another single to left and Charles heads for third. This brings up Al Weis. He had been a second baseman with the White Sox for years, a typical utility man, with fielding skills and no bat. His average for this season was .215. Weis rises to the moment, however, and sends a third straight single to left, scoring Charles with the lead run.

Koosman walks two in the last of the ninth, and reliever Ron Taylor has to come in and get Brooks Robinson to end it. But the 2-1 win convinces the Mets that they can, indeed, play with the Orioles. When they get back to Shea Stadium, pitching, more timely hitting by Clendenon and Weis, and game-saving defensive plays by Agee and Swoboda beat Baltimore three in a row. The Mets win their four straight, just as Gaspar predicted. And baseball is stood firmly on its ear.

The Managers:

Earl Weaver was cast in the mold of all those minor leaguers who had to get by on wit and scrap. A classic umpire-baiter, as well as a motivator, he inherited a talented Baltimore team that was going nowhere and actually turned it around to make a run at the Tigers in the late summer of 1968. After that, he won five division titles and three pennants in the next six years, as the Orioles dominate the league.

Gil Hodges was in his second year with the Mets and one of the most popular figures on the tough New York sports scene. A respected player in his days as the Dodgers' first baseman, he had never finished above .500 in five previous seasons as manager of the Washington Senators and Mets. But his teams improved every year and the patient, 45-year-old Hodges was an excellent handler of young players. His calm exterior, however, hid an inner tension that already contributed to one heart attack.

The Heroes:

The lanky Clendenon had several good seasons for the Pirates in the '60s, but they let him go in the expansion draft to Montreal. When he got off to a slow start with the Expos, New York dealt for him and he bulked up the middle of the feeble Mets lineup. He hit three homers in the Series and every one of them either gave the Mets a lead or brought them back into the game. His two-run shot off McNally in game five cut a three-run Baltimore lead to one and set the stage for the late Met rally that would clinch the Series. His four RBIs led both teams.

If Clendenon had some hitting credentials in his past, the outburst of Weis was totally unexpected. The 31-year-old infielder hadn't even been a regular during the season. He had filled in for shortstop Bud Harrelson when he was on National Guard duty and only started at second against left-handed pitching. But against Baltimore's left handers he hit .455, drove in the winning run in game two, hit the tying homer in game five and generally made a nuisance of himself.

Koosman won both his starts. He overcame one bad inning in the fifth game when he gave up homers to McNally and Frank Robinson—the only time Baltimore's power manifested itself in the entire Series. Aside from that inning, he gave up just 4 hits and his two-hitter in game two got the Mets back in the Series.

FACT:
A .215 hitter during the regular season, Al Weis drove in the winning run in game 2, hit the tying homer in game five, and generally made a nuisance of himself to the Orioles.

The Zeroes:

The mighty Orioles were held to an anemic .146 team average. The only lower mark was the .142 that these same Orioles had hung on Los Angeles in 1966. Brooks Robinson was held to one hit, Powell had no extra bases nor RBIs. It was one of the great collapses of a team known for its hitting.

While the Baltimore pitchers acquitted themselves well, their fielding was something else again. Of the four Orioles errors, three were committed by the pitchers. Richert's throw into a base runner's back gave the Mets the winning run in game four and Watt let a throw get away from him to give New York its final run in the 5-3 finale.

The Aftermath:

No one really expected this to be the start of a Mets dynasty, and they were quite right. New York faded back to third in 1970, although it was a respectable third, just 6 games off the leaders. While Clendenon kept his Series momentum going with a 22-homer and 97-RBI season, Weis faded from sight at .172. He was cut early in 1971 and left the game. The strong, fatherly Hodges kept the Mets in third for one additional season. During spring training of 1972, however, he died of a heart attack.

The Orioles bounced back from the debacle with 108 wins, an easy time in the playoffs and a championship against Cincinnati.

Notes:

Game four ended in a huge argument. The Orioles contended that pinch hitter, J.C. Martin, was running inside the foul line to first base when hit by Richert's throw on a sacrifice bunt in the last of the 10th. The ball bounced into rightfield as New York scored the winning run. Replays showed Baltimore had a case, with Martin clearly outside the boundary on the field side of the first base line. The decision stood, of course, and New York won, 2-1.

Three outstanding plays in the outfield saved the Mets. In game two, Agee raced to the wall to make a backhanded stab of Elrod Hendricks' drive with two on in the fourth. Three innings later, he dove into the left-center alley to grab Blair's liner with the bases loaded. Then Swoboda made a sliding catch of Brooks Robinson's looper down the rightfield line in the ninth inning of game four with two on. If any of those hits had fallen in, the Orioles would have capped a game-turning rally.

Ryan made the only Series appearance of his long career in game three in relief of Gentry. He gave up just one hit in 2 1/3 innings and struck out 3. But he loaded the bases in the 9th on two walks and a single, before mowing down Blair to end the game. A typical Ryan performance.

Line Scores:

Game One, October 11

NY (NL)—000 000 100—1	Bal (AL)—100 300 00X—4
Seaver L, Cardwell (6), Taylor (8)	Cuellar W

Game Two, October 12

NY (NL)—000 100 001—2	Bal (AL)—000 000 100—1
Koosman W, Taylor (9) SV	McNally L

Game Three, October 14

Bal (AL)—000 000 000—0	NY (NL)—120 001 01X—5
Palmer L, Leonhard (7)	Gentry W, Ryan (7) SV

Game Four, October 15

Bal (AL)—000 000 001 0—1	NY (NL)—010 000 000 1—2
Cuellar, Watt (8), Hall (10) L, Richert (10)	Seaver W

Game Five, October 16

Bal (AL)—003 000 000—3	NY (NL)—000 002 12X—5
McNally, Watt L	Koosman W

1970

Baltimore (AL) 4
Cincinnati (NL) 1

Brooks Robinson put on a defensive clinic at third base, demoralizing the Reds in the field and then hitting over .400 at bat. Baltimore had too much balance for Cincinnati and its rookie manager, Sparky Anderson.

The Preview:

The races ended early in both leagues, as the Orioles rolled home by 15 games and the Reds by 14 1/2. Then they each swept their playoff opponents, Minnesota and Pittsburgh. So a sense of anticipation surrounded this meeting of two powerful ballclubs.

Baltimore came back with the same cast of characters that demolished the American League in 1969. They got the same results, too. This time Boog Powell was the most punishing hitter, with a .297 average, 35 homers and 114 RBIs. Frank Robinson, now 35, battled injuries and age, but still led the team with a .306 average, albeit with reduced stats in homers and RBIs. Brooks Robinson perked up with a .276 year and 94 RBIs. Rookie outfielder Merv Rettenmund whaled out 18 homers and a .322 average to add even more punch to the lineup.

The pitching got better, as well. Mike Cuellar, Dave McNally and Jim Palmer were all 20-game winners, the first time that happened on a pennant-winner since the 1931 A's. They all pitched between 296 and 305 innings, too, never missing a start on the march to the pennant. Manager Earl Weaver felt that Palmer (20-10) would be most effective against the predominantly right-handed hitting Reds. The screwball of Cuellar (24-8) also figured to be effective against right-handers, and then there was still the comfort of having McNally (24-9) as the third choice. Again, Eddie Watt and Pete Richert were the bullpen combine, with 25 saves and 14 wins.

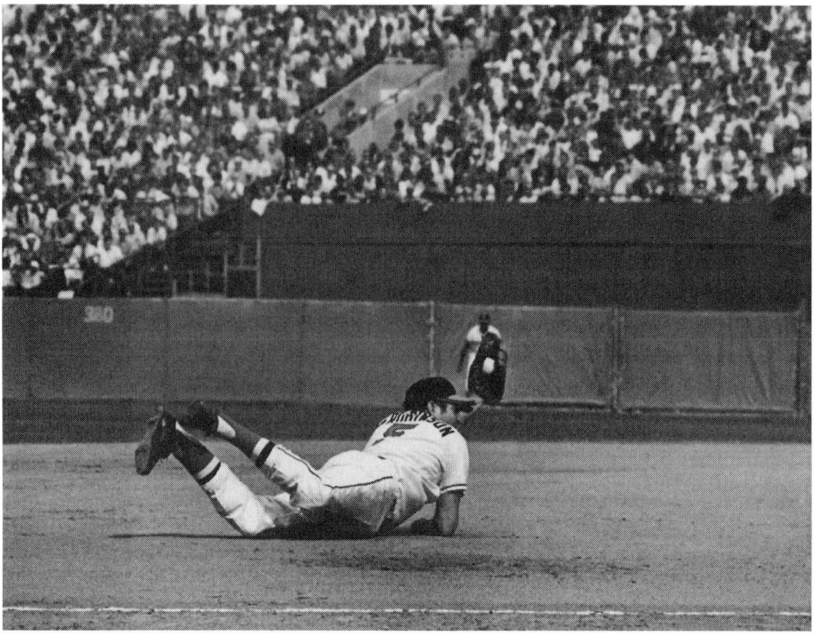

Brooks Robinson lands after his diving catch of Johnny Bench's liner in the sixth-inning of Game 3. Robinson's glovework alone would've earned him the MVP award even if he hadn't hit .429 with two homers and six RBI.

The Reds broke through to their first pennant in 9 years with a fierce display of power. Lacking a consistent long threat since their ill-advised trade of Frank Robinson to the Orioles in 1965, Cincinnati now had a gang of them. The leader was spectacular young catcher Johnny Bench, whose outstanding skills on defense had earned him, at 22, recognition as the best in the game. This was his breakout season, his third in the majors, as a hitter. He led the league with 45 homers and 148 RBIs, while batting .293—power figures that no catcher since Roy Campanella had put up. The Reds got another 40 homers and 129 RBIs from Tony Perez, a first baseman who had been shifted to third. The Reds did that to make room for Lee May, the Big Bopper, who added 34 homers and 94 RBIs. Pete Rose, who had won the previous two batting titles, tailed off a bit to .316, but "Charlie Hustle" still was the catalyst of the Cincinnati offense.

The Reds pitching could not compare with Baltimore's, relying far more heavily on its bullpen. Jim Merritt, acquired from Minnesota two years before, was the top starter at 20-12, while 22-year-old Gary Nolan put together his best year at 18-7. Behind them was confusion. But Sparky Anderson, who prided himself on manipulating his relievers, cajoled 51 saves out of the combination of Wayne Granger (35) and Clay Carroll (16). Another young arm, Don Gullett, joined the staff late in the year to add six saves.

Turning Point: Game Two, Third Inning.

For the second day in a row, the Reds comb one of Baltimore's big starters in the early innings. In the opener, it was Palmer. Cincinnati ran off to a 3-0 lead by the third, only to watch Baltimore inexorably close the margin and win it, 4-3, on a Brooks Robinson homer off Nolan in the seventh.

Game two starts the same way. The Reds' big hitters ring up three on Cuellar in the first inning. An error by shortstop Mark Belanger, followed by a Perez single, a two-run double by May and a squeeze bunt hit by Hal McRae get the runs across. In the third, the Reds continue the attack. Bobby Tolan leads off with a home run and Cincinnati is in front, 4-0. When Bench walks, Tom Phoebus comes in to relieve Cuellar.

May greets him with a bullet down the third base line, heading for the leftfield corner. Brooks Robinson not only manages to make a deft, back-handed stab of the ball off the fast Astroturf, he then starts a double play to end the inning.

That play is the beginning of the end for the Reds. Powell homers in the fourth off Cincinnati starter Jim McGlothlin to cut the lead to 4-1. Then Baltimore moves in for the kill in the fifth. Three straight singles get another run and drive McGlothlin out. Powell makes it four singles in a row off reliever Milt Wilcox, and now it is 4-3. Wilcox retires Frank Robinson, but Brooks then ties the game with another single. When Elrod Hendricks follows with a two-run double, Baltimore has the lead.

Robinson makes another extraordinary play on May in the sixth, cutting off Cincinnati's last threat before it has a chance to develop. The bullpen protects the margin and the O's get out of Riverfront Stadium with a 6-5 win, and take a 2-0 advantage in games back home.

No team ever lost the first two at home and then came back to win the Series. The Reds are no exception. They salvage game four, but the Orioles close it out in five. Robinson's play on May's apparent hit is only one of several defensive jewels. Dismayed by Robinson's second straight diving pickup of one of his liners, Bench throws up his arms in disgust as he runs to first. "I thought I'd seen great third basemen before," says Anderson, "but they were nothing compared

FACT:
So dismayed by Brooks Robinson's second straight diving pickup of one of his shots, Johnny Bench throws up his arms in disgust. "I thought I'd seen great third basemen before," says Sparky Anderson, "but they were nothing compared to this."

to this." Shrugs Weaver: "Oh, we see this all year from Brooks. The only time he surprises us is when he doesn't make the plays." Robinson tops it off with a two-run first inning double in Baltimore's third game win and is voted the outstanding player in the Series.

The Managers:

Weaver is at the top of his game. At the age of 40, he has won pennants in his first two full seasons as manager, and now a championship, too. A rotund little man, he enjoys growing tomato plants in the corners of Baltimore's Memorial Stadium. His devilish twinkle when engaging an umpire in deep disputation over a call becomes a signature of his regime in Baltimore.

This was Anderson's first appearance on the national stage. He, too, won a pennant in his rookie year, and although 6 years younger than Weaver, his white hair made him look far older than his age. Like many slightly built men, Anderson is a tough disciplinarian, a "my way or the highway" kind of guy. He played infield for the Phillies for just one season. Like many lesser-talented players, he learned to find an edge wherever he could, a quality that served well in making him a successful manager. He was on the first step of a path that led to the third greatest win total of any manager in history, behind only Connie Mack and John McGraw.

The Heroes:

Brooks Robinson was installed as Baltimore's regular third baseman at the age of 21 and had been the best at that position in the 12 years since. Even as a teenager, his skills, his ability to move on a ball almost as quickly as it left the bat, put him in a different dimension than most players. He is now 33 and regarded as one of the game's most dangerous clutch hitters. In his third Series, he finally gets a showcase. Turning in one sensational play after another, Robinson dominates these games and breaks down the Reds almost by himself.

FACT:
Dave McNally is the only pitcher in Series history to hit a grand slam; he had also homered in the fifth game in 1969, making him the only pitcher to have homered in consecutive games.

McNally comes back from his disappointing 1969 Series to go the distance in his only start, in game three. He also becomes the first pitcher in Series history to hit a grand slam home run. The sixth-inning clout off Cincinnati's top reliever, Granger, gives the Orioles an 8-1 lead in the game. McNally wins it 9-3.

Carroll pitches well in a hopeless cause for the Reds. He appears four times and pitches the equivalent of a complete game—9 innings,

5 hits, 11 strikeouts and Cincinnati's only win. His stint of 3 2/3 innings of one-hit ball in game four gives the Reds a 6-5 win, as May brings them from behind on a three-run homer.

May is the only Cincinnati slugger who lives up to his billing. Besides the three-run shot that won game four, he also connected in the opener. He wound up hitting .389 and his 8 RBIs led both teams.

The Zeroes:

It was a tough Series for Perez, recognized over the years as the last man in the Reds lineup you wanted to see come up in a tough situation. He was just 1 for 18 as a hitter and suffered the inevitable deleterious comparison with Robinson on defense. This was the only Series in which he didn't play first base, and his hitting improved markedly in later autumns.

Umpire Ken Burkhart had a less than shining performance, too. In the key play of the opener, he not only blew the call but actually blocked off Cincinnati's Bernie Carbo from scoring. With the lead run on third and one out, pinch hitter Ty Cline bounced a chopper in front of the plate. Catcher Hendricks fielded it and turned to tag Carbo, coming down the line. But he tagged him with his glove while holding the ball in his bare hand. Moreover, Burkhart had positioned himself squarely atop the plate and Carbo couldn't get past him to score. Nonetheless, he was called out, and despite enraged protests by the Reds the rally was over. Baltimore then scored in the seventh to win.

The Aftermath:

For the Orioles, 1971 was another 100-victory year and a third straight cakewalk to the pennant. Pat Dobson joined the pitching staff and gave them an unprecedented four 20-game winners, while the rest of the cast rolled merrily along.

The Reds, however, lost centerfielder Tolan for the entire season with an injury. Bench tailed off as a hitter and so did young shortstop Dave Concepcion. Merritt went from a 20-win year to 1-11. The end result was that Cincinnati dipped to fourth in the West, 11 games off the pace. It was only a temporary setback. The last parts of the Big Red Machine were being fitted into place.

Notes:

Baltimore's average of more than 6 runs a game and a .292 batting average were the best marks since the 1960 Yankees went wild against Pittsburgh, in a Series they lost.

Oddly enough, in a Series that belonged to Brooks, the third baseman made an error on the first ground ball he fielded. He threw wide of first on a routine play in the second inning of game one. It was the only mistake he made.

McNally's grand slam was his second homer in the Series. He hit a two-run shot in the fifth game in 1969. No other pitcher had ever homered in consecutive games.

Line Scores:

Game One, October 10

Bal (AL)—000 210 100—4
Palmer W, Richert (9) SV

Cin (NL)—102 000 000—3
Nolan L, Carroll (7)

Game Two, October 11

Bal (AL)—000 150 000—6
Cuellar, Phoebus (3) W, Drabowsky (5), Lopez (7), Hall (7) SV

Cin (NL)—301 001 000—5
McGlothlin, Wilcox (5) L, Carroll (5), Gullett (7)

Game Three, October 13

Cin (NL)—010 000 200—3
Cloninger L, Granger (6), Gullett (7)

Bal (AL)—201 014 10X—9
McNally W

Game Four, October 14

Cin (NL)—011 010 030—6
Nolan, Gullett (3), Carroll (6) W

Bal (AL)—013 001 000—5
Palmer, Watt (8) L, Drabowsky (9)

Game Five, October 15

Cin (NL)—300 000 000—3
Merritt L, Granger (2), Wilcox (3), Cloninger (5), Washburn (7), Carroll (8)

Bal (AL)—222 010 02X—9
Cuellar W

1971

Pittsburgh (NL) 4
Baltimore (AL) 3

Roberto Clemente refused to accept defeat, and his will to win inspired the Pirates to come back from a 2-0 deficit in games. Pittsburgh's maligned pitching staff shut down Baltimore's big bombers to finish off the upset.

The Preview:

The Orioles looked tougher than ever. In fact, they were oversupplied with talent and Earl Weaver had to juggle to get in all four of his outfielders. Frank Robinson's time was cut down somewhat, but he still topped the team with 28 homers and 99 RBIs. Merv Rettenmund, the second-year man for whom Baltimore makes room, was the top batter at .318 and also drove in 75. Leadoff man Don Buford slugged 19 homers and keyed the offense, while centerfiielder Paul Blair keyed the defense. Brooks Robinson and Boog Powell again contributed typical seasons, each getting 92 RBIs.

As if a rotation of three 20-game winners wasn't enough, the Orioles came up with a fourth. Pat Dobson was picked up from San Diego in the off season for some spare change and went 20-8. This fit in nicely with Jim Palmer and Mike Cuellar, both 20-9. Dave McNally worked the fewest innings but won the most games, at 21-5. The Orioles, who have won 9 straight playoff games, make short work of the upstart Oakland A's and turn their attention to Pittsburgh.

The Pirates were no match for Cincinnati in the 1970 playoffs. This year they powered up a bit. Leftfielder Willie Stargell had his best year with 48 homers and 125 RBIs, the biggest numbers ever for a left-handed hitter in Pittsburgh. Slap-hitting Matty Alou was traded, and in his place the Pirates started

Roberto Clemente would not let the Pirates lose. In Game 3, his hustle to beat out a routine grounder ignited a rally that broke open a tight game. Overall, Clemente hit .414 with two homers and four RBI.

Al Oliver, who hit with more authority and also posted a .282 average. The hero of 1960, Bill Mazeroski, reached the end and Dave Cash was moved in at second base. He responded with a .289 year. In addition, Bob Robertson hit 26 homers during the season, then crushed the Giants in the playoffs with a four home run outburst.

The heart of the team was Roberto Clemente. The last remaining starter from the 1960 champions, he was now 37 but still ranked among the game's top hitters. His .341 average was the best on the team and he also knocked in 86. More than that, he drove his teammates with a desire to win that burned in his eyes.

Pittsburgh's pitching was paced by Dock Ellis (19-9), who got away fast enough to be the starter in the All Star Game but then faded in the second half. Behind him was Steve Blass (15-8). Nelson Briles had come over from the Cardinals in the Alou trade but was hurt a good part of the season and not in the regular rotation. Nonetheless, he went 8-4 and had the extra benefit of having pitched in the Series before. Dave Giusti was the top man in relief with 30 saves. It was not a staff that matched up well with Baltimore's, and the Orioles were heavy favorites to repeat.

Turning Point: Game Three, Seventh Inning.

The Pirates look very bad in the first two games and Clemente is enraged. Ellis, who has the habit of talking better than he pitches, can't hold a 3-0 lead in the opener. A three-run homer by Rettenmund brings the Orioles and McNally back to a 5-3 win. Game two is even easier. The Orioles pound surprise starter Bob Johnson, a 9-10 pitcher during the season, and romp to an 11-3 win, even though an uncharacteristically wild Palmer walks eight Pirates.

The Series now is back in Pittsburgh, but the Pirates must contend with Cuellar, the third Baltimore 20-game winner. The home team responds with Blass, probably its most effective starter over the entire year. Pittsburgh starts out promisingly, with a leadoff double by Cash leading to a run in the first. The Orioles can't get a hit off Blass until the fifth, but Pittsburgh is not doing much better against Cuellar. The 1-0 lead holds into the sixth, when a double by Manny Sanguillen and a single by Jose Pagan expands its to 2-0.

The Orioles are a team that erase leads quickly in the late innings. Blass finally shows signs of weakening in the seventh when Frank Robinson pounds a tremendous home run into the second deck in left. Blass gets out of the inning, but now he is back to a precarious one-run lead.

Clemente is the leadoff batter in the Pittsburgh seventh. He is hitting over .400 for the Series, and regards it as his responsibility to seal off this game now. The best he can do is a roller right back to Cuellar, the most routine of outs. But Clemente takes off down the first base line as if he had just driven the ball into the outfield gap. Cuellar, who has fielded the tap languidly, is startled to see the easy out, a hitter who supposedly is afflicted with nagging injuries and cannot run hard, streaking to first. He double clutches on his throw and pulls Powell off the bag for an error. Clemente has turned a simple out into an opportunity and Cuellar is totally discombobulated.

He walks Stargell for the third time in the game, bringing Robertson to bat. The slugger cranks a Cuellar screwball breaking away from him into the rightfield seats for a three-run homer. Suddenly, the Pittsburgh lead is a secure 5-1, and Blass makes it stand up for the Pirates victory.

The restored Pirates topple Baltimore twice more behind the pitching of rookie Bruce Kison and Briles. After losing a tough extra inning game in Baltimore, they close it out on a four-hitter by Blass, with Clemente giving them the lead on a home run off Cuellar. The competitive fury of their veteran star sparks the Pirates to the upset.

The Managers:

Weaver is three for three as a manager; three seasons, three pennants. But there will only be one more in his remaining 11 years in Baltimore and the Series victory in 1970 was his only championship.

Danny Murtaugh had moved to the Pittsburgh front office after the 1964 season. He returned briefly as manager to finish out the 1967 campaign after Harry Walker was fired in midseason. When Pittsburgh continued to achieve less than anticipated, Murtaugh was brought back once more to manage in 1970. In just two seasons, he had them back on top, the only manager to win championships with this franchise in the last 46 years.

The Heroes:

In the early years of his career, Clemente was known to the media as Bob, but by 1971 he made it clear that he wanted to be known as Roberto. He was Puerto Rican and proud of it. There had always been whispers about Latino ballplayers. They lacked heart, wouldn't come through in the tough situations. Clemente heard the talk, seethed and waited for the chance to show it was a lie. Through four batting titles and a Series championship, he had gained respect as one of the top hitters and defensive rightfielders in the game. In 1971 he showed what kind of heart he had. Clemente's .414 average, 12 hits and 2 homers led both sides, and the Pirates were driven to victory by his inspiration.

Through his seven seasons with the Pirates, Blass had never been considered among the league's top pitchers. In most years, he wasn't even the best on the Pirates. He had gone 18-6 in 1968 but had never approached that kind of consistency again. He did lead the league in shutouts in 1971, but his 15-8 record and 2.85 ERA weren't anywhere near the top of the stats in this pitching-rich era. However, he shackled Baltimore twice, giving up just seven hits and two runs in his starts. His first win got Pittsburgh back in the Series, and his second win clinched it.

It was also a comeback for Briles. He had been a starter on the 1967–68 Cardinal teams, but had declined sharply from those years. He started only 14 games for the Pirates in 1971 and wound up pitching mostly long relief. Murtaugh pulled him out of the hat as his game five starter, and he responded with a 2-hit shutout over McNally.

FACT:

Clemente's .414 average, 12 hits and 2 homers led both sides, and the Pirates were driven to victory by his inspiration. He died after the 1972 season in a plane crash carrying supplies to earthquake victims in Honduras. The annual Roberto Clemente Award honors players for community service.

Frank Robinson did all he could in a losing effort. He went 5 for 8 in the first two Orioles wins, then manufactured the winning tenth inning run in game six. He walked, dove head first to get into third on Rettenmund's single and then slid home with the winning run on Brooks Robinson's fly ball to shallow center.

The Zeroes:

Ellis started the opener for Pittsburgh, couldn't get past the third inning and never appeared in another game. The 19-game winner had previously distinguished himself during the season by announcing that he would not be named the National League starting pitcher in the All Star Game against Vida Blue "because they don't want to pitch a brother against a brother." Upon being named the starter he gave up one of the longest home runs in Tiger Stadium history, a massive shot by Reggie Jackson off the base of the light tower on the rightfield roof.

One of the reasons the Orioles were so vulnerable to right-handed pitching in the Series was Powell's inability to get untracked. The big first baseman had 3 singles in 27 at bats and drove in just one run.

The Aftermath:

After winning his second championship, Murtaugh decided it was time for a rest. He had previously suffered a heart attack and while he was just 54, observers noted that he moved like a much older man. The Pirates repeated as division champs in 1972, although losing to Cincinnati in the playoffs. When they faltered the following year, the tremendously popular Murtaugh returned for a fourth time. He went on to win two more division titles, but was stricken with another heart attack after the 1976 season and died at the age of 59.

Clemente reached the 3,000 hit level at the end of the 1972 season. But on a New Year's Eve mercy flight with supplies for earthquake victims in Honduras, his plane crashed on takeoff into the harbor at San Juan. The 38-year-old superstar was voted into the Baseball Hall of Fame the next year. Blass, who had turned in his best season in 1972, was so shocked by the death of his friend and teammate that he developed a mental block, losing his ability to throw strikes. He went 3-9 the following year, walking 84 men in 88 innings, and retired from baseball the following year at the age of 31.

This was also a changing of the guard for Baltimore. Frank Robinson, the catalyst on four pennant-winning teams since 1966, was traded, and the remaining Orioles stopped hitting. The erstwhile terrors of the American League dropped to next to last in hitting. While their deep pitching kept them in the race, Baltimore finished 5 games off the pace in third. But help was already in the pipeline from the farm system, and this bunch of Orioles still had two more divisional titles left in them.

FACT:
Game four was the first night game in Series history.

Notes:

Clemente was not the most popular man in Baltimore during the Series. While in Pittsburgh he said it would be too tough to go back on the road and win "because Baltimore does not have a major league ballpark." The fans at Memorial Stadium took this personally and booed Clemente raucously each time he came to bat.

Baltimore was embarrassed, however, by failing to sell out either the sixth or seventh games in their home park. The sixth game attendance, in fact, was almost 10,000 short of capacity, the second straight season the team could not sell every ticket in the park for the Series.

The fourth game became the first in Series history to be played at night. There would be many, many more.

Because of a rain delay between games one and two in Baltimore, the customary travel date was waived before game three. Fortunately, the two cities were only an hour apart by air.

Line Scores:

Game One, October 9

Pit (NL)—030 000 000—3
Ellis L, Moose (3), Miller (7)

Bal (AL)—013 010 00X—5
McNally W

Game Two, October 11

Pit (NL)—000 000 030—3
Johnson L, Kison (4), Moose (4), Veale (5), Miller (6), Giusti (8)

Bal (AL)—010 361 00X—11
Palmer W, Hall (9)

Game Three, October 12

Bal (AL)—000 000 100—1
Cuellar L, Dukes (7), Watt (8)

Pit (NL)—100 001 30X—5
Blass W

Game Four, October 13

Bal (AL)—300 000 000—3
Dobson, Jackson (6), Watt (7) L, Richert (8)

Pit (NL)—201 000 10X—4
Walker, Kison (1) W, Giusti (8) SV

Game Five, October 14

Bal (AL)—000 000 000—0
McNally L, Leonhard (5), Dukes (6)

Pit (NL)—021 010 00X—4
Briles W

Game Six, October 16

Pit (NL)—011 000 000 0—2
Moose, Johnson (6), Giusti (7), Miller (10) L

Bal (NL)—000 001 100 1—3
Palmer, Dobson (10), McNally (10) W

Game Seven, October 17

Pit (NL)—000 100 010—2
Blass W

Bal (AL)—000 000 010—1
Cuellar L, Dobson (9), McNally (9)

1972

Oakland (AL) 4
Cincinnati (NL) 3

With their top hitter injured and another slugger held hitless, the A's found a surprise source of power in Gene Tenace and managed to upend the Reds. It was a Series in which every game but one was decided by a single run.

The Preview:

The Reds were back in business and this time they were a Machine. They added the parts needed to get faster and deeper and won the divisional title by 10 1/2 games. Pittsburgh pressed them to the limit in the playoffs, but the Reds came back in the ninth inning of the final game to take the pennant.

Second baseman Joe Morgan was the major addition, the player who turned Cincinnati from a very good team into the Big Red Machine. He shored up the infield defense, led the league in walks and runs scored, stole 58 bases, hit 16 homers and batted .292. With Pete Rose (.307) batting in front of him, and the power tandem of Johnny Bench and Tony Perez coming up behind, Morgan galvanized the Reds attack. After a one-season slump, Bench was back in top form, leading the league with 40 homers and 125 RBIs. Perez added 21 homers and 90 RBIs. Bobby Tolan, recovered from injuries that had sidelined him for all of 1971, drove in 82 runs while playing an exemplary centerfield.

Again, the Cincinnati pitching was suspect. Gary Nolan was the best on the staff at 15-5 and a 1.99 ERA, but after him, it got thin in a hurry. Ross Grimsley (14-8) and Jack Billingham (12-12) were the next in line. Not to worry. The Reds had assembled a remarkable

FACT:
This was the first Series since 1959 in which no complete games were pitched, but the whole philosophy of using bullpens had changed since then.

Gene Tenace nearly matched his regular season output with four home runs in the Series. No one else had more than one. He set a record with homers in his first two Series at-bats and collected nine RBI.

cast of relievers, practically one for every occasion. This was the first Series since 1959 in which no complete games were pitched, but the whole philosophy of using the bullpens had altered since then. Sparky Anderson was among the first managers to grasp the new rhythm of baseball. Get six or seven innings out of the starter and then come in every day with the pen. The Reds got 37 saves out of Clay Carroll, 11 from Pedro Borbon and 8 from Tom Hall, who also went 10-1. So 56 of the team's 95 victories were put away by the bullpen.

The A's franchise had waited for 41 years and two moves before connecting with a winner in Oakland. In many regards, this pennant was a personal triumph for the team's abrasive, outspoken owner, Charles O. Finley. He was the epitome of the butt-insky, interfering in every aspect of his team from the radio announcers to trades. He badgered his managers, hectored his players and executives, demanding a winner. He put an end to the club's self-destructive practice of trading promising young players for has-beens. The A's, instead, drafted an outstanding group of prospects in the mid 60s and then stayed with them, allowing them to develop into winners. Finley was an innovator, the first to try colored uniforms and white spikes and colored baseballs. He installed a mechanical rabbit in back of home plate to hand balls to the umpire. He advocated Series games at night during the week so more people could watch them on TV. He also was despised by every other owner in the game.

But Oakland got its winner. Paced by slugging outfielders Reggie Jackson (25 homers, 75 RBIs) and Joe Rudi (.305, 75 RBIs) and a burner at shortstop in Bert Campaneris (52 stolen bases), the perenially laughable A's were now a formidable team. There was power in the infield, too, with first baseman Mike Epstein (26 homers and 70 RBIs) and third baseman Sal Bando (15 homers, 77 RBIs).

The starters were also a superior bunch. Jim "Catfish" Hunter was the top man at 21-7, a pitcher with great command of a variety of curves and the head of a physicist to set them up. The A's traded with the Cubs for Ken Holtzman over the winter and he stepped into the number two spot at 19-11. The trade was doubly fortunate because Oakland's top pitcher the previous season, Vida Blue, ran into arm problems and finished a lackluster 6-10. But he was healthy coming into the Series. They also had John "Blue Moon" Odom (15-6) and a top reliever of their own in Rollie Fingers (21 saves).

The A's won the division by 5 1/2 games, then found themselves in a dogfight with Detroit in the playoffs. They finally won it in 5 but the price was an injury to Jackson, who tore a hamstring while sliding home with the winning run. That injury seemed more than an inexperienced team could overcome. Cincinnati was the heavy favorite to win.

Turning Point: Game Four, Ninth Inning.

No team ever lost the first two games at home in the Series then came back to win. But Cincinnati appears capable of doing it. Behind the surprising slugging of reserve catcher Gene Tenace, the A's take the first two at Riverfront Stadium. Tenace becomes the first man ever to hit homers in his first two Series at bats, and the A's win the opener behind Holtzman, 3-2. Next day it is Rudi's turn to hit the big homer and Hunter muffles the Reds, with ninth inning help from Fingers, 2-1.

When the Series returns to Oakland, though, the Reds rebound behind Billingham and win 1-0. Now in game four, they go with Don Gullett against Holtzman, a battle of young, hard-throwing lefties.

The teams are scoreless into the fifth. Then Tenace jumps up again and bangs his third homer of the Series into the leftfield seats. It is Oakland's first run in 19 innings and the sigh of relief in the Memorial Coliseum is palpable. Cincinnati has hit no homers at all, and through the seventh has scored just 4 runs in 34 innings.

Holtzman has stopped them on three hits, and for the second straight day the teams are grappling in a 1-0 game. Dave Concepcion starts the Cincinnati 8th with a single. He moves around to third on a bunt and Rose's infield out. At this point, manager Dick Williams decides he wants Blue. Knowing that this weapon is available for relief duty is a comfort to the Oakland manager. The move worked in game one, which Blue saved with 2 1/3 innings of shutout pitching. He also appeared briefly in game three. This time he pitches too carefully to Morgan and walks him. Morgan immediately takes off for second and Tolan drives Blue's delivery down the rightfield line. Both baserunners race home on the double and Cincinnati takes a 2-1 lead. The feeling is that the Reds are ready to take control of the Series and sweep away the A's, as Borbon comes in to wrap it up for Cincinnati. He gets Oakland in order in the 8th and retires the leadoff man in the ninth. Then Williams goes to his bench.

Gonzalo Marquez had won a playoff game with a pinch hit and also got a pinch hit single the day before. The rookie bats for George Hendrick and promptly lines a single off Borbon. Pinch-running specialist Allen Lewis is sent in for him. Now the worrisome Tenace comes to bat, and when Borbon falls behind on the count, the Reds bring in Carroll. Tenace singles, with Lewis stopping at second.

Williams now sends up Don Mincher, a veteran left-handed hitter who played first for the Twins in the 1965 Series. He was acquired for bench strength in mid-season by Oakland but hit only .148. This time he whacks a third straight single, tying the game and sending Tenace to third. With the ballpark reeling, Anderson brings in the Reds infield to try for the run at the plate against Oakland's third pinch hitter of the inning, Angel Mangual. A right-handed hitter, Mangual was a utility outfielder with the A's, batting .246; but as a pinch hitter, he was .375. He pokes the ball through the right side of the drawn-in infield and Tenace trots home with the winner. It is a 3-2 decision for Oakland, and the victory gives the A's a 3-1 lead in games.

The Reds win the next two but cannot make the full come-back. The three pinch hits give Oakland just enough margin to hold on for a seventh game. The A's win that one, 3-2, with a single and double by Tenace driving in two of the Oakland runs.

The Managers:

Sparky Anderson earned the nickname "Captain Hook" for his unhesitating removal of starting pitchers. But while he juggles his staff well, even he is baffled by the breakdown of the Reds offense in this Series. With six of seven games going down to the last inning, Cincinnati is always one hit away from taking charge. No matter what he tries, however, Anderson never can find the player to deliver it.

This was Dick Williams' second trip to the Series. After leading the Red Sox there in 1967, he was replaced two years later. Williams sat out the 1970 season before getting a call from Finley. He has delivered two division titles and a pennant, but he lives on the knife's edge with the owner and must deal with a clubhouse constantly in turmoil. Despite the team's success, it is not the most comfortable job.

FACT:
Tenace becomes the first man ever to hit homers in his first two Series at bats, and the A's win the opener behind Holtzman, 3-2. Tenace's entire output for the '72 season was 5 home runs, but his four-homer Series equaled the record set by Ruth, Duke Snyder and Hank Bauer.

The Heroes:

Tenace had never before been known as a power hitter. His entire output for 1972 was 5 homers; certainly not the kind of slugger to challenge the Series marks of Babe Ruth and Duke Snider, or even Hank Bauer. His four-homer performance equalled their records for a seven-game Series and suddenly turned this second-string catcher into a national hero. Tenace stepped into the lineup in August when Dave Duncan went into a long slump. He played every position but shortstop during the season and also knocked in the winning run of the deciding playoff game against Detroit. But nothing in his portfolio gave any warning of this Series explosion. His two homers decided game one. He hit another in game four, and then got the A's off with a three-run shot in game five, which they eventually lost. Overall, his .348 average topped Oakland and his 9 RBIs led everyone.

The handlebar-mustached Fingers saw action in all six of the close games, winning one, saving two and losing one. He stopped the Reds' last gasp in game seven, coming in with the tying run on second and no outs in the 8th. He got out of it with the A's still holding the 3-2 lead they won by.

Billingham also gave a good account of himself. He shut out the A's in game three, going 8 innings in the 1-0 Cincinnati win. He then saved game five and came back to start game seven. He allowed just one run, and that on a misjudged fly ball and a bad-hop single by Tenace. Billingham left for a pinch hitter in the 5th as Cincinnati rallied to tie the game, with the loss going to Borbon. So his final line was 13 2/3 innings, no earned runs.

The Zeroes:

For a while, Tolan seemed like the only Red who remembered how they had won the pennant. He drove in 6 runs and also stole 5 bases, giving Tenace his only uncomfortable moments of the Series. But in the final game he misjudged and then dropped a fly ball for a three-base error that gave Oakland its first run. Then in the sixth he turned late on Bando's drive to center and pulled a muscle as he tried to run it down. It fell for the game-winning double and Tolan was out of the Series. He was never the same player afterwards. While stealing 99 bases in his previous two seasons, he got only 44 in the remaining five years of his career, while his average plummeted to .206 in 1973. He was sent to San Diego the following winter.

The Series was also the end of the road for the slugging Epstein, as far as Finley was concerned. The first baseman, who wore a Star of David on the tongue of his spikes and referred to himself as "Superjew," went zero for 16. He was benched for game seven, with Tenace moving to first and Duncan catching. That was a harbinger of things to come. Epstein was moved to California during the winter and Tenace's Series performance earned him the starting role at first. Epstein lasted just 2 more seasons in the majors and hit a total of 13 home runs.

The Aftermath:

The Reds came back, more machine-like than ever, in 1973, despite poor seasons by Tolan and rightfielder Cesar Geronimo and arm troubles with Nolan. But they were stunned in the playoffs by the Mets, fell back to second place in 1974 and didn't return to the Series until the following year.

The A's traded Duncan for catcher Ray Fosse from Cleveland and a restored Blue once again was a 20-game winner. They returned to the Series, but the turmoil that constantly surrounded the team finally caught up with them there.

Notes:

Tenace's long ball hitting got him into the Series record book. His slugging percentage of .918 was the best ever in a 7-game Series. But the combined team batting averages of .209 were the lowest for a full-term Series.

All three midweek games were played at night for the first time, with only the Saturday and Sunday contests going by daylight.

Although it didn't effect the outcome, the A's managed to embarass Bench in game three. With runners on first and third in the eighth, Tolan stole second with one out. The pitch ran the count to 3-2 on Bench. Tenace then stood up as if to move outside for a fourth ball and an intentional pass. As Bench relaxed, Fingers, instead, fired a third strike past him. To add to the indignity, it was the third time he was called out in the game.

This was the second Series to be played in the San Francisco area. Just as in 1962 the rains showed up along with the ballgames. Game three was postponed by a downpour that hit just before the player introductions. Unlike the previous time, when a monsoon caused a three-day wait, the storm blew over the next day. For the second year in a row, however, the off day for travel was eliminated. This was a substantial trek, too, three-quarters of the way across the continent, which made some wonder why travel days were necessary at all.

Line Scores:

Game One, October 14

Oak (AL)—020 010 000—3
Holtzman W, Fingers (6), Blue (7) SV

Cin (NL)—010 100 000—2
Nolan L, Borbon (7), Carroll (8)

Game Two, October 15

Oak (AL)—011 000 000—2
Hunter W, Fingers (9) SV

Cin (NL)—000 000 001—1
Grimsley L, Borbon (6), Hall (8)

Game Three, October 18

Cin (NL)—000 000 100—1
Billingham W, Carroll (9) SV

Oak (AL)—000 000 000—0
Odom L, Blue (8), Fingers (8)

Game Four, October 19

Cin (NL)—000 000 020—2
Gullett, Borbon (8), Carroll (9) L

Oak (AL)—000 010 002—3
Holtzman, Blue (8), Fingers (9) W

Game Five, October 20

Cin (NL)—100 110 011—5
McGlothlin, Borbon (4), Hall (5), Carroll (7), Grimsley (8) W, Billingham (9) SV

Oak (AL)—030 100 000—4
Hunter, Fingers (5) L, Hamilton (9)

Game Six, October 21

Oak (AL)—000 010 000—1
Blue L, Locker (6), Hamilton (7), Horlen (7)

Cin (NL)—000 111 50X—8
Nolan, Grimsley (5) W, Borbon (6), Hall (7) SV

Game Seven, October 22

Oak (AL)—100 002 000—3
Odom, Hunter (5) W, Holtzman (8), Fingers (8) SV

Cin (NL)—000 010 010—2
Billingham, Borbon (6) L, Carroll (6), Grimsley (7), Hall (8)

1973

Oakland (AL) 4
New York (NL) 3

It was an ugly Series, filled with errors, strikeouts and a foul-tempered owner who embarrassed his team by trying to fire one of his players right in the middle of it. The A's muddled through the madness and won a second straight championship.

The Preview:

Oakland's 1972 championship was looked on as something of a gift, an upset of a good team by a lucky one. But the A's came back to prove that luck had very little to do with it. They fielded an even stronger team this year. It was the first year of the designated hitter and almost every team improved in batting, but the A's jumped by a full 20 points. A fully-recovered Reggie Jackson led the league in homers (32) and RBIs (117), while hitting a team-high .293. Sal Bando had a big season with 29 homers and 98 RBIs. Gene Tenace, hero of the World Series, took over as the regular first baseman and continued his newly-found display of power, with 24 homers and 84 RBIs. Designated hitter Deron Johnson was picked up from the Phillies and added 19 homers.

It was in pitching, however, that Oakland earned its dominance. Vida Blue was once more in the form of his rookie year, with a 20-9 mark. Joining him in the 20-win circle were Catfish Hunter (21-5) and Ken Holtzman (21-13), while Rollie Fingers was again a beacon in the bullpen with 22 saves and a 1.92 ERA. Oakland edged out the Kansas City Royals by 6 games, then defeated Baltimore in a tough playoff, with Hunter pitching a shutout to win it in 5.

Much to everyone's surprise, Oakland found itself facing the New York Mets. The National League's Eastern Division had

Reggie Jackson (right) celebrates his two run homer in Game 7. Jackson, who missed the previous year's World Series due to injury, was named MVP for his nine hit, six RBI performance in the 1973 Classic.

been regarded as a bad joke. Going into mid September, the leader was barely above .500. The final Mets mark of .509 was the worst ever compiled by a winner of any baseball race. Three teams in the West were better. The cream of the jest was the playoffs. New York stunned the Reds and reeled with astonishment into the Series.

The Mets, as usual, had pitching. Tom Seaver was 19-10 with a league best 2.08 ERA and 251 strikeouts. But both the other top starters were under .500, an unprecedented stat for a Series team. Jerry Koosman finished 14-15 and Jon Matlack was 14-16. Tug McGraw was tough in relief with 25 saves, but his 3.87 ERA was not exactly intimidating.

Only one team in the league hit worse than the Mets, too. Rusty Staub was the best in their lineup, with 15 homers, 76 RBIs and a .279 average. His 3 homers in the playoffs had helped sink the Reds. Once past him, the Mets frightened nobody. Third baseman Wayne Garrett led the team with 16 homers and first baseman John Milner drove in 72 runs. Second baseman Felix Millan hit a team-high .290. New York did acquire Willie Mays in mid-season, but he was many seasons past his prime and batted only .211. Moreover, Seaver had to pitch the final game of the playoffs and would not be available until the third game of the Series. The A's did not figure to be in for much of a fight.

Turning Point: Game Six, Third Inning.

The Series has returned to Oakland and the A's find themselves clawing at the wall. After splitting the first two games in Oakland, they score only four runs in the three games in New York and lose two of them. Seaver strikes out 12 in a game the A's pull out in extra innings, but Matlack stops them on a 5-hitter and Koosman and McGraw team up on a 3-hit shutout. The Mets are one game away from the championship with Seaver scheduled to pitch again.

Worse yet, the A's are self-destructing. They commit 5 errors in game two, including two on successive plays by second baseman Mike Andrews in the 12th inning. Three unearned runs score as a result, which turns out to be the margin of defeat in the 10-7 game. Finley hits the roof. He demands that Andrews be placed on the injured list because of a fictitious ailment. When this is turned down, he tells manager Dick Williams to bench the player. But his teammates rally around the humiliated Andrews and even the Mets fans give him a standing ovation when he is sent up to pinch hit in the fourth game. It is the last time he appears in the Series.

Just as it all is coming unraveled, Jackson turns in the first of the performances that would win him the nickname of Mr. October. The A's start their own ace, Hunter, against Seaver in game six and it is apparent that every run will be vital. Joe Rudi singles for Oakland in the first and with two out Jackson lines a double up the left-center alley to score the first run. In the third, Bando singles with two out and once more Jackson comes to bat. This time he finds the right-center gap for his second double, as Bando scores to make it 2-0.

Hunter, pitching his usual crafty game, makes this lead stand up into the eighth. He strikes out just one man, but his control is almost perfect. He is constantly ahead in the count and, as is his style, forces the Mets to hit his pitches. When pinch hitter Ken Boswell singles with one out in the eighth, though, the A's bring in left-hander Darold Knowles. The move almost boomerangs when Garrett and Millan also single. The Mets now have a run over and Staub, their best hitter, coming up. But Knowles manages to find the answer and strikes him out. Now Oakland can bring in its top reliever, Fingers, to face Cleon Jones. Fingers gets him on a fly ball and the A's are still ahead, but only by a 2-1 margin.

McGraw, who already has a win and a save, has pitched effectively every time out, and he comes in for Seaver. It is

McGraw who invented the Mets team slogan: "You gotta' believe." The A's know that New York is uncomfortably close and dangerously confident. Jackson is the leadoff hitter in the Oakland eighth and he smacks his third hit of the game, a single to center. When Don Hahn kicks the ball away, Jackson keeps running and races all the way to third. He then scores on a sacrifice fly by Matty Alou, giving Fingers a 3-1 margin to protect in the ninth. He does, and the A's force a seventh game. Jackson also takes over that one. He and Bert Campaneris put it away with two-run homers in the third off Matlack. Oakland coasts to a 5-2 win and the championship, courtesy of the October Man.

The Managers:

This Series proved to be all that Dick Williams could take of Charlie Finley. After the Mike Andrews incident in the second game, the manager resolved that, win or lose, he was gone. Accordingly, as soon as the Series was over, Williams turned in his resignation. Finley announced that he still had the manager under contract and would block any other team from hiring him. He was signed by California in mid-season of 1974.

This season must have seemed like *deja vu* all over again to Yogi Berra. Just as with the Yankees in 1964, he got his team into the Series, but it didn't seem enough. The Mets had been wallowing in the cellar as late as August of this year and there were frequent reports that Berra would be fired at any time. Unlike his experience of nine years before, though, the Mets brought him back in 1974. But the Mets fell to fifth place and then the following year he was terminated. He never managed full-time again, making his record four full seasons and two pennants. Surely, no manager with that kind of percentage has ever been accorded so little respect.

The Heroes:

Jackson was not exactly a stranger to national publicity. The former Arizona State star had first attracted attention with his quick start in home runs in 1969—a pace that had him way ahead of the record in July. He wound up with 47, but in his third big league season he had become a star. Two seasons later, he slammed an enormous homer in the All Star Game, indicating a flair for the big gesture on the large stage. Missing the 1972 Series with a leg injury ate him up. Now he was missing no chance at taking the spotlight. He won the award for the Series MVP and entertained the national media with his quotable personality. He hit .310 for the Series, and four of his six RBIs came in the last two games, when the A's had to win to survive.

The margin in this Series was the Oakland bullpen, with Knowles setting a record by appearing in all seven games and Fingers making it into 6. They combined to save all four of the A's wins, pitched a combined 20 innings and allowed one run.

Staub led the New York attack with 11 hits and 6 RBIs. Five of them came in game four, a 6-1 Mets win, which he put away practically by himself with his 4-for-4 performance. Staub was playing with an injured shoulder. He had to throw underhand to the relay man, who ran out to short rightfield on almost every ball hit in that direction.

FACT:
The margin of this Series was the Oakland bullpen, with Darrold Knowles setting a record by appearing in all seven games and Rollie Fingers making it into six. They combined to save all four of the A's wins and gave up only one run in twenty innings.

The Zeroes:

It was not a pretty farewell for Mays. The greatest player of his generation announced his retirement right after this Series. He bobbled a single for an error in his only start in the first game. Then, in game two, he opened the door for Oakland's tying rally in the ninth when he lost Deron Johnson's liner to center in the glare and it fell for a double. But in the 12th, his looping, two-out single off Fingers scored the go-ahead run. It was the last hit he would get in baseball. The Series was also the final appearance for Andrews. The 30-year old infielder had come up with Boston and was the regular second baseman on the 1967 pennant winners, hitting .308 in that Series. The A's picked him up late in the season from Chicago for his versatility in the infield. After Finley tried to disown him because of his errors in game two, Andrews played just once more, as a pinch hitter in game five. Not many players can come back after being nationally maligned by their own owner. Andrews called it quits when the season ended, then sued Finley, unsuccessfully, for libel.

The Aftermath:

Williams became the first manager to walk away from a champion since Johnny Keane did it in 1964. Finley just shrugged and hired Alvin Dark, who then led his fractious, feuding ballclub to its third consecutive title.

The Mets fell to 20 games under .500, with mediocre years by Seaver and Staub sinking any chance they had. Those who called 1973 a fluke appeared to be absolutely right. The Mets would rebuild completely before winning another pennant in 1986.

Notes:

Mays played in his first World Series in 1951. The 22-year span between his first Series and the last one broke the record set by Herb Pennock, who played between 1914 and 1932. That is still the longevity mark for pitchers. Mays, the third most prolific home run hitter in the game's history, hit none in four Series.

FACT: The teams combined for 19 errors, the worst Series performance since 1934. The Mets set a team pitching record by fanning the A's 62 times. Individual Series records for strikeouts and walks were tied. That's the kind of Series it was.

Just to show what kind of Series this was, two records were tied in the seventh game—one for strikeouts and the other for walks. By whiffing for the 11th time, Garrett tied the mark set by Eddie Mathews in 1958. And by walking for the 11th time, Tenace matched the mark set by Babe Ruth in 1926.

The teams combined for 19 errors, the worst performance since the Tigers and Cardinals had combined for 27 errors in 1934. The Mets also set a team pitching record by striking out the A's 62 times.

The 12-inning game two took four hours and 13 minutes, the longest game in Series history.

Line Scores:

Game One, October 13

NY (NL)—000 100 000—1
Matlack L, McGraw (7)

Oak (AL)—002 000 00X—2
Holtzman W, Fingers (6), Knowles (9) SV

Game Two, October 14

NY (NL)—011 004 000 004—10
Koosman, Sadecki (3), Parker (5), McGraw (6) W, Stone (12) SV

Oak (AL)—210 000 102 001—7
Blue, Pina (6), Knowles (6), Odom (8), Fingers (10) L, Lindblad (12)

Game Three, October 16

Oak (AL)—000 001 010 01—3
Hunter, Knowles (7), Lindblad (9) W, Fingers (11) SV

NY (NL)—200 000 000 00—2
Seaver, Sadecki (9), McGraw (9), Parker (11) L

Game Four, October 17

Oak (AL)—000 100 000—1
Holtzman L, Odom (1), Knowles (4), Pina (5), Lindblad (8)

NY (NL)—300 300 00X—6
Matlack W, Sadecki (9)

Game Five, October 18

Oak (AL)—000 000 000—0	NY (NL)—010 001 00X—2
Blue L, Knowles (6), Fingers (7)	Koosman W, McGraw (7) SV

Game Six, October 20

NY (NL)—000 000 010—1	Oak (AL)—101 000 01X—3
Seaver L, McGraw (8)	Hunter W, Knowles (8), Fingers (8) SV

Game Seven, October 21

NY (NL)—000 001 001—2	Oak (AL)—004 010 00X—5
Matlack L, Parker (3), Sadecki (5), Stone (7)	Holtzman W, Fingers (6), Knowles (9) SV

1974

Oakland (AL) 4
Los Angeles (NL) 1

Arguing and complaining all the way, the A's made their third straight championship the easiest one of all. They polished off a Dodger team that was not quite ready for prime time in the first all-California Series.

The Preview:

Pitchers Rollie Fingers and Blue Moon Odom prepared for the Series by duking it out in the Oakland clubhouse. Fingers wound up with a gash on his forehead. Catfish Hunter was claiming that owner Charles O. Finley had violated his contract and he threatened to become a free agent. Reggie Jackson wasn't talking to manager Alvin Dark. The A's were so angry at each other that no one seemed to notice the Dodgers.

Oakland simply may have been getting bored. With their third pennant in a row, the A's had a chance to accomplish what no franchise but the Yankees had ever pulled off—three straight championships. It was pretty much the same old formula, power and pitching, by the same cast that had done the job the previous two years. Jackson again was the heart of the attack, with 29 homers and 93 RBIs. Sal Bando dropped off in average, but still had 22 homers and 103 RBIs. Those stats almost were duplicated by leftfielder Joe Rudi, who hit the same number of homers and 4 fewer RBIs. He also batted .293, best on the team. Centerfielder Bill North was acquired from the Cubs, for whom he played 75 games over two seasons; he led the league in steals with 54.

Pitching, though, makes the A's uncatchable. Hunter had his best year, with a 25-12 record and a league-leading 2.49 ERA. The other two starters were not quite up to previous

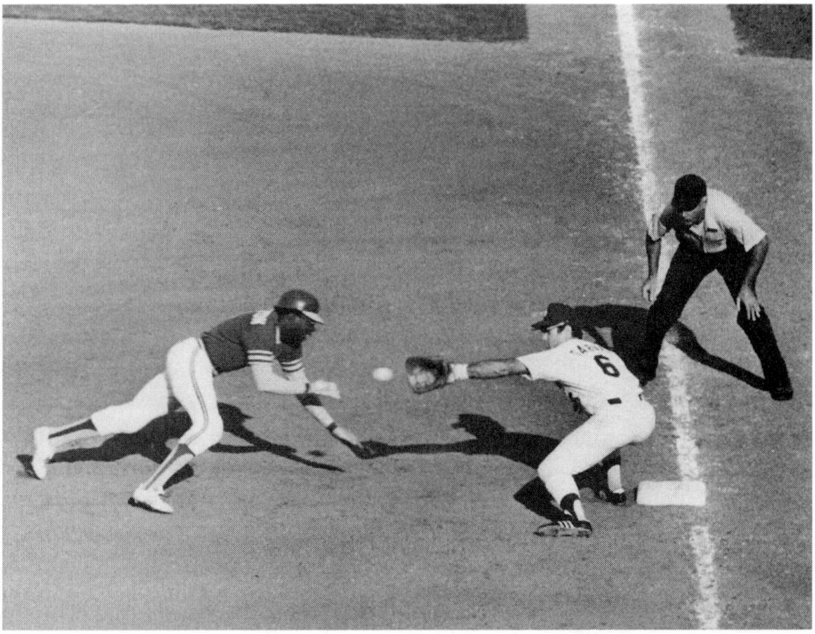

Herb Washington (diving) is picked off at first in Game 2, killing a potential rally. Washington, a former sprinter, was used exclusively as a pinch-runner, never coming to bat during the season or in the Series.

levels. Vida Blue was 17-15 and Ken Holtzman 19-17; the reliable Fingers was around to save 18. They were veterans and they were good. The fact that they were also angry didn't faze the oddsmakers.

The Dodgers swung a major deal with Houston over the winter and wound up with a badly needed power hitter in the middle of their lineup. Jim Wynn, "the Toy Cannon," hit 32 homers, drove in 108 runs and seemed to make the hitters around him more formidable, too. Steve Garvey took over as the regular first baseman and led the team with 111 RBIs while hitting .312. It was the first season the infield of Garvey, Dave Lopes, Bill Russell and Ron Cey played as a unit. It would remain intact for four pennants over 7 seasons, the longest survival rate for an entire infield in history. Bill Buckner, moved out to left field by Garvey, had the team-best average at .314, while the two catchers—Steve Yeager and Joe Ferguson—combined for 98 RBIs.

It was also a fairly typical Dodger pitching staff. Andy Messersmith, in his second year since coming over from the Angels, led the league at 20-6. Don Sutton, the veteran on the team, was 19-9. Tommy John went 13-3 before going down with an arm injury that threatened to end his career. Instead, the Dodgers had to rely on ex-Yankee Al Downing (5-6) as a third starter in the Series. Los Angeles also had an X-factor on its staff. Reliever Mike Marshall had come over from Montreal in another off-season deal and upended all the standard theories on pitching. Following a self-devised physical regimen, the 31-year-old Marshall scoffed at rest. He appeared in 106 games and pitched 208 innings—both absolutely unprecedented marks for a relief pitcher. Moreover, he won 15, saved 21 more and seemed as fresh as April for the Series. The Dodgers staved off a late-season charge by Cincinnati and then wiped out Pittsburgh in four in the playoffs. But few gave them a chance against Oakland.

FACT:
It was the first season the infield of Steve Garvey, Davey Lopes, Bill Russell and Ron Cey played as a unit. It would remain intact for 4 pennants over 7 seasons, the longest survival rate for an infield in history.

Turning Point: Game Four, Sixth Inning.

It is a Series almost devoid of indelible moments. The A's have won routinely twice. First Hunter, in a rare relief role, puts down a ninth-inning Dodger rally in the opener by coming in for Fingers and striking out Ferguson with the tying run on first. Then Fingers does the same for Hunter in the third game, stifling Los Angeles threats in both the eighth and ninth with double plays. The score in both games is 3-2. In between, the Dodgers take their turn and win yet another 3-2 game behind Sutton and Marshall. Game four matches Messersmith and Holtzman, the opponents in the first game. The Dodgers have hung tough against the favored A's and a win in Oakland could get them back into it.

Holtzman, who didn't bat all year because of the designated hitter rule, had doubled and scored in the first game. He improves on that this time. He pounds one over the leftfield wall in the third, and Oakland is off to a lead.

The Dodgers retaliate quickly. A single by Garvey and a walk to Ferguson sets the table for Russell, who drills a triple off the base of the wall in right-center, and the Dodgers lead, 2-1. So far, the team that builds an early lead has won every game in this Series. But the Dodgers know they must expand the margin to give Marshall a chance to come in and save it.

Wynn opens the sixth with a double and the Dodger right-handed power is coming up against Holtzman. But all Garvey, Ferguson and Cey can do is send harmless grounders to third. The Dodgers cannot break through and the A's are ready to roll.

North starts it with a walk. He advances on a wild pitch, and when Bando singles he comes in to tie the game. Messersmith then walks Jackson, and Rudi sacrifices the runners ahead. Trying to stave off the inevitable, the Dodgers walk hot-hitting rookie Claudell Washington. This brings up catcher Ray Fosse, but Dark, instead, sends up Jim Holt. He is one of the lesser A's, a part-time outfielder picked up from Minnesota in mid-season. While he hit just .143 for the A's, the left-hander had already come through with a single in an earlier pinch hitting assignment against Sutton. Holt does it again on Messersmith, driving a single through the right side to bring in two more runs and up the Oakland lead to 4-2. The A's score once more, and Holtzman and Fingers make it stand up for a 5-2 win.

The big inning buries Los Angeles too deep for hope and the A's finish it off the next day, in one more 3-2 game. Rudi jerks a Marshall fastball into the stands in the seventh for the winning margin.

The Managers:

Alston has been at the helm of the Dodgers for 21 years, the longest and most sucessful run in the team's history. He won seven pennants and the first four championships the franchise garnered. An anonymity when he took over, at 62 he is now a beloved icon in Los Angeles. He won with power teams and he won with speed and pitching. Rather than shaping the team to fit his ideas, he adapted to win with what he had. It had been 8 years since his previous pennant and this will be his last one. In only four seasons did he finish under .500.

This is something of a vindication for Dark. He won a pennant with the Giants in 1962, his second season as a manager, then was cut loose after just two more years. He managed awful teams in Kansas City in the mid-'60s, but Finley remembered him fondly from that term with the A's. Now that he finally had the horses, Dark was his choice again to replace Dick Williams. In one of the toughest situations imaginable, Dark fought the pressure, calmed the troubled waters and brought Oakland home again.

The Heroes:

Rudi was one of the few A's who didn't seem to be mad at anyone. Throughout Oakland's disruptive marches to the top, he simply went out, drove in about 80 runs a year, hit about 20 homers and batted around .290. In 1974 he also led the league in doubles. The 28-year-old leftfielder seemed to prefer the relative anonymity, a blue-collar laborer on a team of massive, wounded egos. It was fitting that Rudi's seventh inning homer in gave five produced the run that won the Series.

Fingers was voted the outstanding player of the Series, winning one game and saving two others. He gave up just two runs, on bases-empty homers, and never surrendered a lead.

Marshall was equally effective. He appeared in every game, pitching nine innings, striking out 10 and allowing just a single run. But that run was Rudi's homer in game five and it tagged Marshall with the loss.

FACT:
Buckner made the classic baserunning mistake: Never get thrown out on the bases when your team is behind and you are already in scoring position with less than two outs.

The Zeroes:

Dick Green had seen the worst of times with the A's in Kansas City, then had ridden the championship wave to its crest in Oakland. But he slumped during the 1973 Series. In fact, it was his place that the maligned Mike Andrews was taking when he ran afoul of Finley's temper. The 33-year-old Green could not get going this year, either. He went 0 for 13 in the Series, for a combined two-year total of 1 for 29. He announced his retirement immediately afterwards.

Buckner made the classic base-running mistake of the Series. Leading off the eighth inning of game five, with the Dodgers trailing, 3-2, he singled. North let the ball get through him for an error. Not content with taking one extra base, Buckner tried for two. But Jackson backed up North and fired a bullet to Green, who threw a perfect relay to Bando. Buckner was out and the last Los Angeles chance was over. It may not rank in notoriety with the error he made 12 years later with Boston, but it violated a cardinal tenet: Never get thrown out on the bases when you are behind and already in scoring position with less than two outs.

The Aftermath:

True to his threat, Hunter took Finley to court after the season and won free agency because of a contract violation. In an intense bidding war for the league's best pitcher, the Yankees won his services with a contract calling for $1 million annually. It was a preview of the free agent madness that was taking shape just down the road. In fact, it was the Dodgers' top pitcher in the Series, Messersmith, who brought the case that established the principle for all major league ballplayers. Even without Hunter, the A's had enough to win their fifth straight division title in 1975, but lost in the playoffs to Boston. That was enough for Finley, who fired Dark right afterwards. The A's slowly but surely came apart the following year as their biggest stars jumped ship for rich contracts elsewhere.

The Dodgers could not match up with the two most powerful versions of Cincinnati's Big Red Machine in the next two seasons. Alson retired after 1976. With rookie manager Tommy Lasorda in command, and an overhauled outfield and remade pitching staff, they were back in the Series one season later.

Notes:

Even in victory, the A's kept sniping. At Series end it was Tenace who was furious with Finley. The hero of the 1972 Series was ordered benched by the owner for the last two games and Rudi was pulled in to play first base. Tenace got on the owner's bad side by criticizing Finley's insistence on taking up a roster spot with pinch running specialist Herb Washington.

One of the sideshows of the Series was the duel between Marshall and Washington, both of them graduates of Michigan State University. An Olympic hurdles medalist, Washington was hired on Finley's orders and got into 91 games, never coming to bat once. Like Allen Lewis before him, he was used only as a runner. He did steal 28 bases. But when he was inserted in the ninth inning of game two, with the A's trailing 3-2 and needing to get a runner into scoring position, Marshall neatly picked him off first. Baseball purists cheered.

Line Scores:

Game One, October 12

Oak (AL)—010 010 010—3
Holtzman, Fingers (5) W, Hunter (9) SV

LA (NL)—000 010 001—2
Messersmith L, Marshall (9)

Game Two, October 13

Oak (AL)—000 000 002—2
Blue L, Odom (8)

LA (NL)—010 002 00X—3
Sutton W, Marshall (9) SV

Game Three, October 15

LA (NL)—000 000 011—2
Downing L, Brewer (4), Hough (5), Marshall (7)

Oak (AL)—002 100 00X—3
Hunter W, Fingers (8) SV

Game Four, October 16

LA (NL)—000 200 000—2
Messersmith L, Marshall (7)

Oak (AL)—001 004 00X—5
Holtzman W, Fingers (8) SV

Game Five, October 17

LA (NL)—000 002 000—2
Sutton, Marshall (6) L

OAK (AL)—110 000 10X—3
Blue, Odom (7) W, Fingers (8) SV

1975

Cincinnati (NL) 4
Boston (AL) 3

It ranks among the most dramatic Series ever played, with four of the games decided on the winner's final time at bat. The 12-inning sixth game wrung out the emotions of both ballclubs, and the nation, so thoroughly that the Reds victory in the ninth inning of the deciding game seemed almost like an epilogue.

The Preview:

This time there were no missteps. On their third trip to the Series in six years, the Reds crushed the opposition, winning the division title by 20 games and then sweeping Pittsburgh in the playoffs. No team in the league could come within 100 runs of their total. No team was as fast, fielded as well, had a bullpen quite as deep. The dead spots in the lineup were gone. The starting pitchers went deeper than any previous Sparky Anderson team. Above all, they knew how to win. Led by tough veterans—Tony Perez, Pete Rose, Joe Morgan and Johnny Bench—they carried a public image as popular as the three-time Oakland champions had been negative.

Morgan was the sparkplug, constantly on base (132 walks) and running (67 steals). His .327 average was fourth best in the league and he also drove in 94. One of those he drove in frequently was Rose, who scored 112 runs while batting .317. Bench led the Reds with 110 RBIs on 28 homers, while Perez knocked in 109 with 20 homers. In addition, there were two newcomers since Cincinnati's 1972 Series appearance. It was rightfielder Ken Griffey's first season as a regular and he hit .305. George Foster stepped in as the starting leftfielder, with a .300 average and 23 home runs.

There was no big winner for the Reds, but three starters won 15. Most effective of them was Don Gullett, bothered off and on

Carlton Fisk watches his 12th inning home run clear the "Green Monster" to win Game 6, which some observers say was the best World Series game ever. The blast just barely stayed fair, no doubt helped by Fisk's exhortations.

by arm problems, but finishing at 15-4. Veteran Gary Nolan was 15-9 and Jack Billingham, who pitched so well in the Reds' previous Series, was 15-10. Cincinnati also came out with a young right-lefty combination in the bullpen. Rawley Eastwick and Will McEnaney combined on 37 saves and 10 wins. In addition, former stopper Clay Carroll contributed seven saves.

The Red Sox were a good team and roundly admired for ending Oakland's three-year reign of discord in the American League. In a highly unlikely scenario, two brilliant rookies arrived together to bat Boston to the flag. Centerfielder Fred Lynn hit .331, second best in the league, with 105 RBIs, while Jim Rice was a .309 hitter in left field with 102 RBIs. They also combined for 43 homers. Rightfielder Dwight Evans hit .274 and teamed with Lynn and Rice to give Boston its finest all-around outfield since the Speaker-Hooper-Lewis teams of 60 years before. Carl Yastrzemski, now a first baseman, had slowed significantly since his triumphant 1967 campaign, but still hit .269 with 60 RBIs. Carlton Fisk was hurt for much of the year, but when the catcher could play he was a terror, hitting .331. In addition, there was punch on the bench with Bernie Carbo (a member of the '72 Reds) and Cecil Cooper.

This was also a good Boston pitching staff, always the sore spot on Red Sox teams. The three-man rotation of Luis Tiant (18-14), Bill Lee (17-9) and Rick Wise (19-12) was dependable and durable. Tiant and Lee, especially, were warriors—quirky personalities with tough heads. But the bullpen was a problem. Dick Drago was the best, and he was erratic, at best. This was Boston's most vulnerable point, but the Reds didn't believe it could come down to a test of relievers. They looked to stomp the Red Sox fast.

Turning Point: Game Seven, Sixth Inning.

The country spends three straight days of rainouts between games five and six waiting to see Boston's last gasp. It has been Cincinnati through the first five. Twice the Reds rally on their last time at bat to win, aided once by an umpire's non-call on an apparent interference play. Boston's offense consists of a six-run rally to win game two and a five-run outburst to come away with the fourth game. Otherwise, the Reds hold them in check. The long wait for game six is repaid in multiples.

When the Reds overcome an early 3-0 deficit and take a 6-3 lead in the eighth, the outcome looks decided. But Carbo, a carefree spirit who goes on the road with a stuffed toy gorilla as a companion, stuns the Fenway crowd with a 3-run homer with two outs. The drama builds. The Sox are turned away in the ninth when Foster cuts down the winning run at the plate. Evans races to the rightfield wall to take a certain two-run homer away from Morgan in the 11th, and then turns it into a double play. The country watches transfixed as every pitch, every swing turns the screw another thread. Finally, Fisk leads off the 12th with his blast off the leftfield foul pole, which he wills into fair territory with body language, and Fenway Park goes berserk. It is a moment frozen in time, one of the most dramatic instants in the game's history, replayed a thousand times since.

And now they have to go out and do it all over again the next night. The Reds must rouse themselves for a supreme emotional effort or live with the hollowness of their boasts for an entire year. Game 7 pits Gullett against Lee, two lefties opposing each other in a park famous for destroying left-handers.

The Sox strike first. Carbo, inserted into the lineup after his big homer the previous night, walks in the third. Singles by Denny Doyle and Yastrzemski get a run in, with Yaz taking second on the throw. The Reds want nothing to do with Fisk and walk him to load the bases. But Gullett loses the plate, walking both Rico Petrocelli and Evans to force in two more runs and make it 3-0. With the game on the edge of being blown open, Gullett recovers in time to strike out Rick Burleson.

Both teams threaten and an error by Doyle at second base almost gives the Reds a run in the fifth. Then Billingham, pitching for Cincinnati in relief, has to get Lee with the bases loaded to stop Boston in the fifth.

Cincinnati forces the fatal mistake. Rose singles to start the sixth and stays put on Morgan's fly ball. Bench then sends a grounder to short, an apparent double play given Bench's lack of speed. But Rose goes barreling into Doyle at second. His slide forces a wild throw and keeps the Reds alive. Perez follows with a two-run homer, and now the Boston lead is a shaky one run.

FACT:
Bench sends a grounder to short, an apparent inning-ending double play. But Rose goes barreling into Doyle at second. His slide forces a wild throw and keeps the Reds alive. Perez follows with a two-run homer, and now the Boston lead is a shaky one.

One inning later, the game is tied. Lee has to leave with a blister on his hand and Rose reaches reliever Roger Moret for a single that drives in Griffey. Boston has not had a hit since the fifth but as the game reaches its conclusion it is still anyone's to win. However, the Red Sox bullpen is kaput. Drago had to work three innings the previous night and the Sox are down to a rookie left-hander, Jim Burton, who had pitched in just 29 games all year. In his only Series appearance he had worked just 1/3 of an inning. Now he comes in with everything hanging in the balance. Just as Boston feared, it has come down to relief pitching.

Burton walks Griffey to start the ninth. A bunt and infield out moves him to third. Rose walks and that brings Morgan, maybe the most dangerous hitter in the game, to bat. He loops a pop fly single over second base, and by that margin Cincinnati wins the Series, 4-3. The throwing error forced by Rose on a routine play in the sixth opens the gates. Just like the old Yankees, Cincinnati bursts right through.

The Managers:

Sparky Anderson knows that he cannot let a third World Series get away from him. Yet he proceeds with a serene confidence. After one of the games he admits that he managed "stupidly" and, what's more, that Bench had agreed with him in a postgame discussion. When he wanted to change the lineup for the final game, elevating Morgan from the third to the second spot, he first conferred with his star second baseman to make sure he understood his reasoning. While he is dismissed in some quarters as a pushbutton manager, with the good fortune of having the best talent in baseball, he also knows how to get the most out of the cadre of players who are his leaders. He is unquestionably the boss, but the players who earn his trust are brought into the decision-making process.

In comparison, Darrell Johnson faded into the background during this Series. A former bullpen catcher, he had caught a ride with three pennant-winning teams and learned well from managers like Casey Stengel and Fred Hutchinson. He did a masterful job blending his rookies with veterans like Yastrzemski and Tiant. Unlike Anderson, however, he is not especially quotable and takes a secondary role to Fisk when the media comes around looking for perspective from the Boston side.

The Heroes:

Rose displays the qualities that make him the most feared, and in some quarters detested, competitor in the game. He is, in many regards, a throwback to Ty Cobb, the man whose record for career hits he will eventually break. Equipped with limited physical gifts, neither big nor fast, he willed himself to stardom, playing every game, every time at bat to the hilt. His collision with catcher Ray Fosse in the 1970 All Star Game, a meaningless exhibition, became a classic replay of intensity in action. He came up as a second baseman, played outfield on Cincinnati's previous two pennant winners and switched to third base this year. Later in his career, he will go to the Series again as a first baseman. He had won three batting titles by 1975 and hit over .300 for 10 of the last 11 years. He is now 34, but his zest for the game is undiminished. His slide into Doyle that wiped out a sure double play and set up Cincinnati's comeback rally in game seven exemplified how he plays it.

Tiant gets his lone chance to show his stuff before a national audience. The cigar-smoking Cuban infuriates hitters with his corkscrew, head-rolling delivery, which masks an incredible assortment of off-speed pitches. A thoroughly frustrated Rose yells, "He's got nothing," at the Red Sox after Tiant gets him for the third straight time in game one, a 6-0, five-hitter. What makes him especially effective is that he can still throw hard when he wants. The 34-year-old right hander was picked up from the Twins after the 1970 season as a dead-armed has-been. Boston stayed with him during a 1-7 season and he came back to win 75 games over the next four years. He went all the way in Boston's 5-4 win in game four and also started the sixth game, but left after seven innings with the Red Sox trailing.

Perez showed why he was the most respected hitter in Cincinnati's lineup. While hitting only .179 and striking out nine times, he also slammed three homers and led everyone with seven RBIs. He actually started the Series going 0 for 15, but during the last three games went 5 for 11. His two home runs in game five gave the Reds their margin in the 6-2 win, and his two-run shot in the seventh game brought Cincinnati back into that one.

The Zeroes:

Rice had to sit out the entire Series with an injury. That meant Yastrzemski moved to the outfield while Cooper took over at first base. Because of the shift, Johnson had to use four different leadoff men in an attempt to get some punch at the top of his lineup. They went a combined 4-for-29 and scored 2 runs as Boston struggled to get runners on base for its big hitters.

Umpire Larry Barnett got caught in the middle of the Series' most controversial play. In the 10th inning of game three, leadoff man Cesar Geronimo singled and Ed Armbrister, a sub who had hit .185 during the season, was sent up to sacrifice. Armbrister bunted in front of the plate and when Fisk moved out to field the ball he got all tangled up with the batter. When he tried to make the play at second, the ball sailed into centerfield for an error, while both runners moved up an extra base. The Red Sox were apoplectic, arguing that Armbrister had clearly interfered with Fisk's attempt to field the ball. Several TV replays indicated that he had done so. But Barnett said the key to the interference rule was intent and that Armbrister had not deliberately impeded the catcher. A few moments later, Morgan singled in the winning run to put the Reds ahead in the Series, two games to one. Barnett received death threats, for which he blamed broadcasters Curt Gowdy and Tony Kubek for their analysis of the play.

The Aftermath:

Cincinnati came back with virtually the same team in 1976 and simply annihilated everyone that got in its way. They remain the only team ever to sweep both the playoffs and Series in a season.

Boston, however, wasted little time in giving Johnson the heave-ho. When the team drifted below .500 in the first half of the 1976 season, he was gone. It didn't help that Lee, after three straight 17-win years, came up empty, nor that the bullpen still had no steady closer, nor that several of the young Sox dropped substantially from their 1975 performances. Boston eventually finished third, well off the pace, but was preparing for a pennant run two years later that again would break New England's heart.

Notes:

This was the year that baseball tacitly admitted it did not want to buck pro football for TV ratings. When several days of rain delayed the sixth game, it was rescheduled opposite Monday Night Football. Then that game was also postponed, even though the rain had stopped and most witnesses felt the field was playable, with no standing water anywhere. They suspected that baseball feared it would have won the ratings battle with pro football, but by a margin low enough to be embarrassing. The following year, the Series surrendered and scheduled its Sunday games at night, with Monday as an off day. That left Saturday as the only game played in daylight.

> **FACT:**
> The combined total of 12 pitchers in the sixth game marathon established a new Series record

The combined total of 12 pitchers in the sixth game marathon broke a Series record.

Tiant's first game shutout was the first complete game in the Series since Steve Blass won the final game of 1971. All 19 contests the A's participated in during their three-year run featured the bullpen.

Line Scores:

Game One, October 11

Cin (NL)—000 000 000—0
Gullett L, Carroll (7), McEnaney (7)

Bos (AL)—000 000 60X—6
Tiant W

Game Two, October 12

Cin (NL)—000 100 002—3
Billingham, Borbon (6), McEnaney (7), Eastwick (8) W

Bos (AL)—100 001 000—2
Lee, Drago (9) L

Game Three, October 14

Bos (AL)—010 001 102 0—5
Wise, Burton (5), Cleveland (5), Willoughby (7) L, Moret (10)

Cin (NL)—000 230 000 1—6
Nolan, Darcy (5), Carroll (7), McEnaney (7), Eastwick (9) W

Game Four, October 15

Bos (AL)—000 500 000—5
Tiant W

Cin (NL)—200 200 000—4
Norman L, Borbon (4), Carroll (5), Eastwick (7)

Game Five, October 16

Bos (AL)—100 000 001—2
Cleveland L, Willoughby (6), Pole (8), Segui (8)

Cin (NL)—000 113 01X—6
Gullett W, Eastwick (9) SV

Game Six, October 21

Cin (NL)—000 030 210 000—6
Nolan, Norman (3), Billingham (3), Carroll (5), Borbon (6), Eastwick (8), McEnaney (9), Darcy (10) L

Bos (AL)—300 000 030 001—7
Tiant, Moret (8), Drago (9), Wise (12) W

Game Seven, October 22

Cin (NL)—000 002 101—4
Gullett, Billingham (5), Carroll (7) W, McEnaney (9) SV

Bos (AL)—003 000 000—3
Lee, Moret (7), Willoughby (7), Burton (9) L, Cleveland (9)

1976

Cincinnati (NL) 4
New York (AL) 0

The Reds were at the top of their form in 1976 and swept untroubled to a second straight championship. In much the same manner that the mighty Yankee teams of the past left lesser opponents crumpled wrecks, Cincinnati wiped out New York while hardly working up a sweat.

The Preview:

It had been 12 long years for the Yankees. The greatest dynasty in sports, 29 pennants and 20 championships between 1921 and 1964, lay in ruins. The heroes had left the stage. For two years, the team even left its shrine, Yankee Stadium, while it was refurbished, and played at Shea Stadium, home of the Mets. It was symbolic. The Yanks had become second-best in the city they once owned, being consistently outdrawn by the expansion team. But new ownership was led by Cleveland shipbuilder George Steinbrenner, who proved to be a most impatient man. The new Yankee Stadium debuted in 1976 and Steinbrenner demanded an immediate pennant. A man of similar temperament, Billy Martin, had been installed as manager the previous year with instructions to deliver.

New York had slowly assembled an excellent team. In two horrendous trades, Cleveland turned over the corners of the Yankee infield, third baseman Graig Nettles and first baseman Chris Chambliss. They became two anchors of the 1976 team, with Nettles' 32 homers leading the league, along with 93 RBIs, while Chambliss knocked in 96 runs and hit .293. His dramatic ninth-inning homer also eliminated Kansas City in a taut, five-game playoff.

The Yankees made other swift moves, too. From California came centerfielder Mickey Rivers, who gave them speed at the

Dan Driessen, the first designated hitter in World Series play, raps one of his three hits in Game 3. Driessen collected five hits in the Series for a .357 average, to go along with his four runs scored.

leadoff position and a team-high .312 average. The team leader was catcher Thurman Munson. In his 7th season as a regular, Munson was now a consistent .300 hitter and 100-RBI man, figures he reached this season with a .302 average and 105 runs knocked in. He was also a strong field commander, and his calm demeanor was a useful antidote to Martin's abrasive managerial technique.

Steinbrenner made himself vastly unpopular by raising the ante for Catfish Hunter to levels no one else could match when the pitcher became a free agent. Hunter repaid the compliment by winning 23 in his first year in New York. This time he was 17-15, but never missed a turn, pitching 299 innings. The rest of the New York staff was totally rebuilt over the winter. Hunter got lots of help from Ed Figueroa (19-10), who had ambled over from California with Rivers, and from Dock Ellis (17-8), in a comeback season after his career had fizzled out in Pittsburgh. Doyle Alexander arrived from Baltimore in mid-season and went 10-5. Sparky Lyle was still in top form as one of the league's top stoppers, with 23 saves.

The Yankees were easy division winners and Sparky Anderson pronounced himself greatly impressed with them. But he was even more impressed by his own team. It was as if the close call against Boston in the 1975 Series had challenged the Reds to demonstrate, once and for all, how superior they actually were. They succeeded, winning the division by 10 games and then crushing the Phillies in a three-game playoff. Joe Morgan was the MVP, with a .320 average, 27 homers and 111 RBIs. Anderson anointed him as the greatest all around player he had ever seen. This was George Foster's year to emerge as a top slugger, with a league-leading 121 RBIs, 29 homers and a .306 average. Pete Rose was right on schedule at .323, Tony Perez drove in his standard 91 runs and Ken Griffey topped the Reds with a .336 average. Only Johnny Bench declined somewhat, dropping to .234 with 16 homers while playing in just 135 games, the fewest since his rookie year.

Pitching was the usual Cincinnati scramble. Gary Nolan was again the top winner, at 15-9, and Don Gullett, with more arm pains, still was the most effective arm the Reds had, with an 11-3 mark. Other Series starters would be rookie Pat Zachry (14-7) and Fred Norman (12-7). Anderson's bullpen was a little thinner than usual, with Rawly Eastwick (11-5, 26 saves) his stopper.

Turning Point: Game Two, Ninth Inning.

It doesn't take long for Cincinnati to take control. In fact, this game is their only shaky moment. Gullett wins the opener, 5-1, on a strong-five-hitter against Alexander. Now they face Hunter, tested in three previous Series with the A's. He is opposed by Cincinnati's number four starter, Norman. Anderson feels that if he can steal this one against New York's best there will be no problems the rest of the way.

On a frigid 43-degree night (the first regularly scheduled Sunday night game ever in the Series), the Reds jump ahead early. Designated hitter Dan Driessen leads off with a double and Foster drives him home with a single. Munson cuts Foster down on a steal attempt, but then Bench follows with a double. After a walk to Cesar Geronimo, Dave Concepcion singles and Griffey hits a single for a 3-0 lead.

New York starts chipping away at Norman in the 4th. Singles by Munson, Chambliss and Nettles get one run back. Then they drive out the starter in the 7th and tie the score. A single by Willie Randolph, Fred Stanley's double and a single by Roy White, followed by Munson's infield out, knots the game at 3-3.

Hunter had mowed down the Reds without incident since the early uprising. But the Yanks can't score off Jack Billingham in the eighth and ninth. The game appears headed for chilly extra innings when the first two Reds go down in their half of the ninth. Griffey then sends a roller to Stanley at short. Hurrying because of Griffey's speed, Stanley throws wildly. The ball gets past Chambliss and Griffey scrambles into second. The Yanks decide to walk Morgan and pitch, instead, to Perez. Regarding this as a personal affront, Perez laces Hunter's next pitch for a single, scoring Griffey with the winning run, 4-3, and giving Cincinnati a 2-0 lead in the Series.

Both games in New York go to the Reds, although the finale isn't decided until Bench's three-run homer, his second blast of the game, in the ninth. It is all so perfunctory that even a last ditch temper tantrum by Martin can't stir the Yankees. One observer writes that the 1919 Reds had more trouble in their Series with the White Sox—who weren't even trying to win. The Yankees play like a team just glad to be back in the Series.

FACT:
The Reds took the Commissioner's office to court, trying to block the new Series format, which permitted the designated hitter in alternate seasons. The strategy and decision-making that went into the endgame was rendered unnecessary by the DH, according to Anderson. "You might as well bring in Harvard professors to run ballclubs," he grumbled.

The Managers:

Sparky Anderson was upset over having to use a designated hitter in the World Series for the first time. The Reds took the Commissioner's office to court, trying to block the new Series format, which permitted the DH in alternate seasons. The judge ruled against them. Anderson relished the strategy, the decision-making that went into the endgame, all of which was rendered unnecessary by the DH. "You might as well bring in Harvard professors to run your ballclubs," he grumbled. Still, he adjusted. His DH for the Series (Dan Driessen) hit .357 and Anderson achieved what he felt in his own mind was the hallmark of greatness, a repeat as champions.

Billy Martin's record as a manager had been marked by quick success, followed by acrimony, disruptions and rapid dismissal. He led the Twins to the playoffs in his first year there, got into a fistfight with one of his own players in a Detroit parking lot, and was fired right afterwards because owner Cal Griffith couldn't take him. Hired by the Tigers, he led them to a divisional title in 1972 (his second season) and was fired before the following season was over because of his behavior. After a brief tenure in Texas, and a franchise-best second place finish, he came to the Yankees in the summer of 1975. He and Steinbrenner were made for each other, leading actors in an ongoing psychodrama involving clashing egos and temper tantrums. Martin wound up getting fired and rehired so many times that it became a running joke in New York. He lost all control of himself in the ninth inning of the last game in this Series, throwing baseballs from the dugout at the plate umpire over his calls, and was ejected. A few moments later, Bench put his ballclub out of its misery with his clinching three-run homer.

The Heroes:

In the 1970 Series, Bench was the victim. Brooks Robinson robbed him repeatedly with sensational plays at third for Baltimore. This time it was Bench's turn. He mauled the Yankees for a .533 average. Half of his hits went for extra bases and he also drove in 6 runs. It was the final piece in the Hall of Fame career that he constructed, nailing down his reputation as the greatest catcher in National League history.

Munson almost matched his catching rival, giving the Yankees their only semblance of an offense and batting .529. All his hits were singles, though.

Driessen was asked to fill the unfamiliar role of DH and he came through admirably, with a .357 average. Many good hitters had stumbled in the American League when asked to DH. They found it impossible to keep their concentration level up when not in the field between at bats. But Driessen did much better than New York's two experienced DHs, Carlos May and Lou Piniella. The two of them hit only a combined .200.

The Zeroes:

It was the worst performance by a Yankee pitching staff in the club's long Series history. The team ERA was 5.45 and New York was outscored, 22-8. Only Lyle escaped the conflagration, with 2 2/3 innings of scoreless relief in his two appearances.

It was also a sorry managerial debut by Martin. He belittled the Reds constantly, attributing their crushing success to "bloop hits." Then with New York police officials cautioning about crowd control at Yankee Stadium, he staged a fit in the ninth inning of the last game, with fan frustration at its peak. New York fans had caused an ugly scene after the last playoff game and the Reds had warned Yankee management that the team would be pulled off the field at the first sign of unruliness. Martin, apparently, never got the message.

FACT:
It was the worst performance by a Yankee pitching staff in the club's long Series history. The team ERA was 5.45 and New York was outscored 22-8 by the Big Red Machine.

The Aftermath:

The most common mistake made by winning sports organizations is to hold on to aging stars for too long. With that in mind, along with the imposition of free agency, the Reds decided to start rebuilding while they were still at the summit. They traded Perez, one of the team leaders and a highly respected figure in Cincinnati, to Montreal over the winter. The deal was unpopular with players and fans alike. It seemed to take some of the starch out of the Reds. Even a 52-home run year by Foster and the arrival of pitcher Tom Seaver by trade in 1977 couldn't shake them out of their lethargy. They finished 10 games off the division lead. The Big Red Machine had run its final mile.

The Yankees quickly took advantage of the new free agent structure by signing the best on the market, Reggie Jackson. The league's top slugger gave them the margin they needed in tight division and playoff competition, and their first championship in 16 seasons.

Notes:

Freezing weather in Cincinnati caused some players and owners to reflect on whether baseball was tempting fate by starting the Series so deep into October. But the only alternative was to cut a week off the regular season schedule. A majority of owners wouldn't hear of it, saying they couldn't take the revenue loss.

Executives at NBC were just as happy to see the Series wrap up in four games. Because of a rainout between games three and four, a fifth game would have bumped into the scheduled election debate between President Gerald Ford and Jimmy Carter. NBC said the game might have to be moved to daytime. There was a time when pundits agreed that no serious Presidential campaigning began until after the World Series. But with the Series now running to within two weeks of the election, that was part of a vanished America.

Line Scores:

Game One, October 16

NY (AL)—010 000 000—1
Alexander L, Lyle (7)

Cin (NL)—101 001 20X—5
Gullett W, Borbon (8)

Game Two, October 17

NY (AL)—000 100 200—3
Hunter L

Cin (NL)—030 000 001—4
Norman, Billingham (7) W

Game Three, October 19

Cin (NL)—030 100 020—6	NY (AL)—000 100 100—2
Zachry W, McEnaney (7) SV	Ellis L, Jackson (4), Tidrow (8)

Game Four, October 21

Cin (NL)—000 300 004—7	NY (AL)—100 010 000—2
Nolan W, McEnaney (7) SV	Figueroa L, Tidrow (9), Lyle (9)

1977

New York (AL) 4
Los Angeles (NL) 2

Two old Series foes confront each other for the first time since 1963, and the ninth time in history. Paced by Reggie Jackson's record-shattering home runs, the Yankees win the renewal.

The Preview:

What do you get the team that has everything? The top slugger in the league will do nicely. Oakland, which Reggie Jackson helped lead to five divisional titles, cut him loose in 1976, sending him to Baltimore in a trade made for no other reason than his impending free agency. A's owner Charles O. Finley refused to consider Jackson's demands. He wanted whatever he could get in return for him and sent him off to be someone else's problem. As it turned out, George Steinbrenner was only too happy to load Jackson's pockets with shekels and add yet another massive ego to the collection that would soon be known as "The Bronx Zoo."

Jackson described himself as "the straw that stirs the drink." It is a diplomatic way of saying that while he could not win a championship by himself, he'd make sure that this already-talented team would. He had one of his best seasons, topping the Yankees with 110 RBIs, while hitting .286 with 32 homers. Craig Nettles was the home run leader with 37 and drove in 107, while Thurman Munson hit .308 and drove in an even 100 runs. Chris Chambliss added another 91 RBIs. Mickey Rivers topped the regulars with a .326 average, although DH Lou Piniella cruised along at .330. Finally, the infield defense, which cost the team in 1976, was shored up with a trade for shortstop Bucky Dent.

Jackson was reunited with his old Oakland teammate, Catfish Hunter, the first free agent to follow the money trail to

Reggie Jackson hits the third of his three home runs in Game 6. Jackson's blasts came on consecutive pitches, off three different pitchers. He finished the Series with five homers, eight RBI, a .450 average, and the MVP trophy.

Yankee Stadium. Hunter was on the downside of his career, though, and only a 9-9 pitcher with limited effectiveness. Former Cincinnati star Don Gullett also signed on as a free agent and went 14-4. Returnee Ed Figueroa was 16-11. Veteran Mike Torrez joined his fourth team in as many years, coming over from Oakland in the spring and winning 14 for New York. The most valuable addition, though, was a 27-year-old rookie left hander who got there the old-fashioned way, through the farm system. Ron Guidry had been up briefly twice before and didn't show enough to stick. This year he went 16-7 and became the staff's most dependable starter.

Meanwhile, across the country, the Dodgers were back in business. A new manager, Tom Lasorda, had built around the stability of his infield, which remained intact from the 1974 pennant-winners. Otherwise, it was a brand new team, far more powerful than the Dodgers were accustomed to fielding since the move to L.A. Moreover, the pitching was deeper than ever.

Four regulars hit better than 30 homers—a figure even the powerful Brooklyn teams of the '50s couldn't match. First baseman Steve Garvey had 33 with a team-high 115 RBIs, and third baseman Ron Cey ("The Penguin") added 30 with 110 RBIs. Reggie Smith, who had come over from St. Louis in 1976 in the midst of an off year, rebounded with a team-leading .307 average and 32 homers. Dusty Baker, another good hitter who had tailed off the previous year after coming over from the Braves, snapped back with 30 homers and a .291 average. The Dodgers had languished near the bottom in team home runs during their championship years of the '60s. Now they led the league with 191 in what had always been regarded as a pitcher's park.

There was still plenty of pitching, too. Don Sutton was the top holdover from 1974, with a 14-8 mark. Rick Rhoden, in his second year as a starter, was 16-10, and Burt Hooton, throwing his famed "slurve" (a cross between a curve and a slider) went 12-7 after a sour 1976. The most heartening story was the return of Tommy John. The 34-year-old left-hander had blown out his pitching elbow in 1974 and sat out all next season for reconstructive surgery (now known as "Tommy John" surgery). After a .500 season in 1976, he came back to go 20-7, with a live fastball and the best win total of his 13-year career. Charlie Hough, who came out of the bullpen throwing knucklers, saved 22 games and Mike Garman, a more conventional hard thrower, added 12 more.

The teams were regarded as evenly matched, but the Yankees had to scramble their pitching in order to put away a persistent Kansas City team in the playoffs. The Dodgers, with a better-rested staff, were installed as very slight favorites.

The Turning Point: Game Four, Second Inning.

If the Oakland A's had it right, and hating one another is the best way to play a World Series, the Yankees are proving apt students. This is an angry ballclub from the owner on down and it is enthusiastically despised by most of the country. Jackson isn't speaking to Martin. Worse yet, he openly criticizes the manager's decision to start his old pal, Hunter, in game two. Hunter is rocked early and often and the Yanks lose, 6-1, evening the Series. Gullett had won the opener in New York, 4-3, and then Torrez took game three at Dodger Stadium, 5-3.

Now the Dodgers must stop New York to pull even in their own ballpark and avoid falling into a 3-1 hole. The Yankees will go with Guidry ("Louisiana Lightning"), their most consistent and toughest starter. Lasorda has two choices. He can start Rhoden, who lost the opener in the 12th when he couldn't get anyone out in a very brief relief appearance, or he can name Doug Rau, a left-hander who hasn't worked since a one-inning stint in the playoffs, 8 days before.

He chooses Rau. It is not a good choice. Before he can breathe deeply, the Yankees are climbing all over him. Jackson strokes a leadoff double to the opposite field in the second. It is his first extra base hit in the Series. Until that at bat he hit only .222 and his teammates grumble about how someone doing so little could be mouthing off so often to the media. Piniella also goes the opposite way with a single to right for a run. When Chambliss gets the third straight opposite field hit, a double to left, Lasorda decides this will not do. He comes to get his starter and goes to his alternative, Rhoden. But before the relief man can get out of the inning, a grounder and a single through the drawn-in infield by Dent make it 3-0.

As it turns out, the rally is as significant for giving Guidry a nice lead as it is for Jackson getting himself untracked. Guidry gives two back in the third when Davey Lopes strokes a two-run homer. Then in the fourth, Piniella, who played only 52 games in the field all year as the team's top DH, makes the play of the Series, leaping above the leftfield wall to take a tying home run away from Cey. The Dodgers cannot get any closer than that on Guidry, who finishes with a 4-hitter. Moreover, in the fifth, Jackson cracks his first home run of the Series off Rhoden. More would soon follow. A lot more.

Although the Dodgers manage to send the Series back to Yankee Stadium with a 10-4 combing of Gullett in game five, they then run into one of the great power exhibitions in the game's history. Jackson crashes three homers on consecutive pitches in the clincher and the Yankees win it 8-4 to take the championship they once owned by right in convincing fashion.

The Managers:

For Billy Martin, battling with his stars and his owner and with other demons only he could name, this Series was the pinnacle of a career. But observers said that he looked haunted, as if it were all a horrible ordeal. He would go on to be fired and rehired by Steinbrenner four different times, beginning with the following summer, until their relationship became a bad joke, the punch line of a TV commercial to sell beer. It seemed that Steinbrenner, who enjoyed being called "The Boss," could hardly restrain himself from embarrassing his manager as often as he could. The final humiliation was taking away Martin's chance of leading the Yankees to a second straight championship in 1978.

Lasorda, too, was living the dream of his career. Unlike Martin, he was having the time of his life. "I bleed Dodger blue," he cheerily announced, upon succeeding Walter Alston as manager after 1976. He had been a minor league pitcher for years in the Dodger farm system and loved telling how he was the guy optioned out so the team could keep Sandy Koufax. He rode the buses for years, ate the hamburgers and waited for his moment. Now he was socializing with the Hollywood baseball set and loving every minute of it. Whatever demons he harbored were kept well under control.

The Stars:

When he made his "straw that stirs the drink" remark in spring training, Jackson immediately antagonized Munson. He had been named the Yankees' captain, the first in the team's history, and rather fancied that it was his straw which would do the stirring. During the season, Jackson conducted a raging dugout argument with Martin, seen by a national television audience, when the manager complained about his slow pursuit of a ball that got past him in the outfield. Afterwards, Jackson said that he had saved Martin's job because Steinbrenner sided with him and wanted to fire the manager. When the Series started, he grumped over the location of the tickets he had been assigned. It was the old Oakland A's spirit and his teammates wished the guy would get lost. Then he started to hit. A double and a homer in game four. Another homer in game five. Then in game six, the explosion. A two-run shot off Hooton in the fourth that brought New York from behind and into a 4-3 lead. Another two-run homer an

FACT:

A two-run shot off Hooten in the fourth put the Yankees ahead, 4-3; a two-run homer in the fifth off Sosa extended the lead to 7-3; an enormous drive over the fence in dead center in the eighth off Hough accounted for the last score in an 8-4 game. The drives came on consecutive pitches and each went further than the last. It was Mr. October's finest moment.

inning later, off Elias Sosa, made it 7-3. Finally, an enormous drive over the fence in dead center in the eighth off Hough accounted for New York's last score in the 8-4 game. The drives came on consecutive pitches and each went further than the last. It was Mr. October's finest autumn.

It was also the Series of a lifetime for Torrez, who had bounced from team to team and was regarded as little better than a journeyman. The Yanks got him from Oakland only because his contract was up at the end of the year. He contributed two complete game wins, and then gave Steinbrenner a taste of his own medicine by signing a big contract with the Red Sox.

While the Dodgers managed to bang out 9 homers, New York's pitchers kept their big bombers fairly well contained. The exception was the bat at the bottom of their lineup, number eight hitter and catcher Steve Yeager. He had homers in both L.A. wins, including a three-run job off Gullett in game five, and hit .316 with five RBIs.

The Zeroes:

It was a sad outing for Hunter, who had won four straight Series games while pitching for the A's. Seldom used during the season, Martin started him in game two, hoping that the old knack for winning under pressure would return. Instead, the Dodgers touched him up for three homers in three innings, the Yanks lost 6-1 and Martin was criticized by Jackson for the choice.

New York City was not seen in its best light during this Series. During game one, an arson fire set a few blocks from the ballpark burned out of control for most of the game, as TV cameras focused in from long range. In game two, Dodger right-fielder Reggie Smith was hit in the back of the neck by a hard rubber object fired from the stands. After the clincher in game six, fans ran amok over the field, tearing up large chunks of sod and fighting with police, as an injured man lay on a stretcher, unable to be removed, for 35 minutes.

The Aftermath:

The Yankees lost Torrez to free agency, but then turned around and signed one of the hardest throwers in the game, Goose Gossage, for their bullpen. Since they already had a top stopper in Lyle this was a puzzling move which caused a good deal of acrimony. When the Yanks fell far behind Boston in early summer, Steinbrenner lowers the boom on Martin. Coincidentally or not, they then take off on one of the greatest pennant drives in history.

The Dodgers keep their assignation in the Series, too, fielding fairly much the same cast as in 1977. The major addition for them is also a hard-throwing bullpen ace, left hander Terry Forster.

Notes:

Figueroa, who worked more innings than any other New York pitcher, was completely shut out of Series assignments. To make matters worse, Martin first named him as the game six starter and then switched right before game time to Torrez. Figueroa was not amused.

The return of the championship to New York for the first time in 8 years, since the Mets won in 1969, ended the longest dry spell for baseball in the Big Apple in 56 seasons. It occasioned a tickertape parade down lower Broadway, far beyond what was done when the old Yankees won their titles. Then it was expected. Now it was a gift.

FACT:
The return of the championship to New York for the first time in 8 years, since the Mets won in 1969, ended the longest dry spell for baseball in the Big Apple in 56 seasons.

Line Scores:

Game One, October 11

LA (NL)—200 000 001 000—3
Sutton, Rautzhan (8), Sosa (8), Garman (9), Rhoden (12) L

NY (AL)—100 001 010 001—4
Gullett, Lyle (9) W

Game Two, October 12

LA (NL)—212 000 001—6
Hooton W
Lyle (9)

NY (AL)—000 100 000—1
Hunter L, Tidrow (3), Clay (6),

Game Three, October 14

NY (AL)—300 110 000—5
Torrez W

LA (NL)—003 000 000—3
John L, Hough (7)

Game Four, October 15

NY (AL)—030 001 000—4
Guidry W

LA (NL)—002 000 000—3
Rau L, Rhoden (2), Garman (9)

Game Five, October 16

NY (AL)—000 000 220—4
Gullett L, Clay (5), Tidrow (6), Hunter (7)

LA (NL)—100 432 00X—10
Sutton W

Game Six, October 18

LA (NL)—201 000 001—4
Hooton L, Sosa (4), Rau (5), Hough (7)

NY (AL)—020 320 01X—8
Torrez W

1978

New York (AL) 4
Los Angeles (NL) 2

Same teams, same outcome. But this time the Yankees spot Los Angeles two games before roaring back to win, and the big punch comes from their diminutive shortstop, Bucky Dent.

The Preview:

The new season began with a confident Red Sox team taking control of the divisional race and the Yankees falling far to the rear. As frustrations mounted, the old antagonisms came bubbling up again and Billy Martin was once more feuding with Reggie Jackson and George Steinbrenner. "Both of them are liars and one of them is convicted," Martin said, during a mid-season flare up, referring to his adversaries. The owner had, indeed, been found guilty of falsifying reports on political donations, but it was not politic to remind him of it. Martin resigned to avoid getting fired and the Yankees named Bob Lemon, who had just been fired by the White Sox, to try and salvage the season. He was as calm as his predecessor was antic.

In mid-July, the Yankees were 14 1/2 games behind. Under Lemon, they played better than .700 baseball. The Yanks roared into Boston in September, splattered the Red Sox all over the landscape in a 4-game series, and went into first. But in still a final twist to the drama, Boston came back and caught them, forcing the first divisional title playoff. It was like history caught on the wing. Lemon had been a pitching star on the 1948 Cleveland team, which was involved in the only other such one-game playoff in league history, and that was also in Boston. Just as in that game, it was the slugging of a shortstop that was the difference. Thirty years before, it was Lou Boudreau. This time it

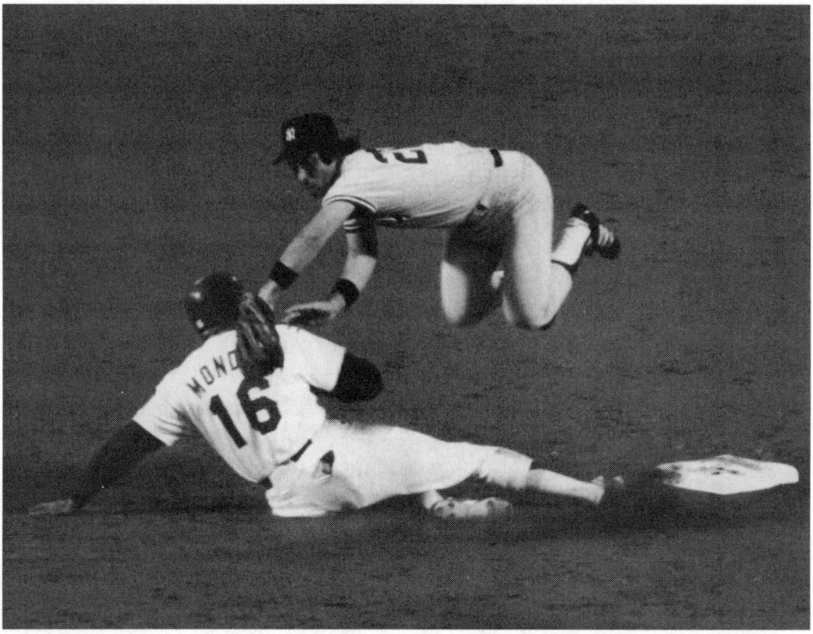

Bucky Dent earned MVP honors with a .417 mark on ten hits and seven RBI, capping a postseason that saw him win a one-game playoff in Boston with a home run and collect four RBI in the ALCS.

was Bucky Dent, the number nine hitter in the lineup, whose two-out, three-run homer wiped out a 2-0 Boston lead and helped the Yankees to a 5-4 win and the pennant.

This New York team did not carry gaudy hitting stats. It was Jackson who led the attack again, with 27 homers and 97 RBIs, and right with him was Graig Nettles, who also hit 27 and drove in 93. Chris Chambliss added 90 RBIs, while the top hitters were Lou Piniella (.314), now the fulltime leftfielder, and Thurman Munson (.297).

It was pitching that took New York to the pennant. Ron Guidry was a sensation, running up a 25-3 mark with a league-leading ERA of 1.74 and 248 strikeouts. Ed Figueroa, who had been scorned in the previous year's Series in favor of free agent turncoat, Mike Torrez, came back with a 20-9 mark. (Torrez, by the way, was the pitcher the Yankees beat in the playoff, which made it all the more satisfying to Steinbrenner.) Rich Gossage, the top free agent addition, came in firing smoke from the bullpen and saved 27 games. This made erstwhile closer Sparky Lyle quite unhappy and he left after the season ended. Catfish Hunter made a small-scale recovery from a disastrous 1977 and finished 12-6 in spot duty. The fourth starter was problematical, but

Lemon was taken with Jim Beattie. The 23-year-old rookie was only 6-9, but he had good control and didn't seem to rattle easily.

The Dodgers were also down in the power numbers, although once more leading the league in homers. Steve Garvey was the chief threat, with 113 RBIs and a .316 average, both team highs. Reggie Smith led with 29 homers and drove in 93 on a .295 average. The other consistent producer in the middle of the batting order was Ron Cey, who had 23 homers and 84 RBIs.

If anything, however, this pitching staff was deeper than the year before. Burt Hooton registered his finest year at 19-10 and Tommy John kept plugging right along with his rebuilt left arm to finish 17-10. Veteran Don Sutton, who would soon eclipse all the Dodger pitching greats to become the top winner in franchise history, was 15-11 in his 13th season. The Dodgers would start only those three in the Series, although Doug Rau also had run up a 15-9 year. In the bullpen was Gossage's mirror image, left hander Terry Forster. The two pitchers broke in together with the White Sox, where both unsuccesfully tried to make the switch to starting. With free agency looming, they were both dealt off to Pittsburgh. And when they were free to move, they signed with contenders. Forster saved 22 games with L.A. The Dodgers also called up a young hard-throwing right hander in mid-season. Bob Welch won 7 games, saved 3 and looked impressive doing it. Tommy Lasorda decided he would not hesitate at putting him in when the pressure went on high.

Turning Point: Game Four, Tenth Inning.

The game comes down to the classic confrontation, the power pitcher pouring it on to the opposition's best hitter. It already happened once before in this Series. In game two, Jackson, who destroyed the Dodgers in 1977, was set to do it again. L.A. won the opener in a breeze behind John, 11-5, and carries a 4-3 lead into the ninth the next day. A win enables them to sweep at home and go into Yankee Stadium with a 2-0 advantage. But Forster gives up a walk with one out. With Munson and Jackson coming up, the Dodgers decide to see what Welch can do. The former Eastern Michigan University star gets Munson on a short fly ball. Then Jackson works him to a 3-2 count. With the memory-haunted crowd screaming at every delivery, Jackson fouls off four straight fastballs. Welch tries one more; Jackson misses and one of the season's most dramatic confrontations goes the Dodgers' way.

FACT:
Game two: Two out, tying run on first, top of the ninth. Reggie Jackson, Mr. October, works the count to 3-2 against the hard-throwing rookie. Then he fouls off four straight fastballs. Bob Welch tries one more: Jackson swings and misses.

Now Welch has to do it again. The Yanks win game three when the Series returns to New York, with Guidry shutting down the Dodgers, 5-1. John and Figueroa, the first game starters, are matched again in game four. Yankee pitching is wearing thin and they desperately need this game to avoid falling into a 3-1 pit. When Smith cracks a three-run homer in the fifth, L.A. is off to the races. New York starts to close in the sixth, though. With one out, Roy White singles and Munson walks. Jackson then lines a run-scoring single to right, the eighth straight Series game in which he drives in a run, tying a Lou Gehrig record. Piniella then sends a liner right at shortstop Bill Russell. It appears to be a double play, since Munson is trapped far off second, but Russell drops the ball. He still has a chance to recover, though. He steps on second for the force and fires to first to complete the double play that way. However, his throw hits Jackson, who is standing a few feet off first base. The ball bounces into rightfield and Munson comes in with the run. The Dodgers scream interference, but the umpires rule Jackson had made no attempt to get in the way of the ball.

It takes Munson only until his next at bat to tie the game, 3-3, on a double off Forster in the eighth. Forster then hits Jackson. Welch has to come in to get Piniella and Nettles and escape the inning. Gossage enters the game for the Yankees in the ninth and now it is all up to the two power pitchers. Both are letting it rip. Gossage has two strikouts and Welch three as the Yanks come to bat in the bottom of the 10th.

A walk to White is sandwiched around two pop ups. Then Jackson comes up again. Immediately, the noise level goes through the decibel limit as fans anticipate a replay of the drama of two games ago. This time it is Jackson who comes out ahead, banging a single through the right side, with White stopping at second.

This brings up Piniella. The 35-year-old outfielder is known as the most intelligent hitter on the team, a student of the art, rather than a hacker. He takes a strike from Welch, then lines a single to center. The hit scores White with the winning run and the Yankees have evened the Series. They go on to sweep the next two in runaways and repeat as champions. The Dodgers, hoping for a while that they had found another Larry Sherry, an unknown who would turn the Series around for them, go home instead with their fourth straight loss in the title round.

FACT:

Game four: Tie game, bottom of the tenth, man on first, two out, Jackson batting, Welch pitching. Fans rise, anticipating a replay of the drama of two games ago. This time Jackson comes out ahead, banging a single to center, then Lou Piniella singles in the winning run.

The Managers:

It had been a long, strange season for Bob Lemon. Not good enough for the fifth-place White Sox, he was just the man the Yankees needed. He calmed the waters, restored the confidence of Figueroa, put a healthy Hunter back into the rotation and got along with Jackson. A good performance for the 58-year-old Lemon, who was already in the Hall of Fame as a player. This was his fifth season as a manager. He got the Kansas City Royals into second place in their third year of existence, then was fired when they slipped back to fourth. He won 90 games at Chicago in 1977, then got the ziggie when they, too, fell back. Given the volatile nature of Steinbrenner, there were not many who gave him much of a chance of survival for 1979.

Oddly enough, Lasorda shared the same birth-date as Lemon, only he was seven years younger. He also had been a pitcher, although he won 207 fewer games than Lemon's career total of 207. Lasorda said that he wouldn't trade his team for any other in the world. Still, for the second straight year, his team was no better than second best.

The Heroes:

One of the stranger rises to stardom in a World Series came to Yankee second baseman Brian Doyle. He had played in just 39 games, mostly as a defensive replacement, in his rookie season, hitting .192, with no extra base hits and no RBIs. All he did in the Series was hit .438 to lead both sides. In the final two games, he went 6 for 9, with five consecutive hits. The 24-year-old Doyle was forced into the lineup when Willie Randolph went down with a leg injury just before the playoffs. The younger brother of Boston's Denny Doyle, who played in the 1975 Series, he lasted just three more years in the majors. His lifetime average was .161—or 267 points below what he hit in this one brilliant week.

Dent got the big hit in the playoff with Boston, then kept right on going through the Series. He hit .417, drove in 7 runs and, like Doyle, came alive in the last two games, going 6 for 8. He was voted the outstanding player award (a choice that rankled Jackson, who led both teams with 8 RBIs). It was the first time a shortstop had won the award.

Longtime Dodger coach Jim Gilliam passed away two days before the Series opened after suffering a stroke. He had played in seven Series with the team and was a mentor to many of the younger players. The closest to him was second baseman Davey Lopes, who dedicated his Series to Gilliam. Lopes did all he could to get L.A. in, with 3 homers, 7 RBIs and a .308 average. Two of the homers and 5 RBIs came in the Dodgers 11-5 win in the opener.

In a fitting valedictory to the Series, Hunter came back to pitch the closing game, going 7 innings in the 7-2 victory. Fighting a sore right arm and diabetes, Hunter gathered his strength for one more big effort and won his 5th Series game over 6 years. Jackson, who had sniped at Martin's choice to start him the previous year, praised Hunter this time as "the greatest competitor I've ever known." Hunter retired the following year after going just 2-9.

Beattie was a minimum-scale Yankees on a team full of millionaires. He had taken over the fourth starter's role almost by default. But when he got his chance, he went the distance to tuck away game five for New York in a 12-2 romp.

The Zeroes:

The Dodger starters were shredded by New York. John, Sutton and Hooton, who started all 6 games for L.A., gave up 25 runs in 35 innings.

Lyle, who had been New York's stopper in the previous two Series, never got out of the bullpen. He was the only man on the Yankee roster who didn't play. The Yanks packaged him up and sent him to Texas a few weeks after the Series. In return, they received Dave Righetti, who became one of the top starters on their next pennant winner, in 1981.

The Aftermath:

Sure enough, Lemon only lasted 64 games into the next season, and Martin was brought back in. The move did nothing to improve the Yankee fortunes, though. Figueroa and Hunter both faded and the addition of two free agents, John and Luis Tiant, couldn't pick up the slack. Then Munson, the team leader, was killed while piloting his own plane in August. After that, the team just finished out the string and came in a distant 4th.

The Dodgers also faded to below .500, with injuries to Smith and centerfielder Rick Monday hurting the outfield defense. Moreover, both Sutton and Hooton tailed off, while John's defection to the Yankees was a major blow. For both teams, however, these were just temporary lapses. They would be back at each other in another two years.

Notes:

Reflecting the increase in salaries and TV revenues, the winning players' share dwarfed all that had gone before. In 1978, it was a record $31,236.

The Yankees had to appeal to the Commissioner's Office to break an impasse on how to divide the team's shares between their two managers. It was decided to give Lemon a full share and Martin one-half. Many of the players, still angry with Martin, wanted to cut him out entirely.

New York's team batting average of .306 was the highest ever for a 6-game Series. It broke the Yanks former mark of .302, set against the Giants in 1936.

Line Scores:

Game One, October 10

NY (AL)—000 000 320—5 Figueroa L, Clay (2), Linblad (5), Tidrow (7)	LA (NL)—030 310 31X—11 John W, Forster (8)

Game Two, October 11

NY (AL)—002 000 100—3 Hunter L, Gossage (7)	LA (NL)—000 103 00X—4 Hooton W, Forster (7), Welch (9) SV

Game Three, October 13

LA (NL)—001 000 000—1 Sutton L, Rautzhan (7), Hough (8)	NY (AL)—110 000 30X—5 Guidry W

Game Four, October 14

LA (NL)—000 030 000 0—3 John, Forster (8), Welch (8) L	NY (AL)—000 002 010 1—4 Figueroa. Tidrow (6), Gossage (9) W

Game Five, October 15

LA (NL)—101 000 000—2 Hooton L, Rautzhan (3), Hough (4)	NY (AL)—004 300 41X—12 Beattie W

Game Six, October 17

NY (AL)—030 002 200—7 Hunter W, Gossage (8)	LA (NL)—101 000 000—2 Sutton L, Welch (6), Rau (8)

1979

Pittsburgh (NL) 4
Baltimore (AL) 3

A bunch of nice guys finally won the Series. Pittsburgh becomes the fourth team in history to come back from a 3-1 margin in seven games. The Pirates Willie Stargell makes this a personal crusade, just as teammate Roberto Clemente had done eight years before against the Orioles.

The Preview:

After years of bickering, bragging and blather, the country has a team that calls itself The Family. Inspired by a hit song by Sister Sledge, "We Are Family," Pittsburgh pulls together. Not picked in the preseason polls as serious contenders, the Pirates assembled a team of veterans. Two of them had won a combined total of four batting titles and another, Willie Stargell, had the last great season of his Hall of Fame career.

The 39-year-old Stargell was called "Pops" by the rest of the team, the father figure of The Family. Pops still had enough pop in his bat to slam a team-high 32 homers with 82 RBIs. Two-time defending batting champ Dave Parker slipped a bit to .310, but he still knocked in 94 runs while hitting 25 homers. Bill Madlock, who won the batting crown for the two years prior to Parker, came over from the Giants at the end of June. He rolled down the stretch with a .328 average. Omar Moreno stole 77 bases to lead the league. The middle infielders, second baseman Phil Garner and shortstop Tim Foli, were a peppery combination who played the game tough.

Pitching was a question mark. No team since the 1952 Dodgers had gone into a Series without a starter who had won at least 15 games. Top man for Pittsburgh, though, was John Candelaria, at 14-9. He was backed up by Bruce Kison (13-7)

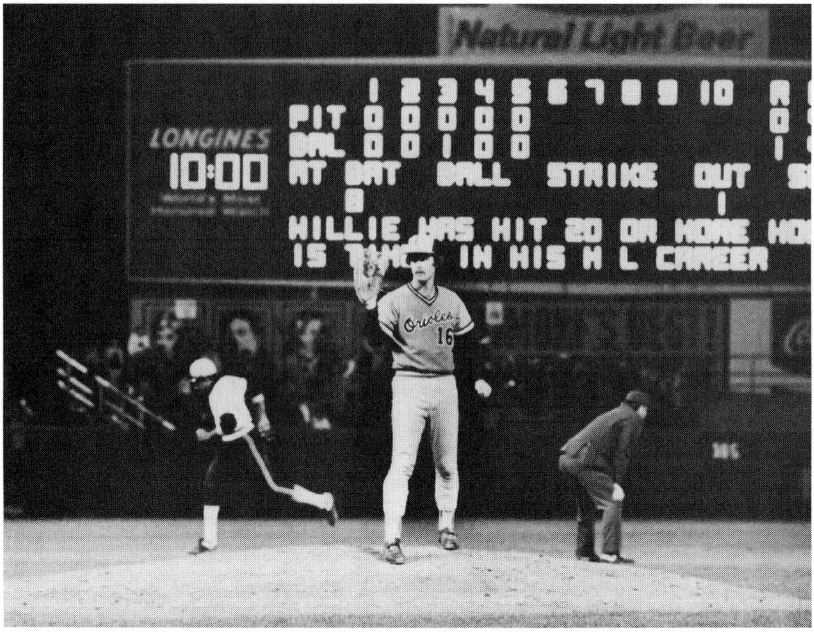

Willie Stargell (left) circles the bases after his sixth-inning homer in Game 7. Like Roberto Clemente before him, Stargell willed Pittsburgh over the Orioles, contributing seven extra-base hits, 25 total bases, a .400 average, and seven RBI.

who had pitched effectively as a rookie in the 1971 Series, and Bert Blyleven (12-5), the hardest thrower on the staff. Another option was six-foot-five Jim Bibby (12-4), a spot starter during the year, but for periods the most effective pitcher on the team. Relief was no problem. Skinny Kent Tekulve, who looked like Ichabod Crane in spikes and made hitters lose their heads swinging at his motion, saved 31 games in 94 appearances. Lefty Grant Jackson put away 14 more.

The Baltimore staff was exactly the reverse. There were no doubts about the starters. Mike Flanagan, the top winner in the league at 23-9, was the Cy Young Award winner. Jim Palmer had won the same trophy three times. He was back for his fifth Series, and while his starts were down he still finished at 10-6. Steve Stone, who would be the Cy Young recipient in 1980, went 11-7. In addition, to those three, there was Scott McGregor (13-6) and Dennis Martinez (15-16). It was in the bullpen that the Orioles had problems. The top choice was Don Stanhouse, who saved 21 games. But he had control troubles that would pop up at the most inopportune moments and drive manager Earl Weaver back into the clubhouse tunnel to nervously puff on a cigarette until the crisis was past.

The hitting measured up well with Pittsburgh. Ken Singleton had the best year of his career, with 35 homers and 111 RBIs, with a .295 average. Eddie Murray, in his 3rd season as the Baltimore first baseman, also produced his best totals to date—25 homers, 99 RBIs and a .295 average. The DH was Lee May, a veteran of Cincinnati's 1970 team. The Orioles also received unanticipated punch from Gary Roenicke. In his first full season in the majors, he platooned in leftfield and slammed 25 homers. It was not nearly as good a defensive team as the Orioles of the previous decade.

Turning Point: Game Seven, Sixth Inning.

The games have followed an all too familiar pattern for the Orioles. They pound the Pirates early. A five-run, first-inning assault on Kison in the opener sets a record, and Flanagan makes it last for a 5-4 win. They clump another 5 runs in game three and win that one, 8-4. Then in game four they improve on that. They score 6 runs in the eighth and carry off a 9-6 win. That gives them a 3-1 lead in the Series.

Then it stops. Exactly as in 1971, the Pirates close down the Orioles almost completely in the next three games, holding them to a total of just 2 runs. There are no more big innings. A man on base is a big inning. Jim Rooker, a desperation choice to start game five, combines with Blyleven to beat them, 7-1. Then Candelaria blanks them in Baltimore, 4-0. The Orioles play like a team waiting to be beaten, while Stargell will not permit Pittsburgh to lose. The forces come together in the deciding game.

The Orioles go with McGregor, who had won game three, and Pittsburgh uses Bibby, a reasonably effective performer in game four. Rich Dauer gives Baltimore a 1-0 lead in the third with a home run, the team's first in four games. Stargell singles in the second and doubles in the fourth. But Pittsburgh cannot move him around, and when Bibby is scheduled to lead off the fifth, manager Chuck Tanner pinch hits for him and brings in Don Robinson. The Orioles quickly threaten, and he switches to the left-hander, Jackson, who ends the threat on an Al Bumbry pop up.

McGregor has a three-hit shutout going when Bill Robinson singles with one out in the sixth. This brings up Stargell, and like the breadwinner of the family he brings it all home. His two-run homer over the rightfield fence, his third hit of the game and third home run of the

FACT:
This brings up Willie Stargell, and like the breadwinner of the family he brings it all home. His two-run homer over the right-field fence, his third hit of the game and third home run of the Series, gives Pittsburgh a 2-1 lead.

Series, gives Pittsburgh a 2-1 lead. It is apparent Baltimore cannot get it back.

The Orioles have one last try. In the eighth, Jackson walks May and Bumbry, which brings in Tekulve for the fifth time. The reliever gives Singleton an intentional pass, which means he has to deal with Murray with the bases loaded. Murray gives it a shot, lifting a towering fly to deep right. Parker seems to stumble as he goes back for it, but keeps his balance and tucks it away near the wall.

Then Pittsburgh breaks it open with 2 runs in the ninth. Weaver uses five pitchers in the inning, a Series record, to try and stem the tide. At one point, he switches pitchers on four consecutive hitters—and two of them end up hitting the man they are called in to face. That makes it 4-1 for the final count, but the game is really over when Pops connects.

The Managers:

Weaver was now 49 and managing was starting to take a toll on him. Three times he had taken a favorite into the Series only to get upset. Twice more he was eliminated at the brink of success in the playoffs. The only thing worse than too many close calls are none at all, but by the end of 1982 he'd had enough. To add to his frustration, the year after he left the Orioles won the championship that had eluded him for so long. He was called back a few years later when the organization began its descent into mediocrity after almost 20 years near the top. But he couldn't stop the decline.

Chuck Tanner had a tough act to follow. He was hired in Pittsburgh to replace local legend Danny Murtaugh, who died after the 1976 season. With roots in western Pennsylvania, Tanner was an immediate hit, and his warm personality was a reflection of the G-rated family entertainment he put on the field. It certainly was an easier job than his previous stint, a one-year stand in Oakland with Charlie Finley, who was in the process of tearing apart his ballclub to avoid the costs of free agency. He finished second and was fired. Pittsburgh was a better place all around.

The Heroes:

Stargell was among the last of his breed. He had come up with Pittsburgh in 1962 and spent his entire 21 years in the majors with the Pirates. With the arrival of free agency, such extended stays were regarded as quaint relics. Star players followed the money trail and Pittsburgh was a small market city that couldn't pay as much. With teams brandishing their free agent payrolls like broadswords, the Pirates were a throwback. Stargell understood that an era was closing. Creating The Family was his way of getting the other Pirates to appreciate what they had. He tied Series records for most extra base hits (7) and total bases (25) while batting .400.

Seven of the eight Pittsburgh starters hit over .300, for a team batting average of .323. That was the second highest in Series history, exceeded only by the .338 registered by the Yankees against the Pirates in 1960. This was done in a year without a DH, too.

Top hitter overall for the Pirates was Garner. He had played for Tanner in Oakland and the new manager traded for him almost as soon as he got to Pittsburgh. Garner batted .500 and matched Stargell with 12 hits.

Tekulve saved 3 of the Pittsburgh wins, worked 9 innings overall and struck out 10.

The most improbable hero was Rooker. The 37-year-old left-hander was nearing the end of a succesful stay in Pittsburgh and appeared in only 19 games all year. But he had pitched 3 2/3 innings of shutout relief in game one, giving the Pirates a chance to get back into it. So when he came up short of starters for game five because of an off day lost to a rainout, Tanner turned to his veteran. With the Pirates staring at extinction, Rooker gave them 5 solid innings, allowing just one run. Pittsburgh came back to win after he left for a pinch hitter, but Rooker held the Orioles down.

> **FACT:**
> Stargell understood that an era was closing. Creating The Family was his way of getting the Pirates to appreciate what they had. He tied Series records for most extra base hits (7) and total bases (25), while batting .400.

The Zeroes:

Stanhouse ran out of close calls, losing one game and compiling an ERA of 13.50. He had smoke coming out of Weaver's ears as well as his mouth. He took a free agent hike to the Dodgers over the winter and flopped there in 1980.

This was one year when the absence of the DH may have been a decisive factor. The Orioles had one of the best in Lee May. Since he could only play first base, Baltimore was not about to move Murray aside to play him. May never even hit a fair ball. He pinch hit twice, walking once and striking out once. Murray had his troubles, too, going 4-for 26.

The Aftermath:

The Orioles got even better in 1980, with more big years from Murray and Singleton, a four-man rotation led by 25-game winner Stone and a more dependable closer in Tim Stoddard. But the Yankees got better than that. So while Baltimore won 100 games, they were still 3 short of the top.

Time finally caught up with Pops, and the Pirate staff went into meltdown, too, with only Bibby winning more than 11 games. The combination sent them down to third place. It would take the rest of the decade to find enough jewels to form another Family.

Notes:

The Pirates also made a fashion statement in this Series. Their gold and black uniform shirts and 19th-century caps became tremendously popular among young African American males. For the next few years, Pirate paraphernalia was the top baseball seller in urban areas.

Sister Sledge's music inspired the Pirates. The young women were even brought in to sing the National Anthem before one of the games. But they had grown up outside of Philadelphia and they admitted that their hearts really belonged to the Phillies.

Besides Stargell and Kison, the other remaining member from the 1971 champions was catcher Manny Sanguillen. Oddly enough, the Pirates had traded him to Oakland in return for the rights to Tanner as their manager. He came back during spring training of 1979 and was used mostly as a bullpen catcher. But in game two, he was sent up to pinch hit in the 9th inning of a tie game, and slapped a single to win it for Pittsburgh. At that moment, Tanner wouldn't have traded him for anyone.

This was the first Series in history in which the opening game was postponed because of rain.

Line Scores:

Game One, October 10

Pit (NL)—000 102 010—4
Kison L, Rooker (1), Romo (5), Robinson (6), Jackson (8)

Bal (AL)—500 000 00X—5
Flanagan W

Game Two, October 11

Pit (NL)—020 000 001—3
Blyleven, Robinson (7) W, T ekulve (9) SV

Bal (AL)—010 001 000—2
Palmer, T. Martinez (8), Stanhouse (9) L

Game Three, October 12

Bal (AL)—002 500 100—8
McGregor W

Pit (NL)—120 001 000—4
Candelaria L, Romo (4), Jackson (7), Tekulve (8)

Game Four, October 13

Bal (AL)—003 000 060—9
D. Martinez, Stewart (2),
Stone (5), Stoddard (7) W

Pit (NL)—040 011 000—6
Bibby, Jackson (7),
Robinson (8), Tekulve (8) L

Game Five, October 14

Bal (AL)—000 010 000—1
Flanagan L, Stoddard (7), T.
Martinez (7), Stanhouse (8)

Pit (NL)—000 002 23X—7
Rooker, Blyleven (6) W

Game Six, October 16

Pit (NL)—000 000 220—4
Candelaria W, Tekulve (7) SV

Bal (AL)—000 000 000—0
Palmer L, Stoddard (9)

Game Seven, October 17

Pit (NL)—000 002 002—4
Bibby, Robinson (5),
Jackson (5) W, Tekulve (8) SV

Bal (AL)—010 000 000—1
McGregor L, Stoddard (9),
Flanagan (9), Stanhouse (9),
T. Martinez (9), D. Martinez (9)

1980

Philadelphia (NL) 4
Kansas City (AL) 2

They were the last of the original 16 big league teams never to have won a championship. The Phillies hadn't even won a Series game in 65 years. They finally caught the brass ring on their third try, upending a favored Kansas City squad.

The Preview:

After three straight division titles, followed by three straight losses in the playoffs, it appeared that Philadelphia's window of opportunity had slammed shut. The Phils fell to fourth in 1979, even with the addition of free agent Pete Rose and second baseman Manny Trillo. Some chemistry was missing and the organization decided the ingredient was a more forceful manager, one who would not blanch from kicking slackers where it would do the most good. Former pitcher Dallas Green was a member of the Phillies organization by employment and by marriage. He was also 6 foot 5, with a toughness to match his height. He took over from quiet Danny Ozark for the last 30 games of 1979 and then kicked the Phils into gear the next season.

Mike Schmidt responded well to the new regime. In his eighth year as the regular third baseman, he had his best overall season, leading the league with 48 homers and 121 RBIs, while hitting for a career high .286. He also played a superb third base. He was assisted by rightfielder Bake McBride, rebounding after two subpar years to bat .309 and drive in 87. Trillo hit .292 and teamed well with shortstop Larry Bowa to give the Phils a steady middle infield, and Bob Boone was a dependable catcher. Rose was now 39 and giving a few signs of slowing down. His average slid almost 50 points to .282, his lowest mark in 16 years. But he started every game at first base and still led the league in doubles.

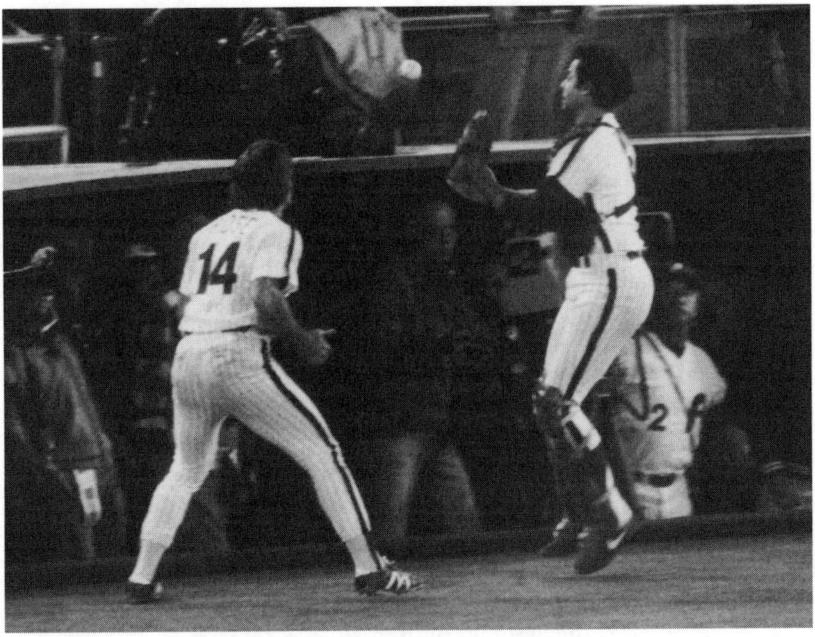

Bob Boone (right) and Pete Rose scramble for Frank White's pop-up in the ninth inning of Game 6. With the bases loaded, the ball somehow squirted out of Boone's glove, right into Rose's.

More than that, the desire he brought to the ballpark, his knowledge of what it took to win, were priceless to the Phillies.

Steve Carlton, who had virtually saved the franchise in its darkest days in the early '70s (he went 27-10 in 1973 for a team that finished 71-91), was the big winner, at 24-9. He was 35 but still threw hard enough to lead the league in strikeouts with 286. Dick Ruthven put together his best year in the majors and went 17-10. Aside from those two, though, the Phillies cupboard was bare. All that was left was Bob Walk, a 23-year-old rookie who went a lukewarm 11-7. Tug McGraw, wit, cartoonist and bullpen stopper, saved 20 games, while compiling a tiny 1.47 ERA. The true believer of the 1973 Mets, McGraw, like Rose and Carlton, and been there before, unlike most of the Phillies. He would not crumple under the Series pressure.

Kansas City was the first of the American League expansion teams to get to the Series. It was also, far and away, the most succesful, winning four of the last five division titles. Each time, the Yankees had been there to block further advancement. This year the Royals ran right over them. George Brett, although injured for more than a month, had an extraordinary year. His

.390 average was the highest in the majors in 39 seasons, since Ted Williams had cleared .400. Besides winning his second batting title, Brett drove in 118 runs in just 449 times at bat. The other key to the K.C. attack was leftfielder Willie Wilson. He led the league in hits and runs, stole 79 bases and upset defenses constantly with his speed. He hit .326. There was more power from first baseman Willie Aikens (20 homers, 98 RBIs) and DH Hal McRae (.297, 83 RBIs). Frank White was an excellent second baseman and while Amos Otis had slowed down some, the 33-year-old centerfielder was still an asset.

There was talent in the Royal rotation, too. Dennis Leonard, a determined righthander with a tight, hard curveball, had his third 20-game season, coming in at 20-11. Larry Gura, who suddenly blossomed as a starter in Kansas City after several aimless seasons with the Yanks and Cubs, was 18-10, his best year. After him was another tough lefty, Paul Splittorff, a touch past his prime at 33, at 14-6. The big advantage was submarining reliever Dan Quisenberry. In his second year in the majors, he had come in 75 times with his unorthodox delivery, saved 33 games and won 12 more. Quisenberry was the X-factor Philadelphia had not seen and could not match.

Turning Point: Game Five, Ninth Inning.

The Series see-saws. The Phillies win twice at home, pounding Leonard in the opener behind the rookie Walk, 7-6, and then landing on Quisenberry for a 4-run rally in the eighth to win game two, 6-4. The Royals rebound when they get home. They beat McGraw in the 10th inning, 4-3 and then even it up, 5-3, with Leonard getting the win.

With the fifth game in Kansas City, the Royals have a great opportunity. They have Gura, who pitched 6 strong innings in game two, while the Phils must rely on Marty Bystrom. The 22-year-old rookie came on at the end of the season and won five in a row as a starter. Green had given him the critical start in the fifth game of the playoffs against Houston and he went 5 tough innings without a decision. Still, this is a touchy spot for a young man with a grand total of 7 games in the majors.

Gura is in good form, ahead of the hitters and keeping the big swingers confused. But with one out in the fourth, Aikens boots a grounder by McBride. The Phils have been held to just 2 home runs in this Series, but Schmidt launches number 3 over the centerfield wall to give Philadelphia the 2-0 lead.

Bystrom starts to wobble, though. He has to pitch out of trouble in the 3rd and 4th. Brett finally drives in one run in the fifth, then Otis starts the sixth with a game-tying homer, his 3rd of the Series. Before Green can react, Clint Hurdle and Darrell Porter pound out singles and the Royals are poised for the kill. Towering Ron Reed, who once played for the NBA's Detroit Pistons, gets U.L. Washington on a sacrifice fly, but that puts Kansas City ahead, 3-2. More damage is averted when Porter is thrown out at the plate on Wilson's double to right on great throws by McBride and Trillo.

Quisenberry, who got a save in game three, is summoned in the seventh to save the lead. Things are apparently under control as the game moves to the ninth, but Schmidt leads off with a scratch hit off Brett's glove. The Phils then send up Del Unser to pinch hit. The 35-year-old outfielder is on his second swing with the team. He had been picked up the previous year after getting cut by Montreal and had rebounded with two good seasons as a utility player. In a similar situation, in the fifth game of the playoffs, he tied the game with an eighth-inning pinch-hit single, then scored the winner after doubling in the 10th. He doubled again during the rally that beat Quisenberry in game two, making it three consecutive clutch hits in a row. In a moment, Unser has his fourth, a smash past Aikens into the rightfield corner for a double. Schmidt scores on the hit and the game is tied. Unser gets to third with two outs, and Trillo drills a hard grounder off Quisenberry's leg. Brett grabs the carom but his throw is too late to get Trillo, as Unser scores the lead run.

McGraw, who entered the game in the seventh, never does things the easy way when there is an option. He manages to walk the bases loaded in the last of the ninth and must face Jose Cardenal, playing in his first Series after 18 years in the majors. McGraw flutters his hand over his chest, simulating a racing heart, and then comes back to strike out Cardenal and end the game. Philadelphia's second throttling of Quisenberry sends them home with the Series lead, and Carlton locks it up for them with a 4-1 win in game six.

The Managers:

Dallas Green looked the part of a man in control. He was imposing, handsome, an individual who appeared to know some really good jokes at the rest of the world's expense. As a pitcher, though, he never could throw that hard and he seemed to be constantly on the defensive as a manager, lacing conversations with heavy doses of sarcasm. He left the Phillies after just two years to take up an even more formidable task. He was hired by the Cubs to remake the front office amd produce a winner.

FACT:
Tug McGraw flutters his hand over his chest, simulating a racing heart, and then goes back to strike out Cardenal and end the game.

Jim Frey was 48 when he got the Kansas City job after a career in the minor leagues and as a coach on other peoples' teams. Given the chance, he brought home a winner first time out of the chute. But the chance didn't last long. When the Royals foundered in the truncated, doubled-up strike season of 1981, Frey was gone 20 games into the second half. Three years later, he resurfaced with the Cubs, hired by Green, the man who beat him in the 1980 Series. In only his second full season as a manager, Frey brought in his second winner, a divisional title, the first thing any Cub team had won in 39 years.

FACT:
When Kansas City's first baseman pounded two home runs in game one, two more in game four and won the third game with a ninth inning hit, some of the Phillies discovered that his full name was Willie Mays Aikens. "This could be a more interesting Series than I thought," said Rose.

The Heroes:

Schmidt seemed to be in the middle of every decisive Philadelphia rally, driving in runs in the last five straight games of the Series. His double brought in the lead run in game two, his single touched off the winning rally in game five, and a two-run single was all the margin Carlton needed in game seven. Schmidt finished with a .381 average and 7 RBIs.

Carlton did exactly what the number one starter is expected to do. He won twice, struck out 17 and kept his mouth shut. Of course, with Carlton that was no big deal because he made it a policy never to talk to the media.

When Kansas City's first baseman pounded two home runs in game one, two more in game four, and won the third game with a ninth inning hit, some of the Phillies discovered that his full name was Willie Mays Aikens. "This could be a more interesting Series than I thought," said an amused Pete Rose. Aikens wound up hitting .400 with 8 RBIs, and his 4 homers were four more than his illustrious namesake hit in the Series.

McGraw gave the entire city of Philadelphia palpitations with his brink-of-disaster performances in the final two games. He struck out Cardenal after walking the bases loaded to end game five. Then he had to repeat the act in game six, fanning Wilson with three on after two hits and a walk.

The Zeroes:

Wilson keyed the Royals attack as the leadoff man and was their top threat to steal. But the Phillies tied him in knots, striking Wilson out a record 12 times and never giving him the chance to use his speed. The whiffs wiped out the record set by

Eddie Mathews in the 1958 Series, but it took him a full 7 games to do it.

Frank White also had a rough time. The Kansas City second baseman went just 2 for 25, and his throw pulled shortstop Washington off the bag in the third inning of game six to set up Philadelphia's winning rally.

The Aftermath:

The Phils made a good acquisition in outfielder Gary Matthews over the winter and got off to a first-place start in 1981. But after the mid-season strike, they tailed off in the second half, and then dropped the divisional playoffs to Montreal. Philadelphia returned to the Series in 1983.

The Royals shared the same fate by a different route. They slumped in the first half of 1981, appointed Dick Howser manager midway through the second segment, and won that half-pennant. Then they lost to Oakland in the first round of the American League playoffs. It would take the Royals until 1985 to get back to the Series, making a more successful visit.

Notes:

Walk was the first rookie to pitch a Series opener since Joe Black did it for the Dodgers in 1952. The choice was more inevitable than surprising since the Phillies had to throw in everyone else to win the last two playoff games. Walk gave up 6 runs in 7 innings, got the win, and never pitched for the Phillies again. He was traded to Atlanta for Matthews in the off season.

It was a painful Series for Brett. Although he hit .375, he had to enter the hospital between games two and three for a surgical procedure on his hemorrhoids. The media made jokes but Brett was a man in agony for most of these games.

As if McGraw's pitching wasn't scary enough, the Phillies pulled off one of the more heart-stopping outs of the Series to help rescue him. With the bases loaded and one out in the ninth of the final game, White hit a pop foul near the seats. The crowd relaxed, anticipating an easy second out, only to gasp as the ball popped out of catcher Boone's glove—right into Rose's first baseman's mitt. "We practice that all the time," Rose laughed later. McGraw then ended the Series with a strikeout.

Philadelphia fans had often been called the nastiest in the game, but Bowa made the mistake of saying that out loud just before the Series. Consequently, he was booed by the home crowd for the duration. During the team's victory parade, Bowa made it a point to give the fans a standing salute and was cheered heartily in return.

Line Scores:

Game One, October 14

KC (AL)—022 000 020—6
Leonard L, Martin (4), Quisenberry (8)

Phi (NL)—005 110 00X—7
Walk W, McGraw (8) SV

Game Two, October 15

KC (AL)—000 001 300—4
Gura, Quisenberry (7) L

Phi (NL)—000 020 04X—6
Carlton W, Reed (9) SV

Game Three, October 17

Phi (NL)—010 010 010 0—3
Ruthven, McGraw (10) L

KC (AL)—100 100 100 1—4
Gale, Martin (5), Quisenberry (8) W

Game Four, October 18

Phi (NL)—010 000 110—3
Christenson L, Noles (1), Saucier (6), Brusstar (6)

KC (AL)—410 000 00X—5
Leonard W, Quisenberry (8) SV

Game Five, October 19

Phi (NL)—000 200 002—4
Bystrom, Reed (6), McGraw (7) W

KC (AL)—000 012 000—3
Gura, Quisenberry (7) L

Game Six, October 21

KC (AL)—000 000 010—1
Gale L, Martin (3), Splittorff (5), Pattin (7), Quisenberry (8)

Phi (NL)—002 011 00X—4
Carlton W, McGraw (8) SV

1981

Los Angeles (NL) 4
New York (AL) 2

For the third time in five years, the two teams meet in a six-game Series. This time the Dodgers turn the tables and win the final four games in a row for their first championship in 16 seasons.

The Preview:

The rhythm of the baseball season was a steady metronome of American life since the first World Series in 1903. In the next 78 years, the nation that gave birth to baseball changed beyond recognition. The game itself was not immune to change. Franchises shifted, grass became artificial turf, arc lamps illuminated the darkness. There were designated hitters and divisional playoffs, expansion and free agency. Through it all, with rare exceptions, each season rolled on as the one before, crowning its champions and matching them in the Series.

In 1981 that came to an end. A strike by the players tore more than 50 games out of the middle of the schedule, stopping the season for two months. When play resumed, the owners decided on a gimmick. They put the games already played in the can and declared it half a season. Then they played a separate mini-season with what was left of the original schedule. The winners of each half season then met in a divisional playoff before advancing to the regular league playoff and the Series.

The results were appalling, breaking the long chain of structural integrity. Cincinnati and St. Louis, the teams with the best overall records in each National League division, were eliminated from the playoffs because they had not finished first in either of the artificial mini-seasons. Instead, the Dodgers, only the third best team overall, won playoffs from Houston and Montreal and sailed into the Series.

Pedro Guerrero, Steve Yeager, and Ron Cey (l to r) celebrate LA's victory and their co-MVP award. The trio combined for 18 hits, five homers, and 17 RBI. Cey returned from a Game 5 beaning to get two hits in the finale.

The same infield from the last three winners was still in place for L.A., with Steve Garvey leading the team with 64 RBIs and Ron Cey adding 13 homers. Another returnee, leftfielder Dusty Baker, hit a solid .320, while Pedro Guerrero took over in rightfield for the first full season and hit .300 with 12 homers.

Burt Hooton was also back from the last winning Dodgers staff and went 11-6. Bob Welch had made the transformation from reliever to starter and was 9-5. Jerry Reuss, the team's best pitcher in 1980, came back with another outstanding year in the abbreviated season, going 10-4. But the big winner was a sensational rookie left hander, Fernando Valenzuela. The 20-year old Mexican with a head-rolling delivery and deadly screwball became a huge hero in L.A., with the ballpark selling out for his appearances. His 13-7 season included 8 shutouts and a league-leading 180 strikeouts. He became the game's top personality in an otherwise dismal year.

The Dodgers bullpen was fairly much a committee affair, with two hard-throwing youngsters, Steve Howe and Dave Stewart, combining for 14 saves.

The Yankees also would have been a non-participant under regular conditions. They finished third in their division overall. A second half skid to a sub-.500 record couldn't keep them out because they won the first season. George Steinbrenner used the slump, however, as an excuse to fire the manager, Gene Michael. He was replaced by the designated Series manager from 1978, Bob Lemon. It made sense only to Steinbrenner.

The Yanks had signed the season's prize free agent, leftfielder Dave Winfield, who led the team in RBIs with 68. Winfield also was a major irritant to resident star Reggie Jackson. He slid to a .237 average, while tying for the team lead in homers with 15 and driving in 54. Jerry Mumphrey, a teammate of Winfield's in San Diego the previous year, rejoined him after a spring trade and hit .307. Veteran shortstop Bucky Dent would miss the Series with injuries, but his replacement, Larry Milbourne, had been one of the team's strongest hitters in the second half, finishing at .313. Veterans Graig Nettles, Willie Randolph and Lou Piniella also returned from the champions of 1977–78.

Ron Guidry was again the team's top winner, at 11-5. Tommy John, who pitched on the other side the last two times these teams met, was 9-8. The big addition was rookie left hander Dave Righetti, one of the few bright spots of the second half, who finished 8-4. Goose Gossage was unhittable in relief, with 20 saves and an almost invisible 0.77 ERA.

Turning Point: Game Five, Seventh Inning.

The Yankees have a chance to win this Series in a rout. They beat Reuss and Hooton in the first two games in New York, with Guidry and John stopping the Dodgers cold. A courageous Valenzuela, struggling with control and not in command of his best pitches, fights off New York in game three and gets the Dodgers in the win column, 5-4. Then L.A. battles back from a 4-0 deficit to win a wild 8-7 thriller in game four. Jackson gets three hits and two walks, but drops a fly ball in his first Series action after bruising a calf muscle.

Now it comes back to Guidry. He pitched 7 strong innings in the opener, giving up only a home run to Steve Yeager. The Yankees, on the other hand, had driven out Reuss in the third. The six-foot-five left-hander does not have an encouraging post season record. He has lost five of six decisions in the playoffs and Series. The one win, though, came against Houston in this year's divisional playoffs, a 5-hit shutout in the deciding game. It becomes apparent in this game that the Yankees are contending with that Reuss rather than the one they saw in the opener.

They get a run in the second on a double by Jackson (his fourth straight hit) and a single by Piniella. Aside from that, however, Reuss gives up just two harmless singles in the first seven innings. Twice he gets catcher Rick Cerone on easy grounders when the Yanks are in position to get a big inning going. The first starts a double play, the second comes with runners on second and third and none out. Even three errors by Davey Lopes don't faze Reuss. But Guidry again is on his game. He gives up a single to Garvey in the first and a double by Yeager in the second and that's it. Going into the seventh he has 8 strikeouts, and while the lead is only 1-0 Guidry seems in total command.

He starts the seventh by getting Baker for his 9th strikeout. Then, with no warning, it all blows up. Guerrero, who had gone 0 for 4 with 2 strikeouts against Guidry, slams the ball into the left-field seats. Bingo, the game is tied. Yeager, who already has a homer and double off Guidry, shows this was no fluke. He knocks a second straight ball over the fence and, with dramatic quickness, the Dodgers have turned the game around, taking a 2-1 lead.

The Yanks go down meekly against Reuss in the last 2 innings. The Dodgers have beaten them three straight. A furious Steinbrenner comes to the New York clubhouse after the game. He rips Cerone. He rips Winfield, who has gone 1 for 18 in the Series. The Yanks dress in sullen silence. They have the look of a team that knows it is beaten. The Dodgers execute that formally with a 9-2 thrashing in game six. The back-to-back homers off the Yankees' ace is more than New York can come back from.

The Managers:

For Lasorda, the final mountain had been climbed. "I never said this before," he said after the final game, "but I had always hoped that when we won our first Series it would be against the club that beat us twice." That would be the Yankees. Lasorda, one of the huggiest men around in normal times, outdid himself for this celebration. He may have bled Dodger blue but this time it looked very much like champagne.

Lemon had become the first man ever to take a team into the Series with less than a .500 managerial record during the season. It was a bizarre season. While Steinbrenner used the manager's office to deliver a diatribe to the press after game five, someone noted to Lemon: "It looks like you've been dispossessed." Lemon shrugged. "It may be worse than that before it's over," he said.

> **FACT:**
> Pedro Guerrero was the Dodgers' driving force in the four games they won. Hitless in the first two games, he went 7-14 from that point, with a double, triple, 2 home runs and 7 RBIs, capping it with 5 RBIs in the closer.

The Heroes:

Guerrero was the Dodgers' driving force in the four games it won. Hitless in the first two games, the 25-year-old Dominican slugger went 7 for 14 from that point on, with a double, a triple, two home runs and 7 RBIs, capping it with 5 RBIs in the closer.

Yeager was one of the rare players with the ability to elevate his performance in big games. In his four Series with the Dodgers, he hit .298, which was 69 points higher than his lifetime average during the season. This year he drove in the tying or lead run in each of the final three L.A. wins.

For Bob Watson, it was his first shot at the Series in a distinguished 16-year career, most of it spent looking up from the second division. He had signed with the Yanks as a free agent in 1980, but slumped badly this year, finishing with a .212 average. He had enough left for one big surge and hit .318 in the Series, leading the Yankees with 7 RBIs and driving out 2 home runs.

The Zeroes:

Winfield had been lavishly praised by Steinbrenner when he came over as a free agent. Now the Yankee owner began referrring to him mockingly as Mr. May and ridiculed his request for the ball when he got his first Series hit in game five. It was also his only Series hit. He went a horrendous 1 for 22. "If he'd hit it [the ball] into the bleachers I'd have gone in and got it for him myself," Steinbrenner snarled. Winfield stayed in New York for the rest of the '80s, but never was on another winner and spent much of his time feuding with the owner.

Lopes wound up making 6 errors, after coming off an injury-filled season in which he hit just .206. He made frequent references to his likely departure and played like a man under sentence.

The big reason the Yankees lost the Series was the collapse of their middle relief. Ron Davis and George Frazier gave up 15 runs in 6 innings. Frazier had been effective during the season as a set-up man for the fearsome Gossage. But he lost all three Series games he appeared in. He became the first pitcher to lose 3 since Lefty Williams, with the Black Sox of 1919, and he wasn't trying to win.

The Aftermath:

Lopes turned out to be quite accurate in his estimate of Dodger intentions. He became the first of the team's long-running infield unit to go, sent to Oakland before the following season. Within 2 more years the entire infield was gone and the Dodgers were being described as a team that "got young too fast." They bobbed in and out of contention but didn't make it back to the Series until 1988.

The five-year Age of Jackson ended in New York when the volatile slugger packed up his free agency and moved to the California Angels. The Yankees dove to fifth place in 1982 and Steinbrenner frantically changed managers three times. The core of the team that had won 4 pennants in 6 years was on its way out and the Yankees were about to embark on a long sojourn in the wilderness.

FACT:
George Steinbrenner followed up his intrusive Series performance by publishing a "Note of Apology" to New York fans for the play of the Yankees.

Notes:

Steinbrenner followed up his intrusive Series performance by publishing a "Note of Apology" to New York fans for the play of the Yankees. Besides criticizing his players in public, he also got himself involved in a fistfight in a Los Angeles hotel elevator with some Dodger fans and wound up breaking his hand when one of his punches hit the door. "Steinbrenner likes to think of himself as being so New York," wrote a commentator afterwards. "But to New Yorkers, he's all Cleveland."

The scariest moment of the Series came when Cey was hit in the head by a Gossage fastball in game five. The third baseman went down and didn't move for several moments. But he only complained of some light-headedness the following day, and when game six was delayed by rain for a day, he was able to start and get two hits.

The one Yankee Steinbrenner had kind words for ("What a pro") was Piniella. The veteran outfielder hit .438 to lead everyone in the Series.

The October 28 wrapup, because of the extra round of playoffs and one rainout, was the latest date in history for a Series game.

Line Scores:

Game One, October 20

LA (NL)—000 010 020—3
Reuss L, Castillo (3), Goltz (4), Niedenfuer (5), Stewart (8)

NY (AL)—301 100 00X—5
Guidry W, Gossage (8) SV

Game Two, October 21

LA (NL)—000 000 000—0
Hooton L, Forster (7), Howe (8), Stewart (8)

NY (AL)—000 010 02X—3
John W, Gossage (8) SV

Game Three, October 23

NY (AL)—022 000 000—4
Righetti, Frazier (3) L,
May (5), Davis (8)

LA (NL)—300 020 00X—5
Valenzuela W

Game Four, October 24

NY (AL)—211 002 010—7
Reuschel, May (4), Davis (5),
Frazier (6) L, John (7)

LA (NL)—002 013 20X—8
Welch, Goltz (1), Forster (4),
Niedenfuer (5), Howe (7) W

Game Five, October 25

NY (AL)—010 000 000—1
Guidry L, Gossage (8)

LA (NL)—000 000 20X—2
Reuss W

Game Six, October 28

LA (NL)—000 134 010—9
Hooton W, Howe (6) SV

NY (AL)—001 001 000—2
John, Frazier (5) L, Davis (6),
Reuschel (6), May (7),
LaRoche (9)

1982

St. Louis (NL) 4
Milwaukee (AL) 3

The Cardinals managed to rein in Milwaukee's power hitters and then got just enough hitting of their own to blow past the Brewers in a Series decided by the bullpens. It was the fourth consecutive National League victory, a Series record.

The Preview:

There was nothing subtle about Milwaukee's winning formula. The Brewers simply hammered you to death. They were called "Harvey's Wallbangers," in tribute to manager Harvey Kuenn, who took over at mid-season and rode the force into the Series. The Brewer lineup contained 3 hitters with more than 30 homers, 4 with more than 100 RBIs, 3 who batted over .300. It was the most impressive collection of power since the Yankee teams of the early '60s.

Gorman Thomas topped the league in homers at 39, and right on his tail were Ben Oglivie (34) and Cecil Cooper (32). Cooper also drove in 121, while hitting .313 and winning recognition, late in his career, as the best first baseman in the league. The MVP of the Brewers was shortstop Robin Yount. An unusually gifted athlete, he had been Milwaukee's regular shortstop since he was a teenager and sometimes pondered the possibility of leaving the grind and becoming a pro golfer. This season he emerged as a superstar, with 29 homers, 114 RBIs and a .331 average, all personal highs. They were enough to get him the MVP award, too. Next to him on the left side of the Milwaukee infield was Paul Molitor, who managed to avoid the injuries that pestered him throughout his career and hit .302 with 19 homers. Catcher Ted Simmons, in his second season since coming over from the Cards in a major trade, drove in 97 runs.

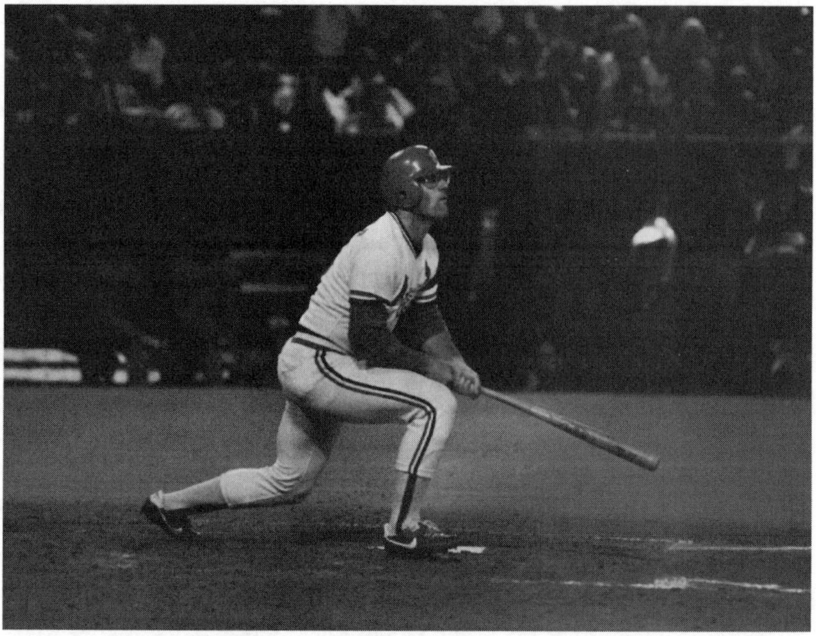

Darrell Porter's MVP performance included a game-tying double in Game 2, as well as a .286 average, a home run, and five RBI. His success was sweetened by the fact that his predecessor, Ted Simmons, played for the opposition.

The pitching was better than anticipated. Pete Vuckovich, who accompanied Simmons in the St. Louis deal, was 18-6 and won the Cy Young Award. Left-hander Mike Caldwell, the team's most consistent pitcher for several seasons, went 17-13. The Brewers had acquired Don Sutton just before the trading deadline. The 37-year old veteran went 4-1 down the stretch, including the clincher against Baltimore, and then added a critical playoff win. The third man in the big trade with the Cards was relief ace Rollie Fingers, and he had been all the Brewers had hoped. This year he saved 29 games in his first 50 appearances before coming down with arm problems. When it became apparent that he would not play in the Series, Milwaukee was left with a gaping hole where a stopper should be. The Brewers decided on Bob McClure to fill it. He had been used as a starter this year and went 12-7. But before the arrival of Fingers, he had been in the pen and Milwaukee thought he could switch back without a major adjustment.

The Cards did not match up well on paper. Playing in a far bigger ballpark, they were built on speed and defense. Their best hitters were first baseman Keith Hernandez (.299, 94 RBIs) and outfielder George Hendrick (19 homers, 104 RBIs.) Rookie

Willie McGee arrived to hit .296. Lonnie Smith, a sub with the 1980 Phillies, stepped into the regular leftfield job here and hit .307, while leading the league in runs and stealing 68 bases. The most vital addition, though, was shortstop Ozzie Smith. He had come over in a trade with San Diego and his defensive brilliance strengthened the entire infield. With the Cards, he would develop into the best shortstop of his generation, with a range that exceeded anyone who ever played the position.

There was weakness in the St. Louis rotation. Joaquin Andujar had been obtained from Houston the previous year and settled in with a 15-10 mark. Veteran Bob Forsch, in his 9th year as a Card starter, was 15-9. After that it was shaky. During the playoffs the Cards chose to start rookie John Stuper. He was only 9-7 during the year but pitched with poise, and manager Whitey Herzog seemed inclined to try him out during the Series, too. St. Louis had its relief intact. After making a trade for Fingers in 1980, the Cards closed another deal within a few days for Bruce Sutter from the Cubs. That allowed St. Louis to package Fingers and send him to Milwaukee. This Series would have matched the top two closers in the game, since Sutter saved 36 and won 9 more for the Cards. But with Fingers sidelined, Sutter had the Series to himself. The difference would prove decisive.

Turning Point: Seventh Game, Sixth Inning.

The Series has been fought in the bullpens. Sutter has a win and a save in the two St. Louis victories, while McClure has saved both of Milwaukee's games, while losing one other. Neither man has appeared overpowering, but both are vital. When Sutter has to pitch more than 2 innings to save game three, the Cards hold him out of game four. That gives Milwaukee all the room they need to rally for 6 runs in the seventh inning and pull out a 7-5 win. But McClure has been thrown in for four straight games and is getting ground down after a full season of starting.

After a 10-0 Milwaukee rout in the opener, each team wins two straight. Then the Cards return the embarrassment by clobbering the Brewers, 13-1, in game six. The rookie, Stuper, gives the staff some critical rest by going all the way, despite two rain delays.

It will be Vuckovich against Andujar in the closer. Andujar beat him 6-2 in their previous meeting in game three. Caldwell, in fact, has been Milwaukee's only effective starter, winning

FACT:
The Series has been fought in the bullpens. Bruce Sutter has a win and a save in two St. Louis victories and Bob McClure has saved two games while losing another. The battle goes to the bigger bullpen.

twice. But he would have to go on two days rest to work again and Kuenn decides to stay with Vuckovich. It is a shaky choice. He is constantly in trouble in the early innings, but the Cards cannot deliver the key hit to take advantage of two walks and four singles. In the fourth, singles by McGee, Tom Herr and Lonnie Smith finally bring a run across, but Oglivie takes Andujar out of the park in the 5th to tie the game, 1-1.

Then in the sixth the Brewers put together an inning. A double by Jim Gantner, singles by Molitor and Yount and a sacrifice fly bring in two more runs, and Milwaukee has a 3-1 lead. When St. Louis comes up in the bottom half, however, Ozzie Smith gets a one-out single and Lonnie Smith follows with a double down the third base line. This normally would be the place where Fingers would walk in. The pitcher had tried throwing on the sidelines earlier in the Series, but the pain from his injured forearm would not allow him to get any speed on the pitches. The Brewers have given up any thought of using him. Instead, the best they can do in this spot is McClure again. It isn't good enough, and the disparity in the bullpens decides the Series. McClure walks pinch hitter Gene Tenace and Hernandez slams a two-run single up the middle to tie the game. When Hendrick follows with another single, the Cards are ahead 4-3 with the lead that will win the Series. McClure can't finish the inning, but the Brewers already are finished.

The Brewers ride Andujar throughout the game. He left the earlier contest when a grounder bounced off his knee. The pitcher went down as if he'd been shot, writhing in agony. The Brewers suspect he was laying on the dramatics and when Gantner calls him a "hot dog" after his at-bat in the seventh, Andujar makes a rush for him. He is restrained, but Herzog figures it is probably time to get him out. It's an easy choice, because he has a rested Sutter. The Cards add 2 more runs in the eighth to make it 6-2 and Sutter mows down the six men he faces to end the game. The battle goes to the bigger bullpen.

The Managers:

Kuenn had never managed in the majors before the Brewers moved him in from his coaching job to give some life to an underachieving team wallowing in 5th place. They leaped to the front under Kuenn's light touch. A hometown guy, who spent the off season working in the family bar, the 51-year-old Kuenn starred for several seasons as a deadly line-drive hitter with the Tigers. He went to the Series as a player with the '62 Giants. Known as a man who would not say no to a beer during his playing career, he is no disciplinarian. The Brewers seem to like it that way.

Herzog, on the other hand, arrived in St. Louis in 1980 and immediately started remaking the team. He pulled off several major trades, stealing McGee from the Yankee system, signing catcher Darrell Porter as a free agent and rebuilding the nucleus of the Cards. He had won three division titles with Kansas City, falling to the Yankees in each instance. He had the best overall record in the Eastern Division in 1981, but the double-season playoff format of the strike year robbed the Cards of a chance at the pennant. There would be such slip-up this time for the tough, hard-driving Herzog.

FACT:
Robin Yount followed his season MVP award by leading the Series with 12 hits. He batted .414 with 6 RBIs. He got 4 hits in the first and fifth games, the first man ever to that twice in the same Series.

The Heroes:

The 29-year-old Sutter no longer threw as hard as he did when he first came up with the Cubs, but he remained the consummate reliever. Even Fingers had carried on a brief fling with starting, but Sutter had never pitched a single inning as a starter in his 7 seasons in the majors. The Series did not show him at his very best, but with two saves and a win it was good enough.

Yount followed up his MVP award by leading the Series with 12 hits. He batted .414, with 6 RBIs. He got 4 hits in both the first and fifth games, the first man ever to do that twice in the same Series.

Use of the designated hitter in this even-numbered year boomeranged against the American League team. Dane Iorg, an occasional outfielder and left-hand hitting utility man, got the call as the Cards' DH. He hit .529, finishing up with a 5 for 7 run in the last two games with two doubles and a triple. His performance intrigued the Kansas City Royals, who obtained Iorg as a DH with unfortunate results for the Cardinals in 1985.

The Series was a personal redemption for Darrell Porter. He had signed with St. Louis after beating an alcoholism problem, but was booed consistently because he replaced longtime Cards hero Ted Simmons. To make it worse, Porter, an outstanding hitter on Herzog's teams in Kansas City, had bad seasons back-to-back. With Simmons catching for the other side, however, Porter came through with several big hits, including a game-tying double that brought the Cards back from a possible second straight loss in game two.

The Zeroes:

Thomas, the American League home run champ, was stopped at 3 for 26 and did not get a single extra base hit. He also struck out 7 times.

This was Sutton's fifth shot at getting a Series ring, after winding up on the losing side four times in Los Angeles. He couldn't get past the 6th in either of his two starts. With a chance to end it in game six he was clobbered for 7 runs in the 13-1 loss.

A total of 14 unearned runs scored in the games, the product of 18 errors. Gantner made 5 at second base for Milwaukee.

The Aftermath:

The Milwaukee power dried up in 1983. Thomas, hitting only .183 on 5 homers, was traded to Cleveland, while Oglivie's home run production dropped from 34 to 13. Moreover, Fingers did not respond to treatment and missed the entire season. Vuckovich developed arm problems of his own, dropped to 0-2, and was out for all of 1984. Through this adversity, the Brewers still won 87 games, but Kuenn was fired.

The Cardinals also fell abruptly, with Hernandez fighting addiction problems and the pitching staff in free fall. St. Louis dropped to fourth place, but would begin a climb back to the Series by 1985.

Notes:

Molitor started off as if he intended to break every hitting record in the books. He became the first man ever to get 5 hits in one game, with consecutive singles in the opener. But he was only .240, on 6 for 25, in the next six games.

Rain forced two delays totaling 2 hours and 39 minutes in the sixth game. Since the outcome was never in doubt after the sixth, when the Cards had a 13-0 lead, only a scattering of fans sat it out in Busch Stadium to watch the affair wind down well past midnight. The official elapsed playing time was 18 minutes less than the delays.

Line Scores:

Game One, October 12

Mil (AL)—200 112 004—10
Caldwell W

SL (NL)—000 000 000—0
Forsch L, Kaat (6), LaPoint (7), Lahti (9)

Game Two, October 13

Mil (AL)—012 010 000—4
Sutton, McClure (7) L, Ladd (8)

SL (NL)—002 002 01X—5
Stuper, Kaat (5), Bair (5), Sutter (7) W

Game Three, October 15

SL (NL)—000 030 201—6	Mil (AL)—000 000 020—2
Andujar W, Kaat (7), Bair (7), Sutter (7) SV	Vuckovich L, McClure (9)

Game Four, October 16

SL (NL)—130 001 000—4	Mil (AL)—000 010 60X—7
LaPoint, Bair (7) L, Kaat (7), Lahti (7)	Haas, Slaton (6) W, McClure (8) SV

Game Five, October 17

SL (NL)—001 000 102—4	Mil (NL)—101 010 12X—6
Forsch L, Sutter (8)	Caldwell W, McClure (9) SV

Game Six, October 19

Mil (NL)—000 000 001—1	SL (AL)—020 326 00X—13
Sutton L, Slaton (5), Medich (6), Bernard (8)	Stuper W

Game Seven, October 20

Mil (NL)—000 012 000—3	SL (NL)—000 103 02X—6
Vuckovich, McClure (6), Haas (6), Caldwell (8)	Andujar W, Sutter (8) SV

1983

Baltimore (AL) 4
Philadelphia (NL) 1

The ragtag, aging Phillies were no match for a young, aggressive Baltimore team, which shut down the Philadelphia attack and outscored them by a 2 to 1 margin.

The Preview:

The Orioles retained a strong core from their 1979 pennant-winners. Eddie Murray, the switch-hitting first baseman, still packed the power. He hit 33 homers, drove in 111 and batted .306. Ken Singleton was now the fulltime DH, with 18 homers and 84 RBIs. Gary Roenicke remained as a powerful, right-hand hitting platoon outfielder, driving out 19 homers and 64 RBIs. Rick Dempsey also continued as the regular catcher, not an especially dangerous hitter but a player with a strong throwing arm and a good head.

John Lowenstein was the left-handed equivalent of Roenicke. Playing in a platoon arrangement in leftfield, he swatted 15 homers with 60 RBIs. In fact, manager Joe Altobelli shifted two complete sets of six outfielders in and out of the lineup. It was a combination of platooning and gut instinct as to who should play.

The focus of the Baltimore team had shifted to shortstop, where 23-year-old Cal Ripken, in his second season, had become a presence. It was the second straight year in which the league's best player had been a shortstop who hit for power. Before Robin Yount in 1982, no American League shortstop had ever topped 20 homers, 100 RBIs and .300 in the same season. Ripken made it two in a row, with 27 homers, 102 RBIs and a .318 average.

A holdover from the previous winners, Scott McGregor, led the pitching staff, at 18-7. Mike Flanagan was also back, but in reduced service with a 12-4 mark. The two other top starters were

Rick Dempsey, known mostly for his defense and rain-delay antics, came up big in the Series. He lead all hitters at .385 on five hits (all for extra bases), and allowed the Phillies only one stolen base.

rookie Mike Boddicker (16-8), who led the league with 5 shutouts, and Storm Davis (13-7), in his first year as a full-time starter. The stopper was left-hander Tippy Martinez, with 21 saves and 9 wins.

The Phillies had undergone a more sweeping change since their last pennant in 1980. In fact, they looked more like a pale reunion of the Big Red Machine. Three former Cincinnati stars—Pete Rose, Joe Morgan and Tony Perez—were in the Philadelphia lineup. But they were well faded from their glory days. Sportswriters, perhaps uncharitably, began referring to them as The Wheeze Kids. Rose, still the regular first baseman, hit just .245. Morgan, the starter at second, was only at .230, although his 16 homers were second high on the team. The 41-year-old Perez hit .241 as a pinch hitter and spot starter. There wasn't much, in fact, that was terribly impressive about this team. Mike Schmidt was still the main man, with 40 homers and 109 RBIs. Catcher Bo Diaz pumped out 15 homers and drove in 64. But the top hitter among the regulars was leftfielder Gary Maddox, and he batted only .275. Just four teams, in fact, hit worse than the Phils and they all finished last or next to last in the two divisions.

Pitching was not much of an improvement. Even Steve Carlton couldn't get above the break-even point with this team, finishing at 15-16. The big winner was John Denny at 19-6. He once led the league in ERA with the Cards, but then went flat and was traded to Cleveland. He did little better there and the Phils picked him up at minimal cost near the end of the 1982 season. Denny didn't win a game, but sometime over the winter it all fell back into place for him. He led the league in wins, was second in ERA and was this team's indispensable man. After those two, though, the top pitcher in the rotation was Charlie Hudson at 8-8. There was some strong relief—there almost had to be with that rotation. Al Holland had come over with Morgan in a deal with the Giants and turned into a stopper. He saved 25 games and won 8. The veteran Ron Reed and left-hander Willie Hernandez added 15 more saves and 17 wins. If you got to the Phillies starters early, though, this was a team in big trouble.

Turning Point: Game Four, Sixth Inning.

It is apparent from the start that the Phillies cannot hit with Baltimore, but there had been some hope that they would hit a little. In the first three games, though, they score just 5 runs. Four of them come on bases-empty home runs and the other is the result of an error. The Orioles win twice and only Denny's five-hit pitching in the opener holds them off, 2-1.

Since then, Boddicker beats Hudson, 4-1, and then Carlton is upended, 3-2, on a late error by shortstop Ivan DeJesus. Now Denny is going again on three days' rest. The Orioles have the luxury of starting Davis, who hasn't worked since throwing 6 shutout innings in the final playoff game with the White Sox.

Both right-handers are strong through three innings, but in the fourth the Orioles bunch four singles. Rich Dauer drives in two runs by getting his with the bases loaded. In the bottom half of the inning, however, it seems the Phillies finally are finding the range. Singles by Rose and Schmidt and a double by Joe Lefebvre bring in a run. Just to show they really mean it, the Phils keep going in the fifth. This time Denny himself knocks in the tying run after a double by Diaz. Rose follows with another double and Philadelphia is ahead, 3-2.

Aside from the outburst in the fourth, Denny is sharp again. The Phils hope to get just one more inning out of him before they bring in their bullpen, but he can't get that far. With one out in the sixth, Lowenstein singles and Dauer, who had gone 1 for 12 before driving in his runs in the fourth, rips a double to left. Now Altobelli goes to his inexhaustible bench. He brings up pinch hitter Joe Nolan, who gets an intentional pass. With Dempsey the next hitter, the Orioles go, instead, for Singleton, who is idle because it is not a DH year in the Series.

Denny is cautious. Moreover, he is tired. He ends up walking Singleton to force in the tying run. That also forces the hand of manager Paul Owens and he has to bring in Hernandez. Altobelli quickly chooses to lift Davis for another pinch hitter, John Shelby, who drives in the go-ahead run with a sacrifice fly. The Orioles will not trail again in this Series. They finish up against Hernandez in the seventh, with a double by Jim Dwyer and Dauer's third straight hit, a single, making it 5-3.

With their best pitcher out of the game and the hits still refusing to come, the Phils roll over for relievers Sammy Stewart and Tippy Martinez. They pitch 4 innings and give up a run only after two are out in the ninth. Too late. Philadelphia loses 5-4 and McGregor ends it the following day by blanking them, 5-0. The Phils are just outmanned in this Series by a far deeper and more talented team.

The Managers:

The 51-year-old Altobelli had been a bench-warmer in his three brief big league seasons as a player. He had coached, managed the Giants for three years in the late '70s, and then landed hip-deep in talent with the top job in Baltimore after the retirement of Earl Weaver. He proved to be a master manipulator of his entire roster, shuttling players in and out of the lineup (with the exception of Ripken, who had already started on his record consecutive game streak).

Paul Owens was an accidental manager. He had worked in the Phillies organization for years after managing them for just 80 games in a dreary 1973 season. When Pat Corrales couldn't get the team much above .500 at the All Star break, Owens stepped out of the general manager's office and into the dugout. So intense he once drove home after a game without noticing that he hadn't changed out of his uniform, the 59-year-old Owens, nicknamed The Pope, may have been the perfect choice for this superannuated group.

FACT:
Joe Morgan did what he could to get Philadelphia going. The 40-year old infielder hit two home runs, stole their only base, and was the only Phillie to score more than once.

The Heroes:

Dempsey had been a combative, hard-working receiver in his eight years with the Orioles, but he had never been anyone's idea of a big hitter. He kicked around as a reserve with the Twins and Yankees before a trade to Baltimore in 1976 gave him the chance to start. His best season had been only a .262 effort. He burst out in this Series, though, with four doubles and a home run, and his .385 average led all hitters. His arm also never let the Phillies running attack get started. They stole only once.

Morgan, playing mostly from memory, did what he could to get Philadelphia going. The 40-year-old infielder hit two home runs, stole their only base, was the only Phillie to score more than once and hit .263. It wasn't nearly enough.

The Baltimore relief combination of Martinez and Stewart was outstanding. Martinez saved two games and the two of them pitched a combined 8 innings while giving up one run.

The Zeroes:

Schmidt had been the dominant hitter in Philadelphia's 1980 Series win, but he was no problem at all to the Orioles this time. They stymied him at 1 for 20, with no extra base hits, no RBIs and 6 strikeouts.

Rose was benched after going 1 for 8 in the first two games and was furious. He came back and went 4 for 7 in the last two, but the episode indicated to him that he would not be signed for 1984 and he took a free agent offer from Montreal in the off-season.

This made two disappointing Series in a row for Baltimore outfielders Roenicke and Al Bumbry. Roenicke was hitless in

7 at bats, giving him a combined total of 2 for 23. Bumbry went 1 for 11, for a two-Series line of 4 for 32.

The Aftermath:

The Orioles, who appeared to be destined for the top for years to come, instead fell apart in 1984. All the outfielders who had come through so stalwartly in Altobelli's shuttle system, tailed off. DH Singleton was ineffective at .215. While the starting pitchers remained effective, the bullpen did not. The result was a fifth-place finish and the dismissal of Altobelli a few games into 1985. By the next year, they were in last place and rebuilding.

FACT:
When Jim Palmer won game three with 2 innings of shutout relief it was a landmark of sorts. Palmer won his first Series game in 1966, which gave him a span of 17 seasons for wins, wiping out the former mark of 12 years set by Whitey Ford.

The Phillies, too, were on a downward cycle, although theirs' was probably more predictable. They disposed of all their old Reds, but no young stars came up to take their place. Denny proved to be a one-year wonder and Carlton, at last, began to wear out. They finished fourth the next year and Owens' brief tenure as manager was over.

Notes:

When Jim Palmer won game three with 2 innings of shutout relief it was a landmark of sorts. Palmer won his first Series game in 1966, which have him a span of 17 seasons for his wins. That wiped out the former mark of 12 years set by Whitey Ford between 1950 and 1962.

The winning player's share of the Series swag was $65,488, which was not only a record but a quantum leap. As recently as 1979, the portion wasn't even half that much. It was an indication of the wealth contained in the new TV contract, which was fueling the free agent feeding frenzy.

Line Scores:

Game One, October 11

Phi (NL)—000 001 010—2
Denny W, Holland (8) SV

Bal (AL)—100 000 000—1
McGregor L, Stewart (9), T. Martinez (9)

Game Two, October 12

Phi (NL)—000 100 000—1
Hudson L, Hernandez (5), Andersen (6), Reed (8)

Bal (AL)—000 030 10X—4
Boddicker W

Game Three, October 14

Bal (AL)—000 001 200—3
Flanagan, Palmer (5) W,
Stewart (7), T. Martinez (9) SV

Phi (NL)—011 000 000—2
Carlton L, Holland (7)

Game Four, October 15

Bal (AL)—000 202 100—5
Davis W, Stewart (6),
T. Martinez (8) SV

Phi (NL)—000 120 001—4
Denny L, Hernandez (6),
Reed (6), Andersen (8)

Game Five, October 16

Bal (AL)—011 210 000—5
McGregor W

Phi (NL)—000 000 000—0
Hudson L, Bystrom (5),
Hernandez (6), Reed (9)

1984

Detroit (AL) 4
San Diego (NL) 1

The Tigers ransacked the American League, winning 104 games and leading from Opening Day through the playoffs. San Diego was no match and succumbed in a rather lackluster Series.

The Preview:

By the middle of May the Tigers were 35-5 and the pennant race was essentially over in the American League East. While Detroit's pace slackened afterward and Toronto did manage to mount some mid-season pressure, the Tigers were never seriously challenged and won by 15 games. It was a team of young veterans that scored lots of runs, led the league in pitching and played a steady defense. While no individuals ranked especially high in any category, there were no significant weaknesses, either.

Catcher Lance Parrish was the offensive leader with 33 homers and 98 RBIs, although hitting just .237. Also high in power numbers were outfielders Kirk Gibson (27 homers, 91 RBIs) and Chet Lemon (20 homers, 76 RBIs). The strength of the team was its middle infield, the best in the game. Shortstop Alan Trammell and second baseman Lou Whitaker had risen together through the Detroit farm system. They came to the majors together in late 1977 and remained as a unit for the next 18 years. It was the longest-running short-second combination in baseball history.

Trammell hit a team-high .314 and Whitaker was at .289. The only shaky spot was third base, where manager Sparky Anderson was not enamored of the defensive play of Howard Johnson.

The top three members of the pitching rotation, all right-handers, wound up with remarkably similar records. Jack Morris

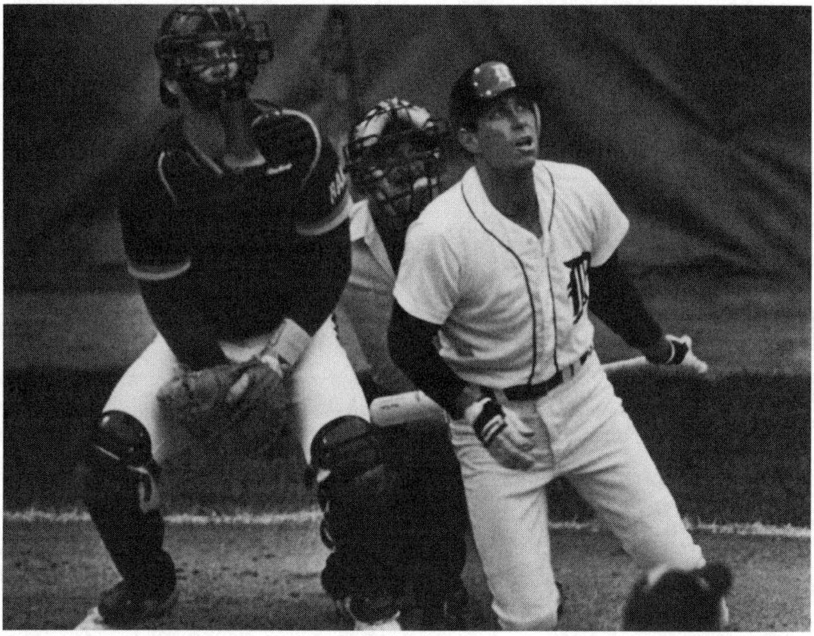

Alan Trammell follows the flight of his first-inning home run in Game 4. Trammell led the Tiger attack, destroying his hometown team with a .450 average on nine hits, two home runs, six RBI, and five runs.

(19-11) had joined the Tigers a few weeks before Trammell and Whitaker and developed into their most consistent winner. He had led the league in strikeouts the previous year and averaged 17 wins over the last 6 seasons. Dan Petry (18-8) was also in his sixth season with the team, while Milt Wilcox (17-8), at 34 the veteran of the rotation, had pitched for Anderson briefly in Cincinnati at the start of his career. The big difference was relief. Detroit had swung an off-season deal with the Phillies to land left-handed reliever Willie Hernandez. The American League found his screwball unhittable. He saved 32 games, won 9 and carted away most pitching awards. To back him up, Detroit had Aurelio Lopez, who threw smoke and saved 14 more while going 10-1.

While Detroit had been favored to win in many pre-season polls, the Padres snuck up on everyone. They had stitched together a team of kids, veterans and free agents around the hitting of brilliant young rightfielder, Tony Gwynn. He led the league in hitting at .351, while driving in 71. Surrounding him was a group that had just enough oomph left to win the big games. Steve Garvey, first baseman on 4 Dodgers pennant-winners, hit .284 and led the team with 86 RBIs. Graig Nettles, the third baseman on four winners with the Yankees, hit 20 homers and knocked in 65. Kevin McReynolds, in his second year in the majors, hit 20 homers, and another young performer, Alan Wiggins, stole 70 bases.

In pitching the Padres didn't stack up well, at all. Top winner on the staff was Eric Show, with his best season in the majors, at 15-9. Ed Whitson and Mark Thurmond, only in his second season, also had their best years at 14-8. The most experienced arm they had was stopper Goose Gossage, who had signed as a free agent. At 33, he was not quite as fast as he was with the Yankees, but Gossage saved 25 and won 10 and still was an awe-inspiring sight as he shambled in to put down a late rally. The Padres had won the division with surprising ease and then shocked the Cubs by winning the last three of a five-game playoff. The country had been primed for a Cubs-Tigers Series, matching two of the old line franchises in their historic ballparks. This seemed like a pretty pallid substitute.

FACT:
The Tigers had a penchant for scoring early all season. In the Series, Padre starting pitchers give up 16 runs in 10 1/3 innings, averaging less than 2 innings per start.

Turning Point: Game One, Seventh Inning.

The Padres know that to have any chance against Detroit they must get off to a fast start in their home park, preferably taking two at Jack Murphy Stadium. But the playoff with the Cubs extended their already thin staff and San Diego must go with Thurmond, who was belted out in the fourth inning of his start in Chicago. The Tigers have a rested Morris ready to pitch.

Detroit is noted for jumping off to quick leads and they are right in form against Thurmond. A leadoff double by Whitaker and a single by Trammell brings in a first inning run before the crowd can comfortably settle. Only a pickoff of Trammell averts disaster when two more singles follow in the inning.

San Diego strikes back quickly. Garvey and Nettles single and then catcher Terry Kennedy bangs a double into the right-field corner to score them both. After that shaky start, both pitchers calm down. Both have slight control problems, but avoid giving up the big hit. In the fifth, though, after Gibson becomes Thurmond's second pickoff victim, Parrish lines a double to left. Then leftfielder Larry Herndon, one of the quieter Tigers, rips a home run into the leftfield seats, and Detroit is back in front again, 3-2.

Morris seems to be gathering strength as the game progresses and San Diego is increasingly desperate for a scoring chance. He strikes out the side in the sixth after two leadoff singles. Then, in the seventh, DH Kurt Bevacqua, leading off as the ninth man in the lineup, drills a wrong-way hit into the rightfield corner. Cognizant of Morris' strikeout capabilities, Bevacqua feels an urgency about reaching third. Since Gibson had been pulled far over towards center on the play, that doesn't seem too difficult. But the speedy Gibson makes a perfect play in the corner on the carom and whips a strike to relay man Whitaker. The second baseman pivots and throws another bullet into the glove of third baseman Marty Castillo. Bevacqua is out by a wide margin and the Padres threat is over before it begins. That is the last hit San Diego can get off Morris, and he closes them out, 3-2. The great relay play rescues Detroit from a possible opening game upset. They lose the next one, but then return to Detroit to pound the Padres three times in a row and close out a quick Series.

FACT:
Sparky Anderson became the first manager to win championships in both leagues, having piloted the Big Red Machine in 1975 and 1976 Series triumphs. Had San Diego won, that distinction would have gone to their manager, Dick Williams, skipper of the A's champs of 1972 and 1973.

The Managers:

Sparky Anderson had been dismissed as Cincinnati's manager after the 1978 season and it still rankled. He had thought that after four pennants he would be given a bit more slack than that. In June of 1979 the Tigers decided to make a change and brought in Anderson to replace Les Moss. Patiently building on a nucleus of young talent, Anderson taught the Tigers how to win. He said later that he got less enjoyment from the 1984 season than any other pennant he had won. After the 35-5 start, anything less than a pennant would have been perceived as a massive choke. He greeted the championship with relief. It also made him the first manager to win a World Series in both leagues.

Ironically, if the Padres had won that distinction would have gone to their manager, Dick Williams. He had also won pennants in both leagues. His last winner had been the 1973 Oakland A's, after which he walked away from the job and abrasive owner Charlie Finley. Since then he had managed in California and Montreal. This was his third year in San Diego, and after two seasons at exactly .500, he guided the Padres on their breakthrough.

The Heroes:

Trammell led all hitters with a .450 average in defeating the team he had grown up cheering in San Diego. He won game four practically on his own, hitting a two-run homer in the first and

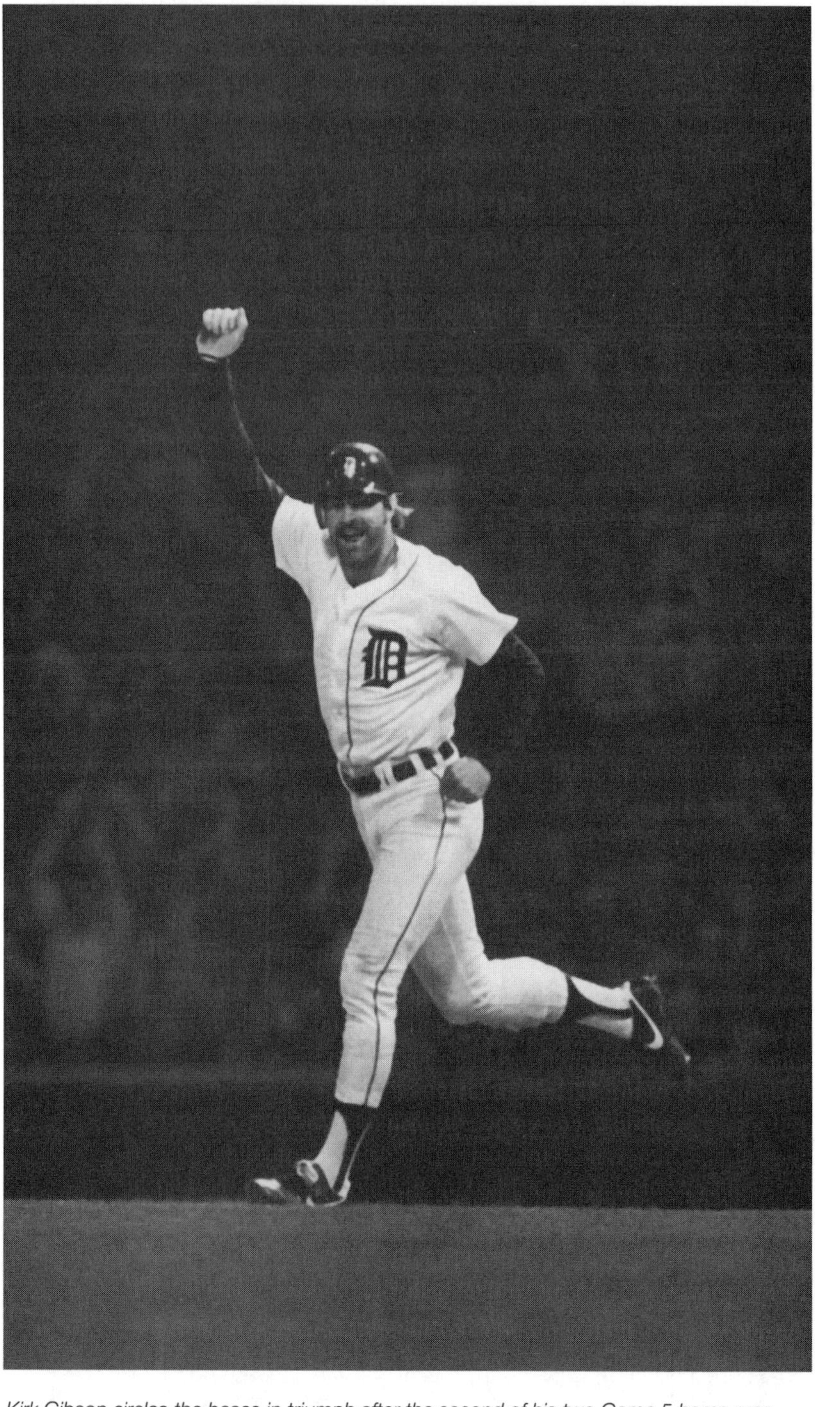

Kirk Gibson circles the bases in triumph after the second of his two Game 5 home runs ices the Series for Detroit. Goose Gossage had unwisely talked manager Dick Williams out of walking Gibson intentionally just minutes before.

another one in the third to give Morris all the margin he needed in the 4-2 win.

Morris was a fierce competitor, whose often surly demeanor was merely the outer form of a desire to win so intense that it would put him in the Series record books. His two complete game victories were the first time that had been accomplished in seven years.

Gibson's 7 RBIs topped everyone and he also played with a ferocity that was the most memorable part of the Series. He dashed home from third to score the lead run in the final game on what was little more than a pop fly to the second baseman. A few innings later, his confrontation with Gossage, in which the pitcher shrugged off an intentional pass to go after Gibson, ended in a three-run homer to clinch the Series. The photograph taken right after the homer, showing the triumphant Gibson bellowing in triumph, his uniform filthy and torn from his slide of a few innings before, still hangs in hundreds of Detroit taverns and homes as a symbol of this season.

Why Bevacqua was named by Dick Williams to be his Series DH was never adequately explained. He hit just .200 during the season, had accumulated a lifetime mark of .235 in his 14 years in the majors and had never given the slightest clue that he could take off in a short series. But he tormented the Tigers with a .412 average, hit in every game and slammed a three-run homer off Petry to win game two.

The Zeroes:

The absence of McReynolds, who was injured in the playoffs, took a major bat out of the San Diego lineup. The Padres had to substitute Bobby Brown and he was held to 1 for 15.

The San Diego starters were completely overmatched by the Tigers. After Thurmond went 6 innings in game one, none of the others got past the third, and two of them were shelled out of games in the first. Their final record was 10 1/3 innings, 16 runs. Even brilliant relief work by Andy Hawkins, Dave Dravecky and Craig Lefferts, who gave up a combined total of just one run in 22 2/3 innings, couldn't overcome the handicap given to them by the starters.

The Aftermath:

Detroit fell to a disappointing third in 1985 as several second-line players departed or declined and a few regulars tailed off just enough to make a difference. Hernandez saved 31 games but developed a knack for giving up key home runs in the late innings, which earned him the wrath of the formerly adoring Tiger Stadium crowds.

The Padres came back to reality, too, even with statistically better years from several starters. But a certain chemistry seemed to be lacking. The base-stealing threat, Wiggins, was sent off to Baltimore and Williams moved on to Seattle at the end of the season. The Padres finished fourth.

Notes:

Anderson and Williams became the fourth and fifth managers ever to win pennants in both leagues. They were preceded by Joe McCarthy, with the Cubs and Yankees; Alvin Dark, with the Giants and A's, and Yogi Berra, with the Yankees and Mets. In their previous meeting in the Series, Anderson had represented the National League with the Reds and Williams was with the A's.

The Series featured one of the ugliest victory celebrations on record. Following the final out on a Sunday evening, crowds began pouring into the Tiger Stadium area, a few blocks from downtown Detroit. They quickly got out of hand. In the midst of the revelry, a police car was turned over and set afire. Since this occurred directly below the ballpark pressbox, photographs of the incident were immediately sent out on the wires. While sports riots in other cities resulted in greater destruction and death, this one took place in full view of the national media.

Line Scores:

Game One, October 9

Det (AL)—100 020 000—3
Morris W

SD (NL)—200 000 000—2
Thurmond L, Hawkins (6), Dravecky (8)

Game Two, October 10

Det (AL)—300 000 000—3
Petry L, Lopez (5), Scherrer (6), Bair (7), Hernandez (8)

SD (NL)—100 130 00X—5
Whitson, Hawkins (1) W, Lefferts (7) SV

Game Three, October 12

SD (NL)—001 000 100—2
Lollar L, Booker (2), Harris (3)

Det (AL)—041 000 00X—5
Wilcox W, Scherrer (7), Hernandez (7) SV

Game Four, October 13

SD (NL)—010 000 001—2
Show L, Dravecky (3), Lefferts (7), Gossage (8)

Det (AL)—202 000 00X—4
Morris W

Game Five, October 14

SD (NL)—001 200 010—4
Thurmond, Hawkins (1) L,
Lefferts (5), Gossage (7)

Det (AL)—300 010 13X—8
Petry, Scherrer (4), Lopez (5) W,
Hernandez (8) SV

1985

Kansas City (AL) 4
St. Louis (NL) 3

The Royals made history by fighting their way back from 3-1 deficits, not once but twice; in the playoffs and then in the Series. Moreover, they lost the first two Series games at home, the first team ever to do that and still win.

The Preview:

Kansas City looked like a team that wandered into the Series in a fit of absent-mindedness. In fact, if it had been one year earlier the Royals wouldn't have been there at all. The playoffs were extended from 5 games to 7 in 1985; under the old format they would have been eliminated by Toronto, 3 games to 1. They survived that round but not many gave them much of a chance against their cross-state rivals in St. Louis.

A small nucleus of players remained from the 1980 pennant winner. George Brett, in fact, had his most productive season since then and ran up his biggest power numbers ever. His 30 homers were a personal high, while his 112 RBIs and .335 average were his best in five years. Frank White was also back for his 12th year as Kansas City's second baseman. His 22 homers represented a high in his career, but his average dropped to .249. Willie Wilson was also in centerfield, but with a fairly ordinary .278 average, 23 points below his career mark. The DH was again Hal McRae, and he drove in 70 runs.

The supporting cast around them, however, was not much of an improvement. The most colorful, by far, was Steve "Bye Bye" Balboni, an almost-bald, hulking first baseman who hit the ball a long way on those occasions when he made contact. Balboni hit 36 homers and drove in 88 runs, but he struck out a league-high 166 times, hit only .243 and moved marginally faster than an iceberg.

Bret Saberhagen and George Brett celebrate Kansas City's first World Championship. Saberhagen earned the MVP trophy with two complete-game victories and ten strikeouts, and became a father before Game 7. Brett contributed a .370 average on ten hits.

Leftfielder Lonnie Smith had come over from the Cards early in the year and spent much of his time griping about how much he disliked the American League, but he and Wilson combined to steal 83 bases. Still, Kansas City was next to the bottom in runs scored in the league and occupied the same place in team batting.

The pitching, however, was tough. Bret Saberhagen turned in a 20-6 year, his second season, and pitched with remarkable control for one so young. Danny Jackson, also in his second year with the team, was 14-12, while Charlie Leibrandt, the old man in this group at age 28, was 17-9. In the bullpen was another returnee from the 1980 team, submariner Dan Quisenberry. He had averaged 40 saves over the last 4 seasons, so his 37-save year with 8 wins was just a run-of-the-mill campaign for him.

The Cardinals had overwhelming team speed along with a batting champion and a guy who accomplished the rather remarkable feat of driving in over 100 runs with fewer than 10 homers. In his 4 previous seasons with the Cards, Willie McGee had hit just below the .300 barrier. This season he went crashing through, finishing at .353 to win the title with 216 hits. Moreover, he combined with rookie Vince Coleman to give the Cards one of the great baserunning combinations in the game's history. Coleman swiped 110 as a rookie, while McGee added 56. The 314 stolen bases for the team had been exceeded only once in the live ball era, by the 1976 Oakland A's, who stole 341. Chief beneficiary of all this running was Tommy Herr, the number three hitter in the lineup. He was constantly coming to bat with runners in scoring position. He drove in 110 runs on just 8 homers, while hitting .302. Other key components were shortstop Ozzie Smith, who hit a solid .276, and Jack Clark, who shifted to first base after coming over from the Giants in the off season and led the team with 22 homers. He also drove in 87 runs. Veteran outfielder Cesar Cedeno was obtained from Cincinnati in August and went on a .434 tear down the stretch.

The Cards also had pitching depth. Joaquin Andujar, who won twice in the 1982 Series, racked up a 21-12 season, his best in the majors. John Tudor, a pickup from Pittsburgh over the winter, was 21-8 with a 1.93 ERA, second best in the league. The third man in the rotation, Danny Cox, was 18-9. The Cards used a variety of closers during the season, but Todd Worrell, who came up in August and threw the hardest, was Whitey Herzog's favorite by season's end.

Even a freak injury to Coleman, who was caught in the automated tarp at Busch Stadium during a rain delay in the playoffs and went down with a bad leg, couldn't dampen the Cards. They were strong choices to run right over Kansas City.

Turning Point: Game Six, Ninth Inning.

When the Cards take the first two games in Royals Stadium, Kansas City is left for dead. No team ever recovered from that kind of start. The way the Cardinals accomplish the sweep is disheartening, too. Trailing 2-0 going into the ninth inning of the second game they score 4 times to win. The last team to overcome a two-run lead in the ninth inning of a Series game was the 1939 Yankees: it is that much of a rarity.

Still, the Royals show some spunk behind Saberhagen to win game three, 6-1. Then Tudor beats them for the second time, an easy 3-0 decision. Even when Kansas City rebounds 6-1, with Jackson stopping the Cards, it seems like just a matter of time.

> **FACT:**
> Trailing 2-0 in the ninth inning of the second game, the Cards score 4 times to win. The last team to overcome a 2-run lead in the ninth inning of a Series game was the 1939 Yankees: it is that much of a rarity.

In game six, time appears to be up. The game matches Cox and Leibrandt and both pitch brilliantly. Cox scatters 7 hits through 7 innings and is never in serious trouble. Leibrant mows down the first 15 men he faces. The spell is broken by two singles in the sixth, then he gets three more in a row in the seventh. In the eighth inning of the 0-0 game, Terry Pendleton singles for the third St. Louis hit. Leibrandt then walks Cedeno, but comes back to strike out Darrell Porter. That brings up Brian Harper to bat for Cox. He batted just 52 times all season, filling in all over the lineup, and even catching two games for the Cards. He now bangs a single up the middle to score Pendleton and St. Louis has a late 1-0 lead.

The game stays that way into the last of the ninth, when Herzog brings in his closer of choice, Worrell, to finish up the Series. The first man he faces is a pinch hitter, Jorge Orta. The 34-year-old Orta, used as a left-handed DH by the Royals, once had some speed, but that was much earlier in his career. So when he sends a grounder to Clark at first base it seems like a routine out, but Worrell breaks late to cover the bag. Orta goes all out down the line and he and Worrell appear to arrive simultaneously. Base umpire Don Denkinger quickly gives the safe signal. The Cards pour from the dugout in angry protest. Televised replays seem to validate the St. Louis viewpoint: Orta's foot comes down on top of Worrell's as they cross the bag. But the Royals now have the tying run on base and that changes the entire inning.

Balboni follows with a pop foul towards first base. Again the Cards blunder. Clark overruns the ball without making a play. Given another chance, Balboni singles to left and Orta goes to second. With these two mistakes, the Cards, instead of having two outs and none on, must contend with the winning run at first and none out. Jim Sundberg tries to sacrifice the runners along, but merely forces Orta at third. Porter then does the job for the Royals, however, with a passed ball, the third St. Louis blunder of the inning. McRae is walked intentionally to load the bases. That brings up another pinch hitter, Dane Iorg. He was the St. Louis DH in the 1982 Series, hitting .529; he served as a utility man with Kansas City for the last two years. In his only previous at bat in this Series he made an out. This time he loops a broken-bat base hit to right. Two runs score, the Royals come racing out on the field to mob Iorg and Kansas City has drawn even in the Series, on the 3-2 win. It is the first time the Cards blew a lead in the ninth inning all season.

Kansas City makes quick work of the Cards the next day, with Saberhagen blanking them 11-0. The second comeback in two weeks is complete and the ridiculed Royals are champions. The umpire's blown call at first compounded by two more mistakes are more than the Cards can overcome.

The Managers:

For Herzog, being beaten by the team he had once managed to three divisional titles, but no pennants, is a bitter pill. "If they were the best team in baseball, how come they won just 91 times during the season," he says afterwards. He even gets himself thrown out of the closing game by Denkinger, with whom he is still unhappy over the call at first base in the ninth inning of game six. After winning the first two in a row, his Cards seemed content to coast the rest of the way, scoring a total of 6 runs in the last five games and making a variety of mechanical mistakes. All in all, it was not a happy Series for Herzog.

For 48-year-old Dick Howser, however, the moment couldn't have been sweeter. A onetime shortstop for the old Kansas City A's, he was fired by the Yankees after his first season as manager, despite winning 103 games and the division title. He was so highly regarded, though, that he was snapped up by the Royals the following year as a replacement for the man who beat him in the playoffs, Jim Frey. Howser guided the team into that year's divisional playoffs and also won the division in 1984. Both of those efforts fell short but now the soft-spoken, well-liked Howser grabbed the big prize.

The Heroes:

Saberhagen became a father for the first time while the Series was in progress. By the end of the Series, the 21-year-old right-hander was also the owner of the sports car given to its top performer. He gave up just one run in two complete games and, equally impressive, walked just one man.

For Wilson it was a nice turnaround from 1980, when he foundered against the Phillies and struck out a record 12 times. This year he hit a solid .367, stole 3 bases and led everyone with 11 hits.

It was also a good comeback for White, his fellow sufferer from the previous Series. Made the cleanup hitter this year (he hit number two in 1980), White led the Series with 6 RBIs. His home run and double knocked in 3 in KC's first win in game three.

FACT:
Saberhagen became a father for the first time while the Series was in progress. By the end, the 21-year-old right-hander was also owner of a new sports car.

While the Cards may have lost some speed because of Coleman's injury, his replacement turned in a solid Series. Tito Landrum led all the Cardinals with a .360 average. He already had his ring. Formerly a member of the Cards, Landrum was waived to Baltimore late in 1983 and was a member of that championship team. Right after the season, though, he was returned to St. Louis where he almost got one for the other hand, too.

The Zeroes:

Andujar had to leave the 1982 Series when he got into a shoving match with a Milwaukee player after charges of rampant hot-doggism by the Brewers. This time he got waved out of game seven by plate umpire Denkinger, who grew weary of his complaints on his calls. The argument was actually an aftermath of the disputed call at first base the umpire made in game six. Since Herzog was also chased, it marked the first time that two members of the same team were thrown out of a Series game since Charlie Grimm and a couple of Cubs turned the trick in 1935.

The Cards were limited to a team batting average of .185, worst ever for a seven-game Series. Most futile of the St. Louis hitters was Ozzie Smith, who went 2 for 23. More noted for his defensive skills than his bat, Smith had actually been riding a hot streak coming into these games. He hit .435 in the playoffs and stunned the Dodgers with a game-winning homer.

The Aftermath:

The Royals pretty much went down the tubes in 1986. After winning the division title 6 times in 10 years, the nucleus of the team had started to age. Moreover, Saberhagen came down with arm problems and plummeted to 7 wins. Then in mid summer, Howser was diagnosed with cancer and had to leave the team permanently. The Royals finished third, a team in definite decline.

The Cards also went into withdrawal the following season. Most of their hitters had subpar seasons, with nobody driving in more than 61 runs. The moody Andujar was dealt to Oakland, and both Tudor and Cox dropped off from their 1985 performances. It was third place for St. Louis, but they rebounded quickly to climb the mountain again in 1987.

Notes:

Tudor had a painful end to his best season in the majors. After beating the Royals twice, he was called on to try a third time in game seven. But he had no control, and after issuing four walks and a home run was taken out in the 3rd inning. He angrily smashed an electric fan in the St. Louis dugout and opened a gash in his left hand, which required stitches. "I made a dumb move," he said.

Buddy Biancalana had become a national symbol of big league futility. The Royals shortstop batted only .188 during the season and TV personality David Letterman frequently joked about his hitting prowess, with Biancalana playing along with the gag on guest appearances. In the Series he hit .278 and reached base more often than any Cardinal.

Line Scores:

Game One, October 19

SL (NL)—001 100 001—3
Tudor W, Worrell (7) SV

KC (AL)—010 000 000—1
Jackson L, Quisenberry (8), Black (9)

Game Two, October 20

SL (NL)—000 000 004—4
Cox, Dayley (8) W, Lahti (9) SV

KC (AL)—000 200 000—2
Leibrandt L, Quisenberry (9)

Game Three, October 22

KC (AL)—000 220 200—6
Saberhagen W

SL (NL)—000 001 000—1
Andujar L, Campbell (5), Horton (6), Dayley (8)

Game Four, October 23

KC (AL)—000 000 000—0
Black L, Backwith (6), Quisenberry (8)

SL (NL)—011 010 00X—3
Tudor W

Game Five, October 24

KC (AL)—130 000 011—6
Jackson W

SL (NL)—100 000 000—1
Forsch L, Horton (2), Campbell (4), Worrell (6), Lahti (8)

Game Six, October 26

SL (NL)—000 000 010—1
Cox, Dayley (8), Worrell (9) L

KC (AL)—000 000 002—2
Leibrandt, Quisenberry (8) W

Game Seven, October 27

SL (NL)—000 000 000—0
Tudor L, Campbell (3), Lahti (5), Horton (5), Andujar (5), Forsch (5), Dayley (7)

KC (AL)—023 060 00X—11
Saberhagen W

1986

New York (NL) 4
Boston (AL) 3

This was the year that Boston fans began to believe that there truly was a curse on the franchise. One out away from their first championship in 68 seasons, and then the Red Sox lost it all.

The Preview:

In their two previous visits to the Series, the Mets were regarded with amused surprise. They were the shock of the nation in 1969 and then emerged from a tangle of mediocrity in 1973. This time there was nothing funny about them. New York was a powerhouse, winners of 108 games, with the strongest lineup and deepest pitching in the game.

The Mets had made a serious run at St. Louis in 1985 with essentially the same lineup. Most consistent hitter was first baseman Keith Hernandez, who had played with the Cards in the 1982 Series. He batted .310 and drove in 83 runs. The power providers were rightfielder Daryl Strawberry (27 homers, 93 RBIs) and veteran catcher Gary Carter (24 homers, 105 RBIs), obtained in a major trade with Montreal two years before. Ray Knight was a disappointment the previous season after coming over from Houston. But this year he won the third base job from Howard Johnson and hit a surprising .298, with 76 RBIs.

The big boost came from two improved players at the top of the lineup. Wally Backman had been New York's regular second baseman for three years. This season he was platooned and his average shot up to .320. Centerfielder Len Dykstra was installed as the leadoff man and was a catalyst to the offense. He hit .295, stole 31 bases and was a constant irritant to the opposition with his aggressive style.

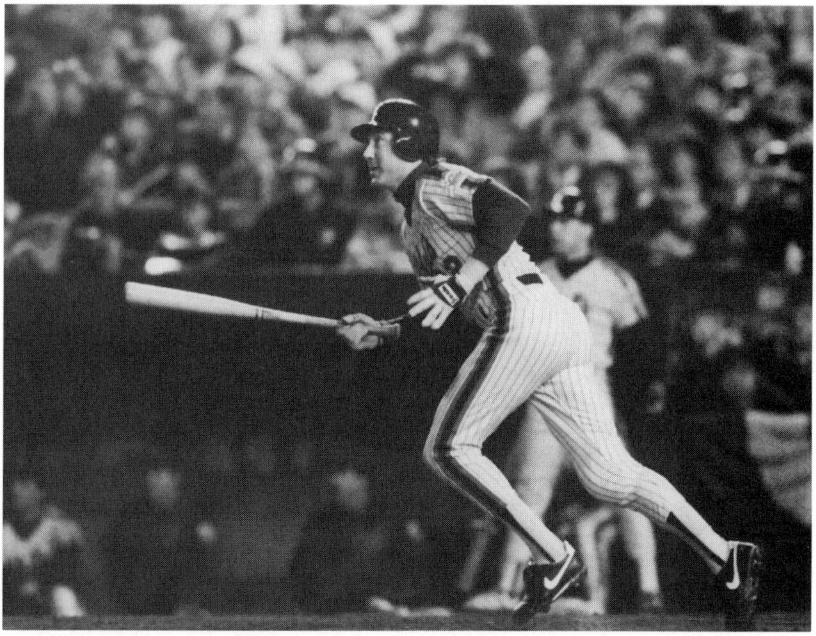

Ray Knight hits a seventh-inning home run in Game 7. Knight won MVP honors with clutch hits in Games 6 and 7, as well as a .391 average and five RBI.

The pitching staff was anchored by Dwight "Doc" Gooden. Only 21 and in his third year in the majors, he was already the dominant pitcher in the league. Not quite as overpowering as in 1985, he still went 17-6. It was the improvement in the cast around him, though, that put the Mets over the top. Left-hander Bob Ojeda came from Boston in the off-season and had the top winning percentage in the league, at 18-5. He had never won more than 12 before. Sid Fernandez, a throw-in on a low level deal with the Dodgers three years before, was 16-6. His previous high was 9 wins. Ron Darling went 15-6, while even the fifth starter, Rick Aguilera, was 10-7. The righty-lefty combination in the bullpen, Roger McDowell and Jesse Orosco, saved 43 games and won 22 more. No team had depth like this.

The Red Sox came close to matching New York's hitting. Wade Boggs, in his fifth year in the majors, won his third batting title, at .357. He carried a career mark of .352 and already was just 22 hits short of 1,000. It had been years since a young hitter had burst upon the majors with numbers like these. On the other hand, 33-year-old Jim Rice was back from the 1975 winners. His home run production tumbled to 20, but he drove in 110 runs and hit .324, his highest figure in 7 years. The Sox had another powerful right-handed bat in the lineup in DH Don Baylor. In his first year since coming over from the Yankees, he pounded 31 homers and drove in 94. Dwight Evans, another returnee from the last pennant winners, was a third long ball threat with 26 homers and 97 RBIs. Finally, 36-year-old Bill Buckner, at first base, knocked in 102 runs. He couldn't run and his body creaked in the field, but he was still a steady hitter.

The Boston pitching was tough at the top of the rotation. Roger Clemens had emerged as a huge talent. The 24-year-old right hander went 24-4 and 2.48 ERA as the counterpart to Gooden in the American League. The Sox also had Dennis "Oil Can" Boyd, a free-spirited fellow who had his best season, at 16-10. The number-three starter was Bruce Hurst. He was 13-8, but may have been throwing better than anyone else at season's end. After that, however, was trouble. The two stoppers, Bob Stanley and Joe Sambito, had 28 saves between them, but were increasingly erratic as the season wore on. Manager John McNamara was turning more frequently to Calvin Schiraldi, a hard-thrower who had come up in mid-season after being acquired from the Mets. He had a glistening 1.42 ERA in 25 games, but not much experience under pressure. The pen was clearly New York's biggest advantage.

Turning Point: Game Six, 10th Inning.

Just as in Boston's last Series appearance, the sixth game turns out to be one of the most dramatic ever played. In 1975 it sent a wave of elation throughout New England; this time it breaks Boston's heart.

The Series returns to New York with the Sox needing one game to win. They swept the Mets here in the first two, on a shutout by Hurst and a pounding of Gooden. But then the Mets awakened in Fenway Park and bounced back with convincing 7-1 and 6-2 wins. Carter keys the attack and Ojeda and Darling stop the Boston bats. The Sox beat Gooden again in game five, as Hurst throws another gem, 4-2. They are closing in now. But the last three times Boston was in the Series, the Sox went 7 games and raised hopes, only to see them dashed. This time they want to close it down in 6. They are prepared with their best, Clemens, to go against his former teammate, Ojeda.

Boston starts fast, as a double by Evans drives in a run in the first and Marty Barrett singles in another in the second. Clemens suffered an allergic reaction to medication during the playoffs and still did not look strong in his game two start. This time he is in peak form, pitching hitless ball through four innings, striking out 6. He starts the fifth by walking Strawberry, however, and after a steal of second Knight picks him up with a single. Mookie Wilson also singles, sending Knight to third, where he scores the tying run on a double play. The deadlock persists into the seventh, when the manipulation of the bullpens begins.

McDowell comes in for New York and the Red Sox quickly produce a run on a walk, a bad throw by Knight and an infield out. The Mets avoid further problems when Rice is thrown out at the plate by Wilson while trying to score from second on a single. McNamara feels Clemens has gone as far as he can. He pinch hits for him during an unsuccessful rally in the eighth and chooses Schiraldi to get the last 6 outs. The Mets manufacture a run of their own. After a pinch hit single by Lee Mazzilli, the Mets drop two sacrifice bunts. Schiraldi, with a clear chance to get the lead runner in both cases, throws to first each time, instead misplaying one into an error. Mazzilli gets to third and a sacrifice fly by Carter brings in the run.

The score stays at 3-3 through the ninth. The leadoff hitter for Boston in the 10th against Aguilera is Dave Henderson. The Sox picked him up from Seattle late in the season, only to have him bat a puny .196. In the playoffs, however, his two-run, two-out ninth inning homer with Boston trailing 4-3 had pulled the Red Sox back from the edge of elimination in game five. Now he is about to become New England's hero again. His leadoff homer gives Boston a 4-3 lead. Just to make sure, the Sox score one more on a double by Boggs and a single by Barrett. They are three outs away from the championship with a 5-3 lead.

Schiraldi gets the first two Mets easily. The Sox are standing on the top step of the dugout as Carter singles. Then pinch hitter Kevin Mitchell gets another single. That brings up Knight, and a murmur of expectation ripples through the ballpark. Schiraldi quickly gets ahead of him at two strikes. But Knight slams the third straight base hit to score Carter and send Mitchell to third.

There is still a one-run lead, though, and McNamara calls for Stanley to get Mookie Wilson. He goes to 2-2 on him and then, as the Red Sox watch in horror, throws a wild pitch past Rich Gedman. The Mets tie the game and Knight is now on second. On the full count, Wilson sends an easy roller to Buckner at first. But his aging body betrays him. Buckner cannot get down on the ball. It rolls between his legs, as Knight dashes home with the winning run and Shea Stadium goes up for grabs.

FACT:

The Red Sox are leading 5-3, bottom of the tenth, one out away from victory, no one on base. Then, three straight singles, and a run scores; another scores on a wild pitch, which moves the winning run to second. On a full count, Mookie Wilson sends an easy roller toward first base . . .

With one of the most improbable rallies in Series history, the Mets tie it up and crush the Red Sox. New York's seventh game win, 8-5, is merely a formality. The Red Sox cannot escape their curse.

The Managers:

This was McNamara's 14th season as a big league manager with five different organizations. He is almost the poster for the old boys network of baseball—managers who always get rehired, no matter what. His only previous success had been a division title in 1979 in Cincinnati, where he was promptly rubbed out by Pittsburgh. He has been under .500 more often than not. But for the 54-year-old McNamara this season was a culmination. His team was loose going into the Series after narrowly surviving defeat by California and fighting back from a 3-1 deficit. It all turned to ashes. "I don't want to hear about history," he said bitterly after game six, "and I don't want to hear about choking." But he had to hear plenty during the off-season about the moves he made in the last two games.

Davey Johnson was in only his third year as a manager and had improved every season with the Mets. He rubbed some people the wrong way with a tongue that could be sarcastic and a manner a bit too abrupt. But he understood Series pressure, having been there four times as a player with Baltimore. And at 43 he had reached the pinnacle of the game.

The Heroes:

Knight was noted as the man who replaced Pete Rose in the Cincinnati lineup (and hit .318 when he did) and the man who married golfing champ, Nancy Lopez. In this Series he finally got recognition on his own as The Man. He hit .391 and his clutch single in game six was the indispensable blow of the Series. He also homered in game seven to give New York its first lead in the seventh inning.

Carter brought the Mets back in the games they had to win in Boston. He went 5 for 9 in those two games, with two doubles and two homers while driving in 6 runs. He also started the winning rally in game six and led everyone with 9 RBIs.

Barrett quietly tied the record for hits in a Series with 13, matching Bobby Richardson's mark in 1964. Both players, oddly enough, played for the losing team.

Hurst pitched valiantly for the Red Sox. He beat the Mets by 1-0 and 4-2 counts. Then, working on two days' rest, he pitched 5 innings of one-hit ball in the 7th game. But the long season finally caught up with him and he gave up a three-run, game-tying rally in the sixth before the bullpen came in and blew up.

The Zeroes:

Buckner was hobbled by ankles so sore that an operation was already scheduled for after the season. They hurt him when he batted and they hurt him in the field. He hit just .188, and at the critical moment his inability to field a routine grounder scored the winning run for New York in game six. The Boston media questioned why defensive specialist Dave Stapleton, on the roster for just such occasions, was not in the game at the time. There was no good answer for that. Buckner carried the weight of his error for the rest of his career.

Gooden could not get it done in the big games. He lasted a total of just 9 innings in his two starts and gave up 10 runs, losing both times.

Schiraldi saved game one for Hurst and then sat for the next six days without throwing an inning. When he was tossed into the maelstrom in game six, and again in game seven, he was out of rhythm, struggling to find his control and a sense of the field. He finished with 2 losses and a 13.50 ERA.

The Aftermath:

The Red Sox dropped to fifth place in 1987 as the pitching disintegrated. The big differences were Boyd's going from 16 wins to 1 and Stanley checking in with a 4-15 mark. But in another year they were back on top of the division once more.

The Mets also tailed off, although not quite as far. They missed a repeat in the division by only 3 games behind the Cardinals. Ojeda could win only 3 times and several other starters came in with ordinary years. New York, too, was back in the playoffs by 1988.

Notes:

Over the first 81 World Series, no team ever came back to win after losing the first two games at home. Now it had happened two years in a row. Moreover, until the Cards did it in 1985, it had been 45 years since a team had come back from more than one run down after the eighth inning. One year later and the Mets did it, too.

McNamara was bitterly criticized for taking Clemens out of the sixth game and opening the gates of disaster. The pitcher reported later that he had been throwing with a blister on his finger from the fifth inning on and had lost confidence in his ability to control his slider.

FACT:
Over the first 81 Series, no team ever came back to win after losing the first two games at home. Now it had happened two years in a row. This was also the second year in a row, after 45 years, that a team had come back from more than one run after the eighth inning.

Red Sox fans rode Strawberry mercilessly, with derisive choruses of "Daryl, Daryl" whenever he came to bat at Fenway Park. Mets fans threw golf balls at Rice and hit the Boston traveling secretary with a bottle tossed out of the stands. The sign outside Shea Stadium read: "Baseball as it ought to be played."

Line Scores:

Game One, October 18

Bos (AL)—000 000 100—1
Hurst W, Schiraldi (9) SV

NY (NL)—000 000 000—0
Darling L, McDowell (8)

Game Two, October 19

Bos (AL)—003 120 201—9
Clemens, Crawford (5) W, Stanley (7) SV

NY (NL)—002 010 000—3
Gooden L, Aguilera (6), Orosco (7), Fernandez (9), Sisk (9)

Game Three, October 21

NY (NL)—400 000 210—7
Ojeda W, McDowell (8)

Bos (AL)—001 000 000—1
Boyd L, Sambito (8), Stanley (8)

Game Four, October 22

NY (NL)—000 300 210—6
Darling W, McDowell (8), Orosco (8) SV

Bos (AL)—000 000 020—2
Nipper L, Crawford (7), Stanley (9)

Game Five, October 23

NY (NL)—000 000 011—2
Gooden L, Fernandez (5)

Bos (AL)—011 020 00X—4
Hurst W

Game Six, October 25

Bos (AL)—110 000 100 2—5
Clemens, Schiraldi (8) L, Stanley (10)

NY (NL)—000 020 010 3—6
Ojeda, McDowell (7), Orosco (8), Aguilera (9) W

Game Seven, October 26

Bos (AL)—030 000 020—5
Hurst, Schiraldi (7) L, Sambito (7), Stanley (7), Nipper (8), Crawford (8)

NY (NL)—000 003 32X—8
Darling, Fernandez (4), McDowell (7) W, Orosco (8) SV

1987

Minnesota (AL) 4
St Louis (NL) 3

For the first time a World Series was played in a dome and the home field advantage was never greater. The Twins rode the noise level to an upset win over the crippled Cardinals, as each team swept its home games, another Series first.

The Preview:

The Metrodome was a power hitter's delight. There wasn't much of a secret about that. In 1986 the Twins had splattered home runs all over the place ... and finished a very distant sixth. This year they returned with the same powerful lineup, the same group of pitchers and one major addition in the bullpen. Jeff Reardon was obtained from Montreal over the winter to become the stopper. The Twins took his 31 saves all the way to first place and then went on to upset Detroit in the playoffs.

This was a team built along the lines of Minnesota's only other pennant winners, the power-laden Twins of 1965. There were home run opportunities all through the lineup. First baseman Kent Hrbek belted 34 of them, with 90 RBIs, and outfielder Tom Brunansky added 32 and 85 RBIs. Third baseman Gary Gaetti led the team with 109 runs batted in and hit 31 homers. The best player in the lineup was Kirby Puckett, the rotund centerfielder, whose stubby legs covered an astonishing range of territory. He also hit .332 with 28 homers and 99 RBIs.

Top winner on the staff was Frank Viola, at 17-10. In his sixth season with the team, he had become one of the most consistent pitchers in the league. He was backed by Bert Blyleven, who broke in with Minnesota 17 years before. He was now 36 and had won over 200 games in his long career with four different franchises. Blyleven, who was deemed washed up a

Frank Viola holds the MVP trophy as Reggie Jackson, no stranger to World Series glory himself, interviews him. Viola won two games, including the finale, in which he dominated after the second inning.

few seasons before, had recovered from serious arm problems and was reacquired by the Twins the previous year. He was 15-12 and seemed to get stronger in the stretch run. Behind these two there was a cavity. Next in line was Les Straker at 8-10 and, of course, Reardon out of the pen. The reliever had an unimpressive 4.48 ERA, but that was inflated by a few poor outings; his ability to keep the free-hitting Twins in close games transformed the team.

The Cards were built around the same formula that had taken them to the Series in 1982 and 1985. Lots of speed, tough defense, bullpen. This team had a little more pop, thanks to Jack Clark, who hit 35 homers, an impressive amount in spacious Busch Stadium. He also drove in 106, to lead Willie McGee by one in that category. Third baseman Terry Pendleton also emerged as a batting threat. His 12 homers were second best on the team and he hit .286, with 96 RBIs. Ozzie Smith turned in his usual spectacular job at shortstop and also hit .303, tops on the Cards. Vince Coleman stole 109 bases, while hitting .289. It was a team very much built to take advantage of its ballpark.

The starting pitchers, however, were as weak as any rotation in Series history. The top winner was veteran Bob Forsch, who was just 11-7. Bunched up with him were Danny Cox (11-9), Greg Mathews (11-11) and Joe Magrane (9-7). John Tudor had recovered from a fractured tibia late in the year and finished strong with a 10-2 record, capped by a 1-0 decision over San Francisco in the playoffs. The Cards also had their big stopper. Todd Worrell saved 31 games and was a mirror image of Reardon. The Cards went in as narrow favorites, despite injuries to Clark and Pendleton, because of previous Series experience and overall team speed. The Twins had heard the same thing entering the playoffs and they were not impressed.

FACT:
Never before had home field been such a factor. With roaring crowds at the Metrodome (aka the Homerdome), the Twins pulverized the Cards twice. Back in St. Louis, the speed game took over, and the Cards won three straight. The Series returned for the deciding games in Minneapolis.

Turning Point: Game Six, Sixth Inning.

Never before had home field been such a factor. With roaring crowds at the Metrodome shattering every noise level known to science, the Twins pulverized St. Louis twice, using big innings to put away the Cards 10-1 and 8-4. But back in St. Louis, the speed game took over and the Cards won three straight rather easily. Minnesota looked like a different team, confused and disoriented. Now the show is back in the dome, where the long ball rules. The Twins had just one home run in St. Louis and feel sure they can rip again in their home field. "We're overpowering at home, and that's a fact, Jack," grins Gaetti.

Still, the Twins must rely on the inexperienced Straker. He pitched 6 shutout innings in game three before the middle relievers came on and gave it away. He is up against Tudor, who stopped Minnesota on 5 hits in that game, 3-1. Neither pitcher is very impressive this time. The Cards batter Straker out by the fourth inning and continue the attack on Dan Schatzeder. By the top of the fifth, St. Louis has a 5-2 lead and finally seems to have the Metrodome measured. Tommy Herr gets the team's first home run there (only its second in the Series) in the first, and four more runs score on assorted singles and doubles and three walks.

Tudor struggles in every inning, but except for 2 runs in the first manages to hold the Twins at bay. In the fifth, though, the Dome falls in on him. Puckett starts it with his third straight single of the game. He races home on Gaetti's double, and DH Don Baylor comes to bat. He played in just one previous game, sitting out all three in St. Louis where the DH was not allowed. He singled in a run in the first inning of this game and now he sends a Tudor delivery into the leftfield seats, tying the game, 5-5. When Brunansky follows with a fourth straight hit, Tudor is gone and replaced by Ricky Horton. With two outs, Vic Lombardozzi comes through with his third straight hit, a single, and the Twins are out in front to stay.

The sudden onslaught seems to deflate the Cards. It seems that no lead is safe in this deafening madhouse. The Twins polish them off the following inning when an infield hit and two walks load the bases. Hrbek clears them with a grand slam, making it a 10-5 Minnesota lead. The Twins win, eventually, 11-5, and then finish off the Cards the next day behind Viola, 4-2. The wall of noise and the sheer relentlessness of the Minnesota offense in the dome shatter St. Louis.

The Managers:

Whitey Herzog had put together a sustained run of success, enough to certify him as one of the game's top managers. In 12 years, he won 6 division titles, 3 pennants and a World Series. His approach was simple. "Casey Stengel once called me aside in spring training and told me how much he liked me, but that he had a kid coming up named Mantle and I wasn't as good," Herzog recalled. "I learned from that. Never let sentiment get in the way of managing." It seemed to work for him.

Tom Kelly was barely known outside of Minnesota. A Twins organization man for years, he had played just 49 games for the big club in 1975. Since then, he served in a variety of jobs with the front office and in the minors and was brought in late in 1986 to take over as manager. It was the job he had been groomed for, but no one expected results from the 37-year-old Kelly quite this quickly.

The Heroes:

Viola had averaged 17 wins over the last four seasons, but because of the overall mediocrity of the Twins that was something of a secret in the outside world. The Series provided him with a showcase. He beat the Cards twice, including a tight 4-2 win in the seventh game, in which he gave up just 2 hits after the second inning. Viola struck out 16 in 19 innings in the Series and walked off with the MVP award.

The Cards were ready for the power in the middle of the Minnesota lineup. They were unprepared for the punch at the top. Leadoff man Dan Gladden led both teams with 7 RBIs. Four of his 9 hits went for extra bases, including a grand slam homer that broke open the opener.

The Twins also surprised St. Louis with the bottom of their lineup. Lombardozzi, the last hitter in the order, finished as the top hitter in the Series at .412, including a two-run homer in the opener and three straight hits in the sixth game.

The Zeroes:

The injuries to Pendleton and Clark took the two most productive bats out of the St. Louis lineup and made their cause almost hopeless. Clark went down in September and batted only once in the playoffs, while Pendleton was injured in the last game with the Giants and was limited to DH duty against right-handed pitching in the Series. He hit .429 in that role, an indication of how sorely he was missed. His replacement against lefties, Tom Lawless, came to bat just 25 times during the season. Although his three-run homer off Viola was the big blow in game four, it was the only hit Lawless got in 10 times at bat.

Coleman stole 6 bases in the first 5 games and was threatening Lou Brock's record of 7 in a Series. But he went 0 for 9 in the last two games and never got on base, which makes it hard to steal. He finished the Series hitting just .143.

The Cardinal starters were completely psyched out by the Metrodome. In the four games played there, they worked 15 innings and gave up 20 runs.

FACT:
Cardinal starters worked 15 innings in the Metrodome and gave up 20 runs.

The Aftermath:

"We had 'em right where we wanted 'em," said Herzog, "but it was in the wrong ballpark." Such is life. St. Louis dropped to 10 games under .500 in 1988 as Clark moved on to the Yankees and no pitcher won more than 13 games. The core of the team that had won three pennants in six years was starting to age and even Herzog couldn't pull them around. He turned in his resignation halfway through the 1990 season.

The Twins improved to 91 wins, but they bumped into the start of a three-year pennant run by a gifted Oakland team. After the A's were through winning, the Twins bounced right back to the top in 1991 and won another championship.

Notes:

Minnesota fans were given "Homer Hankies" to wave during Twins rallies, which they did enthusiastically. It was a shameless ripoff of the "Terrible Towels" waved by Pittsburgh Steelers fans during their run to four Super Bowls in the 1970s, but no one seemed to mind.

The 7-run inning put together by the Twins in the opener, capped by Gladden's grand slam, was the biggest in a Series since the Tigers had slapped the Cardinals with 10 runs in 1968. It, too, had been topped off by a grand slam, in that case by Jim Northrup.

The two Minnesota slams were the first in the Series since 1970 when pitcher Dave McNally cranked one out for Baltimore. That was in the years before the DH.

Line Scores:

Game One, October 17

SL (NL)—010 000 000—1
Magrane L, Forsch (4), Horton (7)

Min (AL)—000 720 10X—10
Viola W, Atherton (9)

Game Two, October 18

SL (NL)—000 010 120—4
Cox L, Tunnell (4), Dayley (7), Worrell (8)

Min (AL)—010 601 00X—8
Blyleven W, Berenguer (8), Reardon (9)

Game Three, October 20

Min (AL)—000 001 000—1
Straker, Berenguer (7) L, Schatzeder (7)

SL (NL)—000 000 30X—3
Tudor W, Worrell (8) SV

Game Four, October 21

Min (AL)—001 010 000—2
Viola L, Schatzeder (4), Niekro (5), Frazier (7)

SL (NL)—001 600 00X—7
Mathews, Forsch (4) W, Dayley (7) SV

Game Five, October 22

Min (AL)—000 000 020—2
Blyleven L, Atherton (7), Reardon (7)

SL (NL)—000 003 10X—4
Cox W, Dayley (8), Worrell (8) SV

Game Six, October 24

SL (NL)—110 210 000—5
Tudor L, Horton (5), Forsch (6), Dayley (6), Tunnell (7)

Min (AL)—200 044 01X—11
Straker, Schatzeder (4) W, Berenguer (6), Reardon (9)

Game Seven, October 25

SL (NL)—020 000 000—2
Magrane, Cox (5) L, Worrell (6)

Min (AL)—010 011 01X—4
Viola W, Reardon (9) SV

1988

Los Angeles (NL) 4
Oakland (AL) 1

In a Series that turned around in one swing of the bat, the Dodgers upset the heavily favored A's. Kirk Gibson's pinch hit homer in the opener became one of the most decisive blows in Series history.

The Preview:

Oakland was back in business after 14 years, with a new ownership and a far less abrasive bunch of players than its champions of the early '70s. The team was built along the same lines as the earlier A's—tremendous power at the heart of the lineup, pitching depth and one unhittable stopper in the bullpen.

Jose Canseco supplied much of the power, and a good deal of the speed, as well. He became the first player ever to hit 40 homers and steal 40 bases in the same season, a guarantee he had made in spring training. He came up in 1986 and hit 33 homers as a rookie, drawing crowds to gape at the distance of his drives during batting practice. This season he led the league with 42 homers and 124 RBIs, while hitting .307, best on the A's. The Miami-born star seemed destined for one of the great careers in the game's history. He was not alone. First baseman Mark McGwire, who was even bigger than Canseco if not as fast, hit 32 homers and drove in 99. They were promoted jointly as The Bruise Brothers. Yet a third slugger lurked in the A's lineup. Centerfielder Dave Henderson had come over from Boston, where he had just missed being the hero of the 1986 Series. He added 24 homers, 94 RBIs and a .304 average. A former batting champion, Carney Lansford, was at third base.

The pitching staff had come together with a rush. Dave Stewart, a reliever with the 1981 Dodgers, had wandered without

Orel Hershiser carried his regular season dominance over to the World Series, winning two games with a 1.00 ERA and 17 strikeouts. Helping his own cause at bat, he added three hits (including two doubles) in Game 2.

much success for several seasons before arriving in Oakland. Then in 1987 he began a run of four straight 20-win years. In this one, he was 21-12. Storm Davis came over from Baltimore and was 16-7. Another ex-Dodger, Bob Welch, arrived via free agency in 1988 and fit right in at 17-9. This trio gave the A's the best rotation in the league and carried them to an effortless sweep of Boston in the playoffs. But the critical acquisition had been Dennis Eckersley. A starter for his entire career, the 34-year-old right hander made the switch to the bullpen in 1987 and became the top closer in the league. He could throw as hard as anyone for one inning and that was all he was asked to do. He saved 45 games and made Oakland uncatchable with a late lead.

The Dodgers, on the other hand, were a major surprise. They had lost Welch to free agency and Fernando Valenzuela had arm problems, which wiped out two-thirds of their rotation from 1987. The team had not hit well that year and finished 16 games under .500, a distant fourth place.

During the winter, though, they signed Kirk Gibson from the Tigers. He had been allowed to leave Detroit because of a clash with management over his scruffy looks and nasty language, but his mean streak was just what the Dodgers ordered. When he was the target of a practical joke during spring training, he blew up in the clubhouse, raging at his teammates who refused to take the game seriously. The incident seemed to solidify the team. Gibson went on to an MVP season, with 25 homers, 76 RBIs and a .290 average. The only other significant force in the lineup, though, was rightfielder Mike Marshall, who hit 20 homers and drove in 82. Otherwise, it was a rather mundane group, although reserve outfielder Mickey Hatcher did hit .293.

This was a Dodger team with pitching reminiscent of the champions of the '60s. Or it was, at least, on the days Orel Hershiser pitched. He carried them down the stretch with a record-setting streak of 59 consecutive shutout innings, then pitched another shutout to clinch the playoffs against the Mets. He was abetted by Tim Leary, a sudden bloomer who went from 3 wins to a 17-11 mark, and rookie Tim Belcher, at 12-6. John Tudor came over late in the year from the Cards to deepen the choices available to manager Tom Lasorda. The bullpen was serviceable, with Alejandro Pena and Jay Howell combining for 33 saves. But when Gibson suffered a leg injury, after slamming two homers to help beat the Mets in the playoffs, it appeared that the Dodgers' very slim chance had disappeared altogether.

Turning Point: Game One, Ninth Inning

Never has a Series swung so early and so suddenly. One moment, Oakland is about to put away a workmanlike win in the opener. In the next, they are sent reeling, never able to regain the initiative or the momentum again. The agent of their defeat is a player so banged up that he can barely drag himself to the plate to bat. With the top closer in the game pitching, the contest seems hopelessly uneven. But somehow . . .

Most of the action is packed into the first two innings. A rested Stewart is the Oakland choice, but he gets off to a rough beginning. After he hits leadoff man Steve Sax, Gibson's replacement, Hatcher, drills a two-run homer for a 2-0 Dodger lead. Hershiser had to pitch the final game of the playoffs so L.A. goes with Belcher. He pitches his way out of a bases-loaded problem in the first, with a walk and hit batsman contributing to his woes. His wildness persists in the second. Two walks follow a single by Glenn Hubbard and load the bases with one out. Belcher strikes out Lansford, but Canseco follows with a grand slam. The star has lived up to his billing.

With a 4-2 lead, Stewart settles into the game. His only rocky inning is the sixth, when consecutive singles by Marshall, John Shelby and Mike Scioscia bring in a run and cut the Oakland lead to 4-3. A double play gets him out of further trouble. Leary, Brian

Holton and Pena blank the A's on 4 hits after the second. When Stewart leaves after eight, he turns just a one-run lead over to Eckersley. It might just as well be 10. Eckersley has been nearly flawless in the closer's role and Oakland prepares to wrap this one up.

He quickly gets outs on a pop up and strikeout. Mike Davis is sent up as a pinch hitter and works him for a walk. Pena is the next scheduled hitter, and when Gibson limps to the bat rack and then from the dugout to hit, an enormous roar goes up from the Dodger Stadium crowd. This is a player with the flair for the big moment and he has delivered one clutch hit after another for the Dodgers, as he often did with the Tigers. He was a college football star at Michigan State and plays the game hard, which contributes to an endless assortment of injuries. He is one of the toughest men, both mentally and physically, in baseball. Still, this may be asking too much of him.

FACT:
The ball arcs towards the rightfield seats, and as the big crowd explodes in joy banged-up slugger Kirk Gibson limps and grimaces around the bases, pumping his arms in triumph as he nears second base. It is an ending out of a movie, and it destroys the A's.

Eckersley and Gibson settle in for the classic confrontation, working each other to a full count. Whenever Gibson swings, the pain is so intense that his face contorts in agony. Summoning one final effort on the 3-2 pitch, Gibson swings. The ball arcs towards the rightfield seats, and as the big crowd explodes in joy the slugger limps and grimaces around the bases, pumping his arms in triumph as he nears second base. It is an ending out of a movie, and it destroys the A's. Hershiser shuts them out the next day. Oakland then manages to win just one game at home before going down to Belcher and then to Hershiser for a second time. Gibson never appears in the Series again. He doesn't have to. His one at bat was all that mattered.

The Managers:

This was probably Lasorda's finest moment as a manager. The 61-year-old ex-pitcher was in his 12th season as the leader of the Dodgers. He had inherited a team with a solid infield, some power and deep pitching and coaxed three pennants and a world championship out of it. But this Dodger team had been brusquely dismissed as a pretender, with its lineup of odd parts and spare change. For Lasorda to bring in a title was an accomplishment that was all his own.

Tony LaRussa had spent most of his career as a player in the A's organization. It wasn't much of a career (lifetime average: .199), but he picked up the knowledge of the game that turned him into a far more successful manager. He brought the White

Sox to a division title in 1983, the team's first win of any kind in 24 years. No sooner was he bounced by the Sox three years later than the A's hired him to lead their promising young team. Within a year and a half he had them in the Series. Only 44 years old, LaRussa was already acknowledged as one of the sharpest minds in the game.

FACT: Orel Hershiser finished the season with a record 59-inning scoreless streak. He became the first pitcher to throw shutouts in both the playoffs and the Series. He stopped the A's in game two, 6-0, then won the final game, 5-2. He had three hits in game two—the first time since Walter Johnson in 1924 that a pitcher got three hits in a Series game.

The Heroes:

Few pitchers had ever caught a hand quite as hot as Hershiser's. He finished the season with 59 scoreless innings, then followed that up with blanks in 26 of his first 27 innings in the playoffs and Series. He became the only pitcher ever to pitch shutouts in both post-season affairs. He stopped the A's, 6-0, in game two, then finished off the Series with a 5-2 decision in game five. Not only did he beat on the A's as a pitcher, he also got three hits in the non-DH game at Dodger Stadium. It was the first time since Walter Johnson did it in 1924 that a pitcher got three hits in a game.

Hatcher had been set for regular service during the Series but he thought it was going to be as a first baseman. He had played there throughout the playoffs, after filling in as a third baseman and an outfielder during the last two seasons with the Dodgers. When Gibson went down, the versatile Hatcher was inserted in his place in leftfield and also in his third slot in the batting order. He came through with a .368 average, slammed 2 homers and led both sides with 5 RBIs. Moreover, first baseman Franklin Stubbs, who had been scheduled to sit in the Series, made the most of his chance to play and hit a solid .294.

One time at bat is rarely enough to make a hero. But aside from Tommy Henrich's blast in the 1949 Series, it is hard to find a home run in a Series opener with such an impact as Gibson's. And Henrich was merely breaking a scoreless tie, not bringing his team back from apparent defeat. Gibson had also struck a dramatic home run for Detroit that wrapped up the 1984 Series. This one happened in L.A. and elevated him to the status of national hero.

The Zeroes:

Canseco's superstar stock plummeted as a result of this Series. His first game grand slam turned out to be his only hit. He finished at 1 for 19 and in the final game, coming up twice with two men on in a close game against Hershiser, he grounded out and popped up. His fellow Bruise Brother, McGwire, was 1 for 17, with his only hit also a homer.

Davis started twice for the A's and was raked for 10 runs in eight innings, with an unfortunate tendency to give up the decisive home run. Marshall touched him for a three-run job, on a two-strike pitch, in game two. Then Hatcher and Mike Davis connected for two-run homers (with Davis' coming on a three-ball count) in game five.

The Aftermath:

Gibson could not recover from his injuries for the 1989 season and spent most of the year on the bench, while Hershiser returned to earth and went 15-15. The combination sank the Dodgers, who dropped back to 6 games below .500

Undeterred by their Series flop, the A's repeated as American League champions, spurred on by the reacquisition of one of their former stars, Ricky Henderson, from the Yankees.

Notes:

The only game won by Oakland was also accomplished with a ninth-inning homer. McGwire's one-out shot off Howell in game three gave the A's the 2-1 victory. But it paled next to Gibson's.

Oakland's team batting average of .177 was the worst in the Series since the 1969 Baltimore Orioles hit .146 against the Mets. They, too, had been heavily favored.

With the outcome decided, LaRussa, in a nice gesture, gave Todd Burns, the only pitcher he had not yet used, the chance to pitch to the final hitter in the ninth inning of game five. He got him on a grounder.

Line Scores:

Game One, October 15

Oak (A)—040 000 000—4
Stewart, Eckersley (9) L

LA (NL)—200 001 002—5
Belcher, Leary (3), Holton (6), Pena (8) W

Game Two, October 16

Oak (AL)—000 000 000—0
Davis L, Nelson (4), Young (6), Plunk (7), Honeycutt (8)

LA (NL)—005 100 00X—6
Hershiser W

Game Three, October 18

LA (NL)—000 010 000—1
Tudor, Leary (2), Pena (6), Howell (9) L

Oak (AL)—001 000 001—2
Welch, Cadaret (6), Nelson (6), Honeycutt (8) W

Game Four, October 19

LA (NL)—201 000 100—4
Belcher W, Howell (7) SV

Oak (AL)—100 001 100—3
Stewart L, Cadaret (7), Eckersley (9)

Game Five, October 20

LA (NL)—200 201 000—5
Hershiser W

Oak (AL)—001 000 010—2
Davis L, Cadaret (5), Nelson (5), Honeycutt (8), Plunk (9), Burns (9)

1989

Oakland (AL) 4
San Francisco (NL) 0

Halfway through this World Series baseball was suddenly rendered insignificant. A killer earthquake tore the heart out of the San Francisco community and turned the Oakland sweep into a mere footnote to disaster.

The Preview:

It had been 27 years for the Giants, the longest gap between pennants in the history of a proud franchise. Two divisional titles in the interim had ended in playoff disappointments. This time the Giants crushed the Cubs and prepared for the first San Francisco Bay Series ever.

This was a team that relied mainly on a one-two punch, but it was the best in the game. Keith Mitchell had a splendid year, leading the league with 47 homers and 125 RBIs while hitting .291. Mitchell had shown promise in earlier shots with the Mets and Padres, but there were attitude problems, and when he had to play third base, as he did for the Giants in 1988, there were fielding problems. He moved to leftfield this season and everything came together. Mitchell led the league in total bases, and right behind him was Will Clark. The first baseman hit .333 with 23 homers and 111 RBIs. Beyond those two, there really wasn't that much to the San Francisco offense. Not much was needed. Leadoff man Brett Butler hit .283 and keyed the attack for the two sluggers. Young third baseman Matt Williams slugged 18 homers in about half a season, although hitting just .202. The Giants were really composed of two big men.

The pitching had a little age on it. Rick Reuschel, in a comeback year, was 17-8, a fine showing at 40. Don Robinson, who had pitched for Pittsburgh in the Series 10 years before, went

Members of the Oakland A's scan the stands for family members after a 6.9 magnitude earthquake strikes the Bay Area just before the start of Game 3. The Series, and Oakland's eventual sweep, was delayed ten days.

12-11. The big move by manager Roger Craig was bringing Scott Garrelts out of the bullpen and making him a starter. He had done some spot starting in the past but was used solely as a reliever in 1988. This year he made the switch, went 14-5 and led the league with a 2.28 ERA, giving the Giants a solid rotation. Craig Lefferts and Steve Bedrosian combined for 37 saves in relief duty.

The A's, in some ways, were more formidable than the crew that won 104 games in 1988. Their win total slipped by 5, but the pitching was even tougher. The three starters were back and all improved on their records. Dave Stewart was still the most dependable at 21-9 and he was backed by Bob Welch (17-8) and Storm Davis (19-7). The big free agent pickup was a fourth right-hander, Mike Moore. Always a promising pitcher with dreadful Seattle teams, Moore broke out with a contender and went 19-11. Dennis Eckersley again was the only man needed for relief. He saved 33, went 4-0 and had a 1.56 ERA.

Injuries plagued Canseco for most of the year, limiting him to just 17 homers and 57 RBIs. The other Bruise Brother, Mark McGwire, contributed 33 homers and 95 RBIs while DH Dave Parker settled into that position and drilled 22 homers with 97

RBIs. Carney Lansford boosted his average 60 points, finishing as the runner-up in the batting race at .336. But the big boost came in June, when the A's wrapped up three players to get back Ricky Henderson. The record-setting base-stealer had worn out his welcome in New York, where the Yankees accused him of faking injuries and comporting himself in a manner befitting a hot dog. Deeply wounded, Henderson returned to Oakland, where his career began, and turned the leadoff spot into the key to the A's offense. He hit .294 for Oakland and helped the A's rip Toronto with a .400 playoff performance. Now there would be the first true subway Series in 33 years, since the last time the Yankees met the Brooklyn Dodgers. It became known as the BART Series (for Bay Area Rapid Transit) and the country tuned in to San Francisco.

Turning Point: Game Three, 5:04 p.m.

The A's make it look easy in the first two games at Oakland. First Stewart throws a five-hitter to beat the Giants, 5-0, and then Moore follows with a four-hitter in a 5-1 win. Some of the media can barely suppress yawns as the Series takes a day off to cross the bay to Candlestick Park. One writer even jokes in print that it may be time for the Giants to unveil their secret weapon, an earthquake. It is a jest that will become macabre in just a few hours.

The teams are on the field before the third game. Robinson will pitch for the Giants and Welch, who has just moved into a new home in San Francisco's Marina district, is the choice for the A's. The teams are finishing their warmups and getting ready for elaborate pregame ceremonies, marking the first Series game here since 1962. Then it happens. A low rumble first, and then a roar. The stands and the pressbox sway sickeningly. Players frantically race into the seats, searching for their families, rushing to the sides of wives and children. People scream in the stands, realizing what is happening.

Across the bay, a freeway has collapsed, burying dozens of motorists in the debris. The Bay Bridge has buckled. The Marina is aflame from ruptured gas mains. Down the coast to Santa Cruz, small towns are suddenly faced with the collapse of homes and office buildings. The quake measures 6.9 on

FACT:

Then it happens. A low rumble first, and then a roar. The stands and the pressbox sway sickeningly. Players frantically race into the seats, searching for their families, rushing to the sides of wives and children. People scream in the stands, realizing what is happening . . . There is no panic, though, and no injuries. The capacity crowd leaves the stadium and gets home as best it can.

the Richter Scale, the most severe to strike this area since the killer of 1906. In a matter of seconds, the World Series has become old business.

There is no panic, no injuries. The capacity crowd leaves the stadium and gets home as best it can. Officials say the highway death toll surely would have been higher if people had not left work early to be home to watch the game. Nonetheless, the heart has gone out of this Series. "I'll play because it's my job," says McGwire. "But I'd rather not be here." "If we win there won't be any champagne," says Parker. "We'll hug each other, but no celebrating. That wouldn't be right." San Francisco's mayor blows up when asked when the ballpark would be certified as safe to play in again. "I don't give a damn about baseball," he says. There are suggestions that the rest of the Series be moved to another site, that the area is simply too wounded to care about who wins or loses now.

After a delay of 10 days the Series resumes in an undamaged Candlestick. The crowd sings an emotional chorus of "San Francisco" before the contest. In two games that are less than perfunctory, the A's finish off what they started the previous week, drubbing the Giants 13-7 and 9-6. It is the first Series sweep in 13 years. No one seems to care. To have lived through it was all that mattered.

The Managers:

Tony LaRussa was being tested. When Oakland resigned Ricky Henderson, the team got a star of the first magnitude and a major headache. Henderson has always gone his own way as a player, getting away with a lot because of his abundant talents. He was superb in the playoffs and the Series. He tests the limits constantly. He skipped a workout scheduled during the long Series delay, explaining that "maybe my phone wasn't working, or something." But he produces and LaRussa is smart enough to know how much slack to cut him.

Craig had appeared in his first Series 34 years before, as a rookie pitcher with the Dodgers. He went on to pitch in three more, then got his first job as a manager with San Diego in 1978. He led the Padres to their best record in history, but when the team backslid next year he was history himself. The experience embittered Craig, who spent the next decade as a pitching coach. His success with the 1984 Tigers, to whom he taught his version of a downward-breaking hard slider—the split-fingered fastball—raised his stock again and he was hired by the Giants the next year. The 58-year-old Craig led them to a division title in 1987 and now into the Series.

The Heroes:

Ricky Henderson went to the Yankees with the purpose of winning a pennant. He sulked and he huffed and he feuded with management, and the pennant never happened. So this flag in Oakland was a personal vindication. This is where he had set the record for stolen bases in a season, with 130 in 1982, and he was determined to make this post season a showcase. He banged out 9 hits in the four games, hitting .474 and repeatedly keying the A's attack. He started the final game with a leadoff homer, a category in which he excelled, pulling it off more times than any hitter in baseball history.

> **FACT:**
> Ricky Henderson bangs out 9 hits in the four games, hitting .474. He starts off the final game with a leadoff homer, a category in which he excels, accomplishing it more times than any hitter in baseball history.

This was also a chance for Stewart to shine. He had won 20 games for three straight years but still was comparatively little known, or recalled, unfortunately, for a bizarre incident with a transvestite police decoy in Texas several years before. Stewart had straightened out his act, become a strong force in the Oakland community (especially evident in his tireless work in the quake aftermath) and also a fine pitcher. In this Series, he pitched a shutout and then left game three with a 13-3 lead after seven innings.

While all the Oakland bats were booming, many of the key hits came from one of the lesser sluggers, catcher Terry Steinbach. He led both sides with 7 RBIs, including a three-run homer that put away the second game and a two-run triple in the closer. Steinbach was also remembered for the gripping photograph of him embracing and calming his family on the diamond as the earthquake rumbled around them. There were many ways to be a hero in this Series.

The Zeroes:

The Giant starters never let the hitters have a chance. None of them lasted more than 4 innings and the combined stat of Garrelts, Reuschel and Robinson was 18 runs in 11 1/3 innings. The staff ERA of 8.21 was the second worst in Series history, better only than the 9.26 of the 1932 Cubs.

Mitchell and Clark had a combined total of 2 RBIs, both of them coming on a Mitchell homer in game four with the Giants already behind 8-0.

Canseco ran his streak from 1988 to 0 for 23, being held without a hit for the first two games. He finally singled in his first time up in game three, and then finished strong at 5 for 9, including a three-run homer.

The Aftermath:

San Francisco's pitching problems continued into 1990; age caught up with Reuschel and the team fell back to fourth place.

The A's, for the third time in franchise history, won three pennants in a row, using another free agent gem, pitcher Scott Sanderson, to get the job done.

Notes:

For the first time since 1960, two pitchers on the same team won two games in the Series, as Stewart and Moore turned the trick.

Moore got the first hit by an American League pitcher in 10 years, a two-run double in game four.

Unsurprisingly, the Series set the record for the longest elapsed time from start to finish. It took 15 days to get it over with.

The combined total of 7 home runs by both teams in game three set a Series record. The A's hit five of them in the first 6 innings, including 2 by Dave Henderson.

Line Scores:

Game One, October 14

SF (NL)—000 000 000—0
Garrelts L, Hammaker (5), Brantley (6), La Coss (8)

Oak (AL)—031 100 00X—5
Stewart W

Game Two, October 15

SF (NL)—001 000 000—1
Reuschel L, Downs (5), Lefferts (7), Bedrosian (8)

Oak (AL)—100 400 00X—5
Moore W, Honeycutt (8), Eckersley (9)

Game Three, October 27

Oak (AL)—200 241 040—13
Stewart W, Honeycutt (8), Nelson (9), Burns (9)

SF (NL)—010 200 004—7
Garrelts L, Downs (4), Brantley (5), Hammaker (8), Lefferts (8)

Game Four, October 28

Oak (AL)—130 031 010—9
Moore W, Nelson (7), Honeycutt (7), Burns (7), Eckersley (9) SV

SF (NL)—000 002 400—6
Robinson L, La Coss (2), Brantley (6), Downs (6), Lefferts (8), Bedrosian (8)

1990

Cincinnati (NL) 4
Oakland (AL) 0

In a major surprise, a young bunch of Reds ran right over the A's, who were making their third straight Series appearance. It was the first time that a team sweeping a Series came back the next year and got swept in return.

The Preview:

This was no Red Machine, big or otherwise. Cincinnati had finished well down in the pack in 1989, 12 games under .500. They were young, short on starting pitchers and untested. Most observers felt that new manager Lou Piniella was in for a lengthy project to build this team into a contender.

At some positions, though, the Reds were brimming with talent. Barry Larkin had come out of the University of Michigan and stepped right in as Cincinnati's starting shortstop, giving the Reds the strongest play at that position in the history of the franchise. A good fielder, aggressive hitter and savvy baserunner, Larkin hit .301 as the anchor of the infield. In leftfield was the multi-talented Eric Davis. He topped the team with 86 RBIs, while hitting 24 homers and catching everything he could reach, plus a few he shouldn't have been able to reach. He was regarded as a player with a reasonable claim at being the best all-around performer in the game. Third baseman Chris Sabo, surprisingly, developed into a power hitter, with 25 homers and 71 RBIs. An even bigger surprise was first baseman Hal Morris, picked up from the Yankees in a minor league deal. He came up in late spring and hit .340 the rest of the way. (Sabo and Morris had been Michigan teammates of Larkin's.) Billy Hatcher, one of the elders of this bunch at 30, was the centerfielder and hit a solid .276.

Billy Hatcher hits a double in the third inning of Game 2, one of his seven consecutive hits in the first two games. He ended up with nine hits after being hit with a pitch in Game 4.

The pitching, as anticipated, was erratic. Tom Browning was the top winner, at 15-9. But Piniella managed to put together a decent rotation behind him. Norm Charlton came out of a limited long relief role to go 12-9, and the serendipitously named Jack Armstrong matched that figure. The big addition was Jose Rijo. He had been loaded with promise ever since coming to the majors as a 19-year-old in 1984 with the Yankees, but he never seemed to settle in anywhere. He was traded to the A's, and then came to Cincinnati in the deal that sent Dave Parker to Oakland as a DH. This season he finally hit his stride and went 14-8, looking at times like the staff's top pitcher. Piniella had a good righty-lefty combination in his bullpen. Randy Myers, who had come over from the Mets during the winter, saved 31 games, and Rob Dibble, thought by many to be the hardest thrower (and nastiest disposition) in the league, added 11 more.

For Oakland, it was the same old same old. Mark McGwire had another big power year, with 39 homers and 108 RBIs, and a healthy Jose Canseco added 37 homers and 101 RBIs. They ranked second and third in the league in homers. A bulked-up Ricky Henderson followed his big 1989 post season by slamming a career high 28 homers and hitting .325, while stealing 65 bases. The other big bat was in the hands of Dave Henderson, with 20 homers.

Dave Stewart was again in the 20-win circle, at 22-11. And this was Bob Welch's career year. The 33-year-old right hander finished 27-6 to lead the league. Mike Moore fell back to a 13-15 record and Storm Davis had left the scene. But Oakland picked up Scott Sanderson from the Cubs as a free agent, following Welch and Moore on that route. He had his best season, at 17-11. Once more Eckersley was tops in the game, with 48 saves. The A's were top-heavy favorites to repeat as champions.

Turning Point: Game Two, Eighth Inning.

All the A's wanted in Cincinnati was a split, a base for putting it to the Reds once they were back in Oakland. They were drubbed in the opener, 7-0, as Rijo got the win and the usually reliable Stewart was belted around freely. Davis knocked in three runs with a two-run homer and a single. Now it is Welch's turn against Danny Jackson. Jackson had pitched for Kansas City in the 1985 Series but was just 6-6 this year, with time out for several injuries and a minor league rehabilitation stint.

Oakland gives Welch an early lead to play with. It manufactures a run on a Ricky Henderson single, stolen base, sacrifice and infield out in the first. The Reds get that back and more on consecutive doubles by Larkin and Hatcher, a fly ball and infield out to take the lead, 2-1.

Canseco homers in the third to tie the game, and then Oakland goes to work on Jackson. A McGwire single is followed by two walks. Ron Hassey brings in one run with a fly ball and Mike Gallego singles to score another and drive Jackson from the game. But the 4-2 advantage is as far as the A's can stretch it. The Reds start coming back with one in the fourth on a Joe Oliver double and pinch hit single by Ron Oester.

Armstrong and Charlton run through the Oakland lineup effortlessly in the middle innings. Welch, too, settles down, and going into the last of the eighth he makes the 4-3 lead stand up. One more inning and it will be Eckersley time. But Hatcher intervenes. He has six straight hits and reached base seven consecutive times, both records for a Series debut. This time up he sends a drive towards right center. The A's bench thinks it will be caught, but Canseco breaks late on the ball and can't reach it. It bounces past him and Hatcher winds up with a lead-off triple. "This is a very strange ballpark, the way the ball carries to right," says Canseco later. To which Tony LaRussa responds: "If you want to win the game, it's a play you have to make. I don't think he got a very good jump." Canseco's feelings are hurt by the criticism and he pouts that the manager is "hanging it all on one play."

Nonetheless, Hatcher's triple changes everything. Welch, working carefully to left-handed hitting Paul O'Neill, walks him, then gets Davis on a short fly ball. The A's bring in lefty Rick Honeycutt to face Morris, only to see the Reds pinch hit right-hand hitting Glenn Braggs. Even with the infield pulled in there is no play at home for shortstop Gallego on Braggs' grounder, and the tying run scores. Canseco's sluggish defense has brought Cincinnati back into the game.

Worse is yet to come. Eckersley finally comes in to pitch in the 10th, but this is not the way LaRussa wants to use him. The game is tied. He is outside his role as the one-inning closer. With one out, pinch hitter Billy Bates, a late-season call-up, gets his first hit as a Red, beating out a chopper. Sabo then drills his third straight single, sending Bates to second. Catcher Joe Oliver hits a harmless looking bouncer right down the third base line. But Carney Lansford cannot reach it and the ball hops directly over the bag. Bates races home on the hit and the Reds have beaten Eckersley to win 5-4. Instead of going home poised to put it away, the A's return in desperation. They can't pull out of it, as Cincinnati pounds them for a 7-run inning to win the third game, 8-3. Then Rijo baffles them utterly to close out the sweep, 2-1.

The Managers:

Piniella was the consummate professional on the discordant Yankee teams of the late '70s and early '80s. While the madness raged around him, Piniella calmly went about his business—which consisted of hitting around .300 while switching between DH and leftfield. It seemed a natural progression for him to manage the Yankees after his retirement. He won 90 games in his rookie year in 1986, but when no pennants ensued the constantly impatient George Steinbrenner lowered the boom on him two years later. The Reds picked him up a year later, with beneficial results. Piniella was known to speak sharply to players he felt were not playing hard and to face down chronic complainers before the situation festered. At 47 he was respected as a tough guy who had been through the grinder.

This Series was a crushing blow to LaRussa. He was convinced that his talent was, by far, the best in the majors. He also knew the proof of that was in the winning. The failure to take two consecutive championships and the mediocre performance of big-name players for the second time in three years left him wondering about how much heart the A's really had. "I don't buy that both teams are winners in a World Series," he said. "I feel a lot like we lost. We could have done a lot better."

The Heroes:

For Rijo, this Series was a revelation. Starting against his former teammates, he was as impressive as any pitcher ever looked in this showcase. He threw seven shutout innings in the opener. That streak ended in the first inning of game four when the A's quickly reached him for a run. He then walked two more in the second inning. But that was all. Rijo sat down the next 20 hitters in a row, striking out 8 of them, until Myers came in to get the last two outs of the game. The Reds rallied for 2 runs in the 8th to give Rijo his second win. The performance won him the MVP award for the Series.

It was a narrow choice over Hatcher, who was unstoppable in this Series. His seven straight hits in games one and two (with nine consecutive times on base) helped the Reds get off to their flying start. There was nothing flukey about the hits, either. Among them were four doubles and a triple. He added two more singles in game three before Stewart finally came up with a way to stop him. He hit him on the left hand on his first time up in game four

FACT:
Jose Rijo was as impressive as any pitcher ever looked in this showcase. He threw seven shutout innings in the opener and gave up only one run in winning the finale.

and sent him to the hospital for X-rays. Hatcher finished with 9 for 12.

He was almost matched by Sabo, who went 9 for 16 while driving in 5 runs. His consecutive home runs in game three helped turn it into a rout, and he collected three hits in two other games.

The Zeroes:

Just as in 1988, Canseco turned up among the missing. The performances were remarkably similar. Two years before he went 1 for 19, with his only hit a homer. This time he was 1 for 12. His only hit—a homer. He couldn't start the final game because of back problems but as a pinch hitter in the ninth inning of the one-run game he topped off a futile Series with a weak infield out.

The Oakland defense was also a problem, with five errors permitting 8 unearned runs to score. The most egregious mistakes were a bobble by McGwire in game three, which opened the way for a 7-run inning, and Stewart's throwing error on a bunt in game four, which allowed the winning run to score in the eighth.

The Aftermath:

While the jubilant Cincinnati entourage headed home from the sweep, Eric Davis remained behind in an Oakland hospital. Diving for a line drive in the second inning of the last game, he suffered a severely bruised kidney and was held over for observation for several days. Davis felt he was not paid the proper concern by team owner Marge Schott and expressed his disappointment with her. The incident led to an irrevocable rupture between the two. Davis eventually went off to Los Angeles and never fulfilled his early promise as a player. The Reds fell back to 74-88 in 1991 as injuries decimated the starting rotation and a brooding Davis was a non-factor.

Oakland's three-year run also ended as the A's sagged to fourth. An injury to McGwire and Stewart's drop to 11 wins after 4 straight 20-win campaigns finally halted the streak, although they were back as division winners in 1992.

FACT:
It was the second consecutive sweep for the Reds, following their 1976 demolition of the Yankees. Their nine straight wins (including the final game of the 1975 Series) is exceeded only by the Yankees, who won twelve in row (1927, 1928, 1932).

Notes:

This marked the first consecutive Series sweeps since the Yankees flattened the Cubs and Reds in 1938–39. It was also the second consecutive sweep for the Reds, whose last Series appearance had been a demolition of the

Yankees in 1976. Their string of 9 straight wins was exceeded only by the Yankees, who had won 12 in a row (1927, 1928, 1932).

Oakland did not score a single run after the 3rd inning in any of these games. The final line for the Cincinnati bullpen was: 13 innings, 7 hits, 0 runs.

Line Scores:

Game One, October 16

Oak (AL)—000 000 000—0
Stewart L, Burns (5), Nelson (5), Sanderson (7), Eckersley (8)

Cin (NL)—202 030 00X—7
Rijo W, Dibble (8), Myers (9)

Game Two, October 17

Oak (AL)—103 000 000 0—4
Welch, Honeycutt (8), Eckersley (10) L

Cin (NL)—200 100 010 1—5
Jackson, Scudder (3), Armstrong (5), Charlton (8), Dibble (9) W

Game Three, October 19

Cin (NL)—017 000 000—8
Browning W, Dibble (7), Myers (8)

Oak (AL)—021 000 000—3
Moore L, Sanderson (3), Klink (4), Nelson (4), Burns (8), Young (9)

Game Four, October 20

Cin (NL)—000 000 020—2
Rijo W, Myers (9) SV

Oak (AL)—100 000 000—1
Stewart L

1991

Minnesota (AL) 4
Atlanta (NL) 3

Time for Domeball again, and, just as in 1987, Minnesota swept all four games at home while losing all on the road. With five games decided by a run, three extra inning games and a 1-0 pitcher's duel in the finale, it was a memorable Series, too, after a run of duds.

The Preview:

There was a time in baseball when climbing from last to first in the course of one season was flatly impossible. This year both Series teams did it. The signing of key free agents transformed ballclubs with a pen-stroke. The maturing of a pack of young players helped, too, but the rapid ascendance of Minnesota and Atlanta was a commentary on the parity that free agency brought to the game.

For the Twins, it was a sentimental journey. Jack Morris, longtime star of the Detroit staff, decided he wanted to go back to his old hometown and finish his career with Minnesota. In the tearful signing of a rich free agent contract he did just that. Morris went 18-12 to add luster to a formerly drab group of starters. He was assisted by youthful Scott Erickson, the most effective pitcher in the league during the first half of the season and 20-8 overall. Also picking up his performance was Kevin Tapani, at 16-9. Tapani had come over from the Mets with Rick Aguilera in mid-1989 in a trade for Frank Viola, the hero of the 1987 Series. It was a calculated gamble by the Twins to rebuild their staff in one swoop, and it worked. Tapani became a serviceable starter and Aguilera, converted into a stopper by Minnesota, became one of the league's top relievers. He saved 42 games this year.

Jack Morris took MVP honors, pitching in three games, winning two. His second win came in Game 7, a ten-inning 1-0 gem which was the fifth one-run game and third extra-inning contest of the Series.

These Twins weren't nearly as powerful as the 1987 collection of sluggers. Another free agent, DH Chili Davis, came in from California and led in homers (29) and RBIs (93). A couple of holdovers also hit well. First baseman Kent Hrbek had 20 homers and 89 RBIs, while centerfielder Kirby Puckett led the team with a .319 average to go along with 89 RBIs. Rookie second baseman Chuck Knoblauch gave Minnesota a steady bat at leadoff, with a .281 average. The two big surprises were Shane Mack and Brian Harper. Both were obtained by the Twins at the minor league level after unsuccessful trials elsewhere. Harper was a utility man with the 1985 Cardinals and nearly won that Series with a pinch hit single in the sixth game. He was able to play almost everywhere but unable to catch on anywhere. Harper turned himself into a fulltime catcher with Minnesota and hit .311. Mack had struggled as a hitter with San Diego, but in his second season with the Twins the rightfielder hit a robust .310 with 79 RBIs.

Atlanta's free agent prize had been third baseman Terry Pendleton. Always a good hitter with the Cards, Pendleton turned into a terror in cozy Fulton County Stadium. He led the league with a .319 average while hitting 22 homers and driving in

86 runs. The Braves also picked up centerfielder Otis Nixon in a minor league deal with Montreal. He thrived at the top of the Atlanta lineup, hitting .297 and stealing 72 bases, adding a new dimension to a club that always had concentrated on power instead of speed. Leftfielder Ron Gant had his second straight 30-homer, 30-steal season and led the Braves with 105 RBIs. Young slugger David Justice was able to move from first base, where he did not feel comfortable, to right field. He chipped in with 21 homers and 87 RBIs.

The Braves rotation was one of the youngest in the majors. When it suddenly came alive in mid-season the pennant race was blown apart. Tom Glavine, 25, wound up at 20-11 and Steve Avery, 21, was 18-8. John Smoltz, 24, struggled in the first half, but after undergoing hypnosis therapy relaxed enough to finish 14-13, and was very strong in September. Charlie Leibrandt, far and away the veteran of the corps at 35, was a solid 15-13. Atlanta's deep pitching enabled the Braves to overtake and beat out Los Angeles by one game and then stun Pittsburgh in the playoffs. The final piece was added when stopper Alejandro Pena joined the team from the Mets in August. He saved 11 games in 15 chances in the last weeks.

Turning Point: Game Seven, Eighth Inning.

No one thought it was possible to squeeze any more drama out of this Series. Puckett wins the sixth game with a leadoff 11th inning homer, giving the Twins a desperate 4-3 decision and keeping them alive to play another day. Four games already have been decided by one run. The Braves win once in the 12th on a two-out single and once in the last of the ninth. The games have been classic confrontations, and now it is once more for the whole shot. The Twins call on Morris, perhaps the most competitive pitcher in the game. For the Braves it will be Smoltz, who grew up in Michigan and idolized Morris when he pitched for the Tigers.

Smoltz was first signed by Detroit but was traded to the Braves in 1987 for Doyle Alexander, who pitched the Tigers into the playoffs. Now Smoltz is the rising young star going against the veteran. Smoltz won twice in the playoffs, pitching a shutout in the clinching game. Morris beat Toronto twice in the American League games and then stopped the Braves in the Series opener. The two battled each other through 7 innings of a 2-2 tie in game four, with neither getting a decision. Now pupil faces master again with everything on the line.

It is a brilliant duel. Through seven innings, Morris gives up just five hits and survives mild threats. Smoltz, however, is touched for just 4 hits and seems firmly in control. It is 0-0 going into the eighth, the longest scoreless tie in 7th game history. It appears the Braves will break through. Lonnie Smith leads off with a single and Pendleton follows with a double to left. Smith is running with the pitch and should score easily, but, instead, he slows down as he reaches second and turns to look for the ball, which has caromed off the wall. He then takes off again but decides it is not worth the risk of trying to score with none out. Knoblauch had faked an incoming relay when Smith got to second and the runner hadn't realized that Pendleton's hit had found the gap. His hesitation cost a run. Still, the Braves have runners at third and second and none out.

Morris, however, is equal to the situation. He gets Gant on an easy grounder, with Smith forced to hold third. Justice then is intentionally walked to get at first baseman Sid Bream. He hits a grounder to Hrbek who throws to the plate to start an inning-ending double play. The Twins escape again.

Now it is Minnesota's turn. The Twins load the bases on two singles and a walk to Puckett. That takes Smoltz out of the game in favor of Mike Stanton. He induces Hrbek to send a liner to second. Mark Lemke spears the ball and doubles Knoblauch off the bag, ending the threat. Then, in the Minnesota ninth, Pena has to come in to strike out pinch hitter Paul Sorrento with two on.

For the third time ever, and the first since 1924, the deciding game goes to extra innings. Manager Tom Kelly intends to pull Morris after nine innings, but the pitcher tells him: "There's no game tomorrow," and walks out for the 10th. He gets the Braves out without a ball leaving the infield.

Dan Gladden decides it has gone far enough. His leadoff pop fly off Pena falls into short leftfield and Gladden, knowing that the ball will bounce high on the Dome's artificial turf, keeps running. He ends up with a fluke double. Knoblauch bunts him to third. The Braves try to stave off the inevitable, giving walks to Puckett and Hrbek, but pinch hitter Gene Larkin ends the drama with a one-out line single to deep left. The Twins win it, 1-0, with Smith's base-running mistake giving them all the margin they need.

FACT:

It is the longest scoreless seventh game in history. Manager Tom Kelly plans to pull Jack Morris after nine innings, but the pitcher tells him, "there's no game tomorrow," and walks out for the tenth inning. He gets the Braves out without the ball leaving the infield.

The Managers:

Very few observers would have put Kelly on the list of the most brilliant managers in the game. Some media cynics write that he resembles an overgrown Boy Scout. Yet he won two championships in five years, doubling the number the franchise had earned in its entire existence. His ballclubs seem to reflect his personality: calm, unflappable, quietly competent.

This was the first Series trip for Atlanta's Bobby Cox, who is on his second time around with the Braves. The first one didn't quite take. He had been an infielder with some of the awful Yankee teams of the late '60s, and got his first job managing some equally bad Braves squads in 1978. He lasted four years, and after being cut loose caught on with Toronto in 1982. The Blue Jays were just starting their rise to the heights of the American League and under Cox they broke through to their first division title in 1985. But the Braves offered him the job of general manager and Cox returned to Atlanta to start putting together the elements of a winner. In 1990, he decided to manage the team he had made. Displaying unlimited patience with his young pitchers, his payoff came in mid-season of 1991. The Braves suddenly jelled and started their rush towards the top, and subsequent dominance of their division for most of the decade.

The Heroes:

Morris ran his winning streak to 4 in a row, two with the Tigers in 1984 and the first and last games of this Series. During his years in Detroit he had been nicknamed Mt. Morris (the name of an outstate town) because of his volcanic personality, always on the verge of eruption. Freed of the expectations heaped upon him with the Tigers, he underwent a temperament change in Minnesota, becoming an elder statesman to several of the younger pitchers. When Erickson could not make his scheduled start in the All Star Game, Morris subbed for him and wore black socks as a tribute to the younger man. (Erickson always wore black when he pitched, as a symbol of the "Day of Death.") His leadership qualities alone may have tilted the Series to the Twins.

FACT:
Kirby Puckett didn't have an outstanding Series, but in the critical sixth game, with his team facing elimination, he took the game over by himself. He drove in three runs and scored the fourth, winning the game 4-3 on an eleventh-inning homer.

The same could be said of Puckett. He didn't have an outstanding Series by his standards—hitting just .250 with 2 homers—but in the critical sixth game, when a loss meant elimination for the Twins, he took the game over by himself. He drove in three runs and scored the other in the 4-3 game, which he won with an 11th inning homer.

Kirby Puckett celebrates his eleventh-inning game-winning home run in Game 6. Puckett was responsible for all four Minnesota runs in the game.

Mark Lemke prided himself on his dirty uniform. It indicated the way he threw himself into the game. He led both sides in hitting at .416. In Atlanta's first two Series wins at home he drove in the winner with a 12th inning hit one day and scored the winner on the next after tripling in the last of the ninth.

The Zeroes:

Leibrandt's Series streak was headed in the opposite direction of Morris'. He lost once with Kansas City in 1985 and took two more defeats in this one. A three-run shot by Greg Gagne beat him in the opener, 5-2. Then Puckett, the first man he faced in relief in game six, greeted him with a homer to tag him with that loss, too.

It was an almost inexplicable base-running mistake by the 36-year-old Smith. He lost sight of both the ball and his coach on Pendleton's double in game seven and then let himself get bluffed out of his socks by a rookie, Knoblauch. Smith refused to talk about it after the game and angrily lashed out at writers who tried to bring it up during the next spring training.

The Aftermath:

After his warm and cuddly return to Minnesota in 1991, Morris decided that business was business. He packed up and moved on to Toronto the following year. His departure left the Twins with just enough of a hole in their rotation to lose first place to Oakland in the division.

The Braves built on this success and came back for a return engagement the following season. It was essentially the same cast except for the addition of two-sport wonder, Neon Deion Sanders.

Notes:

Smith set a record by reaching the Series with his fourth different team. He started with the 1980 Phillies, came back with the 1982 Cardinals and then with the 1985 Royals. This, however, was his first trip home on the losing side.

The teams managed to cram a record 42 players, including 12 pinch hitters, into the 12-inning third game. By contrast, the total number of players in the entire 1905 World Series was 24. It was the longest Series game since the Yankees beat L.A. in 12 innings in 1977, and the 10th in Series history to go that many. Longest in history was the 14-inning game played by the Red Sox and Brooklyn in 1916.

This was the season Atlanta Braves introduced the Tomahawk Chop to an unsuspecting world. Borrowed from Florida State University (whose nickname is the Seminoles), the downward wave of the right hand accompanied by a vaguely Indian-sounding chant became a staple at Braves home games. Despite outraged protests by Native American groups, even liberal activist Jane Fonda, wife of Braves owner Ted Turner, was observed chopping away.

Line Scores:

Game One, October 19

Atl (NL)—000 001 010—2
Leibrandt L, Clancy (5),
Wohlers (8), Stanton (8)

Min (AL)—001 031 00X—5
Morris W, Guthrie (8),
Aguilera (8) SV

Game Two, October 20

Atl (NL)—010 010 000—2
Glavine L

Min (NL)—200 000 01X—3
Tapani W, Aguilera (9) SV

Game Three, October 22

Min (AL)—100 000 120 000—3
Erickson, West (5), Leach (5),
Bedrosian (6), Willis (8),
Guthrie (10), Aguilera (12) L

Atl (NL)—010 120 000 001—4
Avery, Pena (8), Stanton (10),
Wohlers (12), Mercker (12),
Clancy (12) W

Game Four, October 23

Min (AL)—010 000 100—2
Morris, Willis (7), Guthrie (8) L,
Bedrosian (9)

Atl (NL)—001 000 101—3
Smoltz, Wohlers (8),
Stanton (8) W

Game Five, October 24

Min (AL)—000 003 011—5
Tapani L, Leach (5), West (7),
Bedrosian (7), Willis (8)

Atl (NL)—000 410 63X—14
Glavine W, Mercker (6),
Clancy (7), St. Claire (9)

Game Six, October 26

Atl (NL)—000 020 100 00—3
Avery, Stanton (7), Pena (9),
Leibrandt (11) L

Min (AL)—200 010 000 01—4
Erickson, Guthrie (7), Willis (7),
Aguilera (10) W

Game Seven, October 27

Atl (NL)—000 000 000 0—0
Smoltz, Stanton (8), Pena (9) L

Min (AL)—000 000 000 1—1
Morris W

1992

Toronto (AL) 4
Atlanta (NL) 2

The World Series goes international and the Canadian side gets just enough big hits to win. Three games are decided in the last time at bat and for the second straight year it takes extra innings to finish things off.

The Preview:

It was a long, strange trip for the Blue Jays. Part of the third round of American League expansion in 1977, the team had been a contender since the seventh year of its existence. But three times it had been turned away in the playoffs. In 1987, it lost four straight games to Detroit at the end of the season when just one win would have clinched the division. Moving into Sky Dome in 1989, Toronto shattered every major league attendance record in existence, drawing almost 4 million people under the retractable roof. Through all this, the team was completely overhauled while never falling from contention. The big gates also gave Toronto the wherewithal to dip deeply into the free agent market. In 1992 it finally came together.

The core of this team arrived in a trade with San Diego before the previous season. The Jays obtained power-hitting outfielder Joe Carter and second baseman Roberto Alomar. That combination put Toronto over the top. Carter drove in 119 runs on 34 homers this season, while Alomar played a superb infield defense, while leading the team with a .310 average and driving in 76 runs from the number two spot in the order. He was recognized as one of the most intelligent players in the game, a performer with the ability to improve the play of those around him. The other critical addition was DH Dave Winfield. Now 40, the slugger had driven in over 100 runs six times with the

Pat Borders (center, with shinguards) jumps onto the pile of celebrating Blue Jays. Borders, the Series MVP, helped export the World Championship to Canada with his .450 average.

Yankees, but he was constantly at odds with club management and was stuck with George Steinbrenner's characterization of him as a choke artist. He had his finest campaign in years, with 108 RBIs, 26 homers and a .290 average. The other key component was Devon White. A brilliant centerfielder, he came over from California and provided speed at the top of the lineup ahead of Alomar's hit-and-run capabilities. With these players, Toronto could overcome rather ordinary play at shortstop and catcher and a severe decline by third baseman Kelly Gruber.

Jack Morris joined his third team in three years and finished with one of his best seasons, at 21-6. The Jays also received unexpected help from second-year man Juan Guzman, who went 16-5 and was overpowering for long stretches of the year. Third man in the rotation was left-hander Jimmy Key. He was the team veteran, in his 9th season, and with his contract expiring at the end of the season he doubted whether he would be back. Injuries limited him to a 13-13 record, so just to play it safe the Jays brought in David Cone from the Mets for the final month. He went 4-3 and won another in the playoffs over Oakland. Toronto also had the luxury of two stoppers, both of them strapping right-handers. Duane Ward was used mostly as a set-up man for The

Terminator, Tom Henke. At 34 he was still among the hardest throwers in the game and the most reliable closer in the American League. He saved 34 games and Ward added 12 more. The Jays lost few times with a lead after seven innings.

Atlanta returned with almost the same group that won in 1991, but a year older and wiser. Terry Pendleton had another outstanding season, hitting .311 with 21 homers and a team-high 105 RBIs. David Justice had 21 homers, and leadoff man Otis Nixon hit .294. While Ron Gant's power numbers declined he still was second highest on the team with 80 RBIs. Occasionally, though, he sat down against certain right-handed pitchers, which did not make him at all happy. In his place, Atlanta started glittery Deion Sanders. The Atlanta Falcons football star hit .308, ran with abandon, fielded erratically, wore more gold jewelry than the pharaohs and distinguished himself during the playoff celebration by dumping a pail of water over the head of network TV commentator Tim McCarver. They loved him in Atlanta.

Atlanta's pitching kept getting better. For the second straight year, Tom Glavine was the top winner, at 20-8. John Smoltz improved to 15-12 and Charlie Leibrandt seemed to mellow with age. The 36-year-old left hander was 15-7. Only Steve Avery was down from 1991, with an 11-11 record, but that was a reflection of low batting support rather than ineffectiveness. The one dark cloud was that last year's stopper, Alejandro Pena, was not stopping much of anyone. So the Braves traded for Jeff Reardon from the Red Sox. At 37, he was the all-time save leader and was familiar with Series pressure from 1987 with Minnesota. He won 3 and saved 3 down the stretch and seemed to make Atlanta's staff complete.

Turning Point: Game Two, Ninth Inning.

Atlanta rides into the Series on a wave of emotion. Trailing 2-0 in the final playoff game with Pittsburgh, they rally for 3 runs in the ninth to beat the Pirates for the second straight year. Glavine then methodically mows down the Jays on a 4-hitter in the opener and a three-run homer by catcher Damon Berryhill beats Morris, 3-1.

Now the Braves are going for a two-game edge before the Series moves north of the border. Cone gets the start for Toronto, but seems ill at ease, out of rhythm. He walks five men in the first five innings and three of them score. He fails to hold runners on and the Braves steal three bases. One run scores on a wild pitch and Toronto makes two errors behind him. The Jays rally to tie the game 2-2 in the fifth, as singles by Cone and White bring in the runs. In the bottom of the inning, Sanders singles, steals second, goes to third on a wild throw and scores on Justice's single. That gets Cone out of the game and David Wells into it, and one more score quickly comes in on a sacrifice fly. The Braves now lead 4-2 behind Smoltz.

The Toronto bullpen shuts down Atlanta thoroughly. Wells, Todd Stottlemyre and Ward hold the Braves hitless through the eighth. The Jays chip one run off the lead in the top of that inning on a double by Alomar and singles by Carter and Winfield. Reardon stops the bleeding by striking out Gruber with two runners on. Going into the ninth it is still Atlanta's game, 4-3.

FACT:
Ed Sprague batted just 47 times during the season and hit 1 home run. With one on and one out in top of the ninth, his team trailing 4-3, Sprague plants Reardon's fastball into the left-field stands.

Reardon has saved 357 games in his career, plus one in the recent playoffs. He also won the clincher in that series. So this is routine for him. But with one out, he walks pinch hitter Derek Bell, an odd lapse for a veteran stopper against a rookie. That brings up Ed Sprague to bat for Ward. He is Toronto's backup catcher. He also plays a little third base and a little first. Very little. He batted just 47 times during the season with one home run. He plants Reardon's fastball into the leftfield stands. As the Atlanta crowd sits in numbed silence, he circles the bases behind Bell to give the Jays a 5-4 lead. Henke comes on and, despite hitting one man and walking another, terminates the Braves.

Toronto now can go home with some manuevering room. It takes two out of three at Sky Dome before returning to Atlanta and finishing off the Series in a 4-3 thriller in 11 innings. Sprague's homer springs the Jays to the title.

The Managers:

This made two straight Series losses for Bobby Cox, but it hurt a little more this time. That's because he was managing against the team he left seven years before. He also had his share of second-guessers on his decision to let left-hander Leibrandt face Winfield in the 11th inning of game six. "He can get right-handers out," said Cox resignedly. Not this time. Winfield's two-run double was the winning hit of the Series. Unstated was the fact that Cox had lost confidence in Reardon, his bullpen stopper. That didn't leave him much choice.

Cito Gaston was also facing a team he used to be part of. Gaston was an outfielder with the Padres and Braves in the '70s before catching on with Toronto as a hitting coach. When the Jays fired Jimy Williams in 1989 he was named manager in what was supposed to be a fill-in status. But the team responded so well to his tough-minded, light-handed approach, that the job was made permanent. Toronto had started to view the Jays as a team that would collapse in the money situations. This time their hopes were rewarded.

The Heroes:

FACT:
Toronto won this Series in the bullpen. Ward won twice, Henke saved two more, and the Braves managed to get just 2 runs in 18 1/3 innings against Jays relievers.

Toronto won this Series in the bullpen. Ward won twice, Henke saved two more and the Braves managed to get just two runs in 18 1/3 innings against the Jay relievers. David Wells was especially tough in middle relief, getting into 4 games, pitching 4 innings and not allowing a hit.

It was an oddly mixed series for catcher Pat Borders. He was Toronto's top hitter, at .450, and batted safely in all 6 games. But the Braves stole 9 straight bases in the first three games (after Oakland went 16-for-18 on him in the playoffs) before he threw out his first runner. They added 6 more steals later. Much of that was caused by the inability of several Toronto pitchers to hold runners on.

Key pitched as if he knew this was his farewell to Toronto. He stopped Atlanta in the fourth game, 2-1, on a 5-hitter. Then, in an unfamiliar relief role, got credit for the final game, too.

Dizzy Dean had said it at a World Series 58 years before: "If you can do it, it ain't braggin'." Deion Sanders did it. He led all hitters with a .533 average and stole 5 bases, in a performance that left Gant sulking on the bench. Despite his often abrasive personality, Sanders turned out to be the real deal. His first love was football, though, and, in a little more than three years he would add two Super Bowl rings to his jewelry collection.

FACT:
Dizzy Dean had said it at a World Series 58 years before: "if you can do it, it ain't braggin'." Deion Sanders did it. He led all hitters with a .533 average and stole 5 bases.

The Zeroes:

Reardon could not get the job done for Atlanta and a team without a closer usually founders in the Series. He gave up Sprague's game winning homer in game two, then was called in during the ninth in game three and surrendered a game-winning single to Candy Maldonado. Those were his only two appearances.

Morris lost his chance to become the first man in history to win a Series game for three different teams. He came close in the opener, working on a one-hit shutout until Berryhill's three-run homer off a weak forkball beat him in the sixth inning, 3-1. Then he was blasted in game five, 7-2, with a grand slam by Lonnie Smith the final blow. Although he was a member of the 1993 Toronto Series squad, he did not pitch.

Problems continued for Gruber. He broke an 0 for 23 post-season slump with an eighth inning homer in game three, but he finished with just 2 for 19 in the Series and heard ample booing from the home crowd. He left for California as a free agent after the season.

The Aftermath:

The Jays said goodbye to Key, Winfield and Henke through free agency. But they brought in pitcher Dave Stewart from Oakland and DH Paul Molitor from Milwaukee. Molitor, especially, provided the punch for a repeat performance in 1993.

Atlanta snared the free agent catch of the year, adding pitcher Greg Maddux to a staff that already was regarded as the best in the game. Maddux won his first of three straight Cy Young Awards and the Braves took their third straight division title, but were upended by Philadelphia in the playoffs.

Notes:

The first international Series also resulted in an international incident. At game two ceremonies in Atlanta, a Marine Corps color guard marched in carrying the Canadian flag upside down. The gaffe, understandably, irritated Canada. The media ranted, apologies were demanded and street vendors did a brisk trade in upside-down American flags before game three in Toronto. But it was announced before that game that a Marine Corps unit from Buffalo had "requested the honor of carrying the Canadian colors." When they marched onto the field, with the Maple Leaf right side up, they received a standing ovation and the incident was over.

The Series almost saw its first triple play since Bill Wambsganss pulled off the unassisted kind in 1920. In game three, with two Braves on, Justice sent a long drive to dead center. White made a tremendous catch, hurling himself against the wall. Sanders held up between second and third on the play, but Pendleton was running all-out from first and passed his teammate for the second out. Third baseman Gruber then sneaked in behind Sanders and, from all appearances, tagged him out as he slid back into second. But Sanders was called safe and Toronto had to be content with the double play.

The game-winning double by Winfield in the sixth game was his first extra base hit in 44 Series at bats.

Line Scores:

Game One, October 17

Tor (AL)—000 100 000—1
Morris L, Stottlemyre (7), Wells (8)

Atl (NL)—000 003 00X—3
Glavine W

Game Two, October 18

Tor (AL)—000 020 012—5
Cone, Wells (5), Stottlemyre (7), Ward (8) W, Henke (9) SV

Atl (NL)—010 120 000—4
Smoltz, Stanton (8), Reardon (8) L

Game Three, October 20

Atl (NL)—000 001 010—2
Avery L, Wohlers (9), Stanton (9), Reardon (9)

Tor (AL)—000 100 011—3
Guzman, Ward (9) W

Game Four, October 21

Atl (NL)—000 000 010—1
Glavine L

Tor (AL)—001 000 10X—2
Key W, Ward (8), Henke (9) SV

Game Five, October 22

Atl (NL)—100 150 000—7
Smoltz W, Stanton (7) SV

Tor (AL)—010 100 000—2
Morris L, Wells (5), Timlin (7), Eichhorn (8), Stottlemyre (9)

Game Six, October 24

Tor (AL)—100 100 000 02—4
Cone, Stottlemyre (7), Wells (7), Ward (8), Henke (9), Key (10) W, Timlin (11) SV

Atl (NL)—001 000 001 01—3
Avery, Smith (5), Stanton (8), Wohlers (9), Leibrandt (10) L

1993

Toronto (AL) 4
Philadelphia (NL) 2

The Blue Jays became the first team since the 1977–78 Yankees to repeat as champions. The games were marked by the wildest slugfest in Series history and the second time ever that it ended with a home run.

The Preview:

Toronto lost 11 players from the roster of its 1992 champions, the most ever to leave a Series-winning team, but a tide of free agents and young replacements kept the Jays rolling. Chief among them was Paul Molitor. The 37-year-old Milwaukee veteran settled in as DH and compiled his finest overall season. He hit .332, with 22 homers and 111 RBIs, the first time in his 16-year career that he went over 100 in that category. There was enough left in his legs to steal 22 bases, and he became the oldest player to hit 20 homers and steal 20 bases in the same year. John Olerud, regarded as a promising hitter, burst out to become a devastating one. He was threatening the .400 mark late in August before settling back and finishing at .363 to lead the league. His 24 homers and 107 RBIs were personal highs. Roberto Alomar had his second big year as a hitter, with a .326 average, 17 homers and 93 RBIs. Olerud, Molitor and Alomar finished 1-2-3 in batting, the first time in exactly 100 years that the top three hitters came from the same team, since the 1893 Phillies. In addition, Joe Carter led the Jays with 33 homers and 121 RBIs, the seventh time in eight seasons he had driven in over 100 runs. The Jays got their biggest boost, though, with the return of shortstop Tony Fernandez. He went to San Diego in the trade that brought Carter and Alomar to Toronto in 1991. That hadn't worked out for him, though, and Fernandez moved on to the Mets. The Jays brought him back in June and he hit .306, also giving them the best play at shortstop they had seen since he left.

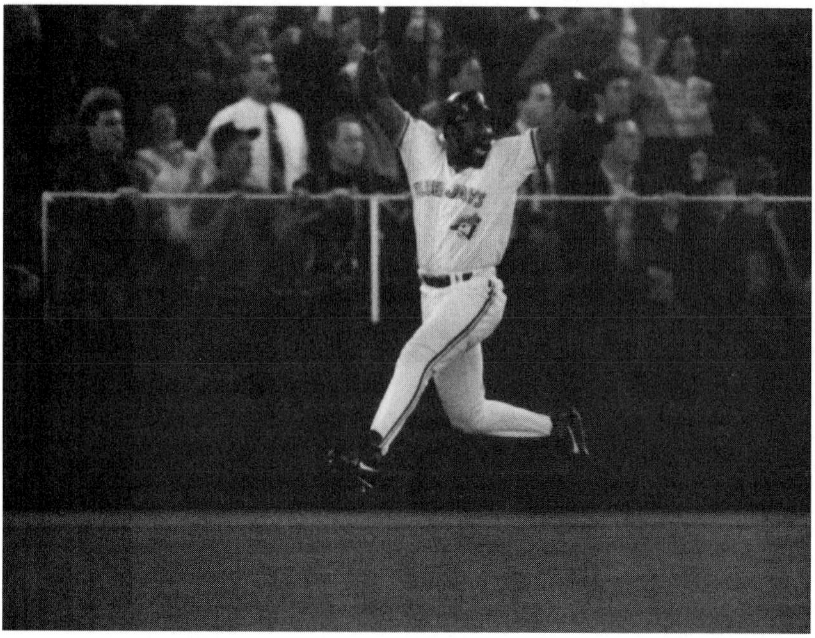

Joe Carter celebrates as his ninth-inning three-run homer reaches the seats at Skydome, ending the World Series on a home run for the first time since 1960. Toronto trailed 6-5 when Carter came to bat.

Jack Morris finally fizzled out at the age of 37, dropping to 7 wins. Rookie Pat Hentgen (a Morris admirer from suburban Detroit) came in to pick up the slack with a 19-9 record. Juan Guzman had his second straight fine season at 16-3. Dave Stewart, a free agent pickup from Oakland, rounded out the rotation at 12-8. With the departure of Tom Henke, the chance opened for Duane Ward to assume the role of stopper by himself. He wound up with 45 saves, surpassing The Terminator's top season.

The Phillies were a major surprise, the third team in three years to go from last to first in their division in a single season. They did it convincingly, too, occupying first place for all but one day. Then they shocked heavily favored Atlanta to enter the Series. The Phils had suffered a near catastrophe two years before when outfielder Len Dykstra and catcher Darren Daulton were seriously injured in an automobile accident. They both missed much of the 1991 season, but led the charge to the top in 1993. Daulton topped the Phils with 105 RBIs and 24 homers. Dykstra was a run-scoring machine from his leadoff position, crossing the plate 143 times, the most in the National League in 61 years. He hit .305, stole 37 bases, walked 129 times, generally made a nuisance of himself and was named the team's MVP. First baseman John Kruk, a fierce, shaggy-haired line drive hitter, finished at .316 with 85 RBIs and cheerfully chided All Star Game voters for selecting "anyone who looks like me." Third baseman Dave Hollins had 93 RBIs. Outfielder Pete Incaviglia, a faded slugger who was picked up as a free agency afterthought, found surprising new life in Philly, with 24 homers and 89 RBIs.

The pitching staff turned out to be even more surprising. Tommy Greene came back from arm problems to go 16-4, and Curt Schilling also had a career best 16-7. Terry Mulholland was 12-9 and Danny Jackson, who had not won more than 10 games since 1988, rebounded from several years of wandering and injuries to go 12-11. The result was an unexpectedly nice little rotation. To top it off, there was the Wild Thing; Mitch Williams, a notoriously erratic lefthander, managed to hold together for the entire season and saved 43 games. He didn't always accomplish this in an esthetically pleasing manner but he usually got it done. It all made the Phillies a fairly formidable bunch.

Turning Point: Game Four, Eighth Inning.

There has never been anything quite like this in Series history. By the seventh inning the record for runs in one game already is gone, as the Phillies build up a 14-9 lead. The fun is just beginning. By the time it is all over Toronto overcomes the third greatest margin in Series history and does it later in the game than any other team. In the process, they shatter the Philadelphia bullpen.

This has been a free-swinging Series right from the start, with both teams ripping richly into the opposition. Each side has averaged 10 hits a game, but Toronto has the best of it in scoring. They won the opener, 8-5 and then pounded out a 10-3 win in game three, with Molitor contributing a triple and a homer. In between, Mulholland managed to calm the Toronto bats long enough to give Philadelphia a 6-4 win, with major assistance from Jim Eisenreich's three-run homer.

Now the Phils send out Greene, their most effective pitcher, who won the clincher against Atlanta in the playoffs. Toronto counters with Todd Stottlemyre, who was just 11-12 as the number four starter during the season. Neither one gives the impression they will linger in the vicinity for long. The Jays hit up Greene for three runs in the first, and then Milt Thompson retaliates with a bases-loaded triple in the

FACT:
There has never been anything quite like this in Series history. By the seventh inning of the fourth game, the record for runs in a game is already gone, as the Phillies build up a 14-9 lead. The fun is just beginning.

bottom of the inning to make it 4-3 for the Phils. Dykstra slams a two-run homer in the second to make it 6-3. Absolutely unfazed, Toronto retaliates by driving Greene from the game in the third by batting around and scoring 4 times, with Devon White putting the Jays in front with a bases-loaded single.

The Phils shake this off, tie the game at 7-7 in the fourth and then land a 5-run haymaker of their own in the fifth. Dykstra wallops his second two-run homer of the game and Daulton launches another. Things get so chaotic during this rally that the wrong pitcher shows up from the Toronto bullpen. Cito Gaston wants a left-hander, Tony Castillo, but gets a righty, Mark Eichhorn. It turns out the phones aren't working and Gaston doesn't know he has only one pitcher warming up. The umpires consider this a case of mechanical malfunction and rule that Castillo can have all the time he needs to warm up. It doesn't seem to do much good. The assault continues against him as the Phils score twice more in the sixth and seventh. That was all right because Toronto gets two of its own off David West.

Going into the eighth, however, Philadelphia holds a five-run lead, which looks reasonably secure. Not a bit of it. With one out, Toronto drives Larry Andersen from the game, with Molitor's double down the third base line (originally scored an error to Hollins, a ruling that many observers felt should have stood) opening the gates. This brings in the Wild Thing to hold a 14-10 lead. A single and walk send in one more before Williams strikes out pinch hitter Ed Sprague. Then, in the pivotal point of the Series, Ricky Henderson drills a two-run single, and White follows with a two-run triple. Toronto fights all the way back to take a 15-14 lead. And that, to the surprise of all, ends the scoring. Mike Timlin and Ward shut down the Phils, striking out four of the last six hitters in the game.

The big comeback destroys the Philadelphia bullpen. One last salvo is left in the Toronto guns, as Carter's three-run homer off Williams in the 9th inning of game six ends the Series. But it was really lost when the Wild Thing let this wild game get out of control.

The Managers:

Cito Gaston becames the tenth man ever to manage consecutive Series winners, the first since Sparky Anderson accomplished it in 1975–76. Gaston's biggest challenge this time was finding a place for his DH, Molitor, to play in the games at Philadelphia. He started him once at first (benching batting champ Olerud against a left-hander) and twice at third. Molitor responded by playing errorless ball and hitting .500 in the three games, making Gaston look terrific.

Jim Fregosi was in his third season with the Phils and in his 10th as a big league manager. Going into this year, though, he had finished over .500 only twice, and that was way back in 1979 when he won a division with California. The 52-year-old Fregosi, a very good shortstop for the Angels in the '60s (and the player for whom Nolan Ryan was traded by the Mets), brought emotional leadership to a team that responded to it. The Phillies widely exceeded their talent level and Fregosi, properly, got much of the credit for that.

The Heroes:

Molitor made one of the most smashing Series debuts ever, with five hits in the opening game in 1982. Eleven years later, he was back and still flailing away. He led everyone with 12 hits and a .500 average, with half of his hits going for extra bases. He also had 8 RBIs as the Series MVP.

The Toronto team batting average of .311 was the best in the Series since the 1979 Pirates. Alomar matched Molitor's 12 hits (as well as stealing 4 bases and playing brilliant defense), Fernandez topped off his comeback with 9 RBIs and White slammed six extra base hits.

Dykstra did his part in inflicting Philadelphia's portion of the damage. From his leadoff position, he whacked 4 homers (making 6 in the postseason) and drove in 8 runs. Even in game five, when he was held hitless, he scored the winning run by walking, stealing second, going to third on the catcher's throwing error and scoring on an infield out. He also made three catches, which even he described as "big plays," to help nail down the game two win.

Carter had been having a fairly quiet Series until his final time up in game six. As it turned out, it was the final time up for everybody. The Phillies held a 6-5 lead in the ninth, with Williams pitching. They had come from four down on a three-run Dykstra homer in the seventh. Carter, Toronto's biggest RBI man for the last 3 seasons, had knocked in only 5 in these games on one homer. After a leadoff walk to Henderson and a single by Molitor, he worked Williams to a 2-2 count. Then Carter sent a low slider into the leftfield seats as the Toronto crowd almost blew the lid off Sky Dome. The only other time the Series had ended in a homer was 1960 when Bill Mazeroski won

FACT:
The Phillies hold a 6-5 lead in the ninth inning of game six. A leadoff walk to Ricky Henderson is followed by a single to Paul Molitor. Then Joe Carter sends a low slider into the leftfield seats—a three-run, series-winning homer. The only other time a Series ended on a homer was 1960.

it for Pittsburgh. That came in a tie game. This was the first come-from-behind shot.

Schilling should get, at least, honorable mention for throwing a five-hit, 2-0 shutout in game five, the day after the wild 15-14 explosion. It may have been that the Jays were too exhausted to hit anymore. Even so, the effort restored a little decorum to a Series that was starting to resemble a sandlot scramble.

The Zeroes:

Mitch Williams described himself as pitching "as if my hair was on fire." He seemed to be consistently in trouble, with men all over the bases, throughout his career with Texas, the Cubs and Phils. In 1993 he left most of them where they were. His season was a case of nature imitating art. The movie *Major League* had come out the previous winter. One of its main characters, on a fictitious Cleveland team, was a wild relief pitcher. As he came in from the bullpen in the film, the crowd would serenade him with a rendition of The Trogs' classic, "Wild Thing." Philadelphia fans identified Williams with the role and he became its living embodiment. But after saving game two of the Series, his collapse in games four and six buried the Phils. He finished with an ERA of 20.25 and two losses.

Williams' ERA was not even close to the worst on the staff. Greene, West and Ben Rivera all had marks of 27.00. It was a meltdown for the Phillies, with a team ERA of 7.39.

The Aftermath:

The Series virtually destroyed Williams' career. The target of death threats and harrassing phone calls by Philadelphia's lovable fans, he had to flee the city and the Phils were forced to trade him to Houston over the winter. Ineffective there, he was out of baseball in another year. Kruk was diagnosed with testicular cancer in 1994 and after attempting a comeback he retired the following season as a member of the White Sox. The Phils dropped back to the depths from which they had emerged.

Time caught up to the Jays in 1994. After 11 straight seasons of fielding a contender, Toronto was never a factor in the strike-derailed season. An arm injury to Ward stripped the bullpen of its closer and the Jays could never find a replacement, while Guzman could not reach his level of the previous two seasons.

Notes:

This marked the first time in history that a National League team scored more than 5 runs in its first two Series road games. The fact that the Phils only got a split out of it indicated what sort of Series this was going to be.

A nationally syndicated columnist wrote that the extremely hairy and very heavy Phillies looked like a "bunch of overweight truck drivers." The head of the American Truckdrivers Association complained before game three that this was "a cheap shot."

When asked the stock question about how he felt after his dramatic homer, Carter responded: "The word for it hasn't been invented yet."

The game 4 marathon lasted 4 hours and 14 minutes and ended just a few ticks short of 1 a.m. in the Eastern time zone. Every Series game had been played at night since 1989, but the TV audience for this work-night game dwindled rapidly and revived calls for playing at least one Series game during the day so children could watch.

Line Scores:

Game One, October 16

Phi (NL)—201 010 001—5
Schilling L, West (7),
Andersen (7), Mason (8)

Tor (AL)—021 011 30X—8
Guzman, Leiter (6) W,
Ward (8) SV

Game Two, October 17

Phi (NL)—005 000 100—6
Mulholland W, Mason (6),
Williams (8) SV

Tor (AL)—000 201 010—4
Stewart L, Castillo (7),
Eichhorn (8), Timlin (8)

Game Three, October 19

Tor (AL)—301 001 302—10
Hentgen W, Cox (7), Ward (9)

Phi (NL)—000 001 101—3
Jackson L, Rivera (6),
Thigpen (7), Andersen (9)

Game Four, October 20

Tor (AL)—304 002 060—15
Stottlemyre, Leiter (3),
Castillo (5) W, Timlin (8),
Ward (8) SV

Phi (NL)—420 151 100—14
Greene, Mason (3), West (6),
Andersen (7), Williams (8) L,
Thigpen (9)

Game Five, October 21

Tor (AL)—000 000 000—0
Guzman L, Cox (8)

Phi (NL)—110 000 00X—2
Schilling W

Game Six, October 23

Phi (NL)—000 100 500—6
Mulholland, Mason (6),
West (8), Andersen (8),
Williams L (9)

Tor (NL)—300 110 003—8
Stewart, Cox (7), Leiter (7),
Ward (9) W

1994

No World Series

The announcement came on September 14, a bit more than a month after the Players Association went out on strike. There would be no World Series. The unbroken thread of 90 years, which could not be severed by war or depression or even earthquake, would be cut by economics.

"It's a very difficult day," said acting commissioner Bud Selig, in announcing the cancellation. "There's an incredible amount of sadness. Nobody wanted this to happen."

Responded Donald Fehr, speaking for the players: "It's almost as if we've been talking to wooden dolls. There appeared to be no urgency, no desire to go to extraordinary lengths to find an agreement."

On the part of the public, the reaction by many was outrage; a disbelief that those who were the stewards of the game permitted this to happen. But to many more, a number that should have terrified baseball, the Series wipeout was a matter of indifference. They had been turned off long ago.

Despite record attendance figures and competitive races throughout the '80s and early '90s, the game was simply not drawing TV ratings, which were the key to its continued profitability. Without big television revenues, the huge salaries paid to the top stars were insupportable.

The owners called for a salary cap as the only way in which teams located in smaller markets could survive. Many formerly solid franchises claimed to be in terrible distress. The players refused to hear of a cap, and challenged the owners to open their books so their financial claims could be examined. The owners refused. So on and on it went.

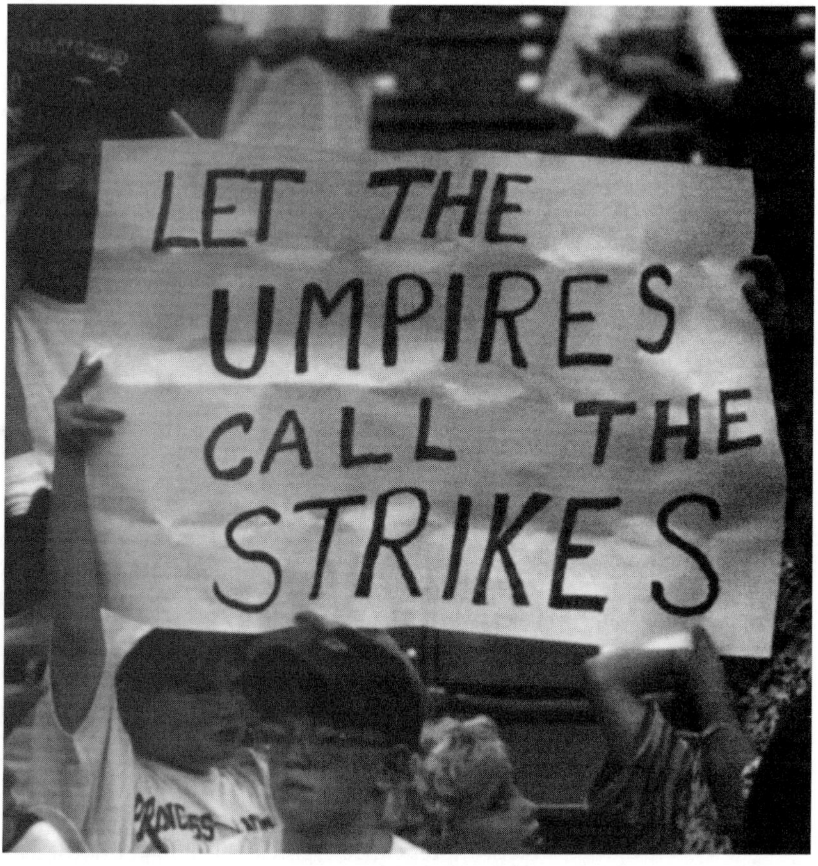

Fans express their opinion of the imminent player's strike, which would eventually cancel the World Series for the first time since 1904. The Series had previously survived two World Wars, the Depression, and an earthquake.

The young audience—the future of the game—increasingly was turning to basketball as the game of choice. Alone of all the major sports, baseball insisted on playing its championship entirely at night, starting at 8:30 in the Eastern zone. The games then dragged on to a time when most young people (and a lot of adults) could not stay up and watch the most dramatic moments.

In 1994 the Yankees were leading the American League with their best team in 13 seasons. It had been eight years since the Series was last held in New York, the longest gap of the century. Every sport knows that healthy teams in the nation's biggest city are a prerequisite to success. But the chance that the Yanks would play for the title was obliterated. Top team in the National League was the long-suffering Montreal Expos, who had never won a pennant in their 25-year history. Their fans, too, would be cheated out of the possibility of watching their team in the Series.

One writer was reminded of the final scene of the classic science-fiction film, *Planet of the Apes,* as Charlton Heston, wandering across the desert of the strange planet, comes across the shattered head of the Statue of Liberty. He finally realizes the horrific place he is trapped on is a post-nuclear war Earth. "The fools," he rages. "The fools." In some degree, that was the emotion one was left with here; a sense that despite all the warnings baseball may very well have gone ahead and destroyed itself.

1995

Atlanta (NL) 4
Cleveland (AL) 2

A classic clash of great pitching against great hitting ends as these things usually do: the side with the best arms wins. Atlanta, with Tom Glavine and Greg Maddux leading the way, broke through to the title on its third try of the '90s.

The Preview:

The road was rough, rocky and 41 years long. Cleveland had won nothing during that time—division, pennant, zilch. The last time the Indians had even been a serious contender (aside from the 1994 strike season) had been 36 years ago. Tiny crowds huddled in despair in the cavernous lakefront ballpark and the game almost died in this city. With the opening of Jacobs Field in 1994 the franchise suddenly came back to life. Capacity crowds jammed the new park for its old-time ambience and, more important, for a competitive team.

By 1995 the Indians were better than competitive. They blew away the rest of the American League, winning the division by an awesome 30 games. Even in the old two division set-up, in effect until 1993, the Indians would have won by 14. Cleveland won an even 100 games, only the second time in franchise history it had reached that figure, and this in a season that lost three weeks to the strike. They did it mostly on hitting. The Indians had assembled the most punishing collection of batters the league had seen in years. Four of them were in the top 10 in average and seven of them hit over .300. Most punishing of all was Albert Belle, who came on like a locomotive in the last two months to hit 50 homers, drive in 126 runs and hit .317—the greatest power year in franchise history. Veteran Eddie Murray hit .323, while adding 21 homers and 82 RBIs. The other big sluggers were second

Tom Glavine, after a season of being vilified by the fans for his prominent role in the strike, took the MVP award and broke Atlanta's Series curse with two victories, allowing a total of seven hits.

baseman Carlos Baerga (.315, 90 RBIs), rightfielder Manny Ramirez (31 homers, 107 RBIs) and third baseman Jim Thome (25 homers, 73 RBIs). Centerfielder Kenny Lofton hit .310 and led the league with 54 stolen bases. This attack was an almost unstoppable force.

Maybe the most significant addition, however, was shortstop Omar Vizquel. He gave the Indians their best defense at that position since the prime of Lou Boudreau and anchored an infield that had been rather shaky before he came from Seattle.

The Indians also brought in a mix of veteran and young pitchers. The Dodgers had given up on Orel Hershiser, whose ongoing arm problems prevented him from returning to the level of his 1988 season. But the 36-year-old right-hander snapped back with a 16-6 year, a record matched exactly by young Chuck Nagy. Forty-year-old Denny Martinez (a teammate of Murray's on the 1979 pennant-winners in Baltimore) went 12-5. But the Indians' real strength was the depth of its bullpen. Jason Tavarez was 10-2 in middle relief and Jose Mesa, who had never given any indication of stopper ability, saved 46 games with a 1.13 ERA.

When it came to pitching, though, the Braves were the standard. In a year when big hitters dominated, their staff stood apart. Greg Maddux was an other-worldly 19-2 with an ERA of 1.63, the sort of stats that hadn't been seen since the era of pitching domination in the '60s. *Sports Illustrated* labelled him flatly "the best right-hander of the live ball era." Tom Glavine, the top winner on Atlanta's two earlier Series teams, was very much around, at 16-7, and John Smoltz went 12-7. The closer was Mark Wohlers, with a rather low 25 saves. But on this staff you didn't get that many opportunities.

The Braves hitting was rather ordinary, though. First baseman Fred McGriff was the chief power source, with 27 homers and 93 RBIs, and David Justice, the only Atlanta player to start every game in the three Series, added 24 homers and 78 RBIs. Rookie third baseman Chipper Jones was a major find, with 23 homers and 86 RBIs, while Ryan Klesko took over in leftfield and hit .310, with 23 homers and 70 RBIs. None of the Braves ranked in the top 10 in any major offensive categories—but they were an evenly balanced club. They scored just enough to win, which is all that was needed with their pitching.

Turning Point: Game Four, Seventh Inning.

The Braves team batting average during the season was .250 and only two teams in baseball were worse than that. They had scored almost 200 fewer runs than Cleveland, too. Even with their decisive edge in starting pitchers, the Indians felt they could control the Atlanta offense well enough to win.

Even when Maddux stops them on two hits in the 3-2 opener, the Indians' faith in their own power is unshaken. But Glavine holds them to six hits in the second game, 4-3. Once back in Jacobs Field, though, the team revives. It takes 11 innings, but the Indians come out on top 7-6, although the Braves put up a more vigorous struggle than anticipated.

Now it is game four and the Indians know they cannot afford to get into a 3-1 hole against Atlanta's pitching. They will face the weakest of the four Braves starters, Steve Avery, only 7-13 during the season. The Cleveland choice is Ken Hill, picked up late in the season from St. Louis. He had won four times for the Indians and was also familiar with the Braves hitters.

Through five innings, the game is scoreless, although Hill is in frequent trouble. Four times the Braves get a runner to second on him and his control is a little wobbly. Avery, by contrast, gives up just two singles and works confidently. In the sixth, both sides find the range. Klesko homers for the Braves, but then Belle comes back and connects for Cleveland. The Indians simply cannot put together a big inning and take control of this game. Instead, it is Atlanta that strikes.

With one out in the sixth, Hill walks Marquis Grissom and then Luis Polonia bangs a double to right-center, scoring the speedy runner. That brings in left handed reliever Paul Assenmacher to try and end the inning without further damage. He cannot do it. Jones is given an intentional pass, but catcher Sandy Alomar lets a pitch get away and both runners advance on the passed ball. Assenmacher strikes out McGriff and that brings another lefty, Justice, to the plate. He is only 2 for 12 so far in the Series, but he connects this time and his single to center brings home two more runs for a 4-1 Atlanta lead.

The rally gives the Braves bullpen a comfortable margin to protect and they seal the victory, 5-2. The Indians are too deep in the trap to recover, even though they beat Maddux the next day. Glavine ends it with a one-hit, 1-0 win in game six. Cleveland proves to be no match for the Braves pitching staff or its opportunistic offense.

The Managers:

Bobby Cox understood that Atlanta was burning. After two Series disappointments, and a third failure in the 1993 playoffs, the once-rabid Braves fans settled into a "show me" attitude. They were noticeably subdued in the first two games in

Atlanta and the Braves players admitted they felt more pressure than ever before. This was the 54-year-old Cox's sixth season as manager and he knew that one more misstep could jeopardize everything he built.

Mike Hargrove was often singled out as one of the chief villains in the problem of lengthening game times. As a player, he went through a mind-boggling ritual of adjustments to his bat, glove and every other part of his uniform between each pitch. Moreover, he was perennially among the leaders in walks. That sort of patience served him well as manager of the Indians, though. He took over a dreadful ball-club and slowly nurtured it for owners who were ready to make the financial commitment to win. Hargrove had a core of veterans who had won before elsewhere and mixed them with some of the best young talent in the game, although the most talented of all, Belle, could be a major irritant. The result was just the sort of heart-warming story that baseball needed after its bitter strike, a flag for long-suffering Cleveland.

FACT:
Tom Glavine's one-hitter in game six was a beautifully realized piece of pitching. The only hit was a sixth-inning single by Tony Pena. Albert Belle, the one man Glavine refused to challenge, got walks his first two times up, then Glavine struck him out.

The Heroes:

Glavine was the rock on which the Atlanta staff was first built. The arrival of Maddux as a free agent in 1993, and his run of three straight Cy Young Awards, pushed him into a subsidiary role. But Glavine emerged in this Series as the bulwark of the Braves. His one-hitter in game six (with a ninth-inning closing job from Wohlers) was a beautifully realized piece of pitching. The only hit was a sixth inning leadoff single by Tony Pena. Belle, the one man in the Cleveland lineup Glavine refused to challenge, got walks his first two times up. With Cleveland trailing by a run and Belle growing impatient, Glavine struck him out on his third time at bat. He never got up again. Glavine also won game two with a six-hit effort, 4-3.

While Maddux missed his chance to close out the Series in five, he set the tone with his two-hit complete game in the opener. The Indians didn't get their second hit until the ninth and both of their runs in the 3-2 game were unearned, the results of Lofton driving the Atlanta defense to distraction. At one point, Maddux mowed down 25 of 26 hitters.

Mesa did what he could to set the table for the Indians. Although his role had been strictly as a one-inning closer, he shut out the Braves for three in the tense, 11-inning third game, which Cleveland had to win to stay in the Series. He then saved game five, although he struggled.

The even-handedness of the Atlanta offense was perfectly reflected in the final stats. Five of the regulars had either 5 or 6 hits, with Justice, Klesko and Polonia all tied for the lead with four RBIs. Klesko hit homers in three consecutive games and Justice got the lone run of game six with his only homer.

The Zeroes:

Lofton started off as if he intended to run the Braves off the field all by himself. In the first three games, he was 5 for 12 with 5 stolen bases and scored 6 runs. In the last three, he went 0 for 13 and got on base once.

It was a continuation of the Series blahs for Murray, who had reached the 3,000-hit mark during the season. Although his single in the 11th won game three, he was just 2 for 19 overall. That brought his career Series total, including his 12 games with Baltimore in 1979 and 1983, to 11 for 65, or .169. Cleveland's other 3,000-hit man, Dave Winfield, was troubled with injuries throughout the season and not placed on the Series eligibility list. He announced his retirement early in 1996.

The Aftermath:

For Cleveland, the sweetness of the season went sour in a hurry. A few weeks after the Series, the owner of the Cleveland Browns, Art Modell, announced that he was moving his football team to Baltimore. Offended at the money that the city had spent on Jacobs Field and the new Rock Museum, Modell declined to wait for the outcome of a vote to raise taxes for improvements to the old lakefront stadium. He accepted a lush offer to move the franchise and all the joy of the baseball season seemed to vanish in a day.

The Braves held the nucleus of their team intact and signed Fred McGriff, who had been their top slugger since coming over from San Diego in 1993.

Notes:

The Series title was the first won by Atlanta in any major professional sport. It had gone more cumulative seasons without winning than any other city in America.

Justice raised eyebrows on the day off between games five and six when he said that if

FACT:
The Series title was the first won by Atlanta in any major professional sport.

the Braves failed to win the Atlanta fans would "burn our houses down." The result was the first noisy crowd of the Series in Atlanta for the final game.

Belle lashed out at print and broadcast media for making too many demands on his time, getting in his way and other sins, real or imagined, during the Series. The club lightly admonished him, but a few months later Indians representatives also complained that the crush of media was so heavy that the team could not get its usual pre-game work in. Curiously enough, this did not seem to affect the Braves.

The Series was the focus of bitter protests by Native American groups because of the team nicknames. Atlanta fans persisted in performing their Tomahawk Chop, while the Indians refused to retire their grinning symbol, Chief Wahoo. "None of that is Indian and it is very demeaning," said the director of the Administration for Native Americans.

This was the first season the triple division, wild card playoff format was in effect. So the Series matched the date for the latest closing ever, on October 28. Weather in Cleveland for game three was reminiscent of a Browns game, with a wind chill of under 30 degrees.

Line Scores:

Game One, October 21

Cle (AL)—100 000 001—2
Hershiser L, Assenmacher (7), Tavarez (7), Embree (8)

Atl (NL)—010 000 20X—3
Maddux W

Game Two, October 22

Cle (AL)—020 000 100—3
Martinez L, Embree (6), Poole (7), Tavarez (8)

Atl (NL)—002 002 00X—4
Glavine W, McMichael (7), Pena (7), Wohlers (8) SV

Game Three, October 24

Atl (NL)—100 001 130 00—6
Smoltz, Clontz (3), Mercker (5), McMichael (7), Wohlers (8), Pena (11) L

Cle (AL)—202 000 110 01—7
Nagy, Assenmacher (8), Tavarez (8), Mesa (9) W

Game Four, October 25

Atl (NL)—000 001 301—5
Avery W, McMichael (7), Wohlers (9), Borbon (9) SV

Cle (AL)—000 001 001—2
Hill L, Assenmacher (7), Tavarez (8), Embree (8)

Game Five, October 26

Atl (NL)—000 110 002—4
Maddux L, Clontz (8)

Cle (AL)—200 002 01X—5
Hershiser W, Mesa (9) SV

Game Six, October 28

Cle (AL)—000 000 000—0
Glavine W, Wohlers (9) SV

Atl (NL)—000 001 00X—1
Martinez, Poole (5) L, Hill (7), Embree (7), Tavarez (8), Assenmacher (8)

Index

C

D

E

H

L

M

N

O

P

Q

R

S

T

U

V

W

Y

Z

Photo Credits

All photos are reproduced by permission.

Foreword, 1968 World Series, Mickey Lolich. AP/Wide World Photos, Inc.
1903, overhead view of first World Series game. AP/Wide World Photos, Inc.
1904, John McGraw. AP/Wide World Photos, Inc.
1905, Christy Mathewson. AP/Wide World Photos, Inc.
1906, "Big Ed" Walsh. AP/Wide World Photos, Inc.
1907, Jack Pfiester. Copyright (c) Brown Brothers.
1908, Joe Tinker. AP/Wide World Photos, Inc.
1909, Charles "Babe" Adams. Copyright (c) Brown Brothers.
1910, Chief Bender. Copyright (c) Brown Brothers.
1911, John McGraw, huddling with others. AP/Wide World Photos, Inc.
1912, "Smoky Joe" Wood. Copyright (c) Brown Brothers.
1913, Frank "Home Run" Baker, batting. Copyright (c) Brown Brothers.
1914, Boston Braves. AP/Wide World Photos, Inc.
1915, Duffy Lewis, Tris Speaker, Harry Hooper. AP/Wide World Photos, Inc.
1916, Larry Gardner. Copyright (c) Brown Brothers.
1917, Red Faber. AP/Wide World Photos, Inc.
1918, Hippo Vaughn. Copyright (c) Brown Brothers.
1919, Ed Cicotte. AP/Wide World Photos, Inc.
1920, Bill Wambsganss. AP/Wide World Photos, Inc.
1921, Jess Barnes. AP/Wide World Photos, Inc.
1922, Heinie Groh. AP/Wide World Photos, Inc.
1923, Bob and Irish Meusel. AP/Wide World Photos, Inc.
1924, Stanley Harris. AP/Wide World Photos, Inc.
1924, Walter Johnson. AP/Wide World Photos, Inc.
1925, Sam Rice. AP/Wide World Photos, Inc.
1926, Tommy Thevenow. AP/Wide World Photos, Inc.
1927, Babe Ruth, Miller Huggins, and Lou Gehrig. AP/Wide World Photos, Inc.
1928, Babe Ruth, Lou Gehrig. AP/Wide World Photos, Inc.
1929, Robert Moses Graves. AP/Wide World Photos, Inc.
1930, Al Simmons. AP/Wide World Photos, Inc.
1931, "Pepper" Martin. AP/Wide World Photos, Inc.
1932, Babe Ruth. AP/Wide World Photos, Inc.
1933 World Series. overview of field. AP/Wide World Photos, Inc.
1934, "Dizzy" Dean. AP/Wide World Photos, Inc.
1935, Freddie Lindstrom. AP/Wide World Photos, Inc.
1936, Vernon "Lefty" Gomez. AP/Wide World Photo, Inc.
1937, Tony Lazzeri, Red Ormsby, Gus Mancuso. AP/Wide World Photo, Inc.
1938, overhead of 1938 World Series game. AP/Wide World Photos, Inc.
1939, Charlie Keller. AP/Wide World Photos, Inc.
1940, Buck Newsom. AP/Wide World Photos, Inc.
1941, Tommy Henrich. AP/Wide World Photos, Inc.
1942, George "Whitey" Kurowski. AP/Wide World Photos, Inc.
1943, Mort and Walker Cooper. AP/Wide World Photos, Inc.

1944, Mort Cooper. AP/Wide World Photos, Inc.
1945, Hank Greenberg, Phil Cavarretta. AP/ Wide World Photos, Inc.
1946, Enos "Country" Slaughter. AP/Wide World Photos, Inc.
1947, Fans swarming onto field after the final 1947 World Series Game. AP/Wide World Photos, Inc.
1948, Lou Boudreau. AP/Wide World Photos, Inc.
1949, Allie Reynolds. AP/Wide World Photos, Inc.
1950. Granny Hamner. AP/Wide World Photos, Inc.
1951, "Lefty" Ed Lopat. AP/Wide World Photos, Inc.
1952, Billy Martin. AP/Wide World Photos, Inc.
1953, Mickey Mantle. AP/Wide World Photos, Inc.
1954, Willie Mays. AP/Wide World Photos, Inc.
1955, Sandy Amoros. AP/Wide World Photos, Inc.
1956, Yogi Berra and Don Larsen. AP/Wide World Photos, Inc.
1957, Hank Aaron. AP/Wide World Photos, Inc.
1958, Bob Turley. AP/Wide World Photos, Inc.
1959, Gil Hodges. AP/Wide World Photos, Inc.
1960, Bill Mazeroski. AP/Wide World Photos, Inc.
1960, Bobby Richardson. AP/Wide World Photos, Inc.
1961, Whitey Ford, Don Blasingame, Elston Howard. AP/Wide World Photos, Inc.
1962, Ralph Terry. AP/Wide World Photos, Inc.
1963, Sandy Koufax and Johnny Roseboro. AP/Wide World Photos, Inc.
1964, Bob Gibson, Tim McCarver, Ken Boyer. AP/Wide World Photos, Inc.
1965, Bob Allison. AP/Wide World Photos, Inc.
1966, Willie Davis. AP/Wide World Photos, Inc.
1967, Bob Gibson. AP/Wide World Photos, Inc.
1968, Mickey Lolich. AP/Wide World Photos, Inc.
1969, Donn Clendenon. AP/Wide World Photos, Inc.
1970, Brooks Robinson. AP/Wide World Photos, Inc.
1971, Roberto Clemente. AP/Wide World Photos, Inc.
1972, Gene Tenace. AP/Wide World Photos, Inc.
1973, Reggie Jackson. AP/Wide World Photos, Inc.
1974, Herb Washington. AP/Wide World Photos, Inc.
1975, Carlton Fisk. AP/Wide World Photos, Inc.
1976, Dan Driessen.AP/Wide World Photos, Inc.
1977, Reggie Jackson. AP/Wide World Photos, Inc.
1978, Bucky Dent. AP/Wide World Photos, Inc.
1979, Willie Stargell. AP/Wide World Photos, Inc.
1980, Bob Boone. AP/Wide World Photos, Inc.
1981, Pedro Guerrero, Steve Yeager, Ron Cey. AP/Wide World Photos, Inc.
1982, Darrell Porter. AP/Wide World Photos, Inc.
1983, Rick Dempsey. AP/Wide World Photos, Inc.
1984, Kirk Gibson. AP/Wide World Photos, Inc.
1984, Alan Trammell. AP/Wide World Photos, Inc.
1985, Bret Saberhagen, George Brett. AP/Wide World Photos, Inc.
1986, Bruce Hurst. AP/Wide World Photos, Inc.
1986, Ray Knight, Ray. AP/Wide World Photos, Inc.
1987, Frank Viola. AP/Wide World Photos, Inc.
1988, Orel Hershiser. AP/Wide World Photos, Inc.
1989, Oakland A's staring at fans. AP/Wide World Photos, Inc.
1990, Billy Hatcher. AP/Wide World Photos, Inc.
1991, Jack Morris. AP/Wide World Photos, Inc.
1991, Kirby Puckett. AP/Wide World Photos, Inc.
1992, Pat Borders piling on top of teammates. AP/Wide World Photos, Inc.
1993, Joe Carter. AP/Wide World Photos, Inc.
1994, baseball fans holding a banner. AP/Wide World Photos, Inc.
1995, Tom Glavine. AP/Wide World Photos, Inc.